CRUSADE TEXTS
IN TRANSLATION

About the volume:

This selection of over 200 texts, nearly all appearing for the first time in English translation, provides a close-up look at the crusades against the Hussite heretics of 15th-century Bohemia, from the perspective of the official Church – or at their struggles for religious freedom, from the Hussites' own point of view. It also throws light on the meaning of the crusading movement and on the nature of warfare in the late Middle Ages.

There is no single documentary account of the conflict, but the riveting events can be reconstructed from a wide range of contemporary sources: chronicles, sermons, manifestos, songs, bulls, imperial correspondence, military and diplomatic communiqués, liturgy, military ordinances, trade embargos, epic poems, letters from the field, Jewish documents, speeches, synodal proceedings, and documents from popes, bishops, emperors and city councils. These texts reveal the zeal and energy of the crusaders but also their deep disunity, growing frustration and underlying fears – and likewise the heresy, determination and independence of the Hussites. Five times the cross was preached and the vastly superior forces of the official church and the empire marched into Bohemia to suppress the peasant armies. Five times they were humiliated and put to flight.

About the author:

Thomas A. Fudge is Senior Lecturer in History at the University of Canterbury, Christchurch, New Zealand. He has published more than twenty articles on Hussite history and religion in addition to the book *The Magnificent Ride: The First Reformation in Hussite Bohemia* (Ashgate, 1998).

For Irv Brendlinger

in lasting gratitude
for unfailing friendship
faithful counsel
and unrealistic expectations

The Crusade against Heretics in Bohemia, 1418-1437

The Crusade against Heretics in Bohemia, 1418-1437

Sources and documents for the Hussite Crusades

THOMAS A. FUDGE
University of Canterbury, New Zealand

ASHGATE

Published by
Ashgate Publishing Limited
Gower House
Croft Road
Aldershot
Hampshire GU11 3HR
England

Ashgate Publishing Company
131 Main Street
Burlington, VT 05401-5600 USA

Ashgate website: http://www.ashgate.com

British Library Cataloguing in Publication Data
Fudge, Thomas A.
     The crusade against heretics in Bohemia, 1418-1437 :
     sources and documents for the Hussite crusades. - (Crusade
     texts in translation)
     1. Bohemia (Czech Republic) - History - Hussite Wars,
     1419-1436 - Sources 2. Bohemia (Czech Republic) - Church
     history - Sources
     I. Title
     943.7'0224

Library of Congress Control Number: 2002101557

ISBN 0 7546 0801 8

Printed and bound in Great Britain by MPG Books Ltd, Bodmin, Cornwall

Contents

List of Documents   viii

List of Maps   xiv

Preface and Acknowledgements   xv

List of Abbreviations   xviii

Introduction   1

1   From the Council of Constance to War   14

2   The First Crusade: Prague, 1420   45

3   The Second Crusade: Žatec, 1421   88

4   The Third Crusade: Kutná Hora to the Sázava, 1421–2   133

5   The Fourth Crusade: Tachov, 1427   192

6   The Fifth Crusade: Domažlice, 1431   262

7   New Tactics: Basel to Sión, 1432–7   341

Select Bibliography   402

Index   406

List of Documents

1. A Hussite comment on the crusades, 1430s 14
2. Report on the affairs in Bohemia, 1416/17 14
3. An emperor pledges allegiance to the Pope, 25 January 1418 17
4. Resolutions against the Hussites, February 1418 17
5. Report that Sigismund intends to suppress heretics, 22 April 1418 20
6. Sermon of Priest Želivský, 30 July 1419 21
7. Proclamation from the hills, 17 September 1419 25
8. Bohemian diet issues demands to the Emperor, August 1419 26
9. First military action: Surprise attack at Živohošť, November 1419 29
10. Apocalyptic climate in Bohemia, 1419 32
11. The beginning of woes, 1419 33
12. A ruling on the use of force to defend the faith, 17 February 1420 33
13. Battle at Sudoměř, 25 March 1420 36
14. Crusaders stopped at Poříčí, May 1420 39
15. Pre-crusade suppression of Hussite heretics, 1419–20 40
16. Letter of Sigismund to the town of Budyšin, 1420 42
17. Song about Archbishop Zbyněk 43
18. The anti-Hussite bull 'Inter Cunctus' of Martin V, 22 February 1418 45
19. Proclamation of the crusading bull, 1 March 1420 49
20. Sigismund promotes the crusade,10 February 1420 52
21. Sigismund orders campaign preparations, March 1420 54
22. An imperial plot revealed, March/April 1420 55
23. Preachers excoriate the Emperor in sermons, March 1420 56
24. Policy and practice on taxes to fund a crusade army, March 1420 56
25. Unrepentant heretics to be executed, 15 March 1420 57
26. Hussite manifesto from Prague, 3 April 1420 58
27. Bohemian nobility side with the heretics, 20 April 1420 60
28. Conquest of towns by the crusaders, late May 1420 63
29. Hussite capture of Hradec Králové, 26 June 1420 64
30. A call to arms 65
31. Battle song of the Hussites 66
32. Crusade legate admonishes the city of Prague, early July 1420 68
33. Czech diplomatic efforts to win allies, 10 July 1420 69
34. Women among the Hussite armies, 12 July 1420 73

35.   Crusaders and heretics in the battle of the Vítkov, 14 July 1420   74
36.   Song of triumph after the first crusade   80
37.   The children's song of victory   81
38.   Conditions in the crusader camps, July 1420   82
39.   Hussite resolve at the end of the first crusade   83
40.   Recruitment of anti-crusade forces, 28 August 1420   84
41.   An heretical denunciation of war, 1420/1   85
42.   Siege of Vyšehrad castle and fortress, 1 November 1420   88
43.   Manifesto after the victory at Vyšehrad, 5 November 1420   93
44.   Persecution at Prachatice, 12 November 1420   94
45.   Hussites strike again, November 1420   96
46.   Truce between Hussites and Oldřich Rožmberk, 18 November 1420   98
47.   Žižka and Táborite leaders address Czech people, 25 November 1420   99
48.   Abbot in Třeboň promises support against Hussites, 25 January 1421   100
49.   Manifesto to the Plzeň Alliance, February 1421   100
50.   Letter of Jan Roháč of Dubá to Oldřich Rožmberk, 3 February 1421   102
51.   A Moravian Tábor, February 1421   102
52.   Mass murder in the east, February 1421   103
53.   Carnage and conquest at Chomútov, 15–17 March 1421   104
54.   Union of German bishops, 23 April 1421   105
55.   Bishops outline anti-heresy strategy, 23 April 1421   106
56.   Support for the episcopal coalition, 24 April 1421   109
57.   Johannes, bishop of Würzburg joins the union, 24 April 1421   109
58.   Crusade alliance with Albrecht, bishop of Bamberg, 28 April 1421   111
59.   Ulm, Memmingen and other cities join the bishops, April 1421   112
60.   Archbishop of Prague supports heretics, 21 April 1421   113
61.   Crusade commander orders death to all heretics, 18 May 1421   114
62.   Hussite league of towns, 20 May 1421   115
63.   Proceedings of the diet of Čáslav, 3–7 June 1421   117
64.   Vanguard of another crusade threat, mid-June 1421   121
65.   Massacre at Most, 5 August 1421   122
66.   Jan Žižka calls for army conscription, 12 September 1421   123
67.   Descriptions of Hussite tactics   124
68.   The art of the wagon fortress   125
69.   Death traps for the crusaders   125
70.   The blind general of the Hussite armies   126
71.   Rewards offered for captured Catholic priests   127
72.   Code of the crusaders, September 1421   128
73.   Atrocities of the crusaders, 1421   128
74.   Crusade armies thwarted again at Žatec, late September 1421   129
75.   Silesian dukes penetrate Bohemia to Chrudim, October 1421   133

76. War on Vladař mountain, 19 November 1421　133
77. Crusade forces march through Moravia, Autumn 1421　134
78. Battle for Kutná Hora, 21–2 December 1421　137
79. Aftermath of the battle of Kutná Hora　141
80. Crusader disasters in the Sázava Valley, January 1422　142
81. Flight of the invaders and the abortive stand at Habry　145
82. Crusader failures in the winter of 1421–2　145
83. Song of victory over King Sigismund at Německý Brod, 1422　147
84. The king's perspective on the situation, 29 January 1422　148
85. Sigismund lobbies support from the bishop of Tartu, 1 May 1422　149
86. Imperial admonition for the city of Frankfurt am Main, 1 May 1422　150
87. Pope Martin V presses for military solution, late spring 1422　151
88. Hussite support for Zygmunt Korybut of Lithuania, 11 June 1422　153
89. A stern warning to prospective crusaders, August 1422　154
90. Protracted siege of Karlštejn Castle, summer/fall, 1422　155
91. Liturgical invocation for launching third crusade, 4 September 1422　156
92. Ceremonies for the crusade expedition, 4 September 1422　158
93. Levying of troops for the campaign　160
94. Žižka writes to supporters in Valečov, 26 March 1423　164
95. Žižka calls for acts of penance, 1 April 1423　164
96. Battle of Hořice, 20 April 1423　165
97. The military rule of Jan Žižka and the Hussite armies, summer 1423　167
98. Bohemia under economic blockade, 8 November 1423　171
99. Assassination plot against Jan Žižka, 24 November 1423　173
100. Martin V, letter to the Archbishop of Besançon, 1 December 1423　174
101. Cardinal Branda orders enforcement of heresy law, 16 May 1424　175
102. An amazing escape from the enemy at Kostelec, 5 June 1424　177
103. Battle of Malešov, 7 June 1424　179
104. Žižka's speech before the battle for Prague, 14 September 1424　181
105. Death of Žižka, 11 October 1424　182
106. Žižka's drum　182
107. 'The very fine chronicle of Jan Žižka'　183
108. Sigismund warns Oldřich Rožmberk, 28 October 1424　192
109. Oldřich Rožmberk affirms loyalty to Sigismund, 12 October 1425　193
110. Response of German cities to crusade proposal, 16 April 1425　195
111. Description of Hussite warriors　195
112. Emergence of Prokop Holý　195
113. Papal legate Orsini rejects diplomacy and urges war, 13 June 1426　196
114. Battle at Ústí-nad-Labem, 16 June 1426　198
115. Song of the Battle of Ústí　200
116. Lamentation on the debacle in north Bohemia　207

117. Franconian knights unite against the heretics, 15 January 1427   210
118. Zygmunt Korybut arrested at dawn, 17 April 1427   213
119. On the capture of Zygmunt Korybut   214
120. Military ordinance of the Reichstag, 4 May 1427   219
121. Reichstag initiatives for the fourth crusade, spring 1427   223
122. A papal nuncio appeals to the 'lost sheep' of Bohemia, 18 July 1427 225
123. Heinrich of Stöffel reports on crusade preparations, 20 July 1427   227
124. Crusaders and heretics clash at Stříbro and Tachov, August 1427   230
125. Poem on the fourth crusade   232
126. Friedrich of Brandenburg's report to Sigismund, August 1427   238
127. A papal legate writes to the city of Lübeck, 26 August 1427/8   241
128. Pope Martin V expresses disgust at crusade failures, 2 October 1427 243
129. A plan to review the fourth crusade, 21 September 1427   243
130. Sigismund urges papal legate to action, 27 September 1427   244
131. A Jewish perspective on the heretics, 1427   246
132. Funding proposals by the Reichstag, 2 December 1427   248
133. Difficulties in raising taxes for the crusade, 18 February 1428   249
134. Hussite heresy threatens distant lands, 9 October 1428   250
135. Beaufort petitions England for crusade aid, December 1428   251
136. Response of the Privy Council, December 1428   253
137. Diplomatic summit at Bratislava, 4–9 April 1429   256
138. A speech which enraged the emperor, April 1429   259
139. The empire strikes again, 10 April 1429   262
140. Sigismund rejects a policy of diplomacy, 16 April 1429   264
141. A call for renewed crusade, 18 April 1429   266
142. Duke of Burgundy prepares for action, 1428–9   268
143. England backs crusade against Czech heretics, June 1429   275
144. Efforts to engage the Hanseatic League against Hussites, 1 July 1429 277
145. Counter crusades, 1428–30   278
146. Hussite invasion of Lusatia, 1429   280
147. Prokop replies to German towns requesting peace, 2 February 1430   281
148. Burgundian crusade preparations, 1429–30   282
149. Joan of Arc threatens the Hussites, 23 March 1430   284
150. Manifesto of the captains of Tábor, 1430   285
151. Defending the Hussite cause, 25 May 1430   294
152. Hussite attempts to neutralize Lusatia, 28 November 1430   296
153. Cesarini's plan for a new crusade, March 1431   296
154. Ceremonies for the fifth crusade, 26 June 1431   300
155. Crusader frustration and foreboding, 16 July 1431   303
156. The Emperor admonishes the Polish king, 21 July 1431   304
157. Heretics propose a basis for negotiation, 1431   307

158. Counter-proposal by the Emperor, 1431   308
159. Hussite manifesto to all Christendom, 21 July 1431   308
160. Disputes over castles, spring/summer 1431   311
161. A call for aid for the crusading armies   311
162. News about the crusader invasion of Bohemia   312
163. Report to the towns of upper and lower Lusatia, 5 August 1431   313
164. City of Basel apprised of crusade strength, 14 August 1431   313
165. Account of the fifth crusade fought at Domažlice   314
166. An abbot files a chilling report, 15 August 1431   317
167. Hussite perspective on the campaign, 15 August 1431   318
168. An uninformed report of the battle, 16 August 1431   319
169. Admission of crusader defeat and disaster, 17 August 1431   319
170. Hussite song of victory at Domažlice   320
171. A crusade commander admits defeat, 19 August 1431   321
172. Poem on the fifth crusade   322
173. Troubles in the crusader camps, 14 December 1431   330
174. Letter of Sigismund to Friedrich of Brandenburg, 26 August 1431   322
175. The Emperor expresses regret to Oldřich Rožmberk, 28 August 1431   332
176. Orphan and Táborite expeditions abroad   333
177. Orphan invasion of Hungary, November 1431   336
178. Manifesto of the entire Czech land, 1431   339
179. Invitation to Hussites to attend the Council of Basel   341
180. Cheb Judge, 18 May 1432   344
181. Persistent anxiety over undefeated heretics, 13 January 1432   346
182. Armistice between Hussites and Silesian authorities, 24 June 1432   347
183. Heretics arrive at the Council of Basel, January 1433   350
184. Speech of Prokop Holý, 18 June 1433   351
185. Gilles Charlier's undelivered reply to Prokop, June 1433   352
186. Plans for a sixth crusade, 31 May 1433   356
187. An Orphan expedition in Great Poland and Prussia, September 1433   359
188. Sorrowful lament on the evil Hussites   360
189. Commentary on the Hussite march to the Baltic Sea   361
190. Compromise and settlement, November 1433   368
191. Prokop's last letter, 6 May 1434   372
192. Report on the battle of Lipany, 1–2 June 1434   373
193. Annihilation of the Hussite field armies   374
194. The end of Prokop Holý   375
195. Defiance by the Hussite remnant, 21 December 1434   376
196. Heretics' philosophy of resistance, 1435   378
197. Hussites denounce Hussites, mid-1430s   379
198. Demands of the St Valentine's Day assembly, early 1435   384

199. The king's concessions to the heretics, July 1435   385
200. Pact made by the emperor with Tábor, 16 October 1436   388
201. Hradec Králové falls to Sigismund, 3–4 March 1437   389
202. The emperor declares war on the Roháč resistance, June 1437   390
203. Gathering of force for the last fight, July 1437   391
204. Fall of the heretics' fortress   391
205. Last stand at Sión Castle   392
206. Execution, Effrontery, Exodus   393
207. Poem about Roháč, autumn 1437   394
208. Death of the crusading king   397
209. Survivors of the crusades, 1451   398

List of Maps

1   Bohemia in the fifteenth century   xx

2   Crusade routes into Bohemia, 1420–31   xxi

3   Battles in Bohemia during the Crusade period   xxii

4   Prague under siege, 1420   xxiii

5   Battle of Kutná Hora   xxiv

6   Counter crusades, 1428–33   xv

Preface and Acknowledgements

The crusade against the Hussite heretics of Bohemia is a rich chapter in European history yet much of its documentation is shackled by sometimes near impenetrable late medieval language. The difficulties and peculiarities of some texts present a formidable obstacle. Professor Norman Housley first approached me suggesting the production of a volume of texts revealing the crusade against the Hussites with the offer of a place for such a volume in the series *Crusade Texts in Translation*. I happily and immediately agreed that such an undertaking was not to be eschewed but doubted that I, even with fifteen years of Hussite research experience, was a worthy person for the project. I am not a translator and only with the greatest reluctance, with no other willing candidate on the horizon, did I apply myself to the onerous task of making heretics and crusaders in fifteenth-century Bohemia speak English. This particular labour has preoccupied me for most of the past five years.

The texts which appear in this collection have been drawn from seven languages: Czech, Latin, German, French, Middle English, Polish and Hebrew. I have received considerable assistance producing these documents. A sabbatical study leave in 2000 made it possible to spend time in Czech and German archives tying up loose ends, while a University of Canterbury research grant enabled me to travel twice to Prague, in 1998 and 1999, to gather materials and consult with Czech historians. I am especially grateful to František Šmahel, director of the Center for Medieval Studies, for the generosity of time and wisdom. He also hunted down more obscure materials on my behalf and saw to it that they were dispatched to the antipodes. Miloslav Polívka was compelled by Professor Šmahel to spend the better part of an afternoon photocopying texts at the Historical Institute for me; a chore well beneath his own scholarly dignity. I am further indebted to Jiří Kejř for his reliable counsel on questions relating to Bohemian towns and legal history. John Smedley and Sarah Charters at Ashgate along with series editor Norman Housley consistently provided good and prompt replies to queries. From a technical point of view it has been a distinct pleasure working with them and their professionalism and efficiency can be commended without reservation.

This book would not have been realized without the valuable assistance of several individuals who wisely and patiently helped me through the linguistic morass: Aleš Pořizka (Prague), bore a very heavy and essential burden with many of the Czech, Latin and German texts, Frieda Looser (Christchurch) and Jim Wilkins (Lee University) with the French, Matthew Gillis (University of Virginia), with almost flawless work on particular Latin texts, Florian Reckermann (Freiburg im Breisgau), Manfred Scherer (Regensburg), and the late Helmut Klingdorffer (Munich) with help on German materials. Lubomír Mlčoch (Lincoln) and Fabrizia Morini (Rome) were especially helpful with various other documents, while my colleague Denis Walker, Head of the English Department, provided valuable assistance with the Middle English texts. I would like to blame them for whatever errors and shortcomings remain but to do so would be knavish, untrue and irresponsible. Gratitude should likewise be expressed to David R. Holeton, my longstanding colleague in the study of Hussitica and the Bohemian Reformation, for answering many queries, especially about the liturgical calendar. Kate Samuel and Helena Blijlevens of the Interloans department in the Canterbury University Library supervised a steady stream of materials from abroad in order to keep this project going. Their professionalism and efficiency has been much appreciated.

Mandi Miller has graciously shared our home for the past four years with Hussite warriors and the occasional crusader and unending stories about deeds done long ago in the medieval Czech lands. For all of her patience and longsuffering, I think she is glad that Jan Žižka and Prokop Holý have now, finally!, moved out. Her cheerful and efficient contribution to the indexing of the book was a gift of no mean value, coming fortuitously as it did, and I owe her considerably for that. My son Jakoub, now precociously all of ten years, affirms that since Žižka 'had no eyes' everything which follows herein cannot possibly be true. His dumbfounded amazement at my tales never fails to amuse. Moreover, he continues to believe that his father must also be a Hussite! The book is dedicated to Irv Brendlinger, now Professor of Ecclesiastical History at George Fox University, one of my early teachers and mentors, later scholarly colleague and very fine friend. He was the first many years ago to encourage my interest and curiosity in Hussitica and he will understand the dedication page better than any. The offering is only a token of gratitude in remembrance of things past. It is deeply regretted that Olga Váchová, whose home in Prague afforded me a place to work for over ten years, did not live to see publication of this book.

Scholars of the crusades, late medieval Europe and the Hussites may be as critical of what has been included as they are of what has been left out of the final 209 documents which comprise this volume. Those decisions, however, remain my privilege and in the end I have done what pleased me. More than ninety percent of the documents herein appear for the first time in English and the others have been freshly translated. Others will be critical of some of the translations. For scholars *au fait* with the late medieval texts in their original languages, this volume was not prepared for you. Be contented with the Czech and Latin. These documents were assembled and put into the English language for those who have either little or no facility with the vagaries of the later medieval sources. Apart from Matthew Spinka's work on Jan Hus, Howard Kaminsky's on Petr Chelčický and Nicholas of Dresden, and Frederick G. Heymann's on Jan Žižka, very little material from Hussite history to 1440 has appeared in English translation. This book is an effort to redress that imbalance. All translation is interpretation. Certain liberties have been taken with certain texts in the interests of readability. While shortcomings do remain, I am confident this volume will prove to be an asset in helping to open the curtain a little wider on the story of the crusade against heretics in Bohemia and at the same time on the larger fascinating Hussite world.

The crusade against the Hussites provides an intimate portrait of the later crusades period, a struggle for religious freedom as well as warfare in the late Middle Ages. There is no single documentary account of the period of crusading fervour in Bohemia but the rivetting events can be reconstructed from a wide range of contemporary sources. These documents reveal the zeal and energy of the crusaders but also their deep disunity, growing frustration and underlying fears. Likewise the heresy, determination and independence of the Hussites is cogently expressed in other documents. Five times the cross was preached and the vastly superior forces of the official church and empire marched into Bohemia to suppress the peasant armies. Five times they were humiliated and put to flight. This is the story of the crusade against Hussite heretics in fifteenth-century Bohemia.

Thomas A. Fudge
May 2002
Christchurch, New Zealand

List of Abbreviations

AČ	*Archiv český čili staré písemné památky české i moravské*, vols 1–6
Bartoš	*Listy Bratra Jana a Kronika velmi pěkná a Janu Žižkovi*
BRRP	*The Bohemian Reformation and Religious Practice*, eds. David R. Holeton and Zdeněk V. David. Prague, 1996–
ČČH	Československý časopis historický
CDL	Codex Diplomaticus Lubecensis, part 1, in *Urkunden-Buch der Stadt Lübeck*, vol. 6
CV	*Communio viatorum*
Decrees	*Decrees of the ecumenical councils*, 2 vols
Długosz	*Historia Polonicae*, in *Opera Omnia*, vol. 13
Documenta	*Documenta Mag. Joannis Hus vitam, doctrinam, causam in constantiensi concilio actam et controversias de religione in Bohemia annis 1403–1418 motas illustrantia*
DR	*Deutsche Reichstagsakten*, vols 8–9
FRA	*Fontes rerum austriacarum*
FRB	*Fontes rerum bohemicarum*
Fudge	Thomas A. Fudge, *The Magnificent Ride: The First Reformation in Hussite Bohemia*
Hardt	*Magnum oecumenicum constantiense concilium*, 6 vols
Hegel	Die Magdeburger Schöppenchronik. In *Die Chroniken der deutschen Städte*, vol. 7
Heymann	Frederick G. Heymann, *John Žižka and the Hussite Revolution*
Historia Bohemica	*Aeneae Silvii Historia Bohemica*
Historia Hussitica	Vavřinec of Březová, *Historia Hussitica*, FRB 5:329–541
Höfler	*Geschichtschreiber der Husitischen Bewegung in Böhmen*, 3 vols, ed. Konstantin von Höfler
Husitské manifesty	*Husitské manifesty*, ed. Amedeo Molnár
Liliencron	*Die historischen Volkslieder der Deutschen vom 13. bis 16. Jahrhundert.* 2 vols
Ludolf of Żagań	'Tractatus de longevo schismate' in *Archiv für österreichische Geschichte*, vol. 60

MC	*Monumenta conciliorum generalium seculi Decimi Quinti,* 2 vols
Nejedlý	Zdeněk Nejedlý, *Dějiny husitského zpěvu,* 6 vols
Nejedlý, 1913	Zdeněk Nejedlý, *Dějiny Husitského zpěvu za válek Husitských.* Prague, 1913
Neumann	'Francouzská Hussitica' *Studie a texty k náboženským dějinám Českým* 3
Papal Registers	*Calendar of Entries in the Papal Registers,* vol. 7
PG	*Patrologia Graeca,* 163 vols, ed. Jacques Paul Migne. Paris, 1857–61
PL	*Patrologia Latina,* 217 vols, ed. Jacques Paul Migne. Paris, 1843–73
POPCE	*Proceedings and Ordinances of the Privy Council of England,* vol. 3
Rynešová	*Listinář a Listář Oldřicha z Rožmberka,* 4 vols
SRB	Stařì letopisové čcšti od r. 1378 do 1527 in *Scriptores rerum bohemicarum,* vol. 3
SRP	*Scriptores rerum Prussicarum,* 6 vols
SRS	Geschichtsquellen der Hussitenkriege, in *Scriptores rerum Silesiacarum,* vol. 6
UB	*Urkundliche Beiträge zur Geschichte des Hussitenkrieges,* 2 vols
Výbor	*Výbor z české literatury doby husitské,* 2 vols
Windecke	Eberhart Windecke, *Denkwürdigkeiten zur Geschichte des Zeitalters Kaiser Sigmunds*

Map 1   Bohemia in the fifteenth century

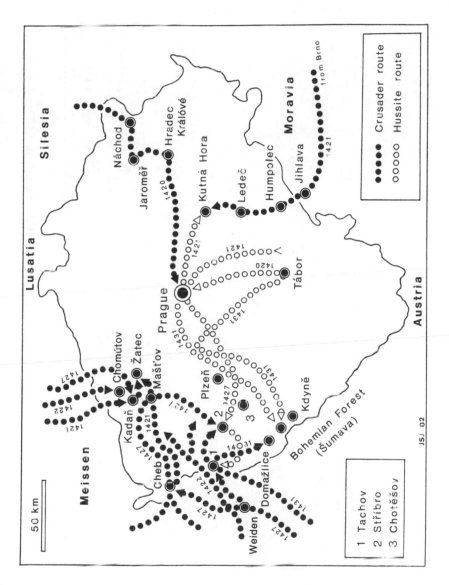

Map 2   Crusade routes into Bohemia, 1420–31

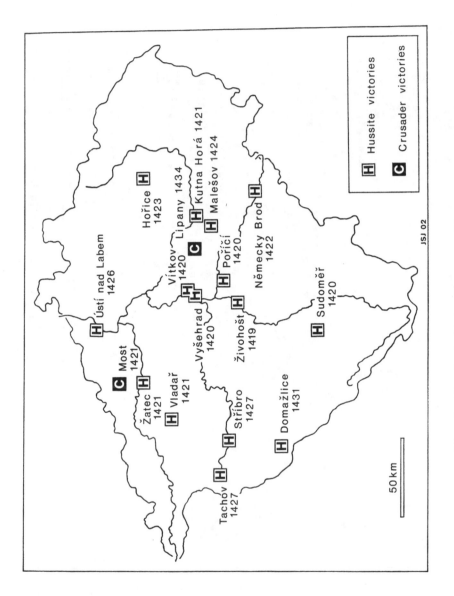

Map 3   Battles in Bohemia during the Crusade period

Legend:
H Hussite victories
C Crusader victories

Úsní nad Labem 1426
Hořice 1423
Lipany 1434
Kutna Horá 1421
Malešov 1424
Vítkov 1420
Poříčí 1420
Německy Brod 1422
Vyšehrad 1420
Živohošt 1419
Sudoměř 1420
Most 1421
Žatec 1421
Vladař 1421
Stříbro 1427
Domažlice 1431
Tachov 1427

50 km

JSJ 02

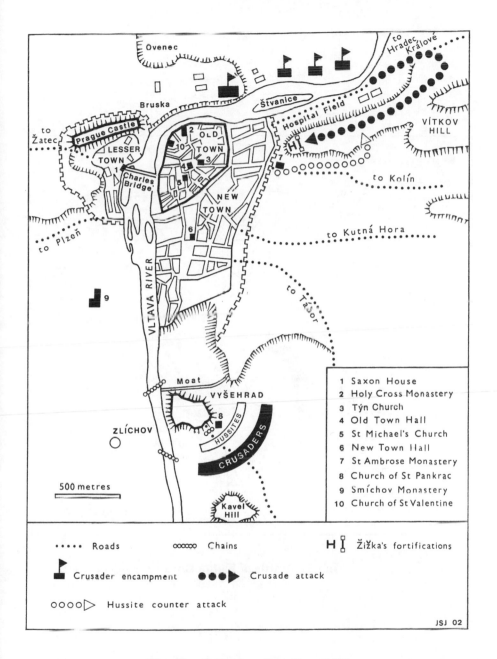

Map 4   Prague under siege, 1420

Key to map labels:

Ovenec

to Hradec Králové

Bruska

Štvanice

Hospital Field

VÍTKOV HILL

to Žatec

Prague Castle

LESSER TOWN

OLD TOWN

to Kolín

Charles Bridge

NEW TOWN

to Plzeň

VLTAVA RIVER

to Kutná Hora

to Tábor

Moat

VYŠEHRAD

HUSSITES

CRUSADERS

ZLÍCHOV

500 metres

Kavel Hill

1 Saxon House
2 Holy Cross Monastery
3 Týn Church
4 Old Town Hall
5 St Michael's Church
6 New Town Hall
7 St Ambrose Monastery
8 Church of St Pankrac
9 Smíchov Monastery
10 Church of St Valentine

•••• Roads   ∘∘∘∘∘ Chains   H Ⅰ Žižka's fortifications

◼ Crusader encampment   ●●●▶ Crusade attack

∘∘∘∘▷ Hussite counter attack

JSJ 02

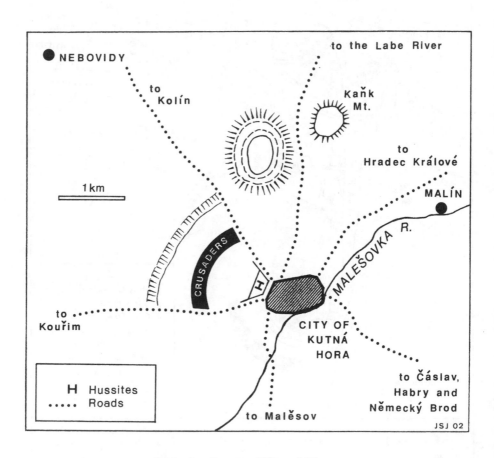

Map 5   Battle of Kutná Hora

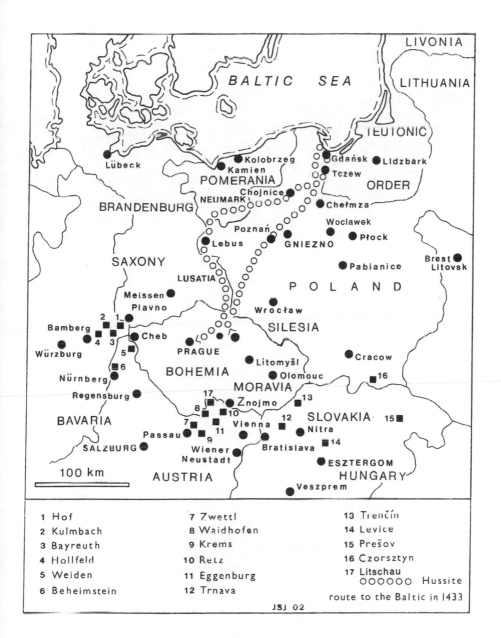

BALTIC SEA

LIVONIA

LITHUANIA

TEUTONIC

ORDER

Lübeck
Kolobrzeg
Kamien
Gdańsk
Lidzbark
Tczew
POMERANIA
Chojnice
NEUMARK
Chełmza
BRANDENBURG
Woclawek
Poznań
Płock
Lebus
GNIEZNO
SAXONY
Pabianice
Brest Litovsk
LUSATIA
P O L A N D
Meissen
Plavno
Wrocław
Bamberg
2 1
Cheb
SILESIA
4 3
Würzburg
PRAGUE
Litomyšl
Cracow
5
Nürnberg
6
BOHEMIA
Olomouc
16
Regensburg
MORAVIA
17
Znojmo
13
8
10
12
SLOVAKIA
15
BAVARIA
7
Vienna
Nitra
11
Passau
9
Levice 14
SALZBURG
Wiener Neustadt
Bratislava
ESZTERGOM
100 km
AUSTRIA
HUNGARY
Veszprem

1 Hof
2 Kulmbach
3 Bayreuth
4 Hollfeld
5 Weiden
6 Beheimstein

7 Zwettl
8 Waidhofen
9 Krems
10 Retz
11 Eggenburg
12 Trnava

13 Trenčín
14 Levice
15 Prešov
16 Czorsztyn
17 Litschau
oooooo Hussite
route to the Baltic in 1433

JSJ 02

Map 6   Counter crusades, 1428–33

Introduction

Hussite heresy in fifteenth-century Bohemia was a result of attempts to introduce ecclesiastical and religious reform. Concerted efforts began in the third quarter of the fourteenth century when the archbishop of Prague, Arnošt of Pardubice, and King Charles IV recognized the need for religious renewal. An Augustinian from Vienna, Konrad of Waldhauser, arrived in Prague in the 1360s preaching reform with the blessing of both authorities. This was followed by the important practical activity of the Moravian priest Jan Milíč of Kroměříž and the intellectual achievements of Matěj of Janov. The single most important, though by no means only, aspect of this reforming movement was the recovery of sacramental piety linked to lay participation in the eucharist. This renewed emphasis on the sacrament of the altar became the focus of ecclesiastical doctrine and religious practice in Bohemia. Czech theologians insisted social ill and church problems were best solved through an active sacramental participation. Initially this meant frequent communing. Departing from later medieval religious practice, reformers urged regular lay participation, perhaps even daily, in receiving the benefits of the crucified Christ and the transformation of God's kingdom which these reformers believed became ever more evident through the celebration of the holy sacrament.

Coupled with frequent communing was the socially significant factor of laypeople and religious standing on level ground, together participating in the community of God with humankind.[1] This communing created social identity, religious reality and in so doing provided the catalyst for reform.[2] Eventually, the implications of eucharistic renewal produced social and theological revolution.[3] Frequent communion gave way to the re-introduction of utraquism, that is the sacrament in both kinds – bread and wine – for the laity as well as priests. In the course of the twelfth and thirteenth centuries the lay chalice had fallen into disuse in most areas in the Latin church. A generation of frequent communion in Bohemian churches set the stage for this next development. According to the ex-

---

[1]   Miri Rubin, *Corpus Christi: The eucharist in late medieval culture* (Cambridge: Cambridge University Press, 1991), p. 2.

[2]   John Bossy, 'The mass as a social institution, 1200–1700' *Past and Present* 100 (1983), pp. 29–61.

[3]   David R. Holeton, *La communion des tout-petits enfants. Étude du mouvement eucharistique en Bohême vers la fin du Moyen-Âge* (Rome: CLV Edizioni Liturgiche, 1989), p. 299 and *passim*.

Hussite priest Jan Papoušek of Soběslav this step placed the Czech Church in greater alignment with the early church. 'In time that sect [Hussites] being greatly strengthened saw that the church was not generally administering communion in both forms of bread and wine to the laity. After attempting to demonstrate this particular article of faith in a most colourful and sophisticated fashion with Scriptural texts, with a type of argument appealing to the simple and illiterate, they introduced the practice of communion in both kinds. . . .'[4] According to other sources, the practice of utraquism commenced in the year 1414 at the instigation of the priest Jakoubek of Stříbro in the Prague churches of St Adalbert (Vojtěch), St Michael, Bethlehem Chapel and St Martin-in-the-Wall.[5] Under fire from critics, Jakoubek claimed the new communion rite was observed on grounds of divine revelation and who would dare withstand the Holy Ghost?[6]

The problem with the claim to divine *revelatio* was that the Holy Ghost ostensibly had a change of mind when eight months later the Council of Constance passed a resolution decreeing the practice 'rash', 'contrary to ecclesiastical practice', manifest 'error', unlawful and those who practised thus were 'to be confined as heretics and severely punished.'[7] The Bohemian reformation movement paid absolutely no heed to the decree and forged ahead contumaciously onto heretical ground. By 1417, the recalcitrant Bohemians introduced communion for all the baptised including small babies.[8] Leading theologians in Bohemia supported the innovation, masters of the university in Prague provided official ratification and the symbol of the chalice became the visible sign of a movement now derogatorily, and erroneously, called 'Wyclifite', or, somewhat more accurately,'Hussite' by its enemies.

This defiance of official church authority was exacerbated by the fact that when the Council of Constance made its ruling it did so in response to developments in Bohemia while at the same time it held within its prisons the leading Czech reformer, a man by the name of Jan Hus. Three weeks after the chalice was banned, Hus was burned at the stake as an incorrigible heretic. Bohemia was inflamed. Less than a year later, Hus' disciple and fellow reformer

---

[4] 'Pro declaracione Compactatorum et decreti in Basilea facti pro communione unius speciei', in Höfler, FRA 1, 7, pp. 158–62 for an overview of the movement.

[5] *Historia Hussitica*, in FRB 5, pp. 329–30.

[6] 'Contra Andream Brodam pro communione plebis sub utraque specie', in Hardt 3, col. 566.

[7] *Decrees*, 1, pp. 418–19.

[8] On the subject in English see David R. Holeton, 'The communion of infants and Hussitism' CV 27 (1984), pp. 207–25, Holeton, 'The communion of infants: The Basel years' CV 29 (1986), pp. 15–40 and Thomas A. Fudge, 'Hussite infant communion' *Lutheran Quarterly* 10 (No.2, 1996), pp. 179–94. The key study is Holeton, *La communion des tout-petits enfants*, *passim*. There is a review essay, Fudge, 'Eucharistic renewal and ecclesiastical reform in Bohemia' CV 38 (No.2, 1996), pp. 185–90.

Jerome of Prague suffered the same fate as his master on the same spot for the same reasons. Opposition to the official church stiffened. In many sectors the Bohemian church regarded both men as martyrs for the faith and went so far as to 'canonize' them. The cult of St Jan Hus was celebrated from the first anniversary of his death. Pictures circulated of both men, now revered, and songs sung their praises. Meanwhile, reform continued and radical groups began to emerge. The Council of Constance warned the Czechs, Pope Martin V sent directives, Sigismund of Luxembourg, king of Hungary and heir to the throne, made threats, while Bohemian clerics faithful to the official church did all they could to curb the growing influence of the Hussite movement. None of these efforts yielded significant dividends. The extent to which this popular movement was prepared to go may be calibrated in part from the activities in Prague on a Sunday morning in late July 1419. On that morning, a congregation from the Church of Our Lady of the Snows, led by a priest, stormed the Town Hall, forced the release of Hussite prisoners, broke into the council chambers, defenestrated the civic officials, and installed a new government, all before lunch.

The crusade against heretics in Bohemia was implemented to avoid permanent schism and to regain control of the church in Bohemia. Rome perceived the movement as rebarbative, heretical, dangerous and requiring more than diplomacy. While Hussites demanded a hearing before all Christendom the church was not prepared to entertain heretics on an international platform. Juridically, Hus had been found guilty, the lay chalice judged non-essential by theological experts. The reform movement was ordered to desist from innovation. All had been in vain. As early as 1416 rumblings about a possible crusade were heard. Crusades against Christians had been preached on either side of the Hussite era. Two centuries earlier the forces of the church marched into Languedoc to militarily subdue the dangerous heresy of the Cathars. In 1488 crusaders confronted Waldensian Christians in alpine passes of the French Alps. By 1418, with no sign the Hussites were going to be any less resistant than Cathars, the language of crusade became more frequent, more vehement and more specific.[9]

It would be erroneous to conclude the Hussite movement was concerned only with eucharistic reform or that the crusade preached against them was simply reaction to doctrinal and liturgical difference. The social implications of heresy were all the more alarming to the official church (doc.101). As early as 1415 more than 450 Czech barons publicly rose up against the decisions of Constance with respect to Jan Hus and the chalice. Going further, they formed both an alliance

---

[9] The preeminent authority on later crusades is Norman Housley, *The later crusades 1274–1580* (Oxford: Oxford University Press, 1992), esp. pp. 234–66; *Documents on the later crusades, 1274–1580* (New York: St Martin's Press, 1996) and *Crusading and warfare in Medieval and Renaissance Europe* (Aldershot: Ashgate, 2001).

against those decisions and a league to defend their cause. Hussites captured a bishop and forced him to ordain priests of the Hussite faith. Churches expelled orthodox priests and replaced them with Hussites. A majority of university masters aligned themselves with the reform movement. Queen Žofie openly supported Hus and used royal patronage to install Hussite clerics in churches. Neither the king, Václav IV, nor the archbishop, Konrad of Vechta, seemed to have either the will or the means to counter the rising tide. Meanwhile, the Hussite cause became codified in the so-called 'Four Articles': utraquism, free preaching, punishment of sins and divesting of ecclesiastical wealth (doc.39). The heretics were resolute. They refused to back down from this programme of reform. Inquisitorial efforts failed and with the sudden death of King Václav in August 1419, the official church prepared to act as did the heir to the throne, Sigismund, who not only played a role in the condemnation of Hus but for many years coveted the Kingdom of Bohemia. As Holy Roman emperor elect, Sigismund was the key political figure in the crusade against heretics in Bohemia.

By 1420 the cross was raised against Bohemia and the crusade was preached. This marked the beginning of protracted warfare in Central Europe. From the crusader perspective, the threat of heresy had grown to intolerable proportions. Sigismund testified he had witnessed personally the birth of the heresy and observed it spin out of control. 'Indeed, I was just a boy when this sect arose and spread throughout Bohemia. Now look at how strong it has already become.'[10] The Hussites were less benighted. The crusade initiative was the work of the Devil through his henchmen the pope, emperor, corrupt prelates, Germans and others who supported the repression of the Bohemians. The struggle against the crusade and the underlying basis of the Hussite wars was a defence of the Four Articles. Accordingly, near the end of the crusade, a leading Hussite summed it up asserting that all the people were united in the cause of the Four Articles and were absolutely unwilling to forsake these truths or abandon the true faith articulated in Hussite doctrine. In one accord, having taken counsel with university masters and priests, they engaged in war out of necessity, not from desire, and they did this only to defend themselves in accordance with the law of God.[11] Since these two perspectives could not be reconciled, swords were raised, banners hoisted, as crusaders and heretics marched out in holy war.

The period of the crusade against heretics in Bohemia technically spans twelve years, 1420 to 1431 during which time there were five separate crusades fought on Czech soil: 1420 at Prague, 1421 at Žatec, 1422 in a scattered and sporadic fashion, 1427 at Tachov and in 1431 at Domažlice. The chronological

---

[10]   *Documenta*, p. 315.
[11]   Mikuláš Pelhřimov, 'Chronicon causam sacerdotum thaboritorum continens' in Höfler, II, FRA 6, p. 481.

scope of this study spans twenty years, from 1418 to 1437. There are three principle reasons for this. First, the crusade did not simply emerge in the course of 1420. As already noted, there had been talk of a crusade for some years prior to the actual declaration of a crusade bull. In one sense any point prior to March 1420 is arbitrary and this book begins with the reply of Emperor Sigismund, at the beginning of 1417, to the suggestion of the Council of Constance that he take military action against the Bohemian heretics (doc.2). Even though Sigismund demurred, three years later he was willing to lead a crusade. Secondly, to end this documentary account in 1431 would be problematic. True, no actual crusading force would again enter Bohemia and no technical crusade battle would again be waged against the Hussite heretics. Those facts aside, it is specious to conclude that the crusade was over. In 1431 Cardinal Giuliano Cesarini decided upon new tactics and urged both emperor and conciliar fathers that the time for the sword should be suspended. When the heretics had their delegates appear before the convocation of Basel, this constituted another chapter in the crusade against the heretics. When that meeting ended inconclusively, plans were brought back onto the table for renewed military action (doc.186). Emperor Sigismund had written immediately following the crusader failure at Domažlice that things could not remain as they were (doc.174), promising the matter would be taken up again (doc.175). There is nothing to suggest the crusade was over in 1431.

Hussite policy of strengthening their borders continued after 1431. The decisive battle of Lipany in the spring of 1434 did seriously impair Hussite military strength, but it would be precipitous to end the crusade here (docs 192–4). The Hussites had been beaten but not exterminated. In fact, the devastation of Lipany had come not at the hands of crusaders but rather those of other Czechs. Resistance went on and surviving documentary evidence suggests Sigismund grew worried. Between 1434 and 1436, agreements were reached wherein Hussite religion appeared to be safe-guarded, demands were placed upon Sigismund, the emperor and aging crusader king made concessions to the heretics, and finally after seventeen long and bloody years ascended the throne of the Kingdom of Bohemia in Prague. The heretics had their excommunication rescinded and were received back into the official church. The crusade appeared well and finished. But the resistance movement continued to gather strength and three years after Lipany posed a threat. In the fall of 1437 two events indubitably ended the crusade against heretics in Bohemia. In September, the last warrior and the last stronghold were destroyed (docs 203–7). Three months later Sigismund died (doc.208). The primary force behind the military suppression of the Hussite heretics was gone. There were no more 'warriors of God' to fight and no crusaders left to march by the cross.

The third reason for taking a wider chronological view of the crusade against heretics in Bohemia is the question of the Hussite wars. These events and the crusades are not synonymous. Indeed, a number of wars waged and battles fought between 1420 and 1431 are technically not conflicts between crusaders and heretics. While that is true, much of the Hussite wars cannot be separated from the crusade. There were no military encounters in Bohemia before talk of a crusade began. The first major outbreak of violence was the defenestration in Prague in July 1419 but that was well after reports had reached the capital that Sigismund was planning to invade for the purpose of suppressing Hussite religious practice. The pre-crusade conflicts at Živohošť (doc.9), Sudoměř (doc.13) and Poříčí (doc.14) were not crusader battles but it is impossible to separate them from crusader mentality, crusade initiative and anti-heresy measures. Likewise, the battle at Ústí on the Labe River in 1426 is technically not part of the crusades (doc.114). Yet three days earlier the papal legate for the crusades, Giordano Orsini rejected all efforts at diplomatic resolution and urged a massive military strike (doc.113). The immediate result was another smashing victory for the Hussites. The crusades are part of the Hussite wars and the Hussite wars are largely part of the crusading ethos and crusade era. They should not be separated and indeed there is no compelling reason to do so, even though appropriate qualifications must always be applied. The wars were principally religious and the crusades were efforts to halt the growth and advance of heresy. This intertwining of motives and militarism marked the history of Bohemia from 1418 to 1437 and for these reasons the crusade against heretics in Bohemia must be considered over the course of these twenty years.

The documentary material for the crusade against heretics in Bohemia amounts to a few thousand documents. There are more than 1,000 texts alone in the two volumes František Palacký edited on the Hussite wars (UB). It would be both impractical and unnecessary to publish all of them in translation. Considerable repetition in the texts would be tedious to all but the few scholars actively investigating the intricate details of these events and these are surely *au fait* with the original languages. This book has been divided into seven chronological units. First, the period between the initial discussion of crusade and the proclamation of the actual crusade bull (doc.19). Second, from the promulgation of the bull on 17 March 1420 to the departure of crusaders from Prague (August 1420). Third, from the battle for Vyšehrad on 1 November 1420 to the second crusade in late September 1421. Third, from the invasion of Silesian forces immediately after the second crusade to the death of Jan Žižka in October 1424. Fourth, from Žižka's death to the conference between Hussite delegates and Emperor Sigismund at Bratislava in April 1429. Sixth, from the emperor's angry mandate signalling a fifth crusade in April 1429 to the days following the defeat of the crusade at Domažlice in the summer of 1431. Seventh, from the invitation to Hussites to be heard at the Council of Basel (1431/2) to the fall of the last Hussite stronghold (September 1437) and the death of Sigismund (December

1437). Surveying the available materials, a conscious effort has been made not to give special weight to any of the seven periods in terms of the number of documents or their length. Hence, there is a substantial number of documents provided for each of the 'crusade' periods in question. The difficult choice of specific text selection rested upon several criteria.

The first criterion was to cover the nominated period of twenty years comprehensively, allowing for the limitations of a one volume work. Hence, there are documents dating from each of the twenty years in question dealing with every event of crusade significance in those years. The second criterion had to do with the categories of documents. Within this criterion an effort was made to obtain and translate materials illustrating tactics, repression, actual crusade battles, diplomacy, propaganda, sermons, narrative chronicles, songs, bulls, imperial correspondence, military and diplomatic communiques, liturgy, military ordinances, court records, trade embargos, epic poems, letters from the field, peace treaties, intercepted intelligence reports, Jewish perspectives, speeches, synodal proceedings, organization of the heretics, causes of the crusades, outcomes, the significance of the crusade itself, counter crusade activities, anti-war perspectives and the roles of leading personalities.

A third criterion aimed at identifying leading characters and making certain their views were recorded and included. There were of course multitudes of men and women involved in the crusade against heretics in Bohemia. Based upon the documents, the following twelve were determined among the most important: Emperor Sigismund, Pope Martin V, Friedrich of Brandenburg, supreme commander of three crusades, papal legates for the five specific crusades, Ferdinand of Lucena (first crusade), Branda of Castiglione (second and third crusades), Henry Beaufort (fourth crusade) and Giuliano Cesarini (fifth crusade). Among the Czech nobility the most important included Čeněk of Vartenberk and Oldřich Rožmberk. Of the numerous and important Hussite warriors there are three seminal names of significance: Jan Žižka, Prokop Holý and Jan Roháč of Dubá. At least one document from the hand of each of these twelve appears and in the case of several there are a number of documents either by them or about them specifically. There are certainly others of note, principally Giordano Orsini, the first legate Jan Dominici, the inveterate enemy of the Hussites Jan 'the iron' bishop of Litomyšl, as well as Jan Želivský, Ambrož of Hradec, Jan Čapek and Petr Chelčický among the Hussites. Most of these are represented as well.

Initially, the focus was on Hussite documents specifically, that is with a view towards telling the story from the Czech side, rather than from the records of the official church and empire. However, as the research deepened and more documents were examined it became clear that both sides needed to be reflected in the book since one without the other would create an insurmountable bias and hopelessly skewed perspective. The fourth criterion, then, was to present a balanced perspective of the overall crusade against heretics in Bohemia. This involved not only authorship perspective but further a revisiting of the genre of documentary materials. Among different perspectives sought, the following have been included: narrative, analysis, Hussite, crusader, hostile, sympathetic, foreign, domestic, ecclesiastical, secular, individual, collective, political, theological, different 'Hussite' opinion, and post-crusade reflections. These four criteria aim to illuminate the central aspects of the crusade period in Hussite Bohemia.

Beyond this, the selection of documents included a fifth criterion which informed the selection of materials aimed at elucidating a number of important elements which resulted either from the crusade or prompted the crusade in the first place. Of initial importance was outlining the nature of the so-called Hussite heresy. The delineation of the Four Articles (doc.39) and the manifesto of the Táborite captains (doc.150) are useful in this regard. Opposition to Hussite religion in general comes into focus in the resolutions against the heretics promulgated at Constance (doc.4), the bull of Martin V (doc.18) and other denunciations (doc.188). The effort to contain Hussites only prompted further instances of resistance to conformity. The defiant messages from the hills in rural Bohemia (doc.7) and the formal demands levelled against Sigismund (doc.8) are indicative. The escalation of violence and the outbreak of open warfare can be seen in the defenestration of the city government in Prague and the surprise attack on pilgrims (doc.9). Of further consequence are the respective theoretical elaborations guiding both sides in this conflict. The crusade bull (doc.19) is similar to those proclaimed in the great crusading era of the eleventh to the thirteenth centuries. The cause of the crusaders is just, holy and honouring to God. Plenary indulgences promised that all who killed the enemy would have all of their sins forgiven and those who died in the cause of the faith would go directly to heaven. On the Hussite side, much the same was declared and the university ratification of the use of force to defend the faith is a seminal document in the history of Hussite resistance (doc.12). Much of this must be viewed against the backdrop of eschatological fervour (doc.10) which seems to have been present in so much of the later crusading motivation. Heretics and crusaders alike fought apocalyptic adversaries in the waning light of the 'night of antichrist'.[12]

The problems faced by the organizers of the crusade with respect to manpower and finance are important concerns and, together with internal strife, may well help to clarify in part the persistent collapse of the initiative (docs 24, 54, 132, 133, 160). Amid open and protracted warfare, there were efforts on both sides to secure diplomatic resolution. The authorities in Prague tried to win over the

---

[12]   A phrase used several times in a sermon by the Hussite priest Jan Želivský on the fourth Sunday after Easter 1419 [19 April] in Amedeo Molnár, ed., *Dochovaná kázání Jana Želivského z roku 1419* (Prague: Československá academie věd, 1953), pp. 37–9.

Venetian government in a carefully worded manifesto (doc.33), while the national diet of Čáslav denounced Sigismund and set up a provisional regency in opposition to the heir apparent (doc.63). Henry Beaufort departed from the usual vitriolic and abusive language of papal legates and tried the method of gentleness (doc.122). When crusades collapsed, the Council of Basel decided to allow Hussites a place on the platform of an ecumenical council (doc.179). Occasionally, in the midst of conflict, the two sides did sit down and talk openly as they did in Bratislava in April 1429 (doc.137). Narrative accounts have been included for each of the major crusade battles. For example, those on Vítkov Hill in Prague (doc.35), at Vyšehrad, Prague's southern fortress (doc.42), Žatec (doc.74), Kutná Hora (doc.78), Tachov (doc.124) and Domažlice (doc.165) as well as for numerous other battles. Descriptions of pitched battles are often suspect but circumspection has guided the choices included here.

During the crusade period while official church and empire expected Hussite collapse and capitulation, it seemed important to note the growth of Hussite strength. The formation of leagues of Hussite towns (doc.62), the conversion of the archbishop of Prague to the side of heresy (doc.60), the offensive of the counter crusades (doc.145) and the triumphant march of the Orphan armies from Prague to the Baltic Sea (doc.183) are among the documents which clarify this phenomenon. Concomitantly, persistent ambiguity and blatant opposition within the Hussite movement to the use of force and involvement in war and bloodshed is noted. The work of Petr Chelčický (docs 41, 197) is representative.

Relentless urging of action by the papacy (doc.85), rejection of strategic talks by the crusade legate Orsini (doc.113), angry letters of Emperor Sigismund (docs 139, 140, 175), and the resolve expressed by Cesarini (doc.153) underscore a huge body of material which reveals the sustained if limited enthusiasm for the crusade. The readiness to fight and the attendant organization and philosophy undergirding that determination is revealed on the Hussite side in Žižka's military rule (doc.97) and the writings of the bishop of Tábor (doc.192), while the crusade military mentality is illuminated in the ordinance for armies drawn up by the Reichstag (doc.120). Beyond all of this, the outcomes of the crusade are underscored in contemporary literature. For crusaders, the re-entrance of the prodigal Hussites into the official church (doc.190), cessation of war and acceptance of Sigismund as king (doc.198) were among positive results. On the Hussite side, one must number the concession of the church to consider the Hussite cause using only Holy Scripture as arbitration (doc.180), ecclesiastical recognition for their programme of religious reform (doc.190), the granting of privileges by Sigismund (doc.199) and the freedom extended to the town of Tábor (doc.200) as outcomes of importance for the erstwhile heretics.

A sixth criterion has been to present lesser known aspects of the period. For example, Jews are mentioned from time to time in the literature and occasionally were involved in aspects of the crusade. Little is known of their perspective with respect to the crusade or the heretics (doc.131). The Hussite campaign through Great Poland and Prussia in 1433 is occasionally mentioned in secondary sources but the only thorough study is in Czech (docs 187–9). There were of course other minor criteria at work. Nothing is worse in historical research than unremitting boredom and the reader of history books cannot be condemned for giving up, overcome with the same frustration. While maintaining a keen effort never to sacrifice substance for sound, essential texts for entertainment, or the heart of an issue for trivia, however thrilling, I have deliberately included unique, unusual and interesting material (docs 34, 106, 209). Similarly, I have not avoided questionable or known apocryphal documents, for their poetical value plays a role even if they should never be taken literally as fact. The simple but bombastic letter from Joan of Arc to the Hussites (doc.149) is representative here as well as the rather far-fetched and outrageous description of the heretics' war wagons (doc.69). Though materials in this genre have been minimized they have historical value which should not be arbitrarily eschewed. Additionally, they are seldom jejune.

Initially, I adopted a policy of including entire documents rather than edited extracts. While this has been observed in the majority of cases it proved untenable in others. In the case of chronicles especially, there is far too much miscellaneous material included and the detail can at times go on interminably. The same can be said with respect to correspondence where late medieval writers seem not to have maintained active interest either in the economy of space or expression. In these cases, discretionary cuts were made based largely on issues of relevance and repetition. The bull 'Inter cunctus' (doc.18) is a good example of an important document containing too much bulk not entirely relevant to the subject at hand. There was no compelling reason to reproduce the final thirty charges against Jan Hus or the list of forty-five 'Wyclifite' articles inquisitors ought to be on the lookout for. Moreover, references to, and digressions into, canon law, did not seem particularly important for this collection and thus were excluded. Notwithstanding length, the preparations of Philip the Good for participation in the crusade seemed relevant enough to leave in their original form and scope (doc.142).

At least nine Hussite manifestos have been included, some in their entirety (docs 7, 26, 27, 43, 150, 151, 159, 178, 195). In certain instances these were deemed essential in order to illuminate Hussite theology (which remained a core issue in the crusade and counter crusade) and their use of religious authorities to argue their case.[13] At least thirteen verse documents (songs or poems) have been

---

[13]   For a brief synopsis of Hussite theology see Thomas A. Fudge, 'Hussite theology and the law of God', in *The Cambridge companion to Reformation theology*, eds., David C. Steinmetz and David V.N. Bagchi (Cambridge: Cambridge University Press, forthcoming).

included despite the severe difficulties associated with finding proper English equivalents (docs 17, 30, 31, 36, 37, 115, 116, 119, 125, 170, 172, 189^c, 207). Even though some of the translations are approximations, the use of songs in the Hussite milieu was profound and to exclude them from consideration in this collection would be indefensible. The other category of very important materials on the Hussite side is sermons. Regrettably, these are fewer than one wishes especially for the crusade proper. Sermons preached on practically a daily basis in the field are regrettably, though understandably, not extant. The several collections of the homilies of Jan Hus are of no value in this context. Most of those of Jakoubek of Stříbro are of commensurate value and those preached by Jan Želivský are extant largely for the pre-crusade period. The one included here at some length is the first of two homilies Želivský delivered on the morning of the defenestration in 1419 (doc.6). In two cases, the battle for Kutná Hora (docs 78–82) and the complete collapse of the fifth crusade (docs 165–9), several related documents have been included. The rationale has been to provide scope for multi-level comparison aimed at achieving goals noted earlier in the criteria of document selection. Beyond this, both events were of singular importance for the crusade.

The majority of documents appearing herein were edited and published in their original languages in collections mainly in the nineteenth century. Some were critical editions, many were not. The collection of documents appearing between these covers does not pretend to be critical editions and the urge to provide commentary, critical apparatus and extensive notes has been largely suppressed. These worthy components were not among the aims of this production. Each of the 209 documents has been given a brief introduction for the purpose of context, explanation, authorship and dating. Footnotes have been used where the reader might usefully be directed to relevant literature or where essential corrections or expansions seemed necessary and instructive, but these have been applied sparingly. I have rarely made references to Czech scholarship on the grounds that most readers would not benefit. The same might be said for the bibliography. Only occasionally have secondary sources in Czech been referenced.

Of the narrative accounts of the crusade period, I have given preference to the *Historia Hussitica* over all others, even though it is regrettably incomplete. The author, Vavřinec of Březová, composed a fairly comprehensive, though uneven, account of Hussite history from 1414 to 1421 where the chronicle ends abruptly (see doc.78). The theories for whether he ceased writing in 1421, was writing later and was interrupted by death, or whether the chronicle was mutilated or lost is not of concern here. The theories and hypotheses have been reviewed elsewhere.[14] It

---

[14]   Though now seriously dated in places, one can still benefit from Howard Kaminsky, 'The Hussite movement in history', unpublished PhD dissertation, University of Chicago, 1952, pp. 18–26.

is sufficient to say that Vavřinec was no mere chronicler but possessed some of the critical qualities of an historian. The value of this source lies in its essential veracity of the events it covers, its judicious use of other documentary sources and its clear exposition. Situated as he was in Prague his horizons are somewhat limited and his unremitting hostility to the cause of the Táborites is evident. Still, there is little direct evidence that he deliberately distorted facts and his own perspective is kept remarkably to one side in most instances. It should be noted that 150 of the 205 pages, in the edition used for this book, deal with the period 1420–1421. For events after 1421 it is necessary to look elsewhere.

The other major narrative chronicle source is a composite work known as the 'old Czech annalists'. There are two dozen texts which comprise this source, with at least twenty relevant to the period under consideration. Of these twenty, sixteen texts were edited by Palacký, though the edition is not without its problems and shortcomings (SRB). Further texts were prepared in the century after Palacký.[15] This source cannot be regarded as one large work prepared by numerous authors. Rather, this is a collection of different works by different authors with different perspectives and different motivations for writing. Despite the work which has been undertaken on this body of source material over the past century, significant problems persist continuing to support the opinion expressed by one of the greatest Hussite scholars of the last century that anyone wishing to use this source for the purpose of scholarship must repair to the manuscripts themselves.[16] I shall be criticized for having ignored the sage advice of Bartoš but the materials drawn from this source for this book are strictly of a narrative nature and as such the intricacies of the manuscript and source problems are not acute. While Vavřinec attempted to deal with Hussite doctrine and theological issues, these sources tend to give such factors a very wide berth. Despite this serious deficit, this is a valuable source for the period after 1421 and I have used it accordingly. Among other sources and contemporary collections there are none to rival these in terms of the Czech perspective and coverage of the Hussite cause.

The interpretation of the crusade against heretics in Bohemia has remained open since the fifteenth century. There has yet to be a definitive history written in a major language either of the Hussite movement generally or the crusade specifically and we are a significant way off from achieving that goal. The complexity and richness of the existing documentation does suggest new avenues of exploration, fresh approaches to old problems and the basis for new and

---

[15]   Published editions include František Šimek, ed., *Staré letopisy české z vratislavského rukopisu* (Prague, 1937) and his later work *Staré letopisy české* (Prague, 1959) and *Staré české z rukopisu křižovnického* (Prague, 1959).

[16]   František M. Bartoš, 'Z musejních i jiných rukopisů Starých letopisů' *Časopis českého musea* 102 (1928), p. 211.

innovative methodologies and interpretation. This collection of documents has been prepared as one tool, among others, aimed at greater awareness, deeper understanding and hopefully suggestive of further work. The substance of the documents can only be revealed in a careful study of their contents in concert with the skill and enthusiasm of those who choose to plumb their depths.

Chapter 1

From the Council of Constance to War

1   A Hussite comment on the crusades

[Of the several extant manuscripts of an altogether valuable chronicle written by Vavřinec of Březová, secretary of the New Town in Prague, university lecturer and conservative Hussite, one bears the following preface which functions well as an introductory comment despite being written just after the crusading period.]

As I consider the varied and great destruction, which is presently everywhere evident in the one-time famous and renowned Kingdom of Bohemia, and see the devastation caused by internal conflict, my senses are dulled and my mind is bereft of sharpness on account of the confusion and sorrow. Nevertheless, so that future generations of the country of Bohemia may not be left without knowledge of this awful tragedy and thereby on account of negligence fall into similar or even worse insanity, and particularly so that the authentic faith and that which is essential be maintained, guarded and preserved, I have written down in this work as carefully as possible the things which I have come to understand as true through trustworthy eyes and ears.

Historia Hussitica, in FRB 5: 329 citing the preface to the oldest manuscript of the chronicle preserved in Wrocław, City Library MS 199, fols. 121^r–199^v.

2   Report on the affairs in Bohemia

[After Jan Hus' death, 452 Czech barons affixed their seals and signatures to a letter defying the council. King Václav IV of Bohemia seemed unwilling or unable to do much to stem the mounting tide of dissent. The Council of Constance urged Sigismund, Václav's half-brother and King of Hungary, to take action against the open defiance. This urging seems to be the earliest indication of a possible crusade against the alleged heretics. Sigismund's reply to the conciliar legates, written either in late 1416 or early 1417, reveals hostility towards the Hussites but reluctance to undertake military intervention.]

To the propositions of the deputies of all the nations of this holy council on the matter of heresy and errors thriving in the Kingdom of Bohemia, we respond most devotedly, saying we are prepared to give all of our effort to the honour of God and God's church for the extirpation of heresies and errors arising everywhere, especially in the Kingdom of Bohemia, for we are committed to the reform of the said realm.

Our brother, the King of Bohemia [Václav IV], directed certain ambassadors most recently to us, whom we have sent back to him with our reply, which is as follows. He should persuade his barons and other subjects, especially the followers of Jan Hus of damnable memory, all of whom defame themselves with their own letters, to desist from errors of this kind, to abstain from the disturbance and pillaging of the clergy, and finally to return cured to the bosom of Holy Mother Church. We will impart [our decision upon] these aforementioned matters and also your petition, which you have made the duty of all nations, by means of this same messenger of our same brother, whom we retain with us. Moreover our brother desired our presence together with the barons of his kingdom, just as he made known to us through messengers. Regarding this desire we decided to send soon our solemn ambassador, to whom we committed to say that we intend the said assembly to be celebrated if they wish to be reconciled to whatever extent to the Church of God, and to obey humbly the decisions and mandates of this holy council – otherwise we do not intend this assembly to meet.

On the contrary, if they do not wish to accept the sound teachings of the holy fathers and dispense with their damned and perverse heresies, we do not intend either to placate them or to meet with them in any way. If, however, they wish to convert to the obedience of the church and do not deviate in this, then with our said brother, or with his counsel and barons, we are prepared to meet in a place and time to be arranged, and following their good appearance and unchanging will we are prepared to lead the leaders, who are said to be from the sect of Wyclifites, to the place of this holy council.[1] We ask for the suspension of opinions and censures, by which they are bound, which we hope to be able to obtain graciously from the holy fathers. And should we find it the case that our brother, as stated previously, has the good will to destroy these errors, but on account of the multitude who support this sect does not have sufficient power to destroy it, then we promise you that we will hasten to help him with all of our power so as to bring about the final extermination of all the mentioned errors and heresies. We

---

[1] 'Wyclifite' was frequently used as a synonym for Hussites in the period up to 1430.

will also procure restitution for the despoiled clergy. Indeed we know that the losses and dangers that have arisen out of this heresy in that kingdom are too many to mention. Indeed that kingdom was Catholic before, during and after the time of our father of happy memory [Charles IV], and was praised for its good faith and devotion. Alas for the wickedness of the present days! We also know that it is defamed among many because of these errors, and is cheated of the most divine clerical ministry, whose priests are robbed. Many other crimes have occurred there, from which the good and faithful of that land suffer and are saddened. For in that realm not all are perverted or unfaithful. On the contrary, many more are honest and devoted men, who hold the true faith.[2]

Our brother, the King of Bohemia, seeing these evils calls upon the judgement of the archbishop, especially against one man [Jan of Jesenice], who is the worst, whom our brother ordered to leave the city, and on account of whom the church and city of Prague have been held under interdict already for so much time.[3] But this man responded that he wished to stand in court before the archbishop, and the archbishop excuses himself [Konrad of Vechta] because he wishes to be a confessor rather than a martyr, and because the business of examining and judging this man belongs to this holy council. And so every day about a thousand masses remain uncelebrated in the churches and in the city of Prague, to say nothing of the Kingdom of Bohemia!, and by this measure so many crimes remain unpunished, while one excuses himself for another.

Moreover may God avert that this holy council might wish to proceed against our brother on account of negligence, or invoke the secular arm against the Kingdom of Bohemia or our said brother. We entreat that, should this be the case, the holy council might wish to commit this duty to another than ourselves; but to whomever it deems to entrust with this duty, we will commit ourselves to defending your precepts for the Church and sacred council as much as we are able. It is, however, not fitting to our honour for us to do these things against our brother and his kingdom. It could appear to many that we were acting not out of piety or favour of the faith, but on account of a desire for the kingdom. Suspicion could also arise against us, by which men might believe that out of the pretext of an attack of the Wyclifites we wish to accept the lordship of the Kingdom of Bohemia for ourselves, and to oppress our brother, at last robbing him of his

[2] Most recently see Balázs Nagy and Frank Schaer, eds, *Autobiography of Emperor Charles IV and his legend of St Wenceslas* (Budapest: Central European University Press, 2001).

[3] Jan of Jesenice (†1420) was Hus' lawyer and conservative Hussite ideologue who opposed both the lay chalice as well as infant communion. He was excommunicated in 1412 but continued to reside in Prague until 1418 when he was forced to leave. According to the 'chronicle of the university of Prague', his presence in Prague was apparently the cause for the imposition of interdict in November 1415 which persisted on and off until 26 February 1418. FRB 5, p. 580.

kingdom. However, since our intention is always to devote ourselves to the honour owed our brother, and to conserve and defend his position, in these matters we seek to have your encouragement and support.

Documenta, 652–4.

3   An emperor pledges allegiance to the Pope

[Among certain acts of the Council of Constance during its last sessions in 1418 was the confirmation of Sigismund as Holy Roman Emperor and his subsequent oath of obedience to Pope Martin V. Both men would play key roles during the crusades against the Hussites.]

On the day of St Paul's conversion [25 January] the lord King Sigismund swore an oath and was confirmed by the empire. . . . The king of the Romans made this oath to the new Pope: 'I Sigismund, king of the Romans, promise and swear to you, Lord Martin V, through the Father, and Son and Holy Spirit and through the wood of the life-giving cross and by the relics of the saints, that I will lift up the Roman Church and you, as the leader of it, as high as I can. I will never damage your honour willingly, or through my descendants or by my counsel, consent or other failure. If I come to Rome, I will make neither imposition nor disposal of anything belonging to you without your consent. Should any part of the land of St Peter come under my power I will restore it. To anyone whom I would commend the Italian kingdom I will cause them to swear to assist you in defending to the best of his ability the land of St Peter.' Given in Constance on the day of St Paul's conversion, [25 January] 1418.

Documenta, 675–6.

4   Resolutions against the Hussites

[In February 1418, the Council of Constance published a list of twenty-four resolutions against the Hussite heretics. The king of Bohemia, Václav IV, was called upon to swear that he would do everything possible to suppress the heresies of Jan Hus and his followers. No distinction was made between the various emerging Hussite factions. From the viewpoint of the official church, they were all the same, equally heretical. These articles underscore the basis for the crusade yet to come.]

The decree of the holy Council of Constance and by the present and only supreme pontiff of the holy Roman Church, elected in the same council, our most holy father and lord in Christ, Lord Martin [V] the pope, to Václav, king of Bohemia on how he should proceed in order to extirpate the heresy of John Wyclif and [Jan] Hus in his land. This ordinance is intended to be observed with respect to those who are to be reduced in the Kingdom of Bohemia.

First, and foremost, the king of Bohemia should swear to preserve the Roman Church and other churches under his jurisdiction in their liberties and should not impose the newly introduced ideas of Wyclif or Hus on either the secular or regular clergy.

Second. All priests, masters and clerics, who have spread errors or heresies through teaching or preaching in the aforementioned Kingdom of Bohemia and have infected others there should abjure those errors of John Wyclif and Jan Hus who have been condemned in this holy council. They should renounce those errors which they have taught or preached and should affirm and proclaim this condemnation of doctrines and persons publicly from their pulpits. If they refuse to do this they should be punished according to canonical sanctions. The relevant names follow.

Third. Likewise, the laity who have not cared to set themselves right in the matter of the faith and who have polluted themselves under the same verdict and those who for a year or many years did not care for the penalties and disdained the authority of the keys should abjure as well.

Fourth. Also, other laypeople who adhered to the Wyclifites and Hussites, protected and defended them, should swear to adhere to them no longer but [rather] persecute them and show no favour to them further. They should affirm and hold as correct the deeds of the council with respect to the condemnation of the articles of John Wyclif and Jan Hus and the condemnation of their persons.

Fifth. Likewise, that the laity who alienated the clergy should be forced to pay restitution because the sin cannot be forgiven until that which has been taken is restored. They should also pledge themselves and swear not to impede ecclesiastical freedom anymore.

Sixth. The ejected [clerics] should be restored to their benefices and the intruders put out and punished.

Seventh. In like manner, each and every one who violates in favour of Wyclif, because of the restoration of temporal properties, should be punished according to canonical sanctions so that contempt of the keys will not be seen to be tolerated.

Eighth. Likewise, that all who promoted the cause of the faith of the papal court should be restored to their benefices and have the security to remain within the kingdom. If the [heretics] refuse to do so, or cannot do so effectively, then it is an indication that they really have no intention of returning. Those trying to convince them to revert shall have to proceed specifically with them if they would truly be forgiven and if they would confess themselves to have been in error and thereby seduced.

Ninth. Relics, payments and other treasures of the church in Prague and other estates or confiscated income of the same church or of other churches throughout the Kingdom of Bohemia and the Margraviate of Moravia shall be restored.

Tenth. So that the university in Prague should be reformed and the Wyclifites who destroyed it might be punished and removed for otherwise the university cannot be reformed. Wyclifites and Hussites cannot remain in the university if they do not relinquish their errors.

Eleventh. Similarly, the principal heresiarchs and founders of that sect should be compelled to come to the Roman court and apostolic see. They include the following: Jan of Jesenice, Jakoubek of Stříbro, Šimon of Tišnov, Šimon of Rokycany, Křišťan of Prachatice, Jan Cardinal of Rejnštejn, Zdeněk of Labouň, the provost of [the chapter of] All Saints', Marek of Hradec, Zdislav of Zvířetice and Michael of Malenice called Čížek.

Twelfth. All of the laity who communicated under both kinds [sub utraque specie] and who forced other lay people to communicate in like manner, particularly after the prohibition of the sacred council, should abjure that heresy and should promise not to promote but rather to impede that communion.

Thirteenth. Those priests ordained by Hermann, the archbishop's suffragan, kidnapped by Čeněk of Vartemberk, should not be pardoned but should be sent directly to the apostolic see.

Fourteenth. Each and every tract of John Wyclif translated into the common language by Jan Hus and Jakoubek, as well as others written by them in the common tongue in which they outlined their errors should be delivered into the hands of the legate or of the ordinary under penalty of excommunication. These should be burned because those which have not been wiped out have not ceased to relinquish error.

Fifteenth. The writings of Jan Hus condemned by the holy council should be handed over under penalty of excommunication and destroyed by fire.

Sixteenth. Likewise, all of the writings of Jakoubek concerning the eucharist under both kinds, concerning Antichrist in which he refers to the pope as Antichrist and says that Holy Writ speaks of him coming personally, should be delivered up and burned. [Also] and specifically the tract edited by him concerning the remanence of the bread after the consecration on the altar.

Seventeenth. In like manner, all of the songs introduced to the detriment of the sacred council and of catholic men of whatever state who resisted the Wyclifites and the Hussites, or the songs which praise Jan Hus and Jerome, the condemned heretics, are forbidden under the heaviest penalty which is to be decided.

Eighteenth. Also, it is forbidden for the clergy to preach in different places unless they have the authority of their superiors including what they will preach when they have not been delegated. Preaching by women and the laity should be prohibited entirely and [violators] ought to be punished.

Nineteenth. Ordinaries and other prelates possessing authority should not be hindered in their jurisdiction by any secular person under penalty of excommunication. This execrable heresy must be exterminated. It [ecclesiastical jurisdiction] must be exercised freely against both clergy and laity suspected of heresy, error or of maintaining favour for the condemned individuals.

Twentieth. Similarly, shall be ordered, under the duty of obedience and under penalty of excommunication, of each and every one who would recognize any Wyclifite or Hussite person, or one promoting their doctrines or who are known to have suspected books, that they denounce them to the bishop or his officials who shall proceed against them *ex officio* according to canonical penalties.

Twenty-first. Likewise, any alliance made between the laity or between the laity and the clergy to the detriment of the holy council, the apostolic see and the Roman Church, in favour of those condemned heretics Jan Hus and Jerome and preachers of that sect, must be dissolved under the heaviest penalty. These alliances are apparent by the letters written to the sacred council.

Twenty-second. In like manner, the rituals and ceremonies of the Christian religion concerning the holy and divine cult, images and the veneration of relics shall be observed and transgressors shall be truly punished.

Twenty-third. Each and every cleric and lay person who would preach, teach or defend the heresies and errors of John Wyclif and Jan Hus, condemned in the holy Council of Constance, and who proclaim or maintain that the persons of Jan Hus and Jerome are saints and holy ones, must be punished as relapsed heretics.

Twenty-fourth. Likewise, the admonished and advised lay people must agreeably provide assistance against all deviants in these aforementioned matters under the penalty of favouring the said heresy.

Höfler, FRA 1, vol. 6: 240–43.

5   Report that Sigismund intends to suppress heretics

[The notary Vojtěch and Dean of the Church of our Lady before Týn, the principle church in the Old Town of Prague, commonly called the Týn Church, arrived from Constance with news that the cross was being raised against the alleged heretics in Bohemia. On 22 April, Martin gave Sigismund full authorization to take action against the Hussite heretics.]

News. In the year of the Lord 1418, on 1 February, the lord king of Hungary was anointed emperor [actually as King of the Romans] by the lord pope [Martin V], invested with the sceptre and oath and constituted lord and ruler of all Germany, upper and lower, and everyone must obey him. We were present on this occasion.

About four weeks ago the bishop of Passau with two dukes were sent to Milan to get the iron crown which they are to bring to Constance during the present feast and once crowned he will be constituted lord of all Italy. Following this, the pope departs to Rome and the king and emperor Sigismund to Bohemia with one cardinal [Jan Dominici], possessing all power from the apostolic lord, and four doctors and an inquisitor of heretics. Should those accused [of heresy] refuse to abjure, they will be apprehended by the emperor through the secular arm and burned to death.

Documenta, 676–7.

6   Sermon of Priest Želivský

[The sermon preached by Jan Želivský in the church of Our Lady of the Snows in the New Town of Prague on 30 July 1419 was the impetus for violent insurrection in Prague.[4] The homily condemns unfaithful Christians and must be understood in the context of anti-Hussite sentiment, culminating in the crusades, and in the popular gatherings which took place throughout that summer in rural Bohemia. See doc.7. The sermon may be regarded as typical of radical Hussite preaching during the crusade period.]

Inasmuch as a great multitude surrounded Jesus and had nothing to eat, Jesus spoke to his disciples and said, 'I have compassion on these people because they have remained here with me for three days and they have nothing to eat. If I send them back to their homes hungry they will be overcome on the trip because some of them have come a long way.' The disciples replied, 'by what means can these people be fed with bread in this remote place?' He asked them, 'how many loaves of bread do you have?' They told him, 'seven.' He then instructed the people to sit down on the ground. Then taking the seven loaves, and giving thanks, he gave them to his disciples to give to the people and they set the loaves before the multitude. They also had several fish. After blessing them, Jesus commanded that they likewise be set before them. They ate and were filled. Seven baskets were filled with the scraps of remaining bread. There were about four thousand who ate and Jesus then sent them away [Matthew 15:32–39 and Mark 8:1–10].

---

[4]   This event is dealt with by Howard Kaminsky, 'The Prague Insurrection of 30 July 1419' *Mediaevalia et Humanistica* 17 (1966), pp. 106–26.

There was a great crowd around Jesus. From time to time our Saviour teaches us through his saving word while at other times he teaches through his gestures and actions. Jesus began to act and teach. The example of a life lived according to a doctrine is more important than words and it encourages many people to perform good deeds. In our own time there are few who teach by the example of their lives and their word and so there is little instruction. The saints support their words through their conduct and so they make significant progress. Last week our Lord instructed us through these salutary words. Today he teaches us by action.

In this case the multitude which followed the Lord were filled. Only those people who labour loyally deserve to be fed with the bread of Christ. Only good people have any right to partake of the bread. Just as the apostle said, whoever will not work, the same should not eat [II Thessalonians 3:10]. 'Come to me everyone who works and is burdened with heavy loads and I will give you rest' [Matthew 11:28]. Only those who labour have the right to say, 'this is our daily bread.' The others who eat this bread are thieves and swindlers. And what shall I say about the bread of the Eucharist? Without doubt, all those who work at useless endeavours eat their bread unworthily. Those who sell on Sundays are not worthy of the bread. Those who give themselves over to sin and strain for a piece of bread are not worthy. Those who commit deeds without any regard for public good, whether they are kings, princes, judges or other idlers of the courts who avoid work and who flaunt themselves in the luxury for which others have greatly sweat and toiled, are also unworthy of the bread. Prelates who do not work with the people according to the commandments of the gospel, but who work hard enough in finding ways to steal from people are not worthy of the bread. And what about all of those ministers of the church who have not been ordained to the priesthood? How can they be worthy of the spiritual bread? They put up the excuse, 'I am not worthy to receive the sacrament frequently.' What am I to say about monks and nuns? They do nothing useful at all, occupying themselves with frivolous trifles. The Lord satisfies only those who follow him as this multitude here. This is why the God of Israel, the Lord of Hosts, says, 'Behold, I will feed this people with wormwood and give them bitter water to drink. I will scatter them among all the nations, who neither they nor their fathers have known. I will send a sword after them and exterminate them down to the very last one' [Jeremiah 9:15–16].

Woe to those who are controlled by pride and lack the bread of Christ. All who acquire their bread through unjust means are without the bread of Christ. Such are the craftsmen, the goldsmiths, painters, butchers, bakers and stone-masons despite the fact that they work hard. Even a thief works with great effort while thieving just as those do who earn their bread sinfully and without faith.

We call to mind three things from the gospel today, First, the all-powerful mercy of Christ. Second, the necessity of repentance and third, the usefulness of his teaching. We are shown initially that Christ is truly human as well as God, capable of satisfying the people of all the world through his grace. It is necessary for us to believe in him, to remain with him for three days and to call upon him for help in time of need in order that he might sustain us. Where are those priests, in this time, who will preach for three days in the wilderness? Where are the prelates who will care for the destitute in love by feeding them so that they do not faint from hunger while on the road? It seems they do not allow themselves to be bothered with such affairs. He does not come to them in spirit in order to ask the disciples how many loaves they have to satisfy the poor of the Lord. But this is precisely to whom the order is addressed. 'Do not hold back! Bring my sons and daughters from the ends of the earth, all of those who bear my name and whom I have created for my glory, those I have made and formed' [Isaiah 43:6-7]. This is what these masters must do. They must multiply the bread and not eat it. The word of Ezekiel is fulfilled, 'the shepherds have fed themselves but have not fed my flock' [Ezekiel 34:8].

Last Sunday I recounted how men need to have a great sense of justice, an unwavering faith, love without treachery and a great hope if they desire to overcome the world and hell. Since it is impossible to acquire these virtues through our own merit, the Lord strengthens us today with the bread of life which will cause us, his elect, to be steadfast. May it please heaven that he might revive us, even though we are weak in faith. . . .

Jerome wrote to Paulinus, 'it is simony to give that which belongs to the poor to people who are not poor. With the exception of food and clothing do not give anything so that it would seem that you are giving the bread of the children to the dogs. The Lord has forbidden one to give that which is holy to the dogs.'[5] Indeed, dogs in our own time eat the consecrated bread and the holy charity which belong to the poor. It is given in tumblers to sorcerers, to their servants, and to their servants and to his dogs. All those who eat the bread of the sons act against the truth just like dogs who pounce on a bone.

'Behold, three days they have stayed with me and they have nothing to eat.' For three days humankind approaches God, but in three nights they distance themselves. The first night is that of pride which causes one to abandon God. Pride begins with desertion, for the heart is estranged from the one who made it. The second night is the desire of the flesh. The third night is the greed which causes one to covet the goods of another. Through pride humans distance themselves from God in order to set themselves up. Through [fleshly] desires, humankind descends beneath dignity in order to become established in the things of the world whereby becoming attached to that which is passing. 'Woe to you who are rich, because you are satisfied'[Luke 6:24]. If we desire to be satisfied by

---

[5]   Jerome, ep. 58, Letter to Paul, in PL 22, cols. 579–86 at col. 584.

the Lord, we must return to doing good and stop doing evil. 'Let the thief steal no more, but let him rather work with his own hands in doing that which is good so that he may give something to those who are in need'[Ephesians 4:28].

He asked them: 'How many loaves do you have?' They said to him, 'seven.' Then he commanded the multitude to sit down on the ground. With these seven loaves he satisfies us. The first loaf is the amending of our wicked lives. . . . The second loaf is a humble and sincere confession of sins . . . . a loaf of sorrow, that is to say of indignation, for the injustice committed. This loaf must be borne because of the sins we have committed. The fourth loaf is the anguish which one experiences in light of the possibility of a relapse . . . . The fifth loaf is a desire to go on in the way of righteousness . . . . The sixth loaf is an imitation of the holy fathers . . . . The seventh loaf is the severe punishment of all wicked deeds. Those who possess these seven loaves will be entirely satisfied by Christ on the mountain. And taking the seven loaves, he gave thanks, then he gave them to his disciples to put before them. According to Chrysostom, in his life he prepared two earthly banquets with seven loaves and two fish, but every day he prepared a spiritual feast.[6] Every time he preached, he offered heavenly food.

They also had seven fish. Having blessed them, he commanded that in the same way they be set before them and they ate and were satisfied. How merciful was the Lord to whom belongs all the earth and everything therein in comparison to the rich people of the world who make a great show of their wealth with banquets but who are never satisfied.

One must marvel greatly at the miracles and not just what is found in the lesson for today. The first and greatest miracle was the creation of the universe, then the salvation of Noah in the ark, the division of languages and nations, the sacrificial ram offered as a victim to Abraham, the parting of the Red Sea, a pillar of cloud by day and of fire by night, the manna which fell down from the sky, water flowing from the rock, quails covering the earth up to two cubits in height, the rod of Aaron which grew two buds and two ripe almonds, the curing of the people at the sight of the bronze serpent, the clothing of the children of Israel which did not wear out in forty years, the stopping of the sun at Gibeon and the moon over Aijalon Valley. [Then] the walls of Jericho which fell down after seven days, the triumph of David over Goliath, Elijah being fed by crows during the famine, which lasted three and a half years . . . . On two occasions fifty soldiers were consumed by fire from heaven at the order of this prophet, the parting of the waters of the Jordan, the widow's oil, the Shunammite's child, the healing of Naaman and the smiting of Gehazi with leprosy, Tobias healed of blindness with the gall of a fish, Daniel saved from the den of lions and Jonah from the stomach

---

[6] Pseudo-Chrysostom, *Opus imperfectum in Matthaeum*, homily 41, in PG 56, cols. 859–61.

of a whale. Christ was born of a virgin, water was changed into wine, three young people were raised: the daughter of Jairus, the widow's son at the town gate and Lazarus from his tomb. Behold, what an abundance of wonders![7]

Prague, National and University Library MS. V G 3 fols. 22^r–30^r.

7   Proclamation from the hills

[Those sympathetic to a more radical form of Hussitism gathered together in several meetings on hilltops in south Bohemia in 1419. A number of these convocations issued manifestos. The following is the manifesto issued by the Táborites as a result of their congregation on Bzí Hora on 17 September 1419. The leading personality was the radical preacher Václav Koranda of Plzeň.]

The community gathered together on the Sunday following St Ludmila's Day, on Bzí Mountain, are united in hope in the spirit of Jesus Christ. We wish that all beloved followers of God like ourselves might now have salvation, peace, unity and truth in the pure faith of Jesus Christ and that unto death.

Beloved, with this letter we wish publicly to inform everyone that our gatherings on the mountains and in the countryside have been for no other purpose than for the free hearing of the true and salutary instruction based upon the Law of God, together with the essential communion of the veritable body and blood of our Lord and Saviour Jesus Christ, which we do in memory of his death and our redemption in order that we might be strengthened, preserved and confirmed in the way of salvation. Each one of us has agreed to ask the Lord God to enable us to be of one law, one heart, one faith and one soul. We ask God that everything wicked and harmful to our souls be destroyed and that which is good be built up.

We are aware that our souls have been imperilled by the hypocritical cunning of false prophets who have been incited by Antichrist against the law of God. We ask God to help us to avoid them with all caution so that they may not dissuade us from the original authentic faith of the Lord Jesus Christ and the apostles. We are witnesses to the fact that during this time as announced by the prophet Daniel the abomination of desolation has settled down into the holy place. Divine truth is ridiculed, abused, rejected and destroyed. The hypocritical wickedness of Antichrist is magnified beyond measure under the guise of holiness and righteousness. Who does not feel pity? Who would dare not be dismayed, to

---

[7]   On Želivský see David R. Holeton, 'Revelation and Revolution in Late Medieval Bohemia' *Communio Viatorum* 36 (1994), pp. 29–45.

complain, to cry out to God with the children of Israel? They lifted up their voices and their petition came to God and God heard their cry. God remembered the promise made to Abraham, Isaac and Jacob and saw the children of Israel and delivered them. With great persistence Judith and Esther prayed to God for the salvation of their people and their prayers were answered. With much endurance, Matthias, at death's door, instructed his children to preserve the word of God for the benefit of everyone. 'But now my sons, be zealous for the law and give your lives for the covenant made by your fathers. Remember the deeds which they performed in that time and great glory and eternal fame will be yours. Abraham, Joseph, Phineas, Joshua, Caleb, King David, the prophet Elijah, Hananiah, Azariah, Mishael, Daniel and many others who trusted God were delivered from numerous dangers. You must understand that as one generation succeeds another generation, all who have hoped in the Lord have never died. Do not fear the threats of the wicked. Today he may be exalted, but tomorrow there may be no trace of him because he will have returned to the dust and his schemes will have come to nothing. My sons, be strong and courageous according to the law. By this you will obtain great glory' [I Maccabees 2:50–64].

Because of these things, dearly beloved, we implore you in the name of God and for your salvation to join us in harmony on Saturday morning of St Jerome's Day near Na Křížkách [At the Crosses], in the field on the road from Benešov in the direction of Prague, on the mountain beyond Ládvím [or Ládvy] for the purpose of uniting with God in order to defend the freedom of the law of God and for the common good of the entire realm. The blatant abuses, scandals and conflicts must be abolished and punished with the help of God, the king, the lords, knights, squires and the entire Christian community. Written on the mountain on the Sunday following St Ludmila's day [17 September 1419].

AČ 3: 205–6.

8   Bohemian diet issues demands to the Emperor

[On 16 August 1419, King Václav died. Shortly thereafter the Bohemian Diet was convened by Čeněk of Vartenberk, Lord High Burgrave of Prague, with the consent of Queen Žofie, and published a list of demands to Sigismund before they were prepared to recognize him as king. It is not clear whether Čeněk or the city of Prague plays the leading role. The first fifteen articles are general demands advanced by the entire Diet: barons, gentry and towns. The last eight items are somewhat more special demands submitted by the City of Prague. Sigismund never directly answered the demands.]

May these articles be handed over to our new king and gracious lord. First, that his royal grace grant freedom to the law of God and God's word, especially in relation to the communion of Lord's body and blood for all Christian people consistent with the liberty bestowed by his brother King Václav [IV] of blessed memory.

Further, that his royal grace accept, as did King Václav, that the communion of the blood of the Lord is the law of God and that this practice neither be censured nor condemned. That priests have served both together and common people attended such masses and whoever attempted to disrupt this practice was not tolerated in the city.[8]

Further, that it has been written by his royal grace to the Pope with the support of barons, squires, the archbishop, the chapter and the entire community, that the kingdom should not be condemned on account of the blood of the Lord, but instead that this practice would be allowed, on appeal to a future council.

Also, that no priest shall be permitted to take up a secular office anywhere in the Czech kingdom. In like manner, priests may not govern in secular justice, acquire estates and income, but shall have their needs met by the people according to the law of God.

Similarly, the simoniacal sale of ecclesiastical sacraments and fees for letters, the archbishop's court and elsewhere in the churches [cannot be tolerated] either privately or publicly.

Furthermore, that Master Hus and Master Jerome were not censured by anyone in the land otherwise a great dissension among the people [would have arisen]. Some people who were against those called Wyclifites or Hussites were forbidden by law to condemn the others. Offenders were not tolerated in the city.

Also, that those exiled from the land or from the city by King Václav are not to be allowed to return. Further, that foreigners are not permitted to occupy any position, office, or dignity, whether ecclesiastical or secular, and particularly in towns where Germans held office when Czechs could and would be able to govern. In all of the courts in Bohemia lawsuits and sentences should be given in the Czech language and Czechs everywhere should have the right of initial voice in the kingdom and throughout its towns.

Also, that any citation of any external secular or ecclesiastical power not be permitted. Similarly, that all bulls and processes from the papal court relative to benefices or interdict, or any other similar documents not be admitted in the land [as valid] until there has been counsel taken by his royal grace with the lords [Bohemian Estates].

---

[8]   This is not altogether accurate. King Václav tolerated the practice of utraquism – communion to all the baptised in both elements of bread and wine – and in February 1418 limited Hussite religion to three churches in Prague. Never had he ratified the legitimacy of the lay chalice.

In like manner, those that are worthy of ordination are to be elevated without simony and any newly invented oaths or renunciations and should have mastered the liberal arts.[9]

Further, that his royal grace makes the land court accessible for all orphans, widows and other workers so that he, together in counsel with the lords [Bohemian estates], may eliminate appraisals, taxation and other disorders through amendment and examination of the Land Tables.

Also, that his royal grace guarantee not to assume property rights except in those cases where there is no clear testament or relative.

Further, that the treasuries of the Czech kingdom are neither removed nor dissipated, without the counsel of the lords [Bohemian Estates] and for the good and honour of the land, for they were gathered and retained for the common good of the Czech language and the kingdom for a long time.

These are the articles from the City of Prague.

Further, that the incidents perpetrated in the city by the community not be remembered by his royal grace. Further, that all brothels, prostitutes and concubines, together with other evil detriments against God the Lord and the community not be allowed in the city.

In like manner, that Jews throughout the kingdom not be permitted to lend money on just any guarantee, but that the security be shown first to the guarantor. This is on account of the fact that many thefts and swindles have occurred throughout the land that the Jews have no recourse and would thus die out.

Also, that there be no hindrance to the reading or singing of the epistles in the Czech language. Further, if there be some error concerning the faith anywhere in the kingdom, or if such was suspected, those teaching these errors should be examined by masters [of the university] in order for them [heretics] to be enlightened and informed by Holy Scripture. Those who refuse to accept such instruction may then be punished.

Also, that his royal grace should praise and confirm all of the acts and articles which the city councillors have enacted following the death of King Václav since these were all for the common good of the land and the city and were not contrary to the honour of his royal grace or his authority. Likewise, that his royal grace promise to uphold the liberties and laws of the land as well as those of the city [of Prague] and confirm this in writing. Similarly, that his royal grace condescends

---

[9]   The sense is somewhat obscure and should be understood that the students should be permitted to hear university teaching despite the fact that many of the masters were Hussite and therefore under ecclesiastical censure.

to give his acceptance to these articles and thus to confirm the law of God for the peace and unity of this kingdom and for the city of Prague.

AČ 3: 206–8.

9   First military action: Surprise attack at Živohošť

[With tensions rising in Bohemia, on both sides, and military action looming, Hussite radicals determined to congregate in Prague. As Hussite pilgrims from the town of Sezimovo Ústí moved through the Vltava River valley in early November 1419 on their way to Prague they were confronted by a superior force led by Lord Petr of Šternberk, a supporter of the crusade initiative. Unable to avoid the ambush a pitched battle ensued near the town of Živohošť. It was the first military engagement of the crusade period. See map 3.]

When the time came for the people to gather together on that day [St Ludmila's Day before St Martin's Day, i.e. 10 November] the barons in the pay of Sigismund, the king of Hungary, together with many castles and towns in the Kingdom of Bohemia, hindered with considerable effort the attempts of the people to come together. Because of this the great wars began. When people from Plzeň, Klatovy, Domažlice and Sušice, a large crowd of people, set off on the journey on the assigned day they let it be known by letters in order that they might come together the first day and lodge in Žinkovy. So it happened that they came together for the first time with weapons, and wagons and wearing armour because they intended to set off on the pilgrimage. The priest Koranda had commanded them to take with them scythes and other weapons to use against the goats saying that the goats wanted to eat the sprouts. 'Brothers! The vineyard of the Lord is flourishing in a wonderful way but goats are coming now who wish to eat the grapes. The time has come when wandering around with the staff is over. Now we march with swords in hand.' Their second lodging was in Březnice and third in Knín. At each stop for lodging the multitude increased until a very large crowd had assembled. That night a messenger from the people of Sezimovo Ústí who had also set off on the pilgrimage came to the people in Knín wishing to know where they could expect to meet up with them in order to join with them and thus come together to Prague or wherever God might direct them. He told them that alone they would hardly be able to get through the strongly held royalist areas. Hearing this, the people at Knín sent to them armed people on five wagons but these had to cross the [Vltava] river. Before they had gone a half mile from the river they spotted two crowds of people. One was very large, well vested and prepared including some 1300 horse with many banners. It was Petr of Konopiště with other mercenaries who had been sent from Kutná Hora. The second crowd of people were the common folk from Sezimovo Ústí along with the five wagons from Knín and perhaps up to 300 men and women. When those who had come from Knín to join those from Sezimovo Ústí saw this they discussed among themselves what they ought to do, whether to return to Knín or to carry on towards those from Sezimovo Ústí. They decided to join with the others from Knín and so they all drew after them together and went forward.

Meanwhile those from Sezimovo Ústí were able to take the hill on which they all gathered. Lord Petr and his men congregated on another hill close to that where the people of Ústí were without hesitation so that those who had come from Knín would not be able to join those from Sezimovo Ústí. Then he and his troops attacked those from Sezimovo Ústí and cut through them in such a way that his cavalry rode right through them. As they prepared to attack them a second time, the people from Sezimovo Ústí asked for mercy from Lord Petr. Those dead and injured lay on the ground. However, during the negotiations more than one hundred of the people from Ústí joined themselves to the company from Knín because they had escaped to another hill and were preparing to defend themselves by building a stone wall so that the cavalry could not get to them so easily. Those with Lord Petr began to negotiate with them and thus they surrendered themselves to the mercy of Lord Petr because they did not want to suffer the same fate as the people of Sezimovo Ústí. They were reluctant to do this hoping that help would come for they had seen the crowd from Knín coming with their banners. Lord Petr and his troops likewise saw this and immediately took the people of Sezimovo Ústí and went away in the direction of Kutná Hora. The other people remained over night at the very place where these things had occurred. On the next day priests celebrated mass and buried the dead before moving on to Prague. Despite the fact that the roads everywhere were strongly occupied, as well as the river crossings, they nevertheless forded the Sázava River near Jílové during the night and on the next morning they proceeded along the river bank to Prague past the New Castle of Kunratice [about one mile from Prague] in which Queen Žofie was staying at that time. I have extended this narrative so that future generations might know how this grievous war began in the Czech kingdom after King Václav died.

Before these pilgrims reached Prague, the people from the Old Town and the New Town had invaded and launched an assault on the Lesser Town on Saturday after All Saints' Day. Already many mercenaries had been placed in the archbishop's court and elsewhere and the Hungarian king Sigismund was paying them all thirty groschen per week plus horse even before he came into the country. The Praguers seized the military gear and horse of these mercenaries on the aforementioned day and caused great damage and burned the archbishop's court and other areas in the Lesser Town. The Praguers took their trophy of plunder from the Lesser Town back to the Old and New Towns. During the entire night they rang the bells admonished and incited by the priests, especially by Priest Ambrož, who had recently been exiled from Hradec Králové.[10] A large number of Táborites, including women, came to help the Praguers with considerable armour under their captain Mikuláš of Hus but were fired upon by the royalist cannon.[11] It was a night of grievance and distress, lamentation and sorrow much like the day of judgement so much so that Queen Žofie and Oldřich of Rožmberk fled from the castle of Kunratice in fear because the mercenaries were ineffectual in resisting. During the tenth hour of the night while few Praguers were still in the Lesser Town the royal mercenaries crept down from the castle and plundered the town hall of the Lesser Town, burned the books and damaged houses situated near the castle. The fires started by the mercenaries as well as by those of the Praguers gradually burned the entire Lesser Town. The Praguers occupied the Saxon house at the end of the bridge on the Lesser Town until the end of all the wars.[12] From this point on, all of the people began to talk about [Jan] Žižka for it was at this time that he began to wage war.

On Tuesday, St Britius' Day [13 November], a truce was agreed upon between the queen, Čeněk of Vartenberk, the Lord High Burgrave of the kingdom, other barons and the captains of the Prague Castle on one side and the community of Prague on the other [which was to last] until the following St George's Day [23 April 1420]. This was approved by senior spokesmen on both sides under a penalty of fifty thousand groschen. As part of the agreement the community of the New Town transferred control of Vyšehrad to the courtiers of the Hungarian king with whom they had made peace but these royal courtiers did not adhere to this.[13]

Žižka left at once for Plzeň and with the people of Plzeň had many military conflicts with Lord Bohuslav of Švamberk which could be described at some length. Lord Bohuslav conducted the war on behalf of King Sigismund and was greatly rewarded for it. Once when Žižka had set off from Plzeň to Nekměř with about three hundred people and seven wagons on which he carried those snakes [cannon] which are used to destroy walls, Lord Bohuslav intercepted him outside of the town with more than 2,000 cavalry and foot soldiers. He attacked Žižka directly, assuming victory, but Žižka and his followers rebuffed him from their

[10] On the important figure of Ambrož see Jan B. Lášek, 'Priest Ambrož and East-Bohemian Utraquism: Hradec and Oreb', in *BRRP* 3, pp. 105–18.

[11] Miloslav Polívka, 'Nicholas of Hus: One of the leading personage [sic] of the beginnings of the Hussite Revolution', trans. Jaroslav Tauer *Historica* 28 (1988), pp. 75–121.

[12] The 'Saxon' House guarded access to the western approach to the bridge over the Vltava River. It had previously been the residence of the dukes of Saxony, hence its name.

[13] On Vyšehrad, see doc.42.

wagons and Hyněk of Nekměř was killed. Žižka retreated through the night as he wished and made three attacks on the garrison.

SRB 3: 29–33.

10　Apocalyptic climate in Bohemia

[The crusades against Hussites were perceived by those under attack in Bohemia as symptomatic of the last days and very definite clues for understanding the deepening apocalyptic climate. This is the essential context for interpreting much of the early theology espoused and articulated by the more radical branches of the heretical movement. The following excerpts from an anonymous Táborite writer draws upon apocalyptic literature and the crises facing the Czech Kingdom mingling the warnings of the Biblical prophets with the words of Hussite preachers.[14]]

Now is the time of great suffering foretold by Christ and the apostles and the prophets in the Holy Scriptures and by St John in the Apocalypse. It has arrived, standing at the gates, and has already begun. During this time God the Lord commands the chosen ones to depart from the wicked as it says in Isaiah 51. Depart from among them my people in order that everyone might save their soul from God's anger and escape punishment . . . . Through St John God says, get away from these things my people and do not partake in this sin for their sins have come up even unto heaven. . . . Now the lion has emerged from his den and the heathen destroyer has come against God and the law of God. In like manner the Hungarian king [Sigismund] . . . has left his own city in Hungary and has come to destroy your land. Cities will be obliterated. No one will live there. Since you know these things you should pay close attention to the Lord God . . . . Do not be distracted by those who do not believe and are disobedient and who assert that such things will not happen any time soon . . . . If you wish to be faithful you must not dismiss sacred prophecies. God the Lord speaks through Amos the prophet in chapter nine saying, those who are sinners among my people shall die by the

---

[14]　On Hussite apocalypticism see Howard Kaminsky, 'Chiliasm and the Hussite Revolution' *Church History* 26 (1957), pp. 43–71, Kaminsky, 'Nicholas of Pelhřimov's Tábor: An adventure into the Eschaton', in *Eschatologie und Hussitismus*, eds. František Šmahel and Alexander Patschovsky (Prague: Historický ústav, 1996), pp. 139–67; Thomas A. Fudge, 'The night of Antichrist: Popular culture, Judgment and revolution in Fifteenth-Century Bohemia' *CV* 37 (1995), pp. 33–45 and Amedeo Molnár, 'Apocalypse XII dans l'interprétation hussite' *Revue d'histoire et de philosophie religieuses* 45 (1965), pp. 212–31.

sword because they maintain that while evil may come it will not fall upon us. In the same way there are those presently who assert that this will not occur in our time or even in the time of our children [Amos 9:10].

AČ 6: 43–4.

11   The beginning of woes

[The anonymous chronicle of the university in Prague, a composite text, contains strident anti-Hussite commentary. The perspective throughout is anti-Táborite and Czech scholars have suggested the chronicle may have been compiled by more than one author. It only goes as far as 1421. The excerpts below cast the Hussites in an unfavourable light.]

[After the deaths of Jan Hus and Jerome of Prague at Constance] their disciples and followers, from that time on in Bohemia, expelled priests from the country, burned churches and monasteries. They did this to such an extent that with the exception of three cloisters, they were all burned down and destroyed. They killed priests by burning them and others also whenever they could and this murdering went on many years both here and in other lands . . . . In the year of the Lord 1419 much secret wickedness increased in every part of the land of Bohemia to such a degree that no one was able to escape the confusion and the awful consequences. I have heard strange and awful things about those people [Hussites] who at one time surpassed all others in the earth in terms of wisdom, truth and in the knowledge of God, and in perfect holiness, justice, glory and honour. Look at how those once enlightened have fallen into error. Even the clerics who ought to know better along with ordinary people, both men and women, who once were standing in holiness and justice have become perverted and are now workers of iniquity. Therefore, do not make an effort to become secure in this world because you will fall. Just as the light of the sun is shadowed by the clouds, even so are the confused by the darkness of error and have gone down the wrong road.

Chronicon universitatis Pragensis, in FRB 5: 579–82.

12   A ruling on the use of force to defend the faith

[Sometime in February 1420 Jan Žižka and Lord Břeněk Švihovský of Skála, of the Rýzmberk family, formally made request of the masters of Charles University in Prague to pass a ruling on whether priests might lawfully use force and under what conditions lay people might be permitted to take up arms in defence of the faith. The answer of the Prague masters was given on 17 February 1420.]

The peace of Christ which exceeds all understanding, Greetings. Dear sir and prominent defender of the law of Christ. Although the brevity of this letter is insufficient to address completely the complexity of the two questions brought to us by your lordship's letter, in order that there may be no accusation of treachery against the revealed truth, or its free proclamation, or any suspicion of carnal fear, we respond in the first instance to your second question wherein you ask whether it is permissible for the secular estates to fight for the honour of God, the building up of the church and the promotion of the truth of the gospel with the use of coercive power and the material sword. It is safer and better and less dangerous to fight for the truth and the law of Christ in the manner that Christ practised patiently all of his life from the moment of birth to the end which he showed by example and through teaching instructed the church to follow. Plainly John 3 says: 'God did not send God's son into the world to judge with coercive power but to save the world through himself through patience and death' [John 3:17]. Similarly, Matthew 5 says, 'You have heard that it was said by the ancients, an eye for an eye, a tooth for a tooth. But I tell you, do not resist evil. Should someone strike you on the cheek, show him your other cheek also' [Matthew 38–40]. Further, 'be perfect even as your father is perfect' [Matthew 5:48]. And he says in the tenth chapter [10:25] if they call the father of the family Beelzebub they will even more refer in like manner to the children. And John 14: 'I give you my peace, I give peace to you' [John 14:27]. The same instruction is demonstrated in like fashion plainly in I Peter chapter 2[:21]: 'Christ suffered for us thus leaving an example to follow his pattern.' And further in chapter 3[:17], 'If we suffer for justice we are blessed. It is certainly better to suffer as doers of good as pleases God, then to be evil doers.' And further in chapter 4[:1]: 'so Christ suffered in the flesh and you must arm yourselves with the same attitude.' In Romans 12[:19] 'Do not defend yourselves, my dear ones, and do not make any provision for anger.' Plainly, in Ephesians 6[:12–13] 'we are not to fight against flesh and blood but against the princes and powers and the rulers of the world of darkness and against spiritual wickedness in the heavens. Therefore, receive the armour of God in order to resist in the day of evil.' Further in I Corinthians 6[:7]: 'Why not suffer wrong, why not rather endure more offense?' Patience is necessary, says the apostle, in order to do the will of God and obtain the promise [Hebrews 10:36]. Every Christian must seek to enter the narrow way, which is secure, and through which everyone fighting patiently in love, even though they may be killed, will nevertheless always win and obtain the crown of victory through which also Christ, the apostles and all of the martyrs have reached the Kingdom of God and this way is the safest to be emulated according to these examples.

However, there is another means of fighting for truth and justice, and even though it is dangerous for the body and also for the soul it is permissible for the secular powers to take up arms which Christ himself did rarely – only once – in using coercive force in ejecting from the house of God through the use of a whip those buyers and sellers. This is an example certainly of those holding secular power and the sword, using weapons against the enemies of the house of God, which is the church, and the law of the gospel, truth and justice, to avenge the evil and praise the good. To such powers, the apostle says, everyone must be in subjection, Romans 13, and whoever serves God does not carry the sword without cause and they have it not only from necessity but also by command [Romans 13:1–5]. The apostle says that such are to be honoured. Neither is it permitted for anyone to receive the sword without guilt. Augustine says plainly in the second book of 'Against the Manicheans': 'It is not right for anyone to take up the sword unjustly or arm themselves for bloodshed without permission or command from a superior and legitimate power.'[15] In the natural body the eyes and the feet do not fight by themselves, even though the eyes control and the feet carry the instruments, so also in the church of God it is permitted to fight with material weapons but this right can only be given by the higher authorities and not from priests, the lower powers or their dependents. Hence, it is permissible only for elevated secular powers to prepare for war either for temporal matters or for the peace of the public good. The same applies to the gospel and the Law of Christ though there are laudable conditions in the law which must be observed. First, that it is for the cause of God, truth or justice. Second, that there is love for one's opponents. Third, that the impulse comes from God and fourth, that it is essential to go to war because it is impossible to avert the enemy from confrontation by any other means. It would be better to retreat from the adversary than to fight quickly.

In this endeavour there are things to be avoided and which are condemned by law relating to war. Augustine says in 'Against the Manicheans' that the desire to harm, the cruelty of vengeance, the insatiable rage of rebellion, the lust for domination are all matters which, if they exist, are condemned by law in the context of war.[16] Because it is difficult in carnal warfare to observe these laudable goals and difficult to avoid these condemnations, it is therefore not easy to fight just wars in love. It seems to us, then, that no one should presume under the pretense of this licence, as some will undoubtedly think, to break down the walls of monasteries, churches or altars, to plunder or abuse priests or anyone else.[17]

---

[15] Augustine, 'Contra Faustum Manichaeum', book 22, chapter 74 in PL 42: 447–8.
[16] Ibid.
[17] This admonition was quickly set aside by Hussite armies and the damages inflicted upon churches, religious houses and the religious were both widespread and severe.

As to the other question which asked whether it was permissible for the faithful adherents of the Law of God to gather together to the honour of God, for the strengthening of the church and the promotion of the truth of the gospel we answer in the affirmative. Since no prior congregation of the faithful seems to be attested in Holy Scripture, such convening for the aforementioned praiseworthy purpose, namely for a good purpose, is to be recommended. Many crowds came together to Christ not just in synagogues and temples, but also in the deserts and on the mountains to hear the word of the Lord. The faithful also gathered together many times during the apostolic age as is described very clearly in the New Testament. Similarly, in the Old Testament, Judges 20, all the sons of Israel like one man from Dan to Beersheba and the land of Gilead came to the Lord and all the tribes of Israel gathered into the church of God to avenge the abomination of pollution. Also in I Kings 7, IV Kings 14, Nehemiah 9 and Joel 2 as well as in many places in Holy Scripture the gatherings of the faithful are recalled.

The assertion of this truth should not allow for any occasion of robbery, rape, murder, destruction of churches, or houses of the clergy, God is the witness of our intention. We intend that all God's people should assemble together in the peace of Christ with the proper respect which churches and temples were consecrated for and that to hear the word of God and the receiving of the eucharist according to the apostle in I Corinthians 11 where he assigns the assembly to gather in churches rather than in the fields and mountains and especially not in such places where there is a threat of scandal and danger.

In replying to your questions, to the extent the brevity of this letter permits, let your lordships be satisfied and may also God the Lord fortify your affection and good intention for the law of Jesus Christ and grant you constant perseverance and progress in his eternal law leading to ultimate happiness. Written in the year of the Lord 1420 on Carnival Saturday.

František Bartoš, 'Do čtyř pražských articulů', in *Sborník příspěvků k dějinám hlavního města Prahy* 5 (1932): 577–80.

13   Battle at Sudoměř

[On March 22 or 23 Žižka set out from Plzeň on a journey to Tábor with about 400 armed men and twelve gun-carrying wagons. Only nine of the men were mounted: Žižka, Břeněk, Václav Koranda, the Táborite priest Markold of Zbraslavice and five other leaders. An armistice signed at Plzeň should have negated the possibility of military engagement. However, the Royalists did not adhere to the truce. Several contingencies of Royalist forces, informed by intelligence reports of Žižka's movements, intercepted the Hussites on the morning of 25 March 1420 and by afternoon a pitched battle was in full force. See map 3. The confrontation buttressed the Hussite movement significantly, enhanced the lustre of Žižka's reputation and was another failure on the part of the Royalists to contain the popular heretical movement. It only served to further ignite the growing Hussite resolve and to bring on the full force of the crusade.]

In the year 1420 after the birth of the son of God, the Hungarian king Sigismund arrived in Wrocław. Here he caused to be burned to death Jan Věnečky of Prague. [Manuscript E reports that] he commanded that two citizens of Prague be burned in Wrocław and before this, that they be dragged through the streets by horse. The first was [Jan] Krása. The second was a house owner from the New Town [of Prague]. He also commanded that twenty-six elders of Wrocław be decapitated.[18]

At the same time, during that winter, the town of Tábor was founded by a student named [Jan] Hromádka together with some other brethren.[19] Hromádka settled there and then sent for Brother Žižka to come with enforcement for the settled area. Žižka sent Chval of Řepice and Machovice with some of the brethren for enforcement. They settled on the mountain and renamed it Tábor. It had previously been known as Hradiště. Many years earlier there had been a town there but the people of that town resisted their lords, the barons of Ústí, and their hereditary lords exterminated them and thus the town remained desolate until this present re-settlement.

From this time, when Žižka had sent the reinforcements from Plzeň, his opponents saw that his position in the town was weaker, they began to rise up against each other in the town of Plzeň and to occupy the houses of each other. And when he [Žižka] saw the rioting in the town, he withdrew on the feast day of Our Lady during the fast. However, plenty of his enemies, along with common folk, followed after him among them Lord Jindřich of Hradec, the soldier of the cross from Strakonice.[20] At the very most, Žižka had 400 people including women and the children of the warriors. He had twelve armed wagons and nine men riding horse. The only baron with him at the time was Břeněk lord of Rýzmberk and Dolany. When he had progressed to Štěkeň and continued on towards Sudoměř, the royalists arrived from Písek in force, many on horse, well supplied and armoured. Because of this armour they were known as the Iron Lords and are [known as] such to this day. These drew near to Žižka in the direction of Plzeň. When they were apprised by their sentries that Žižka was approaching Sudoměř, the soldiers set off to intercept him. On one side of the river, Lord Jindřich of

---

[18] Sigismund's atrocities were outlined and underscored in a letter to the Venetians in July 1420. UB 1, pp. 39–43. See doc.33.

[19] Hromadka was a former sexton or acolyte. *Historia Hussitica*, in FRB 5, p. 357. See doc. 52.

[20] Jindřich was the grand master of the Order of the Knights of St John.

Hradec, the soldier of the cross from Strakonice, gathered together many from the region of Písek constituting an enormous force against such a small group of people. By this time, Žižka had passed by Sudoměř and approached the pond named Škaredý. Since he was unable to go any farther because his enemies had surrounded him, he ordered that his wagons be turned against the dam, for the pond was empty without any water in it, and there he with his little people bravely defended themselves against the superior force. Many people were confident that they would not even have to use their weapons but would be able to crush the Hussites with the hooves of their horse. But the Lord God was with them [Hussites] and an unprecedented miracle occurred. Although it was still early, around about vespers, the sun went down behind the hill and darkness fell so heavily that no one could tell exactly who they were fighting. The aforementioned Lord Břeněk, helper of Brother Žižka was killed and many of the Royalists were either wounded or killed. It is certain they killed each other more than they suffered from the Hussites. When they saw this many voices cried out, my lance does not stab, my sword does not pierce and my crossbow does not shoot. Thus they withdrew in great shame having suffered great damage.[21] Žižka remained on the battlefield that night. At daybreak he ordered his people and his wagons to travel on through the field to Újezdec Castle. He waited there until those of Tábor sent for him. He was welcomed at Tábor with great ceremony and much honour.

Immediately on Good Friday, Žižka with his men came from Tábor and invaded Vožice during the night. He broke through the wooden defences which enclosed the town upon the Iron Lords who had gone to Vožice. With a great shout they set the town on fire and killed many of the Iron Lords. They collected many horse and armour. Žižka distributed the horse and the armour to his men and used these to train his men to ride and fight in the struggle. From this time on, the Táborites rode horse.

Through the summer and winter, older captains and priests amused the peasants greatly because they sold their own villages and placed the money into troughs.[22]

In that same year, Easter Monday, the Praguers dug a moat against Vyšehrad on the New Town side in five days. Priests, students, maids and Jews worked. They occupied the Emmaus Monastery and the Churches of St Apollinaris and

---

[21] Aeneas Sylvius claims Žižka instructed the women to place their long veils on the ground. When the royalist cavalry dismounted to attack the Hussites, their spurs would become entangled in the cloth trains and they would thus be unable to advance properly. The tale is dubious. *Historia Bohemica*, chapter 40, pp. 114, 116.

[22] On these common chests, see Thomas A. Fudge, '"Neither mine nor thine": Communist experiments in Hussite Bohemia' *Canadian Journal of History* 33 (1998), pp. 25–47 and Kaminsky, *A history of the Hussite revolution*, pp. 331–2. For an expression of concern with respect to the social implications of the Hussite heresy see the introduction to doc.101.

Our Lady at Botiče because Vyšehrad was occupied and retained and held with great strength.

In that same summer, on the Wednesday after St Tiburtius, Lord Čeněk of Vartenberk, told Veselí, the burgrave of Prague Castle, that the castle should be turned over to the community of Prague and he promised them that he would stand with them against the king of Hungary. He forced many people out of the castle and robbed them of their goods. Then on the Tuesday before St Stanislav's day, Lord Čeněk holding the castle for the Praguers betrayed them and gave it back to the king of Hungary. And the next day the Strahov Monastery was burned down as were the monasteries of St Thomas and St Nicholas in the Lesser Town.

SRB 3: 33–5.

14   Crusaders stopped at Poříčí

[Other battles in the pattern of Sudoměř were fought shortly thereafter. In marching to the defence of Prague in the spring of 1420 Hussite armies left Tábor on 19 May and reached Benešov where they were intercepted by a small crusader force. The town went up in flames. The crusaders retreated to a monastery nearby. Žižka and his troops marched on to the Sázava River. Here they were engaged by a much stronger force commanded by Václav of Dubá and the Florentine condottiere Filippo Scolari, Count of Ozora, better known as Pipo Spano. Near the village of Poříčí, the Hussite armies drew their wagons into closed formation, dug a moat around the perimeter and proceeded to engage the crusaders. While crusader losses were not substantial they gave up hope of penetrating the wagon fortress. Leaving their dead as well as numerous banners showing the red cross of the crusade on the field, they retired in defeat. The battle of Poříčí went to the Hussites. *Chronicon veteris Collegiati*, in Höfler, vol. 1, p. 80. See map 3.]

Upon receiving request from Prague, the Táborites did not hesitate to march from Hradiště to Prague with their priests, women, children, and a large number of wagons. However, they left many people behind to guard the mountain of Hradiště near Ústí. When they approached the town of Benešov, a large number of infantry and cavalry marched out and tried to prevent them from entering the town. But they entered the town from the other side by force, and all the people ran away from the town to the monastery and into the fields. Then the Táborites burned the church, the monastery, the vicarage and all the rest, and they attacked the monastery so fiercely that they would have uprooted it, had not the flames prevented them from doing so. From there they marched to the village of Poříčí. They crossed the [Sázava] river, and camped on the field near the water with the intention of spending the night there. But when they discovered that their enemies were quite close, they harnessed their horses to the wagons and kept marching without rest. But their enemies organised themselves into three groups, and attacked them, surrounding them from all sides. There were the captains Václav of Leštno and Petr of Šternberk and Konopiště, Janek of Chotěmice, Pipo, and Václav Donínský. Despite nightfall, the Táborites fought mightily against their enemies with their halberds, maces and flails. Their enemies ran and twenty of them were killed. They captured their lances and banners [which had] red crosses with the Passion painted on them. After this, no one obstructed their way.

On the twentieth day of the month of May, Táborites of both genders arrived in Prague by the thousands. Their priests, held high the sacrament on a monstrance pole, marching in front of the people into the town of Prague, which they entered during vespers. The inhabitants of Prague met them with crowds of students and priests and gave them a fine welcome and provided them with provisions in large quantities, since much of it was found in houses of those who had fled, especially various beverages. The women were housed in St Ambrose monastery. The Táborites, with their wagons and cavalry, camped on the island [today called Štvanice] in front of the Poříčská gate, and there they had their temporary accommodation. Their priests preached to them God's word daily and encouraged them to fight as men in the name of God's law, and especially urged them to receive the communion of the body and blood of the lord. And people received the communion of the body and blood of our lord Jesus Christ from them with such zealousness, that they [the priests] gave it to them, so that the people were always prepared to fight.

Of the names of those Táborites, there were the following captains: Mikuláš of Hus, the burgess of the New Town and a member of the great council, Zbyněk of Buchov, Chval of Řepický [of Machovice] and the extremely courageous and brave one-eyed Jan Žižka.

Historia Hussitica, in FRB 5: 370–1.

15   Pre-crusade suppression of Hussite heretics

[Beginning in 1412, heretics associated with the Hussite cause, were executed in Bohemia. After the Council of Constance condemned Jan Hus and Jerome of Prague a strategy of suppression began. In 1416 in Kutná Hora, the German preacher Hermann, appealed to the citizens of that town to kill anyone who took the chalice in communion. The Council of Constance had ruled that the practice was illicit and therefore prohibited. In 1419 the city council offered rewards to anyone who turned Hussites in: one groschen for a layperson, five groschen for a priest. See doc.71. Those captured were thrown into the mine shafts. According to the Hussite chronicler Vavřinec of Březová, in 1419 more than 1,600 Hussites were disposed of in this manner in the numerous mine shafts in Kutná Hora. There is a fifteenth-century illumination depicting this in the Smíškovský gradual which dates from the early 1490s. Vienna, Österreichische Nationalbibliothek suppl. mus. sam. MS 15492 fol. 285^r. Reproduced in Fudge, p. 97. These massacres were long remembered and references can be found with some regularity in Hussite sources.]

During this time both priests and the laity, faithful Czechs, assented to the communion in both kinds and with great reverence received it. They deplored the unjust death of Jan Hus, of holy memory, who died a horrible death on account of the evil priesthood in the Kingdom of Bohemia and the Margraviate of Moravia especially the bishops, canons, abbots as well as parish priests. They had been unable to tolerate his admonishments, exhortations and sermons for he denounced their pride, simony, avarice, lives of fornication and detestable abominations and uncovered the sins they refused to abandon. So they obtained false witnesses against him at the Council of Constance through gifts of money and were aided by the Hungarian king, Sigismund. These faithful Czechs, I must tell you, suffered great trouble, tribulation, grievance and torment from the enemies of the truth and those who blasphemed and they were robbed, and put to the torture of cruel imprisonment, hunger, thirst and death. The enemies of the truth pursued the priests and the laypeople who were zealous for the chalice throughout many different parts of the country. They turned them over to the miners of Kutná Hora and some were sold to them. These people of Kutná Hora, who were German, cruelly persecuted the Czechs, especially those who loved the teaching of Christ. With great blasphemy they tortured them and inhumanly threw them, especially at night, into the deepest pits and mine shafts. Some were still alive [when they were thrown down] while others were beheaded first. This was done primarily at the shaft near St Martin's Church past the Kouřim gate. This shaft was called Tábor. So great was the cruelty of these miners against the faithful Christians who adhered to the law of God that in a short period of time more than 1,600 who supported the holy communion of the chalice were murdered wretchedly by them and thrown into the shafts and the executioners were often exhausted by the exertion of the slaughter. But this inhuman rage against the faithful Christians was followed with divine revenge. As punishment for the numerous murders of the faithful there, this mining city was utterly destroyed and burned down.

Historia Hussitica, in FRB 5: 351–2.

16 Letter of Sigismund to the town of Budyšin

[Sigismund's letter reveals official support for the policies and practices of Hussite repression already in place. This letter is representative of efforts at demonizing the heretics and thereby maintaining popular support for the initiatives aimed at suppressing the Hussite cause.]

Sigismund, by the grace of God, king of the Romans, ever Augustus, king of Hungary, Bohemia, etc. To the noble Wilhelm, Landgrave of Thüringia and Margrave of Meißen, our gracious uncle and prince.

Noble and gracious prince. We have in mind, as probably your grace already has knowledge, the fact that the Bohemian lords together with other knights and vassals along with the common people have adopted a new faith in opposition to God, the holy church, the Christian faith and are opposed to us, as their legitimate and hereditary lord, and to our authority. We have attempted to set them straight again with much effort and with considerable and gracious eagerness but thus far it has, regrettably, done little good. Instead they have become more obstinate and more wicked in their beliefs. Presently we ourselves, together with many princes, knights and vassals, and other pious people, intend to proceed to Kutná Hora to lead a campaign against these same Wyclifites in hopes of suppressing and exterminating them with the help of God. This affair concerns our faith, the whole of Christendom as well as your grace. Additionally, if these people are not subdued in a timely fashion they could easily rise up greater in the land. Therefore we earnestly and urgently desire that your grace would assist us, the holy church and all of Christendom, as soon as possible with your power in dealing with the aforementioned disobedient and contrary Wyclifites so that we might exterminate and eliminate this heresy so that other lands likewise would not be deceived and poisoned by them. For your support and gracious favour you shall merit divine reward and the praise of the holy church and all Christendom. Given in the thirty-third year of our Hungarian reign and in the tenth year of our Roman reign.[23]

UB 1: 28–9.

---

[23] Among recent work on Sigismund: Elemér Mályusz, *Kaiser Sigismund in Ungarn 1387–1437*, trans. Anikó Sznodits (Budapest: Akadémiai Kiadó, 1990), Jörg K. Hoensch, *Kaiser Sigismund: Herrscher an der Schwelle zur Neuzeit 1368–1437* (Munich: Verlag C.H. Beck, 1996) and Thomas Krzenck, 'Zikmund Lucemburský: Liška na trůně' ČČH 95 (1997), pp. 460–72.

17   Song about Archbishop Zbyněk

[Zbyněk Zajíc of Házmburk (1377–1411) purchased the archbishopric of Prague in 1402. Previously he had been awarded the living of the Mělník priory in 1389 when he was twelve years old. He supported the reform efforts of Jan Hus for several years then turned foe. He came into sharp conflict with King Václav over which pope to support during the protracted papal schism and was driven from Prague before the wrath of the king and the outrage of the multitudes supporting Hus. During his later life and after his sudden and premature death, Zbyněk became an object of scorn. This song underscores the Hussite resolve to fight for their faith utilizing the deceased prelate as an example of those resisting truth. The original order of verses two and three have been reversed for the sake of clarity.]

Hear Knights of God
Get ready for battle
Sing bravely and praise God
In order that we might have peace.

Antichrist is already marching around
With a blazing fire
He has given birth to an arrogant priesthood
May God take note of it!

He orders them to prevent preaching
To become lords of the world
To ridicule the apostles
Such is his instruction!

Zbyněk, why did you resist so much?
Speaking harshly against priests
Thus suppressing the truth of Christ
Towards which you were enraged in your heart.

In order to court Antichrist
He took up with the canons
Resisted the humble ones
You who are not enlightened.

In the past the hare
Who forced its way upwards

Did not wish to be concerned
With obeying the orders of the lion.[24]

O God, let the lion rise up,
Tear to pieces the mischief of the clergy
Promote the Law of Christ
Let Hus teach you how.

There is an old and good proverb
Which says, it is impossible
For the honest Czechs to be heretical
This is what all the countries are saying.

Both grass and air flourish
Lament, you silly man
Gold and precious stones
Commiserate with us.

Angels and archangels
You spouses of Christ
Thrones and apostles
Lament with us.

May the holy Trinity
Through the body of Christ
And the work of the saints
Not permit the faithful to perish. Amen

Nejedlý, III: 442–3.

---

[24] Zajíc in Czech means 'hare' and the lion has been a symbol of the Czech Crown since the twelfth century. The lion here means King Václav and the conflict between the hare and the lion refers to the dispute over reform and the papal schism.

Chapter 2

The First Crusade: Prague, 1420

18   The anti-Hussite bull 'Inter Cunctus' of Martin V

[This bull confirmed the acts of the Council of Constance with respect to the decisions made relating to Jan Hus, Jerome of Prague and John Wyclif. This lengthy document includes the final thirty articles of condemnation against Hus and forty-five other articles aimed at detecting Wyclifite or Hussite heresy. The pope addresses his concerns to the ecclesiastical hierarchy and inquisitors in the territories of Bohemia, Moravia, Austria, Germany, Silesia and Poland, arguing that the Devil had incited the followers of Hus and these heretics were to be tracked down and punished. The bull was concluded at Constance on 22 February 1418. In the same year the pope charged the cardinal of Dubrovnik, Jan Dominici with the preparations for a crusade against the Hussite heretics, sending him to Hungary and Bohemia. He died in Buda on 10 June 1419.]

Martin, bishop and servant of the servants of the Lord, to our esteemed brothers, archbishops of Salzburg, Gniezno and Prague, bishops of Olomouc, Litomyšl, Bamberg, Meißen, Passau, Wrocław, Regensburg, Kraków, Poznań, and Nitra, and our beloved children, inquisitors appointed by the prelates named here, as well as to all others to whom this letter might come. Greetings and apostolic blessings.

Among all of the other pastoral duties by which we are burdened the main one which concerns us is this. Heretics with false doctrine and errors must be expelled completely from the fellowship of Christians and uprooted as utterly as God will enable us to accomplish, so that the true Catholic faith might remain stable and unpolluted in order that all Christians might be immovable and unmolested and might be able to remain firm in the sincere faith with all shadow of uncertainty eliminated. However, in certain places in the world, namely Bohemia and Moravia, and in the adjoining areas, certain heresiarchs have arisen against not just one but numerous doctrines of the Catholic faith. They are confiscators of land, schismatics, and seditious, filled with the pride of the devil and the madness of wolves. They have been deceived through Satanic subtlety and in terms of evil have gone from bad to worse. Despite the fact that they arose in different parts of the world they are all one, with their tails joined together as it were.[1] Namely, John Wyclif of England, Jan Hus of Bohemia and Jerome of Prague of damnable memory and they have gathered together no small number of unfaithful [causing] ruin and misery.

When these people and other troublesome persons began to spread their poisonous doctrines and stubbornly disseminated perverse and false ideas, the priests who had the duty and the power of the law behaved like dogs unable to bark. They did not take vengeance like the apostle against such disobedience nor did they physically throw them out of the house of the Lord, as required by certain canons. Instead they tolerated these pestiferous and crafty heretics, together with their wolf-like rage and cruelty and this they did. They negligently permitted their erroneous and wicked teachings through inordinate delays and thus they grew strong and numerous. Many people did not receive the correct doctrine but rather the false, pernicious and damnable seeds which were sown among them. Accepting these things they fell away from the true faith and are now piteously entangled in the putrid errors of paganism. This is now to such an extent that these heretics and their followers have infected the Catholic followers of Christ in various places in the world and have thus caused them to rot in a filthy pile of excrement and lies. . . .

Therefore the aforementioned synod, to the glory of almighty God and the preservation of the Catholic faith and the expansion of the Christian religion and the salvation of human souls, has physically rejected and cast out of the house of God the aforementioned John Wyclif, Jan Hus and Jerome. Among other things they believed, preached, taught and maintained [ideas about] the sacrament of the altar, other sacraments and articles of faith in opposition to what the holy Church of Rome believes, holds, teaches and preaches. They have presumptuously and obstinately preached, taught, held and believed many other things to their own damnation as well as that of others. The said synod has declared them to be obstinate and imprudent heretics, separated from the communion of faithful people and spiritual outcasts. This same council enacted many other wholesome and profitable things relating to the procedures and canonical rules to be followed concerning those who have departed from the house of the Lord on account of these heretics and their erroneous teachings and how they may be returned to the paths of truth and surety.

Now to our grief we hear that not only in the Kingdom of Bohemia and the Duchy of Moravia and in the other places already referred to, but in other places near these areas there are possibly other sectarians and followers of these heretics

---

[1]   Third canon of the Fourth Lateran Council, 1215 condemns all heretics. 'They have different faces indeed but their tails are tied together inasmuch as they are alike . . . .' *Decrees*, vol. 1, p. 233.

and their heretical opinions. They have thrown behind themselves the fear of God as well as worldly shame and have received neither the fruits of conversion nor repentance because of the wretched destruction of the aforementioned Jan Hus and Jerome. Like men drowning in the pit of sin they do not cease to blaspheme the Lord God taking his name in vain, since the father of lies has damnably darkened their minds, and they read and study the books mentioned earlier containing these errors and heresies which the aforesaid synod has condemned to be burned. To their own peril as well as that of other simple minded people, they preach and teach these things in opposition to the statutes, decrees and ordinances of the synod, as well as canonical sanctions, to the great peril of souls, the disparagement of the Catholic faith and to the slander of many others. Considering that when error is not opposed it appears to be tolerated and adapted and having a desire to resist these pernicious and evil errors and uproot them completely from amongst the faithful Christians especially in the places already noted, Bohemia, Moravia and other bordering regions, to prevent their spread and growth, we command your discretion to our apostolic letters. The holy Council of Constance has approved and allowed that you who are archbishops, bishops and other clergy, and each of you individually or through other serious and appropriate persons for spiritual jurisdiction, undertakes to make sure that all persons of whatever rank, office, state or condition, regardless of whom they might be or by whatever name they are known, do not teach, preach or observe the exalted and excellent, wholesome and blessed sacrament of the blood of our Lord Jesus Christ, or the sacrament of baptism, confession of sins, penance, extreme unction or any other sacrament of the church and articles of faith, other than that taught, preached, held and observed by the holy and universal Roman Church. [The same shall apply to those] who dare with presumption and obstinacy, by any way or means, publicly or privately to hold, believe and teach the articles, books, or doctrines of the aforementioned heretics, John Wyclif, Jan Hus and Jerome of Prague, or their teachers, already condemned and damned by the Council of Constance. Those who presume publicly or privately to commend the heretics, their followers or supporters and favour or support the aforesaid errors must be punished severely. You must judge and sentence them as heretics and as notorious heretics leave them to the secular court and power. May the followers and defenders and supporters of such wicked persons, even if they themselves do not adhere to their errors but rather simply receive or entertain them with carnal affection or in friendship, in addition to the punishment due them by law and inflicted by competent judges such heinous acts, [be subjected to] severe pain and excruciating punishment in order to make them an example for others. Thus if the fear of God does not prevent them from leaving off such evil deeds, the severity of our discipline may constrain them.

As for the third type, those infected in any way by this damnable sect, shall be given competent instruction, they must repent and change their ways from these errors and the aforementioned sects and return to the unity of the holy mother church and acknowledge fully, by confession, the Catholic faith. The severity of the judges shall be tempered with mercy according to the facts. Furthermore we command with apostolic authority that you exhort and admonish all those who adhere to the catholic faith, emperors, kings, dukes, princes, margraves, lords, barons, knights and other magistrates, rectors, consuls, proconsuls, towns and villages, universities of the kingdoms, provinces, cities, castles, their lands and other places and all those who have temporal authority, that according to the form and demands of law, that they expel all of these heretics out of their lands, kingdoms, provinces, cities, towns, castles, villages and all other places. [This shall be] according to the spirit and intention of the Lateran Council [namely] that those who are publicly and manifestly known to you by their deeds, as sick and scabbed sheep who would infect the Lord's flock, must be banished and cast out now and always until there be a counter order from ecclesiastical judges or inquisitors holding to the faith and the communion of the holy Church of Rome.[2] They shall not be tolerated anywhere to preach or to maintain a house or family nor yet to hold any occupation or trade nor to associate in any manner with Christians.

Furthermore, if such publicly known heretics die, even if not specifically denounced by the church, they must not be permitted Christian burial, because of their great crime, no offerings can be given or received on their behalf. Their goods or belongings shall be confiscated according to canonical sanctions at the time of death. . . . The rest of them shall be dealt with by the temporal lords, leaders, judges or other officers and shall be put to death without delay. With concern for the prejudice and slander of the Catholic faith and religion through the pretext of ignorance or by excuse of subtle or crafty men pertaining to the apprehending of the aforementioned heretics, their defenders, adherents, those who favour and receive them, and also those suspected of heresy and similar perverse doctrines we give more specific instruction. Concerning the Kingdom of Bohemia and those areas nearby where this doctrine first began to be spread, we have thought it good to send the articles written below regarding the sect of these arch-heretics, for the better information concerning the Catholic faith. . . . [Then follows a list of the final thirty charges against Jan Hus.[3] This is followed by thirty-eight items to be investigated.]

Furthermore, we command and decree that should any person be found, by secret information, holding or suspected of any kind of the pestiferous sect, heresy

---

2   Lateran IV, canon on heretics in *Ibid.*, pp. 233–5.
3   Those brought against Hus at the Council of Constance in 1415. *Documenta*, pp. 225–34.

or teachings of these most wicked men, John Wyclif, Jan Hus and Jerome of Prague, the aforementioned heresiarchs, or of favouring, receiving, or defending the aforesaid damned men while they were living, their false disciples or any that adhered to their errors, or any after their deaths who prayed for them, or considered them among Catholic men, defended their place among the saints, either by preaching, veneration or in other ways, they deserve suspicion. . . .

Beyond this, you are to rise up firmly and with courage against such heretics and their goods, and laity according to the canonical sanctions enacted against heretics and their followers which we will order them and their disciples subject to. Such persons infected with the aforestated heresies and errors, or any of the constituent parts thereof, shall be obligated to purge themselves according to your judgement. The others who are convicted of the aforesaid heresies and articles, either by witness, their own confession or other allegations or proofs, shall be forced to revoke and abjure publicly and solemnly those articles and errors and shall suffer penance and punishment, even to perpetual imprisonment if necessary . . . . you may punish those heretics and those infected with heresy according to the canonical sanctions and traditions, with our authority and office, simply and plainly put without announcement and formal trial. If need be, they may be left and committed to the secular power. . . . Any other edict, indulgence, privilege or exemption, whether general or specific, to the contrary here granted from the apostolic see, for any person or persons not to be interdicted, suspended or excommunicated, or cited to judgement without the boundary of certain limits or any other thing whatsoever which might hinder, stop or impeach your jurisdiction, power and free proceeding by any means notwithstanding. Given at Constance, 22 February, in the first year of our papacy [1418].

The complete bull appears in English in John Foxe, *Acts and Monuments*, vol. 3 (New York: AMS Press, 1965): 557–67.

19   Proclamation of the crusading bull

[On 17 March the papal legate, Ferdinand, bishop of Lucena, publicly read from a pulpit in Wrocław the papal bull, 'Omnium plasmatoris domini', proclaiming a crusade against the Hussites. The usual plenary indulgence guaranteed that whoever took up arms against the heretics would receive absolution of all their sins. The bull was dated 1 March 1420 and had been dispatched from Florence on request by Sigismund. A month before the issuing of the bull, the so-called 'iron bishop' of Litomyšl, Jan Železný, an avowed enemy of Hus and the Hussites, arrived in Wrocław and may well have exerted influence on the king in terms of the crusade. As early as March 1416, Sigismund had spoken of the possibility of a crusade against the Czech heretics (*Documenta*, pp. 609–11). The context of that remark was a letter to certain Czech barons dated 16 March. The following year, on 4 December 1417, he wrote to his half-brother Václav, King of Bohemia, and said, 'we cannot regard you as our brother if you do not, in the manner of our forebears, exterminate all heretics . . . . let every Czech, German and Latin person be aware that I can scarcely wait for the day to come when I shall drown every Wyclifite and Hussite' Höfler 2: 252–4. The bull is an extension of 'Inter cunctus' and provides specific authority for the crusade.]

Martin the bishop, servant of the servants of God, to all venerable brethren, patriarchs, archbishops and bishops, dear elected sons, administrators, abbots, priors and other prelates of churches and monasteries, and to those who profess the Christian faith everywhere, this letter comes with salutations and with apostolic blessing.

Regardless of the lack of merit there might be, we act on earth on behalf of the Lord our creator who did not hesitate to offer himself as a ransom for our salvation and to make us part of the Lord's heritage, we act as guard of the flock in order that we might be called into the royal fold in the favour of our creator. It behooves us then to maintain a careful vigil in order that we might be profitable and with the help of the Lord's grace tend the sheep and not allow the flock to graze in infected pastures filled with the pitfalls of reprobates. We desire to reward the increase of those persisting steadfast and to compel those whose minds reject divine love by force to necessary repentance. We wish to encourage this by a hearty dispensation of the spiritual riches granted to the athletes of Christ with the sign of the cross ratified by our venerable brothers the cardinals of the holy Roman Church.

It is without doubt that our dearest son in Christ, Sigismund, king of the Romans, whom we have acknowledged on the basis of trustworthy witnesses as well as widespread and increasing report, prompted by divine inspiration, has not delayed in undertaking a great and worthy labour for the unity of the church which has been disunited at this time. This was not without great burden and heavy expense but urged by devotion to the faith and the piety of compassion toward an even further propagation of the Christian faith. On the basis of the purest motives and a yearning to use the power granted him as king to the praise of God he has turned against these people of profanity, evil and iniquitous reprobation, the Wyclifites and Hussites as well as others who have become fascinated by the darkness. With their disciples through superstitious assumptions and doctrines they have become maddened through these dogmas, errors and heresies. They study to subvert the true faith and to mislead the flock into danger through errors and devious methods into the outer chambers of hell. They and their adherents, those who accept them and protect them, must be removed and suffer the destruction of their bodies unless they desist from their errors and with sincere heart submit themselves to the traditions of the holy fathers. Emboldened by God, his [Sigismund] hand shall be strengthened and through his authority as protector of the church his arm shall be lifted up for the extirpation of such a lethal virus to souls. This matter shall be undertaken by divine direction, accepted completely by him, humbly imploring our help and that of the Catholic Church which consists of the congregation of the faithful for the joyful consummation of this enterprise.

We exceedingly praise with highest laud in the Lord the plan of redemption proposed by the aforementioned king of the Romans, who is also known as the king of Hungary, Bohemia, Dalmatia and Croatia, and offering our best wishes for the success of it. We fix our eyes on heaven and in terms of the negotiations of that which must be accomplished we admonish all kings, dukes, margraves, princes, barons, counts, administrators, captains, town councils and all other officers and their representatives, together with all towns and cities, universities, castles, villages and all other places and zealous people of the Christian name, of whatever condition, by paternal persuasion. We adjure you through the shed blood of our most holy redeemer, and for the forgiveness of sins, to arm yourselves powerfully and courageously for the purpose of exterminating the Wyclifites, Hussites and other heretics, their followers, protectors and those who receive them, and render support for the happy and successful execution of this task.

Therefore we commission you through apostolic writing and command you and those of your brothers, patriarchs, archbishops, bishops, administrators, abbots and prelates, that should you or any of you be instructed by the aforementioned king of the Romans to take action against these same heretics, their adherents, protectors and those who support them that you would regard this as obligatory, required by virtue of this letter for the execution of this matter. This should be announced clearly in the cities, dioceses and other appropriate places where it seems good to you to preach the word of the cross and have either suitably competent seculars [preachers] or members of one of the orders, chosen by your wisdom publicly present its admirable sign in order that all of those faithful to Christ may hear. Those who respond, through confession and true penance, shall have one hundred days of penance remitted by you on apostolic authority in order that more might be willing to support [the crusade] and be willing to receive the cross on their shoulders after being exhorted and admonished by you or by those chosen by you. Then they receive the cross with reverence and have it impressed upon their hearts in opposition to the perverse teachings and aims of the aforesaid Wyclifites, Hussites and other heretics, along with their followers, protectors and those who tolerate them so that they might proceed against them faithfully and with a fervent spirit.

Hence, in order to inspire the faithful to be more fervent, we refer to the grace they will receive from this with confidence in the mercy of almighty God and in the authority of the blessed Peter and Paul his apostles, and by the power of loosing and binding which has been granted to us by God, we impart that same grace to the faithful who take up the cross and who physically become part of the armies and by their own expense. Those who set out on a journey [to join the armies] should they die on the way shall receive the full remission of all their sins which they would have repented of in their hearts and confessed with their mouths. We promise the fullness of eternal life as a reward to these. To those who cannot go in person but who by their own expense, according to their means, designate suitable warriors, and to those who come personally, we grant the full remission of their sins. Further, so that those strengthened by the sign of the miraculous cross might show themselves taking part in the forgiveness of sin and in an easier indulgence, they shall also be freed from the burden of offene. We concede that the aforementioned king of the Romans and those who become leaders or captains in the army, choose and delegate as many of your brothers, patriarchs, archbishops, bishops, abbots and prelates as you require. Secular or regular priests can be conscripted to hear the confessions of all the crusaders, signed by the cross for those wishing to confess and after having diligently heard those confessions you can, by the same authority announce the absolution, having imposed the penance of redemption even to those guilty by law for their transgressions. All sins and excesses committed by them [shall be forgiven] even if they are violators of the clergy, arsonists, sacrilegious, whatever their fault, even those who transgress the commands of the king of the Romans or the leaders of the army during the process of the armies' movement against the same Wyclifites, Hussites and other heretics, their followers, protectors and those who receive them, as many times as necessary.

Because it is difficult to make this letter known to individuals, we wish that one, two, or as many of you brethren, patriarchs, archbishops, bishops, abbots and prelates as the aforementioned king of the Romans determines, might copy, transmit and announce this letter in the hand of a public notary and affirmed with his seal, to all persons and places where it seems reasonable to do so. To such copies we give the full power of the original. Given in Florence on 1 March in the third year of our pontificate.

UB 1: 17–20.

20   Sigismund promotes the crusade

[Orders for a crusade were dispatched throughout Silesia and Lusatia in March of 1420. German princes and ecclesiastical officials who had gathered at Wrocław for the Reichstag in January gave their backing. Friedrich of Brandenburg, an elector of the empire, left the Imperial diet unwilling to acquiesce in the crusade initiative. Friedrich had been made burgrave of Nürnberg, margrave of Brandenburg and imperial elector in 1415 by Sigismund. Friedrich would later play a key role in the crusades against the Hussites. On 9 April, Sigismund and his army left Wrocław and marched into Bohemia via Náchod. During this entire period he promoted the crusade. The following is an example of the king's letters in which he urged war on the 'heretics'.]

We, Sigismund, by the grace of God, king of the Romans, ever Augustus, king of Hungary, Bohemia, Dalmatia and Croatia, announce to all the prelates, lords, knights, vassals, mayors, councillors, and citizens of all the towns in the region of Žatec, our dear faithful people, our royal grace and good will.

Dear faithful ones. God the Lord commended to us, following the death of the most serene prince, our brother and lord, King Václav, the kingdom of Bohemia for an inheritance. Following this, it has been our duty, by our power and royal order, to uproot all nuisances in this laudable kingdom which causes disorder against the holy Roman Church and to exterminate it. Now that we wish to take up our inheritance we must consider that there are many dissensions, especially within the Christian faith, and also that there is much murmuring about our inheritance which had never been during the time of the most serene prince, Emperor Charles of blessed memory, our dear and gracious father, and such has never been heard of throughout Christendom. Now we must carry our royal duty with dignity and have taken an urgent concern for the best way, according to the advice and with the assistance of the princes, spiritual lords, barons, knights, and vassals, to bring back our kingdom of Bohemia to the order and obedience of the Roman Church and holy Christendom according to law and just as it was during the time of Emperor Charles of blessed memory, our dear father. Just as soon as faith and order can be restored, even with much effort and labour, we wish to carry this burden gladly upon our shoulders in the name of God. Therefore we command you all together under the same penalty to avoid Wyclifism and to provide them neither with advice nor any assistance nor help the people from Plzeň, Písek, Hradec Králové or other towns within the kingdom of Bohemia where they [the heretics] assemble. Do not join them or permit anyone else to. Avoid completely this new faith in order to keep the commandments of the church and this decree without murmuring. But if there should be anyone among you who does wish to do this, then such a person should be punished as he deserves. If you are unwilling to do this then report this to our noble captains: Čeněk of Vartenberk, Burgrave of Prague, Jindřich of Elsterberk, our chamberlain, and Václav of Dubá, our chamberlain, or to any other one of them.[4] We have commanded them to provide

---

[4]   Jindřich of Elsterberk was appointed Lord Chief Steward in charge of royal castles by Sigismund in 1419.

you with help against such disobedience when you notify them in order to correct the crime and disgrace. But should there be some who do not wish to keep this instruction and command, then such a one we condemn to death together with the forfeiture of his property. We wish that this command might be published and proclaimed in all of the towns of the same region of Žatec, and in all of the markets, in order that everyone may know about it, may keep it in mind, and may obey it.

Given in Wrocław on Saturday, the day of St Scholastica [10 February] in the thirty-eighth year of our reign in Hungary and in the tenth year of the Roman one.[5]

UB 1: 15–17.

21   Sigismund orders campaign preparations

[Throughout the crusading period, Sigismund enjoyed wide support in Silesia and Lusatia. The six-town league of Upper Lusatia was particularly important to the crusading cause. These six royal boroughs had traditionally been a league with exceptional power. They owned three-quarters of the land and in the Upper Lusatian diet their vote equalled that of the barons. The six towns are known by their more familiar German names: Bautzen (Budyšin), Görlitz (Zhorjelc), Zittau (Žitava), Lauban (Lubań), Löbau and Kamentz (Kamieniec).]

Sigismund, king of the Romans and for all times defender of the Empire, and king of Hungary and Bohemia wishes to make the following known to the six towns: Because he has the will to punish his opponents within the Crown of Bohemia and has determined to move against them, so now he commands them to prepare the greatest gun they have in their towns [cannon] as he will send for it. The captain, Baron Hlaváč of Lipé will command them to be ready and to accompany him with their weapons and personnel. Given in Wrocław on Thursday after Reminiscere [7 March], in the thirty-third year of our Hungarian reign and in the tenth year of the Roman one.

UB 1: 21.

---

[5]   On the role of the city of Wrocław during this period, see Frederick G. Heymann, 'City rebellions in 15th-Century Bohemia and their ideological and sociological background' *Slavonic and East European Review* 40 (1962), pp. 324–40.

22   An imperial plot revealed

[This anonymous, undated letter warns of the dangers threatening the Hussites and of the resolute attitude of Sigismund to see the heresy suppressed by any means. The letter reflects the king's resolve to exterminate the adherents of the lay chalice either through deception or through violence. It must be dated either to late March or early April, though a conclusive and precise date seems impossible. The carrier of the missive cannot be further identified beyond his name and occupation stated in the letter. There is some possibility that the addressee was Priest Jan Želivský, but this cannot be proven even though it seems likely.]

Honourable Lord Jan. Following the sermon yesterday evening I wanted to tell you what I previously told to Mikuláš the butcher, who bears this letter. I am aware that certain points of the sermon are known by hearsay, other points have actually been heard and in addition other points have been made known through notorious public deeds and this is not just hearsay. It is clear that when the unity agreement was made between the Old and New Towns of Prague shortly thereafter one of the councilmen of the Old Town sent word to Diváček the mint master of Kutná Hora telling him to come, otherwise the city could not be retained for the king on account of the unity within the [Prague] community. This has been reported by a certain squire. Further, according to that same squire, King Sigismund has ordered that all Wyclifites, of whatever state, are to be killed. If the servants of the king are unable to overcome [the heretics] by force and power, then they are to do so by deceit. If this cannot be accomplished by deceit then the same can be done through the use of flattering sermons and false promises and that this should be carried out in Plzeň, Písek, Hradec Králové, Klatovy and elsewhere.

Further, that an official of the Old Town, went through the streets showing a letter and saying, look, the best news we have from our lord the king is that he has abandoned the idea of a crusade against us.

Likewise on this point, I read one such letter which was intended for some lady from a famous squire and the cousin of the same lady or the lady's nephew wrote in this letter that the king recently sent three missives to Litoměřice in order that they should be compelled to force those who receive the sacrament of the Lord's body under both kinds to renounce this. If they are not inclined to do so then they are to be arrested in person and in property. Additionally, they are to prosecute, in the same way, squires and villagers known to them to be of this persuasion. If they are unable to overpower them [heretics], they are entitled to receive assistance from the sub-chamberlain and are to then strangle all such persons. Behold, in addition to the words of the official of the Old Town, I have read the letter addressed to the aforementioned lady.

This has been written briefly to you, not in the fullest manner, but that can be obtained from the carrier of the letter.

UB 1: 24–5.

23   Preachers excoriate the Emperor in sermons

[The role of popular preaching must not be downplayed in the Hussite response to the crusade. Jan Želivský was among the most outspoken of the clerics. As the reality of the crusade loomed, Želivský and others used their pulpits to rally support against the emperor. This chronicler's comment dates from March 1420.]

At that time, priests in Prague and especially Priest Jan, the preacher in the Church of the Mother of God of the Snows, a former monk from Želiv, was stirring up the people to resist the king whom he referred to as the red dragon since the king allowed his favourites to wear a golden dragon on their chests which was the sign of his order.[6] In this way, he denounced the king before all the common people. Large crowds of people gathered and eagerly listened to his sermons. He was eloquent though not a very good teacher. Inspired by his sermons and the preaching of other priests, many faithful people did not hesitate to risk the loss of their lives and properties for the truth of the communion of the chalice. These were brave knights of God mortifying their goods, bodies and the devil.

Historia Hussitica, in FRB 5: 360.

24   Policy and practice on taxes to fund a crusade army

[Václav of Dubá had been appointed Lord Chamberlain in 1419 with jurisdiction over the royal towns. He had been one of two knights who had accompanied Jan Hus to Constance in 1414, though, unlike his colleague Lord Jan of Chlum, he never became a Hussite.]

Václav of Dubá, the subchamberlain of the kingdom of Bohemia, to the honourable and faithful abbots, priors, provosts, convents and monasteries, and

---

[6]   The Sárkanyrend (in Latin *Societatis draconistrarum*), the Order of the Dragon, was founded in 1408 by Sigismund as an institution aimed at his protection. The symbol of the Order was a circular dragon with its tail wrapped around its neck. On its back was the red cross of St George. For a description of the functions of the Order see Windecke, p. 130.

to the wise mayors, councillors, and towns in the district of Žatec, pertaining to the royal chamber, our dearest friends, sincere greetings.

Honourable, prudent and dearest friends. We have decided on royal command by letter the sum of the royal tax presently imposed upon you in the same way as the other monasteries and towns. By command of the most serene prince and lord, Sigismund, king of the Romans, king of Hungary, Bohemia, Dalmatia, Croatia, our gracious lord, [this sum shall be] a means for suppressing and destroying the devilry and imprudence of the delinquents within the kingdom of Bohemia. This is payable to the royal chamber in the terms expressed in that letter to be sent to your university with this letter by a representative. This is a solemn requirement by royal authority to be firmly and strictly followed that each of you upon receiving the letter from the messenger, together with the letter indicating the amount due, affix your seal upon both of them in the usual manner and deliver them to us sealed, or to our notary, as you see fit, within fifteen days from the time of the delivery of the letter according to the content and the spirit of the letter which is made known to you along with this letter. There must be no delay if you wish to avoid severe royal disfavour as well as the seizure of your property and person which shall be done in such cases without delay.

Given at Vyšehrad in the year of the Lord, 1420, on Tuesday during the Feast of St George [12 March].

UB 1: 21–2.

25   Unrepentant heretics to be executed

[Sigismund's utilization of the crusade bull included further special instructions. In a letter to the authorities in Budyšin the emperor made it clear that when the crusade armies entered Bohemia all recalcitrant heretics refusing to submit were to be executed and their possessions confiscated. This order from the king was doubtless intended to be interpreted loosely by the invading force. Crusading armies traditionally had given little quarter to the enemy. The letter is dated 15 March 1420.]

We, Sigismund, by the grace of God, king of the Romans, ever Augustus, king of Hungary, Bohemia, Dalmatia, Croatia, etc., commend to the mayors, councillors and citizens of the town of Budyšin, our faithful ones, our grace and all good things. Dear faithful ones. Since it has been spread widely and known throughout the land, there is no need to describe to you the horrible faithlessness, folly, crimes and dishonourable deeds of the Wyclifites, otherwise called Hussites, which they have been perpetrating for a long time and do so daily by destroying churches and through many other inhuman things against the Christian faith, the holy Roman Church and therefore against us as well. Since we no longer intend to endure such faithlessness, and wishing to extirpate it completely with the help of God from the Kingdom of Bohemia, we have strongly ordered our subjects repeatedly to detain and capture them [the Hussites]. Those ordained or who are clerics should be taken to their bishop to give account. Those who are secular and who wish to convert from their faithlessness and do penance may enter again into the Christian faith and be obedient from now on to the holy Roman Church. Their superiors have the authority to impose such expiation and to receive the penance of redemption which our faith demands and the holy church has ordered. The aforementioned Wyclifites who do not wish to convert and who intend to persist in their faithlessness should be punished in person as well as in goods, exterminated or judged as is fit according to law. They should confiscate all of their assets and estates in our name. It seems to us that the Wyclifites might come to Budyšin seeking trade or business which is what we have in mind.

We command you firmly by this letter to proceed and to take action as necessary and as you see fit in accordance with our love and favour toward you. Given in Wrocław on the Friday after St Gregory's day [12 March] in the thirty-third year of our Hungarian reign and in the tenth year of our Roman reign.

UB 1: 22–3.

26   Hussite manifesto from Prague

[This manifesto was published in the name of the city of Prague and addressed to the Kingdom of Bohemia. It emerged from a meeting held in the city hall of the Old Town. This gathering owed its principal instigation to the efforts of the priest Jan Želivský and was attended by councillors and magistrates from both Old and New Towns, many Hussite priests as well as university masters. Those who were in this session swore to defend their religion and to uphold it without concern for life or limb. A military organization was decided upon and eight captains, four from each town, were elected. The manifesto requested that all towns send delegates to Prague, denounced in strident terms the papal bull, and condemned what was perceived as German aggression. Sigismund is not mentioned, hence the manifesto should be read as a directive against the official church. It is dated 3 April 1420.[7]]

---

[7]   There is a sustained, if not always convincing, analysis of this manifesto in Karel Hruza, 'Die hussitischen Manifeste vom April 1420' *Deutsches Archiv für Erforschung des Mittelalters* 53 (1997), pp. 119–77.

Good men and dear faithful friends. As the grace of God has been given to us so gently and kindly and drawn us to his grace more willingly than to any other, we determined in our hearts that there was nothing more worthy than to obey the will of God and to observe and practice the faith and the law of Christian order with all of our power and to serve our Lord Jesus Christ with all of our ability. We have been burdened with many cares and the evil of the ancient foe who opposes all good things and attempts to destroy all sacred intentions and cast it down into doubt, and cruelly induced the pope and the Council of Constance against us and the Kingdom of Bohemia. This council attempted many times to commit injustice against us and has committed many deceptions in order to stamp out the faithful from the kingdom and this was all on account of the truth of communion in the body and blood of Christ under both kinds by all faithful Christians. The council has already perpetrated many great and grievous injuries against us. Most recently the church has acted, not as a mother, but as a stepmother. That most cruel snake has given birth to a malignant offspring, born of an evil report and the entire poison has been poured out upon us when on Laetare Sunday [Fourth Sunday in Lent,17 March] in Wrocław the church raised the cruel cross against all of the faithful in our kingdom with bloody hands and announced a crusade through corrupted mouth and venomous lips. All of this has been for nothing other than that mentioned above which is the truth of God. There has been neither admonishment, trial, nor an audience but merely a shameful denunciation on account of which the innocent Christ and his pure saints have been disgraced by these detractions of evil people. On this account that council [of Constance] together with the pope have called from everywhere an unjust war, summoning our natural enemies, the Germans, and have invited them, with false indulgences from pain and sin to fight us. Even though they have no reason, they are always antagonistic to our language especially on the Rhine, in Meißen and in Prussia, from where we have been expelled. They wish for us to settle in exile.

Oh evil! Oh much more than evil! Who would not be irate seeing this evil? Who can see it and not be moved to tears? Who, faithful to the kingdom, would not grieve over the fact that the lying priest, full of iniquity wishes to ferment this pus in this golden and most Christian kingdom even to the point of exterminating within us the truth of God which even God has raised up and defends? These people, whose eyes have been turned from all justice are now urged to take up arms against this truth by the cross of our Lord Jesus. Being full of tolerance and charity, we cannot even prepare for war, for weapons, against that which we honour and will always honour. They are trying to take this truth away from us like the godless for the destruction and shame and utter disrepute of the entire kingdom. Therefore, dearest and faithful friends in the kingdom of Bohemia, we appeal to your wisdom and consistent defence of our language, with love and justice that you might be prepared to stand up to resist all of our enemies and we admonish you and encourage you with our whole heart and great sorrow which we have been unable to conceal, with the desire that this great evil not be allowed to grow because of our silence. We earnestly pray that you, like brave knights, may remember our fathers, the old Czechs, fervent lovers of their country, and stand up willingly against this evil and remain with us and with the communities of the great Old and New Towns of Prague. We have agreed with one accord and have completely confirmed this. We advise you and support your stand against anyone who would attempt to promote that malignant cross so that we might avoid such injury to our language and make free this Christian kingdom with the help of our Lord, the almighty God, whose cause we hold, and with the help of the famous St Václav our patron.

Finally, for the accomplishing of this, kindly condescend to send two or more of your leading men from your community to us on the relevant day. Do remember that this will bring you as well as us, great praise, honour and the gratitude of our descendants for the greater welfare and benefit of our fatherland and the kingdom of Bohemia.[8]

AČ 3: 212–13.

27   Bohemian nobility side with the heretics

[The month of April was filled with stirring events in Prague. Hussites put aside their internal disagreements and united in resistence against the crusade. The leading baron in the country Čeněk of Vartenberk, the Lord High Burgrave, had been in Wrocław with Sigismund during the proclamation of the crusade against the Hussites. Thinking that Čeněk was fully in support, Sigismund departed for the Silesian city of Świdnica on 10 April and Čeněk returned to Prague arriving there on the fifteenth. He had already been advised prior to his return that Prague had voted to oppose the emperor. Čeněk then took several dramatic steps to distance himself from the crusading policies of Sigismund. First, the Catholic administrators of Prague Castle, Jan Chudoba of Ralsko and Sigismund of Děčín and Vartenberk were arrested and replaced with Hussite sympathizers. Second, all Catholic priests and Germans were evicted from the castle precincts. Third, he rallied the Czech nobility in support of the anti-crusade measures. Fourth, he formally advised Sigismund that he was opposed to him and with the letter of explanation sent back to the king his insignia of the Order of the Dragon. Fifth, he

---

[8]   On the subject of manifestos from Prague see František M. Bartoš, 'Manifesty města Prahy z doby husitské' *Sborník příspěvků k dějinám hlavního města Prahy* 7 (1933), pp. 253–309.

published the following document on 20 April above his name and the name of Oldřich Rožmberk, another important Czech baron from southern Bohemia. The manifesto was widely circulated within Bohemia and also in neighbouring countries. Three days later an indeterminate number (perhaps hundreds) of barons and knights within Bohemia notified Sigismund of their support for the Hussite cause. While Čeněk's resolve would soon be broken, the impact of this manifesto cannot be underestimated.]

To the noble, brave, esteemed, wise and prudent lords, knights, vassals, townspeople and all the inhabitants of the Kingdom of Bohemia and the Margraviate of Moravia who will see or hear this message being read, we, Čeněk of Vartenberk, supreme burgrave of the Czech Crown and Kingdom, Oldřich of Rožmberk, and other lords, the city of Prague, knights, vassals and other towns, with all those who care about the freedom of the law of God and the well being of the Czech language.

We remind each and every one of you of your obligations to the Czech Crown and Kingdom, and we request that none of you submit to the serene duke Sigismund, the Roman and Hungarian king, or be in subjection to him or obey him as the king of Bohemia and the same in terms of his officials. You must be aware that he has not been elected king by the Czech lords and he has not been crowned. He is the great and cruel enemy of the language and kingdom of Bohemia. This can be demonstrated as follows. First, he abused and insulted us in the eyes of all Christendom, referring to us as heretics chiefly because we receive the communion of the blessed sacrament of the body and blood of Christ, which communion was commanded by God and is recorded in the holy gospel and confirmed by the sacred doctors and practised by the holy primitive church.

Additionally, he ordered his legate [Ferdinand] to proclaim a crusade against heretics which is a great dishonour and disgrace to the Czech Crown and language and contrary to all rules and laws of Christianity. In Wrocław, in the Kingdom of Bohemia, he commanded that an innocent and devout man [Jan Krása] be dragged by horses and then burned to death simply because he communed in the blood of the Lord. This is a severe dishonour and disgrace of the Czech language. He also ordered miners to decapitate and throw into the mine [shafts] any Czech inclined to receive the communion of the blood of the Lord. Already thousands of Czechs – both priests and laypeople – have been thrown into the mines which is a great dishonour and disgrace to the Czech language.[9]

He separated the majestic Margraviate of Brandenburg from the Czech Crown, which Emperor Charles [IV], our gracious lord of blessed memory,

---

[9] An allusion to the horrors of Kutná Hora which are well-documented elsewhere. It is of note that this document accuses Sigismund of having ordered the atrocities.

together with his ancestors conquered with great expense and loss of life. He had no authorization to do this. He gave the bishopric of Moravia to a nasty man, an abuser of the Czech language and against the law and liberties of the Crown. In this way he intended to strip the Crown of her liberties.[10]

In Wrocław, a town of the glorious Kingdom of Bohemia, he put to death many people by decapitation and he confiscated their property to the destruction of the Czech Crown. He entered into a pact with Duke Hanuš, son of Klem, who is a great enemy, destroyer, disturber of the law, and robber of the Czech Crown.[11] He also ordered the death of Master Jan Hus of blessed memory, by burning to death, before the Council of Constance, even though he was innocent and in spite of the safe-conduct he had himself issued. All of this has been done to the dishonour and disgrace of the language and Kingdom of Bohemia. He did all of this and much more and is still doing it to the disgrace and irreparable damage of the Kingdom and language of Bohemia. Which Czech heart is so hard as to not take pity upon the Kingdom of Bohemia? The Crown and the language have been exposed to enormous cruelty and disgrace!

Therefore dear friends, you must understand from this, therefore, that His Majesty has no other intention but to shamefully and brutally wreak destruction upon, and cruelly exterminate, the Czech kingdom and crown as well as and particularly the Bohemian language. We hope that as true Czechs in this hour of crisis that you will gladly stand in defence of the crown and the kingdom just as you have done previously and as your forebears did. However, if after this warning you should ever follow or obey him as the king of Bohemia then you will forfeit honour, life and property, according to law and as individuals who have not maintained the faith with their country and crown. However, we are certain that inasmuch as you are wise, faithful and discerning people, you will not allow something like this to transpire. Instead, you will behave yourselves as true

---

[10] This is a reference to Jan Železný, the 'Iron' bishop of Litomyšl who in the summer of 1415 was appointed special legate against the 'Hussite' heresy by the Council of Constance. He had been an inveterate enemy of Jan Hus. The relevant document is dated 31 August 1415 in *Documenta*, pp. 574–7. He became primate of Moravia the following year when Václav Králík of Buřenic, Patriarch of Antioch and also leading ecclesiastical official in Olomouc, died on 12 September 1416. Jan the 'Iron' bishop was put forth by the canons of that area as successor. The letter of the canons appears in Johann Loserth, 'Beiträge zur Geschichte der Husitischen Bewegung' *Archiv für österreichische Geschichte* 82 (1895), pp. 386–91. Železný closely supported Sigismund in the crusade against the heretics and militated against the Hussites until his own death on 9 October 1430.

[11] Hanuš was duke of Bavaria and count palatine. It was he who had sent Jerome of Prague back to the Council of Constance in May 1416, in chains, after Jerome had been apprehended near the Bohemian frontier. Relevant document in Hermann von der Hardt, ed., *Magnum oecumenicum Constantiense concilium*, 6 vols (Frankfurt and Leipzig, 1697–1700), vol. 4, cols. 215–18.

Czechs in all things and demonstrate your loyalty to, and love of, the Czech language and Kingdom.

Furthermore, we wish for you to know that we stand for nothing other than these articles which follow. First, that the common people might receive the body and blood of the Lord in both kinds. Second, that the word of God might be properly and freely proclaimed. Third, that priests might live lives of exemplary conduct in the manner which our Lord Christ commanded along with the apostles and the institutions of the holy fathers thereafter. Fourth, that the Czech language and kingdom be cleansed from all harmful rumours and slander for the common benefit of our kingdom and language of Bohemia. Should there be anything in these articles which might be deemed improper we have no wish to defend it contumaciously but rather are willing to be instructed by Holy Scripture and be in obedience to that.

Written in Prague Castle in the year of our Lord, 1420, on the Saturday before [the feast of] St George [20 April].

AČ 3: 210–12.

28   Conquest of towns by the crusaders

[In an effort to lure defenders away from Prague and also to strengthen his domestic base, Sigismund actually told the delegates from the town of Louny that the city of Prague had already surrendered to him. Slaný had capitulated to the king on similar grounds. Hussites in Louny were burned to death at the order of the papal legate Ferdinand. This occurred in late May 1420.]

While in Slaný, the Hungarian King Sigismund sent a summons to the town of Louny with orders that they should not delay but come out and appear before him just as the other towns had done under his protection. Therefore, representatives of Louny delegated by the municipality were dispatched to him. Believing they could trust his promises they surrendered to the king. Without the consent of the municipality they allowed his people to enter the town. Many abominable acts were committed against young girls and wives and blasphemies against the sacrament of the body and blood of the Lord Jesus Christ also took place. Those who received the communion of the body and blood of the Lord were subjected to violence by the king's army and the women and young girls were treated so villainously that it is awful even to write about it!

Historia Hussitica, in FRB 5: 375–6.

29   Hussite capture of Hradec Králové

[The crusaders successfully entered Bohemia in the spring of 1420 and in the east took several towns including Jaroměř and the strategically located and important city of Hradec Králové. Command of the conquered city was given over to Aleš of Holice. See map 2. The capture of the city posed a great threat to the Hussite cause and even though Prague itself was under imminent threat, the barons sympathetic to the Hussite cause decided to storm Hradec Králové. That action was consummated on 26 June 1420.]

At the same time Lord Aleš of Vřesov, a great champion of the truth and of the law of Christ, along with Beneš of Mokrovousy and Jiřík of Chvalkovice who were also defenders of communion in both kinds as well as other truths, became aware that in Hradec and in the surrounding area there were monks and priests opposed to the Law of God who grievously oppressed true Christians and most cruelly forced the faithful to renounce the truth. These barons were also motivated by a deep sorrow over the shameful rape of faithful virgins and other women by those champions of falsehoods, some of whom were domestic while others foreign, and being moved of God gathered together from the area a large company of peasants and miners on Kunětice Mountain above Pardubice. They intended to put an end to these intolerable atrocities and to vindicate the righteousness of the communion in both kinds. They were joined by a priest from Hradec named Ambrož whom Queen Žofie and her officials had recently expelled. He had been living in Prague but he set out to join this group paying no heed to the dangers of travel. His preaching and his celebration of the holy body of Christ in both kinds transformed the sorrowful attitude of the warriors into great joy and celebration.

After the feast of St John Baptist [24 June], the priest ordered that ladders be brought and they set out marching with the lords Aleš, Beneš, and Jiřík and all the gathered company, and pretended that their objective was Podlažice. As night fell spies reported to Hradec that the movement was in the direction of Podlažice. The people of Hradec were greatly relieved and let their guard down. At dawn they [the aforementioned troops] approached the city walls and threw their ladders up against the walls. There were only a few defenders to offer resistance, the rest of the city was in confusion, and so the attackers were able to secure the battlements with some ease. Some of the wicked ones in the town fled to the castle or got up into the towers of the gates. When morning fully came, June 26, the attackers were now the masters of the town and were received with great acclaim and joy by those who were defenders of the truth. Those who were captured or who surrendered, enemies of the truth, as well as those who had hidden in the castle and in the towers were expelled from the city. The town was given over to the friends and defenders of the law of God. Following this, those who had triumphed elected the aforementioned Aleš, Beneš and Jiřík as captains. They divided among themselves the goods of those who had been expelled and divided up the property of the same to those who had proven their loyalty to the law of Christ. From then on, the town was carefully guarded both day and night.

Historia Hussitica, in FRB 5: 381–3.

30   A call to arms

[As the capital of the kingdom, the city of Prague wielded considerable power and the nascent nationalism in the Hussite movement tended to regard the city as the 'new Jerusalem'. For much of the crusade period, Prague continued to be emblematic of anti-crusade ideology. The juxtaposing of religious and political themes is representative of Hussite songs and other documents. The denunciation of King Sigismund is a common feature in verse documents of the period and the crusade is associated most prominently with him.]

Arise, arise great city of Prague!
With all loyal subjects of Bohemia,
The order of knights and all who bear arms.

Rise up against the King of Babylon
Who threatens the new Jerusalem, Prague,
And all her faithful people.[12]

Call to your aid the supreme king
Who is all-powerful against his enemies
So great that none is greater in all the earth.

From now on you will please him
Rejecting the vanities of this arrogant world
Feeding on the fruit of everlasting life.

Smash the colossus which has feet of clay
Smash the bronze serpent whom they worship more than God
Revering it, in hopes of being healed.

---

[12] Throughout the crusade period Sigismund was maligned by the Hussites as heretical, criminal, illegitimate, immoral, effeminate and unworthy. With references to the sources see John Klassen, 'Images of anti-majesty in Hussite literature' *Bohemia* 33 (1992), pp. 267–81.

Have no fear of the Hungarian king [Sigismund]
His glory and honour are very frail
He will be overcome by the humble.

Judith the widow defeated the powerful Holofernes
In the humility of her situation
She cut off his head in his tent.

Choose now the gracious king
Whoever is a friend of the Law of God
Will overcome the cruel Holofernes.

This one will defeat God's enemies
And his false master, Antichrist
So that error will cease spreading in the holy church.

Give glory to the God of Israel
Who surpasses all other gods
Implore him to grant peace to the Czechs.

Nejedlý, 1913: 909–10.

31   Battle song of the Hussites

[This was the most popular of many Hussite songs and became symbolic of the movement itself. Hussite armies did in fact sing songs as they marched to battlefields. This song is noted for its ideology as well as its military regiment. Once thought to have been written by the blind commander Jan Žižka, that thesis has now been abandoned on very good grounds. More likely it was composed by the radical priest Jan Čapek, who inclined towards Táborite religion and social views. The song appears in manuscript form in the valuable Jistebnice kancional (Prague, National Museum Library MS II C 7, p. 88) and has been assigned a date around 1420.]

You who are the warriors of God
And of the Law of God
Pray that God will help you
Believe in God
And with God you shall ever triumph.

Christ will reward you for all that is lost
He promises a hundred times more
Whoever gives their life for him

Shall gain life eternal
Whoever stands by the truth shall be blessed.

Our Lord encourages us not to fear
Those who destroy the body
He calls us to lay down our lives
In love for our friends.

You archers and lancers
And those of the rank of knight
Those with pikes and flails
And all the common people
Remember our generous Lord in your hearts.

Do not be afraid of your enemies
Pay no attention to their superior numbers
Keep the Lord in your hearts
Fight for him and fight with him
Never retreat in the face of your enemies.

For a long time the Czechs have said
And have this proverb
That under a good Lord
There is a good riding.

Everyone must remember the password
Just as it was given to you
Always obey your captain
Each one should help and guard his companions
Everyone must stay in his own battalion.

You men keeping the supplies and advance guards
Remember your souls
That you do not forfeit life
Through greed or theft
Never be tempted by plunder.

Now you shall happily shout:
'Charge them, Hurrah, charge them'
With pride hold your weapon in your hands
Attack with the cry, 'God is our Lord!'

Nejedlý, 1913: 910–11.

32   Crusade legate admonishes the city of Prague

[From the Hussite perspective, their struggle against the crusade was nothing other than a defence of their own 'Four Articles' which had been formulated at the beginning of the revolutionary period (see doc.39). During late June and early July, 1420 literally hundreds of copies of these important articles were disseminated throughout the Czech kingdom as well as into neighbouring countries. Copies were also strategetically, though perhaps naïvely, placed in the hands of the crusaders, with the intention of persuading the soldiers of the cross that the Hussite cause was indeed righteous and faithful to Holy Scripture. Ferdinand of Lucena, papal legate for the first crusade, composed a formal response to the Hussite articles in the form of a letter addressed to the city of Prague. As such this document represents the first official ecclesiastical reply to the Hussite cause and is therefore of considerable importance. The letter must be dated to early July 1420.]

Ferdinand, by the grace of God, bishop of Lucena. . . . We are surprised that you people who take pride in thinking of yourselves as dedicated adherents of the law of God and who are prepared to take a stand on its behalf and if necessary lay down your lives for it, have accepted into your ranks, for the purpose of such defence, the enemies of God [Táborites] and that you expect to receive assistance from such people. . . .
    [As far as these articles go] if it means that any individual can preach whenever they wish and preach whatever they desire then this is not proper, particularly if what they preach is in opposition to church doctrine. . . . it is of no value for you to pass judgement on the matter of material possessions on the part of the clergy or to put them out of their churches or confiscate their belongings. It would appear that your motivation is to take their possessions rather than promote the example of a godly life. . . . [However, it is] commendable that you insist upon the cessation and extermination of all mortal and public sins. . . . But [clearing the taint of heresy from the Kingdom of Bohemia] can only be achieved if those people who are themselves infected with error and heresy denounce such [errors and heresies] and be reconciled to the church. They cannot stand in

opposition to the church, rebel against their king and natural lord for this only adds to the disgrace of heresy and the criminal infamy of *lèse majesté*. . . .[13]

[With respect to the eucharist], even if communion under both kinds is better and more meritorious as some doctors claim, it would still be more advantageous to witness to its merit by not receiving the communion of the chalice since it is in opposition to the practice of the Catholic Church as well as the decree of the Council of Constance.[14] [Receiving it] is arrogant and presumptuous and thus adds to the crime and danger. But if you continue to insist upon the greater benefit of communion *sub utraque specie* then you ought to prevail upon the person who alone has the right to intercede in spiritual affairs [the pope] and not press such demands upon His Grace, King Sigismund who has the administration of temporal matters. . . .

With respect to these issues we are prepared to listen to you if you bring them before us. When you made similar request of His Majesty the king he could not grant an audience in such an affair relating to the faith in our absence. We would like to inform you that we have agreed and that His Majesty will grant upon your request safe conduct for an appropriate space of time to those you select as your delegates. Should you desire to take up this offer with sound judgement then forgiveness and grace can be applied. However, if you persist in your contumacy and refuse to walk in the way of true salvation then you will be treated with greater severity since you have now been shown both patience and tolerance.

UB 1: 33–7.

33 Czech diplomatic efforts to win allies

[With the might of Christendom and the empire massing against them, the Hussites found themselves in a perilous position. In the days preceding the unleashing of the first crusade the city government of Prague continued with attempts to secure allies against Sigismund. The following letter was sent by

---

[13] *Lèse majesté* was a legal category in heresy law meaning treason against God. Among numerous studies see, G.G. Coulton, *The Death Penalty for Heresy* (London: Simpkin, Marshall, Hamilton, Kent and Co., Ltd, 1924), Walter Ullmann, 'The Significance of Innocent III's decretal "Vergentis"', in *Études d'histoire du droit Canonique dédiées à Gabriel Le Bras* (Paris: Sirey, 1965), volume 1, pp. 729–41, Henry C. Lea, 'Confiscation for Heresy in the Middle Ages' *English Historical Review* 2 (1887), pp. 235–59 and Peter Diehl, '"Ad abolendam" (X 5.7.9) and Imperial Legislation against Heresy' *Bulletin of Medieval Canon Law* n.s. 19 (1989), pp. 1–11.

[14] On 15 June 1415 the Council of Constance condemned the practice of utraquism. For the text of the decision see *Decrees* 1: 418–19.

Prague officials to the Doge and Council of the Republic of Venice. It is dated 10 July 1420.]

[It is good] to value well-rendered services of all kinds and to believe the truth when it is spoken. Likewise it is fitting to consider and judge equitably about important matters, and for innocent people to suffer with one another. Magnificent prince and lord, beloved and lawful assembly, and ranking patrons! Among the individual cares of men, by which the human race is burdened and ruined, the most potent is the care of the fatherland, embracing every sign of grace. This is so because the most noble of men always love their fatherland and place its safety before their own sweet life, with their eternal name surviving happily among posterity after an illustrious death. Men, however, who neglect their homeland are disreputable, exiled and degenerate, deprived of their very name while living. We know by proof, evidence and the infallible arguments of authorities that Prince Sigismund, King of Hungary – operating under the pretense that the Crown of the most happy and by experience most upright Christian Kingdom of Bohemia, a land whose fame and glory comes from the memory of the magnificent deeds and merits of our fathers, should be his – is the intolerable and cruel persecutor of those celebrating with fervour and devotion the sacrament of the most divine Eucharist under both kinds, the bread and wine, as it was instituted by Christ and the apostles, and of the Bohemian language. The evidence from his own acts and deeds is laid open below for your eyes:

First, the king, who is the originator, patron and director of the Council of Constance, persecutes us as enemies, and judges and damns us unjustly as heretics, because we adhere to the writings of the four evangelists, the letters of Paul, the many decrees of the Church and the writings of the holy fathers, by whose most wholesome authority the primitive church practiced salutarily for more than one thousand years; in fact even today through most Christian kingdoms, that is the kingdoms of the Greeks, Indians and many other eastern peoples, these authorities are still the guides, on account of which these people are damned as we are with extreme dementia. Today, neglecting the love of his native homeland, he orders that injuries and offences be perpetrated against his native land, inciting others and working against the faithful of our kingdom. He does so not within the preserved tradition of divine and human law, with trial and conviction, but by the detestable accusations of men. These same circumlocutions of wicked men are the same reason by which Christ was able to be sentenced. He does so not by the cross of Christ, withholding oppression from the innocent and destroying those who love themselves, but rather by the cross of Antichrist, as a judge from whom justice and mercy are not given. He instructed his own legate to set up and promulgate lies with polluting lips, condemning the very faith of Christ as false and inflaming the nations to fight against the truth of God. It is accepted [by us] that he did these things so that he might attain the Roman Empire by the example of cruelty, and send the Kingdom of Bohemia to flame and ashes. Truly, however, [he might better succeed] by imperial virtue, royal dignity, mercy, and equity of judgement than by the shedding of blood.

Next, he cruelly ordered Master Jan Hus, a man well remembered and acknowledged for his sanctity who lived most admirably among many without equal, to be condemned and burnt at the stake, deceiving him with a royal promise of safety. He did likewise to Jerome, the admirable university master and philosopher. Most recently in Wrocław [Breslau][15] as a disgrace and blemish upon our kingdom, he ordered that the famous citizen of Prague, Jan Krása, pure in faith and most constant in virtue, be drawn by horses until his flesh was off of the bones and his body torn to pieces, and then that he be damned and burnt, because of an incident involving communion. Lastly, he unlawfully alienated from the crown the Margraviate of Brandenburg, which had been included within the Kingdom of Bohemia on account of the sweat, blood, and deaths of our most famous fathers since the reign of our lord, the always august, Emperor Charles [IV]. He did likewise with the old mark.[16] Regarding the bishopric of Olomouc, whose grant pertains to the King of Bohemia, this traitor to our kingdom and most obstinate man, having secretly obtained papal letters, has allowed with approval that the right of presentation of this office, which belonged to Lord Václav [IV], King of Rome and Bohemia, pass from now on to canonical election by the instituted and confirmed chapter. In all of these matters he detracts damnably from the laws, rights and freedoms of the kingdom, which he ought to preserve foremost, and also defend and protect all the way to the shedding of blood. At last, as a grand prejudice against the kingdom, he joined in friendship, made covenants and established pacts and alliances with the Duke of Bavaria, 'Hans', with the perverse offspring of a depraved father, with the Margrave of Meißen, and with the most ancient, ardent persecutors and devastators of our kingdom.[17] He has openly perpetrated anger, hate, injuries, violence, tyranny and other evils, of which humanity recommends to pass notice, with the enemies of the realm and with the counts and barons of the kingdom so much so that through the proof of all of these exploits he shows himself to be an open enemy of the realm and all of its citizens,

---

[15] Frequently in the literature of the period, especially from the Czech perspective, Wrocław is referred to as Vratislav.

[16] The reference to the 'antiguam Marchiam Brutenis' refers to part of the margraviate of Brandenburg, east of the Elbe. Evidently, being strapped for cash, the emperor leased the 'old march' to the Prussian order of the Teutonic Knights.

[17] 'Hanussio' is possibly Heinrich, Duke of Landshut, who, along with other Bavarian dukes, put up strong forces to support Sigismund. The emperor wrote to Heinrich on 15 January 1421 confidently asserting that he would put an end to the Hussite heresy once and for all. UB 1, pp. 57–8.

and the most powerful patron and friend of its enemies. He leads the Hungarians and Germans, the most insolent men in all manners, whose impious hands thus far are soiled with the blood of virgins, infants, pregnant women, and men of the town of Malín in our kingdom. Out of naked hate for [our] language in a short time in the above-mentioned community they threw many hundreds of men, teachers, students, clerics, and humble, unarmed peasants (the order of the justiarship omitted) into ditches and mutilated [them] so much that, as in a most inhuman and abominable pact, just as rumour reports it, he offered one sexagena for laymen and five for priests to those who attacked the Bohemians. So by the trade of Judas and by the stimulation of the said king, these men destroy and devastate the whole [Bohemian] language. Such wickedness! O, even beyond evil! Who can see it and not be offended?

[. .] Behold the mercy of the prince and new ruler! who exists not yet as elected and crowned King of Bohemia, but only through certain demands, and is not yet the accepted, legitimate judge according to the rights of the kingdom [. .] He bound himself by the sacrament to destroy [us] by fire and sword. He also confessed in the presence of some of us that he would destroy the whole Kingdom of Bohemia through and through, turning it to flames and leading foreigners into it. Furthermore, he stated that he could not and did not wish to change or retract [this statement] in any respect. We piously appealed against his cruel pride and subjected ourselves to every humility so that he might at least administer justice to the neglected and give an audience to the inhabitants of the kingdom. However, he made himself too hard when we [came before him] so humbly and modestly [. .] as though he were stung with missiles, he began to move his limbs furiously [. .] Therefore [. .] we are brought against our wishes to resist our king and our lord. [. .] 'just as is declared in the included charter' (the Four Articles of Prague).

Then indeed the cruelty of the king was excited into a rage, so that he inflamed the peoples gathered from different regions against us, leading especially the Dukes of Austria to the destruction of this kingdom. He besieged the capital city, Prague, with the intention of subduing it and destroying the faithful of Christ of both sexes together with innocent children. [However], we do not fear his confessed severity on account of the help of the Almighty. Therefore magnificent prince, together with the noble lords of your celebrated city, our favoured patrons, we humbly pray for your esteemed power and the rival pre-eminence of your famous name and most distinguished glory [as help] against the aforementioned most haughty king [. .] who lately has obtained nothing by the sword, but rather by fraud, deceptions, and the false lies of written promises, by which he has already seduced many barons and nobles of our realm. May you deign to bring the victorious arm of your virtue to our defence, and appoint aid by bringing your armies into Austria and the other lands of the duchies of Austria – those abominable dukes! – lest they become too hard and proud against you as they have against us [. .] and thereby invade and conquer [. .] Should your magnificent authority happily consider these our prayers worth hearing and suited for both your benefit as well as ours, then we will be prepared and obligated to follow equally and serve all of your prayers by just as many or more thousands of armed soldiers.[18] We desire to be consoled with your benign response through the present messenger and in writing. Dated in Prague on 10 July in the year of the Lord, 1420.

UB 1: 39–43.

34   Women among the Hussite armies

[A letter from the Margrave of Meißen to the Duke of Bavaria contains an interesting and somewhat unusual report of an incident during the time of the first crusade (12 July) wherein a significant number of Hussite warriors were captured during a sortie. It was discovered that these warriors opposing the cross were in fact women, armed, and dressed in the military gear of men. The involvement of women in the Hussite armies cannot be regarded as anomalous, even at the stage when the heretics maintained standing field armies. At the battle of Týn Horšův in 1422, women fought openly alongside the men. See UB 1, pp. 197 and 199 and FRB 5, p. 627. Ondřej of Brod commented that Hussite women rode horses and fought like men.]

Our bounden duty to you great prince, dear cousin. We are informing you of news that occurred this past Friday, to whit that his majesty the king of the Romans sent the Hungarians against the inhabitants of Prague. The foot soldiers killed more than one hundred of them and took 156 prisoners, women who had fixed their hair like men and had girded themselves with swords, with stones in their hands, wearing boots. Among these were some high-born.[19]

Hegel, *Die Magdeburger Schöppenchronik*, p. 356.

---

[18] A reference to the fact that Venice had earlier been at war against Sigismund and shortly thereafter the Republic of Venice resumed military action in Dalmatia.

[19] On women in the Hussite crusades see John M. Klassen, 'Women and religious reform in late medieval Bohemia' *Renaissance and Reformation* n.s. 5 (1981), pp. 203–21 and Klassen, *Warring maidens, captive wives and Hussite queens: Women and men at war and at peace in fifteenth-century Bohemia* (Boulder: East European Monographs, 1999).

35   Crusaders and heretics in the battle of the Vítkov

[On 14 July 1420 the first crusade against the Hussites was launched against the heretics at Prague. At least thirty-three foreign states are known to have been involved in the crusade. The Hussite chronicler Vavřinec of Březová hyperbolically estimates the strength of the crusading army at 150,000 men while Eberhart Windecke, Sigismund's confidant and biographer, says 80,000. Aeneas Sylvius makes the extravagant claim that the crusaders had 70,000 cavalry alone. The only major European region not represented was Scandinavia. See map 4 for details.]

On 30 June, following the Sunday of St Peter, the Hungarian king Sigismund approached with a strong army of Czechs as well as many other kinds of people from the fortress of Prague. Following a celebration of the Mass he appeared in a procession, with the great bells tolling, and with hymns and songs. He was welcomed with great ceremony by the clergy and other powerful figures at the fortress of Prague. Meanwhile his army set up tents and took up positions in the fields located in the plain between the Bruska and Ovenec in order to conquer Prague being one of the towns of heresy on account of the communion of the holy chalice and other gospel truths. From one day to the next, many different people streamed to this place in the fields in support of the papal crusade which had been falsely called for against the Czechs and especially aimed at those who supported the communion of the cup. These people came together from different kingdoms, duchies, lands and provinces of the world for the purpose of conquering the famous and magnificent city of Prague. They came also to exterminate and prohibit for all time the communion of the chalice. By this they hoped to obtain an indulgence from their guilt and punishment. This is what their priests had falsely promised them in order to stir them up as much as possible to kill all the faithful Bohemians of either sex.

The size of the army continued to grow until there were more than 150,000 armed people gathered. Among this company were archbishops, bishops, the patriarch of Aquileia, a number of doctors of theology and other prelates. Additionally, there were dukes, and secular princes, approximately forty in all, margraves, counts, barons and nobles, knights with their servants, townspeople from various cities and peasants. They occupied the entire plain of the aforementioned fields and their extravagant tents were situated so that it appeared there were three large towns. From these numerous nations, tribes and languages were the following: Bohemians and Moravians, Hungarians, Croats, Dalmatians, Bulgarians, Wallachians, Szekelys, Huns, Tassyans, Ruthenians, Russians, Slavonians, Prussians, Serbs, Thuringians, Styrians, Misnians, Bavarians, Saxons, Austrians, Franconians, Frenchmen, Englishmen, those of Brabant and

Westphalia, Dutch, Swiss, Lusatians, Swabians, Carinthians, Aragonese, Spaniards, Poles, Rhineland Germans and others in very large numbers.

Every day they stood on the highest hill above the river, opposite the Monastery of the Holy Cross and the Church of St Valentine and howled like dogs across the river to the city: 'Ha, Ha, Hus, Hus, Heretic, Heretic.'[20] If perchance a Czech fell into their hands and was not quickly set free by a Bohemian within their ranks, that person immediately was burned as a heretic without mercy even if that person had never partaken in the communion of both kinds. More frequently they engaged in military skirmishes with the Praguers on the sandy ground below the Bruska. In the archiepiscopal garden many lives were lost as well as a considerable loss in goods. Many times five or ten Praguers, wearing only a coat, put to flight a large number of armed people bearing the best arms. These they pounced upon with iron flails, knocking many down and killing them. Finally they [the crusaders] managed neither to break through the barriers of the mills across from the Monastery of the Holy Cross nor burn those mills down even though they tried to do so several times. They always returned defeated and distraught because they had not been able to accomplish anything.

Now that the King of Hungary, Sigismund, held the fields so completely, as noted previously, together with some local people as well as foreigners who had come against the city of Prague he began to plot to fortify the mountain close to the gallows which was called Vítkov Hill with his soldiers so that he might place a circle around Prague as in a third fortress in such a way that the city of Prague would have its food supply cut off. Anticipating this, Jan Žižka, the captain of the Táborites, immediately, without delay, ordered the erecting of two bulwarks in the form of a building with a small trench dug around it and enclosed by a wall of mud and stones. Through this bulwark, almighty God caused the rescue of Prague in a miraculous way because the enemies who suffered defeat at this spot did not again attempt to invade the town with hostile intent as shall be shown below.

[At this point in the narrative, the chronicler, Vavřinec of Březová, breaks off his story of the first crusade to relate two tales of the atrocities committed by the crusaders as they marched against the Hussite heretics at Prague. Inasmuch as these stories constitute an essential aspect of the crusading mentality they are retained here in the same place where the Hussite chronicler originally placed them in his narrative.]

On the Saturday after [St] Prokop ['s Day], that is to say on 6 July, the duke of Austria rode with a strong army through Miličína to Prague to join the armies

---

[20] Both foundations were located in the Old Town. St Valentine's was demolished in 1794 while Holy Cross was pulled down in 1890. See map 4.

of King Sigismund. About sixty of his men turned off at Arnoštovice. On the grounds of accusation concerning communion of the chalice and in both kinds by certain Czech clerics they arrested the local priest, Master Václav, a man very popular with God and the people together with his vicar. They were placed on a single horse and hauled off to the army of the duke in the village of Bystřice. There they were removed from the horse and presented to the duke as contumacious heretics. Throughout almost the whole of the night they led the frightened men back and forth, this way and that, as in the manner of going from Caiphas to Pilate. They threatened them with fire unless they were to renounce the aforementioned communion in both kinds. Unless they repented, they would burn in the fire. Master Václav answered them with humility saying, 'this is the gospel and the practice of the early church and it is written here in the Mass book. [You must either] erase this part of the Scripture or accept [swallow] this Gospel.' One of the warriors standing there with an iron glove on his hand was not afraid to strike the aforementioned Master Václav in the face whereupon blood gushed heavily from his nose. After they had tortured him and his companion several times, they [the crusaders] went to sleep. When morning came, which was the day of the Lord, they put this Master Václav, together with his vicar and three old peasants as well as four children who had stood firmly for the truth, one of them was aged seven, the other eight, another ten and the last of them eleven, on a pile of wood overlooking the fish pond in the aforementioned village . . . . The people who gathered around appealed to them to renounce [their faith] if they wished to live. In reply, Master Václav, a true shepherd of his sheep, answered with these words saying, 'far be it from us to do what you suggest. We do not wish to die a single death, but if it were possible we would die a hundred of these deaths before we would deny the clear truth of the gospel.' Immediately the executioner set fire to the stack of wood and stoked it. The children who sat in the arms of Master Václav like young apprentices, embraced by him, sang the praises of God and died quickly. The others died much slower so that at the end Master Václav yielded up his soul to God and was received with the martyr's crown as it is faithfully believed. So, we miserable ones, what shall we do? Even those who are not scholars, peasants and children rise up and through a martyr's crown take over heaven. We, however, who live in temptation, every day come close to hell, but we may be rescued by the God we praise who lives and reigns forever.

At the same time, Vojtěch, a priest in the village of Chelčice, which is located near the town of Vodňany, likewise feared God and did not tolerate any deviation from the practice of communing the chalice, even though he was shocked by the pillaging and violence committed by the Táborites. He was captured by Hrzek, an official from Tuřov, a town in the same area, on account of the chalice. Together with another priest he was brought to the town of České Budějovice and handed over to the civil council as heretics and were immediately thrown into the tower.

After three weeks of refusing to renounce [the chalice] they were burned to death outside the town. All honour be yours, O Lord, for allowing to endure to the end those who fear you and who do not shrink back from all kinds of torture.

[The chronicle now returns without further comment to the scene on Vítkov Hill in Prague where the heretics commanded by Žižka have taken up positions against the crusaders headed by Sigismund.]

On 13 July, that is to say, on the day of [St] Margaret, a group of armed people from the army advanced onto the Hospital Field, and attacked the city in order to determine how the Praguers might defend themselves.[21] When they approached the city, the bells of the Town Hall rang out, and a crowd of the Praguers rushed toward them. Failing to maintain order, and against the orders of their commander, they did not wait but instead attacked the superior strength of those mounted even though they were in the minority. Having become involved in the fight, the people of Prague seeing the strength [of the crusaders] fled having killed some and wounding an even larger number. Because an even larger group arrived from the city at that moment, the enemies retreated and withdrew across the Vltava from where they had come. Four peasants killed one knight and while they stood quarrelling over his weapons, others came rushing up quickly and straight away killed these four [peasants] on the same spot and then disappeared.

On the following day, that is on the Sunday immediately after [St] Margaret around the time of vespers, the entire army of the king stood ready in order that several thousand of them would storm [Vítkov] and conquer the wooden fortress which had been erected by Žižka on the mountain above the gallows. After this had been accomplished, the remaining army was to swarm, according to the command of their captains, and set about to invade the city of Prague at three points. From the fortress of Prague [Hradčany], a force of 16,000 would attack the house of the duke of Saxony. From Vyšehrad [the crusaders] would push ahead into the New Town and from the Hospital Field they would surge forward into the Old Town. While these plans were being laid, several thousand horsemen advanced onto the Hospital Field while the king waited with three large armies on the far side of the Vltava in order to watch the outcome of the endeavour. Those from Meißen climbed the mountain with their own troops, while the 7,000 or 8,000 allies, all of whom were mounted, prepared to attack the wooden fortress. At the sound of the trumpet they launched an assault, successfully crossing the moat and taking the watchtower of one vineyard. When they attempted to scale the walls made from mud and stone, two women, with one girl and twenty-six men

---

[21]   The Hospital Field was a strip of land about a mile wide lying between Vítkov Hill and the Vltava River. Through this field ran the main road from Prague to northeast Bohemia. On the other side of the Vítkov lay the main road to the east. Hence, the strategic value of the hill in between.

who had remained in the bulwark, offered brave resistance hurling stones and thrusting with spears and attempted to repulse [the invaders] having neither arrows nor gun powder. One of these women, even though she possessed no armour, surpassed even the courage of the men, stood valiantly refusing to yield a single step saying that no faithful Christian must retreat from Antichrist. Fighting with great zeal she was killed and breathed her last. Then Žižka came quickly to their defence and he himself would have been killed had his own men not come with battle flails and rescued him from the hands of his enemies. Just as the entire city dreaded the fall [of Žižka's defence] and were shedding tears and praying with their children and hoping for a heavenly rescue, a priest approached with the sacrament of the body of Christ. Behind him were about fifty archers and a number of unarmed peasants except for flails. When the enemies saw the sacrament and heard the little bell, together with the loud cries of the people they were stricken with fear. They turned and rushed away, everyone trying to get in front of those before them. Many were unable to keep their balance against the onslaught of the fleeing men and they fell from the high rocks and broke their necks and many more were killed by their pursuers. Within an hour more than 300 of them were slain while others were mortally wounded or captured.[22]

When the king saw what had happened, he retreated in haste to his camp together with the entire army. He was furious, disgusted and full of bitterness but likewise was filled with grief. The soldiers of Prague gathered on the Hospital Field and there knelt and gave thanks to God singing the *Te Deum Laudamus* with loud voices. They were aware that God had miraculously delivered them and had provided them with victory over their enemies and this was not on account of their strength. With great cheering they sang songs and hymns and entered the city stepping lightly. There had been the sounds of mourning of the women, young girls and children, whom the enemies of the truth had purposed to kill horribly as heretics and as the children of heretics. Now their mourning was turned into a sound of happiness, of joy and jubilation. They praised God for divine mercy for having rescued them with a strong hand from the clutches of their cruel enemies. On the following day and ever since that time the children of Prague ran through the narrow streets singing a new song which the priest [Jan] Čapek composed in the common language. . . . [see doc.37].

On Monday, thereafter, following the heaven-sent victory over the enemies, [Václav] Koranda [of Plzeň], a wayward and fanatical priest, together with some nuns from Plzeň and Táborite women entered the holy Church of St Michael in the Old Town quite presumptuously by horse. Having no respect for the sacrament of the body of Christ which was upon the altar, he ordered [his companions] to

---

[22]   Other sources state that 500 were killed. SRB 3, p. 38. The Misnian commander, Heinrich of Isenburg, was also slain.

destroy all of the benches used by the priests as well as the laity, saying they were more useful for the fortifications of the new bulwark which had been raised on Vítkov. In the end this atrocity had been undertaken not for the reinforcement of the bulwark at all, but the scandalous work had been done merely to satisfy his ill-will and deep hatred which he had inwardly fostered against this church and its ministers. As a result only a few of the planks were actually carried onto the hill, whereas most of them were burned by the Táborite sisters at St Ambrose.

Immediately following this wonderful tale of victory over the enemies, the captain Žižka the next day called together a large number of women, girls and laypeople from Prague. He then undertook a strong reinforcement of the frequently mentioned bulwark with a larger number of trenches as well as many walls and a number of wooden huts, as one can indeed see. According to the name of its originator, some people called this mountain as well as the village, 'Žižka's Mountain'. Others called it the 'Place of the Battle' because here the Germans had been defeated. A third group named it, perhaps with more justification, 'the Mountain of the Chalice' or simply 'Chalice'. This was on account of the fact that the enemies of the chalice were killed by those who fought with God's support for the chalice. In order to distinguish themselves these people wore a red and white chalice on their clothes, weapons, as well as on their banners.

Beyond this, when the Germans and the foreigners saw that they had been miserably defeated by peasants, they blamed the Czechs among them and accused them of being disgraceful traitors. Had the king not intervened they would have killed each other that same day. Right after this, on the following day, they burned down surrounding villages and fortifications as revenge for their fallen comrades. While they were doing this, like the heathens, they robbed and quite inhumanely threw women and small children into the fire. In doing this they earned the punishment of eternal hell for themselves, unless they repented, but for those they burned it was for the great joy of eternal reward.

Following the aforementioned, unexpected defeat of the Germans, the city of Prague had peace from hostile attacks. The Germans no longer shouted, 'Hus, Hus, Heretic, Heretic' but instead they reflected peacefully every day about how they might leave the country of Bohemia and return to their own homeland. So the barons of the kingdom, on behalf of the king, entered into a series of negotiations with the citizens of Prague on one side of the bridge. They wanted the city to accept a cease fire in order that they might escape with honour from the hostile armies and also so that the entire country would not be destroyed. The negotiator for the city replied that it was impossible to accept such terms unless they had the agreement of the allied cities. However, for their honour and for the honour of the entire kingdom they would ask for an audience with the king which was to be public for the magistrates and the priests and was to be conducted in four languages, Czech, German, Hungarian and Latin so that everyone could openly present the truth of the Four Articles for which the Praguers had fought with their supporters against the king. They also wished that this might be presented to the armies clearly and without deceit which would indicate to the world their righteousness and this might lead to an elimination of the constant and malicious gossip emanating from their enemies. This would also if necessary allow the negotiator to reply to all the objections raised by the king's theologians. The city managed to accomplish this, as mentioned previously, by legate and barons, with a letter and a promised seal for an audience. However, the barons were seeking for excuses and said they could not consent to give dukes to the city as hostages while the magistrates went to the fortress [Hradčany]. They said it should be sufficient for the city to take barons and knights in their place. Although the community of Prague agreed to this, the lords continuously failed to carry through on the arrangements for the audience noted above.

Because this was the case, the magistrates of Prague, compiled the Four Articles including arguments for their validity, and sent these articles in Latin, German and Czech to the armies in the following form . . . .

Historia Hussitica, in FRB 5: 383–91.

36   Song of triumph after the first crusade

[The whole Hussite period is marked by songs which function as an invaluable genre of material for interpreting the events in Bohemia. This song was written by the radical Hussite priest Jan Čapek. Čapek had been a disciple of Jakoubek of Stříbro early on, but by the time of crusade was affiliated with the Táborites and Jan Želivský. He was probably ordained at Lipnic Castle in 1417 when the suffragan bishop of Prague was kidnapped and forced to consecrate Hussite priests. Later he could be found as priest in the staunch Hussite town of Klatovy.]

Children let us run to meet our brothers
Like Melchizedec we take bread and wine
Now that you have won the battle
Be welcomed our beloved brothers.

After he defeated Goliath
David returned to Jerusalem
The people came out of the city to greet him
Now that you have defeated the enemy
Be welcomed our beloved brothers.

We sung a new song, happy in God
We give thanks to God and greet our brothers
Now that you have defeated the enemy
Be welcomed our beloved brothers.

God gives us what we have wished for our brothers
So beloved brothers be welcomed
Now that you have defeated the enemy
Be welcomed our beloved brothers.

We go together and move toward the house of God
We give thanks to God for God's many benefits
Now that you have defeated the enemy
Be welcomed our beloved brothers.

The honour is not for us, O Lord, the honour is not for us
That which has been done, you have accomplished
We worship your holy name and your eternal glory.
Now that you have defeated the enemy
Be welcomed our beloved brothers.

Nejedlý, 1913: 911–12.

37   The children's song of victory

[The priest Jan Čapek composed another song at the end of the first crusade which was sung by children in the streets of Prague. The following translation is from Heymann, p.140 n.10.]

Children, let us praise the Lord,
Honour Him in loud accord!
For He frightened and confounded,
Overwhelmed and sternly pounded
All those thousands of Barbarians,
Suabians, Misnians, Hungarians
Who have overrun our land.

With His strong protecting hand
To the winds He has them waved,
And we children are now saved.

Faithful Czechs, let's sing our love
To our Father high above,
With the older folks along
Praising God in joyous song!

Historia Hussitica, in FRB 5: 389.

38   Conditions in the crusader camps

[Following the defeat of the first crusade, the soldiers in the crusader camps waited while Sigismund decided on what to do. He was hesitant to attack again and had no wish for the city to be bombarded with heavy artillery. This vacillation prompted rumours that Sigismund secretly was sympathetic to the Hussites. One of the contemporary chroniclers, a canon of St Stephen's Cathedral in Vienna, went so far as to write that 'when Sigismund saw this [the crusader defeat] he returned to his camp smiling because the brave Christians had been defeated and had succumbed to the heretics.' (Thomas Ebendorfer of Haselbach, *Chronicon Austriae*, ed. Bernard Pez, in *Scriptores rerum Austriacarum*, vol. 2 (Leipzig, 1725), cols. 682–987 at col. 849.) On 28 July he was clandestinely crowned king of Bohemia in the cathedral of St Vitus in Prague Castle. Meanwhile, the situation deteriorated in the crusader camps. More than 200 corpses of heretical Hussites had lain unburied and in the blistering heat of summer were rotting. Added to this were the decomposing carcases of numerous horses killed in the futile effort to take Vítkov from Žižka's troops. Rubbish and refuse generated by an encampment of some 80,000 soldiers only added to the problem as it continued to pile up, with no removal, in what is described in some sources as an unusually dry and hot summer. The stench became unbearable and attracted swarms of flies, mosquitoes and other insects. Men began to die in these appalling conditions from a variety of illnesses contracted from the unhealthy environment. Later in July, a fire broke out in the camps and destroyed many tents. The crusading resolve was broken. The sole achievement of the first crusade was Sigismund's secret coronation. Hegel, *Die Magdeburger Schöppenchronik*, p. 354.]

On the 19th of the month of July, the tents of the enemies were burned. Suddenly a very strong wind arose so that many other tents along with their contents burned down very quickly. Then on the day of St Mary Magdalene [22 July], the Táborites along with the army of the Praguers, having learned of the terrible burnings of Czechs by the Germans (see doc.35) marched on the town hall and asked that those imprisoned there be handed over to them so that they could be burned. The councillors were not happy to do this but they could hardly refuse so they agreed. These prisoners, sixteen in all, were burned in barrels outside the town within eyesight of the Germans. Only one monk was spared since he promised to continue to give the communion of the body and blood of the Lord to the faithful people. . . . On 30 July, the third day after Sigismund's coronation, the entire army burned their camps and left. They berated the king as a friend of heretics saying he had betrayed everyone's trust.

Historia Hussitica, in FRB 5: 395-6.

39   Hussite resolve at the end of the first crusade

[Coinciding with the first major effort to suppress the Czech heresy, the Hussites formally promulgated the 'Four Articles of Prague'. They are given here in brief, frequently enumerated in Hussite documents throughout the crusading period, and can be regarded as the *raison d'être* of the Hussite cause. The last paragraph underscores the basis of Hussite resistance to the crusades. These articles have a detailed history of development and articulation in the 1420s and 1430s.]

[First] . . . throughout the Kingdom of Bohemia the word of God shall be freely preached and proclaimed by Christian priests . . . . [Second] the holy sacrament of the body and blood of the Lord, in both kinds of bread and wine, shall be freely given to all true Christians who are not prohibited on account of some deadly sin just as our Saviour did in the beginning and so commanded it. . . . [Third] numerous priests and monks, supported by temporal law possess worldly goods in opposition to the commandments of Christ. This is to the detriment of their office and is also harmful to the lords of the secular estates. These priests shall be deprived of such power, which is unlawful, and in keeping with the Scriptures shall live lives of good repute in accordance with the pattern of Christ and the apostles . . . . [Fourth] all serious sins, particularly those committed publicly, along with other offences against the Law of God shall be prohibited and punished regardless of their estate, by those who possess the power to do so. [This is to be done] so that the evil and slanderous rumours about this country might be removed for the common good of the people and the Kingdom of Bohemia . . . .

If anyone wishes to accuse us verbally or in writing with anything evil, heretical, shameful or unclean, we would ask that such an individual not be believed. For such a one is speaking slander out of hatred and ill-will and is both malicious and a liar. We confess boldly before the Lord God and the entire world that with the help of God we have no other motive than to serve the Lord Jesus Christ with all of our hearts, power, strength and endurance and to be dedicated to the fulfilment of God's law and commandments which is appropriate for all good Christians. Any wicked enemy or anyone else who attempts to compel us away from this good we will withstand in keeping with the law and truth of God. On this position we shall defend the truth as well as ourselves against such violence through the use of secular weapons. Should something terrible happen through the zeal of one of our people, we assert that this is not our intention but we shall stand against all serious sins with God's help. And if someone comes to harm because of us it is because it was absolutely necessary or because that person is an enemy of God as well as of us. It is necessary to protect both ourselves and the law of God from such violence and cruelty. Beyond this, we declare with all solemnity that if it appears that we are incorrect in anything we are prepared to make amends and our hearts are open in all things to be instructed by enlightenment from the Holy Scriptures. Dated in the year of the Lord 1421 [sic].

Historia Hussitica, in FRB 5: 391–5.

40   Recruitment of anti-crusade forces

[Following the victory over the crusaders at Vítkov in Prague, the Hussite general Jan Žižka again retired to south Bohemia where he enjoyed a strong support base. He lost no time, however celebrating his unlikely triumph, recruiting more men for his armies and this letter to his old nemesis Oldřich Rožmberk reflects not only this activity but also the fear in which the old Hussite warrior was held. This brief missive provides a view of the effects of the crusade at the local community level and in that sense reveals a different but important dimension of the crusade era. It is dated 28 August 1420.]

In your service dear sir. Your grace has written to us that Žižka has arrived in Písek and we know for certain that Žižka is in Písek. Furthermore, dear sir, we have been notified by our good friends and by loyal neighbours that he intends to march upon us at midnight. We have also been advised that he camped near Písek. He has a small army but he is recruiting peasants from the neighbourhood. Also, dear sir, we have to complain about the mercenaries who abandoned us immediately as soon as they learned that Žižka was in Písek. Therefore, dear sir, remember that we are like orphans and we beg you to take care of us. Otherwise, if God and your grace will not protect us, we shall perish and also lose the king's castle. Dated on the Wednesday of St Augustine. The mayor, village justice of the peace, councillors and the municipality of Vodňany.

Rynešová 1: 20.

41   An heretical denunciation of war

[Petr Chelčický's tract, 'On Spiritual Warfare', written either in 1420 or 1421, represents a radical Hussite view staunchly opposed to the use of force to defend the faith. It was written with the first crusade firmly in view. As such, the argument of the work constitutes a firm rebuttal of the scholastic just war theory defended by Jakoubek of Stříbro. Jakoubek was Hus' successor as preacher in the Bethlehem Chapel and, along with the priest Želivský, the leading Hussite in Prague. Chelčický makes no distinction between defensive and offensive forms of war; both are illegitimate. His ideology and theological outlook mirrors that of Tábor except on the point that he is utterly opposed to the use of force and regards warfare and authentic Christianity as mutually exclusive. Chelčický technically belonged to none of the Hussite parties for he was opposed to them all. His thought and writings belong among the most significant of Hussite literature.[23]]

We must recognize with much shame and sadness that our brothers have been cleverly deceived by Satan and have been estranged from the Holy Gospel and now hold opinions and engage in strange and inconceivable actions. At first when Satan approached them he did not reveal his true demonic nature. Instead he appeared splendidly to the priests advocating poverty as Christ with a clear view toward preaching and the administration of the holy body and blood of the Lord to the people. But when a great multitude gathered, the Devil changed his appearance and with deceptive action in the name of the prophets and the Old Testament prompted them to anticipate the day of last judgement. Soon they believed themselves to be angels appointed to liberate the kingdom of God from all scandal and that it was their duty to judge the world. To this end they killed many people and dispossessed others of their goods but were not yet judges of the world. As a matter of fact, that time of trouble which they had prophesied in order to cause fear among the people has already passed . . . .

It is not possible to show love for our fellow man with those whom we do love if we do not show love towards those whom we do not love. The apostle invites us to a spiritual war and in order to fight we must put on the armour of God's righteousness and not that of the world. This must be strong and of good quality for the battle. Žižka, that clever knight, will certainly not be the one who attempts to breach it. Rather it will be Satan himself who is much more astute and clever in fighting than the blind Žižka and indeed more perceptive than he. It is a matter of justice that demands of the Christian that he or she shares everything with

---

23   This document might be compared with doc.195. On Chelčický, see Murray L. Wagner, *Petr Chelčický: A radical separatist in Hussite Bohemia* (Scottdale: Herald Press 1983).

everyone he or she meets and in all dealings. This attitude will be one which chooses personal disadvantage and shares everything with everyone as much as possible according to the truth. Such a one prefers to be a hindrance to no one and is committed in every way possible to making the way easier for others. This is the attitude the Lord Jesus commands us to have toward our enemies and it is in this sense that the Gospel is the good news and the law of perfect freedom . . . . The apostle instructs us to take up the sword of the Spirit which is the Word of God [Ephesians 6:18]. We must take possession of this arm and keep it ready for the impending difficult battle. In fact the Devil is prepared to attack on every side. But who is able to take possession of this sword of the Spirit for this impending fight of the Word of God is now being assailed? There are few people today who have a real understanding of the truth and who abide in it. It is entirely inadequate for a single person involved in this difficult battle to simply know that certain educated persons, such as the parish priest or the prelate, have knowledge of the Scriptures. The individual on the street must have knowledge and understanding of the Scriptures. It is clear that in a physical engagement it is not sufficient to know that our friend has a sword, we urgently need one also! Without a weapon we are unable to resist and will therefore be defeated. It is therefore essential that all people personally have a knowledge and understanding of the Scriptures. However, people today are reluctant to believe that God exercises power through those who hold this sword in their hands . . . .

The apostle asks that the Gospel might be preached in its purity. For the cause of this Gospel he is in prison in chains [Ephesians 6:19–20]. This is, dear St Paul, what is disturbing to the game of the priests, of those who believe they can announce the Gospel message while lying on their comfortable pillows and each year receiving pay and if there are two in the same parish they receive 40 coins. This is how they have preached the Gospel, staying in Prague Castle and in other fortifications protected by moats and walls, while the apostle announced the message of the Gospel without protection, chained and in poverty.

With regard to the villages, Vavák takes care of them and the people suffer.[24] They are seduced, victims of theft and are beaten while the priests, evil mercenaries, fled inside the city walls, protected by the moats. From here they wage war on each other using the people as barricades. Completely opposite to this the apostle proclaims the Gospel as well, though in chains and not having a

---

[24]   Oldřich Vavák of Jindřichův Hradec was a Czech baron with ties and connections to Tábor and who lent assistance to Žižka on occasion. He was the only powerful lord in the Jindřichův Hradec area who joined the revolution and had sufficient clout to be named chair of an important meeting in Prague in 1420. He attended the diet of Čáslav in 1421 where he was named to the regency council (see doc.63). He was made mint master of Kutná Hora in August 1421 but fell victim to a plague epidemic and died a month later on 22 September.

feather bed or fine food of meat and fowl. Even though chained he served far better than the prelates who wear long gowns. Despite being in chains he served the people through the Gospel, performing an important service and has therefore introduced a great number of people to an understanding of the Gospel. If our preachers do not have the same desire they will be of no advantage to the Gospel and will not be able in any way to reveal the Lord Jesus Christ and his ways to the people. The majority of these preachers talk a great deal about patience and are able to burden simple people with heavy penance. However, they themselves, most regrettably, do not do penance even with their finger. These prelates are exceptionally greedy!

Eduard Petrů, ed., *Petr Chelčický, Drobné spisy* (Prague: Československá akademie věd, 1966), pp. 41, 77, 89–90, 97–8.

Chapter 3

The Second Crusade: Žatec, 1421

42   Siege of Vyšehrad castle and fortress

[The strategically important fortress of Vyšehrad on the south approach to Prague had been taken from the Royalists in October 1419 by forces commanded by Jan Žižka. Shortly thereafter it was given back to Sigismund against Žižka's wishes. The old warrior withdrew from Prague in anger and did not participate in this siege. Leadership fell to Hyněk Krušina of Lichtenburk and the number of Hussite troops totalled about 12,000. Sigismund was at Kutná Hora with a fair-sized army of approximately 16,000 men. Summoned to assist the Vyšehrad garrison he marched instead to Žatec, approaching Prague from the west, and persecuting all Hussites found along the way. The king hoped to divert the Hussites forces from Vyšehrad with these tactics but did not succeed. Meanwhile the situation had become desperate for the defenders within the fortress, having been reduced to eating nothing but horseflesh for several weeks. Since Sigismund delayed in coming to the relief of Vyšehrad a truce was made with the Hussites to turn over the fortress on 1 November. Notwithstanding this agreement, Sigismund arrived and against the better judgement and advice of his generals undertook a frontal assault on the Hussites. The results were disastrous with many Royalists killed or captured including Jindřich of Plumlov, Lord Petr of Šternberk (the man who launched the attack on the pilgrims at Živohošť a year earlier) and a Russian prince, Georgii, Duke of Smolensk. After the battle, the Hussites took control of the fortress. In addition to this account, there are other details in SRB 3, pp. 38–42 and the best account from the royalist perspective is Windecke, pp. 134–6 who claims the battle was lost when the mint master of Kutná Hora, Mikuláš of Jemniště fled with 1,500 cavalry. See map 4.]

On the twentieth day of October when the king realized that all of his supply lines up to Vyšehrad were barricaded on the riverside as well as on the land side, he dismissed his ships and rode with the food supplies from Karlštejn through the mountains opposite Vyšehrad to the fortress of Prague. He ordered the burning of many villages including the village of Zlíchov as well as the wine presses in the vineyards. He did this so that the mercenaries in Vyšehrad, upon seeing the fire, which he caused to burn very strongly, would take heart in the imminent hope that they would soon be relieved. At the same time other frightened mercenaries yielded up to the king Kněžov and another fortress near Beroun. He started a large fire and burned a priest and some peasants whom he found in Kněžov and whom the peasants had brought to Beroun. But the king himself went from the fortress of Prague by horse to Mělník and thereafter to Nymburk and then on to Kutná Hora and Čáslav. From here he sent for a gathering of an armoured division.

By this time Jan Všemberk [of Boskovice] and the other captains in the castle of Vyšehrad realized that the king was delaying in coming to their rescue with supplies. Many of them were dying of hunger, others had died and they did not have even horseflesh to eat any longer. On the day of SS Simon and Jude [28 October] they held a meeting with Lord Krušina and the other barons and the captains of the Prague army in a place halfway between Vyšehrad and the Church of St Pancrac. While this conference was underway a glorious rainbow appeared in the sky. Some of the masters and bachelors of the liberal arts were sitting on the top of Kavel Hill looking out over the Vltava River waiting for the result of the meeting and were discussing a variety of subjects when this rainbow, like we had never seen before, appeared. Its arc arose practically at our feet in the Vltava River and extended over the city to a spot near St Pancrac's Church where the soldiers were camped waiting for the discussion to end. As it was, the circle [of the rainbow] was not complete only in the area between that church and the hill upon which we were seated. This space was not larger than about one quarter of the entire circle. We sat down again while many views were expressed concerning the meaning of the rainbow which was determined to be that the Praguers would soon be in possession of Vyšehrad. This is exactly what occurred as we shall tell later. By the will of God an agreement was reached between the parties to the effect that if the king did not send sufficient supplies before the fifteenth hour [9:00 a.m.] on the first of November, the day of All Saints, then the castle of Vyšehrad would be handed over to the citizens of Prague honourably and in good faith. The letter regarding this concord was completed and its tenor follows in these words.

'We, Jan [Všemberk] Boskovice of Brandýs, commander, and we a. b. c. d. etc., and all the community of knights, and all others at Vyšehrad, presently under siege, announce by this letter to all those who will see it or hear it read, that we have come to an agreement with the noble lords Hynek Krušina of Lichtenburk, Viktorin of Kunštat and Poděbrady, Hynek of Kolštejn and Valdštejn, Prokop of Ústí, Jan of Lichtenburk and the esteemed lord Mikuláš of Hus, cautious burgomasters and aldermen, together with the municipality of the great and New Town of Prague, as well as with all the community of knights who have been encamped, or are now encamped before Vyšehrad and in front of us or anywhere around Vyšehrad, besieging us. If by next Thursday [31 October] we have not received help from the knights by supplying us with provisions, in substantial quantities or support, it will not be considered as if we receive as little as twenty to thirty bags of provisions. In such a case we, Jan Boskovice and we a. b. c. d. etc. and all the others named above, have promised and are promising by true Christian faith under threat of forfeiting faith and honour, without any deceit, various excuses or other tricks, that tomorrow at the fifteenth hour [9:00 a.m.] we shall hand over without any delay or resistance the castle Vyšehrad, where we are besieged, and surrender to lord Hynek Krušina, the other lords and municipalities mentioned above, together with all guns and gunpowder and other weapons except our personal weapons. We promise to observe a truce with them and not to leave our positions before the aforementioned fifteenth hour, unless King Sigismund arrives. In that case, we would assist him from our side. If we do not fulfil this and did not hand over this castle, where we are under siege, then we demonstrate with this letter that we should forfeit personal faith and honour, and we wish that no one should trust us further, and that we are to be regarded as not having faith and honour. We, named above, put our seal on this letter without coercion by anyone and also on behalf of the community of knights and the others under siege in this castle. Submitted, under the state of siege of our castle Vyšehrad, in the year 1420 since the birth of the Lord, on Monday the day of SS Simon and Jude, apostles of our lord Jesus Christ.'

Even though this agreement was a fine beginning, it displeased Mikuláš of Hus and he retreated from the island with his Táborites to the city of Prague. Beaten by entreaties, however, he led his men over to [the church of] St Pancrac, [leaving] Lord Hynek of Kolštejn to guard the said island. . . . On the vigil of the day of All Saints the king arrived in the New Town early in the morning. However, he was afraid of attacking the Praguers and hoped that further reinforcements might arrive from the Moravian barons. Around evening these [reinforcements] arrived in the New Town but remained in the woods in full armour through the night in order that they would be prepared for an attack first thing in the morning against the Praguers and their supporters. During the night the king sent a message to his troops in the castle [Hradčany] of Prague, with orders to be armed early the next morning and to come down from the fortress and attack the bridge tower and the house of the Duke of Saxony and if possible to burn them down. At the same time with a large force he would drive the Praguers away from the field. But God always opposes the proud and prefers the humble. The messenger and the letter fell into the hands of the Praguers who were now fully aware of the plans of the king. The captains of the Praguers then made plans of where to allocate their men the next morning to most effectively and bravely defend against the attack of the enemy.

Then it transpired that the king together with 15,000 or 20,000 well-armed men approached from the New Town where the armies stood. Standing on the top of a hill where the road comes down in the direction of St Pancrac's Church, he

[Sigismund] drew his sword and brandished it in the air. This was the signal to the Vyšehrad garrison that they should emerge from the castle and attack the enemy since they could see that Sigismund had come with a large army and was preparing to attack the Praguers. But the king, by God's will, had failed to arrive before the hour specified by the agreement and thus the captains of Vyšehrad closed the gates of the castle and did not permit anyone from Vyšehrad to attack the Praguers even though many of them, who were Germans, wished to do so.

When the nobles in the king's army saw that the troops on Vyšehrad did not emerge and that the Praguers were well dug in they advised the king not to launch an attack if he wished to avoid serious damage to his army. But the king said, 'far be it from me to do this. It is absolutely essential that I fight these peasants today.' Then Lord Jindřich of Plumlov addressed the king with great courtesy saying, 'Let it be known to you lord king that you will incur a great loss today and be forced to retreat in disorder for I fear the fighting clubs of these peasants.' But the king said, 'yes I know, you Moravians are cowards and you are not loyal to me.'[1] But Lord Jindřich and other Moravian barons quickly dismounted and said, 'look, we are prepared to go wherever you send us and we shall be in whatever place where you, O king, are not.' Then the king assigned them to the most dangerous post of all and ordered them to advance through the lower part of the field alongside the fish ponds and marsh and launch an attack on the men of Prague while the Hungarians marched along the higher road. So the troops took up this formation and bravely attacked the Praguers in their positions. Initially the Praguers were terrified and began to flee crowding into the Church of St Pancrac. Seeing this, Lord Krušina shouted out, 'Good brethren, return to your places and be brave today as soldiers in the battle of Christ. This is not our war, this is God's fight we are waging. Today you will see our Lord God deliver all of these enemies of ours and of His into our hands.' Even before he had finished what he was saying some one shouted, 'the enemies are running away, they run away.' Hearing this they all rushed forward and drove their enemies back from their entrenchments and turned them to flight. Then the Praguers, together with their barons, chased after them with cruelty and killed some in the marches and in the fish ponds as well as those who were rushing away in all directions through the vineyards and the fields. The peasants struck them down with their fighting clubs and spared none, even though some surrendered and promised to observe the Law of God the rest of their lives. The armoured barons [of the Hussite side] fought valiantly during the battle and

---

[1]   This is reminiscent of Sigismund's attitude earlier when an envoy from Hradec Králové came to the king in Beroun with a proposal from the barons of Hradec Králové that force should be avoided. Sigismund flew into a fit of rage asserting that he would sooner rub the faces of Prague citizens in excrement before he surrendered Vyšehrad and denounced the overture as cowardice. *Historia Hussitica*, in FRB 5, p. 435.

took many prisoners, at great personal risk, and saved many from the battle flails of their brethren. Lord Jindřich of Plumlov was mortally wounded and taken prisoner. He was carried into the churchyard of St Pancrac where he made confession and died asking to receive communion in both kinds. In like manner Lord Jindřich of Lefl died in his tent after confessing and receiving communion in both kinds. There were very few of the Moravian barons who opposed communion in both kinds who survived. Lord Jindřich of Plumlov, the supreme captain of Moravia, who as he promised, joined the king with 2,000 men, Jaroslav of Veseli, Vok of Holštýn, Hyněk of Maleňovice, Albrecht of Chotěnov, Vylém called Zajíc of Židlochovice, Petr of Štemberk, Racek of Rýzmberk, Václav of Clukov, Jindřich Lefl, lord of Bechyně, Aleš Krk Soběšín, Janek the secretary, and many other Bohemian and Moravian barons and knights were butchered like pigs, stripped of all their armour as well as their clothing down to their underwear. What person, unless they were pagan, could walk through these fields and vineyards and view the dead bodies of these brave men without compassion? What Czech, unless he were a madman, could see these rugged warriors, these handsome and curly-haired young men, without being overwhelmed with grief at their fate, especially since many of them on the orders of the [Táborite] priests were left in the fields and in the vineyards and became food for wolves, dogs and birds of the air and were terrifying to those who saw them? Some of them, however, were buried during the night by pious and faithful men. There were about 400 men in armour killed, according to a count, in addition to those who were wounded and killed on the way so that it can be said that about 500 of the king's men were killed. At the same time there were hardly thirty of the Praguers who perished. One of those was Ješek, son of Ješek the goldsmith who fought bravely with Krušina, Bocko and Mikuláš of Hus and who deserved the sword and belt of knighthood. There was on this day a very strong and cold wind which disadvantaged the knights in armour more than the light-clad foot soldiers. There appeared also in the sky a pillar in the form of a rainbow and all who saw it wondered what it meant.

At the time of the battle the mercenaries came down from the castle in Prague [Hradčany] and attacked the Saxon House. But when they saw that their assault had little effect they burned a few houses down in the Lesser Town and retired to the castle from which they had descended.

The king, as already mentioned, stood on the top of a hill during the battle. When he witnessed the pathetic destruction of his men he was struck with terror as well as those with him, and he left in tears. After getting the wounded on carts he moved out of the New Town and took the shortest route to Brod. There he buried one of the Hungarian barons and returned to Kutná Hora with great sorrow. He wanted to cover up the extent of the casualties suffered by the soldiers in his army so he reported that more Praguers had been killed. Then on that day and on the day after, the king and the queen placed green wreaths on their heads and pretended to be happy although in their hearts they were not.

Historia Hussitica, in FRB 5: 435–42.

43   Manifesto after the victory at Vyšehrad

[The very thorough victory at Vyšehrad freed the city of Prague from the immediate threat of Sigismund and the crusaders. A few days after the triumph the city and the leaders of the successful army sent a message to all Czechs castigating the king as an enemy of the kingdom, a destroyer of innocent people and a supporter of an anti-Czech crusade. Of note, is the very clear suggestion that Sigismund deliberately sent Czech troops to their deaths while placing Germans and Hungarians in safer positions. The manifesto can rightly be seen as a means for gathering further support among the barons against the crusade effort. The manifesto is dated 5 November 1420.]

Wishing you all the best, dear friends! We lament over the actions of Sigismund the Hungarian. We wonder whether he even deserves to be called king, this one who has forgotten his noble birth, abandoned the example of kindness and gracefulness of all his ancestors, and is committing unheard-of cruelties. He is perpetrating them in this Crown of the Czech kingdom by atrocious raping of girls and wives, by murdering adults and children and by various iniquities, and with the help of the blood-stained cross, which was never justified in the Christian order, and which the pope unlawfully permitted him to use against us under the pretext of defending the Roman Church. He is cunningly attempting to eradicate the Czech language, which he has defamed all over the world in the most outrageous way, calling us heretics, giving advantage to foreigners in this country and providing them with the positions of expelled Czechs. He proved it quite ostentatiously at Vyšehrad on All Saints' Day, when, after he berated lords, knights and pages, calling them traitors of the Czech language, he placed them in the front line, and in spite of the fact that he could have, he did not want to and did not dare to save them, and so he caused the loss of the lives of more than five hundred prominent people. We lament and regret these Czechs, our brothers, and are sorry that they were seduced to abandon the right faith, and were murdered as a result of his intentions, in order to weaken our Czech language. He spared Germans and Hungarians, the most cruel enemies of our nation, by placing them away from the Czechs, with the eventual intention of weakening the Czechs by making them kill each other, as they were on opposite sides, so that he could defeat them more easily with the help of Germans and Hungarians. He was heard to proclaim in a loud voice that he was willing to give away all of Hungary, if only not one Czech was left in the Czech country.

Therefore, dear friends, out of love and mercy, we beseech you to have pity on yourselves and on your natural language, which this brute wishes to leave in shameful denunciation and to eradicate. Do not help him any further in his atrocities which will lead to your own defamation and final eradication. Instead, do your best, together with us, for the freedom of the law of God represented by all truths, without any oppression, which the king with his helpers is attempting to introduce, by wishing to separate us from our salvation, and to bring us to his heretical faith, proclaimed in Constance, and by doing so to confound us. He did not even want to listen to us, though we often asked him to.

Yet, should you have the intention of assisting him in spite of his obvious atrocities and immense and lawless annihilation of this country, we would be convinced that it is also your wish to eradicate the Czech language, and we would have to take measures against you with the help of God, as against obvious enemies of God and our nation. Remember that we are marching to defend the law of God and the dignity of the Czech nation and the common good. If you do not join us, we will conclude that you too are opposed to the law of God, the Czech language and the common welfare.

Signed on the Tuesday after All Saints' Day [5 November] in the year 1420 after the birth of Christ. Hynek Krušina of Lichtenburk, captain, Viktorin Boček of Kunštát and Poděbrady, Hynek of Valdštejn and Kolštejn, Prokop of Ústí, Jan of Lichtenburk, [together with] the burgomaster, the council and the municipality of the larger New Town of Prague, knights, pages, yeomen, towns and municipalities who adhere to the law of God.

AČ 3: 217–18.

44   Persecution at Prachatice

[The bitter defeats at Prague in the summer and fall of 1420 only caused those sympathetic to the crusade and hostile to the heretics to dig in their heels. This is no where better revealed than in the tensions which prevailed in the southern Bohemian town of Prachatice. The town had promised that the practice of Hussite religion would not be hindered. That vow was not kept. Under pressure from Sigismund's key Czech ally, the powerful Rožmberks, the town implemented repression and purging, including death, of those committed to the Hussite faith. Hussite armies under the command of Jan Žižka made their way to Prachatice to assess and alleviate the situation. The intolerance and violence which went both ways underscores the ethos of crusade.]

In the year of the Lord 1420, on the Tuesday following the day of St Martin, on 12 November, Táborites who were in charge of the town of Písek began to feel compassion for their neighbours in Prachatice who suffered opposition for holding to the law of God. Some of those who had departed following the destruction of the town walls and the fire caused by the artillery of the Táborites returned.[2] Somehow they managed to repair their houses and the walls and they became hostile to all of those who received the communion of the body and blood of the Lord. They captured some of them and forced them to renounce their faith. They confiscated the properties of others and expelled them from the town. Two or three of those who held to the law [of God] were burned. They arrested one of these followers, Ondráček of Vejrov, a former sexton in the church in Prachatice, while he was ploughing and burned him as punishment for stealing pictures [i.e. iconoclasm?].

For this reason, Žižka with his people set out on the journey on the day determined with priests marching in front of them with the body of the Lord with the intention of conquering Prachatice. When the townspeople heard of this they shut the gates and climbed up on the walls in preparation for defence. When Žižka arrived he addressed the people calmly: 'Open the gates and let us come in with the blessed sacrament of the body of Christ, together with our priests. We promise that neither you nor your belongings will be harmed.' But the people of Prachatice replied blasphemously: 'we do not need your body of Christ or your priests. We already have the body of Christ and priests who suit us.' Upon hearing this Žižka replied in a loud voice: 'I confess in the name of God that if I conquer you I will not spare anyone. I will not forgive and I shall order that everyone be killed.' Immediately he ordered his brethren to surround the town. They set up ladders against the walls in many places and forced their way onto the walls. The Táborite artillerymen prevented the townspeople, who were defending their town with cannon, rifles, pitch and stones, from looking out of the balustrade and thus were able to climb the walls in many places. They killed many with their flails on the walls and chased others who tried to escape, slaughtering them like calves in all of the streets. They opened the gates and all of the brothers and sisters walked in singing and carrying the body of our Lord Christ. They went to every house, confiscating possessions, capturing those trying to hide and either killed them or brought them to Žižka. Only the women and children were spared.

Then Žižka ordered that almost all of those captured, with the exception of seven of them who professed the truth of God, be locked in the vestry of the church. The vestry was packed with seventy-five men and he ordered that it be set

---

2   This is a reference to the Hussite offensive at the end of April of that year when Prachatice was conquered and its walls partially destroyed in an effort to eliminate one more place where crusaders might secure a stronghold.

on fire. Clasping their hands together they begged him in the name of God to forgive them and give them the chance to do penance for their sins. [They promised] to follow the Hussites and do whatever they wished, but this was of no avail. The Táborites behaved as though they were deaf. They rolled up barrels of pitch, covered them with straw and threw them onto the heads of the men locked up in the vestry. All of them were suffocated by the flames and the smoke. After this they were covered with stones in the cellar of the vestry as though in a grave and there they were left to rot. Two hundred and thirty corpses lay in the streets. They buried some of them, threw others into the well and expelled all of the women and children.[3] Then they occupied the town themselves surrounded by moats dug with their own hands.

Historia Hussitica, in FRB 5: 443–4.

45   Hussites strike again

[At the same time Žižka was bringing Prachatice to subjection, the backers of the crusade were losing another contest. One of the strongest castles in the possession of the Rožmberks was that of Příbenice in the Lužnice Valley not far south of Tábor. Forces faithful to Sigismund and the anti-Hussite crusade initiative used Příbenice frequently as a base from which to strike at the heretics in south Bohemia. In late September, a number of Táborites including the radical preacher Václav Koranda of Plzeň fell into enemy hands as they journeyed from Tábor to Bechyně. The captives were taken to the strongly fortified castle of Příbenice and held under close guard. The subsequent escape of Koranda and some of his men indicate there must have been Hussite sympathizers in the castle and the willingness of their jailor to actually go to Tábor and summon military help is firm indication of this assumption. As the Hussite armies attacked outside the walls, Koranda and his men holed up in the tower threw stones down upon the defenders. Oldřich Rožmberk in great panic ordered a contingency of mercenaries to hasten to bolster the garrison in Příbenice. They were routed by the Táborites who conquered the castle and also caused the fall of a smaller fortress on the opposite side of the river. Among the new contingency of prisoners was Hermann, bishop of Nikopolis and former suffragan of the Archdiocese of Prague. He had ordained Hussite priests some years earlier after being kidnapped by the heretics. Even though Koranda seems repentant at having possibly killed one of the castle

---

[3]   Sparing the lives of women and children was a consistent policy with Žižka. Since the Táborites immediately occupied the town, the well in question must have been dry.

defenders, he had no compunction about permitting Hermann's death, though the text seems to indicate that Hermann was prepared to join the Hussite cause and ordain as many priests as they required. Despite his promises, he was drowned in the Lužnice River. The fortress of Příbenice remained under Hussite control and served various purposes including that of a prison.]

The same day – on the day of St. Martin (11 November) – the priest Koranda, mentioned earlier, after being captured with other Táborite priests, was in the jail (with Bělobožka) in the castle of Příbenice. Somehow, as God willed it, they freed themselves that night from their shackles and climbed the tower. They forced Odolen, the tower keeper who was watching them, with threats of locking him in the tower, to promise to go to Tábor and to alert them there that the prisoners had freed themselves and now occupied the tower at Příbenice and that help should be sent to them quickly. The aforementioned Odolen wishing to abide by this promise, and not be suspected by his master, asked for permission to go to Tábor on the grounds that the prisoners had asked him to buy fish for them which they could bake. His master said to him, 'hurry up so that the villainous heretics can guzzle baked fish and then I will give the order to burn them.' When Odolen brought the message to Tábor, [Zbyněk] Buchov, who had his people prepared already since he had planned to go somewhere else, marched out immediately. Arriving at Příbenice he began to storm [the castle]. At the same time the people of Soběslav arrived at Příbenice to assist them. So they fought until Buchov, the captain of Tábor, conquered the castle and many of the Rožmberk people were killed there. From this time until his death the priest Václav Koranda did not officiate at mass, because while Příbenice was being stormed, he, together with others, was throwing stones down from the tower as they were defending themselves on the tower. Thinking he may have killed someone, he did not permit himself to officiate at mass, but preached only.

The Táborites, when they found the priest bishop Hermann, (Hermann was a good man who used to be the parish priest in Miličíně), they drowned him. This bishop previously had ordained many of the Táborite priests in Lipnic, at the urging of Lord Čeněk [of Vartemberk], and then he opposed them saying [regretfully], 'I have ordained all those rascals'.[4]

---

[4]   As an example of this tendency, according to a report in 1429, 'they [the Táborites] allowed their bishop Hermann, doctor of Holy Scripture, who ordained many of them, to be drowned. As he was carried away by the river, confessing the truth of God, and willing to do anything, they did not care but allowed stones to be thrown at him, and watched, and while they could stop it by giving the order, they did not do it as they did not wish to.' Jan Příbram, 'The lives of the Táborite priests', in *Ktož jsú boží bojovnici: Čtení o táboře v*

[Later reports embellish this account of Hermann's death, portraying the hapless bishop struggling in the current of the river while Hussite heretics jeered and threw stones at him.]

SRB 3: 42–3.

46   Truce between Hussites and Oldřich Rožmberk

[A daily guerilla war was carried out against the staunchly Catholic and anti-Hussite Rožmberk family in south Bohemia.[5] For twenty years this conflict went on. The court books of the lords of Rožmberk reflect the Hussites from the opposing point of view. From time to time the warring factions reached temporary peace. After the capture of Prachatice, the Rožmberks were amenable to another settlement. The one below was written at Písek and dated 18 November 1420.]

We, Jan called Žižka of Trocnov, Chval of Machovice, Zbyněk of Buchov, Pavlík of Mutice and all the town of Písek acting as guarantors do witness this publicly before all who may hear of it by any means whether through speech or written word, that by the authority in this letter we have undertaken a proper Christian truce with the baron Oldřich of Rožmberk and all of those connected to him up until the beginning of Lent including Shrove Tuesday. We promise on the basis of our Christian faith to maintain this truce, as well as all of those communities under us under penalty of 10,000 groschen in authentic Prague silver currency. We, the aforementioned guarantors, together with the captains, judges, burgomaster, councillors and the entire population of the town of Písek do make this promise individually and collectively under this undivided signature to maintain this agreement under the penalty of ten thousand [groschen].

Alternatively, the aforementioned baron Lord Oldřich Rožmberk has undertaken according to this agreement with us to maintain on all his land and property the following articles. First, free preaching of the word of God. Second, that without exception the holy body and blood of the Lord is to be given to all faithful people regularly. Third, that clerical wealth be abolished and fourth, that in as much as possible all serious sins shall be eliminated on all of his properties. To these agreements he is bound under the same penalty as mentioned above.

---

husitském revolučním hnutí, ed., Josef Macek (Prague: Melantrich, 1951), p. 283. According to this view, the bishop was essentially a martyr.

[5]   On Rožmberk, most recently John Klassen, 'The Public and Domestic Faces of Ulrich of Rožmberk' *Sixteenth Century Journal* 31 (No. 3, 2000), pp. 699–718.

Should we fail to observe the truce, God forbid, it then becomes our obligation and sworn duty to hand over within one month after notice, the aforesaid penalty at Krumlov or New Castle or wherever our creditors require. If we fail to do so within one month, then we give complete authority to the aforesaid baron, Lord Oldřich Rožmberk and his burgraves to reprimand, curse, arrest, place in prison or put us and all of our people under contribution for as long as the penalty is unpaid. To confirm this agreement we affix our seals to this letter.

Given in the year 1420 after the birth of the Lord, on Monday of the octave of St Martin.

Bartoš, pp. 7–8.

47 Žižka and Táborite leaders address Czech people

[This letter, written from Prachatice on 25 November 1420 by the elites of the radical anti-crusade cause, underscores the basis for Hussite resistance but at the same it also introduces a coercive tone in relation to the Czechs who did not support the active, radical programme. As the crusade period progressed, there was even less toleration for those in Bohemia who chose not to support the Hussites.]

Our Lord Jesus Christ who has in grief shed his blood for us be with us and with you all amen.

Dear brethren and friends, we send you this message to say that should it be told to you that we have become your enemies we make affirmation and beseech you as beloved neighbours that you not believe this. Instead, you will find out who our enemies are. They are the wicked priests and laity who have taken a stand and who write against the holy gospel. Beyond this we wish for you to know that on account of these Four Articles we despise all false Christians. First, that God's word be preached everywhere throughout Christendom which is not the case. Second, that the true body and holy blood of our Lord be given to all authentic Christians, both young and old. Third, that the power of priests from the highest level, even the papacy, to the lowest not be tolerated. Neither may they own estates or collect tithes and that any power of these church lords assisted by secular barons be eliminated. Fourth, that all clear sin be driven out whether by king or lords, squires or priests, or ecclesiastical or secular people.

We hope that you, our dear brethren, will accept the truth and will assist us to stand against every false and unbelieving Christian, whether ecclesiastical or secular, who is in opposition to this holy sacred truth. Please reply to this letter in writing. Should you fail to do so we will take the view that you are willingly enemies of God as well as of the Táborite brethren.

Given at Prachatice, on Friday before St Catherine's Day. Jan Žižka, Chval, leaders and directors of the Táborites. Jeník, captain at Prachatice.

Bartoš, pp. 8–9.

48   Abbot in Třeboň promises support against Hussites

[After crusader defeats at Vítkov and Vyšehrad, communities loyal to the official church and to the claims of Sigismund began to fear backlash from the Hussite armies. Buoyed by their successes at Prague, Žižka's armies continued their daily war against the powerful Catholic coalitions. The abbot of the monastery in the southern Bohemian town of Třeboň wrote to Oldřich Rožmberk on 25 January 1421 reporting on agreements between southern towns to oppose the Hussites.]

First, a faithful prayer. Dear Sir. Please be aware that I have negotiated with Budějovice about guns and other assistance. Following some consideration, Lord Krajíř [of Krajku and Landštejn, a captain at Budějovice] together with the councillors and elders have given us this answer. 'We are anticipating that our enemies will attack us at any time now, therefore we must look out for ourselves in the first instance. However, soon we will have more soldiers and guns. If we have more than we need we will be pleased to supply Třeboň with guns, men to fire them as well as other soldiers. Therefore, dear sir, take care in the meanwhile so that you suffer no harm.' Also, some of the elders spoke with me saying, they wondered what the lord has in mind and why he does not inform us concerning his intentions. Then I told them that your grace intends to notify them and they were pleased to hear this. They promised to send Jaroš and others to the town to help them. Dated on the conversion of Paul, Ondřej, abbot of the monastery in Třeboň.

Rynešová 1: 32–3.

49   Manifesto to the Plzeň Alliance

[The political unit represented by the west Bohemian city of Plzeň was the strongest point of anti-Hussite sentiment in the country. This manifesto of February 1421 argues the righteousness of the Hussite cause, castigates the policies of Sigismund and affirms continued resistance to the crusader initiative. The counter charge of heresy is noteworthy.]

We, Jan Žižka and Chval of Machovicc, captains and leaders of the Táborites, true Czech people hoping in God, warn all of you by the death of our Lord, specially you knights and squires, both people in the cities and peasants belonging to the Plzeň Landfríd to cease opposing the Lord God and God's holy law as well as the worthy Four Articles. It is for these matters that we fight with the help of God. But you stand in opposition to them and you attempt to detract us from their righteousness and from the salvation of our souls. The first of these is the liberty to hear the word of God. The second is to receive the body and blood of the Lord. You refuse to receive it and yet you try to prevent us and other faithful people from receiving it. The third pertains to the wealth and opulence of the clerics. This constitutes heresy. It should have been destroyed by you. Instead you defend it against our Lord God and you are even willing to die for it and to suffer the awful sentence of death as heretics. Fourth, you should have put down and eliminated those guilty of committing deadly sins. Instead, alas, you offer them support.

Among those you assist is the Hungarian King Sigismund, a heretical king, who has betrayed our Lord God as well as his sacred word. He is the violator of young girls and women, a murderer and arsonist. He intends to destroy our Czech nation. Along with him is the baron [Bohuslav] of Švamberk, barons of Švihov, Jindřich of Elsterberk and barons of Kolovraty. You have helped these men oppose the Lord God, to cause the reading of God's word to cease, and to thwart the establishment of divine order in this land as God wills it. Their will is to deceive you in order that you lose your souls and forfeit your property as well. They seek to win the praise of the king and be honoured by him for forcing you eventually to serve him and labour on his behalf. Thus you will lose your souls and everything else also. We are not surprised that people who keep not faith with God do not keep faith with men either.

Therefore we must warn you to be aware of these men otherwise they will betray you and worse than this, your souls will be lost. They would like to do this to us as well were it not for God's help. However, we trust that our Lord God will save us from their nefarious purposes. May God our Lord also grant you the ability to be able to escape from the traps set by the enemies of God so that you might be able to find your way to God, the one who gave you body and soul.

You wish that we would not destroy your land and burn your houses down. Why have you not given liberty to God's word and to the worthy Four Articles noted above when you were among the first to hear them? Is it not true that you told us you were willing to grant freedom to these articles and agreed that this was right and proper? But you were speaking lies to us and in the face of God.

Bartoš, pp. 10–11.

50   Letter of Jan Roháč of Dubá to Oldřich Rožmberk

[Jan Roháč of Dubá was one of Žižka's chief lieutenants who played a key role in
the anti-crusade resolve from the beginning to the very end. His letter underscores
the persistent Hussite frustration with the powerful Rožmberks of south Bohemia.
Sigismund had no greater ally within Bohemia throughout the crusading period.
The letter is dated 3 February 1421.]

Noble lord! As I wrote previously admonishing you out of love not to oppose God
and God's holy truths, so now I would like to see that you do not perish in soul or
in property. I have received no reply from you. Therefore I cannot understand why
you do not desire to spread the truth of God and God's holy law and defend them
with the sword. It is proper for every Christian knight to put on his belt and sword
and do his best in order to spread the truth of God and to praise the holy writings
so that the knaves of Antichrist might be destroyed.

I have written to you in an earlier letter, in a reasonable manner, but I have
received no answer from you. Therefore you must know that either in time of war
or peace I am remaining near to our Lord Jesus Christ together with the faithful
Táborite brotherhood and I desire to remain so, along with my brothers and
servants and other helpers and with all those who wish to help. I do not want to
be guilty in anything I have written with respect to you, your servants and
subjects.

Dated in Lomnice the second day after the Feast of Purification. Jan Roháč
of Dubá, commander at Lomnice.

Rynešová 1: 33–4.

51   A Moravian Tábor

[In February 1421 a 'new Tábor' was established in Moravia near the town of
Strážnice in a region around the lower Morava River. Here the Hussite influence
was stronger than anywhere else in Moravia. The strength of the 'new Tábor' was
sufficient to repulse an assault by Austrian dukes and the bishop of Olomouc in
1421 and later withstood the efforts of a Hungarian army, under orders from
Sigismund, to destroy it.]

In the same year, 1421, in the month of February, a new Tábor began in a village
called Nedakunice near Strážnice which is situated on an island in the Morava
River. These Táborites, together with peasants, a few priests and barons, occupied
the Velehrad monastery. They burned the monks, the abbot, many books and the

entire monastery. Fearing that they would suffer the same damages as in Bohemia, the bishop of Olomouc and the barons and cities of Moravia moved quickly, with some Austrian forces, and attempted to conquer the island. In the attack many Austrians and citizens of Olomouc were killed. Following this, they burned their military equipment and withdrew. Hungarians also tried to take the island but suffering defeat as well they withdrew.

On this island were some bloodthirsty priests wearing beards but no tonsures, who fought like laymen. They paid no heed to the rites of the church but celebrated [the eucharist] after saying only the Lord's prayer and wearing only their own clothes. Their two principal leaders were Bedřich and Tomáš of Věžonice.

Historia Hussitica, in FRB 5: 473–4.

52   Mass murder in the east

[Early in February, Táborites established bases in eastern Bohemia to support their adherents in the upper Labe River valley. Such bases would also be an asset in defending against crusader invasion from Moravia. The leader was Jan Hromádka of Jistebnice (see doc. 13). His troops were divided into the towns of Přelouč, between Pardubice and Kolín, and Chotěboř, which was situated northeast of Německý Brod. Not long after they established themselves they were attacked by forces loyal to King Sigismund led by Lord Jan Městecký of Opočno and Mikuláš 'the fierce', the master of the mint in Kutná Hora. Přelouč was taken easily and numerous Hussites were executed. Chotěboř was then assailed by the same forces but with the help of Půta of Častolovice, another baron firmly committed to the crusade against heretics. After a siege lasting several days, the defenders asked for terms and were promised safe conduct on the honour of the lords. Hromádka agreed. Acting on the time worn principle that faith need not be kept with heretics, three hundred Táborites were burned to death on the spot.[6] The rest were marched off to Kutná Hora. Some were burned alive on the way, the rest were thrown alive into the mine shafts upon arrival. Hromádka was burned at the stake in Chrudim the next day.]

In the same year [1421], three weeks before Shrovetide, miners conquered the church in Přelouč and the people were taken to Kutná Hora. Then on Shrovetide

---

[6]   'Et cum juxta sanctorum Patrum canonicas sanctiones ei qui Deo fidem non servat fides servanda non sit. . . .' PL 215: 1357, a statement from a circular letter of Pope Innocent III in 1208. This attitude is noted in the *Historia Hussitica*, FRB 5, p. 429.

Tuesday [4 February], miners conquered Chotěboř. At the time Hromádka was the captain in Chotěboř. Lord Opočenský convinced them [to surrender] and made honest promises that their lives would not be endangered [by doing so]. However, he rounded them up and herded them into three barns and burned them. [Manuscript L adds: One woman, seeing that her husband was burning jumped into the flames and burned along with her husband. In Horky, forty were driven into a cottage and burned. . . .] Some 700 of them [Hussites] died here thanks to the dishonourable lord. On 5 February they executed Hromádka in Chrudim. . . .

SRB 3: 44.

53   Carnage and conquest at Chomútov

[The betrayal and mass murder of more than 700 Hussites at Chotěboř could neither go unnoticed nor unavenged. The siege was raised against the town of Chomútov and for two days the defenders repulsed the Hussite armies. On the third day, the town fell and wholesale slaughter followed. The normal rule of sparing women and children was contravened. From other sources we learn that the Hussites offered to spare the Jewish community in Chomútov but the Jews preferred to perish rather than renounce their faith. *Chronicon veteris Collegiati*, in Höfler, 1:83. The result of the offensive at Chomútov was the securing of several important towns for the Hussite cause in opposition to the crusade threat. The news spread widely and fear struck the hearts of the intending crusaders. According to other sources 'this was the first time they [Hussites] committed a cruel act and it was a most horrible one.' SRB 3, p. 44.]

In the same year, 1421, when an agreement with Plzeň had been reached, as noted earlier, the entire army moved towards the town of Chomútov which they surrounded on the 15th of March, on the Saturday before Easter Sunday. When the Germans looked over the walls and saw the army they cursed them and thwarted their attack. However, on the following day, that is on Easter Sunday, the army attacked the town from all sides, crossing the moat and scaling the walls. They ignored the hot water and melted pitch which the inhabitants of the town poured down on them from the walls. The castle was taken from one side by the Prague army and from the other side by the Táborite army and they climbed into the castle and conquered the town. When they entered they looted everywhere and they killed all of the men in the town, some with the sword, others by burning. They spared only forty of them and these people buried the corpses. At least 2,015 were buried by them in addition to many yeomen, priests and Jews who were burned.[7] But the villainous Táborite women committed a horrible crime. They took women and young girls out of the town, all of them crying out, with the promise of releasing them and allowing them to depart unharmed. However, when they got out of the town they stripped them, took their money and jewellery and locked them into a shed in the vineyard where the grapes are pressed and burned them, not even sparing the pregnant women.

After the Prague army took control of the town they marched off towards Žatec and many strongholds and castles, driven by fear, surrendered to them. The inhabitants of Louny, being frightened, sent their delegates to Žatec and surrendered to the Praguers. The army from Prague took over Louny and appointed as councillors those who previously had been expelled from the town on account of their [Hussite] faith and then marched on to Slaný. While they prepared to attack, the inhabitants of the town surrendered, opened their gates and let the army enter. The army appointed their own people and after achieving these tremendous victories, returned to Prague on Easter vigil, conquering on the way Makotřasy and Okoř.

Historia Hussitica, in FRB 5: 476–7.

54   Union of German bishops

[In light of the perceived growing Hussite threat, and in the shadow of the terrifying retribution in eastern Bohemia, the archbishops of Mainz, Trier and Cologne along with the palsgrave, Ludwig of Wittelsbach organized a union against the Czech heretics on 23 April 1421 during the Reichstag in Nürnberg.]

We, Conrad of Mainz, Otto of Trier, Dietrich of Cologne, archbishops by the grace of God of the Holy Roman Empire in German and foreign [French and Italian] lands, and through the kingdom of Arles and in Italy archchancellors, and Ludwig, count palatine of the Rhine, the Holy Roman Empire's lord high steward and duke in Bavaria, all four of us electors of the Holy Roman Empire, declare and publicly announce with this letter to all those who learn of its content by hearing or reading it: that, with regard to the matter of heresy and infidelity, which unfortunately have arisen in the Kingdom of Bohemia, and with regard to which it has to be feared that if we do not counteract them in good time, that they will

---

[7]   The figures killed vary but all accounts make the number substantial. Texts in the 'old Czech annalists' collection give the figures of 2,200 and 2,300 in addition to the 2,105 plus others noted above. SRB 3, p. 44. 'The very fine chronicle of Jan Žižka' (doc.107) numbers 3,000 among the dead.

also occur in other lands, that in order to remain even more united and to be able to resist them the more excellently and the more powerfully together and in cooperation with the support and help of other Christian princes, dukes, barons, knights, squires, cities, and communities of Christian associations, as we are obliged to as electors and the highest and the closest members of the Holy Roman Empire, so we all have associated and united, for the glory of Almighty God and for the strengthening of all Christianity and the Christian faith and for the honour, benefit and profit of the most serene prince and lord master Sigismund, Roman etc. King, our merciful dear master, and of the Holy Roman Empire – we all associate and unite by virtue of this letter.

If it were the case that the same, our merciful master, the Roman King, should demand and request from us, the aforementioned electors, together or separately, help in order to go to Bohemia on account of the aforementioned heretics, then we shall and will consult with one another and hold council on this in order to give an answer to his request. And we shall and will give him such an answer together and from all four of us, and we shall not separate or be separated from one another with regard to this matter in any way without any reservations. Furthermore, none of us, with regard to such help and support, shall seek or accept any special advantage from the abovementioned King our master, without the knowledge and the consent of the others among us, all reservations and malicious intent completely excluded. All that is written above we, the aforementioned electors, promise, say, and swear to on our Christian loyalty and our princely honour and worthiness, that we shall at all times honestly and firmly keep to it and implement it and do it and do nothing against it, neither clandestinely nor openly, through ourselves or through someone else, in any way and without any reservations. All this to record and firmly to testify to, each one of us has attached his seal to this letter in the proper manner, which is given in Nürnberg in the year 1421 after the birth of Christ, on the day of St George [23 April], the holy knight and martyr.

DR 8: 28–9.

55   Bishops outline anti-heresy strategy

[Sigismund's absence from the Reichstag caused the balance of crusading power to move into the hands of the Rhenish electors. This was a move fully supported by the papal legate for the crusade, the aging Cardinal Branda. While the union promised undying support for Sigismund in his actions against the Hussites, the electors seized the opportunity to move ahead with their own plans which included rooting out heresy at the grass-roots level. In one sense this complimented Sigismund's policies but on the other the Emperor was somewhat eclipsed by the

German electors in the crusade against the heretics in Bohemia. Sustained bickering in the higher echelons of imperial politics later had a negative impact upon the crusade initiative. While Sigismund's authority was not overtly challenged, his frequent, and sometimes unexplained, absences from the crusade process itself did little to enhance his reputation in Germany and in some cases created no lack of ill will.]

We, Conrad of Mainz, Otto of Trier, Dietrich of Cologne. . . . and Ludwig, count palatine of the Rhine. . . . that we have seen and observed such heresy and infidelity, which unfortunately have arisen in the kingdom of Bohemia, and with regard to which it has to be feared that if we do not counteract them in good time, that they will also occur in other lands. And therefore, we as Christian princes, to whom such things and defects are a great pain, in order to resist them, for the glory of Almighty God and for the strengthening of all Christianity and the Christian faith and for the honour, benefit and profit of the most serene prince and lord master Sigismund, Roman etc. King, our merciful dear master, and [for the honour, benefit and profit] of the Holy Roman Empire, have associated and united, with well-thought-out firm counsel of our councillors, – we all associate and unite by virtue of this letter in the form as is written hereafter.

First, we shall and will resist such infidelity and destroy it wherever it may develop or arise, and we shall also firmly help and support each other against all those who deliberately support or help the same infidels, with our knights, cities, castles, lands and people and with our subjects and with all our might without any reservations.

Furthermore, we shall and will in each and every one of our cities, castles, markets, villages, lands, and areas earnestly and strongly decree to our officials, servants, and our people [the following]: where one becomes aware of such heretics and infidels or of such persons who are suspected of this, be it men or women, clerics or secular persons, that one shall stop and apprehend them and hand them over to us or a senior official, as is required. And we shall and will, at all times, also have all of them tried on the basis of the given facts in order to destroy the aforementioned heresy and infidelity, as is required, without any reservations.

Furthermore, we shall and will decree that each and every one of our citizens and subjects of male gender in our cities, markets, villages and lands, who are more than twelve years of age and who are of sane mind, promise and swear by the saints to resist such heresy and infidelity, and also to reprimand and to report such infidels and heretics, when they become aware of them, and to help to get hold of them and to hand them over to their masters and officials, without delay. To this effect, we shall and will decree to each and every one of our dukes, barons, knights, squires and those who belong to us, over whom we have legal power and who do what we want them to do or not to do, that they shall decree to each and every one of their citizens, poor people, and subjects that they shall also promise and swear by the saints in the same way as is written above.

We, the aforementioned electors, shall and will, for the sake of the preservation and strengthening of the Christian faith and in order to destroy the aforementioned heresy and infidelity, consult and negotiate with other princes, dukes, barons, knights, squires and cities of the Holy Empire, where we deem this necessary, and will bring them on our side with regard to this matter. And every one of us shall and may on behalf of all four of us invite and receive princes, dukes, barons, knights, squires and cities into our alliance. And those princes, dukes, nobles, knights, squires and cities who are invited and received into our union described above by all or one of us above-mentioned electors shall give to all four of us their letters with their seals attached to support and to help us against such heresy and infidelity and to destroy them, as is written above, truthfully and with all their might, without any reservation, and also against all those who might interfere. By the same token, we will faithfully help and support them with regard to this matter and against them, and if they so wish, we shall give them our sealed letters, without any reservations. And if it were the case that many princes, dukes, barons, knights, squires or cities will come into this alliance not through all of us, the aforementioned electors, but through one of us, then that one of us, through whom they join this alliance, who invites and receives them into it, shall announce this to us and inform us. And also, if we, the others, demand of the same among us who invites and receives them into our union to help us on behalf of our alliance against whom it may become necessary, then he shall extend the same demand to them. And the one of us who will invite and receive them into this coalition, may also demand on their behalf that we help them if that is necessary.

Also if it were the case that someone wished to display ill will or do harm to us, the aforementioned electors, or our dukes, barons, knights, or squires or our subjects or princes, dukes, nobles, knights, squires or cities, who shall join our alliance, all of us or individually, because of our Christian union, in whatever way that may be, then we shall and will not abandon each other and we shall faithfully help and support each other against this in the same way and to the same extent as if we were concerned ourselves and if it were our own matter, all reservations and malicious intent completely excluded. All that is written above we, the aforementioned electors, promise, say, and swear to on our Christian loyalty and our princely honour and worthiness, that we shall at all times honestly and firmly keep to it and implement it and do it and do nothing against it, neither clandestinely nor openly, through ourselves or through someone else, in no way, all reservations and malicious intent completely excluded. All this to record and firmly to testify to, each one of us has attached his seal to this letter in the proper manner, which is given in Nürnberg in the year 1421 after the birth of Christ, on the day of St. George [23 April], the holy knight and martyr.

DR 8: 30–1.

56   Support for the episcopal coalition

[There was some response to this episcopal union throughout the German territory. The bishropic of Speyer is an example reflected in this incomplete document dated 24 April.]

We, Rabann, bishop of Speyer by the mercy of God, declare. . . as a Christian prince. . . to the venerable and highborn princes and lords, master Conrad of Mainz, master Otto of Trier and master Dietrich of Cologne, archbishops, and master Ludwig, count palatine of the Rhine etc., electors of the Holy Roman Empire. . . that they will invite and receive to them into the aforementioned alliance. . . by the above-mentioned, our masters, the electors or a single one of them. . . by the above-mentioned master Albrecht [bishop of Bamberg]. . . with all our power. . . the aforementioned, our masters, the electors, or other princes, noblemen or cities, whom they shall take into this coalition, together or individually. . . . We, the aforementioned Rabann, bishop of Speyer, promise on the Thursday after the day of St George, the holy knight and martyr. . . .

DR 8: 32.

57   Johannes, bishop of Würzburg joins the union

[The electors met again in May at Wesel in an effort to obtain formal military support from other sympathetic princes, cities and barons. This effort was moderately successful. Even prior to the meetings at Wesel, there were powerful additions to the growing coalition. The membership of the bishop of Würzburg must be viewed as significant. The union promised to defend and assist all of its members against all threat or enemy in return for their loyalty against the Hussite heretics.]

We, Conrad of Mainz, Otto of Trier, Dietrich of Cologne. . . . and Ludwig, count palatine of the Rhine. . . . Unfortunately, grave heresy and infidelity have arisen in the Kingdom of Bohemia, with regard to which it has to be feared that if we do not counteract them in good time, that they will also occur in other lands, and therefore, we as Christian princes, to whom such things and defects are a great pain, in order to resist them, for the glory of Almighty God and for the strengthening of all Christianity and the Christian faith and for the honour, benefit and profit of the most serene prince and lord master Sigismund, the Roman King, ever Augustus and king of Hungary etc., our merciful dear master. . . .

We have, for the preservation and strengthening of the Christian faith and so that we may be able to destroy and suppress the aforementioned heresy and infidelity more strongly and more powerfully, invited and received the venerable master Johannes, bishop of Würzburg, our dear special friend, who is also a member and prince of the Holy Roman Empire, into our aforementioned union – we invite and receive him to the alliance by virtue of this letter. And he has joined us with regard to the same matters and he will faithfully support and help us against the aforementioned heresy and infidelity and to destroy and suppress them with his and his foundation's knights, castles, cities and lands and with all his might, as is shown in his letter, which he has given to us with his seal attached.

And therefore we, the four aforementioned electors, promise, say, and swear to the aforementioned master Johannes, the bishop of Würzburg, and again by virtue of this letter, that we shall and will faithfully support and help the same master Johannes, bishop of Würzburg, in order to resist and destroy such infidelity wherever it may develop or arise, in our or in his and other princes', dukes' or masters' lands or also in cities which we will invite and receive to us into this alliance, and also against all those who deliberately support and help the same heretics and infidels, if he is in trouble and if he asks us for help, with our knights, castles, cities, lands, people and our subjects, with all our might, without any reservations. And none of us shall ever decline to help the other, without any reservations.

If it were the case that somebody wanted to display ill will or do harm to the aforementioned master Johannes, bishop of Würzburg, or his or his foundation's dukes, barons, knights, or squires or his subjects or other princes, nobles, or cities, who shall join our coalition, all of us or individually, because of our Christian alliance for the destruction of such heresy and infidelity, in whatever way that may be, then we shall and will faithfully help and support him against this in the same way and to the same extent as if we were concerned ourselves and if it were our own matter, all reservations and malicious intent completely excluded. All that is written above we, the aforementioned electors, promise, say, and swear to on our Christian loyalty and our princely honour and worthiness, that we shall at all times honestly and firmly keep to it and implement it and do it and do nothing against it, neither clandestinely nor openly, through ourselves or through somebody else, in no way, all reservations and malicious intent completely excluded. All this to record and firmly to testify to, each one of us has attached his seal to this letter in the proper manner, which is given in Nürnberg in the year 1421 after the birth of

Christ, on the Thursday [24 April] following the day of St George, the holy knight and martyr.

DR 8: 33–4.

58   Crusader alliance with Albrecht, bishop of Bamberg

[In June, the electors again convened, this time at Mainz and here they met with even greater success in securing military backing for a proposed crusade into Bohemia. Prior to this the bishop of Bamberg declared in favour of the union and yet another powerful ally was won. The following document is similar in nature and content to that relating to the bishop of Würzburg and is dated 28 April.]

We, Conrad of Mainz, Otto of Trier, Dietrich of Cologne. . . . and Ludwig, count palatine of the Rhine. . . . have associated and united, with well-thought-out firm counsel of our councillors, and in the right way, with the venerable father in God master Albrecht, bishop of Bamberg, our special good friend – we associate and unite with him by virtue of this letter as is written hereafter.

First, we shall and will faithfully help and support him, in order to resist and destroy such infidelity wherever it may develop or arise, in his or other princes', dukes' or masters' lands or also in cities which will associate and unite with us with regard to these matters, and also against all those who deliberately support and help the same heretics and infidels, whenever we are asked for help by the aforementioned master Albrecht, with our knights, castles, cities, lands, people and our subjects, according to our ability, without any reservations.

Furthermore, we shall and will in all and every one of our cities, castles, markets, villages, lands, and areas earnestly and strongly decree to our officials, servants, and our people: where one becomes aware of such heretics and infidels or of such persons who are suspected of this, be it men or women, clerics or secular persons, that one shall stop and catch them and hand them over to us or our senior officials, who are under our orders, as is required. And we shall and will, at all times, also have all of them tried on the basis of the given facts in order to destroy the aforementioned heresy and infidelity, as is required, without any reservations. . . . All this to record and firmly to testify to, each one of us has attached his seal to this letter in the correct fashion, which is given in Nürnberg in the year 1421 after the birth of Christ, on the Monday [28 April] after the Sunday when one sings in church the Vocem jocunditatis [Fifth Sunday after Easter].

DR 8: 35–7.

59   Ulm, Memmingen and other cities join the bishops

[By the end of April, even before the assemblies at Wesel and Mainz had convened, the energetic episcopal initiative had successfully secured sufficient support not only to undertake a further crusade campaign against the recalcitrant heretics, but also to exert further pressure upon Emperor Sigismund. The following document guaranteeing urban support must be dated shortly after 23 April.]

We, the mayors, councillors, and citizens of the cities of Ulm, Memmingen etc., which are associated, declare. . . with the venerable and highborn princes and lords master Conrad of Mainz, master Otto of Trier, and master Dietrich of Cologne, archbishops etc., and master Ludwig, count palatine of the Rhine, lord high steward of the Holy Roman Empire and duke in Bavaria, electors of the Holy Roman Empire, our merciful dear master with well-thought-out, firm and appropriate counsel of our councillors with ourselves, our fellow-citizens, subjects and according to our ability. . . .

We shall and will also earnestly and strongly decree to ourselves with our fellow citizens, officials and subjects of the city of Ulm and the other cities etc. which are associated with us, and also to each and every one of our citizens and the citizens of the same cities and the cities, castles, markets, villages, lands and areas belonging to us, with our and their officials, servants, and subjects. Where one becomes aware of such heretics and infidels or of such persons who are suspected of this, be it men or women, clerics or secular persons, that one shall stop and catch them and, if they are priests, monks, or clerics, hand them over to our highest prelates and bishops or their officials, who will act in their name, also we shall have all of them, at all times, tried on the basis of the given facts in order to destroy the aforementioned heresy and infidelity, as is required, without any reservations. . . .

Furthermore, we shall and will decree, that we ourselves and also each and every one of our male fellow citizens and subjects in the city of Ulm and the others which are associated with us, and also each and every one of the fellow citizens and those belonging to us of our and the same cities, over whom we have legal power in cities, castles, markets [shall] hand them over. . . . [as] if we, our fellow citizens and the city of Ulm and those which are associated with us were concerned ourselves.

All that is written above we, the aforementioned mayors, councils, and citizens of the city of Ulm and those associated with us etc., promise, say, and swear to on our Christian loyalty and honour in lieu of an oath, that we shall at all times [fulfil this obligation]. All this to record and firmly to testify to, we, the mayors, councillors, and citizens of the city of Ulm and of those associated with us, have attached our seal to this letter, which is given etc.

DR 8: 37–8.

60   Archbishop of Prague supports heretics

[In a serious blow for the crusading cause, Konrad of Vechta, Archbishop of Prague, declared his allegiance to the Hussites on 21 April 1421. This move had significant implications for both sides. The Saxon religious Ludolf, abbot of an Augustinian house in the Silesian town of Żagań, noted the event with shock and condemnation in his chronicle in the spring of 1421.]

Konrad, the Archbishop of Prague, although he suffered the destruction of his archiepiscopal court in Prague, and many other kinds of misfortunes in the beginning from the Hussites, in the end, however, turning towards Satan and away from the correct faith and rite, and foully going apostate from the observances of the universal Church, joined himself to their sect and perfidy. He did not persevere in the end with the good work he had begun, and likewise he cannot be saved without penitence. What earlier he admirably attacked, afterwards he approved in shame; the heretical error from which earlier his soul shrank is drunk by him like sweet wine. He either asked the leaders of the Hussites and Wyclifites in his city of Roudnice to preach in public their false doctrines regarding the taking of communion under both kinds, or he allowed them to do so, and some estimate that he decreed that others should take communion in this way. Indeed either adhering to or unable to resist their other venomous rites, assertions, and doctrines, he permitted the laity of his city of Roudnice to be deceived and seduced by himself, either appearing converted from a pastor into a wolf or seeing the wolf coming into his flock he fled like a mercenary, while in the upheaval of this time he hid himself in silence.

Therefore he is held in great reverence by the Wyclifites and Hussites, from which he stood out with hate previously, as now they write 'our most reverend father and archbishop in Christ.' Now through him they make whom they wish excommunicated, under interdict, and suspended, while earlier they cared nothing for excommunication, and said that other kinds of ecclesiastical censure were also nothing. Perhaps they were unaware what his opinions prior to his adherence with them were, for they were not promulgated by heretical or schismatic manifest, or by a supporter, harbourer, or even a defender of theirs. Moreover, the custom among the Hussites is corruption, for when he wished to unite himself to their perverse congregation, he had to make a confession that he had erred previously in the true and immaculate profession of Christianity. Furthermore he confessed that he abjured the faith in the future with an oath on account of their perfidy, which they say is the true, orthodox, and Catholic faith, wishing to continue in their wickedness until the end of his days. Whether he performed this promise, guarantee, and confession, deviating himself from us to them, only he knows.

I do know, however, through a most upright man that regardless of this oath, confession, and promise the regular canons ruling the parish of Roudnice wish to make known that they remain unperverted by the Wyclifites in their affairs, goods, and substance; or at least that even though they were harmed they were not harmed as gravely as the archbishop. For scorning to perform such an oath, promise and confession, their monastery was burnt (9 May 1421) in a large part by those impious and perverse men, and they found solace only in flight; and not without the danger of death or great injury did they flee, and not without the verbal reproach of their persecutors.

Ludolf of Żagań, pt. 2, chap. 10, pp. 496–7.

61   Crusade commander orders death to all heretics

[The crusader resolve was damaged but not broken by the disastrous events at Prague in July 1420. The next year, Sigismund forged ahead with a new plan to exterminate the Hussite heretics and their defenders. On 18 May 1421 the king wrote a letter to various officials in Lusatia urging all available men to join with the Silesian dukes and forces for the purpose of wiping out the Hussite menace.]

We, Sigismund, by the grace of God king of the Romans, for all time, commend to each and every lord, knight, vassal, mayor, councillor and citizen in general, as well as to the entire region and the common people of our land and the towns of Budyšin, Zhorjelc, Žitava, Lubán, Löbau and Kamentz, our dear and faithful ones.

We have no doubt that it has come to you what inhumanity the Wyclifites and the heretics in Bohemia have perpetrated in many towns: murder, arson, robbery, destruction and many other disastrous acts. In this way they have destroyed, burned and grievously put to death many pious Christians and they intend to do likewise wherever there are people who do not wish to join with their heretical faith. This business concerns souls, bodies, honour and possessions and it should rightly move all Christian people to resist them at this time.

All of the vassals, knights and towns of our princedom in Wrocław, Świdnica, Jawor, Środa Śląska and Namysłów have united on this. All who are able, young and old, wish to march towards them and against them and they plan to be in the field on the border with the noble Albrecht of Kolditz on the following

Wednesday [21 May]. On this account we are also moved and we shall gather all of our force which we can assemble and will march through Moravia and we intend to join together with those from Silesia.

Therefore, we desire also to remind all of you of your honour that you are obliged to Almighty God, the Christian faith and to us, to take this matter to heart which concerns souls and that you would rise up and draw into the field with all of your might, all who are able to stand, young and old, on horse and on foot, together with the high-born Heinrich called Rumpold, duke of Głogów, our dear uncle and prince, as well as those aforementioned from Silesia, in order to resist and exterminate the aforementioned heretics. Make no delay in this. [By such action] you will win a reward from God, honour before the whole world, gratitude from the church, and we will never forget this goodness. Given in Trenčín on Trinity Sunday in the thirty-fifth year of our Hungarian reign, in the eleventh year of our Roman reign and in the first year of our Bohemian reign.[8]

UB 1: 95–6.

62   Hussite league of towns

[In the early 1420s with the wrath of the official church and the empire descending upon them, Hussite towns banded together for the cause of defending their beliefs. On 20 May 1421, the chief administrator, mayor, and councilmen of the town of Čáslav accepted the Four Articles of Prague, rejected Sigismund as king of Bohemia, and allied themselves with the so-called Hussite heresy. There were similar letters from the cities of Nymburk, Kolín, Kouřim and Litoměřice. By the mid 1420s numerous towns in Bohemia had allied themselves with the Táborite and Orebite faction of the Hussite movement.[9] This aspect of the Hussite resolve against the Crusades must not be underestimated. These 'leagues', which anti-Hussite writers referred to as 'monstrous alliances' and 'the Devil's fraternity', also enjoyed support among the Czech clergy, barons, knights and some of the university masters. The coalitions provided political, military and economic

---

[8]   Trenčín is in present-day Slovakia on the Váh River about halfway between Brno and Banská Bystrica.

[9]   These included the following: Prachatice, Česká Lípa, Ústí-nad Labem, Bílina, Bělá, Trutnov, Dvůr Králové, Jaroměř, Mladá Boleslav, Chomútov, Kadaň, Slaný, Louny, Žatec, Žlutice, Prague New Town, Písek, Horažďovice, Sušice, Klatovy, Domažlice, Stříbro, Beroun, Tábor, Kostelec-nad-Labem, Kouřim, Kutná Hora, Čáslav, Český Brod, Kolín, Nymburk, Přibyslav, Hradec Králové, Vysoké Mýto, Litomyšl, Polička and Rokycany.

support against the crusades.[10] There is an edition with a scholarly introduction in Jiří Spěváček, 'Nález významného dokumentu z počátků husitského revolučního hnutí' *ČČH* 8 (1960), pp. 733–4.]

We, the chief administrator, mayor, councillors and the entire community of Čáslav, confess by this letter to everyone who might see it either by reading it or by word of mouth, that after considering the holy and just cause engaging the discreet lords, mayor, councilmen and the entire community of the revered city of Prague, capital of the Crown of the Kingdom of Bohemia against Sigismund the Hungarian king and his helpers, we are united against that king on account of his conduct and are his enemies. Not wishing to resist the authority of Prague and the just controversy we have voluntarily, without any compulsion, joined ourselves with this letter to the four honourable, worthy and salvific articles and to the aforementioned city of Prague. Trusting ourselves to the grace of God, we commend ourselves because of the disorderly riots against them we promise in good faith, without deception, never to rise up against that city in any way or otherwise to offer resistance. Instead, we shall give assistance and advice to them with all of our power, goods and lives to the best of our ability and endurance standing for the truth of God enumerated in the Four Articles and for the honour and good of the commonwealth of the Crown of the Kingdom of Bohemia in all useful matters in which they might engage against any one of whatever status, order, rank or dignity whoever he might be. We do not and we will not accept that King Sigismund as king or hereditary lord of the Czech crown because he is unworthy in every way. We will resist him along with the capital city and its adherents until the very end. We will not accept another person as king of this Crown unless he is accepted by the city of Prague, the aforementioned capital, together with its supporters, even in the future, when this kingdom is fatherless through the deprivation of the king.

We promise further neither to accept any officials to our town, nor to obey them, except those sent, approved or set up by the lords of Prague. We shall obey them and see to the collection of remunerations belonging formerly to the king and his officials. We shall not make any appeal or protest to a higher law in any cause anywhere outside the land in opposition as long as the Almighty Lord God shall give a lord and king to this Czech Crown and that he might be properly crowned and in the traditional way in this land with the consent of the entire community of the Czech kingdom.

Each of us vows to hold, keep and observe in their entirety these articles written above, without any suspension under [penalty of] loss of honour and faith.

---

[10]   On towns in general see especially Heymann, 'The role of the towns in the Bohemia of the later Middle Ages' *Cahiers d'histoire Mondiale* 2 (1954), pp. 326–46.

To this we bind ourselves with this letter lest we transgress anything, God forbid, written herein. May we be found proven and precise by worthy conscience. In witness and guarantee of this testimony we affix the large seal of our town to this letter in good will and conscience. Given in Čáslav on the Tuesday after Holy Trinity [20 May] in the year 1421 after the birth of God's son.

AČ 1: 203–4.

63   Proceedings of the diet of Čáslav

[This crucial convocation met between 3–7 June 1421 in Čáslav, a town about 45 miles southeast of Prague.[11] Important documents from the sessions convened there bear the date 7 June 1421. This document constitutes a formal record of the growing opposition on the part of the Bohemian Estates towards Sigismund and underscores the considerable strength of the Hussite movement within the Czech Kingdom. Even more importantly, it also set forth a provisional government and constitution for governance in light of the refusal to recognize Sigismund's claim to the throne.]

We the mayors, councilmen and communities of the Old and New Towns of Prague, Konrad [of Vechta], by the grace of God archbishop of the church in Prague and legate of the papal see, Oldřich Rožmberk, Čeněk of Vartenberk, and Veselá, Jindřich Berka of Dubá residing in Húska, Oldřich of [Jindřichův] Hradec, Hyněk Krušina of Lichtenburk, Aleš Škopek of Dubá also of Dražice, Jan of Ralsko, Mikeš of Žampach, Jindřich of Vartenberk, Viktorín and Jindřich of Kunštát, Heřman and Jan of Landštejn, also of Borotín, Jan of Lichtenburk called Krušina, Jindřich Lacembok of Chlum, Václav of Zvířetice, Ernst of Richemburk, Jan of Chlum residing on Pihle,[12] Vaněk of Jenštejn, Mikuláš Šlechta of Valdštejn, Mikuláš of Mochov, Zdeněk Medek of Týnec, Jan Žižka of Trocnov, Zbyněk of Buchov, Chval of Machovice, Jan Roháč of Dubá, administrators of the people and towns of Tábor, Petr of Svojšín, mint master of Kutná Hora, Janek of

---

[11]   For a full discussion of this convocation see Frederick G. Heymann, 'The national assembly of Čáslav' *Mediaevalia et Humanistica* 8 (1954), pp. 32–55.

[12]   This is one of the two knights who accompanied Jan Hus to Constance in 1414. At least fourteen letters exchanged between Hus and Lord Jan survive. Born in Svojkov Castle near Česká Lípa he spent much of his early life in military affairs. After Constance, he was a member of the king's council. For several years he had control of the town of Mělník until 1420 when it was seized by Sigismund. After 1422 nothing is known of him and he was dead by 1425, possibly a casualty of war and evidently a Hussite to the end.

Smilkov, Mikuláš of Barchov, Oneš of Měchovice, Milota of Chřenovice, Jindřich of Boharyně, Jan Košík of Lomnice, Markvart of Soběšín, Vlachen of Slatina, Prokop of Talmberk, Jan Kyjata of Zásada, Zdeněk of Lipka, Markvart of Chvalonice, Jan of Markvatice, Diváček of Kladruby, Jan of Roudnice, Dobran of Kochovice, Zdeněk of Levín, Mikšík of Ulibice, Uzík of Bašnice, Jan Lemberk, Straník of Kopidlno, Jan Ohnieštko of Smidary, Jan Biskupec of Třebovětice, Pavlík of Hoříněves, Procek of Třebnúševes, together with other barons, knights, squires, towns and villages, faithful to us and which adhere to the law of God. We profess by this letter in general to all who will see this or hear it read that we have in mind the several and significant difficulties, tumults and destructions, burnings, violence, and other problems which have arisen in our kingdom of Bohemia on account of a disunity in the desire, comprehension and a striving after the truth as is clearly evident in Holy Scripture. Because of this our duty urgently requires us to see that these disorders are transformed into order and that these dissensions give way to peace and harmony and that here we establish again and enforce this for the common good of the kingdom. Therefore we have made arrangements and convened this public diet of the Czech country and we have, each of us gathered together, made a single resolution at this meeting to agree to and maintain the following contract which we confirm by the direction of this letter.

We intend to be united in mind and with all purpose to protect and defend the truth of God as laid down regardless of who might wish to prevent this or harm us with respect to any or all of these truths in whatever fashion and the same applies to those who intend to take us away from this by force. Furthermore, we shall faithfully uphold these articles together with our subjects until we are better instructed by the Holy Scriptures, in such a way which does not contradict those Scriptures, by the Prague masters and our priests. These truths are as follows:

First, the word of God is to be proclaimed and freely preached by Christian priests throughout the kingdom of Bohemia without opposition.

Second, the venerable sacrament of the body and blood of our Lord Jesus Christ shall be administered, in both kinds of bread and wine, to all faithful Christians, both young and old, in accordance with this constitution.

Third, inasmuch as many priests and monks rule over temporal property with secular power, against the commandment of Christ and in defiance of their priestly office and to the detriment of the secular state, we insist that such improper domination be taken away from the priests and the practice stopped. They are to live exemplary lives in accordance with the example of Christ and his apostles in keeping with the Scriptures.

Fourth, all manifest deadly sins and other transgressions which are repulsive to the Law of God must be stopped and properly punished by those who have authority in every state so that the wicked reputation of the Czech land might be purified for the common good of the Czech language and the kingdom.

Fifth, the Hungarian king Sigismund, and his supporters have done the most damage and through whose injustice and cruelty the entire kingdom of Bohemia has suffered very serious harm. We have never accepted him as our king and not as hereditary lord of the Czech Crown. By his own worthlessness he has demonstrated that he is unfit to bear this [responsibility]. As long as we live and as long as he does, we will not accept him unless it is God's will and ratified by the will and vote of the glorious city of Prague, the barons of Bohemia, the community of Tábor, the knights and squires, towns and communities of Bohemia that accept or will accept the truth of the articles noted above. This king is an infamous despiser of these holy truths which are clearly shown in Holy Scripture. He is the murderer of the honour and the people of the Czech nation. Should any lords or squires, towns or communities, separate from those lords and squires adhering to the truths of God and thus offer assistance and relief to that king either through advice or deed without the permission of the Prague community, its lords and squires and the aforementioned communities, and should it be proven in good conscience that this activity does not cease upon being warned by a messenger or through letters, then they shall be subject to penalties noted hereafter.

Sixth, together we have with one accord consented to the election of twenty wise, steadfast and faithful men among us for the administration, establishment and due process of the Crown and Kingdom of Bohemia: Oldřich Rožmberk, Čeněk of Vartenberk, and Veselá, Oldřich of [Jindřichův] Hradec, Hynek Krušina of Lichtenburk, and Jindřich Berka of Dubá from among the barons. Jan of Kněževes, Lideř of Radkovice, Pavlík, Jan Charvát of the lords of Prague and the community. Jan Žižka of Trocnov, Zbyněk of Buchov, Janek of Smilkov, Mikuláš of Barchov, Milota of Chřenovice, Oneš of Měchovice, Jindřich of Boharyně, Franca of Rosental, Vacek of Žatec, Matěj Praguer of Hradec on the Labe, and Petr Hostic of Kouřim. To these officers, administrators and governors we have given, and we confirm by virtue of this letter, full power and authority to establish peace and to cause the Czech land to be at rest putting an end to all disunity and separation and for bringing to an end any problem existing between communities and individuals within the kingdom of Bohemia. In good faith we promise without deceit that we shall faithfully and without delay not only execute but be obedient to everything arranged by the aforementioned governors and administrators and we shall, with one accord, proclaim, taking into account both sides whatever they command us or anyone else, particularly if admonished by these officers and administrators to assist in the defence of this land or another country. We promise to do this personally to the best of our ability and to continue to obey these instructions whenever we are so commanded. It is the duty of every one of us, unless there is some worthy reason, to accept these governors. This power, constituted by us, is to be observed. There has also been a significant decision that should someone not wish to unite with this agreement and the previously noted articles, they are to be compelled to do so and we are therefore to regard such persons or communities as our enemies and this is the judgement of the aforementioned governors.

Further, it has been jointly asserted that should God not preserve any of these governors, or the community did not approve of them at any time, then a new governor could be elected from the community of the former. With respect to the aforementioned officers in terms of their more difficult task which cannot be resolved except according to the law of God they have appointed two priests, Jan Příbram and Jan the preacher, in order to assist them and to effect order and justice for everyone.[13] Further, it has also been decided that these governors and administrators are to have supreme power given to them by us all together until the following St Václav's Day [28 September] but not beyond this. If we have a king during this time through our Lord God, then every provision made above shall remain insofar as the liberty of the four articles for our salvation shall be preserved at every level until there is unanimous assent by all of the aforementioned lords and communities.

It has been agreed together to call a common assembly of the senior priests within the Kingdom of Bohemia who administer the law of God among the people. This is to be constituted by the entire church upon order of the archbishop, masters and priests for the purpose of defeating and eliminating excesses and problems. Such an ecclesiastical order is to be adhered to by the entire priesthood and clergy in the kingdom of Bohemia unanimously and in unity. Should any priest be in violation of this order and wishes to preach in some other fashion, his excesses must not be tolerated by the lords or the communities in any way. He must rather be sent to the officials of the archbishop at once.

Similarly, it has been agreed, assented to, and constituted, that all lords, knights, squires and communities which are not named and written in this letter, but who would like to be part of us and the truths of God at a later time, shall be required to submit themselves to every aspect of this letter and to pledge themselves by letters, with their seals, in order to be acknowledged. They shall affirm their intention to teach, uphold and preserve each of the points set down in this agreement wholly and entirely under a penalty of loss of faith and honour. This letter condemns without an objection so that their goods and estates would then come to the common collection, as though such were inscribed on the Land Tables. There shall be perpetual banishment from the kingdom of Bohemia should there be any violation, God forbid, of any article written here, and an unwillingness to correct that according to the judgement of the aforementioned

---

[13] The appointment of these two men to the position of mediation is remarkable. The two were not only incompatible but implacable enemies. Příbram was among the most conservative of the Hussite priests while Želivský was the leader of the radical faction in Prague.

governors and clearly substantiated by witness. To confirm all of this we have attached our seals to this letter in good conscience. Given in Čáslav by the common assembly in the year of the Lord 1421, on Saturday after [the feast of St] Marcellinus [7 June].

AČ 3: 226–30.

64   Vanguard of another crusade threat

[Sigismund's letter of 18 May (doc.61) called for the extermination of the heretics under the auspices of the crusading cross. The dukes of Silesia with a strong army took the directive literally. While the Diet of Čáslav was still sitting in session (doc.63) the Silesians struck by surprize attack in northeast Bohemia. This action must be regarded as the precursor to an even more powerful crusade offensive already in the planning stages. The cruelty of the crusaders was regarded by Sigismund as entirely appropriate conduct against unrepentant heretics. The views of the Lord High Burgrave, Čeněk of Vartenberk, and those of the priest Ambrož, usefully underscore the diverse responses to the crusade threat within Hussite Bohemia.]

At the time of the assembly, the dukes of Silesia, with an army of 20,000 strong, arrived and began inflicting harm in the Czech kingdom. They conquered Polička, Náchod and Trutnov, killing many men and women. They cut off either the right foot and left hand or the left foot and right hand of forty children and also cut off the noses of some. Therefore, the lords at the assembly decided that all of the barons with knights and ordinary people from the villages in the region of Hradec Králové should gather near Náchod on St Vitus' day [15 June]. Hearing of this, the Silesians left the country. However, many thousand barons, knights and common people gathered at the appointed time which struck fear into the Silesians and on this account they sent a letter stating they wished to come to an agreement with the Czechs. Because of this Čeněk [of Vartenberk] and [Hynek] Krušina [of Lichtenberk] did not permit their people to invade Silesia.

The priest Ambrož, leader of the people of Hradec as well as a vicar, stirred up the people and had the lords not departed hastily they would have been smashed to pieces by the flails of the common people. After they had been calmed down, they dispersed and went to their homes. But when Priest Ambrož arrived in Prague he spoke vehemently against Lord Čeněk saying that they could have conquered Silesia had not Čeněk ordered them to disperse. At the same time, Lord Hynek Krušina arrived in Prague and defended Lord Čeněk as well as the other barons saying that they were innocent. Because of this, the people were divided and held conflicting opinions, with some on both sides.

Historia Hussitica, in FRB 5: 491–2.

65   Massacre at Most

[The ill-fated Hussite expedition against the northern Bohemian town of Most, led by the priest Jan Želivský was a disaster. See map 3. The report by the Silesian abbot Ludolf of Żagań greatly exaggerates Hussite losses in the battle of 5 August 1421.]

Such a number of tares have sprung up in the Bohemian field, that it is as if countless locusts from one city and village to the next have passed, demolishing everything in fields and pastures. They abandon no castle, place, or meadow unsullied by their tyranny and cruelty. Of the multitude of religious orders that once made Bohemia glorious none remain intact or nearly so, as their buildings are all destroyed. For all of the monks and other religious have fled or were put to the sword, and their buildings destroyed by the Wyclifites. And would that they had spared those monks, most of whom they are said to have killed disgracefully, when they refused to hand over their churches, cloisters, houses, and goods.

There is a city, however, in the Kingdom of Bohemia which is called Most, located on the borders of Bohemia and the Margraviate of Meißen. The inhabitants of this city, putting themselves under the protection of the illustrious and magnificent lords of the Margraviate of Meißen, received soldiers, nobles, and armed men from those lords for their protection. Therefore the schismatic, heretical, Wyclifite, Hussite, Bohemians in a great multitude came to besiege the city. They had, moreover, such a force of cavalry and foot soldiers that, dividing themselves into many battalions, they made an assault upon that city with some of their forces, while others went through nearby areas to wreak havoc. And behold the army of the Margraviate of Meißen, which was not small, did great harm to those who were wandering through the fields. They spread great ruin, killing and capturing many thousands of the enemy, and destroyed their goods and supplies. Once this was heard, those attempting to assault the city turned in flight and gave up the siege.

After this Jan Žižka, captain of the forces of Prague, with many others (including a certain Pole, who wrote that he was sent to Bohemia to protect it in the name of a certain prince from Poland [Zygmunt Korybut], whom the Bohemians are said to have elected or accepted as their king against Sigismund) sent letters of public defiance to the lords of Meißen, indicating that they wished to vindicate themselves in a just war [see doc.89]. Lord, help your faith and your Church lest your people be oppressed and the mouths of those praising be closed.

Ludolf of Żagań, pt. 2, chap. 61, pp. 531–3.

66   Jan Žižka calls for army conscription

[This letter from Žižka's pen was written from Orlík Castle on 12 September 1421. It should be noted that there has been some scholarship preferring to place the date in the following year.]

May God grant that you may be able to again return to the state of original grace and be the first to come to such an honourable state.

Dear brothers in Christ. I ask that for the sake of our Lord God that you remain in the fear of God inasmuch as you are the beloved sons of God and that you make no complaint when God punishes you. Remember the one who brought about the foundation of our faith, even our Lord Jesus Christ, and bravely defend yourselves against the evil deeds committed by the Germans. Follow the example of the old Czechs who with pikes firmly planted defended themselves as well as the cause of God. Now dear brothers, we are in search of the law of God as well as the good of all. We will do everything possible so that everyone capable of swinging a club and throwing a stone may be prepared.

Furthermore, beloved brothers, we are now conscripting men everywhere against these enemies and those who destroy the Czech land. You should also command your priests to stir up the people to take up arms against the forces of Antichrist. All of the people should be summoned together in the marketplace in order that all of them, from the youngest to the oldest, those who have sufficient strength, should be armed and prepared at every hour of the day.

If God wills it, we shall soon be coming to you. Therefore, prepare beer, bread, food for the horse and all of the weapons for war. It is the time to fight against these alien enemies every bit as hard as we have against those enemies within our own country. Keep in mind the first battle when little people were taking on the great ones of the land. There were few against many, men without armour fighting those in iron, and yet you fought bravely to victory.[14] The arm of God has not become shorter. So, be prepared and let your hope remain in God. May God the Lord give you strength. Given at Orlík Castle on Friday, after the

---

[14]   Either a reference to the Hussite victory over the 'iron lords' at Sudoměř in March 1420 (see doc.13) or to the battle on Vítkov Hill in Prague in July of that same year (see doc.35).

nativity of the Virgin Mary, Jan Žižka of the Chalice and leader of the people of Tábor.

Bartoš, pp. 14–15.

67   Descriptions of Hussite tactics

[Aeneas Sylvius Piccolomini, later Pope Pius II, was the first to write a history of the entire revolutionary period (1458). His sources were materials obtained from the Czech utraquist priest Jan Papoušek of Soběslav, but also from his own experiences in Bohemia in 1451. Among his associates must also be numbered Kaspar Schlink, a German imperial official from Cheb, the Czech humanist Prokop Rabštejn, the notaries František of Břánice and Václav of Bochov, the chancellor of the Old Town of Prague, Jan Túšek, and the university professor Jan Ondřejův Šindel, all of whom could have provided Aeneas with various information. He had also personally witnessed the Hussite arrival in Basel on Sunday, 4 January 1433. See doc. 183. The description of this system of waging war from the wagon-fortresses is historical and factual information available only in Aeneas.]

They seldom go inside walled cities except to buy food. They spend their lives in camps together with their wives and children. They had as many wagons as they could possibly get and these they used as a defence. Whenever they advanced into battle, the two lines of wagons functioned as their flanks with the soldiers in between. Mounted troops were outside the fortification close at hand. When it seemed an appropriate time to get involved in the fighting, after part of the enemy forces had been closed off, the drivers of the wagons ordered that the flanks be drawn together at the signal by the commander. The enemies, now cut off from their fellows, were captured and killed. Some were cut down by the foot soldiers, others by the missiles of the men and women within the wagons. Outside the wagons the cavalry fought and if things went badly for them, the wagons were opened up and they were able to retreat safely. Then these wagons were defended much like a walled city and through this strategy they won many victories. The nations nearby were unfamiliar with this method of war and the area to the north being much exposed was regarded as very well suited for the deployment of two and four horse wagons.

Historia Bohemica, chapter 47, pp. 138, 140.

68 The art of the wagon fortress

[Along with the peasant flails the most unique feature of Hussite warfare was their deployment of the wagon fortress. Though not original with the Hussites the war wagons were successfully and regularly used against the crusaders.]

In the Czech land one finds considerable level ground with few ditches and they [the Hussites] enclose both cavalry and foot soldiers within wagons. They gather together armed men within these wagons as if they were on walls and they rebuff the enemy with missiles. As they commence to fight, they arrange two flanks of these wagons and they bring them into service in proportion to the number of warriors they have as well as in relation to the immediate terrain. Being covered behind and along the sides, they fight from the front. While this is happening, the drivers of the wagons begin to move forward and they make an effort to surround or enclose the battle lines of the enemy. If this is accomplished then they will without doubt be the winners because now, they can attack from every side. Additionally, this linking together of the wagons is an art and can be executed upon the order of a commander whenever and wherever he wishes, either for the purposes of retreat or for chasing the enemy, whatever the situation requires.

Aeneas Sylvius Piccolomini, *Commentarii ad Alphonsum regem*, Bk 4, chap. 44, in *Opera Omnia*, Basel, 1571.

69 Death traps for the crusaders

[The wagon-fortresses were armoured vehicles, protected by movable wooden shields. Behind each shield were perhaps twenty soldiers with war clubs, halberds, fails, maces, hand-cannon, crossbows and other firearms. When the wagons were moved into their circular formation, the wheels were chained together and the gaps filled with other shields to protect the wheels as well as to prevent entry to the wagon-fortress by the enemy. Medium sized cannon – *tarasnice* – were mounted on stands while larger cannon – *houfnice* – were mounted on the wagons. The density of firepower across the parapets of the wagons could be very dense. There are numerous chronicle accounts which refer to the many guns of the heretics fired from the wagon-fortress as well as the halberds which were used to pull knights and soldiers from their horse to their deaths. Such stories, though based in apparent fact, at least in isolated instances, soon gave way to myth, legend and propaganda of grand proportions. The following extract is representative of tales about the Hussites warriors.]

As soon as the signal for battle was given, the drivers coordinated their movements against their enemies by a previously agreed upon system of figures or letters and thus formed passageways that the Táborites understood quite well but which to the enemy appeared as a hopeless labyrinth. There was no escape and they were caught as if in a net. If it was possible to break the enemy up and cut them off from each other and thus isolate the troops, then the foot soldiers were capable with some ease of completely defeating them with swords and flails. Or the enemies could be utterly beaten by the marksmen standing on the wagons. The armies of Žižka were quite like a monster with numerous arms which very quickly and without warning snatches its prey, crushes it to death and devours it in pieces. If anyone was successful in escaping from the wagon labyrinth they quickly fell into the clutches of the cavalry waiting outside the wagons and were killed there.

Bohuslav Balbín, *Epitome historica rerum bohemicarum* (Prague, 1677).

70   The blind general of the Hussite armies

[From his youth, Jan Žižka apparently had only one eye. This did not seem to limit his ability as a soldier for numerous sources make clear that his military career, both before the revolution and during the Hussite period, was one lived in the forefront of battle. At the Prague defenestration in July 1419, a Hussite chronicler comments upon the soldier's apparent disability. 'Jan Žižka the one eye, formerly servant of the king and zealous defender of the law of Christ.' (Vavřinec of Březová, 'Historia Hussitica', in FRB 5, p. 362.) Tragedy struck Žižka in the summer of 1421 as he directed a Hussite offensive and it appeared that the end of a brilliant career had come. Aeneas Sylvius makes clear in this brief extract that such was not the case.]

[During the siege raised by the Táborites and Orebites at Rabí Castle in June 1421, Žižka]. . . . was struck with an arrow and lost the one eye with which he still saw the light of the skies. He was borne from there to Prague where doctors treated his wound so that he survived but he did not regain his sight. Notwithstanding this, he did not retire from his work as a conqueror of castles nor from directing military operations. These blind people were delighted to follow a blind leader. Generations to come will be amazed by this tale and will not believe it.

Historia Bohemica, chapter 44, p. 124.

71   Rewards offered for captured Catholic priests

[In a report reminiscent of German initiative at Kutná Hora (see doc.15), Abbot Ludolf claims that Žižka offered rewards to anyone who captured priests of the official church. Žižka's wrath against priests and monks is well established, but this report is not so well corroborated. It is impossible to date many of Ludolf's assertions but 1421 or 1422 seems most likely.]

Those, who once followed the elect of the Lord, decided to hand them over to stand in judgement and to suffer death by kings, princes, and judges of the land, and to stand in submission before God. They were induced to do this by threats, terrors, flatteries, and even by gifts and honours. And those judges, kings, and princes decided who would suffer torture or the humility of death. And behold! the o [omega? end?] revealed to the a [alpha? beginning?]; so also in the days of these worst of men, if men they deserve to be called, seizing those believers of Christ, and especially the priests, and in my opinion other well-established clerics in the sacred rights. They say or believe themselves to exhibit a submission agreeable to God in doing this, and they do not doubt beyond this that they pursue the proper end unlike other men. For indeed the captain of that diabolical sect, whom the Hussites have placed as their head against God, named or surnamed Žižka made it known publicly that whoever presented an orthodox priest, or even as I believe a deacon or subdeacon, to his commander would receive the sum of sixty-two Bohemian groschen as a reward. Soon he handed over many of those presented to be killed and especially to the flames unless they would renounce the Catholic faith, take up the errors of the Hussites and Wyclifites, and promise to know and courageously defend the said errors. He told them if later he discovered that any of them had receded from this perfidy, he would soon deprive them of life without any threat or warning. And he went against those things which were instituted for the Christian faith by the Roman pontiffs, emperors, and kings, thinking that only he and his men had the true, holy, and immaculate faith. And all the others must be merited as unbelieving sons of despair, because their errors are false! The water of the Scriptures, the effusion of the martyrs' blood, and miracles all confirm the faith for all eternity, in which the promise of the Church always exists, along with all truth and recognition of truth. The gates of hell, errors, and heresies will all be condemned, as nothing can prevail against the faith.

Ludolf of Żagań, pt. 2, chap. 3, pp. 494–5.

72   Code of the crusaders

[Authorities in Nürnberg wrote to the city of Ulm concerning the second crusade effort which was already underway. The armies had set off from Cheb on 28 August and had entered Bohemia from two directions (see map 2) with orders to kill everyone in the Czech lands they encountered with the sole exception of small children. Judging from other extant contemporary records this seems to have been the principle under which the crusaders dealt with the heretics. The letter is dated 1 September 1421.]

Dear friends. As you have written and desired of us concerning the development of the campaign against Bohemia, you letter was delivered to us last Saturday morning. Your messengers have remained with us so that if we had further information we would be able to write more to you. Thus we wish to let you know that our good friend has let us know and has written a letter with this message. Our graceful lords [. .] the electors have decided to march on two separate routes, one through the forest towards Kynžvart and the other in the direction of Loket. Our graceful lords [. .] the electors have set off to march last Thursday from Cheb and they intend to meet on the other side of the forest next Sunday to speak together among themselves and to arrange everything.

   Furthermore, our lords [. .] the electors have announced at a public fair in Cheb that everyone must be killed in the land of Bohemia, with the exception of children who are not yet at the age of reason. No women are to be taken or are to march with the army. Provisions must be procured since they are expensive and will not be available for sale later. Also, let it be known that one of your mercenaries rode with your weapons as far as Cheb and he will come again to you and will be able to tell you these things and more news besides by word of mouth. For the love and service of your honour. Given on Monday, the day of St Giles.

UB 1: 144.

73   Atrocities of the crusaders

[The following document written by the authorities in Nürnberg to their counterparts in Ulm relate the conquest of the town of Mašťov, twelve miles from Žatec, by the German electors and also the atrocities perpetrated by the crusaders in Bohemia. It is dated 12 September 1421.]

Dear friends. . . . As you have desired of us about the course of the expedition into Bohemia we wish to let you know that a message from one of our good friends came to us yesterday. He writes to us that our gracious lords the electors camped in front of a castle called Mašťov on the Tuesday prior to the birth of Mary [2 September] and called for our cannon and equipment and these were brought on the next Wednesday [3 September]. Then our gracious lord [..] the palsgrave himself rode and pointed out the place where our cannon were to be placed. This was very close to the castle, against the tower and gate. When everything was ready, on the following morning the cannon were prepared and ready to operate. When those in the castle saw this, they called out at once for negotiations desiring peace saying they would surrender. The captain in the castle and eight others with him were spared and were taken captive by the princes. The others were killed and burned grievously. Eighty-four were hanged while three priests, discovered in a house, were thrown over the wall and also burnt.

Also, the people on foot who rushed out of there who could not speak German or were thought to be Czech were captured, struck down or burned because the people did not wish for the leaders to control matters, [saying] the lord is great and powerful. Last Saturday [7 September] they attempted to decide on which town or castle to march on next. [We have written] out of love and service to your honour. Given on the Friday before the elevation of the holy cross [12 September].

UB 2: 145–6.

74   Crusade armies thwarted again at Žatec

[The aftershocks of the crusaders' crushing defeat at Prague resulted in further military encounters. A Hussite army led by the priest Jan Želivský was defeated at Most in northern Bohemia on 5 August 1421 by a German force led by Friedrich of Wettin, Margrave of Meißen who had invaded that part of the country (see doc.63). This set the stage for the first half of the second crusade which was fought near Žatec. There was the usual opposition to the crusaders entering Bohemia. Peasants near Mezilesí made efforts to block the German–Silesian army from entering the country (SRS 6, pp. 15–16). The siege of Žatec lasted three weeks involving an estimated 125,000 crusaders. Several ineffectual assaults were made against the town walls but each was repulsed. Some later sources note some military technological innovations, namely a pivoting shield. 'Herr Arkinger had this shield before Žatec. A hundred men can easily go safely behind it. The winch is inside and when one arrives at the city, he raises the shield and shoots and then lets it fall shut again. Then he turns the winch inside again so that the shield departs from the place and the soldiers stand behind it without harm.' (Bert Hall, *The Technological Illustrations of the so-called 'Anonymous of the Hussite Wars'*, p. 55.) When news that Žižka was approaching with a relief force reached the crusaders they were seized with panic, burned their tents and fled. They were chased by the Hussites and suffered heavy losses. A German joke circulated about the Catholic soldiers at Žatec who were so pious they could not bear to even look upon a heretic and thus they took to flight. See map 3.]

On the day after the nativity of the blessed virgin, the cities of Chomútov and Kadaň were occupied [having already been evacuated] by the Praguers. Thus it happened that the captains in charge of the army of the Misnians and Germans already in the area making conquests, partly destroyed the city walls without even waiting for the Praguers to appear. They did this to their own damage and to the shame of the Praguers and also burned some houses and then proceeded on to Žatec. After the previously mentioned Germans of Meißen had, together with some Czechs sympathetic to them, conquered the towns of Chomútov and Kadaň, they laid siege to the fortress of the town of Bílina which belonged to the lord of Koldov. They destroyed the surrounding fortresses and villages and did not spare either peasants or women at all but inhumanely slaughtered many pregnant women. When the Praguers heard of these wicked acts, the thirteenth of September, that is to say on the Saturday before the raising of the cross, two communal divisions of soldiers left Prague on foot together with a large number of peasants in order to drive those Germans from the field. When the Germans heard of the approach of the Praguers, they abandoned the siege of the fortress of Bílina. Likewise, Sigismund of Děčín [and Vartenberk], together with his allies, abandoned the siege of the new fortress called 'Chalice' at Litoměřice before the citizens of Prague arrived.[15]

At this same time a large number of Germans, together with the prince-electors of the empire had invaded Bohemia through Cheb en route to Žatec (see map 2). They expelled those of Prague waiting in Slaný and sent them off to the allied barons. Word came to Žižka and to the other Táborites that they should advance to Slaný with the largest possible army in order to move against the Germans and expel them. This was on account of the fact that it was rumoured that the prince-electors of the empire, along with the ecclesiastical and secular lords and the Bavarian and Rhineland electors, dukes, counts, barons and knights, together with an even larger number of armed people, on the initiation of the papal crusade, had crept clandestinely into the kingdom of Bohemia. When they reached the Czech borders, the bishops dismounted and in front of them all expressed humility, false though it was, in order that God might grant good success in terms of defeating the Bohemian heretics, then they walked across [the border]. Among

---

[15] In May 1421, Žižka conquered a small wooden fortress on the top of a hill near the town of Třebusín near Litoměřice. The fortress belonged to the Knights of the Teutonic Order. He named the fortress 'Chalice' and made it his own.

the bishops of great esteem included the following: Johannes, archbishop of Mainz, the archbishop of Cologne, the archbishop of Trier, Duke Ludwig, the son of Klem, the Count of Nassau, together with many others whose names we do not know.

When they had laid siege to Žatec, they made six attempts on the Friday before [the day of] St Matthias to storm the town. However, they were badly beaten and with considerable damage were repulsed by the help of God's grace. It was reported by those living in the town that about sixty of them had been killed, although many wounded had been carried off by the enemy. At least sixty prisoners had been taken into the town. At this time an enormous crowd, of more than 6,500 had congregated at the town on behalf of the German tyranny. There were more than 5,000 warriors on foot and four hundred cavalry. Many people had come from all over Christendom to join the German army, people with different languages from far away. They had come to join in the great remission of all guilt and sin which had been offered and extended by the pope. Even these people who saw the [crusading] army claimed they had never before seen such a numerous, well-equipped army with so many tents gathered together. According to a common consensus there were some 200,000 warriors. Day after day they burned down country villages, towns and castles and eager to receive the [aforementioned papal] indulgence they were even crueller than the heathens and they killed and burned those of both sexes, young as well as old. Fear and trembling seized the hearts of many people in the area of Žatec. Because of this some forsook the fortresses and fled to the cities. While there some of them were subjected, without mercy, to burning like the rest.

In order to maintain their forces as well as their honour, they sent off a contingent to King Sigismund and urged him, with reference to his oath at Constance, to come with the largest possible army in order to prosecute the heretics. If he would not come the prince-electors [threatened] they would arrange to have another king of the Romans. But before King Sigismund of Hungary was able to leave where he was at to join the army, the Lord Jesus heard the weeping and wailing and shouting of the women and the virgins and the widows and the anger of God and a just vengeance came over all of the armies of the enemies. In some miraculous way, Almighty God put those inhuman armies to flight without so much as another attack. On October 2, in many places the tents of the army caught fire by the coincidence of God. Above the tents one could see a single yellow and brown pillar which went from one tent to the next and wherever it went a bolt of fire shot down into the tent. Abandoning their goods they [the crusaders] fled, some barely escaping with their lives. When the people of Žatec saw what was happening, they pursued the crusaders with about a thousand men and killed several hundred. They captured others alive and cast them into prison.

Then they gave God praise with great thanksgiving because God had scattered their enemies and the persecutors of the truth had been put to flight.

Historia Hussitica, in FRB 5: 511–13.

Chapter 4

The Third Crusade:
Kutná Hora to the Sázava, 1421–2

75 Silesian dukes penetrate Bohemia to Chrudim

[Even though the crusader offensive at Žatec had been scattered, Silesian dukes continued their campaign. In the face of the crusading force a number of Czech barons switched sides including Jan Městecký who had surrendered to Žižka in late April, pledged allegiance to the Hussite cause and had been treated very leniently. The Silesian invasion occurred in late October 1421.]

On the same day of the same month, the dukes of Silesia invaded the kingdom with a large number of soldiers. They killed people and burned villages and towns on properties belonging to Lords Boček and Žampach in the area near Chrudim near the castles of Litice and Žampach. Some of the Czech barons joined with them, including Půta, Janek of Svídnice and Jan Městecký [of Opočno] who abandoned his faith even though he had sworn when the town of Chrudim was under siege that he would hold with the citizens of Prague and the Four Articles determined by them and faithfully defend them.

Historia Hussitica, in FRB 5: 516.

76 War on Vladař mountain

[This important battle was fought around 19 November 1421 just outside the village of Žlutice (see map 3) on a hill known as Vladař ('the ruler'). The commander of the forces opposing Žižka and his warriors was Heinrich of Plavno, one of the richest lords affiliated with the Plzeň Landfríd. Heinrich was an implacable Hussite foe and figures repeatedly in the crusade period. He can be found also at the fifth crusade in 1431. See doc.172.]

At the same time the men of Plzeň, with all of their supporters, besieged the Castle of Krasikov which was held by Žižka. Having heard of this, Žižka, even though he lacked both of his eyes, prepared to relieve the castle quickly with his forces. He led away the supplies from the plundered villages and towns that were adjacent to the castle against the will of the besiegers. The only nobleman to come to the aid of Plzeň was the Lord of Plavno [Heinrich], who brought a multitude of his forces. Most of the army of Plzeň, however, turned and fled from the enemy and were destroyed. After the Lord of Plavno's force of several hundred horsemen were attacked, Žižka hastened against Žatec with his own force. The lord of Plavno's force and the remainder of the people of Plzeň pursued Žižka's troops so that both sides frequently drew themselves into battle formation on the road. Once Žižka and his forces reached the mountain called Vladař and climbed it, he surrounded himself with his wagons, and manfully defended himself from his enemies. Intemperate weather, that is the cold temperature and wind storms, together with hunger, however, certainly contributed to his success. Nevertheless, for three days they [the Hussites] courageously defended themselves, and the enemy was unable to gain a position on the mountain. On the third day, on account of hunger, they descended the mountain and drove through [the enemy] in a powerful force of men and animals towards Žatec.

Historia Hussitica, in FRB 5: 524–5.

77 Crusade forces march through Moravia

[Emperor Sigismund planned to undertake an invasion of Bohemia from the east in concert with the crusader attack in the western part of the country which came to fruition at Žatec (see doc.74). However, he delayed and did not enter Moravia until 16 October and even then paused, for no known reason, for a period of eleven days at Brumov near Trenčín. From there he marched on to Brno. There he rescinded his prior pledge not to militate against the 'four articles' and demanded that all of the barons renounce the Hussite agenda and regard it as a serious heresy. He remained in Brno from 1–17 November before going on to the border town of Jihlava where he stayed for yet another another ten days. The delays were absolutely inexplicable and very costly for the crusaders. It gave the Hussites valuable time to organize. Finally, in early December the king entered Bohemia from a point north of Jihlava and marched to Humpolec. Žižka's troops reached Kutná Hora on 9 December but the king lingered in Ledeč for several more days. Altogether, he took three weeks to cover fifty miles from Jihlava to Kutná Hora. See map 2.]

At that time, Pipo Spano from the Hungarian king's side arrived in Moravia with thousands of armed people, destroying and burning properties belonging to lords Petr of Strážnice and Lacek of Ostrov, and others who supported the inhabitants of Prague in their defence of the Four Articles. In the manner of the heathens they murdered ordinary working people. Knowing this, the aforementioned Petr of Strážnice, turned his very strong castle of Heštejn over to a Silesian duke with the understanding that the duke, Přemek, would not surrender to the king, unless the aforementioned Lord Petr settled an agreement between him and the king. Duke Přemek signed and confirmed this by leaving hostages with Lord Petr. In the meanwhile, the aforementioned Lord Petr, knowing that King Sigismund was about to arrive with a large army, asked Master Zikmund and the other priests who were giving the body and blood of the Lord to come out of the town. And Master Zikmund with the venerable sacrament of the body of our Lord Christ, walked together with all faithful people to Ostroh to meet Lord Lacek. And the aforementioned Lord Lacek, was as firm as a rock and held with the truth of our Lord Christ, even though he suffered great damage from the Hungarian army. During the night, along with his people, he attacked some of the battalions of the king's army. Several times he charged through them, killing many hundreds, but lost many of his people, those who were held up by looting. Also the young son of Lord Petr Strážnice, Václav was his name, refused to abandon the Four Articles, made friends with the aforementioned Lord Lacek and became his ally, promising to die with him for the truth of the Holy Scriptures.

King Sigismund with large numbers of Hungarians and Tartars, though not too well armed, marched through Moravia, destroying and burning both friendly and unfriendly properties. Finally arriving in Brno, he summoned all lords, knights and pages, issuing to them a safe-conduct. In the meantime, he set a trap, surrounded the town with armies, and only then announced to the lords and knights what his intentions and demands were, saying, that he had summoned them because he wanted them to abandon the Four Articles [on the grounds that] they were false and heretical. As soon as they renounced them, he expected them to accept penance from the deputy legate who was then present. While they were considering what to do, and seeing that the irascible king was asking them to answer without delay, and also seeing the Hungarian army ready to obey the king's orders, they became fearful and bowed to the will of the king and renounced [the Four Articles]. At the same time they promised to aid the king in the struggle against the Four Articles, which previously they had defended so resolutely. These are the words of the oath:

'I swear by the passion of the Lord, that I will no longer cling to those Four Articles, which I have falsely observed along with others. That is, the preaching of various priests about taking the communion of the body and blood of the Lord, committing obvious sins, confiscating the belongings of priests, demolishing churches, annihilating priests and the people who are lawfully in their positions. I will no longer adhere to any heresy, deviating from the holy Roman Church, and in particular, I will not hold to the preaching of Master John Wyclif and Master Jan Hus and their followers, nor disseminate them by word, deed or advice.

Further, I also swear that I will hold with the Christian beliefs in all articles, as the holy Roman Church instructs us. I will obey the pope and my bishop and the priests appointed by them, in matters of faith and in other matters, to which they are entitled.

I also swear that I will vilify and fight against all heretics and people who are ignorant about the Christian faith using all my force, and especially those who hold with the aforementioned heresies, whether they are clergy or laity, whenever I find them on my property or learn about their whereabouts anywhere else. [The same] as well for all of their accomplices or those who accompany them. I will not shelter them, help them or defend them, even if I should lose my life. May God help me through his holy blood and the Holy Scriptures!'

Then followed a type of absolution. 'I, the legate etc. through the power of almighty God and the holy apostles Peter and Paul (they will not admit it) and through the power of the Holy Father in Christ, our lord pope Martin V, and also Lord Ferdinand, bishop of Lucena, his delegate, given me in this matter, free you from any excommunication or condemnation you were subject to, because you held with dishonourable heresy, remove the interdiction inflicted upon you because of this, and because you held with the articles of John Wyclif, Jan Hus, or with any heresy or articles accepting them, practicing them, or defending those who held with heresy, or any other articles, which were prohibited by man or by law. Also, I free you from the condemnation, excommunication or anathema and burden imposed upon you because of your recalcitrance which you demonstrated when you were asked to add your seal to the letters sent to Constance as a response to the pope's order and the decision of the Council of Constance, by not refusing to do so, and also for any other recalcitrance and disobedience.[1] Further, I free you from all sins which you repent of and which you confess to me, and I return you to the pale of our mother the holy church, to associate with people and also to your dignity and honour. All of this in the name of the Father and of the Son and of the Holy Spirit. Amen.'

---

[1]   This is a reference to the protest of the Czech nobility against the execution of Jan Hus. In September 1415, at least 452 barons formally protested the action of the Council of Constance in the Hus case. This followed a series of protests commencing in January of the same year when Moravian nobles convened at Meziříčí and appealed to Sigismund to act. *Documenta*, pp. 580–4 for the text of the September protest and pp. 584–90 for a list of the names.

But because Lord Václav, son of Lord Petr of Strážnice, did not obey the summons of King Sigismund, and neither came, nor did he wish to take the oath, the king at the court in Brno, condemned Lord Václav's paternal inheritance for eternity and ordered that [this decision] be entered into [both] the provincial and baronial registers to the memory and eternal damnation of those disobedient sons!

Historia Hussitica, in FRB 5: 526-8.

78   Battle for Kutná Hora

[The battle at Kutná Hora was, originally, part of the second crusade initiative which collapsed in western Bohemia with the debacle at Žatec. Sigismund had entered the country from the east through Moravia, but characteristically made slow progress while the crusaders under his command engaged in gratuitous destruction, murder and rape. One of the notable military men among the ranks, mentioned in some of the accounts, was the Florentine condottiere Filippo Scolari, Count of Ozora, often referred to as Pipo Spano. While Sigismund remained supreme commander, tactical details were left to Pipo. The Hungarians forces were joined by a small army raised by Bishop Jan 'the Iron', troops led by Bishop Conrad of Wrocław from Lusatia and Silesia, and Austrian forces under the command of Albrecht of Habsburg. The four confrontations which frame this event, Kutná Hora, Nebovidy, Habry and Německý Brod, resulted in the deaths of several thousand crusaders with the Hussites capturing almost all of their supplies. The battle for Kutná Hora was fought on 21-2 December 1421. See maps 3 and 5.]

About the same time Hungarians and Tartars conquered the city of Polička through deceit. They brutally killed about 1,300 people, both men and women. Because of this, the barons and nobles of Moravia, who had been supporters of the truth, now denounced the Four Articles, with the exception of Hašek of Ostroh, Master Václav, son of Master Petr of Strážnice, lords of the same country. Meanwhile, King Sigismund was approaching with a large army, estimated to be some 60,000 cavalry and foot soldiers. He turned near Jihlava in order to be unseen and by deceit to enter Kutná Hora. The Prague army heard about this as they were camped in Čáslav and Kutná Hora. They reasonably concluded that it would be impossible to march against such a major force on account of its own inferiority. Therefore, on St Catherine's Day [25 November], following the securing of the cities they returned [to Prague] by way of Hradec Králové. Straight away the city councilmen dispatched a delegation with letters to Žižka and his Táborite brethren as well as to other barons, citizens and peasants who supported the truth. They asked that they not refrain from coming to Prague as soon as possible in order to fight against the heretical king for the sake of their faith, and the honour, and liberty of the law of God.

While numerous legates, mentioned previously, were swarming out in all directions, on the first day of December, Brother Žižka although blind in both eyes arrived at the city of Prague along with his brothers and sisters, his troops of horse and his wagons of war. He was received by everyone as though he was a prince-elector and was provided with plenty of food so that he would loyally support the Praguers and expel that inhuman king from the country. The large bells in the city hall were rung as well as those in the churches. As usual the priests carried before them the blessed sacrament of the body and blood of Christ and all the clergy and the people walked along with them. Then Brother Žižka reached an agreement with the Praguers and on the day of the glorious virgin's conception, with all of his men, started out on the march from Prague to Kutná Hora. The next day the Praguers with their army began to march.

The citizens of Kutná Hora, however, noted the arrival of Brother Žižka along with the Táborites and rode out towards him on horse. As they did this they kept to one side as though the arrival of the Táborites were welcomed. However, inside they were quite angry and not without good cause. They knew that the unrestrained people of Tábor tended to rob, that they were uncontrollable when it came to murder and that their priests did not observe the proper ecclesiastical order in matters pertaining to divine service. Thus it happened on the following day that the Táborite priests entered the Church of St John and held the service in their usual manner. Many of the people of Kutná Hora flocked together with a desire to gape. However, both men and women took offence at them when they saw what happened. Only one of the priests held the church service, as was their custom, wearing only his own clothes without any of the ecclesiastical vestments. He completely disregarded the usual order, only bowing his head, as opposed to kneeling on the ground and praying only a short time as though it were the Lord's Prayer. After straightening up, right away he spoke the words of consecration over the broken host and the wine which filled a chalice of iron or tin: 'the Lord Jesus, after he had held the meal took bread and blessed it and broke it,' and so on. And in this manner, breaking the host, which he held in his hands, he communicated first himself which is, as far as the people were concerned, an unheard of consecration. Then the other priests stepped up to him and each communed himself. Finally, the brothers and sisters, knelt down and were separately communed. That is to say, one of the priests administered the venerable body of Christ to the people, while a second [administered to the people] the sacred blood without any reverence as is proper for such a sacrament of such elevated dignity. Seeing this, the people of Kutná Hora, both men and women, spat on the ground and left the church railing [against the Táborites]. They spoke to each other saying, 'now we believe what thus far we have only heard. That is, that these Czechs are indeed the real and worst heretics and they deserve to be persecuted by every faithful Christian.' Because of this, they continued to favour King Sigismund all the more and earnestly desired his arrival. . . .

At the same time while King Sigismund was staying in Jihlava with his armed men, Čeněk of Vartenberk, Jindřich of Rožmberk, Vílem Zajíc, Jan Městecký, Půta and a number of other barons of the kingdom of Bohemia came to the king under safe conduct. They vowed loyalty to him as king and also promised to support him in word and deed. At the same time they desired that he would cease the burning and destruction of the kingdom and its inhabitants. It is said that the king promised to do this but it was his nature neither to have regard for that nor to fulfil his promise. Instead, he multiplied evil by evil while he marched with the aforementioned barons leading his army to Kutná Hora by way of Humpolec and Ledeč. His dishonest and inhumane army burned everything, friends as well as foes, villages, marketplaces and castles. They raped girls and women until they died or they killed them. They cut off the hands and feet of children and threw them in front of their mothers. They stripped the mothers, together with other women, and drove them like cattle before hanging them up on fences by their breasts from which their children had sucked. Such sinful and sacrilegious people could be moved neither to mercy by the moans of the women nor by the great streaming tears and cries of the children. This was more cruel than the heathens and all this blasphemous evil they did with pleasure believing that the sins of the Czechs demanded it. All the while they believed that by committing such great evil they were demonstrating to God their obedience and by doing so would gain an indulgence for their sins.

You heartless prince! Why do you behave like a heathen and persecute the children of the country whom you ought rather to protect? Why don't you stop fouling your own nest? Why do you not cease to shed the blood of the innocents? Why do you desire to exterminate these people, who oppose you only because they fight for the law of God? Wait just a little while and take heed because the Lord will uphold those who hear him and with a small group will defeat you and put you to flight, you who trust in having a great number of people. In the place of the true chalice of the blood of Christ, whose adherents you persecute and whom you seek to destroy, very soon vicious dogs will lick the blood of you cruel monsters. So take it to heart and realize that it is difficult for you to kick against the thistles. Cease to do evil and perhaps God will have pity on you and forgive your evil deeds.

When the king arrived in Ledeč word got around in Kutná Hora that Brother Žižka, together with his Táborites and the Praguers were camped on the battlefield. Above Kutná Hora they camped with their divisions at a wooden hut which had recently been set up by the king and there they waited for the king to arrive. But as the king delayed his coming they marched to Čáslav and gained reinforcements by acquiring additional armed forces. Lord Boček, Lord Hašek, Lord Václav [of Kravař], the son of Lord Petr of Strážnice, barons of Bohemia and Moravia came to Čáslav. They fortified Čáslav and then returned to Kutná Hora. On the day of [St] Thomas [21 December], Sunday, the aforementioned lords, together with Žižka and the Praguers at the conclusion of the morning church service, announced through the priests in the pulpit and by heralds in the streets, that they should all be prepared to march against the king, maintaining the faith, which they had vowed to God and to the citizens of Prague in defence of the truth of the gospel. They were not to be fearful of the king's arrival, they should keep faith with the captains, lords and knights, as well as the entire army [who] would rather lose their necks together with them than desert them. After a small meal and the ringing of bells, they left a group [of warriors] with the mint master [Mikuláš of Prague] and marched through the gate leading in the direction of Kouřim.

When they had barely covered a half mile from the town the king and his army began to approach the Praguers in squadrons. In the larger squadron of the king, however, among the armed cavalry were also hundreds of cows and oxen in order to frighten and put to flight whoever might see them. However, God always provides support and never lets his warriors down but granted to all who fought for the truth courage and bravery. Being fearless of the strength of the armies they [Hussites] entered the battlefield and enclosed themselves within the wagons on all sides. The infantry, as well as the citizens of Kutná Hora who had joined them, some to actually fight, others to observe how the battle would go, were put into position within the wagon fortress with their flails and weapons. Numerous guns were prepared. After a short exhortation, everyone knelt down on the ground and humbly prayed to God. After they had finished praying and stood up they appointed new recruits in order that they might defend the truth even more courageously and arm themselves against the king. Although some of the squadrons attempted to storm the wagons they were beaten back by the guns and suffered a high number of casualties. These kinds of attacks characterized the early stages of the battle and continued until night fall.

As these skirmishes continued, in the manner of knightly combat, at the same time the people of Kutná Hora treacherously allowed many hundreds [of the king's men] into the city through the Kolín Gate. As these troops entered the town, the citizens of Kutná Hora who had allied with them and were hiding in the cellars of the houses, came out and began to kill everyone [Hussites and their supporters] who did not know the password. They entered houses and killed as heretics everyone who supported the Praguers. A very ugly fellow ran into the rectory and asked repeatedly for the parish priest and the magistrate Petr. When he was told that he was with the army he proceeded to eat and drink there. At length he ran off and returned with a very brutal robber and with the sword they murdered the administrator and all of the priests they could find. Some of them escaped to the church tower in an effort to save their lives. They were not, however, spared and together with the priest Master Matěj of Slovakia were killed and thrown down from the tower. Another priest, an old man with white hair who deserved more respect, was found kneeling in front of an altar and the body and blood of Christ. Without so much as blushing they wounded him until he expired and thus they killed him. Then they carried out of the church the newly made handsome tabernacle and smashed it to pieces. One does not know what became of the body and blood of Christ but it was rumoured that someone came and shoved a spear through the body of Christ. Nevertheless, a monstrance was found in the Chapel of the Mint with the body of Christ but it was reported to the great offence of all Christians that the body of Christ was trampled upon. As the citizens of Kutná Hora, previously noted, murdered people in such inhuman ways, others had set up pictures, which had previously been hidden, of Christ and the saints in many houses as an indication that they were not and had never been part of the sect of the heretical Praguers. With great pleasure they again set these pictures up on the altars in churches while they cursed the Táborites, together with the Praguers as supporters of Wyclif.

As noted previously, the fighting continued on in the field by both armies until night fell. The army of the king had camped close by the Praguers because now they would be supplied with food from Kutná Hora. The Táborites and Praguers, however, had few supplies and in the cold fasted before God. Then they got up and marched forward towards the place where the king was ensconced with his army. Shooting at the enemy with their guns they drove the king, together with his entire army, from their positions. When morning broke . . . .

[The chronicle breaks off at this rather dramatic moment and must be attributed to the sudden death of the author. For what happened thereafter, other sources must be consulted.]

Historia Hussitica, in FRB 5: 528–34.

79   Aftermath of the battle of Kutná Hora

[Inasmuch as Vavřinec of Březová did not live to finish telling the story of the battle at Kutná Hora, the end of that conflict and the ensuing attempts by the crusaders to exterminate the heretical Hussites in early 1422 must be accessed elsewhere. One of the important accounts of this whole period is that written by Eberhart Windecke, a German merchant who became associated with Sigismund in 1411. He was a confidant of the king, his biographer, and possessed first-hand knowledge of the wars up until 1424.]

[Retreating], King Sigismund drew back to Český Brod and even deeper into Bohemia. One of the Hungarian lords who was with him, whose name was Pipo, whom the king had elevated as a lord, was an instigator of the people and quite equal to it. After all, it was said that he was the son of a shoemaker from Florence. Evidently he asked the king why he wanted [to wait for] more Germans, those sons of bitches. He was already strong enough. So the king returned to Kutná Hora and conquered it again on Christmas Eve. He announced that he would not hold it longer than eight days. Following this, on New Years' Eve, because there were many traitors, both Bohemian and Moravian, in the army even though they had sworn [allegiance] the king was forced to avoid them. Pipo was blamed for the flight from the field as well as from the town. Hence, the king pulled away from them and ordered that they come along with him as many as who wished. Quite a number of pious people who were faithful Christians and who had been oppressed in Kutná Hora went with him. Then [as he retreated] the king set Kutná Hora on fire and a good portion of it burned. But the Hussites [who had just arrived back] extinguished the blaze and put the rest of it to use.

So the king retreated to Německý Brod with many devout people, men and women, with their children, as well as rich and poor all following behind him. When the Czech heretics saw where the king was heading, along with the Serbs, Tartars and Hungarians with him, because many of these were in his company, these Czech heretics pursued after [the king] to Německý Brod and conquered the town (see map 3). They burned it down and beat to death many men, women and children, both young and old and thus caused great grief and suffering to the Christian German people there. It is thus no wonder that the people lost faith in God and that the Bohemian or Moravian language was no longer honoured. Then the king came on to Uherské Hradiště, while the Hungarians and Tartars went on to Hungary. Duke Rumpolt, Duke Kantner, the Bishop of Niße went to Jihlava. What happened thereafter can be found described further on in this book.

Windecke, p. 120.

80   Crusader disasters in the Sázava Valley

[Our only source on Nebovidy is the Polish chronicler Jan Długosz who made extensive use of a report filed by Black Záwiš of Garbów to King Władysław. Záwiš was on hand and was captured with several other knights after the siege of

Německý Brod. Windecke omits many details of the battles and the extended flight of the king from the Czech lands.]

Intending to marry Queen Žofie, Władysław, the king of Poland, sent Black Záwiš of Garbów to Bohemia. However, he was captured by Jan Žižka and thus that marriage was prevented. Having gone through the lands of Russia, Władysław, king of Poland, came on the day of St Martin [12 November] to Niepolomicze and held a council of his prelates and barons to discuss the offer made by Sigismund, king of Hungary and of the Romans. It was decided that the offer made by King Sigismund of the queen of Bohemia along with the dowry of the lands of Silesia was worthy and very useful to the kingdom. This was praised very highly and affirmed by all of the councillors. The burden of the concluding negotiation was placed upon the knight Black Záwiš from Garbów and he was dispatched at once to King Sigismund to confirm the details of the arrangement of the aforesaid marriage under the conditions offered. When he arrived to see the Roman king, Sigismund, to arrange the matter in accordance with the instructions given him, he found Sigismund already occupied with the expedition against the Czechs and prepared for the campaign. He communicated the message he had been entrusted with. Sigismund ordered him to remain with him a bit longer until he had concluded the campaign against the Czechs and worked out some of the negotiations involved in his mission. Considering it disgraceful to leave a king preparing for war, he [Záviš] set off for Bohemia as well.

King Sigismund collected a great multitude of Hungarians, Poles, Germans, Czechs and other peoples and entered Bohemia around the feast of the birth of Christ. He set out immediately for the mountain town which is called Kutná Hora in Latin.[2] He captured the town on his first attempt as the town was neither easy to defend by reason of location nor fortification. Many of the Czechs and Germans who had lived many years in Bohemia had suffered the unworthy disgrace of being thought of as heretics. They joined the king together with all of their equipment and goods, as much as they could carry. They were welcomed and the materials collected. Then he commanded them to be of good cheer and to put their faith in him. Meanwhile the forces of the Czech heretics consisted of Táborites, Praguers as well as other Bohemians who were accustomed to living by robbery and [had endured] injury through the alienation of the mines. These gathered from all over with their leader Žižka who, although blind, arrived with the fortified wagons. King Sigismund, being stronger and far superior in number surrounded the Hussite army in a circle and closed in with his warriors. This, however, did not have any great impact upon the Czech army who stood ready by day and night.

---

[2] Kutná Hora in Czech, Kuttenberg in German, while the Latin designation for the mining town was simply *Montem* (mountain). In other sources the town is known as Chuthnis.

Thus when the Hussite army had been neither invaded nor threatened by the army of King Sigismund, they grew bolder and moved their positions from within the encirclement which was like the points of a fence. At the same time Sigismund and his men retreated. Seeing this, King Sigismund fled in horror together with many of his forces. Then surmising that he was safely removed a secure distance, gave orders to form his men into ranks of faithful soldiers and familiars. He did not suspect any hostile assault and thus the king's forces were dispersed throughout the fields and across the land. All at once the Czech warriors appeared and suddenly, with a loud shout, attacked the dispersed and unprepared soldiers beating them down. The first line attempted to resist but a great massacre and bloodshed resulted. Numerous outstanding knights, considering it disgraceful to flee, were either captured or killed. In order not to fall into the hands of his enemies, that king Sigismund ran together with a great number of his army towards the town of Německý Brod, a town of his own language.

The Czech heretics obtained an exceedingly great victory from the hand of God through a short and easy fight. They likewise made off with the royal tents and wagons as well as many spoils of war. Having annexed Kutná Hora on the day after the conflict they surrounded the town of Německý Brod thinking that King Sigismund was inside. But he had secretly fled the previous night dreading capture. The Hussites assaulted the towers and the ramparts with their cannon. Black Záwiš of Garbów, the honourable Polish knight, could also have escaped before the town was surrounded by the Czechs. But taking heed to his responsibilities he did not release the knights of King Sigismund's army, with whom the town had been entered and in whom the citizens trusted, he elected to remain and in so far as possible to defend the town along with the other knights against capture. Some of the citizens however betrayed them and the enemies gained the town and took captive Black Záwiš, the Polish knight as well as other captured Poles, Czechs, Germans and knights and took them off to Prague where they were kept in prison in chains for a long time.

During the captivity of Black Záwiš the negotiations surrounding the marriage of Władysław, king of Poland and Žofie, queen of Bohemia came to an end because of this unfavourable star [i.e. bad omen]. Following the struggle, Žižka the leader of the heretics was greatly honoured and from that time became even more famous. He began to rage at the Catholics and their churches and did not tolerate any statue or picture of the saints any longer. Neither did he tolerate anyone following the ancient patterns who dressed in vestments during divine service.[3] Additionally, he set fire to the town of Německý Brod and it remained

---

[3]   Długosz is quite wrong on Žižka's attitude towards vestments. The old warrior took a more moderate view than the Táborites and had no compunction about Orebite priests wearing vestments for divine service.

desolate for fourteen years.[4] Pipo the Florentine who had led 15,000 horse in the expedition from Hungary across the ice [of the Sázava River] collapsed on account of the weight and many men were drowned.

Długosz, *Historia Polonicae*, book 7: 279–81.

81   Flight of the invaders and the abortive stand at Habry

[This version of the crusader disaster at Kutná Hora and its aftermath provides valuable details on the battle at Habry omitted in the other sources.]

In the year of the Lord 1422 on Tuesday after the Lord's epiphany, the aforementioned King Sigismund with a large army entered Bohemia. He burned Kutná Hora and many villages and towns in the district of Čáslav, killing many priests and people who lived in Kutná Hora. At the same time many children were plundered by the Hungarians and women and virgins were raped until they died. The Praguers and Žižka, with their followers, prepared their army against them and marched out. The king fled from Kolín [sic], having set the town on fire. They followed him and on a hill near Habry the army of the king put its troop into battle formation. The standards were raised. Then there was a great blast of trumpets and the Czechs attacked forcefully. The Hungarians turned their backs for what help could the royal power be when God had sent great horror into their hearts? They left their standards and urging their horse with their spurs they fled straight away like those who can only be saved by fleeing. Those unable to flee quickly enough were captured, drowned or in other ways delivered their bodies to death.

Chonicon veteris Collegiati, in Höfler, I: 85–6.

82   Crusade failures in the winter of 1421–2

[Sigismund's defeats during December and January drove him from Bohemia. He would not set foot there again for more than fourteen years. It is a gross exaggeration on the part of the chronicler to say that the town of Německý Brod remained uninhabited for seven years. Notwithstanding this, the crusade initiative was in serious jeopardy following these events. It is estimated that Sigismund lost 12,000 men in the winter battles between Kutná Hora and Německý Brod. Quite

---

[4]   A gross exaggeration as Žižka called for important meetings there early the next year.

a number of ranking crusaders who survived the battles were taken prisoner. The crusader defeat was thorough.]

In the year of the Lord 1422, the Hungarian king Sigismund with secrecy invaded Bohemia with a very large force of about 50,000 Hungarians, Germans, Czechs and Moravians and he approached Kutná Hora. At that moment Brother Žižka was near Kutná Hora and when he heard that Sigismund was approaching he came out from the city. There they encircled him under Kaňk [Mountain] from all sides and drove oxen before them on account of the guns. When night fell, Žižka cut through them with hand to hand fighting and went to Kolín and all of this happened before Christmas. Immediately after Christmas Žižka together with all the people around Jičín and the immediate area set off against King Sigismund once more. At the same time the people of Žižka gathered themselves to Kolín as the king still had hold of Kutná Hora. Žižka's people marched out from Kolín on the Tuesday of the Lord's baptism and set against the king's people at Nebovidy.[5] But the royalists stood everywhere upon the hills so thickly that they looked like a forest and they burned forts and buildings and villages all around Kutná Hora. There in Nebovidy they found a young girl who had hidden herself in a barn, but the vile Hungarians raped her until she died. The Czechs were very remorseful about this and said, 'we must avenge this and we pledge to give our lives for this.' On Tuesday and Wednesday night at three o'clock in the morning, Sigismund commanded that the town of Kutná Hora be set on fire and he retreated with his men in the face of Brother Žižka and Žižka pursued him but the king continued to retreat before him. Then on the Thursday after the baptism of the Lord, Brother Žižka managed to run him down at Habry near Německý Brod.

Here Žižka drew into formation and attacked the royalists and at once they fled towards Německý Brod and attempted to make a stand there in formation. But the king did not even pause there but retreated still further. Those who remained [to fight] were beaten, captured or killed while others fled beyond the town. Some tried to cross over the Sázava River, but fell through the ice and drowned while some reached the other side. They abandoned here in front of the town more than 600 wagons, full of supplies with various goods including money, clothing, chests full of various books, both Jewish and Christian, the number of which made it impossible to gather together into three wagons. Here they remained overnight and early in the morning, after hearing Mass, they attacked the town throughout the day of Friday. Stones were shot over the walls and cannon were used on both sides to a great degree. When evening came, the assault ceased. On Saturday morning,

---

[5]   During the Middle Ages this holy day was observed on one of the free days after Epiphany. Alternatively the author may have had in mind the Epiphany itself (6 January) as the baptism of the Lord is an older theme for the Epiphany than the Magi.

following Mass, they began to negotiate. While this was going on others [succeeded in gaining] entrance to the town. Thus they invaded the town and they killed several hundred people, throwing many down from the town hall onto swords, lances and pikes. There are still indications of this to be seen to this day because blood splattered all over the walls. The town was laid waste for seven years and wolves and dogs ate the dead bodies in the square while others were buried by some of the peasants. A large number of people were killed in Německý Brod, of the royalists and Hungarians, along with people in the surrounding vicinity during that campaign beginning in Kutná Hora all the way to Německý Brod, about 12,000 not including those who fell through the ice and drowned of which 548 heavily armoured bodies were found.[6] On Sunday, before the octave of the baptism of the Lord, Brother Žižka was made a knight. Then on Monday morning they gave to the knights the banners which they had captured in that battle and there were six or seven banners.

SRB 3: 48–50.

83   Song of victory over King Sigismund at Německý Brod

[The text which follows has been reconstructed from a verbal Polish translation and even this reconstruction leaves gaps in the text itself which clouds the meaning in several places. It reveals a Hussite perspective on the triumph at Německý Brod underscoring the king's distress, his low morale, the anti-royalist sentiment in Bohemia and the idea that since Žižka's warriors are invincible the Hungarian king might just as well leave the country once and for all. The song itself appears to have been contemporary with the events, therefore 1422 or shortly thereafter.]

We have received the news about the Hungarian king,
We had to laugh when we heard what the Czechs told us.
Žižka marched in between the mountains
The king marched to the mountains, [..]
[..] burned, no one opposed him.
You unfaithful inhabitants of Prague,
[..] damn you,
[..] must you engage in betrayal because of hunger (?)

---

[6]   There is some dispute about whether the Sázava River is deep and wide enough below Německý Brod to have caused this disaster. My own visit to the site did not convince me either way and it is of note that more than one contemporary source included this event.

[..] Oh, you unfaithful king, do not become involved in this.
Žižka will turn around and many Germans
Will jump over the flails [i.e. will be slain].
The king [..] [was standing] on the mountain
Dear God, do not [..]
Now he [Sigismund] has a headache
Things are not as he would like them to be in the Czech lands.

[When] the inhabitants of Prague learned about this,
They quickly gathered and wherever they saw the king
They ran after him. And what about you Lord Hašek [of Valdštejn] and Ostrov:
Do not talk about it, you Hungarian king,
It was easier for you to hand it over by words in Constance(?),
Rather than try to conquer Prague with the sword.
What about [..] Lord Jan Kravovský:
Therefore go away, O Hungarian king, do not remain here any longer,
You can not expect anything good here.
And you Lord Janíček, do not let them kill you,
Come with us to Constance [..]
[..] we will drink enough Svinice beer
But the armour and equipment must be ours.

Paul Diels, 'Ein Hussitenlied auf K. Siegmund' *Archiv für slawische Philologie*
42 (1928-9), pp.97–108, the Polish text on pp. 98-99, the Czech on pp. 101-102.

84   The king's perspective on the situation

[Now at a safe distance from the Hussite armies, the thoroughly humiliated king
threatened renewed crusade. The letter is dated 29 January 1422.]

Sigismund, God's grace, king of the Romans, ever Augustus, king of Hungary,
Bohemia, etc. I commend our grace and all good things to all of the mayors,
councillors and citizens in general of the towns of Wrocław, Namysłów, Środa
Śląska and to all the others and those who belong to them, our dearly beloved.

   Dear beloved and faithful ones. We have come to Brno and have given
thought there and have taken counsel with our ecclesiastical and secular princes
and with our advisors, concerning how peace might be obtained and kept between
our people and throughout the land, including the principalities of Wrocław and
Namysłów, against the Wyclifites and heretics in Bohemia. We intend to call a
war against them when summer comes and then we can set out on a campaign and

then be able to find sustenance in the field. Therefore we desire with all earnestness and diligence that you send your people for the sake of our friendship, with as much force as possible to Olomouc on Tuesday in three weeks without delay. This way we can bring to completion these matters and organize our business. We are writing to all of the princes and prelates in Silesia and also throughout the lands and towns of Świdnica and Jawor as well as to other places bordering Bohemia so that they might all come to Olomouc on the aforementioned day. This will enable us to make a complete end to those matters mentioned above. Do not neglect this for any reason because we have placed trust in you and believe in you completely. Given in Brno on the Thursday after the conversion of St Paul [25 January] in the thirty-fifth year of our Hungarian reign and in the twelfth year of our Roman reign and in the second year of our Bohemian reign.

UB 1: 174–5.

85   Sigismund lobbies support from the bishop of Tartu

[This letter was sent by King Sigismund to the bishop of Tartu[7] after it was clear that Prince Zygmunt Korybut of Lithuania was going to defend the Hussite heretics with the support of his uncle the Grand Duke Witold (†1431). Sigismund wrote to encourage the bishop, together with all his servants, to prepare to assist the Knights of the Teutonic Order in Prussia and to withstand the defenders of heretics. The courier and the letter were intercepted on the Polish frontier. Earlier, Witold, Grand Duke of Lithuania, had written to Pope Martin V on 5 March stating he would take charge of leading the heretics back to the church and was sending Korybut to Bohemia as his representative (UB 1: 186–7).]

Venerable prince, our dearly beloved. We have no wish to be unaware of your piety or to be absent from your mind even though malicious lances have come against our faith through false and erroneous doctrines which have been written down and which endeavour to extinguish the orthodox faith in clever ways. I speak of the hypocritical and fictive elements meaning the communion under both kinds as well as the tyrannical and atrocious cruelty of fire and sword through which they seek to convert everyone they can in order to spread their sect by false brethren. Not satisfied to have infected Bohemia entirely they have sent their

---

[7]   Referred to as Dorpat in certain sources and located in present-day Estonia. The see of Tartu had a history of hostility towards the Hussite heretics. For example, in 1417 the bishop attempted unsuccessfully to persuade Witold, grand duke of Lithuania, to punish a Czech baron who publicly defended the Hussite faith.

followers to foreign countries in order to deceive souls. They have invited Zygmunt, the duke of Lithuania in whose shadow they desire to hide their sect, to take up the crown of the kingdom of Bohemia. They wish to teach him in order to strengthen the heretics in their perversity which they call a brotherhood and thus to praise and give authorization to their errors. They have taken up, together with him, a great multitude of Poles and annexed Tartars who have been designated by Duke Witold for the support of the aforesaid heretics. They have set off for Bohemia, having no mind for his honour and completely abusing it. They wish to swallow even more of that lethal poison and thus vomit that virus which has been received and spread it around even more. We have considered all this with respect to the Highest, in whose hand everything is and by whom the empire is controlled and maintained. Carrying a fervent zeal for the defence of the Christian faith, as well as preservation by the sword we have invited for this defence, the venerable Paul [of Rusdorf], general master of Livonia and master of his order for Germany [1422–41], the athletes of Christ and warriors of the cross of Christ, against those heretics previously noted, together with their adherents and patrons.

Now you and your vassals are obliged by the duty, of which you enjoy ecclesiastical liberty, as do other Catholics and leading churchmen, to crush the heretical pestilence and all its followers. Therefore we require and advise you carefully in terms of your devotion, that it is most solemnly commanded that you require all of your vassals and servants most strictly to be prepared with you to take up weapons, arise, and proceed with all force against the enemies of the order, those adherents of the heretics, along with the venerable master of Livonia and his people and invade their lands and domains.

If you neglect to do this, which we cannot believe, from that moment on we shall regard you not as friends of the faith but as fervent supporters of heretics and followers of heresy. We trust that you will not spare any force, expense or danger for the suppression of this malignant mischief of the enemies of Christ in this matter. For this you shall obtain the abiding favour of God, the praise of the people, and for your service we shall compensate you with worthy rewards and remuneration. Given in Devín, on 1 May in the year of the Lord 1422.

UB 1: 194–5.

86   Imperial admonition for the city of Frankfurt am Main

[Sigismund writes to the city fathers of Frankfurt noting that the Reichstag had already been called to assemble in Regensburg on 1 July. The Hussite problem is at the top of their agenda. The letter is dated 1 May 1422.]

Sigismund, by the grace of God, King of the Romans, ever Augustus, king of Hungary, Bohemia, etc.

Dearly beloved. We have notified and determined a common assembly at Regensburg of all the electors, princes, counts, barons, knights, vassals, and cities of the holy empire on account of a considerable and significant matter concerning the holy empire, the Christian faith and the common good. This is to consent and unify together in force in a campaign against Bohemia for the suppression of the heretics and an extermination of their heresy. We have written to you about this previously in our letters and called the assembly. We are certain that these letters have reached you and desire that you would wish to come to Regensburg on the appointed day should God will. We likewise desire that you diligently send your envoys to Regensburg on the eighth day immediately following the Day of St John Baptist [2 July]. In the meantime, prepare yourselves and get ready, as best you can, to join with the electors and princes against the heretics of Bohemia. For this you shall obtain an eternal reward from God, honour and praise from all Christendom and special gratitude from us which we shall never forget. Given in Devín on the day of SS Philip and James [1 May], in the thirty-sixth year of our Hungarian reign, the twelfth year of our Roman reign, and the second year of our Bohemian reign.

UB 1: 196.

87   Pope Martin V presses for military solution

[Martin V informs Sigismund that further action against the Hussites is essential. He urgently requests that the king prepare to act in concert with the German electors in formulating a policy which can be implemented aimed at the extermination of the heresy. Sigismund called for the Reichstag to be held at Regensburg but the electors withstood him and assembled in Nürnberg. This disunity set the tone for the third crusade. Martin wrote many letters to those involved in the crusading initiatives: Sigismund, Władysław, King of Poland, Witold, Grand Duke of Lithuania, Michael Küchmeister, Grand Master of the Teutonic Knights [1414–22], Albrecht, Duke of Austria, to name a few. There were no fewer than 511 such missives. This one, addressed to Sigismund, was composed before July 1422.]

We have no doubts about your Grace's willingness to move quickly and zealously in order to eradicate the Czech heresy and that this holy task is foremost in your mind and that you have no need to be admonished further in this respect. Nevertheless, we are aware that you are soon to assemble with our venerable brethren, the archbishops, and the dearly beloved noble imperial electors and other German princes and that this convocation is going to discuss many significant and difficult matters pertaining to the holy faith. This is a priority and is to be preferred to all other [points of business]. We wish to encourage you by letting you know through this letter that this matter is most urgent in our hearts. To be sure, we are convinced that if you, together with the faithful princes and German people whom this heresy threatens with grievous injury as well as God and the church, take this matter into consideration and provide a remedy this summer by coordinating an army to enter Bohemia it would be easy to put down and exterminate the heretics, these rebels against yourself and God.

Certainly we have heard that several towns were conquered through force, or capitulated out of fear and that nearly the whole of the Margraviate of Moravia has been restored. From this laudable beginning it can be possible, if the timing is right, to achieve a complete and perfect victory. Therefore, dear son, we ask that this matter be undertaken principally by your office which has the obligation to suppress such militant heresy through the use of weapons just as your predecessors, the most Christian emperors, did in times past. If a heresy arose under different circumstances among Christian people which sought to pollute the Christian faith and religion with false and sophisticated arguments, as it happened in the time of our fathers, the church was able to remove it through the holy instruction and arguments of true doctrine and the chastisement of justice without recourse to the secular arm. But this disgusting heresy violates not only the Law of God and the precepts of the church but destroys the holy temples, murders priests, violently plunders the decorations of the churches which have been designed for the worship of God. This heresy dishonours all that is sacred and after polluting divine law, it subverts human law and the human estates, removes political authority and thereby alters the lives of people which have been instituted by reason and law. All of this is transferred into the irrational grossness of beastly license and continues in such a criminal manner that what else are we to do, who have been constituted in the apostolic power by the Lord to preserve our religion and Christian faith. We implore therefore the help of your Grace and of faithful who are capable of defeating militarily this nefarious pestilence which is close by to the German princes and people and who are the neighbours of this mad disease.

Therefore we have written to these princes whom we know will be present at this assembly so that they might demonstrate themselves ready to undertake the final extirpation of this most befouling heresy in the proper time with all of their power. You must encourage them in this regard through your authority as well as your example in order that they might see that you are the leader and the most zealous in this matter and that you wish to labour in this cause with all of your might. This can only be done by setting aside and delaying other matters temporarily with the greatest consideration to this holy task. It is clear that if you undertake all of the other duties you might reasonably enjoy it but you would have to neglect this. This would satisfy neither God nor the common welfare of Christendom which expects and demands that you provide assistance for while the Christian faith is disturbed and offended in other lands, it is also being violated in your own house together with your royal rights. Therefore, dear son, implement a plan in order that the aforementioned assembly above all discusses the idea of an expedition into Bohemia. Turn all of your attention to this resolution and undertake it being persuaded that nothing could be done or regarded as more acceptable by God, more gracious for us, more glorious for you and more beneficial for Christian people. Given in Rome.

DR 8: 119–21.

88   Hussite support for Zygmunt Korybut of Lithuania

[Hussite opposition to the claims of Sigismund for the throne of the Czech kingdom is supported well in this letter written by Jan Žižka while in Čáslav on 11 June 1422. It calls for comparison with the decisions made a year earlier at the national assembly. See doc.63.]

With God's help, amen. Do be aware, barons and brothers, that we support and accept his Highness the prince as our helper and as supreme regent in this country. We have done this with the support of the brothers at Tábor, the towns of Domažlice, Klatovy, Sušice, Písek, Prachatice and Horažďovice, together with other barons, knights, squires, and some other towns, all of which have freely been followers of myself, as well as Chval and Buchovec and they have put their trust in our direction. We intend to gladly obey his Highness and will faithfully assist him and provide him with counsel in everything that is good and proper, as God enables us. We ask that all of you likewise obey him just as you have committed to do so before God.

Beyond this we request that from this time forth all of you might harmoniously, in good faith and for all time, be forgiving in terms of all of the problems, conflicts and ill will which you had one for the other either relating to last year or more recently. With a proper conscience you should pray the Lord's Prayer and be able to say, 'forgive us our transgressions even as we forgive those who have transgressed against us.'

However, if you are unwilling to do this and seek to stir up animosity, disputes, riots or other conflagrations, aimed at creating factions, then with the help of God and together with the prince, his Highness, and our lords the councillors as well as with the help of other barons, squires, knights and the faithful communities, we shall take action and punish these deeds together with those responsible and no one will be exempt from this. Can we rely upon you to assist us in these matters?

Should someone have difficulty with another person over matters of goods or anything else besides, than that person should go to the magistrates, councillors and judges, without causing great unrest, and seek justice from them in a proper fashion. The elder officials, such as the magistrates, councillors and judges ought to be respected and everyone should love each other as if they were brothers. In this way our Lord God will be among us with his holy grace and God will give us the victory in everything which is good and proper.

Bartoš, pp. 12–13.

89   A stern warning to prospective crusaders

[Sometime in August 1421, Jan Žižka and Diviš Bořek of Miletínek, wrote letters to the margraves of Meißen who, in support of the bishops' union, were preparing to invade Bohemia on another crusading sortie. Žižka's letter threatened severe retaliation should they set foot on Czech soil. Abbot Ludolf who reports on the now lost correspondence records his shock at Žižka's language and message.]

Therefore in a letter of defiance, which Jan [Žižka] sent to the margraves of Meißen and to Friedrich the Younger, Landgrave of Thuringia, he named himself captain of the community of Tábor. The Bohemians, that is the Hussites, reach such madness, imagining foolishly that they will obtain a certain, special, spiritual or temporal safety on the height of certain mountains, that they climb these heights in an unrestrained multitude. Reaching the top they find comfort in defending with a cruel sword their sect and this same Jan Žižka, whom the forces of Prague had for a captain. Having climbed their mountains, they have named the place Tábor, hence they are called Táborites. The community of these men, corrupt in mind, words, and deeds, together with their well-known captain made a sign on which they carved the image of a chalice, which is the same image depicted on their battle standard. They also made known to the peoples of the surrounding nations that they use this image, because they maintain the impious and faulty assertion that all of the faithful people need to take communion under both kinds in order to obtain salvation. By this they mean taking up the body of the Lord under the form of bread, and the blood of the same Lord under the form of wine. Indeed such wine is typically drank from a chalice. In defending their error most tenaciously, they think themselves to be gloriously carrying out the mandate of God. They say that the entire family of Christ that does the opposite of them in this matter is heretical and in error. For this same reason, Jan Žižka, in his letter of defiance to the princes of Meißen and the landgrave of Thuringia, calls these same magnificent, illustrious, and venerable princes obstinate heretics and murderers, who shed the blood of those fighting a most just war for the true faith, those Hussites, Táborites, and Wyclifites. They consecrate their hands in the blood of the slaughtered heretics.

Ludolf of Żagań, pt. 2, chap. 62, pp. 533–4.

90   Protracted siege of Karlštejn Castle

[During the summer and autumn of 1422, Hussite armies attempted unsuccessfully to conquer Karlštejn Castle, the well-fortified royalist stronghold, southwest of Prague. While this siege was going on, there were other military activities within the kingdom and the time of the third crusade was marked by numerous skirmishes.]

In the same year [1422] the prince Zygmunt Korybut, for whom the Czechs regarded highly [in hopes] that he would come to the Czech land against Sigismund, the king of Hungary, in order to defend and protect the land from domestic as well as foreign enemies, arrived first at Uničov and here he received the holy sacrament of the body and blood of the Lord Jesus Christ under both kinds. Previously he had promised the lord envoys, who had gone to him before he came to the Czech land, that he wanted to fulfil the truth which he recognized by action and so he did. Being then in Moravia he wrote to Žižka's army asking them not to plunder and destroy the land. Žižka answered him in writing with great cruelty, as he alone could do, letting him know his mind, and calling him a murderous prince and a damned incendiary. The prince was astonished at this. But being informed that he [Žižka] was victorious and brave in battle and undefeated in the wars, the prince overlooked it. Later when they became acquainted with each other and were united favourably, the prince called Žižka 'father' and Žižka called the lord prince 'son'. . . .

In the same year, Žižka conquered Krasíkov Castle and captured the great pest Lord Bohuslav of Švamberk and put him in prison in Příběnice. When he [Bohuslav] saw that the king had no concern to set him free from the prison he agreed with the brethren of Tábor and remained faithful to them until his death.

In the same year, on Whitsuntide Tuesday, Prince Zygmunt with the Praguers and Poles laid siege to Karlštejn Castle but they did not conquer it even though they had been attacking it excessively and had been shooting many kegs of ammunition with the catapult. In the castle were five Czech knights along with many other squires. They shot 932 stones into the castle with the catapult, 820 barrels of dirt which they had brought from Prague, along with carcasses and excrement. Also, they were shooting the Pražka [a type of cannon] seven times daily as well as the Jaroměřka [another cannon] seven times a day and the Rychlice [a rapid fire cannon] thirty times per day. But they caused little damage to the castle. Then the Poles began to eat the meat of donkeys rather than venison.

In the same year, the electors and the margrave of Meißen invaded Bohemia with great force and laid siege to Žatec. They acted treacherously, catching pigeons, swallows and other birds and attaching flaming sulphur candles to their feet hoping in this manner to set fire to the town. Then on the day of St Jerome the Czechs defeated them during the watch and they rushed off in great shame.[8]

Also in the same year, the Silesians invaded Bohemia with great force during the drought prior to St Wenceslas day and they called the Czechs to follow them. But they turned around against them and killed about 300 Czechs.

SRB 3: 52–4.

91   Liturgical invocation for launching third crusade

[On 4 September 1422 at St Sebald's Church in Nürnberg, Cardinal Branda gave the crusade banner to King Sigismund, which had been blessed by Martin V thus officially inaugurating another crusader effort against the Hussite heretics in Bohemia. Sigismund in turn gave the banner to Friedrich of Brandenburg who would be appointed chief commander of the crusader expedition.]

This is the manner in which the banner representing the living cross shall be bestowed upon those in opposition to the faithless heretics.

Antiphon: Through the sign of the cross I have lifted up my soul to you. In the name of God I have lifted up my eyes. Through this sign of the cross deliver us from our enemies, O God. Lord have mercy. Christ have mercy. Lord have mercy. Our father.
[Versicle] We worship you and praise you O Christ.
[Response] Through your holy cross you have redeemed the world.
[Versicle] Save your servants.
[Response] May hope be in you.
[Versicle] Let the enemy have no triumph over him.
[Response] May the son of iniquity be unable to do such a one any injury.

---

8   This is a reference to the second crusade in September 1421. See doc.74.

[Versicle] Be a tower of strength to that person.

[Response] In front of all enemies and persecutors.

[Versicle] Send that one divine assistance.

[Response] Protect that one in Zion.

[Versicle] Lord, hear my prayer.

[Response] Let this cry come to you.

[Versicle] The Lord be with you.

[Response] And with your spirit.

Let us pray. It was according to your will, O God, that this banner of the life-giving cross was made holy and exalted through the precious blood of your only begotten son, even the Lord Jesus Christ. We give this banner to this prince of the Christian people and to every one of the faithful who have upon their chests the sign of the holy cross. This we do for the honouring and glorifying of your sacred name and for the preserving of the Catholic faith. Also, [we do this] for the defeating of the unrighteous heretics in order to secure the safety and peace for all Christendom. May these have your protection in all places and may they overcome their enemies decisively through faith in your all powerful goodness through our Lord.

As the banner is given, the following words are to be spoken. Take this banner which has been sanctified by the blessing of heaven. May it cause terror to the enemies of the Christian people. May the Lord grant peace to you that you may be able to penetrate the ranks of the enemy without harm in safety and thus bring glory and honour to his name. Amen.

Prayer: O God, our defender and sustainer of Christian people. We give this banner of the sacred cross to your servant by the authority of the holy church. May it be lifted up in opposition to the vicious enemies of the cross and of the correct faith. May this servant have wisdom in order to achieve victory through your goodness so that together with the assistance of divine help, he might be able to powerfully defeat these heretics who treacherously and with great arrogance persist in following in their unteachable faithlessness. Take heed to us, our protection and merciful God, defend those who defend the faith and your faithful people against every danger presented by the heretics who have no faith and who blaspheme your glorious name. May these be liberated from the burdens of the [heretics] as well as from that of those who support and defend them. May they succeed in conquering and exterminating them through your great goodness.

Merciful and mighty God, do not neglect your Christian people who in confidence have turned to you and who beg you in their time of trouble. Be gentle and sustain those who are in difficulty in the sake of your glorious name. With grace, give regard to their difficulties and, in mercy, turn aside any indignant rage which they might well deserve. Ever living and all-powerful God, you who comforts those who weep, who provides strength for those who labour and to those who are in need, may the prayers of all these Christian people come before you.

In their pressing needs may your mercy be joyfully received and for which they ask in humility in a humble attitude against these enemies of the blessed cross. Almighty and everlasting God, all things are in subjection to your authority, no one can withstand what you desire. Positively regard your Christian people and cause that they shall always be steadfast in the proper, true and Catholic faith. May all the world see and know that such faith is indeed undergirded by your goodness and all who insistently oppose it by persecuting your faithful people shall be brought low through your very great goodness.[9]

Andreas von Regensburg, 'Chonica Husitarum', in Georg Leidinger, ed. *Andreas von Regensburg Sämtliche Werke*. [Quellen und Erörterungen zur Bayerischen und Deutschen Geschichte n.s. 1]. Aalen: Scientia Verlag, 1969, pp. 377–8.[10]

92   Ceremonies for the crusade expedition

[There was considerable disunity in the third crusade. Friedrich of Brandenburg, supreme commander, made enormous efforts to keep the initiative together. On 1 December 1422, Martin V ordered the German clergy to tax themselves to pay for the crusade (DR 8: 181–2). Though launched officially on 4 September 1422, the third crusade evaporated, despite some local skirmishes. See map 2. It would be the only crusade against the Hussites not to end in a smashing defeat for the crusaders. The day after Sigismund accepted the crusade banner, 5 September, he published a detailed, written instruction giving supreme command for the third crusade to Friedrich of Brandenburg.]

We Sigismund, by the grace of God, king of the Romans, ever Augustus of the empire and king of Hungary, Bohemia, Dalmatia, Croatia, etc., announce and make known publicly by this letter to all those who read it, see it or hear it [read], that we have now ordered, on the advice of the imperial electors, other princes,

---

[9]   On liturgical matters in Bohemia the leading authority is David R. Holeton whose principal work *La communion des tout-petits enfants: Étude du mouvement eucharistique en Bohême vers la fin du Moyen-Âge* is supported by a number of shorter studies published in *BRRP*, vols. 1–3, *CV*, *Studia Liturgica, Ephemerides Liturgicae, Studie o rukopiesch* and elsewhere.

[10] For Andreas see most recently, Norman Housley, 'Explaining Defeat: Andrew of Regensburg and the Hussite Crusades', in *Dei gesta per Francos: Etudes sur les croisades dédiées à Jean Richard*, eds. Michel Balard, Benjamin Z. Kedar and Jonathan Riley-Smith (Aldershot: Ashgate, 2001), pp. 87–95.

counts, barons, and faithful people, and also many of our lords, nobles and faithful people of Bohemia, to undertake, with a numerous and powerful army, a campaign into our Kingdom of Bohemia against the Wyclifite heresy and the Wyclifites who are called Hussites, as well as to force a daily war against them. We have further taken into consideration the righteousness, wisdom and solidarity of the high-born Friedrich, margrave of Brandenburg, Imperial archchamberlain and burgrave of Nürnberg, our counsellor, dear uncle and elector, and especially the respect, love and faith he has shown to the Christian faith, to us and to the empire. Therefore, having reasoned together, taking the good advice of our aforementioned electors, princes, barons, banner lords and those faithful to us, both of the empire as well as of the Crown of Bohemia, we have appointed and constituted him our supreme captain in the aforenamed campaign and daily war against the previously mentioned Wyclifites. We are making this appointment on the basis of our Roman and Czech royal authority by virtue of this letter. On the basis of this letter we have given him also full power and authority to raise and lead our banner, and that of the empire and of the Crown of Bohemia, against the aforementioned Wyclifites to press the war and siege against them and to undertake, and allow to be undertaken, whatever is necessary in this matter just as we ourselves would do and allow to be done if we were present.

We have given him power, by virtue of this letter, to negotiate and to come to agreement with all barons, banner lords, knights, vassals, and the inhabitants of all towns, castles, small towns and villages, who are the promoters, helpers and adherents of the Wyclifites named above, and also with the Wyclifites themselves, in terms of returning to obedience and subjection to the holy church and to us as their legitimate hereditary lord. Further, to guarantee them with their movable and immovable goods and assets, that should they receive and accept us and our [claim] to the Crown of Bohemia and to give to them, collectively or individually, peace, safe-conduct and security. But if they persist in their faithlessness [he has authority] to punish them in body and in property, to torture and put to death by burning or otherwise. [He may] capture them and do with them as he wishes, whether to examine the captives, to set them free, to hold them as prisoners, or to put them to death, as his will and reason advises and as he desires. Whatever he deals, makes, negotiates, does or concludes, according to what is written in his letters, to undertake and allow to be undertaken, just as we would do and allow to be done if we were present, to the extent that is necessary to do in the previously mentioned campaign and daily war. Whatever he does or will do, promises or imposes, instead of us, remains our will and word.

We have sworn and we are swearing by this letter and by our royal word to keep and to fulfil constantly and firmly and where there is need, to add to our royal letter without delay. We command also seriously and firmly, by this letter, all of our imperial princes, counts, barons, knights, vassals, officers and inhabitants of all towns, small towns and villages of the above named crown, to faithfully support, assist and obey the previously mentioned Friedrich our captain, instead of us and because of us, in each and every matter and issue since we have complete confidence in him and our love, grace and favour belong to all of them. The captainship of Friedrich is to continue from the date of this letter and the next Whitsuntide and beyond that until we revoke it or until either we or he so desire. The writing of this letter, sealed by our royal majestic seal, is given in Nürnberg in the year 1421 after the birth of Christ, on the Saturday before the birth of our Lady. In the thirty-sixth year of our Hungarian reign, in the twelfth [year] of our Roman [reign] and in the third year of our Bohemian [reign].

UB 1: 236–8.

93   Levying of troops for the campaign

[The assembling of soldiers to engage Hussite heretics in the third crusade provides a useful picture of the size and importance of those powers (mainly German) opposing the Czech heretics. A great concentration of military power came from the Rhineland and the contributions from respective cities and towns sheds some light on the importance of the city in question in the fifteenth century.]

The electors
    Archbishops: Mainz with fifty swords, Cologne with forty swords, Trier with forty swords, the count of the Palatinate with fifty swords, Saxony with twenty armed cavalry, Brandenburg with fifty swords.
    Bishops: Archbishop of Magdeburg, thirty men with swords and ten archers, Bishop of Hildesheim, five men with swords and five archers, Bishop of Würzburg, twenty men with swords, Bishop of Bamberg, twenty men with swords, Bishop of Eichstätt, ten men with swords, Bishop of Strasbourg, five men with swords, Bishop of Constance, eight men with swords, Bishop of Basel, two men with swords, Bishop of Chur, two men with swords, Bishop of Besançon, six swordsmen, Bishop of Augsburg, two men with swords, Bishop of Metz, six men with swords, Bishop of Toul, three men with swords, Bishop of Verdun, six swordsmen, Bishop of Lausanne, six men with swords, Bishop of Speyer, eight men with swords, Bishop of Worms, two men with swords, Bishop of Verden, three swordsmen and six other armed men, Bishop of Schwerin, eight men with swords and eight other armed men, Bishop of Halberstadt, six men with swords and six other armed men, Bishop of Bremen, ten men with swords and ten other armed men, Bishop of Kammin, six men with swords and six other armed men, Bishop of Regensburg, five swordsmen, Bishop of Münster, ten men with swords.

Dukes and secular princes: Duke of Lorraine, twenty men with swords, Duke of Bar, twenty men with swords, Duke of Savoy, fifty men with swords, Margrave of Baden, ten men with swords, Landgrave of Hesse, twenty men with swords and ten other armed men, Duke Otto of the Leina, ten men with swords and ten other armed men, Erich of Brunswick, five men with swords and five other armed men, Duke Otto of Hirschberg, five men with swords and five other armed men, Bernhard and Wilhelm of Brunswick, together with their cities, Brunswick and Lüneburg, ten men with swords and ten other armed men, Johannes of Mecklenburg, ten men with swords and ten other armed men, Albrecht of Mecklenburg, ten men with swords, and ten other armed men, children of Duke Ulrich and the country of Stargardt, ten men with swords and ten other armed men, Otto and Casimir of Stettin, twenty men with swords and twelve other armed men, Vladislav of Wolgast, fifteen men with swords and twelve other armed men, Erich of Saxe-Lauenberg, three men with swords and six other armed men, Louis of Ingolstadt in Bavaria, sixteen men with swords, Ernst and Wilhelm of Bavaria, ten men with swords, Heinrich of Bavaria, twenty men with swords, Johannes of Bavaria, ten men with swords, Stephen of Bavaria, five men with swords, Otto of Bavaria, five men with swords, Adolf of Cleve, twenty men with swords, Duke of Berg, six men with spears, the bishop of Utrecht, with Deventer, Kempten, Zwolle and Utrecht, forty men with swords.

Dutch Barons: Duke of Jülich, and knights of Jülich and Guelders and the four cities of Romunde, Nymwegen, Arnheim and Zutphen, sixty men with swords, the three cities of Brabant, one hundred men with swords, the cities of Liège, one hundred men with swords. Those carrying banners, knights of Holland, sixty men with swords, those carrying banners, knights and men of Hainault, the cities of Hainault and the count of Namurs, twenty men with swords, lords and knights of Flanders and Flemish cities, twenty men with swords.

Counts and lords: Gerhard, Count of Mark, three men with swords, Wilhelm, Count of Ravensburg, two men with swords, Count of Teckelnburg, two men with swords, Count of Riedenburg, one man with a sword, Lord of Lippe, two men with swords, Lord of Dippoldswald, one man with a sword, Count of Bentheim, one man with a sword, Count of Schaumburg, one man with a sword, Count of Oldenburg, one man with a sword, Friedrich and Wilhelm of Henneberg, four men with swords, Count of Rheineck, two men with swords, Count of Kastel, two men with swords, Count of Hohenlohe, two men with swords, Count of Weinsberg, two men with swords, Count of Heideck, one man with a sword, Otto Erich of the Heust, six men with swords, Count of Württemberg, twenty men with swords, Count of Schauen, fifteen men with swords, Margrave of Rotelen, three men with swords, Margrave of Toggenburg, five men with swords, Conrad of Freiburg, five men with swords, Hugo, master of the Order of St John, ten men with swords, Christopher of Wenden, six men with swords and six other armed men, Albrecht and Georg of Anhalt, five men with swords and five other men with swords, Bernhard of Anhalt, four men with swords and four other armed men, Bernhard of Rheinstein, three men with swords and three other armed men, Count of Wernigerode, four men with swords and four archers, Emich of Leinigen, three men with swords, Friedrich of Leinigen, two men with swords, Philip of Nassau, four men with swords, Johannes of Sponheim, five men with swords, Friedrich of Veldenz, three men with swords, Johannes and Friedrich, counts of the Rhine, two men with swords, Philip and Emich, barons of Oberstein, two men with swords, Lord of Hohenfels, one swordsman, Nicholas Vogt of Honolstein, one swordsman, Johannes of Katzenellenbogen, eight men with swords, Adolf of Nassau, two men with swords, Wilhelm of Wied, three men with swords, Philip and Salentin, barons of Ysenburg, three men with swords, Johannes of Wied and Reinhard, baron of Westerburg, two men with swords, Dietrich, baron of Runkel, one swordsman, Johannes and Heinrich, counts of Nassau and baron of Bilstein, two men with swords, Bernhard and Johannes, brothers and Count Solms, three men with swords, Johannes of Wittgenstein, one swordsman, Ruprecht of Virenburg, two men with swords, Gottfried Eberhard, baron of Epstein, four men with swords, Reinhard, baron of Hanau, three men with swords, Dieter, baron of Büdegen, three men with swords, Michael of Wertheim, one swordsman, Wilhelm of Eberstein, one swordsman, the barons of Arbergen, three men with swords, Wilhelm of Blankenstein, one swordsman, Johannes, baron of Schleiden, one swordsman, Friedrich of Moers, four men with swords, Wilhelm Craft, baron of Saffenburg, one swordsman, Johannes, baron of Heimsberg, four men with swords, Walgrave of Moers, one swordsman, Johannes, baron of Rodemachern, two men with swords, Johannes and Gottfried, barons of Ziegenhain, two men with swords, Heinrich of Waldeck and others from Waldeck, four men with swords, Johannes Heinrich of Vinstigen, two men with swords, the baron of Wibelkoben, one swordsman, Shenk Eberhard, Schenk Conrad and Schenk Conrad the Younger of Ehrenpach, three men with swords, Conrad, baron of Bickenbach, one swordsman, the baron of Neuenahr, one swordsman, Eberhard of Lineburg, baron of Hartenburg, two men with swords, Count of Limburg, one swordsman, baron of Harn, two men with swords, Johannes of Saarwerden with one swordsman, the Bitsch brothers, one swordsman, and the Count of Salm having one swordsman.

The Abbots: Abbot of Fulda, six men with swords, Abbot of Weißenburg, two men with swords, Abbot of Zelle, one swordsman, Abbot of Mürbach, three men with swords, Abbot of Maulbronn, five men with swords, Abbot of Einsiedeln, two men with swords, Abbot of Biebenhausen, three men with swords, Abbot of Salem, five men with swords, Abbot of Alb, two men with swords, Abbot of Kempten, two men with swords, Abbot of Schaffhausen, two men with swords, Abbot of Petershausen, two men with swords, Abbot of Kinzing, two men with swords, Abbot of Weingarten, four men with swords, Abbot of Elchingen, two men with swords, Abbot of St Blasien, two men with swords, Abbot of Balbcuren, two men with swords, Abbot of Zwiefalten, two men with swords, Abbot of Isni, one swordsman, Abbot of St George, one swordsman, Abbot of St John, one swordsman, Abbot of Pfaeffers, one swordsman, Abbot of Königsbrünn, one swordsman, and the Prior of Schußenried, two men with swords.

The cities: Cantons of Berne, Lucerne, Zurich, Freiburg in Vaud, 250 horse, Constance, Lindau, Buchhorn, Ravensburg, Überlingen, Zelle am Unter See, Dießenhofen, fifty men with swords and 200 cavalry, Schaffenhausen, Waldshut, Lauffenberg, Sächingen, Rhienfelden, Winterthür, Rapperswil, Frauenfeld, twenty-six armed men, Kempten, Isny, Wangen, Leutkirch, Memmingen, Augsburg, Biberach, Pfullendorf, Kaufbeuren, Ulm, Giengen, Nordlingen, Bopfingen, Aalen, Gmünd, Dünkelsbühl, Esslingen, Reutlingen, Rottweil, Weil and Buchau, one hundred men with swords and one hundred other armed men, Halle, twelve men with swords and twelve other armed men, Heilbronn, Wimpfen, Weinsberg, twenty-four armed cavalry, Basel, sixteen men with swords, Strasbourg, Muhlhausen, Colmar, Münster in St Gregorienthal, Kaiserberg, Dürkheim, Schlettstadt, Oberehnheim, Roshein, Hagenau, Weißenburg, thirty men with swords, Freiburg, Neuenberg, Breisach, Kenzingen, Endingen, ten men with swords, Verden, ten men with swords, Kaufmansarburg, three men with swords, Trier, four men with swords, Metz, twenty men with swords, Toul, ten men with swords, Speyer, Worms and Mainz, twenty-four men with swords, Cologne, Aix la Chapelle, thirty men with swords, Dortmund, six men with swords, Frankfurt, fifteen men with swords, Friedberg, two men with swords, Gelnhausen, three men with swords, Wetzlar, two men with swords, Nürnberg, thirty men with swords and thirty other armed men, Rothenburg, twelve men with swords and twelve other armed men, Windsheim, five men with swords, and six other armed men, Weißenburg in Franconia, five men with swords and five other armed men, Schweinfurt, five men with swords and five other armed men, Regensburg, fifteen men with swords and fifteen other armed men, Lübeck, thirty armed men and thirty other armed men, Hamburg, fifteen men with swords and fifteen other armed men, Mühlhausen in Saxony, three men with swords and six other armed men, Nordhausen, fifteen men with swords and ten other armed men, Aschesleben, ten men with swords and six other armed men, Halberstadt, ten men with swords and ten other armed men, Quedlinburg, ten men with swords and ten other armed men. Total: 754 men with swords and 777 cavalry from the cities.

DR 8: 157–65.

94   Žižka writes to supporters in Valečov

[By 1423 Žižka had shifted his base of operations from Tábor to eastern Bohemia. The tranquillity of relations between the two centres is of historical importance. The reference to an assembly at Německý Brod is taken up in more detail in doc.95. This letter was written from Vilémov on 26 March 1423.]

May the grace of the Holy Spirit be with you as well as with us, illuminating our hearts and our minds in order to fulfil the will of the all-powerful Son.

Dear brethren in the name of God our Lord. I wish for you to know that presently I am at Vilémov. I sincerely wish that one of you would join me here so that we might talk about those things which must be accomplished for the honour and glory of our almighty God and Lord. You should also know that I am still in full agreement with the Táborites and they have without coercion made it clear that they intend to follow my orders just as they have always done. I have ordered them to assemble their troops for the battle and they have undertaken preparations. Also I am sending letters to the towns in order that all faithful leaders might appear either on Wednesday or at the very latest Thursday of Easter [week] in Německý Brod. There we must do penance at the place where we sinned. We must stay there according to the God's will, united together as one, in accordance with his holy law. In the agreement of both rich and poor we must prepare ourselves in the truth of the Lord, our almighty father in order to do battle against all faithless deceivers both here at home as well as foreign. I also bring news that the Prince [Zygmunt Korybut] has departed from the country. Do not enter into any treaty agreement with the baron Čeněk [of Vartenberk] unless it involves your neighbours as well. If God so wills, when we get together we can talk about this matter. Given at Vilémov, on Friday following the annunciation of the Blessed Virgin Mary [25 March]. Jan Žižka of the Chalice to the most worthy and steadfast brethren in God's hope, Bartoš and Bernard of Valečov, members of little Tábor.

Bartoš, pp. 15–16.

95   Žižka calls for acts of penance

[The lapse of discipline among the Hussite warriors at Německý Brod in January 1422 was a rare occurrence in armies commanded by Žižka. The old warrior regarded the lapse seriously and the troops were ordered to repair to Německý Brod and make amends before God. Žižka's orders were dispatched from Vilémov on 1 April 1423.]

Jan Žižka of the Chalice, with the help of God a humble servant who hopes in God. May the grace of the Holy Spirit remain with you as well as with us, illuminating our hearts and our minds, together with all the faithful who have committed their lives to the truth of our Lord, the almighty God. To everyone, without exception, in the towns of Skalice and Náchod and to everyone else in the country of Bohemia who are faithful to the truth of the Lord, our almighty God. Humble greetings and best wishes.

Dear brethren, I draw to your attention the goodness of our Lord, the almighty God, who has aided us considerably and has given us liberation from strong enemies, for example at Německý Brod where God overpowered those enemies and indeed, God fought on our side. However, we did not acknowledge this assistance with proper thanksgiving and neither did we on that occasion properly praise God for that beneficial favour. Rather, we engaged in pillage and greed and undisciplined arrogance as well as betrayal. In so doing we angered our God considerably. Ever since that time we have accomplished very little of note. Hence, our Lord God justly punishes us. With regard for the death of our Lord and for the freedom of all his holy truths, I suggest that all of the leaders congregate in order that the programme of the faithful might succeed in the holy church and that the wicked and faithless heretics might be exterminated. Those who gather together with the help of God should come to Německý Brod on Easter Wednesday. At the precise place where we committed sin we shall undertake repentance and penance. Following this, we shall offer up thanksgiving to the Lord God for the great and wonderful gift which was given to us by our most gracious father despite the fact that we were surely not worthy. To God we give praise forever. Amen.

Likewise, while we are there, we shall discuss and make resolution with all of the faithful ones, taking advice from rich and poor alike, how we might remain unified as one against those faithless deceivers, both foreign and domestic. This we shall do as directed by the Lord our God and in harmony with the holy Law of God. We shall fight with the aid of the holy Trinity, our one Lord, who sets free all those who put their trust in him. Given at Vilémov on Maundy Thursday in the year 1423 after the birth of the Lord.

Bartoš, pp. 16-17.

96   Battle of Hořice

[This report on the military engagement at Hořice (20 April 1423) provides another important glimpse at Hussite war tactics (see map 3). The subsequent battle at Strachův Dvůr (August) reveals internecine conflict among the Hussites and their supporters which can be attributed in part to the exacerbating element of the crusade.]

In the year of the Lord, 1423, on Tuesday following [the day of] St George when Žižka was marching through the region of Hradec Králové subjecting the people there to his authority, the barons prepared to attack him. Learning of this he marched on towards Hořice since he had no more than two columns of wagons. He took up position along with his men near the Church of St Gothard in order that he might mount his cannon on the small hill so that the cavalry attacking would have to dismount and they would have nothing to tie their horse to. When they approached they dismounted and moved in to attack. However they were under great burden from their heavy armour than were the [Žižka's] foot soldiers who were accustomed to this. As they neared the top of the hill and made an effort to attack the wagons, he [Žižka] fired upon them with his cannon and his fresh troops and before they had any chance to capture the wagons he repulsed them as he pleased. As they retreated he sent fresh soldiers in pursuit. Here the Lord God helped him so that Lord Čeněk [of Vartenberk] and Lord Arnošt [of Pardubice], together with the other barons were defeated and also lost their wagons and weapons. Lord Čeněk fled from the field with only a few of his men. Then they [Žižka and his troops] proceeded on to Kozojedy [Castle] and conquered it and they burned sixty people.

In the same year, Lord Viktorin of Pardubice and Diviš [Bořek of Miletínek] went to Moravia and conquered several forts and castles [Přerov, Kvasice, and Kroměříž]. They took up positions near Kroměříž, beyond Olomouc where Germans had gathered together against them. The battle was fought and the Czechs took the victory.

In the same year, on the Tuesday before St Peter's [Day], large hailstones fell while [Bohuslav of] Švamberk and his men went from the Castle of the Virgin, near Litoměřice, around Prague because Brother Žižka was waiting there at that time.[11] Lord Diviš ruled Hradec Králové and placed his brother Lord Jetřich over the town [while he went off to Moravia]. The citizens informed Brother Žižka and he marched from Litoměřice to Hradec Králové. The citizens gave him entrance to the city, he expelled Lord Jetřich from Hradec Králové and destroyed the castle. Then Lord Diviš returned from Moravia and taking some Praguers with him sought revenge against the people of Hradec Králové because they had driven his brother away. Together with the Praguers he marched to Hradec Králové. Brother Žižka marched out to meet him along with the citizens and a battle took place near

---

11   Panna Castle, also known as 'New Castle', was owned by Sigismund of Vartenberk and was one of the strongest castles in the region. It seems to have been recently named for the Virgin in opposition to the Castle of the Chalice (Žižka's nearby fortress).

Strachův Dvůr and there went ark against ark.[12] And the Praguers fled having been beaten on the field by Žižka. Many people were killed and about 200 were taken prisoner. Diviš escaped with his men to the hill.[13] The priest who had carried the ark on the side of the Praguers was killed by Žižka with his battle club. All of this happened on the Wednesday before St Laurence [4 August].

From here Žižka went to Čáslav and here he was surrounded but not defeated. Matěj Lupák, a Táborite captain set out with reinforcements to assist Žižka at Čáslav. On the Sunday after the Assumption of Our Lady, Hašek's troops set off from Kolín against them [Lupák's men] and attacked them near Týnec near the ferry crossing and they defeated them, killing some and taking others captive. [Jan] Černín [of Mlazovice] killed Matěj of Lupák. Then Brother Žižka marched off toward Moravia near Jihlava. The people of Jihlava came out after him into the field. But Brother Žižka .. [the manuscripts are corrupt here] and they [the people of Jihlava] fled and were pursued right up to the moat [city walls].

In the same year on the Friday after St Bartholomew, Lord Jan Městecký [of Opočno] and Lord Půta of Častolovice invaded the suburbs of Hradec Králové and burned the street of the Knights of the Cross and then entered the Church of St Ann killing the priest Jan and trampling the sacrament of the body of the Lord.

SRB 3: 56–7.

97   The military rule of Jan Žižka and the Hussite armies

[This important document, both in terms of European military history as well as the Hussite crusades, was drafted and signed in the summer of 1423 at the Castle of the Chalice, Žižka's own fort, northeast of Litoměřice.]

By the grace and bounty of the Lord almighty God, our Father, we have received and we do affirm the illuminating, steadfast, revealed, proven and everlasting truth of the Law of God. First, that the Word of God is to be free, preached in all places, without exemption and that it be received in one's heart with love in order that it may be fulfilled and observed, so that others might be brought to it and taught. Second, that we all partake of the body and blood of our Lord Jesus Christ, with piety, reverence and devotion, both young and old as well as children immediately

---

[12] Hussite priests of all parties – Praguers, Táborites and Orebites (later Orphans) – carried a consecrated host in a monstrance during all of the battles in full view of the warriors. As time went on it became common to refer to the monstrance as an 'ark'. This motif is featured in Hussite iconography.

[13] Kunětická Hora, a hill close by, where Diviš had a castle.

following their baptism and throughout their childhood. Everyone is to be involved without exception. This we urge at least on every Sunday each week. Third, that we direct the clergy in the way of the lives of God's son, the Lord Jesus Christ and the apostles. That they cease and abolish their wealth and simony with the help of God. Fourth, that we suppress, put an end to, and exterminate all sins, both mortal and venial, in ourselves in the first instance, after this in kings, princes, barons, townspeople, artisans, peasants and all other people, both men and women, no one being exempted, whether they are young or old and this consistently with the aid of our Lord, the almighty God. Whoever does not wish to observe and faithfully obey the articles written above, or who does not desire to protect and defend them shall not be tolerated among us, without any consideration of who they are. Neither shall they be allowed to fight with this army with God's help either in the castles, or fortresses, in cities or towns, walled or open, in villages or small communities, in any place without exception. Everyone shall be advised, warned, prodded and encouraged toward this righteousness with the aid of God our Lord.

Being inspired by a good attitude and aware that worldly things are set to fall and be eliminated, and knowing the truth of the Lord Jesus Christ, our almighty God, will last forever be it known that we, Brother Jan Žižka of the Chalice, Jan Roháč of Dubá, Aleš of Risenburg and Vřešťov, Jan of Potštain and Žampach, Boček of Kunštat and Jevišovice, Bartoš and Bernard, brothers from Valečov, Bartoš, Jan and Martinék, brothers from Vysoká, and the mayors, councilmen and the entire communities of Hradec Králové on the Labe [River] and Čáslav with Beneš of Mokrovousy, Jaroslav of the Chalice, Václav Horyna of Honbice, Křišťan of Žernoseky, František of Litožnice, Jindřich of Řečice, Jan of Studená, the mayor, councilmen and the community of Jaroměř, together with Zdislav the squire, Vavřinec of Paňov the Pole, Blažek of Kralupy, Jakob of Březová, Petr Kralovec of Příbram, Jan of Domažlice, Jan of Tehov, Martinék of Borovnice, Gallus the Orebite and the mayor, councilmen and the entire community of Dvůr. And we, Chústní of Košov, Ondřej of Studená, Sárka of Slavné, Kříž the captain, Beneš the captain, Mikát Brada Odraný, Aleš of Hostačov, Polévka of Hoštka, Mikuláš the Orebite, Veta of Chlumčany, Litobor of Trubeč, Linhart of Sleza, Beneš of Horošovice, Jan Baštín, Mařík Velek, Šeňk, Jíra, Roh, Mikuláš Brada, together with the captains, barons, knights, squires, mayors, councilmen, and townspeople without exception. All of us request, demand and insist that all of you be in proper obedience. Through disobedience, disorder and excess we have sustained great loss both in terms of the life of our brothers and also in goods. We have suffered humiliation from those who are the enemies of God and of us.

From now on, with the aid of God and with the help of the faithful, we intend to take note of such things in the following manner.

First, when we intend to depart from a town or relocate from the place where we have camped in the fields, no one shall be permitted to ride on ahead of the rest to the town in order to obtain lodgings. No one shall be allowed to stay camped in the field without the permission or order of his superior captain or of the several commanders appointed to this. If anyone should make such a camp or go on elsewhere without permission from these superiors we desire and we require that such individual shall be punished through the loss of goods and life regardless of who he might be, to which rank he might belong, without any exception.

Second, when it is time to move on from the area where the camp has been in the field with the permission or order of the proper elders, they shall march until a proper place has been found and they shall await the entire army to move out.

Third, no person shall start a fire or light anything on fire during the march or while they are in the camp, unless they have been specifically told to do so. No one else may undertake this without great penalty.

Fourth, when they move out from any place before engaging in some aspect of war, they shall pray to the Lord God on their knees before the body of the Lord and the face of God. Whenever they leave the camp or a town, they should pray that God, the almighty Lord might give help in order that war might be waged to the praise of his holy name for the glory of this aid and for the salvation and betterment of all the faithful.

Fifth, following this, all people shall fall in proper formation under their banner. A password shall then be given. After this and without delay, they shall begin to march behind the leading troop under its banner designated for that day. No one shall interfere with them, create an obstruction or go a different way. Once they have been assigned to a particular battalion or placed in formation beneath a banner, battalions shall not mingle with each other. They shall march taking due care to protect the van, the rear as well as the flanks in such a way as ordered by their superiors.

Sixth, if God does not protect us so that we suffer harm through the carelessness or negligence of the military captains whether in the field, at the guard points or on the watch towers entrusted to them either by the commanders or the community, be it resolved that the commanders and the entire community will find out who is responsible and they shall be punished with the loss of possessions and lives. It does not matter if they are prince, baron, or any other person, there is no exception.

Seventh, whenever the Lord God permits us to conquer and defeat our enemies, to capture towns, castles or fortifications, and thus to obtain loot whether by movement in the field or through an operation from the camp, all of those items which are captured shall be brought together to an appointed place, chosen by the superiors, whether it is considerable or very little. Elders shall be chosen from every community, barons, knights, townspeople, peasants, and they shall be charged with fairly dividing the goods among rich and poor in a just and proper fashion. No one must take anything for personal use or keep anything. If someone does take something for himself or keeps it, and is found guilty of this on the basis of good witness, then that individual, whoever he might be, shall be decapitated, without exception, and his possessions taken away on the grounds that he has robbed God and the community. This according to what happened to Achan for the hat and the robe of the king's daughters [Joshua 7:16–26]. If he is some other type of person, say a prince, baron, knight, squire, townsman, artisan or peasant he shall suffer death perhaps by another means. Without making any excuse or having regard to who it is, that person, with the help of God shall have vengeance taken out upon him.

Eight, no quarrels, fighting or rioting shall be tolerated in our army or among our people. Ninth, if anyone should hit, wound or otherwise injure someone, or kill that person, there shall be retribution brought upon that person in accordance with the law of God and as the Lord our God allows. No one is exempt and there shall be no consideration for who it is.

Tenth, likewise it shall be made clear that if anyone were to sneak off, or in any way depart from the army while we are marching in the field, or in camp, not having the permission of the superiors mentioned above, or not having the authentic password, regardless of whether they are baron, knight, squire, townsman, artisan, or peasant or any other person, such a one shall be arrested, punished by decapitation and his goods taken from him on the grounds that he is an unfaithful robber who has crept away from the Lord's battle and away from the faithful brethren of the army wherever the army might be marching or in camp.

Eleventh, we shall not tolerate among our ranks any faithless person, disobedient one, liar, thief, gambler, robber, plunderer, drunkard, blasphemer, lecher, adulterer, prostitute, fornicator, or other definite sinners, either men or women. All such persons shall be banished and sent off or otherwise punished with the aid of the Holy Trinity according to the law of God.

Twelfth, in like manner Brother Žižka together with all the other barons, captains, knights, squires, townspeople, artisans, and peasants referred to above, along with all their communities, shall punish all crimes with the help of God and the community, in the following ways: flogging, banishment, beating, beheading, hanging, drowning, burning and by any other means which fits the offence according to the Law of God. There are no exceptions regardless of rank or sex.

If we obey, keep in mind and fulfil these worthy articles written above, the Lord God shall be with us in grace and aid. It is fitting that we behave in God's fight in this way. Live as good Christians in love for God's order and in the fear of God and to put faith for all needs and requirements and hope in God our Lord, and have no doubt but expect an eternal reward from God.

Therefore we urge all dearly beloved communities from all places, all princes, barons, knights, squires, townspeople, artisans, peasants, workers, people from all ranks, but especially faithful Czechs, to join with us in this salutary struggle and provide us with advice and assistance. For our part we will observe and fulfil our duty to you on behalf of our beloved Lord God in view of his sacred death in order to free the truth of the law of God. This we do for the saints and their exaltation to aid the faithful everywhere in the blessed church especially in the Czech and Slav country, but also throughout Christendom in order that the faithful might be lifted up and the stubborn heretics, hypocrites and workers of iniquity might be brought to disgrace. May the Lord our God permit us to gain the victory over God's enemies, with God's help, and fight for us against our enemies, with God's power. May the Lord not hold back his grace from us and from you. Amen.

May the Lord our God be with us and with you wherever you are and in whatever circumstances it pleases the blessed Trinity. For a better witness, affirmation and in security of these things, and to demonstrate our exceeding determination with the clerics in standing above the debased thinking of the world, all of those named above herewith in good and deliberate conscience give witness to this pronouncement and writing. We promise to keep, defend and preserve it with the help of the eternal and ever blessed Holy Trinity. Amen. May the Lord our God grant these things.[14]

Bartoš, pp. 18–24.

98   Bohemia under economic blockade

[The continued build-up of resistance within Bohemia to the crusade initiative, along with three successive Crusader defeats, caused the official church to consider further action against the recalcitrant heretics in an effort to secure their submission. The abortive council of Pavia – Siena took the step of imposing an economic blockade upon Bohemia during a solemn session on 8 November 1423. Sigismund supported the initiative and tried to enforce it. See his letters to the city council of Regensburg, Silesian cities and the exchange between the civic authorities in Nürnberg and Regensburg in UB 1, pp. 339–41 and 344.]

---

[14] This document invites comparison with two other contemporary documents as well as historic military doctrine. See doc.120 for the ordinance ratified by the German Reichstag. For the military statutes and ordinance of Henry V, see N.H. Nicolas, *History of the Battle of Agincourt* (London, 1870), pp. 31–40 and Flavius Vegetius Renatus, *Epitoma rei militaris*, ed., Leo F. Stelten (New York: Peter Lang, 1990).

The holy general synod of Siena, legitimately gathered together in the Holy Spirit representing the universal church under the presidency of Peter, archbishop of Crete, James, bishop of Spoleto, Peter, abbot of Rosacio in the diocese of Aquileia and Leonard, master and general of the Order of Preachers, the specifically delegated envoys of the most holy father in the Lord Christ, lord Martin V the only true and supreme pontiff. With the intention of reforming the same [now the church] commencing with the basis of the faith against which no one can gainsay, [the council] approves and confirms the condemnation of the Wyclifite and Hussite heresies together with their adherents and followers as declared by the holy Council of Constance. [This council also approves] of their extirpation which has been provided for by the aforementioned most holy pope Martin according to his ability together with an admonition and appeal to the princes, lords and other people and the conferring of a plenary indulgence to those hunting [the heretics] and the appointment of a legate *de latere* for the complete abolition [of the heresy] regarding this as proper and correct.[15] In order to continue the process against them the synod decrees that all those prosecuting and providing for the extirpation of the aforementioned sect shall enjoy all of the rights, privileges and licences with respect to the remission of sins, granted to those who proceed against the heretics. Further, [the synod declares] that those infected by the contamination of the aforesaid heresies and all those who assist them with advice, help or favour in defending or receiving them, in delivering any food, spices, clothing, salt, lead, gunpowder, weapons, military equipment, or any other items, or entering into negotiations or business with them, either publicly or privately, as well as those who allow such things to be delivered or brought to the previously mentioned heretics, completely or in part, through the domains, lands, districts or localities under their jurisdiction, or [permit] their dependents to negotiate with them, shall come under the penalties and condemnations announced against the heretics and shall be delivered to the judges concerned with the eradication of heretical perversity. There shall be no regard given in terms of privilege, exemption, immunity or safe-conduct granted or proposed to be granted by any ecclesiastical or secular individual even if they were to surpass the papal, imperial, royal, ducal or any other ecclesiastical or secular dignity.

Additionally, the synod exhorts, challenges and admonishes all princes and lords of the Christian faith, ecclesiastical as well as secular, by the bowels of divine mercy, that if they wish to avoid the wrath of God and punishments of the law, to stand up with all eagerness for the extermination of such error condemned

---

[15]   The reference is to the bull 'Inter Cunctus' promulgated by Martin V on 22 February 1418. See doc.18.

by the church. Notwithstanding, it has been constituted that this holy synod will before its dissolution provide for an effective fulfilment of this decree.[16]

Walter Brandmüller, *Das Konzil von Pavia–Siena 1423–1424* (Münster: Verlag Aschendorff, 1974), vol. 2: 20–2.

99   Assassination plot against Jan Žižka

[The stature and significance of the supreme captain of the Hussite armies, Jan Žižka symbolized the strength of the Hussite resistance in the face of crusade and repression. His almost legendary career provided much of the military motivation for the anti-crusade efforts. The discovery of an assassination plot at the height of his career is not surprising. His death might well have changed the course of Czech history had the plot been successfully carried out. The letter is dated 24 November 1423.]

May the grace and aid of the almighty Lord be with you, all your loyal brethren, and with us other sinners as well. Brother Žižka and other dearly beloved brethren. Do know that we have taken a prisoner of rather high rank from the party of Opočno, who has asserted that there is within your troops a man who intends to murder you. He will receive as a reward 1,800 groschen. One third of this sum has already been paid to him. The bearer of this letter, Pavel, with the curly dark hair, knows who the assassin is. This is why we have dispatched him to you. He shall reveal in detail how this plot was hatched, who the conspirators are, and will reveal to you who was going to carry it out. We implore you to extend to Pavel your trust in all matters of which he will reveal to you on our behalf. May the almighty Lord preserve you for his praise and the well being of the communities of the faithful.

Given at Hradec Králové, on the Labe [River], at three o'clock in the morning, on the eve of St Catherine, by the hand of your priest Ambrož. Jan Hvězda, the mayor, town councillors and your priest Ambrož.

AČ 3: 302–3.

---

[16] The council went on to admonish all inquisitors and bishops to deal swiftly and decisively with the heresy. They were ordered to curse the heretics with bell, book and candle every Sunday in all principal churches. See Cardinal Branda's specific application of the bull in doc. 101.

100　Martin V, letter to the Archbishop of Besançon

[The following document reveals the persistent eagerness of the papacy for the suppression of the Hussites and underscores the preparations by Sigismund and the Reichstag for yet another crusade effort. The alleged preparations were in reality plans on paper only. Numerous heads of government pledged support but only one actually implemented those promises. The ruler of the kingdoms of Scandinavia, King Erik, brought troops to Germany but returned to Copenhagen immediately when he learned that no one else was coming. King Erik's aborted expedition is reported in a letter from Martin V to Witold, 14 February 1424 (UB 1: 321–3). This letter is dated 1 December 1423.]

We have received from the celebrated assembly of princes held in the city of Nürnberg in the presence of our most dearly beloved Sigismund, illustrious king of the Romans, Hungary and Bohemia, the prince-electors of the empire, together with other prelates, priors, and envoys and delegates of many cities and with them our dear son Cardinal Branda, priest of the title of St Clement, our apostolic legate who has been specially designated by us to the negotiation concerning the faith. Having obtained their advice concerning this matter of the faith, it was concluded and resolutely ordered that a tax be exacted from all of the prelates and ecclesiastical officials all over Germany. This is so that it can be determined the number of warriors according to the ability of each so that a constant war may be waged against the heretics which must persist until that plague has been exterminated. Therefore we have asserted that some taxes collected there were perhaps unfair given the brevity of time and the occupation of the agents and perhaps they were not utilized as diligently as they might have been. We wish neither to be lacking in our bounden duty to assist in these negotiations nor to be unfair but rather to provide inasmuch as possible the progress of the matter of the faith.

We request by brotherly mandate, in apostolic writing, that you together with the priests and other honourable God-fearing men, aware of the possibilities of your church and other ecclesiastical benefices, tax all nonexempt ecclesiastical persons in your city and diocese under your jurisdiction to provide either military personnel or other support and that you make every effort to complete this as quickly as you can with the utmost care so that the aforementioned cardinal, occupied with other negotiations concerning this matter, will not be obliged to compensate for your neglect.

We have written to him, of course, and submitted an estimate of the tax to be expected and also to supervise you and the other prelates, those determined to be nonexempt according to our mandates and to watch over the taxes and if there are any improprieties to correct them with the help of God. We cease not to admonish by our letters the faithful ecclesiastical and secular people to send envoys for the holy expedition that so malignant a heresy may be brought to conversion or placed under excommunication. Given in Rome on the feast of St Mary Major on the kalends of December [1 December] in the sixth year of our pontificate [1423].

DR 8: 181–2.

101 Cardinal Branda orders enforcement of heresy law

[The social implications of Hussite heresy figures in the motivation of the crusade against them. On New Years' day 1424, the papal legate, Branda da Castiglione, Cardinal of Piacenza (1341–1433) wrote to the Polish king Władysław Jagiełło: 'The purpose of my mission is for the glory of God, the cause of the faith and the church as well as the salvation of human society. A significant proportion of the heretics hold that all things should be held in common and that no tribute, tax or obedience should be given to a superior. This is an idea which would destroy civilization and abolish all government. They intend to destroy all human and divine right through force and it will happen that not even kings or princes in their own kingdoms and dominions, or even people in their own houses will be safe from their insolence. This terrible heresy not only attacks the faith and the church but it also, under inspiration of the devil, makes war upon humanity in general, attacking and destroying those rights as well' (UB 1, pp. 309–14). Branda's concerns continued to be raised throughout the crusade period. Six months later, in the spring of 1424, Cardinal Branda ordered the bishop of Regensburg to announce in his diocese the punishments which would be meted out to any person entering into any relationship with the heretical Czechs. The legate – an expert in canon law – made his declaration on the basis of the decree issued by the Council of Siena (see doc.98) the previous autumn and appealed to existing legislation concerning heresy. The letter is dated 16 May 1424.]

Branda, by the grace and mercy of God, cardinal priest of the holy Roman Church, of the title of St Clement, popularly called Piacenza, the legate of the apostolic see. To the venerable father in Christ and lord by the grace of God and apostolic see, the bishop of Regensburg. Eternal salvation in Christ.

Previously the holy Council of Siena congregated legitimately in the Holy Spirit representing the universal church under the presidency of the venerable lords and fathers in Christ, lords Peter, abbot of Rosacio in the diocese of Aquileia, Leonard, general master of the Order of Preachers and the specially delegated envoys of the most holy father in Christ and our lord, by divine wisdom, Pope Martin V. Beginning with *Fidei fundamento* [the council] approved and confirmed the condemnation of the heresies of the Wyclifites and Hussites, together with their followers, believers and adherents, as mandated by the holy synod of Constance considering it right and valid.[17] Continuing the process themselves and in order to provide for the extirpation of the aforementioned sect, [the synod] decreed that all those arising against the heretics should enjoy all the privileges and licences provided by law and by men. Then the council decreed that those infected with the contamination of the aforementioned heresies and each and every person assisting them with advice, help, or favour, defending them or receiving them, or delivering any food, spices, cloth, lead, salt, gunpowder, weapons of war, military tools or any other thing to them, or making some other negotiation or business, whether publicly or secretly with them; together with those who allow such things to be delivered or brought to the heretics either completely or partially through domains, lands, districts or localities under their dominion, or permit their dependents to negotiate with them, shall come under the penalty and condemnation promulgated against the heretics. [There shall be no consideration given] to privileges, exemptions, immunities, safe-conducts, either granted or forthcoming by any ecclesiastical or secular person, even if they should go beyond pontifical, imperial, royal, ducal, or any other ecclesiastical or secular dignity. In addition, the synod calls for and admonishes all princes and lords of the Christian religion, both ecclesiastical as well as secular, by the bowels of God's mercy, to stand up with all vigour for the extirpation of such error as condemned by the church if they wish to avoid divine wrath and the punishments of the law. Nevertheless, it has been constituted that this holy council will provide prior to its dissolution a more effective fulfilment of this decree.

We, as obligated by duty of our office and desiring to guarantee the salvation of souls in that part as much as we can with God, have ensured every help, counsel and business be eliminated entirely from the perverse heretics. The aforementioned decree of the holy council [should] be announced to you so that relayed by you to your parishioners and subjects, the [decree] might discourage them for fear of the punishments from providing any help, counsel or favour to the heretics and from having any business with them whatsoever, especially if you stress that the penalties of the law are aimed at the heretics as well as their supporters, so that they cannot pretend to be ignorant of this. We bid you by the tenor of this letter, in virtue of holy obedience and under the penalty of excommunication, to announce, or cause to be announced, the aforementioned decree publicly or in the cathedral church and in other collegiate and parish churches of your city and diocese, especially in the neighbouring and contiguous

---

[17] *'Fidei catholicae fundamento'* was a lengthy decretal promulgated by the Council of Vienne (1311–12) and utilized and applied to the Hussite problem by the Council of Siena. Text in Decrees, 1, pp. 360–401.

areas to Bohemia and Moravia. [This should take place] on Sundays and feast days when the people have gathered to hear divine service and [you should] declare specifically the punishments described below, as well as others of more significance you might find in law or in your provincial or diocesan constitutions. You should notify them that such persons also come under the Imperial ban recently promulgated by the most serene prince, Lord Sigismund, favoured by divine graciousness, king of the Romans, always victorious, and king of Hungary and Bohemia, etc.

These are the penalties of the common law against heretics and their supporters. The receivers of heretics, defenders and promoters of such are *ipso facto* excommunicated. They are neither permitted to be buried in a cemetery nor it is allowed that prayers be made for them. Likewise, those condemned for heresy, their receivers, defenders, and promoters are to be regarded as infamous, neither can they make testimony, nor inherit, nor shall they be heard in a judicial court. They are to be deprived of all dignity, honour and jurisdiction, whether ecclesiastical or secular. Similarly, their good are to be confiscated by law, even though they have Catholic sons, because of *lèse majesté*. Further, all subjected vassals and any others who are bound by an obligatory contract of faith to the aforementioned heretics are hereby released on the authority of the law. Likewise, the dowries of women which are to be used to seal the marriage are to be confiscated because of the heresy of the men. In like manner, when the war against them as public enemies is declared, all heretics and those who defend and promote them in any way shall become the slaves of those who capture them as declared by the Holy Roman Church and the Holy Roman Empire.

For this testimony we have ordered this letter to be made and to be guaranteed by the affixing of our seal. Given in Visegrád, on Wednesday, the sixteenth day of May in the year of the Lord 1424, in the seventh year of the pontificate of the afore named most holy lord, by divine wisdom, Pope Martin V.

UB 1: 336-8.

102   An amazing escape from the enemy at Kostelec

[Leaving the staunch Hussite town of Žatec, Žižka marched east to Louny. Both towns were firmly loyal to the old warrior. Prague leaders, those loyal to Sigismund and the crusade cause, including the Karlštejn garrison and the forces of the Plzeň Landfríd, decided to oppose Žižka. Meanwhile Žižka continued east to the Labe River near Roudnice. Turning in a southerly direction, he crossed the Vltava River near the confluence with the Labe at the town of Mělník. Continuing in a southeasterly direction, the Hussite armies neared the town of Kostelec on the

Labe River, a spot some fifteen miles from Prague when he was, without advance warning, intercepted by a superior force. Caught within a fairly small bend of the river there was only one escape route which lay to the south but that route was utterly blocked by the enemy. As he had on so many occasions, Žižka formed his wagons in a circular fortress formation. The siege lasted a week until 4 June. News of Žižka's predicament was reported to Sigismund at the royal court in Buda where several Czech barons loyal to the king, including Oldřich Rožmberk, were present. Confidence ran high that this time the old warrior was outwitted. Sigismund, more than once the victim of Žižka's schemes and genius, seems to have been the only skeptic. In what defies any thorough explanation, when the crusaders awoke on the morning of 5 June they discovered the Hussite wagon fortress gone and the camp of the heretics empty. Somehow, Žižka managed to transport his armies and their equipment across the Labe River in the middle of the night. The amazement among the opposing army and at the royal court in Buda cannot have been inconsiderable. The event magnified the image of Žižka both among his supporters as well as among his foes, helping to provide him with almost mythical status.]

On the same day a message came of how the Praguers in Bohemia had surrounded Žižka, the captain of the Hussites and heretics and that it would be impossible for him to escape. Then some of the barons, especially the Lord of Rožmberk said to the king, 'my lord king, that fellow Žižka is surrounded and cannot escape.' But the king said, 'he will get away.' The lord of Rožmberk said, 'my lord, he cannot escape.' The king replied, 'he will get away.' Then the lords of Bohemia all said together, 'he cannot escape.' But the king reproached them in this manner for the barons had done nothing in this matter and had made it possible for such an abominable man of gross manners to have governed even though they might well have prevented it. So the Czech barons said, 'Gracious lord, would you bet a young horse that Žižka will not escape?' Then the king of the Romans, Sigismund, said, 'well sure. You want me to gamble so that I will lose.' The king did this to the barons in order to mock them because he knew very well that they had no intention of keeping their word but to the contrary reneged on practically everything. Just then the message came to his ears that Žižka had escaped. And when Žižka escaped from the encirclement he thrashed those of Prague and their supporters and killed more than 1,200 of them who remained there and he did immeasurable damage to those honourable Christians. Then he marched on to Kutná Hora and conquered it and burned down the major part of it. Following this he caused additional injury as well and permitted young and old, men as well as women to be killed and thus he devastated Kutná Hora.[18] May God in heaven be merciful.

Windecke, pp. 197–8.

103   Battle of Malešov

[This battle, which put an end to domestic hostilities against Žižka was fought on 7 June 1424 (see map 3). Its outcome determined the course of Bohemian domestic history for the next decade (Heymann, 414). While it was Czech against Czech, even Hussite against Hussite, the impetus was the ever-present crusader initiative. There are at least seven extant contemporary accounts of the battle.]

In the year of the Lord, 1424, on the day of the baptism of our Lord, Brother Žižka and the men of the castle [Tábor] defeated the barons, Lord Jan [*sic recte* Hynek] of Červenohorský, Lord Arnošt of Černčice [other mss. have the Lord of Opočno, Lord Půta of Červenorhorský and Lord Arnošt of Černčice] and they killed some and captured others in Skalice near Jaroměř.

In the same year Brother Žižka marched on with his people to Hostinné. By attacking the towns he conquered them, killing many and wounding numerous others. Then he marched away from here. Soon after this Brother Žižka captured a nobleman, Černín of Mlazovice and they killed this Černín. Then they went down to Smidary, conquered it and burned it down.

In the same year before the Holy Ghost [Pentecost], Brother Žižka was surrounded by the Praguers and their supporters in Kostelec on the Labe [River]. But Lord Hynek Boček of Poděbrady came to help him and led Žižka with his people out of there. And they went side by side with the Labe River between them until Lord Boček transferred them across the Labe. Following this, there were some negotiations and at this time Lord Boček was taken prisoner and held first at Nymburk, then later at Mělník and then at Smiřický. But Žižka went to Malešov near Kutná Hora. The Praguers wishing to defeat him, followed along allied with some of the barons. But Žižka arrived first before them very quickly in order to find an adequate place for putting up his forces in battle order. He got his wagons up on one hill and there closed himself in [the wagon fortress] and waited for the Praguers who had been pursuing him already thinking to themselves that he was in full retreat. They gathered together their troops but did not wait for those

---

[18]   This is doubtful since Žižka maintained a fairly consistent policy of sparing women and children.

coming in the rear. They came through the valley where Žižka was waiting for them. He had prepared for battle and had set up his wagons in this manner: he put the wagons wheel to wheel and he placed his battalions in order, first the cavalry, then the foot soldiers. Then he ordered that several of the supply wagons be loaded with rocks and these were placed in the midst of the troops so that the Praguers could not see them. He allowed about half of the enemy to cross through the valley and then ordered his cavalry to move out towards them while the foot soldiers rolled the wagons forward. When the enemy troops approached and it seemed that the two armies would meet, he ordered that the wagons be rolled down upon them so that their formations were divided. Then he ordered the cannon to be fired and commanded his troops to charge. The [opposing] troops were unable to use their battle order and could not adequately deploy their forces. So they fled. But they ran into their own men coming in the rear and soon all were running away. And thus Žižka won the victory and he confiscated all of their guns, wagons and other weapons, even though he was blind in both eyes. Many citizens of Prague were killed and a high number of those of the knightly rank. It is generally said that 1,400 people died on that day. These included Petr Turkovec, the knight who had carried the banner of the Praguers, Lord Ondřej of Dubá, Žižka's son-in-law, Lord Čeněk, the son of Lord Vikeř of Myslív, Lord Hlas the knight and many other knights. Immediately thereafter Žižka invaded Kutná Hora and burned out the rest of it.

In that same year, Žižka, with those of Žatec, Louny, Klatovy and many other towns, came to Prague and stopped by Libeň [prepared to take up arms] against Prague. On Wednesday, the day of the Holy Cross [14 September], an arrangement was reached between Prince Zygmunt [Korybut] and the Praguers on one side and Žižka on the other . . . . This peace was confirmed by a security payment of 14,000 three scores of Czech groschen. On the Hospital Field they piled up a large bunch of stones near St Ambrose in the New Town as a sign of the peace symbolizing the fact that if either side violated the peace they should be buried beneath the stones. But Žižka said that the peace would last only as long as it had following the treaty made at Konopiště.[19]

SRB 3: 62–3.

---

[19]   In the spring of 1423, the Hussite parties reached an agreement at Konopiště which bridged their differences. This concord was short-lived.

104   Žižka's speech before the battle for Prague

[This historically dubious speech was apparently delivered on 14 September 1424 as Jan Žižka and his 'warriors of God' stood poised to militarily confront the city of Prague. The content is doubtless the creation of the imagination of Aeneas Sylvius Piccolomini who seems to have maintained a keen though horrified interest in the old soldier. The monologue does accurately underscore the serious internal tension within Bohemia at this time. Open conflict was averted at the last moment.]

'My brothers do not be angry at me and do not accuse the one who has spent his lifetime on behalf of your well being. The laurels of the victories you have achieved under my leadership are still fresh. I have never taken you anywhere you did not return from in triumph. By this you have become well known and rich. But I, on the other hand, have lost the light of my eyes in this cause and already must walk in unending darkness. Despite all these wars undertaken so successfully there has been nothing for me except an empty name. It has been for you that I have fought. It has been for you that I have won. I have neither regrets about this work nor do I regard blindness as a burden too difficult to bear as long as I have been able to labour, principally, for the extension of your cause. I do not fight the people of Prague for my own desire and they want your blood anyway, not mine. It would not do them much good to destroy me since I am already an old man and completely blind. Instead, it is your powerful arms which they are afraid of and your spirit which knows no fear in the face of danger. Certainly either you or they shall perish. While they set an ambush for me, it is your souls they hope will fall into their hands. Our enemies with weapons inside our country are more dangerous to us than those enemies outside the land. Therefore, it is essential to put down domestic rebellion. Unless we defeat Prague, that rebellion will remain at liberty to exterminate our people well before Sigismund even hears the news about our schism. Then with even less people, but having the same attitude, it can be anticipated without any doubt that the attack of the emperor can be repulsed [easier] than if the people of Prague, whom we cannot depend on, were to fight alongside us.

'I give you permission to decide for yourselves in a free council what you wish to do so that you cannot accuse me any longer. If you wish to make peace with the people of Prague I shall not object and there shall be no deception in my stance. On the other hand, if you think it best to go to war then I stand prepared to help you. Regardless of the decision you make, Žižka will assist you in reaching your goal.'

They decided for war and a great number of them rushed to get their weapons. Then they marched in haste toward the city walls in order to challenge their enemies and to contest the gates in an effort to push the defenders back into the city. Žižka took charge of preparing for the conquest of the city.

Aeneas Sylvius, *Historia Bohemica*, chapter 44, pp. 134, 136.

105   Death of Žižka

[Because of the significance of Žižka to the Hussite movement and especially in the history of the first three crusades against the Bohemian heretics, two accounts of his death are given below. Following his death, the Hussites took Přibyslav, Třebíč, (a strongly fortified monastery), Ivančice, Boskovice, Letovice and Mohelnice. They returned home in November.]

In the same year immediately after peace had been made between the prince [Zygmunt Korybut] and the Praguers with Žižka, he started off for Moravia with his brethren. En route he stopped at the castle of Přibyslav intending to conquer it. There Brother Jan Žižka fell ill with a sickness unto death. Making his last will be known he instructed his beloved and faithful brothers and Czechs, Lord Viktorín, Lord Jan Bzdinka [Hvězda] and Kuneš [of Bělovice] that they ought to continue on fighting in love of God and that they should faithfully and without wavering defend God's truths in order to obtain everlasting reward. Then Brother Žižka commended his soul to God and there he died on the Wednesday before St Gall [11 October 1424]. There his followers took up the name Orphans for themselves as though they had lost their father. Then they conquered the castle of Přibyslav and they burned to death those who opposed them in the castle. These were about sixty armed men. They burned the castle down as well and demolished it. After this Priest Prokůpek and Priest Ambrož took him, since he was already dead, to Hradec Králové and there he was buried in the Church of the Holy Ghost near the main altar. Later he was removed to Čáslav and buried there in the Church [of SS Peter and Paul].

SRB 3: 64.

106   Žižka's drum

[Following his death, the story circulated that the old warrior ordered his body flayed and his skin stretched onto a drum. There are different versions of the tale as well as visual representations.]

Now Žižka had appointed a time to assemble for the purpose of attacking Sigismund when, near the castle of Přibyslav, by divine inspiration, if you will, that detestable, cruel, horrible and savage monster was stricken with an infectious disease and died. The one whom no mortal hand could destroy was extinguished by the finger of God. As he lay ill, he was asked where he wished to be buried after his death. He ordered that his body be flayed, the flesh discarded for the birds and animals, and a drum be fashioned from his skin. With this drum in the lead they should go to war. The enemies would turn to flight as soon as they heard its sound.[20]

Aeneas Sylvius, *Historia Bohemica*, chapter 44, p. 138.

107 'The very fine chronicle of Jan Žižka'

[This anonymous short chronicle is a record of the career of Jan Žižka and may have been written as early as 1435. It provides valuable details on the crusade against the Hussite heretics.]

In the year 1410 after the birth of God's son there arose a man named Master Jan Hus. He preached, denouncing the people for their wicked lives. The clerics spoke well of him and said that God's spirit spoke through him. He began to preach about the sins of the priests, from the pope to the lowest cleric, about their concubinage, simony, arrogance and greed saying they ought not to have either secular power or civil estates. He likewise preached that holy communion should be given to the people in both kinds of the body and blood of Christ.[21] Then the clerics raged against him and asserted that the Devil had taken possession of him and that now he was a heretic. All of this came about in the Czech kingdom when Václav, the son of Emperor Charles, was the king and a priest named Zbyněk was the archbishop of Prague.

In the year 1415 a council of the higher clergy requested Master Jan Hus to come under safe conduct to Constance. He went there along with Master Jerome [of Prague] under the protection of the Hungarian king, Sigismund. But when he arrived in Constance with some of the barons of Bohemia, he was arrested and degraded from the priesthood. Some of the higher clergy caused him to be condemned to death. When he was thus sentenced, King Sigismund was sitting in

---

[20] For an earlier version of the story told by Aeneas Sylvius, see doc.209.
[21] Jan Hus did not practice utraquism and it did not originate with his thought. It began while he was in Germany though he did approve of it in a letter addressed to two Czech barons, from his cell in Constance in June 1415.

judgement and it was he who had given safe conduct to Master Hus. Thus he was commanded to be burned at the stake as was Master Jerome about a year thereafter. These things happened when Konrad [of Vechta] was the archbishop of Prague.

When these things transpired, the Bohemians and the Moravians were outraged. Many priests in Prague and in other towns throughout Bohemia and Moravia started to give the body and blood of Christ to the lay people in both kinds. They lifted up the host in a monstrance and it became customary for multitudes to walk behind the host giving praise to God. But the people were rebuked and were called abusive names like Hussites or Wyclifites, and even heretics, when they took communion in both kinds. So the people were divided into two groups. This included clerics as well as the laity. Both groups were of considerable size and were led by priests. They fought with each other and the struggle became so intense that even the king could do nothing about it.

When the king was absent from Prague and in the New Castle [1419], it happened that some priests with the host and a large multitude following went from the Church of St Stephen to the town hall in Prague's New Town.[22] Someone threw a stone from the town hall at the priest. The crowd was outraged and cried out, 'they are throwing stones against the body of Christ and against the priest.' Then they launched an attack on the town hall and broke in. Then they threw the councilmen out of the windows and killed them.

When the king heard about this, he was greatly upset and suffered a massive stroke and then King Václav died. The people in Prague became enraged against some of the priests as well as the monks and the Germans and they expelled them from the town. Others fled on their own accord. Up until this time it was usual for Germans to sit on the council and to be in the town offices. Because of the uproar, it became impossible for the barons to carry the body of King Václav through the city of Prague. Hence, it was that he was taken clandestinely to the castle of St Wenceslas. There he was left unburied for quite a period of time. He had wished to be interred in the monastery at Zbraslav. Later, the barons conducted him, secretly by night, to Zbraslav and the monks buried him there.

After these things [in 1419], the king of Hungary, Sigismund, King Václav's brother, went to Brno and called for the Bohemian and Moravian barons, as well as Praguers and others who followed the law of God [to come there]. When they arrived, he asked them what it was that they adhered to which caused such disturbance. The Bohemian and Moravian barons spoke to the king as in one voice. 'We adhere to the Four Articles. First, that the body and blood of the Lord be given in both kinds to all people everywhere. Second, that all serious sins are

---

[22] The defenestration of civic officials on 30 July 1419 at the behest of priest Jan Želivský. For details, see Kaminsky, 'The Prague Insurrection of 30 July 1419'.

put to an end. Third, that there be liberty for the preaching of the Word of God. Fourth, that clerics are not permitted to have secular power or to have an accumulation of material goods.' Sigismund replied that since the body and blood of Christ had been given in this manner in the beginning it should be so again.[23] Then he asked those of Prague if he were to come to Bohemia would they permit him to enter the city of Prague. The Praguers answered the king and said that if he did not wish to come through the gates, they would make a passage through the walls in order to shame themselves so that he might enter as their king. So the king told them to remove all of the chains which blocked the streets and to remove them from the Old Town to the castle of Wenceslas and those from the New Town to Vyšehrad. The people of Prague did this. But then in that same year [March 1420] the pope made a proclamation against the Czechs saying they were heretics on the grounds that they partook of the body and blood of Christ. Indulgences were given to anyone who murdered a Czech or killed him one way or the other and promised forgiveness for all sins to that individual. So they began to kill the people and to put them to death in many different ways.

There was one Czech, by the grace of God, who arose from among the rank of the knights. He was a very brave man, who had but one eye, whose name was Žižka. He took stoically to the field to do battle against those who did not take the body and blood of Christ in both kinds. He regarded such people as his enemies and he likewise considered them to be heretics. The two groups fought each other and whichever group had more power they killed and unmercifully burned or murdered the others in many ways. Only those whom God wished to save survived. Above all, the Germans wanted to kill the Czechs and the Czechs desired to kill the Germans. These wars went on without mercy for fourteen years.

Žižka and the other Bohemians fought for the law of God both in Bohemia as well as in other lands. They conquered Sezimovo Ústí and then Hradiště and they settled in the castle on the hill. There they built a town which was called Tábor. Then Žižka marched all over the land with his warriors and they took towns and castles by conquest. He waged many battles against powerful enemies but he was never defeated. Then Sigismund, the King of Hungary marched from Hungary into the lands of the Czech Crown. He came to Wrocław and there ordered that a citizen of Prague [Jan Krása] be dragged by horse and said this ought to be done to other Czech heretics. When this came to the attention of the citizens of Prague they set up their barricades again but where there had previously been one chain in the streets they put up two and so they secured themselves against him. Now the king established garrisons of many knights in the castle of St Wenceslas as well as in the Vyšehrad castle in opposition to the people of Prague. When Žižka

---

[23] A misrepresentation since Sigismund never expressed that view.

heard of this, he went straight to the Vítkov Hill and fortified it against the king. The people gave this fortress the name Žižkov.

At that time the Hungarian king arrived with his army and camped in Zbraslav while Žižka and the Prague army laid siege to the castle of St Wenceslas. The knights defended themselves bravely but they were so hungry they were forced to eat boiled rye. When the king learned that they would have to surrender the castle on account of hunger he arrived with a large army with the intention of saving them or supplying food. He killed some of Žižka's men, those who ventured outside the wagon-fortress and thus he was able to fend off the Prague army from the castle.

The Duke of Austria, the margrave of Meißen and numerous other princes with multitudes of knights came to assist the king. So the king came and set his battalions against Prague. There he was crowned king in the castle of St Wenceslas and at the same time many Germans were made knights.[24] Following this [14 July 1420], they marched with all strength against Žižka and his fortress to take it by force. When Žižka was in much difficulty, a priest came out of the city with the body of Christ. The Germans were panic-stricken and tried to run away with their horse but they fell down the hill and broke their necks. After this, whenever the Germans saw a Czech and got hold of one, even if he or she was in agreement with them, they burned them without so much as asking the person about it. This went on until the Bohemians within the ranks of the king grew disgusted with it. And many other Czechs were encamped near Hradec Králové at this time. The lord of Rožmberk was encamped with other Germans near Tábor and he was defeated there to his great shame and loss.

When the king dismissed the foreign armies [end of July] and sent them away from the land, Žižka went on the offensive and marched throughout the land. He burned down monasteries and exiled the monks. He commanded that all priests who insisted on giving communion under only one kind be burned.

Then the Praguers with other barons laid siege to the castle of Vyšehrad when there were a considerable number of knights therein. The defenders were brave but they had no food to eat so they ate their horse. On the morning of All Saints' Day, the king drew near with a great army in an effort to save Vyšehrad. The barons of Bohemia and Moravia fought with the king and many were killed. The king sustained a serious loss of stalwart men and was defeated. Then the people of Prague took over Vyšehrad and demolished the castle.

Žižka fought for two weeks against strong enemies, both Czechs and Germans. He conquered Bor and inflicted much damage on his enemies and emerged as the victor. Then he laid siege to Zbraslav Monastery. His soldiers

---

[24] Chronologically wrong as Sigismund was crowned after the crusader defeat on Vítkov.

broke open the tomb and removed the body of King Václav [IV] and took it with them. When Žižka ordered the monastery burned the soldiers went away and left the king there.[25] Now a fisherman by the name of Můcha took the king's body, because the king had been kind to him in the past, and hid it secretly in his vineyard where he kept it for over three years. Then Žižka, together with the Prague army, conquered Říčany. Then [at the beginning of 1421] Žižka marched to Lom and conquered Chotěšov, Kladruby and Krasíkov where he took lord Bohuslav Švamberk prisoner.

After this, the Hungarian king marched against Žižka with a very powerful force. He laid siege to some of the followers of Žižka at Kladruby. The king was there himself armed with strong siege guns. Žižka assembled his warriors and marched to Plzeň in order to save his followers at Kladruby. While Žižka was yet six miles off from Kladruby, the king retreated and departed from Bohemia and went to Hungary. But Žižka laid siege to Plzeň where he suffered a great loss of life and did not conquer it. Then Žižka marched to Chomútov and on Easter Sunday [16 March] he attacked it. Here in this place about 3,000 people were killed and burned [see doc.53]. From here, he marched to Beroun and attacked it and here, as well, a considerable number of people were killed and burned. But Žižka went to Prague and during this time they surrendered up the castle of St Wenceslas to the Praguers. From Prague Žižka went on to Český Brod with a strong contingency. The Germans there shut the gates against him but he stormed the town and conquered it. Some of the Germans fled into the tower of the church. They set fire to the church under their feet, some died in the flames and other Germans leapt down from the tower. Those who did not break their necks were killed with flails. Other towns surrendered, among them Kouřim, Nymburk, Kolín, Kutná Hora, Čáslav, Chrudim, Litomyšl, Polička, and Dvůr Králové. The town of Jaroměř had to be taken by force since the defenders thought that the town was strong enough to withstand them. All of these towns, along with a number of others, were faithful to the law of God.

After this, Žižka went on and besieged the castle of Rabí. Here his second eye was shot out and he barely survived and was now completely blind. [Elsewhere] the margrave of Meißen arrived, liberated Most, and defeated the Prague army. However, he took only a few of them prisoner [see doc.65].

Some time later the German electors invaded the land with a powerful force

---

[25] Žižka was not present during these events, the chronicler notwithstanding, rather the warriors were under the direction of Václav Koranda. The beautiful monastery at Zbraslav was a Cistercian house and traditionally the burial place of kings. According to one source the soldiers raided the wine cellars, got drunk, disinterred the king's body, propped him up, placed a crown of straw on his head, poured wine over him, and implored him to drink with them. FRB 5: 399. The entire episode was very much uncharacteristic of Hussite soldiers.

and they had with them numerous princes, counts and bishops along with the Margrave of Meißen. They perpetrated innumerable brutalities and whenever they captured a Czech that person was immediately killed or burned every time. They marched on to Žatec with as much force as they could muster and they put the town under heavy siege [September 1421]. They stormed the town three times but could not take it. Many of them were slain. The electors sustained significant injury and in great shame and humiliation left the country leaving all of their supplies behind. Many tents were burned down and they barely managed to march away from the country.

Then Žižka, having recovered though now completely blind, marched into the region of Plzeň. There both Czechs and Germans attacked him ferociously. Žižka fought near Planá. When he began to fare badly he continued to march ahead. Fighting all the while, he beat back his enemies. Then he advanced with his army to a very high mountain [Vladař] and here many people from both sides were killed [see doc.76]. Then Žižka and his army marched off to Žatec. From here he attacked the Pikarts [Adamites] and took them by force on an island near Val and ordered that they be burned.

Then the king of Hungary returned with a great army to Bohemia. He had with him Turks, Wallachians, Croats, Hungarians, Cumans, Yassyans, Germans and people from many other lands. Žižka marched against him with his armies to Kutná Hora. When the king heard that Žižka was in Kutná Hora he marched there in hopes catching him there. So Žižka marched out from Kutná Hora to fight the king and he camped with his wagons of war in the field before Kutná Hora and there the battle lasted all day. When night fell, the king surrounded the camp but he stayed out of range of Žižka's warriors. At five o'clock that night, Žižka moved out against the army of the king. There he fought his way straight through the army because there was no other way out for his men. He marched on for a quarter mile until day broke and there he ordered that the war wagons be drawn into a defensive position. However, the king chose not to join the battle but waited for reinforcements to arrive because he knew they were close by. Žižka commanded his men to march on to Kolín and there he assembled more soldiers because he was still intent on fighting the king. The king occupied Kutná Hora and ordered his men to camp close by. His soldiers went about raping women and young girls until they died. Everywhere the king ordered that people be burned.

When Žižka had assembled his soldiers, he moved with great speed to Kutná Hora in order to engage the king. But when the two armies were close at hand, the king commanded that Kutná Hora be burned at three o'clock that night. He retreated in the face of Žižka towards Německý Brod but Žižka was in hot pursuit. As the army of the king passed the village of Habry, Žižka caught up with them. He defeated them and crushed them, all the while they tried to get to Německý Brod. They tried to cross the river on their horse but the ice gave way and many were drowned. Žižka captured all of their wagons together with a wealth of booty. The next day [9 January 1422] Žižka commanded that the town be attacked. They assaulted it throughout the day but were unable to take it for those defending it fought with great courage. The following day they managed to capture the town and they killed all of the defenders except three knights whom they took as prisoners: Lord [Black] Záwiš from Poland, and the barons Borovský and Mrtvice. Then Žižka left with his army and marched to the region of Plzeň and on Easter attacked and conquered Žlutice. From there he conquered Kukštýn [Gutšejn] and then marched towards the town of Týn [Horšovský]. They attacked it and defeated it and during the battle they killed many brave people.

At this time [May 1422] a prince [Zygmunt Korybut] with a retinue of knights came with a cavalry of some four thousand. He was accepted in Prague and the city submitted to his authority. Žižka called him 'son' and he called Žižka 'father'. At this time the Praguers were laying siege to Karlštejn Castle. The prince was fighting Opočno but was not able to conquer it. At the same time the Táborites came to Prague with a powerful contingency and set up in the New Town. From there they attacked the Old Town even though there was no animosity between them. Some of the people who lived in the Old Town, were wary and they took captive more than a hundred of them and the others were driven out of the town in shame. The prince did not wish to take communion in both kinds so the Praguers as well as Žižka left him and he went back to Lithuania [1423].[26] Some time thereafter he returned [1424] thinking he would be received as he had previously but this was not the case.

After this [May 1424], a dispute erupted between the citizens of Prague and Žižka. When Žižka went to Kostelec on the Labe [River], the Praguers went after him with a very great army. When he saw how powerful the army was he departed but the Praguers followed.[27] When he came near to Malešov, Žižka turned around and began to fight with them and he defeated them. On account of that battle there were many widows and orphans in Prague and throughout the land.

Four years after the death of King Václav, the people of Prague realized they were in a bad shape and more than ever lamented the death of King Václav. They searched for anyone who had knowledge about him [his body] and they offered a large reward because they wished to give the king a proper royal burial. One fisherman called Múcha, when he learned that they wanted to bury the king with all dignity, announced that he had him in his vineyard. So they brought him to Prague and gave the king a solemn royal funeral. They buried him [25 July 1424]

---

[26]   This is quite incorrect inasmuch as Prince Zygmunt Korybut did in fact receive communion in both kinds. See doc.90. His departure was political, not religious or theological.

[27]   This rather bland comment should be balanced with detail provided by Windecke. See doc.102.

in a grave next to his father, the emperor Charles, in the castle of St Wenceslas, and that is where he lies. After this, Žižka marched with his warriors to the Hospital Field near Prague where he came to terms of peace with the citizens of Prague [14 September].

Then Žižka marched to Moravia and besieged Přibyslav. By this time the Táborites hated Žižka.[28] This was mainly because the priests with Žižka celebrated mass in the proper manner wearing vestments, tonsure and surplice while holding the body of Christ in a monstrance.[29] On this account the Táborites referred to the priests with Žižka as linen weavers, but Žižka referred to the priests of Tábor as cobblers. The Táborite priests celebrated mass in a simple fashion without tonsure and some had grown beards so that they were quite different.

It happened that at Přibyslav, Žižka was seized by the plague and he died [11 October 1424] and they took him to Hradec Králové and buried him and that is where he is. His soldiers took the name Orphans and they have been called this ever since. The people of Hradec Králové mandated that Žižka be painted upon their banner, sitting on his white horse, in the armour of a knight, holding his battle club just as he looked when he was alive. Whenever the people of Hradec Králové went into battle with this banner they were invincible.

Then the people of Hradec Králové elected a captain but the priest Prokůpek was thought to be the best and he remained in charge most of the time. The Táborites also had a large army and this force was in the field continuously. This army of the Táborites was under the command of a priest called Prokop Shaven. In battle he was always at the front of the army wearing a heavy coat.[30] These two armies [Táborites and Orphans] were on the field frequently and they fought in Bohemia and Moravia, in Austria, Hungary, Thuringia, Brandenburg, and Lusatia. These Czech soldiers marched far and near and they came also to Ruthenia and Prussia and there they fought as well. They were in Denmark [sic] and they watered their horse in the distant [Baltic] sea.[31] Every time they returned they had earned more fame and esteem. However, in the end, many of them were lost, when

---

[28] A gross overstatement because as Žižka's own letters and other contemporary documents show, the Táborites continued to obey the old warrior and much was accomplished among the Hussite groups under the leadership of Žižka.

[29] This opinion of Táborite hostility is countered by Žižka's own statements. See doc.94. It should be noted in marked distinction to this account that priests with Žižka during the battle of Kutná Hora apparently wore no vestments. See doc.78. The matter of ecclesiastical vestments remained a point of contention for many years among the various Hussites groups.

[30] Also known in the sources as Prokop Holý, Prokop the Great, Procopius Rasus (Prokop Shaven, wrongly Prokop, the Bald). After Žižka, he was the dominant Hussite military personality despite being a priest. See doc.112.

[31] A reference to the Hussite counter-crusade of 1433 which took them all the way to the Baltic Sea above Gdańsk. See doc.187.

they fought against each other between [the Czech towns of] Český Brod and Kouřim.[32]

Bartoš, pp. 36–44.

---

[32] The battle of Lipany fought on 30 May 1434. See docs.192–4.

Chapter 5

The Fourth Crusade: Tachov, 1427

108 Sigismund warns Oldřich Rožmberk

[Even with the feared Žižka dead, Sigismund was no closer to solving the Hussite problem. Writing from the Tata Castle in Hungary near Ezstergom on 28 October 1424, the king urged the powerful Rožmberks not to enter into any agreements with the Hussites. The king had intelligence reports which suggested that the Rožmberks were coming to an agreement with the Hussites. The king had also not forgotten that Oldřich had been among the signatories of the documents emerging from the diet of Čáslav in 1421. See doc.63. Sigismund could ill afford to lose the complete support of the Rožmberks.]

Sigismund, by the grace of God king of the Romans, ever Augustus, king of Hungary and Bohemia, dear gracious sir. We have received your letter along with copies of the arrangements you have made and these have been considered along with the barons. We are amazed and regretful that you have been deceived and betrayed so naïvely by the other side and drawn into such matters which are contrary to your honour and soul as well as in opposition to all Christendom. Particularly in the first article, as you write, that you wish to purify the Czech land from the unfair denunciation, and the second pertaining to how the Czech Crown be purified from the violation of villainous rumour and undeserved wrong. May God have mercy. You must understand this one thing. To purify them from their wickedness and to confess to their innocence is to make yourself guilty in this matter with respect to them. Further, that you allowed a meeting to assemble in Kouřim in the middle of the fast and made yourself judge of the Christian faith which neither is your right nor do you have the power to judge Holy Scripture being a layman but this you did to your own dishonour. Likewise, the safe conduct which you have arranged in the town hall in Prague for you and your guests who were to come for that meeting. Consider this. What kind of security can you expect from such people, when you arrive, against something terrible happening to you as well as to those accompanying you? Where will you find suitable masters to go along with you to negotiate about the Christian faith in the territory of the heretics? We are amazed that you allow yourself to be deprived of your rights to the point where ordinary people and peasants may judge you.

Similarly, you have made a commitment that should the other side militarily defend themselves against foreigners that they may have access to your goods to satisfy their needs and beyond this, if any castle or garrison on our side in the Czech land does not wish to abide in these arrangements or would seek to contravene them you are then prepared to force them to obedience. It now appears that while you were negotiating with these heretics, they marched against us and our son, the margrave of Moravia, in great strength because they no longer had to be concerned with you. Your supporters, as we understand it, were helping them.

You must appreciate that this commitment and these arrangements are entirely in opposition to us, against all of our supporters, and faithful Christians everywhere and contrary to Christendom. It seems to intend to help the heretics. We have found many other improper, dishonourable, unworthy and unChristian articles against the faith, against Christian order and also against your rank and liberties and all of these aim entirely at your extermination and to your irreversible dishonour. We have not made an effort, because of their length, to write in reply to all of them. Therefore, it is impossible to comment on everything, but should you continue with these arrangements you shall cause yourself to be dishonourable to the whole of Christendom and it would be impossible to reverse this. Therefore it seems good to us to advise you and order you to get out of these arrangements any way you can and not to fulfil them on any wise. It would be better and more honest to abolish such indecent vows than to fulfil such obligations which are contrary to God and to honour.[1]

Given in Tata on the day of SS Simon and Jude [28 October] in the thirty-eighth year of our Hungarian reign, in the fifteenth year of our Roman reign and in the fifth year of our Bohemian reign.

Rynešová 1: 68–70.

109   Oldřich Rožmberk affirms loyalty to Sigismund

[The reply of the Czech baron denies any and all suggestion that he may have entered into an agreement with the Hussites. This affirmation must have allayed considerably Sigismund's fears. However, even if the king received the letter in

---

[1]   Such contravening of prior agreement was consistent with Sigismund's own political policies. The king may well have had in mind the oft-repeated statement made by Innocent III when dealing with the Cathar heretics in the early thirteenth century: 'there is no obligation to keep faith with those who keep not faith with God.' PL, 215, col. 1357.

this light, nevertheless Rožmberk provides clear testimony to the strength of the heretics. The letter is dated 12 October 1425.]

As your grace has written to me not to have an armistice, may you understand that I neither have one nor do I intend to have one. These [Táborites] congregate in my district and I suffer great damage in attempting to resist them. I do not have sufficient money which your Grace granted me in Wrocław and I endure great injury and I do not foresee the end of these troubles. You must also know that they demand negotiation, wishing to come to me whenever I give the word. Therefore, give me some indication of whether or not I should do this. I pray your Grace to remember me with assistance as I am your servant. I have no wish to cause your Grace anxiety and thus I endure these damages while trusting in your Grace as in my Lord that you will condescend to aid me in this misery for I am sorely troubled by my enemies.

I have sent several letters but the messengers were captured. Other letters have reached your Grace but you have not responded so I remain expectant of hearing from you and have no intention of acting in any other way than as a servant of your Grace. You must also know that some of the most powerful castles in the area of Plzeň have made a truce [with the heretics]. I do not wish to name them as your Grace will receive knowledge of it fairly readily. It would be better that we wage war together rather than some making a truce. I am continually fearful of being denounced by them to your Grace. I therefore beg you, as I have done many times previously, not to believe it. I am prepared to defend myself before your Grace against whatever guilt they ascribe to me and vow never to act as anything other than a servant of your Grace.

Furthermore, I am unable to oppose these enemies successfully any longer owing to their great power as I do not have as many people as heretofore. However, I have ordered them to do what they can in secret around the army and elsewhere. We cannot any longer hang them [Hussites] publicly even though they drown or secretly murder anyone they capture.[2]

AČ 3: 7–8.

---

2   The records of the court books of the Rožmberks make the point about Hussite guerrilla warfare. František Mareš, ed. *Popravčí kniha pánův z Rožmberka* [Abhandlungen der Königlichen böhmischen Gesellschaft der Wissenschaften, 9] (Prague, 1878), especially pp. 25–52 covering the period 1420–9.

110   Response of German cities to crusade proposal

[On 16 April 1425, imperial representatives met at Ulm to discuss another crusade against the heretics. The tentative nature of crusade plans at this time are reflected a year earlier in Sigismund's vague proposals mentioned in correspondence with Władysław of Poland and the Regensburg city council (UB 1, pp. 333–4 and 342–4). The shadow of three successive defeats kept a damper on enthusiasm. This brief comment is part of a contemporary record found on a scrap of paper.]

There has been discussion about the commitment which our lord the king wishes to be accomplished. The opinion of the delegates of the cities is that a common campaign must be undertaken in the service of him [the king]. However, they determined that it would be too difficult for them to undertake a daily war throughout the entire year. [It was recommended] that this must be brought to Constance and discussed among the common cities and from there an honourable embassy sent to our lord in Mainz.

Neumann, p. 89.

111   Description of Hussite warriors

[The rather fanciful and demonizing portrait of the Hussites gave credence to their alleged invincibility going all the way back to their stunning victory at Sudoměř in March 1420 when it seemed the weapons of the 'Iron Lords' were useless against Hussite flesh. See doc.13.]

The Táborites and Orphans were men exceeding black from the sun and the wind and also from the smoke of their camp fires. Their very appearance was frightful. Their eyes were like those of an eagle, their hair wild and stood on end, their beards long and their stature prodigiously tall. Their bodies were hairy and their skin so hard that it appeared able to resist iron as though it were a piece of armour.

Aeneas Sylvius, *Historia Bohemica*, chapter 51, p. 162.

112   Emergence of Prokop Holý

[Žižka's death left an enormous vacuum in Hussite military affairs. Even though the field armies were divided at this point in history, Žižka had always been able to exert supreme command and control. Zygmunt Korybut became general commander following the death of the old warrior in October 1424. This would not last. In 1427 Prokůpek (known also as Prokop the Short or Prokop the Lesser) assumed command of the Orphan armies and remained in this role until his death in battle in 1434. In the Táborite camp there were a series of transitions until one emerged who would dominate the anti-crusade effort almost as completely as Žižka had. Jan Hvězda of Vícemilice became commander of the Táborites but was killed in September 1425 during the siege, but eventually successful conquest, of Vožice Castle (near Tábor). He was succeeded by Bohuslav of Švamberk, the former commander-in-chief of the Plzeň Landfríd. He had been converted to the Hussite heresy by Žižka in 1420. Bohuslav's tenure as general captain was brief inasmuch as he died of wounds received in November 1425 while besieging the town and castle of Retz in Lower Austria.[3] The next leader was Prokop Holý. Born in the 1370s, Prokop travelled widely outside Bohemia in his youth and had later taken holy orders and spent some time at a Minorite house in Hradec Králové. He was also married by the time he came to prominence in the crusade period. Both Aeneas Sylvius and Jan Długosz suggest that Prokop had been an intimate friend of Jan Žižka. Prokop adopted a policy, after 1426, of strengthening the borders of Bohemia by invading neighbouring countries hostile to the Czechs. Unlike his predecessor he consented to diplomatic meetings with Sigismund. He adopted and successfully utilized Žižka's military tactics and strategies and was the dominant leader of the Táborite branch of the Hussite movement from 1426 until his death in battle in 1434. In the war period he is second in fame only to the blind general, though it should be said that unlike his predecessor he did not engage in warfare personally. The only documented case of his actual taking up the sword was at the Battle of Lipany in May 1434 when Prokop was forced to fight, unsuccessfully, for his own life.]

113   Papal legate Orsini rejects diplomacy and urges war

[In March 1425, Cardinal Branda, now more than 80 years old, retired as papal nuncio for the crusade against the Hussites. He had led two crusades. His replacement was the canonist Giordano Orsini (†1438). Though a superb propagandist and ruthless defender of the official church, Orsini was not sufficiently *au fait* with either Hussite military power or the reluctance of Central European princes to undertake another campaign against the resilient Czech

---

[3]   On the Hussite presence and military activity throughout Austria, see especially the succinct study authored by Silvia Petrin, *Der österreichische Hussitenkrieg 1420–1434* (Vienna: Heeresgeschichtliches Museum/Militärwissenschaftliches Institut, 1982).

heretics. Hence, he advised Sigismund against further diplomatic considerations but instead to undertake an immediate military expedition. His letter is dated 13 June 1426.]

To the sacred, royal and most invincible imperial majesty. My most serene prince and only lord. After my humble recommendation the letter of Your Majesty was delivered to me in which you referred to having received a letter from the baron, your faithful Oldřich Rožmberk, directed to him from the Praguers. To this I answer by first thanking Your Majesty for allowing me to reply to this and offer advice to Your Grace. In order to be faithful to your commands let me say directly what I think, which is more of an answer rather than advice. First, I wonder greatly and deplore their [the Hussites] foolishness, even their devilish suggestion, that they wish to dispute about the articles of faith which have been arrived at long ago and approved. These are of such long standing that nothing can be added to, or detracted from, without indication of heresy. I think they ask this with the intention of deceiving Your Majesty, which they have done many times, as you know. They are afraid of a campaign of the faithful against them and by these demands are attempting to subvert [or delay] it.

However, I would like to say something even more concrete concerning this matter and will show more clearly that their requests must be refused just as the foolishness of simple minds. My opinion is, namely, that they wish to argue about the articles of faith decreed by the Council of Nicaea in the time of Constantine in such a manner that imperial as well as canon law indicates is not [permissible] to argue about the faith. If they wish to speak about the articles of [the Council of] Constance, [it must be said] that the most reverent fathers and venerable men, endowed with knowledge and wisdom have declared them to have been certainly approved unanimously in the Holy Spirit and nothing can be disputed. I recall that we, our most holy father, Your Majesty, and others have promised by oath never to oppose the articles determined by the same [Council of Constance] but rather to hold to them unto death. Surely all of those articles, if they are judged correctly, do not search for light in the darkness, do not favour their heresies, but disprove them from the root up.

But as I said, these sons of perdition, twisted by a devilish harness, propose tricky expositions with the intent to deceive. Of this I judge that such mad people are not to be listened to in any way but are to be avoided completely, [especially] when their infamy is so great that they work to subvert the faith; the faith of which nothing is more worthy as I call the divine matter. What remains? I strongly admonish Your Majesty and I desire, as much as I can, that you would not cease from the laudable and worthy undertaking [i.e. the crusade] which you have begun. What I hope foremost of Your Majesty, who has always been a defender of the faith, the cause of the unity of the church and the one who expels schism, is that you would suppress these heresies, those lethal thorns.

I determine, then, that the authority exists and the need involves the will, and the princes are ready. It remains finally to execute the matter so that such heretical iniquity might be eliminated from our most Christian faith by the attention and work of Your Majesty, both by word and action, as soon as possible. It will be beneficial to the Most High, for the advancement of the faith and the Apostolic See, and significant beyond all else for Your Majesty, for the salvation not only of the kingdom, but also of the entire fatherland, and finally the most enjoyable thing which could happen to me. [Given] in Nürnberg, in the diocese of Bamberg, on 13 June. The servant of Your Majesty, Giordano Ursini, Cardinal bishop of Albanus, legate of the Apostolic See.

DR 8: 491–2.

114   Battle at Ústí-nad-Labem

[Technically, this battle was between Germans and Czechs and as such is not part of the crusades. In practical terms, however, it was very much related to the efforts to suppress the heretics by military force. Hussite nobles had made attempts to secure a hearing before ecclesiastical and imperial authorities. The papal legate for France, England, Hungary and Bohemia, Giordano Orsini, flatly refused these overtures. Three days later his crusade collapsed in ignominious defeat. Overall, the Hussites were under the command of Zygmunt Korybut, but Prokop Holý was in charge of the Táborite troops while the Orphan army was commanded by Žižka's old comrade, Jan Roháč of Dubá. The engagement took place on 16 June 1426 in northern Bohemia near the town of Ústí on the Labe River. See map 3.]

In the year of the Lord, 1426 on the Sunday following St Vitus, the Praguers with the prince Zygmunt [Korybut], along with Táborites, the Orphans and other Czechs besieged the town of Ústí on the Labe [River]. To this town the Margrave of Meißen, with many princes, counts, barons and knights from the German lands, came to help. The Czechs set up their formations and engaged them in the field. The Germans were beaten completely and driven out of the land. Many counts, barons, and knights of them [Germans] were killed while others fainted in their armour on account of the heat and from thirst and thus died. Immediately following the battle, the Praguers conquered the town of Ústí on that same day, confiscated goods, mercilessly killed many people and then burned the town down completely. During the battle only one eminent person from the Prague side was killed, Jan Bradatý, a citizen of the Old Town. [Manuscript D notes that] Wácha, a knight of Popovice carried the banner in that fight and bravely went wherever there was need. [Manuscript E notes that] Lord Bohuněk of Rabštejn said that if all of the people killed in the battle had been taken prisoner instead they could have been used by those on the borderland as hostages for ransom and made a good thing out of it.

[Mss LM] In the year of the Lord 1426 on the Sunday, the day after St Vitus, there occurred a great battle near the town of Ústí by the village called Předlice. On one side was the prince, Zygmunt with the Praguers and other Czechs. The town had been settled by the Margrave of Meißen and from this town they had been causing great damage and destruction in the Czech kingdom and capturing and burning people. The Czechs were unwilling to endure this any longer and following Easter, Lord Jakoubek of Bílina with other good people diligently undertook the difficult task of conquering Ústí. The margrave, together with a multitude of people from Saxony, Thuringia, Serbia and Lusatia as well as other regions as far away as the Rhine, marched in an effort to save Ústí and drive the Czechs away. When Lord Jakoubek heard that the Germans were assembling in this manner and wishing to expel him from the town, he sent word to the barons, the knights and to the towns, as well as to the Táborites in the field, asking them to come and not permit such damage and shame to be inflicted on the Czechs. The prince of Lithuania, Zygmunt, the baron Boček of Kunštát, Lord Smiřický and other barons, the Praguers and towns which were affiliated with the Law of God, along with the Orphans and Táborites drew near to Ústí. According to Lord Jakoubek the Czechs had about 25,000 forces.

When the Germans approached through the forest, they proceeded along three roads: under the Osek Castle, along the Janov road and along Krupka. They had in all about 70,000 troops. While the Germans were approaching Ústí the Czechs sent gracious letters to them to the effect that if God aided them they would capture us [Hussites] and if God aided us again they could expect the same. But the Germans trusting in their superior numbers proudly replied in a message marked by arrogance and high-handedness, that all would be killed.[4] So the Czechs moved out from Ústí towards them and began to beseech the Lord in great humbleness and piety that God might condescend to help them. They encountered the enemy before midday but the Czechs did not wish to fight on Sunday. But the Germans thinking that the Czechs intended to flee on account of their superior forces rushed at them without any hesitation on the holy Sunday. They reached the wagons and crashed through the first line of defence. At that moment the Czechs

---

[4] This seems to have been the consistent policy of the crusaders. See, for example, the letter of the Nürnberg city council to Ulm, 1 September 1421 wherein it is noted that all of the heretics – men and women – must be killed. Only small children were to be spared the carnage. See doc.72.

clamoured up and began shooting from the wagons using the main cannon and the fortress cannon until they had achieved major breaches in the enemy. Then with a great cry that the Germans were fleeing they leapt from the wagons and utterly thrashed the Germans. [They chased the Germans] from the battle field of Ústí all the way to the mountains of Meißen so much so that they laid dead in the fields like sheafs in the time of harvest. The stream flowing through Ústí turned red on account of the great slaughter of people and horse.[5] Thus the Czechs won the battle and they spared no one's life and took no captives. They captured thirty-seven three scores of German wagons, three three scores of cannon [and] sixty-six tents. So many thousands of Germans were killed there that they laid unburied for a long time and stacks of bones lie there to this day. They managed to kill no more than nineteen Czechs and no one of significance save for Jan Bradatý, a citizen of Prague. There is no old person who can remember such a battle in Bohemia.

Following the battle, near the village of Hrbovice, there were forty counts and barons kneeling under their banner in surrender having thrust their swords into the ground indicating they wanted to live. Notwithstanding this, the Czechs killed them all because of the promises and obligations made to each other and so they were not permitted to live. Those who had fled to the villages of Předlice and Hrbovice were on fire in the surrounding villages and no one was able to escape. Lord Jakoubek of Bílina wanted to save Lord Walkenberg of Wolfstein. So he took him on his own horse but this did not work for the Táborite soldiers saw this and shot him while he was on the horse behind Jakoubek. While the dying German was falling from the horse he pulled Lord Jakoubek down with him and he was also nearly killed.

After that defeat, on the same day, the Czechs marched again to the city of Ústí and they conquered the town, defeating the Germans there. Of the leading men, Jakoubek ordered that they be freed from the prison and the city was burnt down and destroyed and it remained deserted for three years. Thereafter Jakoubek rebuilt it and settled there and it remained so until the time of Emperor Sigismund.

SRB 3: 66–9.

115   Song of the battle of Ústí

[The overwhelming victory by Hussites was cause for celebration. Chroniclers reported that 10–15,000 royalists were killed. This figure could only have any

---

[5]   The stream ran down a hill into a fish pond. Up to the present time the fish pond has the name 'the pool of blood.'

relevance if it includes those who fled from the battle and took refuge in towns west of the city, such as Hrbovice and Předlice, where they were pursued, and then slain in the resulting conflagration. Hussite sources reported losses of thirty men.]

It is fitting for the Czechs
To recall the victory which God granted them
Over their enemies at Ústí
When they fought for their faith.

On the Sunday
Following the Feast of St Vitus
In the year 1426
They put the Germans to flight.

There were great crowds of people
Present at this battle
Who would not help the Czechs
Hoping to see them beaten.

Thanks be to our God
All glory and honour to God
For God condescended to aid us
In expelling the Germans from our country.

The princess of Saxony was a powerful woman
Together with barons, princes and knights
She assembled a mighty army
And marched into Bohemia.[6]

The army captured Ústí
Intending to murder Czechs
And exterminate their race
They reduced the land by fire and bloodshed.

Upon hearing this news
Prague barons, lords and knights

---

[6] Princess Catherine was the wife of the Saxon elector Friedrich of Wettin, margrave of Meißen, who had gone to Nürnberg to consult with Sigismund and the Reichstag. He left Catherine in charge. She inspected the troops at Freiburg on 11 June and gave them an extravagant send-off.

The two armies of the Praguers and Táborites
With Zygmunt, Prince of Lithuania,

Marched toward Bavaria
To resist the crusaders
Sent by the pope from the German kingdom
To kill the faithful.

They repented of their animosity
And went to their aid saying
The faith of the Czechs
Consists also in helping one another.

At Předlice, the armies camped
On the battlefield with the equipment
The Germans were full of valour
The Czechs were as brave as lions.

When the initial forces attacked
The Czechs were advised
To give up their faith and submit
Otherwise they should prepare themselves.

They said you are not able to defend yourselves
Behold our strength
There are more of us
Than poppy seeds filling a barrel to the brim.

The Czechs replied saying
They would not surrender their faith
They wanted to defend their homeland
Even if that meant dying on the battlefield.

Certainly we are but a few men
As a spoonful of mustard seeds
You must deal with us
As Christ our Lord will grant.

Let us always honour this agreement
If you capture one of our people

Do not kill them
We will do the same.

They [the Germans] said we will not do this
The pope has ordered excommunication
Therefore we must kill everyone
Women, young girls, children and the aged.

So the Czechs agreed
Not to take prisoners either
Everyone must call on God
Remembering his faith and honour.

The Count of Meißen warns
If the Czech armies combine
Our cause is lost
We must stop them from joining.

Fear seizes me when I see the lancers
As well as those vicious peasants over there
Those whom they will work to death
With their weapons after losing their tongue.

Lord Vaněk of the Black Mountain
The military captain
Says whoever makes war on the righteous
Must first make peace with God.

On Friday morning, two days earlier,
The Czechs assembled
Communing the body and blood of the Lord
So that they might fight for his law.

Prince Zygmunt does the same
He tearfully begs God
Encourages his people to fight
Gives instructions to his barons.

But the Germans poked fun
Riding their horse in front of them saying

We shall use our pikes, daggers and maces
To kill those Hussites like geese.[7]

More than one woman
Will be left alone
Losing brother, father or husband
Orphans will grieve.

When the armies began to fight
The Czechs call upon God
Then the cavalry will appear
The like of which has never been seen.

Then Táborites begin to fight
Their foot soldiers throw themselves into the attack
Wherever the Orphans go
Streams of blood begin to flow.

At the beginning of the battle
– So say the popular accounts –
Prince Zygmunt exerts himself so much
That he is bathed in sweat.

The Poles, Czechs and Moravians
The brave lords of Prague
Fearlessly follow his example
In attacking the enemy.

Lord Václav of Kravař
Behaved himself heroically
It is fitting that he praise God
May he recover.

Those with Janěk of Smiřice
With Čeněk Mičan of Klinštejn
With Albrecht of Kamyk
Fought bravely against the Germans.

---

[7]   The Czech word for goose is 'hus' and was often punned upon beginning with Jan Hus and
used derogatorily by crusaders and other enemies of the Hussite movement.

My lord, Václav of Říčany
Took the banner of the prince
Holding it high with courage
Until the outcome of the divine battle.

Lord Hynek called Valdštejn
Acquitted himself as a hero
As did Bavor of Pernštejn
And Hynek Krušina with them.

Viktorin of Kunštát and Lord Boček
It should be known
Are true knights of valour
Those who saw their exploits can testify.

My Lord Burda Trčka of Lipnice
Threw himself into the fray
He was believed to be lost
But he reappeared with a banner.

Lord Jaroš of Chlum, Čeněk of Vartenberk,[8]
Petr Kuneš, Hanuš Kolovrat,
Jan Vrbata, Chlum of Markvart
And their battalion,

Should be compared
With the most noble and brave in the fight
Škopek, Záruba Dohalsky,
Beneda of Bohdanec.

My lords Jošt of Blankštejn
Jan of Gořka with Prince Frederick of Russia
And Václav Vřezovec Maštovský
Head up the rear guard.

Many other loyal servants and knights
Demonstrated their courage

---

[8]   This is not the aforementioned Lord High Burgrave of Prague and mercurial baron active
      during the first three crusades. That individual died in 1425.

It is not possible to name them all
May God reward their children.

During the battle
They courageously defended the truth
And gave their lives
In order to be with you in heaven.

In the middle of this holy battle
The wind blew against the Germans
Immediately they turned away from the Czechs
And fled for the forests and hills.

Those who managed to escape
Reported to the Margrave
That the mad heretical Czechs
Remained firm in their faith.

Fourteen dukes and lords
Dismounted from their horse
Thrusting their swords into the ground
They ask for mercy.

The Czechs pay them no heed
Scorning their gold and silver
They remain true to their agreement
And spare no one.

Fifty and two thousand enemies fell
Young squires wearing their helmets at their side
Were spared in order to give account
And testify to the princess and her friends of the holy battle of Ústí.

The message comes to the Margrave
He informs her [Catherine, the Saxon princess] that her people have been defeated
She falls to the ground in shock
Alas, bad news.

She tears her golden curls
From her beautiful head and says

Have pity, O Lord,
On my people and on their virtue.

Other beautiful women
Mourn the loss
Of brothers, uncles or fathers
Killed in the battle.

Another message reaches
The palace of the Hungarian king
Asking that he advise those of Meißen
Immediately he speaks to the lord [Heinrich] of Plavno.

My friend tell me
What can be done in order to save the honour of the princess?
He replies, the one who wishes to fight in Bohemia
Must have strength, good fortune and righteousness.

Seven years I waged war in Bohemia
Not once have I gained anything
If one wishes to avoid dishonour and injury
He should leave the Czechs alone.

Let all faithful Christians
Whether barons, knights, or burghers of Prague
Follow the faith of his fathers
And prove that he is of their blood.

Remain firm in your faith
So you will be praised and blessed of God
The Lord will bless your descendants
And give them life everlasting.

Nejedlý, 1913: 912–15.

116   Lamentation on the debacle in north Bohemia

[This curious piece seeks to lay the blame for the debacle of the battle at the feet
of the Saxon supreme commander Boso of Fictum who was one of the few high-
ranking officers to escape from the carnage. He was denounced in his own country

as a traitor. He was however exonerated by the Elector of Saxony. This anonymous lament underscores the thoroughgoing Hussite triumph.]

Boso [of Fictum], Boso the Younger
Meise the Younger and Little John
I note quite clearly
Are four great gluttons.[9]

Even though new wine would age
They would not be comparable to an idiot
They had sex with many women
And carried off money from the land!

They accepted bribes
Perverted judgement
Through greed and iniquity
By devilish counsel
Very many men have been destroyed
They have become great miscreants by this!

I cannot write of this at all
Nor can I tell it
But I want to let it be [known]
To be remembered against old Boso
How he stepped out from the ranks
And ran off with the banner.

He sacrificed his honour to the extent that he ran off without respect
We should lament this to God in heaven
Because of the cowardice of this one
Many good people were killed
Great lords, knights and vassals
Citizens, peasants and many houses.

Now we often hear and much is to be told
The pious ones are degraded all their days
The evil ones must be recompensed
In many towns and fields.

---

[9]   It is possible that the author is referring to four officers of the prince of Saxony.

They have dressed themselves in infamy
In pride and in the appetite of usury
In impurity they have cleaned out money from the people
As he [Boso] did in the land of Meißen.

Such great infamies are told in all the lands
It is apparent so that he cannot deny it
He has also supplied the heretics
Against God and the holy creed
By the tributes they have given to him
So that he might live in Thuringia.

He has received one gulden for a wagon
So that food has come into Bohemia
Trampling the good works
Selling the faith for tributes
This is the sign which reads
He is a perfect trickster in his evil.

He has done even more evil
Which I cannot enumerate here specifically
How he allowed the Wildenstein to be climbed
Against his faith and honour.[10]

This evil was too little for him
So he undertook greater iniquity thereafter
When he injured many good people through his flight
By which he caused them to be killed before Ústí.

He would fall into great misery
Because of the knights and vassals
Who have rejected him
I hope he will be knocked down to the dust because of it.

Who would like to avenge such infamy?
That one would free himself from the Devil
Therefore each and every one
Both poor and rich are praying.

---

[10] The meaning here is not clear.

All the princes and princesses
Should take this to heart
Think of their profit and piety
So that their land would not come to grief.

They should declare themselves
Appoint good people to their positions
So that advisors might love virtue and piety
That people not be seduced as it is written in the books.

But live honourably
Not offend one another
Not break agreements
Or supply anyone of their own.

If they do it, then they do well
They shall be filled with the grace of God
So that all might come into the kingdom of heaven
With the help of God.

Now I want to report to you
When these things happened
It was, when it was written,
After the time when Jesus was a child
[Fourteen hundred and twenty-six years
This is true.]

Liliencron 1: 293–4.

117   Franconian knights unite against the heretics

[Following the crushing failure at Ústí, the Franconian knights published a decree specifically indicating their intention to form a league in order to more effectively oppose the Hussite heretics in Bohemia. Deploring their perception of the corruption of Christendom within the Kingdom of Bohemia they declared themselves prepared to dedicate their resources to war against the heretics under the banner of the Blessed Virgin Mary and St George, their patron saint. The manifesto was dated 15 January 1427 at Bamberg and distributed throughout Germany.]

To the glory, honour and service of almighty God, the source of all good things and to Mary, the glorious queen of heaven and of all heavenly hosts. Let this be known to all who see, read or otherwise receive this letter. Concerning the great and persistent contempt of the glory and honour of the holy Catholic faith in God and the Mother of God, the Virgin Mary, and the entire heavenly hosts caused by the outrages, violence, spilling of blood, murder, injury and scandal close by in Bohemia. Even though the Christian authorities and power provided the means in many ways for the express extermination of this iniquity, the Most High permits this, after all, to test the constancy of the holy Catholic faith in the hearts of the good and pious faithful Christians which to this point could not be known. These disturbances against the Christian faith, contempt, and abominable damages and scandals have grown daily and furthermore they are getting worse up to the present time. Some remedy of redemption must be provided through means of counsel and action by good and pious lovers of the Christian faith and zealous people. We must defend the honour and glory of God, the Virgin Mary and the entire heavenly host. Those who should have handled these matters up to now and extirpated these errors have not done this. It might possibly be understood that the almighty God in the depths of God's wisdom has intended that the holy Catholic faith is aided in some other way. In these days all the power of good Christians has been stopped and the struggle against the aforementioned heretics has been suspended, namely the work of extirpating their errors.

Therefore almighty God has inflamed some of the godly hearts of the pious and defenders of the orthodox faith to come together in an assembly for which purpose the princes of the province of Franconia, which is otherwise known as eastern France, have come to the city of Bamberg for these negotiations. Further, the reverent fathers, Friedrich, Bishop of Bamberg, Johannes, Bishop of Würzburg and the blessed Friedrich, Margrave of Brandenburg, prince-elector of the empire and its archchamberlain and Burgrave of Nürnberg, together with a notable multitude of counts, barons, knights and warriors of the same Franconia who arrived here with the aforementioned lords and princes brought to remembrance the disturbances against the Catholic faith, the errors, and scandals. It was the will and agreement of those princes that the most reverent Christian fathers and barons, lord archbishops and other serene lord princes of the holy empire, together with the prince-electors determine how the aforesaid errors and scandals might be most effectively exterminated. An assembly shall be gathered, together with other princes of the holy empire and imperial communities, in the city of Mainz on the Sunday following the feast of the Blessed Mary's purification. The aforementioned counts, barons and knights, having entered into mutual debate and discussion, with prudent consideration, for the honour and pleasure of the named lords and prince-electors and with a desire to conform themselves with each other in their agreed praiseworthy intention, provide each other with favours and services honourably and usefully in those points written below. They have reduced themselves into one accord into a league having firm trust in God who illuminates the hearts of many that when this letter comes to others they may with the same fervour join themselves to us and follow the patterns and intentions of this league.

First, in the beginning of this present and, with the help of God, happy new year, in the praise and service of our newly born Lord Jesus Christ and the most glorious lady the Virgin Mary, we unite in defence of the devout Christians remaining to this time in Bohemia who have suffered severe and varied pressure and distress on account of their allegiance to the Catholic faith to this hour and who have bravely fought against these errors. The aforementioned counts, barons, and knights have united and decided to convert their military exercises, plays and other amusements which they have been accustomed to performing in tournaments and jousting, into the struggle against the aforementioned heresies and errors namely in the following way. The sign of the army, its ensign and banner shall be the image of the aforementioned glorious lady the Virgin Mary with an image of her most blessed little child and in front of them the blessed and glorious knight George kneeling and holding the garland of his knighthood. Whoever would desire to join this military court or spiritual tournament must do so at their own expense in terms of equipment of horse, weapons, servants, and other items for their force and should come to the town of Cheb on the Sunday after Whitsuntide which is the feast of the Trinity. This is where the aforesaid court or spiritual tournament is to be formed and where the captains and other vital matters are selected. Then after the journey, this exercise or spiritual tournament shall be fought for an entire six weeks and is to be performed strenuously and bravely against the previously mentioned faithless ones.

As soon as the army reaches the land of the enemies, the newcomers who have been determined as fit according to their merits, shall be decorated with a knightly waistband and a festive celebration in which there shall be an honourable knightly table on which the awards shall be distributed to those individuals according to their military merits. This shall be called in the German language 'die Ehrentafel' [the honourable table]. Those who are not of the knightly status, but are from a community or of another estate and have acted bravely shall receive a similar insignia of praise and these merits are to be distributed proportionally. Furthermore, there is to be some consideration for what might be done in the future either in this way just written or in another better way for the final extermination of those heresies and errors.

Therefore let it please the princes, counts, barons, knights, warriors and to those from other cities, towns or other places, and to everyone, who has the spirit, virtue and force of action and who love to defend the honour and praise of that child and his mother and the good condition of the Christian faith. Those who desire to reach eternal honour and joy in heaven must be diligent in order to be regarded worthy of being invited to this laudable court and spiritual knighthood and to deserve such honour and heavenly reward through brave and strong acts maintaining a firm faith. May the most glorious woman with her holy little child, on whose behalf these deeds are undertaken, grant freely the wisdom, virtue, power, protection, grace and salvation to all who gather for their service and would fill their houses with praise, glory and salvation. As heralds, the administers of this letter will narrate all of this more completely by living voice.

For the testimony of all that is written above, we, the undersigned, here present, have appended our seals to this letter. Johannes of Wertheim, Wilhelm of Castel, Conrad, baron of Limburg, Erkinger of Saunsheim, Arnold of Sekkendorf, Conrad of Aufsatz, Witus of Rotenhon, Eberhard of Scauenberg, knights Karl of Hessburg, Matthias of Liechtenstein, Eberhard Fursch of Turnau and Heinrich Fox of Eltmain, warriors of the will and provisions of that knighthood written above. Given in Bamberg on Wednesday before [the feast of St] Anthony in the year of the Lord 1427.

UB 1: 478–81.

118 Zygmunt Korybut arrested at dawn

[In an effort to gain political control of the Czech kingdom, Korybut entered into secret negotiations with Pope Martin V. He promised the Holy See that if he were supported by the conservative parties in Bohemia he could lead the Hussites to reconciliation with the official church. Should this have occurred, the papacy may have been willing to recognize Korybut as king and refuse to acknowledge the claims of Sigismund of Hungary. When these plans were uncovered nearly all of the Hussite parties regarded the plan as treachery and Korybut was seized on charges of treason. The only ones to defend him were the arch-conservatives Křišťan of Prachatice, Petr of Mladoňovice, Prokop of Plzeň and Jan Příbram and they were sent into exile from Prague. The regent was placed under arrest on 17 April 1427. He was later expelled from the country.]

On Maundy Thursday, during Easter week, right after the morning sermon, there were great disturbances in Prague among some of the priests. A plot had been hatched against Prince Zygmunt Korybut of Lithuania who, at the time, was at the royal house. This action was initiated by Jan Rokycana, the preacher at the Church of the Mother of God before Týn, along with some of the secular lords of Prague as well as some knights, especially Svojše of Zahradka and Rozvoda called Rameš (because he [Zygmunt Korybut] would not receive the communion under both kinds).[11] They arrested him and took him under the cover of night in disguise to the castle of Prague. From there he was taken to the Valdštejn Castle. Thereafter he was expelled from Bohemia. The people of Prague did this as a reward to him for the way he had supported their enemies. However, the Lord God did not fail to punish these traitors. Rozvoda called Rameš was soon thereafter killed by one of his servants. Before his death Svojše went insane. The others likewise ended their lives rather miserably.[12]

SRB 3: 70–1.

119　On the capture of Zygmunt Korybut

[This incident had fatal consequences for the Hussite movement and positive results for the crusade against them. In the first instance, it effectively severed formal political ties with Poland and Lithuania. Emperor Sigismund stood to gain most from the fall of his rival and he wasted no time reappearing in a bid to sway public opinion. It is not a great exaggeration to tie the implications of the event to the final conflict at Lipany. See docs 192–4. There is an edition of the song in Výbor, vol.1, pp. 327–31.]

All Czechs of good reputation,
Always esteemed heroes,
Lament the events in Prague
And the irreparable mischief!

Because our mother, Prague
Always guarded our honour
Now the inquisitive clergy
Have left her at the mercy of defamations.

Master Jakoubek [of Stříbro], priest [Jan] Rokycana
[Martin] Lupáč, [Jan Biskupec called] Ožeh, priest Jaroslav[13]

---

[11]　Again, a point of inaccuracy. Korybut was an utraquist communicant. See doc.90.

[12]　Rokycana was elected spiritual head of the Hussite church by a synod in Prague in 1427 and made senior preacher in the Týn Church in Prague. The Bohemian Estates elected him Archbishop of Prague in the fall of 1435. He died in 1471, never consecrated.

[13]　Jakoubek of Stříbro († 1429), successor to the martyred Jan Hus, and Jan Rokycana, later the long-standing but unconsecrated Hussite archbishop of Prague, are well-known figures in Hussite history. Ožeh had been serving as rector of St Peter's Church in Prague in Poříčí

Committed that frightful act
On that day of Easter Thursday.

They plotted a conspiracy against the honourable duke
Good people are lamenting it,
Because it did not happen with their consent,
And they are grieving.

Already we are experiencing
What the clergy has arranged for us:
They dishonoured many respectable people
In an awful, treacherous way.

And so they brought things to the extent
That we are enemies with all the world
Now we have lost even Poland
Which previously we could rely on for help.

They do not care a damn about it
They are well hidden in Prague
They are not interested to know
How the peasants live.

They criticise abuses
While the community supports them
They put themselves in a danger of death
But they are in no hurry to leave Prague.

If a priest should leave Prague
Without being accompanied by troops
He instantly argues that he can do nothing useful
Even if he died for God.

He can find countless excuses
Saying: my time has not come yet!
That is what people say
When they are afraid.

---

and Jaroslav served as the administrator of the Church of St Nicholas in the Old Town of
Prague.

They offer advice in town halls,
But between themselves they fight:
It is obvious
That when there are two, they cannot agree.

Rather than accepting that things are not as they wish
They would rather like
People to betray each other
And continuously kill each other.

Of the lay participants of the plot
Let us first name Rozvoda
He was the leader, and Svojše,
Who played the role of the late Judas.[14]

Sitting at the dinner table
With the honourable duke Zygmunt,
They were busy conferring with him
About how to get meat for Easter.

He confided in them
Because he trusted them:
Whatever you do
Will be as I want it to be.

In the evening they left the town
Knowing all his plans
In the morning they returned to Prague
Bringing his enemies with them.

They ordered an attack.
They began to stir the people up
Priests from the Týn [Church] did not hesitate
But rushed into the square with the sacrament,

---

[14] Jan Rozvoda (Rameš) of Stakor and Svojše of Zahrádka were his foremost officials, the latter serving as the regent's vice-chamberlain. On 16 April both men had been invited to dine with Zygmunt. The regent then sent them to the Prague commanders Heník of Kolštejn and Jan Smiřický with instructions but the two went instead to Rokycana.

Shouting: Good people,
They are plotting against us!
And they called to the people, saying,
They had intercepted a letter of treachery.

Víšek Polák and Šrol Jeroným
Were helping them a lot
Shouting at the crowd:
It is your life, the lives of poor people that are at stake![15]

The saints
Never lied or betrayed
When they were convinced that it was right
They did not hesitate to die for it.

And I can certainly say
About these new prophets:
If somebody wants to reproach them
Let him order their expulsion from the town.
The same thing happened
To the virtuous priests
Of St Michael and their followers
When they did not approve of this evil.[16]

They led them to the prison
Calling for their [execution by] drowning.
But then it turned out for the better
They were expelled from the town!

Whoever does not admire the priests
Is wasting his time:
Whether widow or orphan,
They have no chance of being heard, not even in the town hall.

---

[15] Víšek was a Polish baron living in Prague and Jerome was a town councillor in the Old
Town of Prague and a follower of the deceased priest Jan Želivský who had been murdered
five years earlier.

[16] The priests of the Church of St Michael in the Old Town were opposed to the arrest of
Zygmunt and rather than accept the authority of Rokycana they were expelled from Prague:
Master Křišťan of Prachatice, Jan Příbram, Petr of Mladoňovice and Prokop of Plzeň.

The brave František Šilink
Is very cautious in this matter
He trims his sails to any wind
He will never leave Rokycana![17]

Hedvika, the master tailor,
Was once a humble man
Now he only waves the mace
And lines pretence with lie.[18]

Matěj Smolař the just
Looks after orphans and widows
He interprets the law of God
And seizes their houses.[19]

The Devil himself sent us the Englishman [Peter Payne],
Stealthily he walks around Prague,
Issuing laws from England
Which are not good for Czechs.
Vavřinec fits in well with them
Correcting matters in their favour
He knows how to interpret literature
And turn truth into abuse.[20]

Štraboch would welcome peace
Because he fears for his properties
He sits hidden like a hunter
Together with his colleague Zdeněk.[21]

Then the whole community burns
And teeters as if on the sea
There is no good advice on how to resist them
Neighbour fears neighbour.

---

[17] František Šilink, councillor in the New Town of Prague and one of Zygmunt's antagonists.
[18] Václav Hedvika was an Old Town councilman in Prague.
[19] Matěj Smolař was also a councilman in the Old Town.
[20] The reference here is to Vavřinec of Březová, the Hussite chronicler.
[21] Václav Štraboch was the owner of the houses called 'At the stork' and 'At the sickle' in the Old Town Square. Zdeněk Svícník was the owner of the house of Lazarus the Jew situated behind the Church of St Nicholas in the Old Town Square.

The people are fed up
If it lasts for a long time
It will come to a bad end
If priests continue to behave like this.

Behold this, Lord God
May the people understand it quickly
So that they might take away their power
In order to avoid unreasonable actions! Amen.

Prague, National and University Library XXIII F 2, fols. 428^r–430^r.

120   Military ordinance of the Reichstag

[A meeting of the lesser nobility in Bamberg formed an alliance against the Hussites. Detailed arrangements were drawn up by the Reichstag in Frankfurt in April and May. With direct reference to the crusade, this latter meeting adopted a military ordinance similar to Žižka's. It bears the date of 4 May 1427.]

Be it known that our lords the electors, all princes, counts, barons, free knights, vassals, towns and others, wishing to strengthen the holy Christian faith, to the praise and glory of God, and preserve the holy Roman Church and comfort all Christian people, have decided to act against heretics in Bohemia and those who support them. All who wish to resist these heretics must come to Cheb or to the vicinity on Sunday, the day of SS Peter and Paul [29 June], especially the following.

The captains of the campaign, also the princes who are obliged to them may accept if they think it necessary six or more true, honest men of the other princes and lords which have come and these will determine and direct how it shall be planned and executed. They shall also manage and take charge as the occasion dictates. All who follow and come must be completely obedient and disposed to the same princes without any contradiction, without exception.

Likewise everyone shall come at their own expense without depriving other people. However, when they are not in the towns or in the field, they may obtain enough hay and straw to meet their necessities for room and board. They may obtain this where they will but it must be paid for properly according to what is determined by their captain when they make arrangements for it.

Every prince, count, baron, and town must purchase ammunition, especially those who live in the Czech land. This is essential above all things and they must be imported and all of those importing must take care to avoid damage.

Similarly, anyone who seizes or steals something belonging to another without permission shall be beheaded without mercy. Whoever conceals this shall also be subject to a penalty and this shall be carried out and no one may either resist or defy this.

In like manner, no woman or any other recruitment, whatever they are called, may be followed or withdrawn. Further, everyone must go to confession at least once a week. Every prince and captain must compel his people to do this. They must also hear Mass daily so that God may be truly and with humility served with one's whole being.

Further, whoever would purposely take issue with another on some assertion, oath or false accusation shall be flogged openly on the pillory at the mercy of the captain or shall be whipped naked for an hour.

Also, whoever would take his sword, knife, axe, or other weapon out against another, without cause, shall have his hand cut off without mercy. Should he wound someone additionally he shall be beheaded.

Also, if there are quarrels, dissensions or attacks among the princes, lords, towns or any others, then the chief captains may appoint other princes who are not involved in it or such captains might delegate themselves to intervene if they do not wish to hand the affair over to others. They would have to judge such matters and what they adjudicate should be upheld and observed.

Also, no one must go to procure food or feed unless they are so instructed and have the banner which is sent at the command of the captain. No one shall undertake to burn or [launch an] assault without the direction of the captain or the banner which has been determined for that.

No one must put to death any person without due cause unless they are one of those heretics or someone who supports them. In that case, their throats may be cut. Further, when the captains extend safe conduct by their authority to any person it must be observed by all persons on pain of the aforementioned penalty.

Further, anyone who is directed by the captains or on their authority to stand watch or guard or move out must do so without refusal. Likewise, no one must go ahead or lag behind unless directed to do so by command of the captain. When one is directed to go ahead or stay behind or draw out the attack, escape, or stand, at the order of the captain, one must do so obediently.

Every elector and city must provide stone-cutters, carpenters, warriors, guns, gunpowder, stone, ammunition, battering rams, ladders and other commodities.

Likewise, every elector must send 200 armed men on foot or by wagon from his towns, with the exception of the archbishops of Trier and Cologne which must supply 100 armed men.

Similarly, the electors shall march in from one side (i.e. Bohemia), the duke of Saxony on the other side, those of Silesia on a third front, while the duke of Austria on the fourth. All of them must set off on the same day.

Further, the Bohemian lords, as well as others there, who have remained faithful must be summoned and asked if they would like to participate in this campaign and join us with their forces.

Similarly, all of the armies must wait for the orders of the captain under whom they serve before they march out and they must be obedient to this. If the same forces get into trouble and are in need of assistance then they shall send a message and following this the captains shall come to their aid with advice at full speed.

Likewise, every lord shall provide for his own people so that no one, either lord or vassal, has more than one assistant unless such a one is a prince, count or knight. Further, he is to see to it that this agreement is declared to everyone not once but three or four times or as often as there is need in order that it might be followed and that everyone knows how to conform to it and does not violate it.

In like manner, every lord shall vow and likewise provide guarantees that all those in his army shall swear to his captain to keep all of the articles of this agreement faithfully and honourably on pain of a penalty.

The towns, villages, territories, goods and roads belonging to all of the princes, counts, lords, knights, vassals, and of every city, especially of those who are affiliated with us in these matters, are to be maintained, secured and undamaged by all in whatever state, rank, or character as they might be. If someone were injured by this, we, the electors, princes, lords, and cities shall in one accord, help and advise against the one who has caused the damage so that the one injured receives proper restitution and compensation. We shall consider those delinquent to be banned people and in no case offer them pardon of our own will or allow them to be protected. They shall be pursued in life and in goods as an evil and marked person.

Further, every lord, city and all others shall keep the peace and undertake no attack. No prince or lord or city may excuse himself by exceptions in order to avoid the campaign or through some other neglect or by lack of will in the matter because the campaign must take full priority.

Also, the lords, with the help of the cities, shall guarantee that when they march out the next castle or town lying within the land of Bohemia shall be occupied and prepared for a daily war by the Christians in order that there be sufficient supplies and that there will be no support for the needs of the heretics.

Also, every bishop shall require that all religious and secular people shall serve God together on the same day of the week and those who are not so inclined shall have a stiff penance placed upon them.

Likewise, no prince or lord shall in any way patronize or attempt to protect or shelter any goods, villages, or territories in the land of Bohemia, or allow any of his people to do so. Neither shall they attempt to take preference before the others in terms of food or feed or in any other consideration. Should someone find feed or food he may take that for his needs but also share it.

Also, no one is to look for provisions in any way except by the order of the captain. Then some shall be sent by all the lords so that all may be shared fairly.

Also, when any castle, town, village or fortress is conquered, or surrenders, all things must proceed according to the decisions of the captains and to those who have been sent and in agreement with the majority.

Similarly, whatever is gained or captured by anyone in the field, who has come at his lord's expense in terms of wages and allowance, must be handed over to the lord without hesitation. Whatever is captured by knights or vassals or the cities who have marched to Bohemia at their own expense may retain what is taken for themselves or they can dispense with it according to their own wishes.

Further, anyone who wishes to leave the army must obtain from the captain a proper declaration or letter. Also, anyone who becomes a criminal, swindler, offender, or deserter must receive no recognition in the land, in towns, villages, or the territories of any lord, anywhere, but shall be brought to account according to the nature of the penalty as it has been written above.

Further, the two lords and archbishops of Trier and Cologne must bring with them four large cannon,[22] twenty other cannon and each of them 10,000 bullets and 200 fire arrows[23] and gunpowder along with stone[24] and tools according to the need and each shall supply three master gunners.[25]

Also, the archbishop of Mainz, six chamber cannon, thirty main cannon, four other cannon, 10,000 bullets, stone and equipment according to the need as well as 200 fire arrows and three master gunners.

Also, the count Palatine of the Rhine shall bring, or send, just as much as the archbishop of Mainz and in addition one great stone-cannon which shoots one and a half quintal along with three master gunners.

Further, the margrave of Brandenburg one great stone-cannon, four fort-cannon, 10,000 bullets, 200 fire arrows, powder, stone, and other needs as well as one master gunner.

Likewise, the barons of Bavaria in low countries, one stone-cannon, which shoots two quintal, four small stone-cannon, twenty-two main-cannon, 10,000 bullets, 200 fire arrows, powder, stone and other adequate necessities and tools together with his master gunners.

---

[22] Cannon used against fortifications. In Czech these were called *houfnice*, in German *Karrenbüchsen*. There were of course even larger calibre cannon than these.

[23] These were the frequently used incendiary weapons employed against flammable roofs of buildings or wooden battlements, but not Greek fire.

[24] Cannon-balls.

[25] Men trained specifically in firing the cannon.

Also, the bishops of Bamberg and Würzburg must bring a small gun as well as a large gun with ammunition, powder and other tools, such as they have, and each of them three master gunners.

Likewise, the city of Nürnberg, one great stone-cannon, which shoots two quintal, six small stone-cannon, twelve fort-cannon, sixty main cannon, 20,000 bullets, 600 fire arrows, and tools as needed along with six master gunners.

Also, Regensburg shall bring one great stone-cannon, and four small guns, powder, munitions and tools according to capacity along with master gunners.

In like manner, Cheb, one stone-cannon and some guns, powder, munitions and equipment according to their ability with their master gunners.

Similarly, those of Loket [Elbogen], the burgrave and the town must come with their force and bring one great stone-cannon and other great and small guns, powder, stone and munitions, with tools, as they are able, and master gunners.

Also, every city must have guns, powder, stone, and equipment according to their ability. Likewise, if any significant defects are detected in this agreement, they must be amended by the captains of the campaign.

Further, the three archbishops of Mainz, Cologne and Trier must personally join the campaign. The archbishop of Cologne should be a captain, if he does not come then the archbishop of Trier or if neither of them is able to come then the archbishop of Mainz must be so and remain as such. If none of them are able to come and then none can be captain, then it shall be one or more of the secular princes according to the need and they shall then submit to one captain. Whoever becomes captain, the others must agree to this and submit themselves to the agreed upon captain without dissent.

UB 1: 503–9.

121   Reichstag initiatives for the fourth crusade

[The strategy underpinning the fourth crusade called for the assembling of four armies to simultaneously attack the heretics from four directions. One army consisted of forces from the Rhineland, Alsace, Swabia, Franconia and Bavaria, another of the Saxons, a third of the Silesians and the fourth was assembled from the Habsburgs and the archbishopric of Salzburg. This strategy was never fully implemented. The plan emerged from the Frankfurt Reichstag in the spring 1427.]

By the grace of God, the electors of the Holy Roman Empire, Conrad, archbishop of Mainz, Otto, archbishop of Trier, Dietrich, archbishop of Cologne, Ludwig, palsgrave of the Rhine and duke of Bavaria, Friedrich, duke of Saxony and margrave of Meißen and Friedrich, margrave of Brandenburg and burgrave of Nürnberg, send favourable greetings.

Dear, wise, honourable colleagues. In times past and even now you have been aware of the significant injury and desecration which the Hussites and Czech heretics have with great malice caused to the sacred faith of Christians as well as Christendom through the shedding of the blood of Christians, the burning and otherwise destruction of churches, monasteries as well as priests. Without ceasing they have blasphemed almighty God, our Lord Jesus Christ, his beloved mother Mary, the hosts of heaven, the holy church, the blessed Christian faith, all of Christendom, the holy sacrament, the crucifix as well as all other images with wanton contempt. It is dreadful that they persist in this all the more as time goes on. This they do to the destruction of their own souls and all of those who believe in Christ must now resolve to put an end to it. We have taken the step of discussing these matters at length with the princely electors of the Holy Roman Empire and other imperial officials along with King Sigismund at whose order and suggestion we did so.

We called other princes, counts, barons, knights, vassals and towns to join with us. However, inasmuch as we are sinners, along with other Christians, this has caused nothing to have been done in terms of punishing and exterminating the aforementioned heresy and wickedness. At this time, according to the dating of the letter, we have gathered together in Frankfurt many personally present and others who could not come have sent representatives, either appointed friends or councillors. The prince lord Duke Albrecht of Austria, the advisors and associates of the Silesian lords, the cities of Wrocław, Cheb [Eger] and elsewhere have come together with numerous other lords, counts and princes of the holy empire and we have discussed at length taking advice from these as well as other advisors here present. We have come to an agreement to mount an expedition of force into the Czech land in opposition to the Hussites and heretics to take action toward their retribution and this for the praise and glory of almighty God, the heavenly queen, the beloved Mother of God and the whole host of heaven. [This expedition is also aimed at the] strengthening and benefit of the holy church, the Christian faith, all of Christendom as well as His Grace, the lord King of the Romans and the Holy Roman Empire.

We have outlined the expedition as follows. On the feast day of the apostles SS Peter and Paul we will march into the Czech land against the heretics with four armies from four directions in four different places. The prince-electors, counts, lords, other princes and towns of the holy empire from the Rhine area, Alsace, Franconia, Swabia and Bavaria shall be in one place. Friedrich, duke of Saxony and margrave of Meißen with others shall assemble in another area. The Silesian lords, princes and towns in another place. Lord Albrecht, duke of Austria with the people of the king of the Romans, His Grace our lord, along with the bishop of

Salzburg and others shall assemble in another area. With this plan the heretics may be attacked and punished in a way that ought to put an end to their wantonness and wickedness for all time. This we hope and trust almighty God for. You will understand that all of those who believe in Christ must contribute, without coercion, to these godly plans and campaigns with the assistance of supplies as well as counsel. To this end we make urgent request to you as faithful Christians that you support the expedition as fully as possible and to best of your ability with equipment, arms and troops.

On the feast day of the apostles SS Peter and Paul [29 June] you must come to Nürnberg and gather there in that vicinity with all the people, the princes, counts, barons and all of the believers in Christ. Please come on time. Together we shall march from that place, in keeping with the plan, into Bohemia to undertake the destruction and extermination of heresy. Everyone should look to this matter as faithfully as possible without delay or neglect for the praise and glory of almighty God, his mother Mary and all the hosts of heaven and for the strengthening and benefit of the holy church, the Christian faith, all of Christendom as well as His Grace, the lord King of the Romans and the Holy Roman Empire. Allow nothing to prevent this for in consequence you will obtain from almighty God an everlasting reward as well as the gratitude and honouring of all Christendom. A map has been drawn up of the arrangements for this campaign and a copy is being sent to you for your information.

Given at Frankfurt on the Sunday in which we sing the Misericordia domini in the holy church [second Sunday after Easter]. To our very beloved, wise and worthy mayor and town council of Passau.

DR 9: 41–44.

122   A papal nuncio appeals to the 'lost sheep' of Bohemia

[Henry Beaufort was appointed by Martin V on 18 March 1427 as papal legate for Germany, Hungary and Bohemia and nuncio for the fourth crusade replacing Giordano Orsini. Beaufort would have no more success than his predecessor but it is of note that he undertook a different tact with the Hussites. The following letter, written to the Praguers on 18 July 1427, avoids the use of threat, coercion and all vitriolic language. There is an edition of the letter in František M. Bartoš, 'An English Cardinal and the Hussite Revolution' CV 6 (No. 1, 1963), pp. 52–4.]

Henry, by divine permission, cardinal of England and bishop of Winchester. Little children, of whom I am in the pains of childbirth until Christ is reformed in you [Galatians 4:19]. Grace to you and peace from the one who being born gave peace to all people of good will and being immortal died for the people and left his peace to the faithful. How many times has the sower of weeds and the seducer of the entire world, detesting the great magnificence of the king of peace, divided the temple of the Lord since the beginning of the early church? How many times has the fury of war invaded the peace of the Christian people? We are unable to narrate it without our heart groaning and our minds galled. Alas, the world, already growing old perhaps will not endure the ancient lies of his deceit to which the latest divisions have added additional miseries. Alas, his fury has [already] slain many sinners with more to come at dawn anticipating the chains of the darkening age and the destruction of the real Lucifer. Then we, to whom the end of the ages has already come, constrained by the dignity of the assumed order and urged by an ardent flame of the apostolic legation to all of Germany and the kingdoms of Hungary and Bohemia, desire and wish especially for the peace of those to whom we have been sent. The author of peace not only attests but also commands those entering the house to first offer peace to the sons of peace [Luke 10:5]. Therefore, we offer to you the gift of peace. May you not reject it. We invite you to general unity. May you come. May you see that the most blessed father and shepherd of the church militant loves you with great desire and how that by numerous means his most holy legation has been called up to this by him. May you regard the holy mother church as opening her arms to you and may you regard us, however small compared to those great, and our zeal and how we act for your benefit in the way of peace having neither spared nor sparing grace, resources or efforts in this matter. If this does not move you, may your hearts be moved at least by the spilling of human blood which is certainly going to happen. Of course if you remain alone and separated from the others you will provoke all of the Christian powers and princes to exterminate your community which we regret to report will happen. We advise you to return, we require you to do so and we extend the arm of humanity as far as possible. The dwelling of Christ will not be gripped by any anxiety if you enter considering how that in former times the Kingdom of Bohemia and its neighbouring areas shone and through its far-flung reputation to all those situated around them brought forth the light of admirable life and the examples of the most obedient behaviour. Now this reputation is failing and the standards of the kingdom and empire while persisting to the present is undermined and the order of spiritual and secular authority is dissolved. Do not allow in these times this region which for so long was practically the teacher of virtue to become the cultivator of errors in such a lethal manner.

But we have all made mistakes and each of us have gone away from the path of the Lord. Nevertheless, as others revert, may you also return as sons and assume the form of the penitent so that the good shepherd might find the lost sheep [John 10:1–16] and the neighbouring people might rejoice in the return of them and human and angelic voices might applaud the penitents. As much as we are able, we would set the virtue and the desire for the reduction and reformation of the Lord's flock from all areas, may God give witness to our conscience. Concerning the present matters, we expect a kind response from your people and we pray that your hearts might be inspired by the great Comforter so that the woman bearing you, namely the holy mother church, being prostrate during this birth might rejoice so that we remaining within the only fold of Christ might in one accord praise and glorify with one mouth the one shepherd even the God and father of our Lord Jesus Christ. Written in Nürnberg on the eighteenth day of the month of July in the year of the Lord 1427.

Prague Castle Archive MS. A 59.3 fols. 208^v–209^v.

123   Heinrich of Stöffel reports on crusade preparations

[Heinrich of Stöffel made this report to the city of Ulm just before the siege of Tachov. He comments on the march to Bohemia, the negotiations among the princes, the relative power of the crusading armies as well as the spirit and attitude within the army of the bishop of Trier. There is further detail about a dispute among the mercenaries. The report is dated 20 July 1427.]

My willing and friendly service as before, Discreet and wise [men]. I wish to let you know that my lord Duke Hans and Duke Otto marched through the forest, we were with them, on St Margaret's Day [20 July]. My lord, the bishop of Trier, marched through in the direction of Tachov on the previous Friday with those from Nürnberg. Thereafter all of the lords and people set off from Tachov on Saturday and marched toward Planá where we set up in the field. There the lords ordered a march on the following Tuesday which brought us within eyeshot of Stříbro. There was Master Hans with a battalion of sixty horse and Master Hans was of the opinion that this Stříbro could be conquered as well if the cannon were used against it but the barons had few of them. Nevertheless the first soldiers of Duke Hans came as well as those of Nürnberg and of Regensburg and they had some cannon. Furthermore, as I understand it, we have thus far been welcomed here and no one has made any effort to treat us with iniquity in any way. Also, when I arrived in Nürnberg, I consented with the advisor of the lord of Württemberg to march with them. I went to Duke Otto and told him that we wished to join the battalion of His Grace and that of his brother. This we did and so my lord Duke Hans led the banner of St George through the forest. Much was said about this but nonetheless it was accomplished inasmuch as we Swabians wished to have the banner of St George and so the bishop of Augsburg and the advisor of my lordship and the Swabians agreed that we wished to remain with it.

This came to pass and was graciously permitted. There is nothing else to write about. Given on Sunday before the day of St James in the year 1427.

[These details follow] So the three princes decided on the captains, namely, the bishop of Trier put forth one captain by the name of Friedrich of Stein. Duke Hans put forth another, that of Labern while Duke Otto that of Weinsberg. Then the lords together with the army had to be divided into three parts. Those of Nürnberg are with those of Trier. Those from Regensburg with Duke Hans. The bishop of Speyer and of Augsburg, together with the battalion of my lord of Württemberg and me with your battalion and the German master [of the Order of the Knights] with Duke Otto. Then the margrave [of Brandenburg] separated from the lords of Weiden because he, together with the bishops of Würzburg and Bamberg, wanted to march on to Cheb and wished to join with the lords of Plavno on the following Saturday though the margrave has not yet come. Meanwhile we wanted to take Stříbro but then a message from the margrave of Brandenburg arrived. The young duke of Saxony did not think he meant to effect this and in fact planned to retreat if the margrave of Brandenburg did not join him. Additionally, a letter of warning came to him that the heretics wanted to assault Karlštejn. He intended then to turn against the enemy and with many clever words tried to persuade the lords to do this also. But the young duke of Saxony, on the contrary, did not draw back. So the princes sent for all the captains with this news and asked for their advice. Then the advisor of my lord and the bishop of Augsburg, along with myself, gave this counsel. We should march on towards him halfway and also turn against the enemy and commend him [the margrave of Brandenburg] to come to us and unite together on the matter of which direction the march should take. They did not like this, but they remained there so that my lord of Trier and Duke Otto had to ride to him in Teplá and commend the margrave to come there. Meanwhile we remained still while it was decided what else should be done.

The bishop of Augsburg and the councillor of my lord and I regarded this as a very bad thing that the lords were not united. It was much discussed as well as the agreement made in Frankfurt that every lord should remain in his place and keep in mind his area but the lords have not come forward yet. Also I should let you know that we have a very small battalion and I think that my lord Duke Otto has about 500 cavalry together with that of Speyer. My lord of Württemberg has a good brigade but I would guess that it is not more than 300 horse or thereabouts. The bishop of Augsburg has about one hundred horse and the German lords [the Order of the Knights] have about 130. Those of Nürnberg have about 130 or perhaps a few more, so it is said, those of Regensburg have about fifty as do those of Augsburg having about fifty and the same for us. They want us to remain with them but I cannot write anything about that yet. The bishop of Constance is said to have about fifty and beyond this there is no one else of the lords or from the cities to write about save for a romantic bishop of Besançon. I have heard that there is no one with the margrave save for the two bishops of Würzburg and Bamberg. The schedule and the letter have been written. The lords have returned from Teplá and sent for everyone and reported that there had been no envoy of the margrave to give account. So they held a council and this advice emerged: they would send another legate to the margrave in order that he might come to them and they were united on this for the benefit of Christendom and the common good. So they sent the bishop of Speyer and a representative of the bishop of Trier to him to admonish him to undertake the march on their behalf. I am not sure where they went except that they were to meet in the vicinity of Švamberk.

Meanwhile we are to march on farther this Sunday and the lords intend to go to Stříbro because then the margrave will have returned. It is then intended, but I do not know much about it, to run and attack Stříbro on Tuesday before St Jakob's Day. However, I cannot write anything except that we only have a small battalion and that the bishop of Trier is said to have as many as 700 horse. Duke Hans is reported to also have 700 horse or perhaps more, so it is said. Now I cannot write you anything more because we have heard absolutely nothing about the heretics and I have already written so much. It is thought that Stříbro will resist but that there are many Christians inside. If they were persuaded they might surrender, but I do not know how it will transpire but some say that those of Klenové are inside with 500 servants but others say that he is outside. I do not know anything else but if it were arranged it would be good if we had not gone there. It seems to me that the princes wish the same thing as does the advisor of my lord. I am afraid that if the margrave and the two bishops do not come to us then we will have to return home soon but only if Duke Heinrich of Bavaria comes. It is said that he is coming with a powerful force of 300 lancers. I do not know if this is true. Also the bishop of Constance has fifty horse and when I closed the letter I went to my lord Duke Hans and he told me that the margrave rode to the duke of Saxony and he meant that he wanted to go personally and also to bring the duke to us.

[Following this report of the dispute between the crusaders the following status is given.] Also, I should let you know that the margrave of Brandenburg and the two bishops of Würzburg and Bamberg also have no more than 1,500 horse or so it is said.

Further, the captain [Heinrich of Stöffel] has nineteen horse, master Felber has two horse, Buhler has four horse, Jörg of Rietthain has four horse, Jörge Schilling has four horse, Hörlinger has four horse, Wolf of Asch has four horse, Hölenstein has four horse, Conrad Eckinger has four horse: Ulm. Hans Rott of Aulun has four horse, Ulrich of Baißwil has five horse: Kempten. Those of Bopfingen have three horse, from Nördlingen Hans of Lierhain, Lutz of Zipplingen, Jerome of Böppfinger and Hans Haintzel have eighteen horse. For Gmünd, Eberhard of Freiberg has six horse and for Giengen, Conrad of Sunthain has four horse. Eberhard of Rischach, Hans Warthauser, Conrad Ottmar has fourteen horse:

Bibrach. Ulrich Beßerer has four horse: Pullendorf. Steuber Ulrich with Johannes has six horse: Ravensburg. Those from Isne have six horse. Hans Mellinger, Märklin of Hausen, Conrad Ungelter have twelve horse: Rüttlingen. Albrecht Tumme, Albrecht of Bergwangen, Werner and Hans of Neuhausen, Rutger Staiglin have twenty seven horse: Esslingen. Heinrich of Althain has nine horse: Dinckelsbühl, Ulrich Türlacher, Anthony Stuber have eight horse: Kaufbeuren. Hans of Hohenried, Ulrich Scharenstetter, Hans Keller, Huninger have twenty four horse: Memmingen. Those of [Schwäbisch] Hall have ten horse and joined with me, arriving late, on the Saturday before St Jakob. Those from Wil have four horse and they likewise came late on the Saturday before St Jakob. Those of Leutkirch have one horse.

DR 9: 51–4.

124   Crusaders and heretics clash at Stříbro and Tachov

[The fourth crusader invasion was set for July 1427. Only two of the four proposed armies actually materialized. One, led by Otto, archbishop-elector of Trier, marched into Bohemia near Tachov and moved in the direction of Stříbro (see map 2). A protracted siege was raised against that town. The whole enterprise was another crusader failure. The crusaders attempted to utilize a large number of Hussite-style war wagons based upon information supplied by spies. The operation collapsed in the face of the Hussite onslaught. The papal legate for the crusade, Henry Beaufort, arrived late and was met at Tachov by the crusaders in full flight. He planted the cross in front of them and ordered their halt. It worked momentarily, but when they saw the Hussites coming in force they again fled. Beaufort tore the imperial banner to pieces and threw it to the ground. Crusaders tried to run for Germany through the mountain forests into the upper Palatinate, but were cut down relentlessly. The Augsburg Chronicle puts the number of dead crusaders at 100,000. That figure is greatly inflated. The crusaders were not pursued over the border. Instead, Prokop Holý turned to take Tachov. Second only to Plzeň, Tachov was a strong royalist position in western Bohemia and as such functioned as a convenient base for crusades. Siege artillery was used as well as incendiary missiles. In less than a week Tachov fell, on 14 August, to the Hussites. See map 3.]

From Žlutice. In the year of the Lord 1427 the margraves with the people from Meißen and those of Brandenburg, the landgrave of Thuringia, the duke of Bavaria Hans, Friedrich the landgrave, with the other princes, the count of Schwarzburg, the bishops of Mainz, Trier, Bamberg and Würzburg and many other bishops and princes with the people from the imperial cities came into Bohemia in the week following the feast of the apostles SS Peter and Paul [29 June]. They came to the town of Žlutice from where Jakoubek, the captain of the Wyclifites, and his collaborators had fled because they were fearful. The Germans entered the town and returned it to Lord Aleš of Šternberk, also of Holice. On Wednesday before St James they surrounded the town of Stříbro which had been gained that same year, before the carnival, by Přibík of Klenové and the people of Zmrzlík [of Svojšín] who, at night, scaled the walls and then with the same Přibík and 200 cavalry, and other helpers, bombarded the town with large cannon.

The Praguers, together with the priest Prokop and the other groups of the Táborites and Orphans and their captains and assistants, among whom were no significant barons, gathered up to 1,500 cavalry and 16,000 foot soldiers from the towns and villages together with their wagons and cannon. They marched against the aforementioned princes who were said to have more than 80,000 cavalry and as many or more foot soldiers. With the German side were the lords Krušina of Švamberk, Vilém of Švihov and other knights and warriors from the district of Plzeň and people from Plzeň and Tachov. When the aforementioned Táborites and Praguers had drawn to within three miles or so of the Germans, those princes mentioned previously rushed off from Stříbro in the direction of Bavaria. During this flight the princes mentioned earlier lost the great cannon of the lord King Sigismund which had been lent to the people of Plzeň in Tachov. They returned home alone with their wagons through the forest.

It was said that among them was present the cardinal [Henry Beaufort] appointed by the lord pope with orders to proceed with them into the field of battle against the heretics and Wyclifites. This cardinal unfurled and raised the banner before them, to be certain the banners of the pope, the empire and the crusade, during the flight to escape, endeavouring to encourage them not to flee and admonished them with many words. At length seeing that he could not prevail he tore down the banner and threw it to the ground in front of the Germans whom he cursed, and not just a little. One of the knights named Kamrovec [said]: 'I do not know from whom we are fleeing, I do not see any enemy.' Thus they rode with lord Vilém of Švihov into Tachov. This occurred after St James [25 July].

Then on the Monday following the feast of James, the aforementioned Táborites with the Praguers came to Tachov and made a circuit around that town and made camp there for several days, but not for a whole week. They bombarded the town with fire from their catapults and set the town ablaze. Having dug tunnels under the walls they violently invaded the town and killed the previously mentioned knight, Kamrovec with fifty of his companions, both German and Czech, in the streets. Then the aforementioned lord Vilém of Švihov with lord Jindřich [of Jivjany], who was called Žito, with their squires and people escaped into the castle. There they defended themselves for three days until 900 of them surrendered to military capture.

They obtained there the great cannon called Chmelík. After many days the aforesaid lord Vilém and Master Arnošt and twenty-two of them escaped from captivity. They went to Roupov Castle and the lord of the castle made an agreement with the Táborites and they joined their camps and went with them. Then they moved towards the town of Plzeň. Not being able to take it they reached an armistice which lasted until the feast of St George [23 April].

Chronicle of Bartošek of Drahonice, in FRB 5: 596–7.

125   Poem on the fourth crusade

[This lengthy verse is a lament on the disunity, failure and, as the author characterizes, disgrace of the crusade armies. The poem puts the defeat down almost entirely to the internal squabbling among the crusader princes. The Hussites are mentioned only in passing but they never figure in this interpretation of the fourth crusade. The author of the verse is Hans Rosenblüt, a Nürnberg poet and war reporter who wrote as though he were an eyewitness.]

O eternal God, may you be gracious
And hear the worried complaint of we poor people
The plaintive and woeful heartache
Of what has happened to poor Christians
In the land of Bohemia.

Many nobles, princes and brave knights
Conducted themselves disgracefully
When they rode before Stříbro to attack and fight for the name of Christ
The devil seduced them and sowed his seed
Into the counsel of the wise princes!

It [the town of Stříbro] should have been attacked and taken easily
But they could not agree
Everyone wanted to take the town for himself
Even before it was conquered.

Afterwards one wise prince remembered
That they should not pray and expect more
They should use the cannon on the wagons

To break down the resistance of the walls
In order to reduce the number of defenders inside
This happened in three days.

Then it has been truly said
The Hussites marched against them there
With great ambition
Intending to strike them all down to death
This came to the attention of the princes
They began to be troubled and afraid.

Then they sent the one of Plavno [Heinrich]
To see how many there were
This he did willingly with gladness
He rode without delay night and day.

In the meanwhile one fellow suggested
That they should construct a wagon-fortress
In which to overwhelm the Hussites
Hearing this, it got under their skin.

Then all the princes became foolish
And began to flee before seeing the enemy
Should not God disregard them
Even though they had come on account of God?
These pious ones sought further
How everyone might fill his purse.

Therefore we must pray to God
Not to punish Christendom because of this
Many princes fled disgracefully
They all became unfaithful to God
So much so that the Hussites mocked them
[Saying] How they trusted in God and the angels!

Then I saw many people on foot
Wishing to save their lives
And desiring shelter
They fled as far away as Tachov
There I saw many men and women
Lamenting and crying with great woe.

I do not understand what the princes mean
That they camped in the field
But afterward left their tents again
And gathered together for counsel.

The cardinal [Henry Beaufort] ordered them there
That they should return again
He commanded with faith and honour
That all princes, lords, knights and vassals
Should contend with the Hussites.

Who wishes to remain with God
And help drive out the Hussites?
[Beaufort] cried out in a woeful voice
There he admonished the princes to such an extent
That they gathered together again
Advising each other they became unified
[Saying] no one should go home again
To this they affirmed their faith with an oath.

Those born of noble stock
Should remain here
And help in expelling the Hussites
This was the council of one prince.

'It seems to me a good idea
That we march on again
Burn down everything with roof, frame and gable
And cause such smoke in the land
That their resistance would break down.'

All of the princes liked this very much
And all said: 'this is just our thing'
They swore together with their lives
That they wished to march on again
Not staying two nights in any place.

The cardinal liked this very much saying
'I must help with body, goods and all my might
Day and night I want to be ready
To die and to be together with you!

'I need neither shield nor armour
I wish to be in the vanguard
When you march onwards again.'
All of the princes agreed.

Then they caused a herald to proclaim
To all the tents and huts
When the trumpets blew on the morrow
Everyone was to make ready
Expecting the supreme princes and prepared to follow their lords
Who wished to turn towards Bohemia once more.

In the morning when they should have ridden out
There was horror and terror among the princes
Such that they secretly overturned their plans
But only gathered to themselves more shame.

The cardinal fell pained and said:
'Let it be damned forever by God that ever I entered this land!
Now the pious ones will be overcome
Christendom will become as small as a dwarf!'

The he rode out from them onto a hill
And raised up the Roman banner and said:
'Whoever rides away from here today
Will forfeit the name of Christ
And was never born a noble!

'Whoever wants to be a pious Christian today
And free his soul from the pain of hell
Will come here under this banner
Thus it will be seen who is a pious Christian!'

This plaintive cry and clamour
Was heard by the counts, princes and freemen
All these turned around again because they heard his plaintive cry
Which sounded far and wide
Then they rode toward the cardinal and talked with him.

One knight said: 'If God does not avenge us for our needless and disgraceful flight
Then it would not be a true God

When we will be faithless to him today
And still we all wish to be Christians!
How can we keep the Christian order?
Let it be damned by God that I ever became a knight!'

The noble and precious blood of Saxony
Who grew up into nobility
The one I wish to praise with my tongue
That young noble prince of Saxony.[26]

He said to the princes, knights and vassals:
'Whoever wants to dismount and fight on foot
I wish to be at the front with him.
I would rather never have been born
Then to forsake the poor people like this
Who came with us here on foot.'

Therefore he desired from all the lords
That everyone should saddle his horse
Half a mile from him
So that no one should take to flight
When it came to [a time of] real necessity
In this way the rich had to remain with the poor.

But one prince said
(I shall not name him but God knows who he is)
'No, I do not want to dismount for a man can lag behind easily
And be captured quite unworthily!
A bird can be taken with ease when it loses its wings!'

Then the young [prince] of Saxony said again:
'The one who wants to do battle on horse
Is the one who always intends to ride away
When he is fearful for his life
Such a one intends to take flight with shame!'

After the words of both
The cardinal took the Roman banner

---

[26] Friedrich (II) of Saxony, son of the Saxon elector Friedrich who was ill and did not participate in the crusade.

And gave it to one of the lords commending him with faith and honour
That they should march again into the land.

This one was Duke Johannes[27]
He wanted to do his best fulfilling this obligation
So that God would hear the pious ones
The right time has not yet come!

Then one prince there on the journey
Whose name might have been Neithart said:
'Could no one else be found than this fellow?
Could there be anyone found more noble than me to take the banner?'

Many came to Duke Johannes
He became angry and very upset and said:
'Does everyone envy me because of this?
I mean, we should all be brothers.

'It seemed to me in my heart
That there would be no faith among us
Envy and hate always avert us!'
Then he threw the banner away
Thus the expedition against the Hussites ended.

Then the lords fled
Everyone tried secretly to turn back
So they tried to hunt the animals
Which are the Hussites which they killed.

Then I saw Friedrich the Margrave of Brandenburg begin to weep
And the sorrowful cardinal
Whose tears flowed down to the valley
Because of his great heartache.

I said: 'If as many prostitutes had been sent to the land of Bohemia
As the men which were sent
They would have worked out a plan
And conquered Stříbro and defeated those inside
Who would not tolerate the Christian faith.

---

27 Elector-Palsgrave Johannes of Neumarkt, a young and zealous anti-Hussite crusader.

How should I praise the princes?
Their fame I would like to gladly show
But I have not seen one of them
To whom I can render praise.

Is it not a great disrepute
That all of the princes withdrew from the land
Before they had won any castle or town?
I am afraid they have stretched out a clothesline
Upon which lament and heartache are hung.

Mother Mary, pure virgin
May you look down upon our distress
Bring peace to the defeated
May you pray to God the Lord for us
That he would grant grace to his Christian army
So that we might not multiply our sins
And drown in the false faith!

When the enemy wishes to steal our souls
May you revive us, Eternal father, with the hosts of heaven.
Send upon us divine favour
Do not take vengeance upon us for our guilt
Which we carry from place to place.

Lord, may your blood cleanse us
May you lift us from the filth of sin
For this I pray the Lord Jesus Christ
Through your fatherly goodness.

Hans Rosenblüt has thus written.

Liliencron 1: 296–9.

126   Friedrich of Brandenburg's report to Sigismund

[Following the crusader defeat at Stříbro and Tachov, the supreme commander of
the crusade sent the following report, dated 24 August 1427, to the emperor. The
communication was written at Plassenburg Castle in the principality of Bayreuth.]

To the most serene prince and graceful dear lord. My prompt submission and obedient service is ready for Your Grace as before.

The most gracious lord. When Your Grace wrote to me, sending a message and requiring through Lord Michael, provost of Boleslav, your proto-notary, to proceed with all other princes, lords and cities against the unfaithful ones in Bohemia because an assembly in Frankfurt should be called later, a common declaration was made to draw together at once. As required by Your Grace, I promptly obeyed with great steadiness and with reference to the announcement as Your Grace may have been informed principally by the aforementioned Lord Michael and perhaps might know well from the writ of the announcement itself. I wish to make Your Grace to know that when such a campaign was announced and decided upon in Frankfurt, I dispatched myself with all my power in person for the praise of Almighty God and for the honour and service of Your Grace and Christendom. I drew together with my lords and special friends, the bishop of Bamberg and of Würzburg, to Cheb where we remained some days in order to find and determine which places the other princes, lords and cities intended to gather to invade Bohemia.[28] When I discovered that my lords the archbishop of Trier, the bishop of Speyer, the bishop of Augsburg, my uncle Johannes and Duke Otto of Bavaria, together with some imperial cities were near Weiden, I rode there personally to meet them and there took counsel. The aforementioned princes, lords and cities marched into Bohemia in the direction of Tachov and the lords of Bamberg and Würzburg and I went towards Ostrov [on the Ohře River] with a considerable number. In the meanwhile, the aforementioned lords of Bamberg and Würzburg and I undertook a mission of importance to our uncle the duke of Saxony to admonish him and to plead with him to dispose himself together with his people in the direction of Mašťov in order that we might all proceed together farther and thus become even stronger. However, he sent back a message that all the princes, lords and cities allied with him according to the announcement had renounced him entirely because they did not wish to deal and negotiate with him with respect to Bohemia and beyond this he was in such illness that he could not have marched himself though he wished to send his eldest son [Friedrich II] with his people and force to us near Kadaň. Therefore, we lords rode ourselves towards Kadaň and farther in the direction of Žlutice with the mission that we lords wished to unite all together in order to march more powerfully and more securely.

---

[28] Friedrich's actions and motivations are subtle at this stage and he is not being entirely forthright with the emperor. He had deliberately ignored the decision of the diet at Frankfurt for the crusade armies to gather at Nürnberg. Friedrich's principal loyalty was not to the Reichstag but to the proclamation made by the Franconian knights on 15 January 1427. See doc.117 which called for the crusaders to gather at Cheb.

During our riding and mission, back and forth, the aforementioned princes, my lord of Trier, my uncle of Bavaria and the others with them, moved towards Stříbro, an announcement and action which I disapproved of as well as my other lords and associates. However, we put it aside for the profit and honour of Christendom and of Your Grace and we trusted in God that if such advice did not occur that such matters might have turned out for the good. Then proposals from Stříbro arrived and we were admonished by the aforementioned princes and lords to draw towards them. We did not desire to refuse them our assistance on account of the other lords' fear of defeat, and so we worked farther towards our uncle of Saxony, the young one, and towards his captains in order to come on towards Stříbro. After this, my brother-in-law, Duke Heinrich came to the same place and camped some days. During this time, it happened that some weakness [occurred] in my body and I was advised and ordered by that one of Trier [Archbishop Otto], who was also here, and by other associates, to go to Tachov to the doctor for my restoration and then later follow them and to leave the one of Plavno [i.e. Heinrich] who was in Bohemia with me, with my other advisors and people with the army before Stříbro. Meanwhile, the aforenamed barons and associates sent out spies to determine whether the enemy wanted to draw out the forces or attack us. Then the warning and also the report reached them that the enemy had been reinforced and was approaching. Consequently, my previously mentioned barons and associates who remained before Stříbro dispatched [Heinrich of] Plavno with 300 horsemen to observe the enemy and after him my brother-in-law, Duke Heinrich with 3000 horsemen [went to determine] whether there might be any profit to be taken from it. During the observing of the enemy's army they moved farther [away]. Therefore, the lords in the army before Stříbro took counsel in our absence [and decided] to march against the enemy, to take away the cannon in front of the town during the night and to move into a nearby castle.

At daybreak the next morning, the army standing in front of the town of Stříbro were fired upon. At this, they broke away en mass to a nearby hill in order to draw farther against the enemy. In the rush there was disorder among those with the cannon and the wagon-drivers so that some of them drove one way and the others went in the opposite way and they struck each other to the extent that the army came as far as Tachov where the cardinal from England [Henry Beaufort] and I were. We were shocked as you can imagine. They [the army] were panic-stricken beyond what might be regarded as proper. Then all of the lords, together with the aforenamed cardinal, held counsel together and determineded to move onto a hill nearby to Tachov and from there to approach nearer towards the enemy. So we came onto the hill and looked out over our people. There were so many people on horse and on foot and also the wagons of which there should have been made a wagon-fortress according to the order of battle as had been planned and ordered.[29] [However,] during the night the army was diminished in so far that the cardinal was advised by the majority, as well as the other princes and lords, that under the circumstances we should neither march against the enemy nor engage them without the wagon-fortress. Consequently, we all drew up through the forest. My lord the cardinal knows that when I came towards Wundsiedel [near Bayreuth] the other princes and barons wrote to me that the unfaithful ones [the Hussites] had surrounded Tachov and requested that I should come with all force and help to rescue it [Tachov] along with them. I promptly ordered all of my people, old and young, to prepare. However, another message reached me that in the meantime the town had been conquered by fire in various places and a number of the knights, vassals, citizens and poor people had come up into the castle. Then my uncle, Duke Otto wrote to me [asking me] to help rescue them to which [request] I was entirely willing and I instructed my people. Before we were able to convene together those in the castle at Tachov had surrendered and were led off and the town of Tachov was occupied by the Orphans, as it was communicated to me by my previously mentioned uncle, Duke Otto. Also our lord the cardinal has called an assembly in Frankfurt eight days after the birth of Mary and he has written to the princes. I would like to go in person if I could, in spite of the illness, but since I am quite weak I cannot go there myself on account of the illness though I wish to send a significant delegation with my authority as will be written about. This will be made known later and reported to Your Grace when and where I can or may be ready for the will and service of Your Grace. Your Grace will find me always willing and obedient. Also, I wish to make Your Grace to know that the aforementioned cardinal has shown himself to be quite courageous and honourable in the negotiations in Bohemia. He has overseen all things willingly and assisted in every way. I would have trusted by God that if he had come earlier to Bohemia all of these matters may have been settled and turned out well. Given in Plassenburg on [St] Bartholomew's Day. To the king and no one else.

UB 1: 539–42.

127   A papal legate writes to the city of Lübeck

[The papal legate Henry Beaufort revealed plans for a fifth crusade in this letter written to the northern German city of Lübeck. Herein, he mentions active involvement of English troops. This document is important for the detail on

---

[29]   This was an effort to fight the Hussite heretics using Hussite war tactics. This document suggests that the attempt was not even made to assemble a Hussite model war wagon-fortress while other sources assert that the effort was made but came to naught. See doc.125.

crusade preparations as well as the European-wide thrust of the anti-Hussite initiative. The letter is dated 26 August without specific year, but either 1427 or 1428.]

Henry, Cardinal from England, legate of the Apostolic See, to the excellent and illustrious men, masters of the citizens and consuls of the entire community of the city of Lübeck, our beloved friends in Christ. Excellent and illustrious men, our beloved friends. Since it [i.e. the Hussite heresy] cannot be pardoned in your judgement, it must be destroyed not without compunction. These most faithless heretics, who increase their abominations more and more daily, are not only the most notorious enemies of the Holy Church, but also are attempting to subvert the universal political structure. God knows how we have worked for their extirpation, and how diligently we have attempted to work out the matter, although human deliberation has not proven useful. Our sins demand it. We concluded immediately to enter Bohemia next summer, to the shame of the heretics, and in all possible ways and means to attack the aforementioned heretics under the protection of divine mercy, together with the assistance of the catholic princes, you and the other faithful sons of the Church. Archers of England will be among the other nations on this expedition. It has proven necessary to make this decision, and it will soon be announced publicly. And since we fear that a shortage of bows, the sort of which our English archers are most skilled and experienced at using, might hinder the effort our forces shall make, as we have written to Prussia, we have decided to send and have sent our great friend, the Master of the Blessed Order of Mary of the Teutonic [Knights] of Prussia, to that same region for the purpose of transmitting without delay two ships laden with wood and materials suitable for the making of bows to the Port of London. We pray asking your charity, but nevertheless, by the apostolic authority by which we discharge the virtue of the legation committed to us, we strictly mandate that you do not cause violence nor permit violence to be caused upon the mariners and commanders leaving and boarding the said vessels in the course of this present business, because we pursue the cause of faith with their aid. We also mandate that you shall not hinder, impede or cause them any grievance on account of some conflict weighing between you and another party. On the contrary, if it is needed, you should provide safety and security for the said ships and their commanders, as you should desire to be distinguished as faithful helpers of the cause of the faith, which is the cause of these men. The universal good and the welfare of Christ is distinguished to reside in defending these men. May you always fare well in Christ. Dated in Calais, under our sign, on the 26th of August.

CDL, 6: 36–7.

128 Pope Martin V expresses disgust at crusade failures

[This letter of 2 October 1427 expresses deep papal chagrin at yet another failure to defeat the Hussites. Henry Beaufort had been employed by Martin V in 1420 and then again in 1427/8.[30] During this latter period he served as legate to Germany, Bohemia and Hungary. He was appointed cardinal-priest of St Eusebius on 24 May 1426.]

To Henry, cardinal of England, legate of the apostolic see. The pope has with grief heard, from the legate's chancellor, Nicholas Bildeston, of the disgraceful flight of the army of the faithful in Bohemia from the siege of Stříbro to Tachov where it was met by the legate, and from Tachov to the frontier on August 4. He commends the cardinal for promptly betaking himself to Bohemia, and for his efforts with the princes and the army. The cardinal must persevere with his enterprise, and is to strive in season and out of season with the princes and prelates of Almain. There is no need for the pope to give him detailed instructions. One thing of importance the pope may mention, namely the alleged evil life of some of the prelates and clergy of Almain.[31] These, and notably the archbishop of Cologne and the bishop of Würzburg, he is to admonish. The archbishops of Cologne and Mainz, too, he is to order to cease their warfare, and turn their forces instead against the heretics. For if they had joined those in Bohemia as they ought, and as had been arranged, the army would not have retreated with such disgrace.

Papal Registers 7: 35–6.

129 A plan to review the fourth crusade

[Following a fourth overwhelming failure, desperate and dejected crusade leaders met to review alternatives and discuss revised strategy. Despite their losses there was still considerable resistance to diplomacy. The following document, reflecting that convocation, is dated 21 September 1427.]

First, there needs to be consideration about how to help the Czech Catholics inasmuch as they have requested monetary and military assistance until such time as an army can be sent. [If this does not happen] the faithful may feel deserted and

---

[30] On Beaufort see František M. Bartoš, 'An English Cardinal and the Hussite Revolution' *CV* 6 (1963), pp. 47–52 and G.A. Holmes, 'Cardinal Beaufort and the crusade against the Hussites' *English Historical Review* 88 (1973), pp. 721–50.

[31] Principally the region of Upper Germany.

thus enter into an arrangement with the faithless. Second, an investigation must be carried out into the ordinance which was drawn up not long ago. It must be changed in those aspects where problems have arisen. It is most important that caution be exercised to ensure that everyone agrees on what is to be done. It is quite evident that disagreement has caused great problems for the holy endeavour. Third, it must be decided when an invasion of Bohemia should be undertaken and who should be informed, how this is to be done, and what penalties. Preparations to attack the faithless must be made without excuse unless the people wish to be suspected themselves of heresy. Fourth, should precise numbers be levied on each one. Fifth, what route should the expedition take. Sixth, it must be decided who will be the commander of the army which will gather in the name of Christ. Otherwise everyone will do whatever they wish and, just as it has happened before, the cause of Christ is left off and a disgraceful retreat transpires. Seventh, what should be done if someone negotiates with the faithless or takes castles or towns from them. Eighth, should many princes personally go on the expedition. Their numbers and diverse opinions have been of little profit or honour thus far. Ninth, on the matter of a general arrangement of peace for the region of the country which is referred to as the peace of the land [landfrieden].

DR 9: 70–1.

130   Sigismund urges the papal legate to action

[Lamenting the collapse of the fourth crusade, and unprepared to undertake much personally, Sigismund called for greater resolve and urged Henry Beaufort to pursue a further crusading course of action. The letter is dated 27 September 1427.]

Revered father in Christ and dear friend. We have been apprised from reports made by several individuals of the fact that the electors of the empire along with those who went into the field in Bohemia to oppose the heretics, gave up the expedition, without any reason, and for unknown reasons rushed out of the Czech land all together. We have been deeply bothered by this in heart and in spirit. We are aware that it brings great cheer to our enemies, makes a mockery of Christianity and causes great disgrace, scandal and sorrow to the German people. We have been informed that the princes and electors of the empire not long ago discussed these matters again at Frankfurt. They did this evidently so that the pestilence [Hussite heresy] while increasing even more significantly might be put down to a greater degree than has been the case in the past. This caused us great joy. We remain hopeful that this may be the way forward for the relief of all

Christendom, that the heretics might be exterminated and that God might enable us to overcome what has been lost through this affair. It is time, revered father, for your Grace to observe with the utmost caution the imperial princes and the Czech Crown and to persuade them, together with all other faithful Christians, that the will of God is to put all other matters aside, issues like petty disputes, and work hard with great zeal on behalf of the Christian faith. As [Christ] did not hesitate to accept death on the cross for us so now these ought not to hesitate to expose themselves to risk for him. Those unwilling to defend the one who was crucified are not worthy of life. We are ready to do so with our lives and possessions in order that this business might be ended.

In order that these concerns we have are known to you, it is good for you to appreciate that we have been working against the Turks, those infidels and the enemies of the cross of Christ all summer. We are still engaged in this matter. They attacked our castle of Severin in Wallachia and made a great effort to conquer it. We made haste to defend it and by God's strength to fight. However, the Turks learned of the death of the ruler of Serbia, who was to us a faithful prince and one well known. They started for Serbia, leaving the siege and filled with greed, with their whole army. They did not expect us to come. Djuradj Branković who was appointed duke in Serbia by us asked us to send aid against the Turks so we straightaway commissioned a large contingency. We took possession of the Belgrade castle as well as the key to the Hungarian kingdom and we armed other castles in the kingdom without Hungarian troops as needed. Each day we undertook advances and having arrived we accepted the submission of the Serbian kingdom together with the duke. Each day we trust that everything will work out and so far our ambitions have been met.

Revered father, you should know that we are dispatching a good sized army to Lombardy to give assistance to our dear son the eminent duke of Milan. This is related to one of our closely kept secrets. Once we are able to stabilize matters with the Turks, which we hope in the help of God will be soon, and the kingdom has been ordered appropriately we are planning to enter Lombardy as soon as possible and from there to Rome in order to accept the imperial crown. We do not arrogantly seek after glory or dignity in the ceremonies, God knows this since nothing is kept from God. In doing this we seek only a complete understanding with our most holy lord, the High Pontiff. Along with him we can unite the two earthly swords for mutual benefit as is necessary in order to bring peace to Italy as well as to all Catholic kingdoms. We place our trust in the king of peace that peace may prevail and when it does we can turn our attention fully to crushing the faithless Czech heretics and to causing great distress to the barbarians and taking back the tomb of the Lord and the land which has been turned red with the blood of Christ. We call upon you, most revered father, and with great love ask that you not cease to defend the correct faith of almighty God for it is to his glory that these matters are upon us and it is for the good of all Christians, not just ourselves but also the holy empire. The electors, princes, vassals and subjects of the empire, as well as the faithful in the Bohemian Crown, must continue to apply force with even greater zeal, Persuade them to maintain their attention on the matters in Bohemia even more fully and with great care. Their neighbour's wall is on fire and to ignore this will be harmful. If due care is not taken, this fire will spread and in the end shall be a fire which cannot be put out.

Beyond this father, I trust you will forward reports on all these affairs and your decisions to His Holiness as well as to us in order that we shall be able to take advice with His Holiness when these things are concluded. We shall do the same and in this way our combined counsel may help to being about an agreeable method and means for acting against the aforementioned heretics. Whatever has been neglected in the past and left undone may yet be brought about and acted upon in the summer to come through the efforts of the orthodox people to the glory of God and for the extermination of the heretics.

Given on the hills near Belgrade in the camp, on 27 September, in the forty-first year of our reign as Hungarian king, in the eighteenth year as king of the Romans and our eighth year as king of Bohemia.

DR 9: 72–4.

131   A Jewish perspective on the heretics

[There were efforts among some Hussites, namely Jakoubek of Stříbro, to subvert the idea that Jews should not own property. Jakoubek proposed that Jews might possess land and be permitted to practice their way of life. These ideas noted, it is quite impossible to assert that Jewish life was substantially changed on account of the Hussites.[32] The Táborite conception of universal justice caused some Jews to perceive parallels with their own messianic ideals. Some contemporary Jewish documents refer to the Hussites in this connection. An example would be Jakob ben Moses ha-Levi, rabbi in Magonza, better known as Maharil who died in 1427. Similar views were held by some Jews living in German-dominated cities who based this view on personal experiences during the crusades against the Hussites. This theme was taken up by Joshua ha-Kohen in his work *Emek habacha*. Jewish sources referred to the German territories invaded during the counter crusades in

---

[32]   Ruth Gladstein, 'Eschatological Trends in Bohemian Jewry during the Hussite period', in *Prophecy and Millenarianism*, ed., Ann Williams (London: Longman, 1980), pp. 241–56 and I.J. Yuval, 'Jews, Hussites and Germans in the Chronicle of Gilgul bnei Hushim' *Zion* 54 (1989), pp. 275–319 (in Hebrew).

1428–33 as Edom. In Biblical literature the term Edom refers to the area southeast of the Dead Sea inhabited in ancient times by people hostile to the Jews who refused to permit Jews to pass through their borders. The following extract refers to the fourth crusade.]

Behold a miracle: Suddenly at midnight a cry was uttered in the midst of the large army of Edom which had pitched its tents over a three-mile range near the city of Žatec in Bohemia about ten miles from Cheb and everyone fled before the sword.[33] It was but the sound of a falling leaf that caused them to run away even though they were not pursued by anyone. They left behind all of their wealth and riches and they no longer cause destruction in this country. These evildoers were most disappointed and went back, each of them where they had come from, but many were killed. They were killed by others with the sword because they were pillaging and looting since they were in need of supplies. I saw them going back to Cheb begging for a piece of bread even at the door of Jews. But, glory to God, they no longer caused destruction any longer, not even in word or even to a child.

Time and time again the Hussites got the upper hand for many years and began to send a large expedition against the people of Edom. On one occasion they went out of the country some distance until they arrived at the city of Nürnberg and they threatened to burn it down. In the end, the people of that city paid a large sum of money and reached an agreement so they [Hussites] returned to their country and left them alone.[34]

So the priests and princes from the country of the Rhine joined together and imposed taxes on the Jews. Everyone, even infants one day old, were obliged to pay as ransom a gold coin of the Rhine for each person.[35] Even the poorest people had to pay for themselves and for their children this coin of ransom. In this way, they obtained a great deal of money and by imposing this tax were able to recruit armed soldiers to send back in order to attack the Hussites.

When the Hussites no longer had a leader they gave up their agenda and most of them returned to the errors of former times. But the land of Bohemia remains divided over the faith and in some places they have neither churches nor crosses. Some Hussites who do not believe in Jesus live on a mountain which is called Tábor.[36] They have neither church, nor cross, nor priests.

---

[33] It is about 40 miles from Cheb to Žatec.

[34] See doc.145.

[35] See the documents on the plan of taxation drawn up by the Reichstag at Frankfurt on 2 December 1427 in DR 9, pp. 91–110.

[36] This curious statement is inaccurate with respect to the Táborites proper. The christology of the radical Hussites was effectively orthodox. The author may have in mind fringe elements such as the Adamites or the various strands of the so-called Pikarts who became, incorrectly, identified as Táborites.

[The Jews, in large measure, seem to have escaped the carnage of the crusades against the heretics in Bohemia.]

G.I. Pollak, *Sefer halichot kedem* (Amsterdam, 1846), p. 80.

132 Funding proposals by the Reichstag

[Meeting at Frankfurt, the Reichstag passed several decrees on 2 December 1427 aimed at financially underwriting the cost of a subsequent crusade. The war effort stated specifically that it was essential to wipe out the Hussites and Czech heretics in any way possible. The Reichstag noted that it was pointless to undertake another crusade unless provision could be made to ensure that such an effort could be brought to successful conclusion. A scheme was then introduced and ratified for the raising of money to fund the expedition. The money was designated initially to supply salaries for the soldiers and for the maintenance of a daily war against the heretics. The clergy were to be subjected to a tax of five percent of their income. All laypeople with means, over the age of fifteen, were asked for a particular sum based upon the value of their belongings. Barons, knights and other elites were also taxed proportionally. Every Jewish person, regardless of age or gender, were also required to contribute financially to the crusade effort. Crusader tax collectors, in teams of six, were commissioned to carry out the collection. Several collection locations were nominated and ratified: Cologne, Nürnberg, Erfurt, Salzburg and Wrocław. The collected monies were to be gathered into chests and locked with six keys (one key held by each of the tax collectors) and stored in cathedral sacristies or other secure locations. Duplicate records of the proceeds were to be compiled at each of the collection points. Letters announcing papal indulgences were ordered to be publicly explained from the pulpits of parish churches. Each of the Imperial prince-electors were required to send a representative to Nürnberg on the second Sunday in Lent when an account of the collection would be considered and specific plans outlined for the crusade. It was decided that a crusade army would likely undertake a general invasion of Bohemia around the feast of St John Baptist after having amassed on the Czech frontier at locations to be specified at a later time. While there are a number of relevant documents devoted to the problem of funding the crusade the decisions summarized here are among the most comprehensive of the extant documents. The text of this lengthy document in question has not been provided here since most of it is readily available in English. See Norman Housley, *Documents on the Later Crusades, 1274–1580* (New York: St. Martin's Press, 1996), pp. 123–28.]

DR 9: 91–110.

133 Difficulties in raising taxes for the crusade

[The archbishop of Mainz, Conrad, in this general letter sets forth a number of the attendant difficulties in collecting the general taxes levied to pay for the renewed crusade against the Hussites. The letter is dated 18 February 1428.]

By the grace of God, Conrad, to all of the provosts, deans, archdeacons, chapters and other persons of the cathedral in Mainz as well as to the other collegiate and parochial churches, leaders of the people, arch-presbyters and town counsellors in and around the city and diocese of Mainz wherever they are and who receive this notice, everlasting salvation in our Lord and great striving in defending the true faith against the spread of heresy. Not long ago our revered father in Christ, the illustrious prince and lord, Henry, cardinal of England and legate of the Apostolic See and our beloved lord along with ourselves gathered at a diet in Frankfurt where, along with the renowned electors of the Holy Roman Empire other ecclesiastical and secular princes, notable and illustrious counts, barons, noblemen, knights and cities, we discussed the possibility of exterminating the poisonous plague of heresy which is still increasing in Bohemia. Good advice and a sound method for taxation of all faithful Christians, men and women, ecclesiastical and laypeople, were decided upon. According to his authority as a legate, the lord legate promulgated some letters about indulgences and other holy matters, incentives of free gifts from the mystical treasures. This was designed to stir up in fullness zeal with respect to the holy faith, a defending of that faith and an expected putting down the heretics who are rebellious against God and the Church. All of this was made known in copies sent out in times past to you.

As we understand it there have been some people, particularly laymen of different estates who have stated they doubt they must pay the tax by obligation and the requirements of the church which was explained clearly in the letter from the legate. Because of these views there has been hesitancy and reluctance to pay the required allotment in the matter of the faith. There are reports that the letter of the legate is inconsistent with the decrees from Frankfurt. Such a significant godly matter, concerning the faith, the holy Catholic church and the good of the community must take precedence over all else and must be seen in this light. It is of concern to all Christians and must be given assistance inasmuch as possible by all Catholics.

It is our thought that the best way to proceed is on the advice of our pious and beloved faithful counsellors, especially with respect to the letters from the lord cardinal concerning indulgences which are very generously offered in this matter of the faith. This should be announced by each of you to the faithful on Sundays and feast days without penalty, censure, or excommunication. Rather, kind encouragement and pious exhortations should [point out] how serious this matter is and how swiftly it must be undertaken. The laity must not be treated as outcasts from the church if they are slow to pay the tax nor should they be denounced unless it comes to your attention by letters from the lord legate. It is held that the laity will be more ready to pay the tax willingly than if coerced through an ecclesiastical penalty since nothing of this sort was included in the Frankfurt decrees.

DR 9: 117–18.

134   Hussite heresy threatens distant lands

[On 9 October 1428, Pope Martin V addressed a letter to the church hierarchy in England warning them of the danger of the Hussite heresy, pointing out the old assumption that the Czech heresy had arisen in England in the first place – Wyclifism transplanted – and also putting forth his own opinion that England was already full of heresy and suggesting that there was some underground conspiracy between Bohemia and England. John Wyclif had died on 31 December 1384 and was posthumously condemned by the Council of Constance on 4 May 1415 and his body ordered destroyed. In1428, the bishop of Lincoln, Richard Fleming, had Wyclif disinterred and his remains burned. In this excerpted letter the pope calls upon the English church to do all it can to aid in the crusade to exterminate the Hussite heresy.]

. . . . Inasmuch as this wretched and terrible heresy has its roots there [in England] and has created so much scandal and evil throughout Christendom, for the sake of your honour and reputation the English ought to give this matter the highest priority. There ought to be due consideration given as to how this plague can be exterminated. Everywhere when this is discussed it is frequently noted that it originated in England and that is where it came from. Beyond this, there exist in England not a few offshoots of this heresy which will continue to grow up quite significantly if they are not quickly cut down. One wonders if England may not suffer the same fate as Bohemia. May God mercifully prevent this. If this was not apparent in times past, it is certainly evident now. Throughout England, heretics have been detected and captured. A very likely rumour indicates that they have many associates and followers who daily infect and seduce others. This will increase and become the basis for destruction of the entire kingdom. As long as the heresy persists in Bohemia it will multiply. Similarly, we have been informed by a reliable source that frequently representatives of the Wyclifites, hiding in England, go to Bohemia to strengthen them [Hussites] in their pestiferous ways and to provide them with hope in terms of assistance and support. You ought to know about this . . . .

Edward Brown, ed. *Fasciculus rerum Expetendarum et Fugiendarum* (London, 1690), vol. 2: 616–17.

135   Beaufort petitions England for crusade aid

[Inasmuch as Henry Beaufort had been appointed cardinal and papal legate for crusade initiatives against the Hussites, it is not surprising that England, despite being caught up in the Hundred Years' War in France, would play some role in the crusades. Beaufort's main challenges included manpower and finances. The following documents clarify the negotiations which took place in early December 1428 over what is referred to as 'God's quarrel'. The formal records are dated six months later (see doc.143). The texts are written in a form of legal English and the use of Norman French terms interspersed with Middle English present peculiar difficulties for clarity and translation.]

[In] remembrance of things that I, Henry, cardinal legate, etc. request and desire of the king, my sovereign lord, and of his noble council on behalf of our Holy Father for the well sustaining defence and exaltation of our Christian faith.

First, since it has pleased my sovereign Lord previously [concerning] the initiation and desire of our holy father to grant unto Master Cuntzo, his ambassador, people and notable captains out of his land, concerning the aforesaid matter, as clearly evident by the answer given to him in writing by my sovereign Lord's council, may it please my sovereign Lord to grant that the number of people might reach to the number of 500 spear men and 5000 archers and that I may have captains to lead them as I may arrange.[37]

Secondly, that I may publish and do publish in all places of his land where I think necessary the *cruciat* which is committed unto me by our holy father and

---

[37]   A reference to Kuneš of Zvole, later bishop of Olomouc, who preceded Beaufort to England with the financial concerns of the crusade. On 10 May 1428 he appeared before the council with a papal request for clerical assistance. On 9 July he petitioned convocation held at St Paul's and that meeting adjourned without a decision. Kuneš was present at the fall convocation on 23 November with the letter of Martin V (see doc.136) accompanied by Jacob Cerretano, another papal envoy. Cerretano was a notary in the papal chancellory where he was involved in the negotiations at the Council of Constance. In 1429 he became bishop of Teramo and remained there until his death in 1440.

execute all that belongs thereto.[38] Considered that crosses have been seen recently in this land where the cause was not so great.

As touching the first, that is to say, the obtaining of people to which many other things depend as accessories to the principal, I ask and desire that I may proclaim in all places of the land what wages I would give to such as will go in the expedition of the faith.

Also, that such as shall go in this expedition and cause of God may stand in the king's protection as they do that go over in the king's voyages just as was promised and granted unto the said Master Kuneš.

Likewise, that such constable and marshal as I shall depute and assign for the rule of the king's people that shall go, may make such statutes and ordinances as shall be thought necessary and expedient for the good governance and salvation of them. The said constable and marshal and their ordinances and statutes [shall] be obeyed under such pains as shall be thought convenient to be executed freely and lawfully in all of them who disobey or that be punishable according to the extent of the offence. Considering that to lead over any multitude of people without law to rule them by, would be to lose all or a great part of them, which God forbid.

In like manner, the admiral or his deputies [should] have sufficient charge and authority to ordain and bring shipping and navy sufficient for the said people at such ports and at such times as shall be advised and thought necessary and at such wages as the king allows.

Similarly, in relation to the second [matter], that is to say the publication and the execution of the crusade, if any man will only of devotion and for the health of the soul go over in the said expedition that he may have freedom and license to do so and under similar protection as above. However, it is not my intention under the colour of the said crusade to allow any religious men, especially in great number or those whom I have any suspicion would take the benefice of the said crusade rather to walk in apostasy than for desire of merit, to go over in the said expedition.

Also, that those who will only go to rejoice in the benefice of the said crusade without wages stand under the laws, statutes and ordinances to be made by the constable and marshal as is noted above, as well as they which shall go for wages. Considering that since all are the king's people it is as necessary to maintain good rule and preserve from all mischiefs and inconveniences [both] one and the other.

Likewise, I trust that my sovereign Lord and the noble lords of his council granting these articles as I trust to God you will, will not deny me other things

---

[38] The noun *cruciat* derived from the medieval Latin *cruciata* indicates the papal bull authorizing a crusade. Such document sets forth the privileges granted to crusaders. In this context is refers also to the actual crusade. Hereafter the word is translated as 'crusade'.

needful for the furthering thereof, if any such come to mind hereafter, for peradventure it comes not to remembrance now that will hereafter which shall always be necessary for the good and effectual speed of them. [December 1428]

POPCE 3: 330–32.

136   Response of the Privy Council

[Before convocation dispersed in December 1428, Beaufort's negotiations with the council had advanced sufficiently to merit a formal response by the Privy Council. The results were mixed. He would not be allowed to obtain financial support for the crusade from the clergy of England and his petition for armed forces from England had been modified by the council. Despite this partial setback, the cardinal-legate was permitted to preach the cross in the realm, to collect whatever financial support he could and also to advertise wages for prospective crusaders.]

This is the answer given to my Lord the cardinal, etc. concerning the requests made by him unto the king on the behalf of our holy father the pope, for the well sustaining defence and exaltation of the Christian faith, etc.

First, concerning the publication of the crusade and freedom of licence to be given to the king's subjects to [the] execution of the means comprised therein to obtain by the benefice of the same crusade, it is conceived that the said means rest in two things. One is the gift of goods to be made by the king's subjects in promotion and furthering of God's cause and quarrel against the heretics. Another is the going personally of the king's subjects out of his land, on account of their own devotion in the said God's cause and quarrel.

And as to the first, the king with the advice of his council agrees that if his subjects, out of their devotion, would give of their goods to the furthering of the said cause, they shall freely do it with the following provision. That is to say, that these delegated persons, notable and sufficient, who shall receive all the goods so to be given of devotion by the king's subjects. Such persons shall faithfully and truly certify to the king and his council all their receipts, from now on, as it shall stand in gold and silver not to pass out of his land, but to be employed according to the king's laws in merchandises in such ways as it shall be, by way of exchange, delivered in payment to them by the king's subjects that shall be waged in this land to go over in the cause of the faith against the said heretics.

Also, concerning the personnel going, of the king's subjects out of his land, of their [own] devotion in the said quarrel, it is considered that part of the number of them that shall go, my said lord the Cardinal has desired to have with him, by licence of the king, 500 spear men and 5,000 archers on wages. And it is also considered that the people of his land have been diminished and decreased in recent times by deaths, wars and in various other ways, especially of defensible men and persons suitable for the war and because of this [there is] great necessity that the king has such persons for the defence, keeping, [security and] safe guard of his realms, lands, lordships and subjects, especially in his realm. Therefore, it is thought quite perilous and dangerous to allow the king's people to pass out of his land on some other cause, to any other strange country that is not of the king's dominion. Nevertheless, for the praise of God and promotion of his said cause, and at the reverence and request of our holy father, the pope, and special contemplation of my said Lord the Cardinal, who has taken upon him the soliciting of the said cause, whom, whose estate, whose worship, person, and surety, it is well thought that the king and his land for many great and evident causes owe especially to careful consideration [so that] the king, with advice of his council, is agreed to license his subjects as well such as will go of devotion, as such as will go at wages to the number of 250 spear men and 2,000 archers in all to pass out of his land to employ their persons in God's service in the quarrel noted above under the conditions which follow.

First, that our holy father the pope be a good, gracious and tender father unto the king, to his land and to the king's subjects of the same, and generally to all the king's lands and subjects.

Also, that our said holy father, being gracious to the promotion of the said cause, be contented that the king's subjects of the same land would give them of their special devotion, and in all ways to defer any common charge to be borne of any of the estates of this land, be it by the clergy or any other.

Likewise, that before the king's subjects depart out of this land, it be shown and demonstrated to the king's council the guarantee of reasonable ways and means of passage for these subjects of the king out of his land to the place that they shall go to, and their return back into his realm.

In like manner, that the king's subjects presently in his realm of France intended for his service there and to the defence [and] safeguarding of his realm, be not removed, admitted, nor allowed to go from there by my said lord the cardinal, or any other as far as he may allow it, considering his great peril and danger that might fall to the king in his kingdom, by the destitution, departing or withdrawal of his subjects from the same.

Similarly, that my Lord the cardinal shall do his effectual and notable diligence and duty toward the king of Scotland to make the king sure that the said king of Scotland shall hold him in friendship and stay with the king, his lands and subjects and namely with this land, and to make him truly and duly observe and keep, as well, this and other appointments made with the king to which he is bound as well by his oath made in this land and when he was free in Scotland and by his [..] and seal. And so, in conclusion, the king agrees to the execution of the said crusade with and under the conditions and provisions before mentioned and to the publication of the same to be made in all the places of this land where it shall be thought expedient by my lord the Cardinal. In this publication it shall be openly declared that the crusade is published with the king's assent and licence. And moreover that in the publication of that part of the crusade that relates to those who go on it and expose her persons in God's quarrel, it shall be openly declared that the king has granted permission and licence to the subjects of his land to go in this said quarrel for the good of their souls in great and notable number.

Also, with respect [to the fact] that my lord the Cardinal wishes to have granted to him captains which he would cause to lead the king's subjects that shall go out of the land, the king is agreed that my lord the Cardinal shall name to the king such persons here as he desires to be captains and those that the king will agree with him to appoint them in his wisdom.

Likewise, the king agrees to this, that my Lord the cardinal, according to his request, shall proclaim in all places of his land where it shall be thought expedient to him, and the wages he will give to those who will go in the said voyage.

In like manner, the king is agreed that my lord the Cardinal shall name to the king those he desires to be constable and marshal of the company of the king's subjects that shall pass out of this land and that these [persons] the king shall be pleased to agree with him to be the constable and marshal shall have authority and power from the king to rule and govern his people and to chastise and punish those who disobey or offend against the law of arms.

Similarly, the king is agreed that his subjects of this land, that as it is before rehearsed, shall go out of this land to expose their persons in the said God's quarrel, shall stand in his protection with the provision and in the manner and form contained in the answer given to Master Kuneš sent to the king from our holy father the pope.

Also, the king is agreed that the admiral or his deputies shall have sufficient authority and charge to order and bring shipping and other vessels sufficient for passage of the people at whichever port and at whatever time as it shall be advised at the same wages as the king gives for his own voyages.

And if it happens that the said journey against the heretics, before rehearsed, does not take place, for one cause or another, then the money collected may in no wise be employed in another use without the advice and consent of the king and his council. [December 1428]

POPCE 3: 332–6.

137 Diplomatic summit at Bratislava

[At a mid-winter (January) diet convened at Český Brod, the Hussites discussed and eventually accepted an invitation from Sigismund to meet at Pozsony [Bratislava] in western Hungary. The negotiations began on 4 April and lasted six days (4–9 April 1429). The occasion was convened and agreed upon by both sides in hopes of securing a peaceful solution to the crusade crisis.It is notable that diplomatic efforts on the part of the Hussites prior to 1424 would almost certainly not have gone to this length.]

This is a record of the meeting between the Hussites and the king in Bratislava on Monday after the first Sunday in April in the year 1429 and how they are divided.

It should be known that the Hussites did not wish to come to Bratislava even though they had a safe conduct. There also had to be extended to them as a guarantee Duke Mikuláš of Opava as well as in credit Duke Přemek of Opava, Wilhelm Ebser, burgrave of Brno and another noble. As it turned out the Hussites came to Bratislava [including] Prokop of Jindřichův Hradec, the English master, many lords, knights and vassals and two hundred Táborites on horse.[39]

Of the ecclesiastical princes there was the cardinal of Olomouc, the archbishop of Ezstergom, bishop of Zagreb, chancellor, bishop of Brixen, bishop of Nitra, bishop of Rab, bishop of Veszprém, bishop of Erlach, bishop of Wrocław, and the bishop of Freising.[40]

From the secular princes and lords were Duke Albrecht of Austria, Duke Wilhelm of Bavaria, Duke Ruprecht of Lubin, Duke Bolek of Opole, Duke Kentner of Olsen, Lord Oldřich, the grand duke of Rožmberk, Půta of Častolovice and many other barons from Bohemia.[41]

The duke of Burgundy [Philip the Good] was there with his delegation as well as Duke Ludwig of Bavaria, his advisor and two lawyers from the school of Paris, Duke Wilhelm, three doctors and the king had four doctors.

On Tuesday following the first Sunday after Easter, our lord the king held a conference with all of the ecclesiastical and secular princes as well as the learned doctors on how best to carry out the business with the Hussites. It was advised by the common council that he had to speak to them of how they had strayed from the holy Christian faith and did not observe it as their fathers did and which they themselves had done in the past. If they wished to desist from their beliefs they

---

[39] Principally, Prokop Holý and Peter Payne.

[40] The archbishop of Ezstergom [Gran], at this time, was the old adversary of Jan Hus at Constance and the inveterate enemy of the Hussites, the 'iron bishop', Jan Železný, former prelate of Litomyšl.

[41] Bolek of Opole, a Silesian baron, joined Hussites on military operations.

could then receive enlightenment in order to be heard out and then receive instruction through which they might return to the mother of holy Christendom. Our lord the king did this through wise and kind words.

The Hussites replied they would gladly be heard before the whole world in a trade off with Christendom on account of the faith so that it might be seen which faith was more correct.

It was advised that this could not be done and it was doubtful that our faith was not authentic since our Lord Jesus Christ had established it and taught us the faith and it had flourished and been approved through the holy prophets of the gospel and other holy teachers. The faith of the Hussites had been condemned by the holy father, the pope, and the general Council of Constance. If they really wished to be heard, it was accepted that they should be heard out kindly and given instruction and this would be best done in the presence of the ecclesiastical and secular princes and the doctors who understand such matters rather than publicly because there would be many unlearned people who would not understand such things at all. They are to be granted two days to appear and be heard out though without agreement and it shall be kept quiet.

It was further advised that in terms of the extermination of heresy in Bohemia there could be no better way of doing this than by the sword. Since this could not be done temporarily, it should be kept in mind and the peace reached with them might be until the next council. They should come to that council and be heard and accept the decision and instruction made by the council. The rabble in Bohemia would be divided by that and it might be supposed that they might never be united and many things would transpire in the meantime and things might improve. Our lord the king and all the other princes and lords liked this advice very much and it was reported to the Hussites.

They replied that they would be glad to be heard before the council. When all ecclesiastical and secular princes and all other people were reformed, they will also be reformed. In the meantime they will remain in their faith. They can do this only for a short time since there is no one who can rest until the whole world is reformed.

Following this, our lord the king spoke to the effect that he wished, in hope, to become their ruler and that they should follow up the peace and consent to it until the next council which must be held within two years at Basel and to which the holy father, the pope, wishes to come. That which has been seized belonging to the Crown of Bohemia – considerable goods – must be relinquished. That pertaining to monasteries, priests and laymen which has been conquered must be returned. No one was to be forced into another faith for the time being but must be tolerated just as other faithless people are tolerated within Christendom. Many of the princes and lords and the doctors liked this very much and the matter was arranged in this manner. Then our lord the king brought the report forward to the

Hussites and succeeded in getting some of the Czechs to undertake negotiations with the Hussites in this way and let them discuss it with each other to see if they could find something amenable and then do the right thing.

The Hussites answered that they wished to have peace with no one except those who were of like faith since they had the true faith. They would answer to God with their conscience if they did nothing against such impious matters. Our priests lead in this matter and have already drawn their swords in defence of the faith and they will not put them back until all have been brought to the faith.

On the following Friday, after the meal, the Hussites answered our lord the king and promised that if he wished to adopt their faith and hold to it, they would be pleased to receive him as their king. Otherwise they would prefer another lord and gladly give him the kingdom and the goods of the crown of Bohemia and help him to bring it into subjection and march with him wherever hc wished and help him subdue all his enemies. But if he did not wish to do this they spoke as before saying they had drawn their swords and they did not wish to put them away until they had rallied everyone to their faith.[42]

This made our lord the king very angry and he spoke with all of the princes and the lords and implored them on behalf of the holy Christian faith and the holy cross on which the lord died, that they might help him exterminate the faithless in order that he might come into the inheritance of which he is the rightful heir. But he wanted to be patient a while yet as he desired to personally march against the heretics along with his son of Austria and to make war against them quickly with the help of God. Following this, all of the princes and lords, together with their advisors, gave him counsel and advised him thus, promising their assets and their persons to come to the field with him and he thanked them all.

When they ate on Friday, Prokop and some of his brothers came to our lord the king and asked him when the next council was held who would hold the power, the pope and the cardinals, or the king and the princes together with them. Our lord the king told them that the power other Roman emperors and kings had in councils would be the same as he would have. One of the doctors asked why they inquired about such a matter saying they had many learned people among them they should ask themselves. The Hussites also demanded to have a written answer to this question which would please them. The king took advice on this.

The Hussites also wished to take their leave, as soon as the answer was given, on Saturday and ride from Bratislava to their brethren who were in force about six miles away. [There follows this report an undated note from April 1429 simply titled 'News'. The substance of the report though interesting is completely specious. See doc.139.]

---

[42] This statement, noted twice, seems to indicate counter-crusade mentality among the Hussites. The sentiment has sometimes been attributed to Prokop Holý.

To the venerable W, dear lord. I make a report of this news. The priest Prokop came from the king and into the Táborite army with the news that our lord the king had reconciled wholly and completely with him and wishes to remain so in all matters wholly and completely and act according to his advice. On the forthcoming day of our dear Lady, the royal counsel will come to Prague and all the Czech barons will come as well. There will be a complete reconciliation there as well. This news was brought by our young lord from Prague. Those of Meißen and of Pirna remained outside the negotiations and are the enemies of the king and the Táborites have them also as enemies. The Lichtenberk castle has no tax, etc. You should also know that our lord the king became friendly with the Praguers which they did not expect but he has ordered it. The aforementioned castle must remain unconquered until the day of our Lady's birth [8 September], even though they are in need of reinforcements and supplies. No one of our army is to plunder any further. Whoever does and refuses to cease, the rest must be against him. May you also know that the house near Dubá [or Český Dubá] which Lord Štěpán, Lord Vaněk and Lord Peke had occupied, Smiřický and Czetko have conquered.

UB 2: 22–6.

138   A speech which enraged the emperor

[Peter Payne was the chief speaker at the Bratislava conference and he gave this address, excerpted here, following some preliminary remarks by Prokop. Sigismund was enormously annoyed with this speech.[43]]

. . . Our Lord Jesus Christ is a most invincible soldier and Prague warrior . . . . Since no one has ever vanquished God or defeated the truth, it is futile, O mortal king and your princes, whose days are numbered, to attempt to destroy this immortal and everlasting truth which God defends and to which God grants authority. I maintain that this portion of truth which we have and for which we fight, surpasses all the sons of men in terms of virtue, greatness and dignity. Since it triumphs over everything, it will succeed against kings, princes, popes, legates and masters. In accordance with the witness of Esdras it overthrows, overturns,

---

[43]   Payne was the former Wyclifite principal of St Edmund's Hall, Oxford who left England *c.* 1412 in the wake of the anti-heresy initiatives of Thomas Arundel, Archbishop of Canterbury and went to Bohemia. He was active in the Hussite movement from about 1414 until his death around 1456. The most extensive treatment of Payne in English is William R. Cook, 'Peter Payne: Theologian and Diplomat of the Hussite Revolution', unpublished PhD dissertation, Cornell University, 1971, 413pp.

overcomes, vanquishes, confounds, overwhelms and brings to ruin all the powerful [1 Esdras 3:12]. Unjust rulers, bad wine, crazy women and corrupt popes will likewise perish together with the sons of men along with their works of iniquity. On the other hand, the law of God is powerful, great and victorious. It ever lives and continues forever. To be faithful to this noble truth is to live with God. To serve this truth is to reign . . . . To die for it is to gain life. To be mocked on its behalf is to be glorified. To endure innumerable dangers is to enjoy bliss.

For these reasons we have been willing to serve this blessed truth in contempt of our bodies and our own lives even unto death. We have no desire to entertain any other thought than the solemn promise made to our Lord Jesus Christ to keep his commandments, obey his law and participate completely in his humility. Rather than taking pleasure in worldly wickedness we would rather suffer ill treatment with him to the extent of slander, humiliation, cursing, torment, crucifixion and death if this is what pleases him.

So what troubles you, O king of Israel? Think about your own behaviour and of those you persecute. What evil can you and your princes possibly do to us, when those things which you regard as harmful we accept as blessing. That which you scorn we value highly. Those things counted as value to you, we mock. With Christ as our help we consider all of your instruments of torture as toys and indeed as pleasure. That which you regard as terrible we see as mild as honey. So what wrong can you cause to people who are prepared for anything? What will you bring against those who mock everything? What can you use to threaten people who fear nothing?

You foolish and unreasonable men who make promises to us of the worst punishments. Rather than effecting evil you actually do us the greatest good. Your apparent success indicates your defeat. In a stand-up fight you descend into hell . . . . Even if you were to succeed through spying and through warfare, you will be defeated by your sins and by your criminal activity.

Therefore you must know, O mortal king, that we will wage warfare against you, not for personal gain, but on behalf of the truth of Christ. Before you will be able to take this from our hearts, your life will be taken from you. Before you are able to take this glory from us, your own body will be mutilated. Before you succeed in besmirching our dignity, you will lose your own soul and your name will become a name of infamy throughout the world.

Pause now and stop illustrious king. Allow me to steer you away from the conflict perpetuated by you and your lords against Christ. Do not bring ill upon your name, do not cause it to become opprobrious. Do not cause an evil to come upon your house which is marked not by grandeur and majesty shining forth knightly even to the heavens. As long as you have kept on God's side, you have been victorious over the heathen. But when you departed from it, you suffered defeat at the hands of peasants. This is an incredible thing, sire, have you not been astounded that your armies, ten times more numerous and much better equipped have been on numerous occasions, overcome, thrashed and put to flight by a bunch of peasants? And this has been done causing much sorrow and shame to you. We do not take credit for these successes, instead we attribute them to God; to the God whose truth we have no shame in serving. The one who possesses both heaven and earth is our witness that neither pride, gain nor fear motivates us to fight. I pray you to reflect on these things. Leave us and you gain the affection of the Praguers and all Czechs. Grant to us equality and your kingdom will prosper. Make us a promise that you will faithfully serve the Lord and we will be prepared to obey you. We commit to you before God that which is just and right as well as our desire to serve you. Everything can be set in order if you agree to this. But should you refuse, everything becomes more difficult. There should be no doubt, even if your spirit refuses to understand, truth will triumph over everything.

František M. Bartoš, ed., *Petri Payne Anglici: Positio replicca et proposition in concilio Basiliensi a. 1433 atque oratio ad Sigismundum regem a. 1429 Bratislaviae pronunciatae* (Tábor: Taboriensis Ecclesia Evangelica Fratrum Bohemorum, 1949), pp. 81–90.

Chapter 6

The Fifth Crusade: Domažlice, 1431

139   The empire strikes again

[The meeting at Bratislava in 1429, and especially the cutting comments made by Prokop and the inflammatory speech by Peter Payne incited the King to renewed wrath against the persistent heretics. No sooner had the Hussite delegation departed, then Sigismund committed his wrath to paper urging the armies to move expeditiously into Bohemia to again attack and this time exterminate the heretics. The document is dated 10 April 1429.]

Sigismund, by the grace of God, king of the Romans, for all times Augustus, king of Hungary, Bohemia, etc. commend to you, venerable Conrad, bishop of Regensburg, our prince and dearly beloved, our grace and all good things.

Venerable prince and dearly beloved. How many years it has been til now that these raving heretics have committed an unfortunate and great nuisance, inhumanity and misery in our Kingdom of Bohemia. They have put aside all law and order of the holy church and the Christian faith and have committed so much evil through killing, arson, destruction of churches, the violence against priests, nobles and many devout Christians. Every day they perpetrate what no human can adequately describe. God knows and their notorious deeds are known throughout the surrounding areas so there is no need in this letter to express the great nuisances committed which is disgusting also to be seen and heard. We and other Christian princes, lords, cities and others struck at it and undertook a campaign in order to root it out and to exterminate such calamities from the midst of Christendom. But no human effort had any effect because of the fate of almighty God and the same heresy becomes stronger day by day so that it will be more difficult to put down. I am afraid that when it gets more mature, if we delay in striking it, it will be very difficult. With our people and money we act against these same heretics daily without any significant [financial assistance] with all our diligence and strength with the help of everyone who is opposed to them. It is evidently known that we have just concluded a meeting with the captains and the senior heretics who have been sent to us by them in the presence, and with the advice, of many prelates, princes, and lords of us as well as the holy empire and the kingdoms of Hungary and Bohemia, teachers of Holy Scripture of the universities of Paris and Vienna as well as many other learned, excellent people and advisors. We proposed to them all what we could do for God and honour. We have done this in all things, neglecting nothing, in an effort to end the bloodshed and to bring them into the pale of reconciliation and obedience to the church.

However, this has been to no avail. They perpetuate more trouble and calamity on a daily basis more now than before in a manner which seeks to erase and extinguish the Christian name. Therefore we have risen up and resolved with the advice of the aforesaid prelates, princes, lords, teachers and so on, that we can no longer tolerate it but wish to turn against it with all force and with all possible assets for the praise and glory of almighty God, for the strengthening of the Christian faith and for the salvation of all pious Christians who are oppressed and destroyed every day by these same heretics. [I announce] a personal campaign of force into Bohemia this summer to confront the heretics with the help of God and we intend to be in the field without delay on the forthcoming day of St John Baptist [24 June]. We have admonished and ordered, through our representative, and also through letters to other princes, lords and our cities and those of the holy empire to commit themselves to this as a great and necessary matter of holy Christendom and to assist us with all of their assets. We trust in God that they will not avoid this, because every Christian person must defend the name of the divine father of Jesus Christ from whom he has body, life and essence until death and who did not avoid death on the holy cross for us. Therefore we require your devotion and pray that with all diligence and admonish you as best we can, not to delay on such a duty which you owe to almighty God, the holy faith and we, as king of the Romans as to yourself, but to join with us with all of your equity against the aforementioned heretics for the sake of the divine and hereditary matters noted above. Come with cavalry and foot soldiers, wagons, large and small cannon and other equipment which you should bring and you are to join us in the field on the aforementioned day of St John. Therefore we refer you to our delegate, the noble Wilhelm and Hans, counts Palatine of the Rhine and dukes of Bavaria, our dear uncles and princes in Nürnberg on the Sunday before Whitsuntide. If you do not wish to come personally, send your delegates with full powers and the representatives of your church, an abbot or provost, or if they cannot come personally they should send a legate with full powers. He [Wilhelm, Sigismund's envoy] will instruct you and all of these on our behalf of how we have resolved and arranged this. We also need a final answer about your strength, when and in which number you wish to come so that we can know how to plan. For this you shall obtain a great reward from almighty God, praise and honour from the world. We shall also be gracious to you forever.

Given in Bratislava on Sunday, misericordia domini, in the forty third year of our reign in Hungary, in the nineteenth year of our Roman [reign] and in the ninth year of our Bohemian [reign].

UB 2: 27–9.

140   Sigismund rejects a policy of diplomacy

[Stung by the arrogance (both perceived and real) of the Hussites, the king set his face to a revised policy of military action against the heretics and prevailed upon others to abandon resolution through channels of diplomacy. The following representative letter clearly setting forth Sigismund's renewed strategy was written on 16 April 1429. There is no ambiguity with respect to the king's determination and intention.]

We, Sigismund, commend to noble Friedrich, margrave of Brandenburg, archchamberlain of the Holy Roman Empire and burgrave of Nürnberg, our dear uncle and elector and to our generous and dear nephews and uncles, advisors and servants of the elector of the holy empire who are appointed to our aforenamed uncle, the margrave, in the matters according to the tone of the resolution, to the dearly beloved and faithful of the holy empire, our grace and all good things.

Dear noble uncle and elector, beloved and faithful ones. We have now concluded a meeting with the elders and captains of the heretics who had been sent by them here. With the advice and in the presence of many prelates, princes, lords, among us as well as those of the holy empire and the Crowns of Hungary and Bohemia, especially also teachers of Holy Scripture from Paris and Vienna, together with many learned people and advisors we proposed to them all what could be done with God and honour in order to stop such misery, nuisance and inhumanity which have been perpetrated for many years now by wild heretics through killing, the shedding of blood, robbery, and arson, known to God and throughout the adjacent areas. This year alone they have considerably devastated our lands of Silesia, the six towns, and the land of our dear son the duke of Austria as far as Trnava. We have tried to bring them to reconciliation and to the obedience of the church but nothing has worked. They persist in their dark ways without ceasing all the more destroying devout Christians in the same way as though they wish to erase and eradicate the Christian name. Now they have laid a siege to the castle of Eggenburg of the aforementioned duke Albrecht of Austria, our dear son. They work, press through, control and destroy the surrounding land. Together with our princes, prelates, and lords we have decided that we can tolerate this no longer and we wish to personally and forcefully confront them this summer with the help of God and intend to undertake a campaign against them. We remain convinced that there can be nothing more urgent then to organize a strong war against them at both ends of Bohemia and Moravia until the time of the expedition. Thus it would be necessary that the heretics are compelled to return home and their assembling again more difficult. Now we send to our dear son Duke Albrecht of Austria a great host of people into the land of Moravia, namely to Brno and Olomouc at our own expense and we are determined that there must be a thousand in Znojmo, a thousand in Jihlava, and in České Budějovice likewise a thousand horse. Hence we have assigned to our aforementioned son the money which has come from the archbishopric of Salzburg and its churches and dioceses so that people might be able to have the proper equipment in order to assault and damage the heretics. Also, we have put at his disposal some Bohemian lords.

We have further resolved that the region of Plzeň must have at least 3,000 horse with the same for the assistance of the region of Žatec. Thereafter we have arranged allowance for the six towns of Silesia and we trust that they do not set out on the campaign but remain at home so long as we plan the campaign. When sufficient money is collected against the same heretics according to the resolution, it shall be applied to a strong war particularly in such difficult circumstances suffered on account of the heretics in the surrounding lands. The proposal in [..] which you sent to us by the venerable provost of Hayn, Hans of Seckendorff and Peter Volkmer of Nürnberg, how the war [..] is to be organized in several regions in Bohemia is understood. This is why we need from you, and we pray and admonish you to follow such duty which you owe to almighty God, the holy faith and to us as king of the Romans, and we command you seriously and resolutely by this letter that you arrange the money which you now have in Nürnberg and elsewhere for the magnates, knights, vassals and towns in the region of Plzeň who have properly held themselves with God, to the faith and to us until now and have committed themselves to help us and Christendom. You will see later the schedule for 3,000 horse. Should they not want so many in their region then the surplus should be sent with the German people for their assistance in order to confuse the heretics everywhere in the intervening time until our campaign.

You should have no doubt that this plan when followed will mean a relief and the way to all good things and the expedition and other business will be accomplished rather easily if God wills. You should do this for God, the faith and for us so that there is no delay in this on your account so that such an honourable undertaking does not fail because of a lack of money and we believe and trust that you will do well. Should this not happen, God forbid, then all plans, resolutions, work and endeavours thus far which we have done, together with the campaign to which we have invited and summoned all the German lands should remain unrealized, and the damage to all of Christendom would be added to as well as to the barefaced audacity of the heretics. You must know that we wish to be excused before God, and all the world, that we have done this with all diligence and arranged the matter as best we could if someone would follow us. We have also committed the noble Johannes, count Palatine of the Rhine and duke in Bavaria, our dear uncle and cousin, and the generous Heinrich of Plavno, burgrave of Meißen, our advisor and dearly beloved to ride ahead as our embassy to inform you about this matter and our desire. You should believe them in all things as you would us. Given in Bratislava on Saturday after the day of St Tiburtius, in the forty-third year of our Hungarian reign, the nineteenth of our Roman [reign] and the ninth year of the Bohemia [reign].

UB 2: 30–33.

141   A call for renewed crusade

[This report summarizes the precipitous diplomatic failure at Bratislava. It accurately reflects Sigismund's attitude in terms of the crusade option. It also reiterates the perceived necessity of another military campaign Finally, it underscores the continued support for the emperor in Silesia and Lusatia. The letter is dated 18 April 1429.]

Our willing and unwearying service, dear venerable lords and good friends. May you know that peace with the heretics is over. They have refused everything which our gracious lord the king proposed to them. The Hussite representative came to our gracious lord the king and indicated that the Hussites wanted to convoke an assembly in Brno and they wish to unite. If they desire to send [a representative] to the general council for reform that is up to them. When the Hussites hold the assembly then they shall send a message to our lord the king whereupon his Royal Grace shall send an embassy and at such time a peace begins. It should be noted that it seems good everywhere that there is doubt that they will not enter the general council. Our gracious lord the king came to the council with all the Hungarian lords, the imperial cities, Bavarian princes, embassy of Burgundy, with the Silesians and all his other subjects. It was resolved that they would all assist him with all of their power against his enemies and would commit body, property, honour and life to His Grace. Then the king wished to know from everyone what exactly this assistance would be. Those from Świdnica promised to help him with 12,000 men and all their vassals personally. The six towns wished to vacate themselves and all would take to the field with His Grace if necessary. Then the king asked us what would be the assistance from Wrocław, both city and land and clergy. We replied: Gracious and dear lord, we do not know the number of the people but we wish to help your Royal Grace with all of our property. Then the king turned to the princes, knights and those of Świdnica and the six towns and spoke among other things these words. I thank the dear people of Wrocław who have behaved themselves well towards us and have done by all means what was pleasant for us. Thereafter on another day the king spoke to all vassals and towns in the presence of the princes. I thank the towns, and if the princes have answered me like the towns and vassals, I wish to thank them too.

Thereafter, the king called all the princes, vassals and towns from Silesia and said, we want to undertake a better campaign and we have determined that it is useful for three men to equip the fourth one. That is, ten men have a wagon and a captain. Further, one hundred men, one captain, a thousand men one captain and so on. We want there to be among all of them a supreme captain. We would like to occupy the towns and the border for the daily war along the border and he named for defence of the border all those who reside on the border, namely Tíšín, Duke Mikołaj of Racibórz, Duke Přemek, the baron Půta, the land of Świdnica, the six towns and the king will help all those with soldiers as they require. The king wishes to have the other princes, vassals, and towns with him in the field and wants to take the campaign with all his Hungarians and march into Silesia. There he wants to join all of the aforementioned princes, vassals and towns and wishes to come to Wrocław. From there to march on to Lusatia and there to meet with the duke of Saxony, the younger of Brandenburg and of Thuringia.[1] Then to march into the land of Bohemia with his army where the imperial cities, Burgundian, Bavarian lords and those of Austria will be met. Those who were sent to the border must remain on the border and the king does not intend to stop until he exterminates the evil completely or he sheds his own blood even unto death. Take notice that he wishes to come to us in Wrocław and wants to assemble there. We are to march with him into the campaign with our best equipment everyone who is able, both old and young. In accordance with this you will know how to manage yourself. Take note that the Turks will now come to the king in Bratislava where peace with the Turks has yet to be approved. Also, the king has forbidden under penalties of body and property that no one shall make peace with the Hussites and all negotiations are to be completely avoided. Whoever, to the contrary, undertakes this shall be banished and lose life and property. Given in Bratislava on Monday before the day of St George.

UB 2: 33–5.

---

[1]   Friedrich, margrave of Brandenburg's son, of the same name.

142   Duke of Burgundy prepares for action

[The following document reveals the proposals advanced for a crusade against the Hussites with respect to the duke of Burgundy, Philip the Good.[2] This lengthy document outlines the difficulties and complexities associated with undertaking a crusade. The relevant section of the French manuscript has been transcribed in Neumann, pp. 89–98. The text refers to the period 1428–9.]

For setting right it is this that it seems my lord the Duke of Burgundy has to do and is able, if God gives him grace and the will, to go in strength of arms at this new season against the disloyal unbelievers of the Kingdom of Bohemia, that one calls Hussites. This notice is comprised of eight parts.

First, and before all things, he is disposed and intends to marry. If he were allied,through marriage to some worthy princess all of his good and loyal subjects would be full of joy and comforted in their good fortune, hoping that from him would come a noble generation to rule after him the worthy tenants which God had sent to him and in serving more freely to serve of the body and in feudal dues. Further, in haste my said lord must send at least one knight and one priest, worthy and expert men, to our Holy Father in the court in Rome, and indicate to him through our said lord, how my lord has heard the very reverend father in God, my lord the cardinal of England [Henry Beaufort], who came from the parts of Germany where, according to our said Holy Father, he was commissioned legate to have authority and to resist the false and detestable enterprise and heresy that the people of the Kingdom of Bohemia maintain and believe, which is called Hussite, [as well as] the great inhumane acts and dishonour which they commit against our Christian faith. Because of these issues, he begs my said lord of Burgundy that he would dispose and place under arms to encounter the aforementioned heretics. Even though he had important business, nothing must take precedence above the needs of the faith. The people of the German lands most desire this prince that he would go there in arms.

Further, my lord the cardinal said, that he was confident of leading four to six thousand archers, from the Kingdom of England, on this expedition in the company of my lord of Burgundy. Also, during the time my lord cardinal was before my lord duke, the prior of Pont-Sant-Esprit, representative and messenger of our holy father, arrived, having been sent to my lord. Among other things, he spoke with my lord about whether he would undertake this [expedition] for the benefit and relief of the Christian faith. He wished indeed that God might give him

---

[2]   For other relevant details see, Yvon Lacaze, 'Phillipe le Bon et le problèm hussite: Un projet de croisade bourguignon en 1428–1429' *Revue historique* 93 (1969), pp. 69–98 and docs 148 and 186.

grace and honour in order to have good results before all the other princes. My lord had strong views on this himself.

Similarly, since my lord duke had heard the said cardinal and prior, with the complaints that several great princes, prelates, cities and good towns of the German lands had made and make known daily, my lord, was moved by faith and genuine love for his blessed Creator and for his Christian Church. He strongly desired and declared that he could not do more than go into combat and put all that God had granted him in order to resist the aforementioned heretics leaving aside all his other affairs.

Also, after these things have been pointed out to our Holy Father by the said ambassadors, it shall be required by my lord concerning this holy and worthy enterprise that all the other princes see that the Emperor did not do this, that is giving command through bulls to all other princes and men of whatever estate they may be, in order that they in this group obey my lord duke and aid our Lord to do well there in order to benefit Christianity as well as his honour.

Further, it will be pointed out by the said ambassadors, that with respect to the great wars that my lord duke had for a long time, sustained on account of the death and murder perpetrated against the person of the late my lord Duke Jehan, may God pardon, and during these wars it has been necessary for him to guard his inheritances in Hinault, Holland and Zealand. He has spent a great amount, including his feudal taxes. Even though he had such good will as has been noted, he could not put together quickly at his own expense, such a force of men needed for this enterprise. This is why it is necessary to have the assistance of our said Holy Father and of the Church.

For the reasons stated above, my lord begs our Holy Father that, in order to hasten and advance the need of Christianity and her army, he would grant him the sum of [. .] which our said Holy Father could recover through all of Christendom, for no one must pretend to be exempt in such a case.

Also, in reply to our Holy Father and, to aid our Lord, my lord duke will lead this great and worthy army, be it made known three to four thousand gentlemen and four thousand archers or more, and to hope that he will lead men of such estate that he will well find strength of 15,000 combatants or more.

Further, that our Holy Father will send some worthy prelate as legate to the King of France on his behalf, obedient to the King as well as to the lands of Savoy, Brittany, Brabant, Liège, Namur, Holland, Zealand, Hinault and the county of Burgundy. This legate must assemble the princes and prelates of these places together in order together to advise all that will be expedient for the conduct of this holy enterprise, both financially and otherwise.

Further, to carry by the said legate letters from our Holy Father to my lord the Regent of the Kingdom of France, the Duke of Bedford and the men of the three estates to whom the Kingdom submits its government, requiring immediately this same lord that if he wishes to aid Christianity and to take part in the encounter against the aforementioned heretics in the company of my lord the Duke of Burgundy, his brother-in-law, leaving aside all other things, and to induce him for the good of Christendom, that he should participate in person, and could if it pleases him, find the time during some truce or abstinence of war against his adversaries and with a common working accord, saying to him that the same request is made by our Holy Father to the Dauphin.

Also, and if through my lord the Regent puts forward an excuse citing the business and wars which are at present in the Kingdom of France, that he would at least employ and stay his hand in order that through the aforementioned men of the three estates any worthwhile assistance of men and finances may be to help Christianity and to sustain the army which my lord of Burgundy is raising.

Also, similarly may be sent by our said Holy Father a legate carrying bulls to the Dauphin and to him and the men of the three estates obedient to him to propose a similar request as that made to my lord Regent, as has been mentioned above.

Further, a similar request to be made to my lord the Duke of Brabant, my lord the Duke of Brittany, my lord the Duke of Savoy and the three estates of their countries. Likewise, that for the increase of finances that bulls and indulgences are granted by our Holy Father and carried by my lord the legate commissioned to the said Kingdom and to other aforementioned countries. These bulls shall follow that form which copy the reverend father in God, my lord the Bishop of Tournai, will provide.

Also, to appropriately ask our said Holy Father his advice concerning whom conquest should be that, pleasing God, will be made over the said heretics. Also, my lord must send a very worthy ambassador to the country of Germany in order to carry out, on behalf of my lord, that which follows:

Item, to speak to the princes, prelates and governors of cities and good towns neighbouring and bordering the enemies of the faith and let them know that my lord is quite willing to come in this new season in great strength of men at arms and archers. In this way [my lord alerts them] and wishes to know from them in what manner they are making war against the said enemies, and in what help my lord could find there in terms of armed men and finances for paying the men at arms and archers which he will lead in his company which will be very great and sufficient as has been noted.

Further, to ask the princes, prelates and governors of good towns [noted] above, how my lord the duke and his men at arms in going, on the said journey may have open lodging and passage among the good towns and fortresses and also, how one would have recourse to provisions and the price one would put on them.

Also, to ask the aforementioned princes, prelates and governors which road my lord and his force should take through there, for the easiest route and finding an abundance of provisions, and through which place it seems to them that one should enter the country of the enemies.

In like manner, to enquire of the state of the said adversaries, how they maintain themselves in their war, what number of men, of cavalry they are, how they are armed and equipped, how many foot soldiers they have, how many men at arms they have, and what clothing and supporters they have when they take to the field of battle.

Further, to ask the said princes, prelates and people of the country, what remedies seem to them to be suitable and necessary for resisting the engines and evil attacks of the said enemies. [Also] of those of the country to seek through advice on what sort of clothing to protect against the encounter with the said adversaries, and that the said ambassadors be allowed to see whoever is there.

Also, to ask the said princes, how one would govern if the said adversaries would not dare come to battle but retreated into towns and fortresses, and how one might besiege them and continue the sieges and also have provisions. Likewise, to have discussion with those of the said country through those of them who have knowledge, how much money and gold my lord and his people should carry there for their greatest benefit. In this case to find some good means with the princes, countries and good towns.

Further, that my lord sends with his aforementioned ambassador some wise and knowledgeable gentlemen to inspect two or three roads for going there, especially the rivers and routes, and what lodging one would find for entering into the country of the said enemies. If there are rivers to examine, how one would navigate them, and if one must go by carts, how one will obtain them. This will be thoroughly and religiously examined by my lord's men so that he will be dependent for nothing on the people of the country and also that they will inform themselves truthfully, how one would find provisions and how the army could be cared for.

Third, during the time that the abovementioned things are done, to send to the emperor and make him aware, how our holy father has persuaded my lord duke to apply himself to the destruction of the perfidious Hussite heretics, and also the goodwill and love of our Christian faith, that my lord has for this holy struggle.

Also, to advise the emperor, how my lord proposes to go against the said enemies. My lord would have great joy if the affairs of the said emperor should be so arranged so that he might apply himself against the said heretics in this next season. In this case my lord would go to accompany him with all force, because he is the prince of the world that my lord would most willingly see in his conduct of arms, for it seems to him that he would always wish it so.

Further, in another request to the said emperor in order that my lord may do the deeds stated in this part, he wishes to have for his pleasure and for recommendation, by giving him his letters patent by which he commands princes, prelates and guardians of good towns, said fortresses and passages of the empire that to my lord and to his men to make all aid, comfort and assistance, giving him opening and passage during this present armed expedition administering to him provisions for his money at a reasonable price. Such letters should be most beneficial to my lord as one will be able to obtain.

Fourth, knowing the intention of our Holy Father and of the Church concerning the aforementioned requests which must give to my lord the leading function of his enterprise and particularly in the matter of finances, my lord could accordingly make his mandate, great, medium and small.

Also, it seems that the legate coming from parties of that place and meeting with the princes and prelates and other worthy people considerably involved in this matter as much the Church and the nobles, worthy sermons should be commanded to be preached in all the churches and parishes on several solemn days. Through these sermons one could aid the princes and prelates and their officers and the laws, of the cities and good towns to put aside finance which would be levied, without exception of person, on each a certain tax of money borne by their devotion, and if this could be undertaken, there would be raised quite an appropriate amount.

Similarly, this said finance could be raised from each parish by two proof givers with the priest, these going from house to house, making request, and it would be put in writing what each would give and during these three days of solemn fast to read it publicly, so that each could know that the money was safeguarded and how much had been raised.

In like manner, that the indulgences which will be published by my lord of Tournai and of which the above is publicly mentioned many of good devotion and in order to be absolved should source large sums of money. Further, that one could have a great finance of the tenth of the annual income of the Church.

Likewise, also it could happen that several lords, knights, gentlemen, merchants and wealthy burgesses would wish to go there at their own expense or to send men at arms or archers and in this way cost less.

Fifth, however, if my lord raises the number of 3,000 men at arms and 4,000 lancers and archers, as is said above, the wages of these men at arms will require twenty écus and forty gros. Lancers and archers half of this. Landholders and knights according to their estate, in the future will require 100 thousand écus per month which being said, the estate of my lord not encompassing any of these and seeing the long road and that he must pay everywhere, one could not give lower wages.

Also, and if they could be found, the said men at arms and archers in the following way: Be it known, my lord of Brabant 300 men at arms if he came in person, and if he cannot go, that he commits some worthy person of his country to lead the above number with 200 crossbow men or other appropriate number.

In like manner, my lord, the duke of Brittany, similarly unable to come himself, that he would send 300 crossbow men or archers, or other similar number as above. Also, reverend father in God, my lord bishop of Liège, has 200 men at arms and 200 crossbow men. Further, that my lord the duke of Savoy wishes to send the prince his son, accompanied by 300 men at arms and 300 crossbow men, and if the aforementioned princes wished to send the number of men at arms and archers as requested above, which amount to 1100 men at arms and a thousand archers, my lord would have considerably fewer men to raise in his said lands.

Similarly, in order to pay the men at arms and archers of the aforementioned princes and prelates, the money could be found in their particular countries using the ways and means cited above.

In like manner, could my lord command to come with him the count of Verneburg, who is a well-loved lord and known in all the German lands and is very brave in war and has granted to him a certain retinue of men.

Further, if any of the said princes do not come or send by the way declared above, it would mean that my lord must find the aforesaid 3,000 men at arms and 4,000 archers within the lands of Burgundy, Artois, Flanders, Hinault, Holland or Zealand and Namur. At the least, those that are needed to make up the said number. To be quite certain, it would be advisable to order by a certain day the men of the said countries and the other gentlemen and to put down from memory the names of those who in such case are commanded; but this could delay so much that one would hear news from the ambassadors sent to Rome.

Also, when the said lords and gentlemen come to my lord in good manner they must go on the said journey and indicate what number each will lead, how many men at arms, [and] archers, and the means by which obedience can be maintained for the duration of the journey and also broadcast several good ordinances necessary for the conduct of the said men at arms.

Further, that the men at arms and archers that my lord will lead in company, as has been said, from those lands of my very noble lord John of Luxembourg must have the charge of them and lead them under my lord the duke of Burgundy.

In like manner, my lord the prince of Orange, similarly will have charge of those from the duchies and counties of Burgundy and the neighbouring lands. Also, my lord the marshal of Burgundy they will use as general of his office also that which belongs to the marshal.

Sixth, that my lord must equip himself with great and sufficient artillery, namely handbows, arrows, ropes, crossbows mounted on a stand and *agmudas* [sic] and arrows to serve this. Also, lances, axes or mallets of lead.

Further, large and small pieces of protective clothing to provide against the projectiles of the enemies. Similarly, of cannon, bombards, gunpowder and materials and other supports according to what one will find necessary by means of the report of the ambassadors which my lord will send to the parties in Germany, especially those who will have charge of knowing the state of the said enemies and of the way they conduct war in order to have appropriate provisions.

In like manner, in order to find good artillery of handguns and arrows, seeing that it is for Christianity, one should find out from my lord Regent and obtain them from the Kingdom of England.

Similarly, for cannon, tents, pavilions and other equipment of war of which mention is made above, one could enquire if one could obtain them from the good towns of Germany, from the closest places to the said adversaries and on this matter to have good advice so as to have the greatest financial benefit.

Likewise, to order two worthy men, expert men and wise, who will organize the matter of the artillery mentioned above.

Seventh, that my lord, for the conduct of his person and of his household and generally of all his affairs, must provide himself with ten or twelve worthy men of council, even though from the Church, such as former knights knowledgeable through experience in the affairs of the world and others. Above all, [these must be] men on whom he can rely for assistance in such a great matter as this present enterprise, with the lords and captains named above to help in leading this work and business.

Further, that my lord provides for the conduct of his person during the said journey garments suitable to his high status, clothing, armour, horse and other such things as he requires seeing the great enterprise and the foreign places where he is required to go in order to maintain his honour and credit, and what is more, his good reputation. Also, that during the journey which my lord is bound to make, one must choose his household officials from all estates, the most skilled and expert and the most qualified to endure the labours and to provide in each case what is appropriate.

Likewise, it seems that one should send to the parties of Germany where my lord is bound, to converse with the best men in order to purchase wheat, wines, wagons and other things in order to maintain his estate of which one could have many thousands marching. This should be done beforehand as though my lord were there and as he would have a large number of people.

Similarly, that in order to undertake and sustain the estate and expenditure of my lord himself, how to have great finance which could be found in the countries of my lord, but he wishes to refer to the first article in which he speaks of his marriage.

Eighth, that my lord provides for the lands of Burgundy, Duke and Count of Autun and others, who in his absence have the government to whom one could appeal should anything arise, and similarly be provided for from the lands of Flanders, Artois, Hainault, Zollen and Zealand and other lands of which my lord has the government.

Further, that in order to guarantee the said lands, my lord takes, truces and abstinences to all his enemies and evil seekers during the time that he is bound to be out of his lands. Also, if the finances are sufficient to pay the number of 3,000 men at arms and 4,000 archers and lancers (as has been said) which one could calculate with the household of my lord duke to the number of 15,000 combatants (as has been said) which is a worthy strength of force. If God wills to benefit them with his grace, again my lord the cardinal goes in strength with him 5 to 6000 combatants from the King of England and [this] without having calculated anything of the strength of the lords of Germany.

Likewise, humbly request him who of good affection according to his small understanding, has hastily made this advice that one seeing it takes it well (for if there is anything of fault) and it is not through the lack of good will, but one can ask to fault the meaning always ready to begin again and defer to better opinion and also prepared to declare all these things written more fully with understanding which is not presently put in writing.

Paris, Bibliothèque nationale MS franç., no. 1278, fols. 49ᵛ–57ʳ.

143   England backs crusade against Czech heretics

[Six months after his initial advances to the Privy Council, Henry Beaufort secured final and formal approval for English involvement in a crusade against the Hussites. There were a variety of stipulations and conditions imposed by the council, but in the end a fairly large military expedition aimed at Bohemia began to take shape.]

This agreement made between the king, our sovereign lord on the one part, and the most worshipful father in God, Henry Cardinal of the title of St Eusebius, named Cardinal of England, on the other part, witnesses at initiating reverent request of our holy father the pope and for the well being and defence of the Christian faith, our said sovereign Lord has given and granted his royal licence and consent to his subjects of this land to the number of 250 spear men and 2,000 archers, or within the moderation of the said Cardinal, to pass out of this land in the campaign of the Cardinal for the reduction or chastening of the heretics in Bohemia, the which licence aforementioned and also the captainship and leading of the aforesaid spear men and archers the king has granted unto the aforesaid Cardinal and ordained and deputed him captain and leader of those with and under the provisions that follow.

First, that the Cardinal shall effectively fulfil his duty and diligence toward our holy father the pope, in order that he be a good and tender father to the king our sovereign lord, and to this land and to the king's subjects of the same and generally to all the king's lands and subjects. Also, that the Cardinal shall sufficiently provide and arrange for the sure and safe passage of the king's subjects out of this land to the land of Bohemia and for the re-passage and return of them into the same under the rule, governance and leadership of a captain or captains sufficient and suitable thereto as the Cardinal shall agree or as far as he can as to permit the king's aforementioned subjects to be withdrawn, led or drawn to employ them in any other service save only the reduction or chastening of the heretics of Bohemia, before rehearsed, except that the Cardinal may, if it please him, have accompany him to the court of Rome 200 persons of this number.

Also, that the aforesaid Cardinal shall not, for any reason, move or disturb the king's subjects that are presently in his realm of France intended for the defence and safeguard of the same nor, as far as he may prevent it, allow any other to stir or move them to depart or to withdraw them out of the realm of France nor admit nor receive them to go from there with him or his in this present voyage. Likewise, the aforesaid Cardinal shall not take with him nor allow to go with him out of this land in this aforesaid passage except the number before rehearsed or within which shall show themselves before their departing in the presence of the king's commissioners that shall be deputed thereto. Their names shall be recorded and brought in writing to the king's council, the which captainship and leading in the manner, form and under the provisions previously rehearsed which the Cardinal has taken upon himself and by this present agreement binds him unto the king truly and duly after the grace that God will give him to execute that which relates to the office of the said captainship as far as it may accord with his estate. And our said sovereign Lord wishes and declares that neither the aforesaid Cardinal nor any of his executers or deputies by virtue of these agreements be bound to any manner of account or to answer or compensate the king or his heirs of one third or other gains of war or to any proof as therefore.

In witness of which they as party of this agreement disposed toward the said Cardinal our said sovereign Lord the king has consented to be put to his privy seal.[3] Given at Westminster the 18th day of June [in] the eighth year of the reign of the king our said sovereign lord [1429].

POPCE 3: 337–8.

---

[3]   It is not clear whether this is a reference to the document itself or to the privy seal.

144 Efforts to engage the Hanseatic League against Hussites

[Cardinal Henry Beaufort writes to the towns of the Hanse deploring the previous ineffectual action against the Hussites and isues a strong call for the Hansa to abandon its war with the Danish king and instead unite together with the crusaders against the abominable Czech heretics. The letter is dated 1 July but does not specify which year. Considering Beaufort's movements, 1429 seems the best possibility.]

To the illustrious men, masters of the citizens and communities of the city of Lübeck and the other cities of the Hansa, our dearest friends. Distinguished men and most dear friends. Among the many disasters that Christianity suffers these days, we know nothing to be more against the faith and the church than the plague of division and factionalism which is held in emulation of peace by so many Catholics. They are occupied with civil wars so much so that their men are weakened and their lands are plundered to such an extent that they are not only too few to destroy the infidels, but they also lack courage and are not dependable. They have been rendered merely petty and foolish. Formerly only one prince, attended by a great army of Catholics, would boldly attack a great mob of enemies with a magnanimous, warlike face, and in the virtue of the Most High he would be accustomed to triumph. But now, on account of weakness caused in part by inexperience of war or lack of faith in our princes, the Catholic people are unmanly. The result of this weakness is that even when nearly all of the forces [of Empire and Christendom] have been gathered together against the infidels, especially those of Bohemia, they are still unable to resist and they complain. These men [Hussites] are not nobles or skilled in arms, but instead a feeble rabble that strives to subvert and reject not only the faith, but the whole republic of humankind. Therefore the war, to which we refer sorrowfully, that has thrived for some time between that most serene prince, the king of Hungary, etc, and you together with some other cities is such an impediment to the devotion of most Catholics, who might [otherwise] bring the greatest force against the heretics and destroy them. Henceforth, if they are not freed from these wars, which no doubt offend the majesty of the Almighty, then blame and scandal may be attributed to you for continuing these conflicts out of negligence and for causing the wilful destruction of Catholics.

We ask your friendship with affection, and even more so in the body of Jesus Christ, so that you will desire an opportune and peaceful concord with the aforementioned king and his subjects. We ask that you make this peace and perpetuate it in praise of the omnipotent God and the orthodox faith, knowing that without a doubt if the power of the said king, of the other Christian princes, and of your cities were united against the heretics, then they will see that the division of the Catholics is at an end and they will lose their determination to resist further. If indeed we have conducted ourselves most willingly regarding this cause, and if we having been impeded did not strive enough for peace and tranquillity in the negotiations of the kings of France and England and in the concerns of my king in this case, these things we mention sorrowfully. But after these realms are pacified, the Most High permitting, we will be able to gather the forces of the Catholics to exterminate the said heretics of Bohemia with all diligence through the grace of God. For the Most High knows and would that the entire world was aware of how much bitterness of mind we sustain and how much the faithful suffer, even recently as we have heard, from the unusual and unheard-of kinds of torments of such obstinate heretics. To this purpose, our beloved brother in Christ, Johannes Wynnepennyng, bachelor of sacred theology, the bearer of the present letter, will take care to discuss our affairs and concerns with your friends. We hold him in the utmost confidence, as we do your friends, and you may place faith in him without any hesitation. Illustrious men and most dear friends. May he be considered worthy to conserve your friendship for a long time and prosper in favourable mercy. Written in Calais on the first day of July. H[enry], Cardinal of England. Legate of the Apostolic See.

CDL 6: 25–7.

145 Counter crusades

[Under the new policies of Prokop Holý, Hussite armies expanded their military portfolio and no longer waged defensive warfare only which had been Žižka's forté. After 1426 and the battle at Ústí when Prokop assumed the mantle of supreme commander, his policy had been to strengthen the Czech borders by waging warfare outside of Bohemia. See map 6. During the winter of 1426/7 the Hussites invaded Silesia and Austria. In March 1427 a Táborite army commanded by Prokop defeated Austrian forces at Zwettl, an Austrian town halfway between České Budějovice and Vienna. Between 1428 and 1434 there were three separate Hussite invasions into the Duchy of Silesia in retaliation for previous anti-Hussite military action. The heretics burned churches, rectories, taverns and the estates of barons as well as monasteries. The author of the chronicle of St Mary's monastery on the Sand, Abbot Joss von Ziegenthal, blamed the Hussites for the famine and shortages in the Duchy of Wrocław in 1433/4. From 1429 to 1433 the Hussites fought many times outside Bohemia. The climax of these 'magnificent rides' came in late 1429 and early 1430 under Prokop's command. Saxony, Meißen, Upper and Lower Lusatia were overrun. Five armies consisting of 40,000 infantry, 4,000 cavalry and 3,000 battle wagons were involved. Grimma, Leipzig, Altenburg,

Plavno, Bayreuth, the lands of the Hohenzollerns and the bishoprics of Bamberg, Kulmbach and Bayreuth seemed in danger as did Nürnberg. Friedrich of Brandenburg hastily met with Hussite leaders at Beheimstein Castle, three miles from Nürnberg, on 11 February 1430 and was able to negotiate a temporary truce (UB 2, pp. 109–29). Orphan armies under the command of Prokůpek went into Moravia and Slovakia and fought against Hungarian forces at Trnava in March 1430. The battle was fierce. Windecke tells us that 2,000 Hussites were killed and 'nearly 6,000 Christians. May God have mercy on us' (Windecke, p. 280). Four crusades against the heretics had accomplished little beyond inadvertently enabling the Hussites to strengthen their borders. Now the theatre of war was expanding.]

In the year of the birth of the son of God 1430, in the week before our Lord's birth, many Czechs and Moravians gathered together in great force and marched as warriors toward Meißen to avenge the dear ones murdered by the Misnians during the reign of King Václav in the forest before Prague. They marched also to other lands through Meißen where they first quickly conquered Plavno and the castle because that one of Plavno [Heinrich of Plavno] had not observed the agreement with the Praguers when they released him from prison. They sinfully murdered many people in the town and they destroyed the town as well as the castle by fire. The Germans were frightened by this and fled from castles, towns and also from well fortified places not wishing to oppose the Czechs. The Czechs riding through those lands, in Franconia and elsewhere, burned several thousand villages and small towns. When the Czechs invaded their land, the prince of Meißen gathered in force near Grimma. Hearing this, the Czechs marched straight towards him and drew into formation willing to engage him on the field. And they marched in formation for ten days. When they came to the town of Grimma they had to cross the stream which flows beneath the town. When three lines of wagons entered the water, the water swelled on account of the wagons and upset the other wagons. At this moment some of the people jumped into the water to assist the other wagons, dragging them out one after the other using ropes without horse. In the end they had to cross over the water in a single line. When half of the wagons had crossed, a shout went up in the army that the Germans were marching upon him. The Czechs were in great danger because half of the wagons and people [were still on the other side]. Those who had crossed, however, drew into formation and marched on against the Germans. The Germans had only sent out a few hundred cavalry to take a look at the Czechs. The Czechs, expecting them all at once, attacked them and thrashed them, capturing many others. The other Germans hearing of this, fled to their homes and the following day the margrave of Meißen dismissed his troops while he went on to Thuringia by way of Leipzig.

Then Jan Zmrzlík [of Svojšín] was highly praised for attacking the Germans so bravely and encouraging the others. Meanwhile night came and the Czechs waited for the second half of their wagons. They did not sleep all night and were guarded on account of the Germans. On the next day they marched near to Leipzig and saw that the Misnians had ordered the buildings set on fire and the army had retreated. So the Czechs were able to ride freely throughout the land, divided into five armies. Having burned a great deal of the land of Meißen they marched on towards Franconia and from there to Bayreuth. From there the Germans fled and the Czechs turned towards Bamberg.[4] Hearing that they [the Hussites] were entering those areas, the people of Nürnberg sent the margrave of Brandenburg with a safe conduct to the Czechs and reached an agreement, paid several thousand gulden, so that the Czechs would not march onward and they would deliver the money to Domažlice on the designated day. There Prokop Holý and Lord Kostka, received the gulden and divided it among themselves.

Never before had the Czechs engaged in such a magnificent ride as that into Meißen. No one could remember anything quite like it and nothing of the sort had ever been recorded in the chronicles. According to common opinion, there were about 40,000 men. Had their intention been simply to obtain glory, in the manner of their predecessors, they could have marched all the way to the Rhine and utterly conquered numerous nations. But having accomplished their purpose, they returned to Bohemia.

SRB 3: 78–9.

146   Hussite invasion of Lusatia

[This brief report supplements the previous document noting the invasion of Lusatia but also highlighting the blitzkrieg Hussite campaign through Meißen. The chronicler does not attempt to explain how or why the Hussites managed to invade, plunder and advance through the German lands relatively unhindered but the anti-heretical bias is clear.]

In the aforementioned year of the Lord [1430] and in the preceding year 1429, the Hussites came pouring out of the mountains from Bohemia and attacked the six towns of Upper Lusatia as well as Lower Lusatia and they destroyed Gubin [27 October], that commendable and wine producing town right down to the ground

---

[4]   See Gerhard Schlesinger, *Die Hussiten in Franken: Der Hussiteneinfall unter Prokop dem Großen im Winter 1429/30, seine Auswirkungen sowie sein Niederschlag in der Geschichtschreibung* (Kulmbach: Stadtarchiv, Freunde der Plassenburg, 1974).

by fire, plunder and killing. Additionally, they directed their forces into the land
of Meißen where they devastated almost the entire land beyond the Elbe River.
Although innumerable armies of the neighbouring princes and barons were
gathered together there, namely those of the duke of Saxony, of the margraves of
Meißen, of the margrave of Brandenburg, of the duke of Brunswick, of the
archbishop of Magdeburg, with a great host of people, notwithstanding this, they
[the Hussites], led by a spirit of confusion and blinded by a cloud of error,
accomplished nothing good at all. However, they were able to obtain free passage
as they willed through all the land of Meißen and Thuringia. They came without
hindrance as far as Bamberg and from there they returned to Bohemia with a very
great plunder. The end.

SRP 3: 492.

147 Prokop replies to German towns requesting peace

[As part of the so called 'magnificent rides', the Hussite armies stormed across the
Lusatian lands before heading for Franconia. Friedrich II of Saxony, with a
powerful force, intercepted the Hussites at Grimma but the heretics put them to
flight. Prokop's armies conquered Altenburg and at the end of January 1430 they
took Plavno. Then, in quick succession, they conquered Hof, Bayreuth and
Klumbach. As they pressed into the diocese of Bamberg efforts were made to
secure peace.[5] Friedrich of Brandenburg hurried back from the Imperial diet at
Bratislava. Bishop Friedrich fled from Bamberg but representatives from Bamberg
and two other towns offered to pay the Hussites not to sack their communities.
The Hussite answer, written perhaps appropriately by Prokop Holý, is dated 2
February 1430.]

Priest Prokop, the military captain of the field armies of Tábor to the famous lords
Swirpold of Brandenstein, Johannes Kastner of Weismain and to the mayors of the
communities of Bamberg, Scheßlitz and Hollfeld. The offer of my services as time
permits and as you desire. I desire and wish for the salvation of your souls.

   Dear friends! As you have given notice through your letters which were sent
to me by your messengers, you ask that your estates not be plundered by the
armies in the way in which other regions have been plundered, and that a peace
might be entered into between you and our forces. Therefore, you offer yourself

---

[5] On these events see Schlesinger, *Die Hussiten in Franken*, pp. 76–81 and Thomas Krzenck,
'Die große Heerfahrt der Hussiten 1429–1430 und der Bamberger Aufstand in Februar 1430'
Mediaevalia Historica Bohemica 2 (1992), pp. 119–41.

voluntarily to give a certain amount of money to our armies. I wish to advise you that I have already communicated your proposal and offer to the armies, namely the Táborites and Orphans, for consideration, and also to the lords and barons, Praguers, knights and warriors who belong to the Kingdom of Bohemia. The will of the aforementioned armies and lords is that you be notified by letter. They ask first, that you return to the truth of the gospel. For these truths they have been leading a daily struggle up until the present time. If you agree to this, then the plunders will cease immediately and they will under no circumstances extort money from you. They would rather defend you from those who would assault you than plunder you in the manner of war.

However, if you do not decide to agree to the truths of the gospel for which our forces contend, but should you wish to think it over for some time, may you be assured that the will of the aforementioned armies and all of the lords who are of the Kingdom of Bohemia is this: if you desire to save your lives and your goods you are to provide them with a certain amount of money such as an advancement or subsidy for their labours.

Thus, our aforementioned forces require that the town of Bamberg, with all of its garrisons and communities, villages and so on, as well as the town of Scheßlitz and herewith the town of Hollfeld, give them 50,000 Rhine guilders.[6] Should you agree to do this, you should confirm this through worthy guarantors and letters that you will give them half of the amount in cash now and the second half soon. When you do this, all of your assets will remain safe and secure in accordance with the arrangement with the aforementioned armies. Do not neglect, either by night or day, to reply according to your common and united will. Given on Thursday, the day of the purification of the Virgin Mary. Priest Prokop, director of the Táborite field armies.

Josef Macek, ed. *Ktož jsú boží bojovníci: Čtení o Táboře v husitském revolučním hnutí.* Prague: Melantrich, 1951, pp. 197–8.

148   Burgundian crusade preparations

[In response to calls for renewed crusade, Philip the Good, duke of Burgundy, is representative of positive responses. While the manuscript gives the date as 1429, there is some chance it should be dated to 1430.]

---

[6]   Since the two smaller towns had already been captured by Hussite armies, the fee for Bamberg was reduced to 12,000 florins.

Philip, Duke of Burgundy, Count of Flanders, Artois, Burgundy, Palatine of Namur, Lord of Salins and of Malines, to the governor of our sovereign domain of Lille, Douay, Orchies and its appendages, and to the governor of our domains of Arras, Bappaulmes, Aubigny, Hannin-Lietard and Quiery, and to all of our countries, lands and lordships, and to those of which we have government, and to their lieutenants, greetings.

In order to take precautions against the very great and damnable evils, dangers and irreparable consequences, which to the reviling, scandal and enormous injury of our Catholic faith and of our holy mother church, to our great displeasure was seen to occur in our country and within our lordships, especially in our town and stronghold of Lille, caused by that which several of our subjects in next to no time, through the seduction of the enemy, have held, believed and taught several damnable errors which the false heretics of Prague hold against our Christian faith and our holy mother church; and in order to deceive other simple people by the said errors in the damnable and perverse sect of the Praguers, have held several secret meetings in suspicious places and at suspect hours.

After having had information on this fact several times before the judges of the faith, and several of our said subjects as suspects and charged in the aforementioned cases (in particular Aleaume Polet, Thomas Vuemel, Pierart du Puch, Pierart Estoquiel, of Lille; Colart Gulant, Jehan Hacoul, Piat Morel, Jacot de Goutieres, Mahieu Quedin, of Seclin; Jehan du Pire, Gillot Flament, Jehan de Hellin, Henri Des Mons, of Avelin; Jehan Dannetieres, Pierart le Maire, of Annevelin; Jehan d'Egrement called the Brown, of Fretin; Jehan Tart, from Torquiong; Vincent Blahuer, Pierart Brassart, of Landas; and Jehan du Breuch, of Avechin) who thus accused, neither wished to return to obedience to our said holy mother church nor to be reconciled to her, being obstinate in their wickedness. There were others of them who absented themselves and made themselves fugitives, and others are in hiding in secret places in our said towns and countries [. .] and in concealment.

For what is it that we, as a Catholic prince for the maintenance of our true faith and of our holy mother church, would wish for our person and for our vassals [. .] and even villeins [. .], and that this matter we have much to proclaim and would not wish it for anything to tolerate giving way – we order and commit and to each of you as will belong to him, very seriously and clearly that the said Aleaume Polet, Thomas Veumel and others named above, wherever they can be found, in a holy place or outside, you will approach them in order to immediately arrest them and deliver them to the priests and inquisitors, judges in this matter in order to do what is right. And yet all others, whom by the same judges will be required and that they affirm to you to be guilty of the aforementioned errors, or having received, favoured, harboured or defended the above named or other similar people, in the same way, wherever they be found, take by authority forthwith and deliver them to the said judges without query or delay, in order to proceed against them as must be right; and so that in fact this damnable sect can be in every way eradicated and prevented from arising again through negligence. For the favour of our faith and of our holy mother church this would certainly please us.

In order to accomplish this, we give full power, authority and a special commission to you and to your officers and deputies. We order and command all our judicial officials, officers and subjects, requesting and requiring of all others, that they obey and understand carefully both you and your commissioned officers and deputies. That they hasten and give advice, comfort, help and assistance and render service of what they have and of what is required of them.

Given at our town of Lille, the 11th day of March in the year of grace 1429, under our secret seal in absence of the great seal. For my lord the Duke: (Lancelot Savarre?).

Neumann, 'Francouzská husitika', pp. 113–15.

149   Joan of Arc threatens the Hussites

[The authenticity of this letter has always been in dispute. The document purports to be a missive from Joan of Arc to the heretical Hussites threatening to turn her attention on them if they do not cease and desist from their errors and heresies and resistance to the church and return to the orthodox faith. The letter is almost certainly apocryphal and may have been part of a strategy of propaganda aimed at intimidating the Hussites. Nonetheless, its importance may be gauged in part from the fact that František Palacký, the leading nineteenth-century historian of Hussitica, discovered a copy among the documents of the Imperial Chancellory referring to Sigismund. It is worth noting that Henry Beaufort, papal legate for the fourth crusade, was one of Joan's jailers. The letter is dated 23 March 1430.]

Jesus Mary. Long ago the rumour of your fame was brought to me, the girl Joan, that you, becoming heretical from true Christianity, and similar to the Saracens, have wrecked the true religion and have accepted an ugly and godless superstition and you persist in this and attempt to extend it. There is no perversity or cruelty which you have not entered into. You pollute the sacraments of the church, tear apart the articles of faith, destroy churches, smash images of good remembrance, and kill Christians in order to maintain your faith. Where does your fury come from, or what obsession of rage drives you? What the almighty God, the Son and the Holy Spirit brought to life, appointed, established and illuminated in a thousand ways by a thousand miracles, that faith you persecute, overturn and work to exterminate. You are blind, and not as those who have no eyes and cannot see. Do you really think that you shall escape punishment? Do you not consider that God does not put an end to your nefarious tendencies and allows you to remain in darkness and be overturned by error so that the longer you are in error so much more are you intoxicated with sacrilege, the greater will be the punishment and execution God prepares for you?

I confess truly that if I were not occupied in war with the English I would have already come. But really, if I do not see that you have amended your ways, I will leave off the English and turn against you in order to exterminate that vain and obdurate superstition [of yours] by force. I shall rid you either of heresy or of life. But should you prefer to return to the Catholic faith and to the former light, send your envoys to me and I will tell them what is proper for you to do. But if you wish to resist in any way with stubborn will against this suggestion, remember that you have perpetrated damnation and crime and thus you can expect me to be prepared to take vengeance on all of you with both human and divine force. Given in Sully [on] 23 March.

UB 2: 132.

150   Manifesto of the captains of Tábor

[This manifesto argues for the abandonment of the official church on the grounds that the clergy are most dangerous. The document outlines a sixteen-point agenda of grievances against the Roman Church. The letter refers to Hus and Jerome and includes the Four Articles of Prague in its concluding sections. The principal author is Prokop Holý and the manifesto can be dated to 1430. A revision was published the following year. See doc.151.]

We desire that the almighty Father would reveal and confirm to all Christians the knowledge of his son Jesus Christ through the Holy Spirit and that he would illuminate your hearts with divine justice. We desire that you would remain strong and persevere to the end and be saved.

Venerable and worthy lords together with the whole community, both rich and poor, listen carefully to the words of this letter which is addressed to you from the land of Bohemia.

You well know, just as it is known to everyone, in numerous cities and foreign regions, to kings and princes and lords, that a number of years ago a great dispute and discord arose between us and you to the extent that you have engaged in warfare against us in an effort to destroy us. As a result – and this is painful to say – both common men and nobility have lost their lives unnecessarily both from your side as well as ours. All of this has happened and you have never actually heard from our mouths what our faith is and whether or not we can prove it and defend it from the Holy Scriptures. Due to this inattention, kings and princes, lords and cities have been heavily damaged. For this reason we are most astonished by the fact that you put your faith in the pope and believe him and his clergy who give you a pernicious, silly and vacuous comfort and this is exactly what it is. They promise you the remission of all your sins and offer you great grace as well as indulgences if you will go to battle against us and annihilate us. But their indulgences and grace are nothing other than pure lies and a monstrous seduction of souls as well as the bodies of those who believe thus and rely on it.

We desire to attempt to persuade you on the basis of Holy Scripture, in the hearing of all those who wish to listen, that the pope and his clerics are doing to you precisely what the Devil has done to our Lord Jesus Christ just as Luke wrote in his fourth chapter: 'The devil took him up on a very high mountain and in a moment showed him all the powers of the world and said to him, I will give to you all of this power as well as the glory which has been given to me which I can give to anyone I desire. If you will perform an act of worship before me, all of these things can be yours' [Luke 4:5–7]. In the same way the Devil has enchanted the pope and his clergy with the riches of this world and temporal power. They think they have the authority to dispense grace and indulgences to anyone although they themselves will not find grace before Almighty God if they do not repent and provide satisfaction for their enormous seduction of Christianity! In what manner can they really give to others something they themselves do not possess? The Devil who is rich in promises but impotent and poor in gifts has given them assurance. If the Devil is not afraid of lying, so likewise are they of promoting something which is not the truth and for which they cannot adduce a single proof from the Holy Scriptures.

As a matter of fact they instigate kings, princes and lords, as well as cities, to fight against us not on behalf of the Christian faith but instead so that their hidden crimes and heresy would neither be revealed nor spread abroad. If they had a true and proper godly predilection for the Christian faith they would take the books of Holy Scripture in their hands and would then do battle with us using as their only weapon the divine word. This is something we have earnestly desired for a long time. The apostle of our Lord Jesus Christ did this with a gentle spirit as it has been written in Galatians [6:1]: 'Brothers, if an individual has been involved in some fault, you who have the Spirit should instruct them with a kind spirit.' In this same way should our enemies behave if they are truly right and we are wrong and we refuse instruction then at that point they could call then for the help of kings and dukes and all imperial cities against us and persecute us according to the rule and proper procedures of Holy Scripture. But the bishops and priests have an excuse and a cunning reason for not doing this. They say that Masters Hus and

Jerome were found to be in manifest error by the holy father the pope and the entire council at Constance and were therefore burned at the stake. So thus it can be answered that they were not convicted of error by Holy Scripture but instead on the basis of trifling and violence. But those who have given this advice and who aided in this affair will be punished severely by God.

Moreover they affirm that it is not possible for them to hear us out concerning our faith. In what way can they prove that they do not have to listen to us except by using the Holy Scriptures? This is something we have desired for a very long time. Even Jesus Christ, our Lord, listened to the Devil, just as it is recorded in Matthew chapter four [vss. 1–11]. Apparently they are better than Jesus Christ and we are worse than the Devil!

If they are righteous men who have truth in themselves as they indeed affirm, and we are unrighteous, why then are they afraid of us since the truth does not have to fear falsehoods as it is written in the second book of Esdras where Zerubbabel says, 'the truth is great and stronger than all other things.'[7] Christ our Lord is truth and the announcement of it as he says in the fourteenth chapter of the Gospel of John [John 14:6]: 'I am the way and the truth. No one can go to the Father except through me.' But the Devil is the cause of falsehoods as it is written in John [8:44]: 'He was a murderer ever since the beginning and he did not remain in the truth because the truth is not in him.'

Therefore, if the pope and the entire clergy have truth, there is no doubt they will be superior to us and will defeat us with the word of God. However, if they are on the side of lies, it will be impossible to prove their conviction and intention. For this reason, beloved and sincere people and lords, rich and poor, we exhort you and all Imperial cities together with the king, dukes and the lords in the name of divine justice to come to a written agreement among yourselves for a day of negotiation which shall be certain and opportune for both you and us. At this time you may bring your bishops and scholars and we shall bring our scholars. We will permit them to do battle using the word of God before all of us and no one shall triumph using violence or evil cunning, but shall use only the word of God! If your bishops and doctors demonstrate the superiority of their faith from Holy Scripture and our faith pronounced unrighteous in that case we will desire to correct ourselves and repent according to the Holy Gospel. On the other hand, if your doctors and bishops are the ones defeated with reasoning from the Holy Scriptures, then in that case you will repent and unite with us and remain with us. If your bishops, doctors and priests do not wish to cast aside their spiritual

---

[7] I Esdras 3:12 states 'truth is victor over all things.' I Esdras 4:13–40 is an oration in praise of truth delivered by Zerubbabel which points out that 'truth endures and is strong forever, and lives and prevails for ever and ever.' This became a slogan of the Hussites during the crusade period and can be found throughout Hussite literature, songs and iconography.

arrogance and correct themselves or do acts of repentance we will then exercise our power in order to force them to correct themselves and be converted; otherwise we will expel them from Christianity.

If your bishops and doctors say that it is not the responsibility of the laity to interfere and demand a hearing this is to be understood to the effect that they are fearful of defeat and embarrassed before the people and thereby to forfeit public respect. But if they thought they could win there is no doubt they would want many people to listen because it would increase their honour and glory as well as their reputation across the land.

On the other hand, if your bishops and doctors advise that you should have nothing to do with us or listen to us and gladly abide by this you should do at least this one thing: Do not allow yourself to be deceived in such a silly manner as it will happen with their false indulgences. Instead, stay at home with your wives, children and property and let your Roman pope with his cardinals and bishops and all the clergy face us personally in order to do battle. In this way they could gain for themselves these indulgences and remission of their sins as well as the grace they offer to you since they themselves apparently have no need of the remission of sins, of grace or of indulgences! We will have almighty God to help us and we will give them indulgences!

They excuse themselves wickedly saying that the priests are not permitted to make physical war. It is true that this is as much their task as it is to incite others to fight, to give advice and to encourage others when the blessed St Paul says in Galatians [sic] chapter one [Romans 1:32], 'all who do such things, deserve death and not only these who do so but also those who approve what is done.'

However, if they are always making war against us then we wish to protect and defend the truth with the help of God until death. We do not fear the threats or excommunications of the pope, his cardinals and bishops. We know well that the pope is not God no matter how much he behaves as though he were and as if he were permitted to damn anyone and excommunicate him, or to the contrary, redeem anyone he wishes. He has asserted this through denunciation and excommunication. Nevertheless, God has not failed to help us. May all thanks be given to God's grace. You might object of course [and say], we know from our own experience that the bishops and priests are malignant sinners. However, we do not wish to do away with them because we need them. Who would baptize our children? Who would hear our confessions and serve the holy sacraments? We would fall into the papal and episcopal ban. Dearly beloved! Do not be fearful of this! The papal excommunication cannot hurt you, but you should be on your guard in terms of God's ban. God can certainly manage, if you exclude the malignant bishops and priests, and you can obtain as compensation good priests who will baptize, hear confessions and serve the sacraments. Wherever the Devil is expelled, a place is made for the Holy Spirit and where evil bishops and priests are ejected, good ones take their place.

Your bishops and priests announce today that we are unfaithful and that we hold to heresy in that we do not believe in purgatory, the Virgin Mary, the mother of God and in the saints. They do not speak the truth. We wish to prove from Holy Scripture that on account of divine grace we know better than they are able to learn what we ought to believe about purgatory, Mary the mother of God and the dear saints. They assert, in opposition, that we should submit to the holy father the pope. If he is truly holy and just, we know we are obliged to be obedient and subject to him in all good things. They also assert that we destroy and ravish the holy and divine offices by uprooting them and demolishing the monasteries, expelling the monks and nuns from them. Previously we assumed that they were holy and piously rendering service to God. But as we have gotten to know them closely and watched their lives and actions we have come to understand that they are holy hypocrites of artful humility and vacuous show-offs, sellers of indulgences and requiems, living off the sins of people.

They say that it is necessary to provide for them because they get up even in the middle of the night while other people are sleeping in order to pray and to intercede for the sins of the people. But their prayers, intercessions and requiems are done for gifts and nothing other than hypocrisy and the heresy of simony. If we drive them away and demolish their monasteries we do not disturb the true divine service, only the fortifications of devils and heretics. As soon as you recognize them as well as we have, you will destroy them with the same zeal as we do. Since Christ our Lord has established no monastic order by his word it is essential to abolish them sooner or later according to the statement of the Lord in the fifteenth chapter of Matthew's gospel: 'every plant not planted by my heavenly father shall be pulled up' [Matthew 15:13]. Therefore we require you to devote careful attention to the articles which we give to you concerning these matters and to what your bishops and priests have not prepared.

The first article: When your bishops accede to the ordination of priests, they grudgingly ordain the candidates of holy orders who do not have a sufficiently large stipend on which to live. However, Christ ordered the priests to be poor. Matthew writes in the tenth chapter: 'you should have neither gold nor silver' while the bishops declare their need to have dominion over the land which is iniquitous against the righteousness of God [Matthew 10:9].

The second article: The bishops require payment and money from their ordinands even though St Peter castigated Simon Magus because he wanted to buy spiritual value with worldly goods as it is written in the eighth chapter of the Acts of the Apostles [Acts 8:18–24].

The third article: Those running for the priesthood enter the priestly state not for divine justice, namely intending to preach and to spread the Christian faith among the people, in order to teach and to correct, but for aspiration of lazy life and plenty of food and drink, and for worldly honour and dignity. Everyone who creeps into the priesthood with such intentions is a thief and a robber just as the evangelist John writes in the tenth chapter [John 10:1].

The fourth article: The pope and all his clergy appropriate to themselves the ban of excommunication, by means of which they violate and enslave Christian people, deciding themselves who shall be excommunicated and damned before God. But we wish to prove by Holy Scripture that they themselves are damned before God because they do not keep the commandment of God's love of which Paul writes in the first epistle to the Corinthians in the sixteenth chapter: 'whoever does not love the Lord, let him be damned' [1 Corinthians 16:22]. This means until the Lord comes because they cannot excommunicate and enslave you while they themselves are excommunicated and bound before God and all the saints. Why are you afraid of their ban?

The fifth article: Receiving gifts for their prayers for the dead and for requiems is a naked heresy before God. Therefore the wrong is perpetrated by all who give them anything for this purpose and thus make merchants of the priests trafficking in prayers and requiems. By this abuse the entire Roman Church is poisoned today by this venom. If they wish to pray and read the requiem for the dead, on this account no one sins if they do not take anything for it, whether much or little. However, to take gifts in order to redeem souls from purgatory they help their own souls into hell. Those giving to them lose everything they give. The pope with all his clergy have swindled through this devilish deceit and have stolen the rights of kings, princes, barons, knights and squires. He has subjected them to vassalage through the heritage by which in times past their fathers and mothers founded institutions, monasteries and churches, in order to remember their souls and pray and sing and read the requiems for their delivery from purgatory. From these goods the power of bishops, canons, and monasteries have been enriched and built up to the point where today they are able to fight against imperial cities, princes and lords. Although they should mediate peace between lords and cities, they are those who violate the peace. They possess these goods wrongly and should surrender them. But as long as they do this they will not cease fighting and struggling with the cities, princes and barons. Therefore, they do not encourage the right foundation of truth with a single word but are rather like dogs who gnaw bones and are silent and do not bark. Until these people have the sweet bone of riches and delights for themselves, it will never be well in the world. Therefore all the kings, princes, barons and the imperial cities would cause a great goodness if they wrested that sweet bone out of their mouths caring not if they awakened their anger as the dogs rave when the bone is taken from them.

So dear lords, kings, princes, imperial cities and all people, rich and poor, if you have slept until now, awake and open your eyes and see the glaring deceit of the Devil and may you understand how the Roman Church has been blinded by that and take what belongs to you and not to the church. If you wish to have your souls in good memory, you should act according to the statement of Solomon who says in Ecclesiasticus 29: 'close the alms in the heart of the poor man and he will pray you out of everything bad' [Sirach 29:15]. May you fulfil for the poor those six acts of mercy of which Matthew wrote [Matthew 25:35].

The sixth article: They are full of pride and arrogance when they appear in public in long, expensive and useless habits in which they walk quite differently from our Lord Christ who was satisfied with one seamless robe and the dear John Baptist who had sufficient with a robe of camel hair. It was the sermon which taught us true human worth. They want to instruct us to honour their priesthood, as it suits and becomes but far and wide no one does more damage to the priestly state, no one makes a greater disgrace and shame, than they do by their wicked deeds, evil way of life and bad words which they carry on in front of the eyes of all. Paul writes in the first epistle to Timothy in the fifth chapter [17]: 'let the priests who regard themselves as superior, be considered worthy of double honour.' Take note that he emphasizes 'the ones who approve themselves' and not 'who have not approved themselves.'

The seventh article: From the highest to the lowest they are always avaricious and from their greedy gold-digging they fabricate vain myths, wilful lies and they traffic in the holy sacraments which is the greatest heresy because God has given to them and commanded them to serve without charge. Though St Paul writes in the first letter to Timothy [6:10]; 'avarice is the root of all evil, for because of the desire for money many have gone astray from the faith' and therefore they have lost the faith.

The eighth article: Most of them are public fornicators, everyone can see their concubines and children which they themselves show openly in the streets. They incite the wives of many men to adultery and they deflower their virgin daughters and make them concubines. St Paul writes against that in the epistles to Romans [2:2–9] and Galatians [5:19–21] and in the first epistle to the Corinthians [6:9], that the publicly impure ones do not obtain the kingdom of heaven unless they give it up, repent and do penance.

The ninth article: They are full of devilish envy and especially in the monasteries they fret with jealousy and animosity if one monastery or institution obtains a gift or alms. Then the other institutions and monasteries become envious and hate them on that account because they wish to have everything for themselves. They behave like dogs. If you give to one and not to another they all growl and they want to eat everything themselves. Therefore it would be proper to release them from this great sin of jealousy and give them nothing. And it would be even better to take from them what they have. And the best would be to expel them all out at once and say to them what the Lord said to his disciples: 'let you go and preach the gospel of the kingdom to all the world' [Matthew 16:15].

The tenth article: They are lazy, especially the bishops, canons and other prelates. They do not want to study diligently Holy Scripture of which they should care for holy Christendom like the teachers as they are obligated. They eat their bread as do the idlers. While other people are getting up early and working to sustain themselves and their children, they lie about with their concubines or go walking around whenever they want. Some of them have been carrying hunting birds, or sitting in pubs with good wine and playing dice with whores, singing, playing the lute and [eating] sumptuous meals. All who bring and volunteer worldly goods will obtain their part in the same damnation by which they will be confronted by God because they eat the bread they have not earned. St Paul speaks of it in the second epistle to the Thessalonians [3:10]: 'whoever does not work, should not eat.'

The eleventh article: They lie knowingly. Because they want to be liked by the people they spread any lie which has no basis or foundation in Holy Scripture. John writes about such people in the twenty-first chapter of the Apocalypse [v.8]: 'the share of all liars will be in the lake of burning fire and sulphur which is the second death.'

The twelfth article: They do not serve the Christian people, as they should, the holy body of our Lord Jesus Christ and they do not do so in the way that God constituted and commanded presuming it to be a devilish sin. We want to convince the pope and all his clergy and persuade them by the holy evangelists, Matthew, Mark, Luke and by Paul's first letter to the Corinthians, and we wish to invite to this audience the kings, princes and barons and all who care about this.

The thirteenth article: When they sit in ecclesiastical judgement they deliver a verdict according to their patronage and not according to God's justice. They accept bribes and gifts and do not judge according to law but instead they concede the right to the one who has no right before God and they damn as wrong the one who has right on his side. Woe to such judges! The prophet Isaiah writes in the fifth chapter: 'woe to you who say good is bad and bad is good, who replace darkness with light and light with darkness, the bitter for sweet and the sweet for bitter' [Isaiah 5:20]. Solomon says in the second chapter of the book of Proverbs: 'whoever excuses the godless one and condemns the just one, both are an abomination in the sight of God' [Proverbs 17:15].

The fourteenth article: When they hear the confessions of extortioners, robbers, thieves and merchants, they receive gifts from them and forgive them and tolerate all public sinners with bribes even though God has forbidden it.

The fifteenth article: They accept tithes from people and exact them through their sermons as they would be paid in accordance with the law and they assert the people are obligated to pay them. They have been announcing falsehood in this matter and they cannot prove by the New Testament that the Lord Jesus Christ ever commanded one to give tithes. On one hand it is true that in the Old Testament there was a commandment about giving tithes but on the other hand they cannot derive from that Christian people are obliged to pay them now as. This Old Testament commandment of tithes lost validity through the death of Christ just as the commandment of circumcision lost validity. Pay attention dearly beloved and consider how much your bishops and teachers seduce you and how they pour dust into your eyes by their requests and statements which cannot be proven. Yet our Lord Jesus Christ tells us in the second chapter of Luke: 'let you give alms' but he does not say 'let you give tithes' from your assets. As soon as you hear these words, in all probability they say with the expert in the law in the eleventh chapter: 'Master, when you say this, you offend us also' [Luke 11:45].

The sixteenth article: From the ends of the earth they accept money from payment and usury on villages and towns and they have their temporary or perpetual payments and income as powerful governors and agrarian lords. They have opposed presumptuously the commandment of the tenth chapter of Matthew's gospel: 'do not have either gold or silver' [Matthew 10:9]. In opposition to this gain from payment and usury God says in the twenty-third chapter of Deuteronomy: 'you will not lend to your brother for usury neither money nor corn nor any other thing, but to the foreigner; though to your brother you will lend without usury whatever he needs' [Deuteronomy 23:19–20].

Honourable, prudent and dear lords, we are willing to explain to you all of these articles described here and to demonstrate them against the pope and all his clergy through many witnesses of Holy Scripture which we have not quoted here for the sake of brevity. Finally you must consider closely and with special attention the four articles for which we fight and for which we wish to protect and defend them with our whole heart until death.

The first article requires that all public mortal sin of the priests and laity be forbidden according to the commandment of Holy Scripture which is corroborated by many testimonies of Scripture and so on.

The second article requires the pope and all the clergy, from the highest to the lowest, to have their wealth taken away in order to be reduced to poverty and to be like the holy apostles of our Lord Jesus Christ who were poor and owned nothing. They had no worldly estates, did not govern and had no secular power.

The third article requires that the word of God be proclaimed free by anyone who would be established and constituted for it. This does not depend on the existing government. Preaching must not be inhibited, either publicly or secretly by anyone and must not be forbidden either by an ecclesiastical or secular person.

The fourth article requires the holy body of our Lord Jesus Christ be given to every Christian according to the institution and commandment of God as written by the evangelists.

Further, we have been informed that the council is to be convoked in Basel. Do not let anyone be happy and joyful about this, but let each one prefer rather to guard diligently his wife, daughters and servant girls from the bishops, priests and monks. Do not believe that they convoke a holy gathering or that the bishops, priests and prelates would perhaps like to work for the common good and the reformation of Christendom. Their intention is to hide and to cover their secret blasphemy and error under the blanket of hypocrisy and to empty and deceive by intrigue divine justice which is utterly against them. Therefore may you carefully realize that they do not convoke a holy assembly but a satanic and devilish one. Let the people of Basel pay attention so as not to end up like the citizens of Constance. Although they obtained gifts from the bishops and prelates they had to allow their wives to sleep with them.

Dear honourable lords, if you find some hard words in this letter which we write, you should know that we have not used them to offend or displease you but to make you realize better and more attentively what the state of Christendom is under the watch and care of the contemporary priests. May our Lord Jesus Christ give you health in body and soul. Amen. Written in the year of the Lord 1430. [Signed] Prokop, Markold, Koranda, Záviš and Smolík, captains of Bohemia.

Husitské manifesty, pp. 156–70.

151   Defending the Hussite cause

[This manifesto to the inhabitants of the Kingdom of Bohemia, dated 25 May 1430 consists of a protracted recitation of authorities in extenso: among them, the Hebrew Bible, New Testament, Clement, Origen, Jerome, John Chrysostom, third council of Carthage (397), Augustine, Gregory, Isidore, Ambrose, Peter Lombard, Esdras, Ecclesiasticus, and Paschasius. All of these are cited in support of the main thrust of the manifesto which comes at the end which is simply that the four articles are salutary and the Hussites will defend them until death.]

In hope the faithful Christians and inhabitants of the Kingdom of Bohemia have recognized that considerable sin, both serious and minor, have originated on account of the sin of the better situated people especially the priests. We can indeed repeat what the prophet Jeremiah said in chapter four of his lamentation: 'kings of the earth and all the inhabitants of the regions of the world have not believed that the enemy could enter the gates of Jerusalem on account of the sins of the prophets and the iniquity of the priests' [4:12–13]. Similarly Jeremiah speaks in his prophecy [23:11]: 'a prophet and a priest are polluted and I have found dishonesty in my house, says the Lord.' And further we read: 'therefore the

Lord is telling the prophets, look, I will feed them with sage and imbue them with gall because the pollution comes from Jerusalem into the whole earth' [23:15].

In the hope that these circumstances can be made better through the use of opportune means and moved by the Spirit of God, the Czechs have understood that the public nuisances in the militant church do not stop until the clergy is returned to their original evangelistic state. It is our opinion that the fulfilment of the following demands contributes to the correction of them. Let the secular goods as well as secular dominion be prohibited to the priests of Christ in the time of the law of grace in accordance with divine and human law and in the sense of ancient teachers and of reasonable statements. Let the priests return to the rule of the gospel and to the ordinary life which Christ lived with his apostles . . . .

[Here follows a long citation of authorities.]

If anyone wants to regard our right and holy views as dishonourable and inexpressible vice let that one be considered by believing Christians as an unequal and unrighteous witness. We have nothing in our hearts but readiness for our Lord Jesus Christ with all our might and to the best of our ability to keep and fulfil his law, his commandments and these four articles. Therefore we wish to oppose every evil person who attacks us on account of these truths and who attempts to turn us from God and from this decision and to persecute us. Under the bulwark of the truth of the gospel which binds everyone, we will stand and resist with the utmost force these wretches and the most cruel man of Antichrist. And if it happens that someone of our community perpetrates some injury or vice we declare that it has been done against our will. Our intention is to eliminate all vices and to suppress them. Additionally we confess that many evil disorders within Christianity come forth from this. That is, the secular and ecclesiastical powers do not acknowledge the aforementioned evangelical four articles. We accuse them plainly of working to extirpate us through various and sundry ways and means full of sinister intentions. But we hold to the aforesaid four articles by the grace of God even at the cost of being damned by this world.

We proclaim our constant readiness to be instructed according to Holy Scripture, should anyone be able to prove to us any fallacy in any of these things which we or our people hold. Given in the year of the Lord 1430 on the day of the ascension of Christ [25 May].

Husitské manifesty, pp. 128–46.

152   Hussite attempts to neutralize Lusatia

[This short communication underscores the Hussite willingness to limit the war as well as their concern for neighbouring communities, especially in terms of securing support. The document is dated 28 November 1430.]

We, captain Jakob of Březovice, Zygmunt, by the grace of God, prince of Lithuania, the lord of Glivice, Lord Prokop, barons, knights, yeomen, and senior warriors of the Táborite armies, working in the field in the name of the Lord, to the prudent counsellors, mayor, and the entire community of Namysłów.

Because we desire your welfare, we are puzzled that you stubbornly neglect to avoid these damages which have come to you and to the surrounding communities and that you do not inquire as to why this damage and plunder happens to you. You should know that such damages to you and the surrounding communities, which you seem not to be too concerned about causes us pain. Since we intend good for you, we desire to meet with you following the campaign so that we could notify you, in kindness to you and your dependants, of what we plunder. We are willing to provide a guarantee to confirm that you will come to the meeting and also to return from it. However, if you do not wish to do this, your damages will be increased.

Given in the field near Namysław on Tuesday following the feast of St Catherine [25 November] in the year 1430 under our common seal.

SRS 6: 99.

153   Cesarini's plan for a new crusade

[On 14 March 1431, Cardinal Guiliano Cesarini, papal legate for the fifth crusade, outlined his proposal for the anti-heresy undertaking in Nürnberg to Sigismund and the Reichstag which was in session at that time. His urgency and commitment for the campaign was communicated by Jan Stojković of Dubrovnik to the officials gathering in Basel for the council in the document which follows. While his envoy went to Basel, Cesarini commenced a three month tour to 'preach the cross'. He travelled throughout Germany, met Philip the Good of Burgundy and went as far as Flanders. Of note is Cesarini's lack of sympathy for any suggestion of diplomatic solution to the Hussite problem and also his reasons for not immediately coming to the council. The fathers at Basel understood Cesarini's decision and were supportive. MC 1, pp. 76–7.]

To the venerable men, the lords, ambassadors of the gracious university of Paris, our dearest friends, Guiliano, cardinal of St Agnolo, legate of the Apostolic See. Venerable men, our dearest friends! We send to your reverence, the venerable man, Master Jan [Stojković] of Dubrovnik, professor of Holy Scripture, our associate and servant, who knows everything of our intention and of those who have until now been acting in the cause of the catholic faith. May you have faith in him, whose goodness, knowledge and virtues are very well known to us, in whatever he might reveal to you in our name, just as you would towards us. We offer ourselves to you with gratitude. Given in Germersheim on 25 April [1431].

Then the aforementioned master reached Basel with the trusted letter on the penultimate day of April. On the following day, in the Dominican cloister, the said ambassadors, many canons, masters of various orders and many citizens gathered to listen to the solemn mass of the Holy Spirit being sung. After the mass, he explained the intention of the aforementioned lord legate [Cesarini] to one and all gathered in the great hall. His comments contained two points: The first one had to do with the expedition of the army against the heretical Czechs while the second related to the matter of the council which should be celebrated in Basel.

In terms of the first point he related that Martin, the lord pope, had sent the lord legate primarily against the perfidious heresy of the Czechs and that he had gone directly to Nürnberg to the most serene king of the Romans [Sigismund] and to the other princes of Germany who had gathered in Nürnberg at that time. He admonished them with great urgency and supreme diligence so that the most serene emperor and the princes would condescend to provide for the salvation of the faith and the whole of Germany by ordering an army against the said heresy immediately. It was finally decided among the princes after considerable negotiation and examination of a variety of modes of action, that a powerful army of the faithful would gather around the feast of John Baptist in opposition to the heretics. Having decided on this, it was determined that the princes should depart for their own lands in order to make preparations so that they could appear near the border of Bohemia at the agreed time. So it was done.

Then the aforementioned most serene king of the Romans and the princes prevailed upon the lord legate in the meanwhile to ride around Germany soliciting the princes, cities and people to make ready for the campaign and to preach the cross everywhere in Germany and this he did. Specifically, he immediately began to preach the cross in Nürnberg and he sent solemn preachers into various parts of Germany to do the same. He went quickly throughout Bamberg, Würzburg and Frankfurt to the Rhine and to Mainz urging peace, truces or at least a pause in conflicts, during the period of the campaign, in every place where there was division and war. He also stirred up and exhorted the people to prepare for the expedition and he caused the cross to be preached in his presence in all cities and significant places. He came from Mainz to the lord Palatine of the Rhine admonishing him in a similar fashion. Then he went down to Cologne, Liège and as far as Flanders. When the feast of John [Baptist, 24 June] drew near, he intended to return to Nürnberg and if God permitted the army of the faithful to enter Bohemia he also determined to go with them since this seemed to be the view expressed by wise counsel.

No one can express how great is the necessity of the army. To wit, if this campaign were to be omitted this year, all of the lords and communities neighbouring the heretics will make arrangements with them and gradually so will others. For example, they declare expressly that they will not be able to resist them and they will come to arrangements with them unless they are given assistance this summer. From this, the destruction of the faith in those places would follow. Likewise, those heretics, if they cannot be broken by an army, will enter Germany with great power and will devastate and conquer the lands of the faithful. It was decided by the aforementioned deliberation, and the planned army, that this must not happen and the conclusion by the full and composed counsel in the assembly was that if such a thing transpired it would be hopeless. What would follow would be the audacity and triumph of the heretics and the terror and despair of the faithful since there can be no other solution. Therefore, it is viewed as necessary by all judicious ones that negotiations to consider the matter with all capabilities and diligence is essential since there is no other hope for the defence of the faith and their [Hussite] extirpation except through the means of a [military] campaign.

On this basis, the proposal deduced from the foregoing that the necessity of the said army was implied since the salvation of the faithful and of the entire church seems to depend upon it. Therefore the lord legate had done and is doing everything possible with the greatest diligence for the preparation of the army. It would have been to no avail for one to do anything directly or indirectly which might impede the progress of the army's preparation. Surely the aforementioned most reverent lord legate knew of and had seen with his own eyes, and read the letter sent by the fathers and lords, especially by the envoys of the gracious university of Paris to various princes concerning the celebration of the Council of Basel. This letter could have caused, albeit indirectly but nonetheless, some detriment to the preparation of the said army. For example, the princes and communities and people, hearing these admonitions concerning the council may have taken another view: 'Because the council begins let us see what the council will do. The council will provide adequately and will impose remedies. It will provide the way so that we might have the support also from those who are outside of Germany' and so on. Since they are considerably lax in this matter and also afraid and encumbered by the expense, burden and danger of war, they might wish to have some occasion to avoid it. The lord legate was well informed of this.

The same master admonished those who were in Basel for the council on behalf of the legate so that they would write, without delay, to the princes and particularly to the king of the Romans. He did this to provoke and admonish them both suitably and inopportunely to prepare for the aforementioned army. The council can be delayed but the preparation of the army must have little or no delay. When the council is congregated there will be many issues, but first the cause of the faith. Nothing must be undertaken which might impede the preparation of the army. It must be so that all impediments are eliminated. Namely, the extermination of the aforementioned Czech heresy must be ensured even if that means delaying the council. [The council] either way will condemn the heresy but this has been done sufficiently by the Council of Constance and also of Siena as well as through the way of peaceful reduction. But as far as humankind can guess, this cannot be hoped for because those heretics call for nothing else but that they wish to be judged and they are already obdurate and irreversible. Even some of the faithful in Bohemia report in writing that no policy of reduction can be used against them unless an army is sent first because they can only be reduced by fear. There is no other hope but through the fact of ordering a campaign. And if it, thus, is finally ordered and is being prepared it must not be inhibited in any way but supported in all possible ways and means since it is to counter the evil as quickly as possible. Besides this, if the council should give assistance to the campaign, the army cannot be prepared except by a common subsidy and the collection of this requires at least two years though much less is necessary. [There will be debates] on how to proceed, many secular lords will put their hands on it [the collected subsidies] in their domains just as experience has taught us. In the meanwhile, the heretics will devastate and conquer everything and the army will arrive too late. Therefore, when such a powerful army is ordered through the will of God it must work entirely for the progress and preparation [of the expedition].

Therefore the aforementioned most reverent lord legate admonishes and desires of your paternities and lordships that, as mentioned, you would write to the king of the Romans and to the other princes as soon as possible, exhorting them for the preparation of this army. Then, if it seems good to you, send one or two of you to the most reverent lord legate to promote this preparation together with his paternity and for the presence of the army because many things could transpire. This is what was said with respect to the first point.

As for the second point concerning the celebration of the council, he [Jan Stojković of Dubrovnik] expressed the fervent desire which the aforementioned lord legate had for the celebration of the council and for that which should be done. Namely, the extirpation of heresies, the reformation of behaviour and the pacification of the Christian people. He insisted on this, persuading [them of] the necessity and celebration of the said council and narrating what evils in the church would follow if the celebration of the council was omitted. Thereafter, he provided the reasons why the lord legate did not come directly to Basel even though he ardently desired the progress of the council [to go ahead]. He [Cesarini] had been sent principally in the cause of the faith against the heresy of the Czechs and hearing the princes assembled for the same cause of the faith in Nürnberg he would not have been as effective in the negotiation of the faith if he had disposed himself with anything else. However, even though he had been in Basel it seemed better to him to agree with the princes and delay everything else. At the time he had departed from Rome he had no written commission from lord Martin concerning the matters of the council. Therefore, it would not have been honest or convenient to dispose himself to something else thus delaying his legation and engaging in matters not committed to him. Although Martin had committed to him the legation of the council verbally in Rome prior to his departure, nevertheless he did not have the bull and thus did not feel secure in engaging [in the business of the council] since Martin could change his intentions for any number of reasons. Thus the letter of the mission of the council was delivered to him by the lord bishop of Olomouc [Konrad of Zvole] in Nürnberg after having received the news of Martin's death as was said earlier.

MC 1: 73–5.

154   Ceremonies for the fifth crusade

[On 20 February 1431, Pope Martin V died. One of his last acts had been to appoint Cardinal Guiliano Cesarini as papal legate to lead a renewed crusade effort. On 20 March, a new crusade was announced against the Hussites at Nürnberg. The Reichstag was well attended: electors, princes, Sigismund as well as Czech Catholic barons. On paper, the strength of the committed army was 33,000 men. The planned use of artillery and battle wagons appears to have followed the Hussite model quite closely (DR 9, pp. 517–35). As the time for the implementation of the fifth crusade effort against the Hussite heretics neared, the same ceremonies were observed on 29 June at St Sebald's Church in Nürnberg. Emperor Sigismund once again appointed Friedrich of Brandenburg as the supreme commander of the crusade armies and invested him with the authority to proceed or negotiate according to the circumstances. As for the emperor, Sigismund excused himself from active involvement in the crusade, as he explained to Pope Eugenius IV in a letter dated 17 March 1432, on the grounds that he had suffered a painful injury (UB 2, pp. 275–7). Cesarini opened the proceedings for the mobilization of the crusade and conferred upon Friedrich the crusade banner and sword according to Sigismund's wishes. Sigismund's trust in Friedrich's ability as supreme commander was over-estimated. The margrave had been in the forefront of three imperial crusades against the Czech heretics. In 1422 he had a clear purpose and was a determined leader. In 1427, he was restricted and disadvantaged by some of the other leaders and eventually fell ill and was therefore ineffective. In 1431, now sixty years of age, his crusade objectives seemed rather vague and his actions throughout the preparation and the campaign itself suggest that Friedrich was not convinced he could win. The following constitution is dated 26 June 1431.]

We, Sigismund, announce and make known that we have taken to mind and considered the righteousness, wisdom and solidarity of the high-born Friedrich, Margrave of Brandenburg, archchamberlain of the empire and burgrave of Nürnberg, our counsellor, dear uncle and elector and especially the serious love and faith he has shown through a variety of services to the Christian faith, to us and to the empire. This he is prepared to continue and to approve with good will. Therefore, we have appointed him, with good reason and on the sound advice of our imperial electors, princes, nobles, banner lords and all the faithful among us, in the empire and in the Crown of Bohemia, to be our supreme captain in the campaign which we have resolved and decided upon in accordance with the advice of the aforementioned imperial electors, princes, counts, barons and faithful ones and also of our banner lords, nobles and those faithful within the Crown of Bohemia, to undertake into the Czech land against the heresy and the unfaithful ones in Bohemia. We are appointing and constituting him with our Roman and Bohemian royal authority by virtue of this letter. We have also given to him our entire and complete power and authority to do or to have done, as though we were present ourselves. We are also commanding him at this time to elevate and lead our banner, that of the empire and of the Crown of Bohemia against the aforementioned unfaithful and disobedient ones in Bohemia, to press the war and siege against them and to undertake and allow to be undertaken everything which we would do or allow to be done if we were present.

Specifically, we have given him complete power, and we are indicating this by virtue of this letter, to enter into negotiations with each and every noble, banner lord, knight, vassal, and inhabitant of each and every town, castle, small town and village, who are the promoters, helpers and adherents of the aforementioned unfaithful and disobedient ones as well as with the faithless ones themselves in Bohemia, to accept and negotiate peace or other settlements with them, to receive them into grace and to guarantee them with their moveable and immoveable goods and assets and who accept us [as king] of the aforementioned Crown of Bohemia, and also to provide them, one or all, with peace, safe-conduct and security. If they persist in their unbelief and disobedience [he has power] to punish them in person and in goods, to torture or put to death by effective means such as burning or other examination. [He may] capture them and do, or cause to be done to them, as he wishes. The captives may be held or set free, or put to death in accordance with whatever his own reason, will, advice or pleasure determines. Whatever he deals, makes, negotiates, does and concludes with these people, secular or ecclesiastical, noble or low-born, whoever and however they are called in the aforementioned Crown of Bohemia, written down in his letters, he shall do and allow to be done in all things, without exception, just as though we were present.

Whatever he does, or will do and promises to do, imposes or negotiates instead of us, shall be entirely our good will, word and command and we shall not consent to the least alteration of this [policy] in any way. We also give him the authority to impose punishments on body and goods in all matters whatsoever he negotiates, wherever and however the need occurs to him and if necessary to pronounce the consequences [either] by law or according to grace on those who fall into such penalty. Should it happen that our aforementioned uncle the margrave becomes ill or weak and is unable to execute the [work of captain] we give him full authority to order and appoint another prince or someone else who seems to be good and useful to the captainship in his place. We command that individual, who is appointed by him, according to our Roman royal power, seriously and firmly by this letter, to accept such captainship for the consolation of Christendom and to our honour and the holy empire and to do nothing else. This individual shall have the same authority as our aforementioned uncle, the margrave himself.

We have sworn and are swearing by this letter according to our royal word to uphold and fulfil [all obligations] constantly, firmly and irrevocably now as then, and wherever there is need to give our royal letter without any requirement, contradiction or delay. We command also quite seriously and firmly, with this letter, each and every prince, count, noble, knight, vassal, officer, city and faithful one of whatever condition or substance, whoever they may be, in the holy empire, to come to the service of the Christian faith and of us against the aforementioned unfaithful and disobedient ones and also each and every banner lord, noble, knight, vassal, officer and inhabitant of every town, small town and village of our aforementioned Crown of Bohemia to faithfully support, assist and be obedient to the aforementioned Friedrich our captain, rather than us and on our account, in each and every issue and matter mentioned above just as they would to us. We have complete confidence in him and everyone who wishes to avoid our displeasure should likewise.

This letter is sealed with our royal majestic seal, given in Nürnberg in the year 1431 on the Tuesday following [the feast of] John Baptist. In the forty-fifth year of our Hungarian reign, in the twenty-first year of our Roman reign and in the eleventh year of our Bohemia reign.

UB 2: 218–21.

155   Crusader frustration and foreboding

[Cardinal Cesarini sent the following letter to his colleagues at the Council of Basel in the month preceding the launching of the fifth crusade. It is filled with frustration and foreboding. The papal legate underscores the lack of unity within the crusade. Several key sources of support, including that of Philip the Good, have failed to come to fruition. According to Cesarini, the matter of the fifth crusade is indeed doubtful. The letter is dated 16 July 1431.]

To the venerable men, Lord Juan of Palomar, delegate judge of the holy palace, doctor of canon law, and to Master Jan of [Dubrovnik] Ragusio, professor of sacred theology, our most beloved friends, etc. in Basel; Cardinal of St Angelo, legate of the Apostolic See. I congratulate you as our partners in so many disputes, as so many continue to be necessary for the army; I considered my misfortunes finished, after I read of your enduring troubles. I rejoice again that you are in a safer and quieter place, first because it brings you rest, then because of the matter for which it was necessary to send you. You are now further away from dangers and labours, and you ought to pray piously for us, who sent you there, and for the faithful defenders of the Christian Republic, because we are certainly acting in every respect for your sake.

We received a letter yesterday from the Lord Duke of Burgundy [Philip the Good], not the kind for which we were hoping. He said that he did not wish to assent to any subjection or compromise, unless previously the tower will have been torn down. Because of this every hope is born in the arrival of the Lord Bishop of Liège to the army, who already, as he wrote to me, has made preparations. The same lord duke wrote also that because we were never concerned that defiance had been shown to him by Friedrich, Duke of Austria, he could in no way send the force that he had promised to me for the Bohemia expedition. I am frustrated by a great and certain hope! See how our affairs are arranged! See also the misfortune that has afflicted me! For the Count Palatine of the Rhine has failed, he who had preserved constantly for us. A force about to be sent to us, the count wrote us, was sent to the Duke of Baranja under the hope and condition that on the feast of St John it be returned to Bohemia; but after the war was waged between this duke and a certain count, whom you, Lord Jan, seen in Isel seeking absolution, the duke himself and the force of the Lord Count Palatine fell in battle and were captured, the force was destroyed. Here we are much fewer than is said in Nürnberg, because those princes hesitate greatly to enter Bohemia.

The matter is doubtful, not only regarding victory, but worse yet because we are only at the beginning. We are not, however, so few that we are unable to enter Bohemia with a bold spirit. I am very anxious and greatly dejected. For if the army leaves with the affair unfinished, it will bode ill for the Christian religion in this region; a great terror will be born to our lands and the heretics will grow more daring. We will inform you about whatever else occurs, and you should do likewise to us as the opportunity presents itself. Farewell, most beloved brothers, and pray to God for me and the whole army. Dated in Weiden, near the Bohemian forest, on the sixteenth day of July.

MC 1: 98–9.

156 The Emperor admonishes the Polish king

[Sigismund warns the Polish king about the Hussites, suggests that the heretics will eventually invade Poland, advances the argument for renewed military action, and asks Władysław to put an end to all forms of Hussitism and indicate support for such measures within Poland. The emperor was clearly still annoyed that collusion had existed between the Czech and Polish kingdoms with respect to the regency of Zygmunt Korybut. The letter is dated 21 July 1431.]

Serene prince Władysław, king of Poland, our brother and godfather, greetings and brotherly love be multiplied.

Our dearest brother and godfather, most serene prince. When the most recent general assembly was celebrated by the barons, nobles, communities and other ecclesiastical and secular people in the Kingdom of Bohemia on the feast of Philip and James in Prague [1 May], some of the leading men informed us secretly that if we so desired to accept the arrangements made at Bratislava we could have sent our envoys on the aforementioned occasion in the firm hope that this would have led, God willing, to a better end. However, at the next assembly of the electors, and other princes, nobles and cities of the empire in Nürnberg, on the basis of their advice and approval we have constituted a powerful army to proceed for the suppression of the insolence of those Czechs with the help of God. Yet we adhere to our usual gentleness and natural inclination, which we have always had, for the reduction of that Czech nation. To this end we have spared neither goods nor people but have sent our significant envoys and knights towards Prague to prepare the most convenient methods which could be found for their reduction so that nothing which might be provided in this matter would remain untried by us considering this a great service to God in every case by their conversion so that slaughter, bloodshed and the great oppression of the faithful might be avoided in this way. Our envoys led all armies, barons and their communities, excluding only the Orphans and the New Town of Prague, to the city of Cheb under our security.

So dear brother, upon arriving in Bamberg after the journey there, the letter of your fraternity was presented to us in which you describe to us how these same

Czechs had their envoys at your fraternity who were also admonished by your fraternity in the proper way to give up their errors, return to obedience of the holy Roman Church and to the unity of the Catholic faith. Having deliberated they responded to Your Grace saying they would like to come to the next celebrated general council with a sufficient and secure safe conduct, though with certain conditions which you and your advisors did not like. However, Your Grace required them again to abandon these dubious conditions and to accept the conclusions of the forthcoming sacred general council and to make that agreement certain by their letters and seals. Concerning what Your Grace also sent your knights with them according to their demands under a good hope because those, as you wrote, we instructed not to have full power for negotiation. Although we did not receive your letter before we sent our envoys off to Prague, nonetheless we had heard a rumour spreading around that the Czechs had negotiated with you on this matter. We gave them your letter to read so they would understand the refusal of their dubious and conditional offer which we also had simply refused in Bratislava, through the advice of four doctors of our University of Paris and others of the University of Vienna and other experienced men, since they would decline the honourable conclusions of the sacred council at this time even though we were prepared to give up the idea of invading them. Nevertheless, these obdurate people shamelessly in public before the electors and other princes, prelates and barons, would not accept this matter and were completely contrary to the tone of your letter. They proposed again some other plan in which they offered to come to a future council under certain fraudulent means and added outrageous clauses full of trickery which we have been unable to find in the schedule offered to you. When we required explanation and clarification of their elusive words they added also that in the council all of Christendom should be present including Indians, Greeks, Armenians, schismatics and all those who confess Christ, along with plenty of others which would be rather more ridiculous than useful to write about . Then we, in order to have tried everything in terms of efforts at their reduction, offered them two schedules, one from the doctors of Paris and Vienna in Bratislava and the other proposed by doctors who were present with us, while different in wording they are consistent in meaning to the effect that they should accept the judgement of the sacrosanct council about the questions which would come up. We admonished them to accept these salutary and honourable offers in order to avoid numerous evils which had been perpetrated on account of their obstinacy to this time and even worse which would follow if they persisted thus and assumed that the agreements made in Bratislava of them coming to the council and whether they reached agreement or not they might return home and temporarily keep the armistice with the faithful of Christ. They replied in brief that they were not prepared in any way, nor did they wish to submit themselves to the judgement of a general council when it had already condemned them and incited many princes and people against them in establishing the cross against them. Rather than submit themselves to the sentence and judgement of their enemies they preferred to die all together on a single day. They also stated that they did not want to accept a safe conduct to the council unless we would demonstrate how things would be discussed in the same council. This was strange enough for us and even impossible to impose some restriction on the sacred council and on Holy Mother Church.

So, dearest brother, having discussed these possibilities back and forth with the prelates, doctors of the university of Paris and other more experienced men present among us as to how we might move them to piety, we were as successful now as in the past. Now it is necessary to take up arms in order to repulse with force that lethal power which is impossible to be mollified by gentleness and to eliminate this calamity and pollution from the midst of the most sacred faith. Additionally, we again required the electors of the holy empire and other princes, nobles, cities and communities, which are to invade Bohemia following the upcoming feast of St John, to accelerate their transfer so that the brashness which cannot be inclined through piety might be exterminated by a powerful arm, with the grace of God. We admonish you as much as we can, dearest brother, who as a Christian prince is concerned by these negotiations not a little. The aforementioned Czechs have already made themselves neighbours in Silesia and in other places bordering you and your country. Without doubt, having obtained these completely they will spread further in accordance with their custom, God forbid, and will not leave you or your kingdom without attack. You should rise up with the other faithful of Christ for the praise of almighty God, for the establishing of the faith and the Christian religion and for the extirpation of that perversity and to participate in this worthwhile matter which must be assumed by all Christians out of reverence for God and the faith. You will receive for this the payment of divine reward and the praise of the world and the same gratitude from us. You must also abolish their supporters in your kingdom who have been protected daily by Zygmunt Korybut, the descendants of Puchala and many others.[8] It is manifestly well known to you, and we have no doubt, that the garrisons taken by the heretics in Silesia were held by Poles and everything which is taken from the faithful of Christ is being sold freely in your kingdom. They are provided with free arms, horse, and other things in Kraków and daily business is carried out with them. They have brought not a little favour to those heretics to the present time to the point where they are glorified in front of others. Without doubt, this terrible rumour has originated in many provinces of Your Grace. May Your Grace uproot

---

[8] A reference to the Polish-Hussite captain Dobeslav Puchala and also to the meeting between Hussites and Polish officials at the king's castle in Kraków in spring of 1431. Perhaps an allusion to Jan Sziafraniec, lord chancellor, one of the strongest Hussite supporters in Poland.

this from your midst for your honour and provide more vigilant watch and show your power effectively for the support of Christians against that plague so that the world may know the good fervency which you have for the Catholic faith and the holy church of God. Given in Cheb in the year 1431.[9]

UB 2: 209–13.

157   Heretics propose a basis for negotiations

[The following proposal was composed by Hussites, after extended consultation, and presented to King Sigismund at Cheb in 1431. Needless to say, it was rejected without qualification or protracted consideration.]

In the same way as we, the barons, captains, knights, squires, cities and communities of the kingdom of Bohemia and the margraviate of Moravia and adherents of the Law of God, wish to remain with the most serene prince and lord Sigismund, king of the Romans, on the proposal offered to us by him in Bratislava, we are here present as envoys prepared to come to agreement in the statement which follows: 'We the afore named wish to come and stay at the next celebrated general council of all Christendom, this we intend, without deceit, having a secure and sufficient safe-conduct. However, we add that whatever might be deduced and proven from the writings of divine law or the statements of the holy doctors, founded truly and clearly upon the same must be accepted without any contradiction. If some person of any state, rank, dignity or preeminence rejects or refuses to accept what has been proven, he is to be forced to give assent and accept it on the authority of the secular arm.'

UB 2: 213–14.

---

[9]   On the Hussite influence in Poland see most recently the work of Paweł Kras, 'Hussitism and the Polish Nobility', in *Lollardy and the Gentry in the Later Middle Ages*, eds., Margaret Aston and Colin Richmond (New York: St. Martin's Press, 1997), pp. 183–98, *Husyci w piętnastowiecznej Polsce* (Lublin: Towarzystwo Naukowe Katolickiego Uniwersytetu Lubelskiego, 1998) and essays by Kras and Wojciech Iwańczak in *Christianity in east central Europe: Late Middle Ages*, eds., Paweł Kras and Wojciech Polak (Lublin: Instytut europy środkowo-wschodniej, 1999), pp. 232–43 and 244–7.

158   Counter-proposal by the Emperor

[Sigismund made a counter-proposal which was refused equally and adamantly by the Hussites.]

Whatever would be deduced in the general council from the sacred writings of the doctors accepted by the Roman Church must be acknowledged. If there should be any doubt or controversy concerning the statements of the writings of the doctors we insist that these controversies and disputes be resolved by the aforementioned general council. [Dated] 21 July 1431.

UB 2: 214.

159   Hussite manifesto to all Christendom

[In this manifesto the utraquists of Bohemia note they have offered on numerous occasions to negotiate. However, they had always been required to submit to the judgement of their enemies in a council. This they refused to do. They assert that should force be used in an effort to compel them to submit they would defend themselves. The manifesto is dated 21 July 1431.]

To each and every one of those faithful to Christ, kings, dukes, margraves, counts, barons, nobles, knights, squires, citizens and people of every state and condition: magnates, nobles, knights, squires, governors of communities, prefects of castles, judges, councillors, assessors and citizens, and the entire community of the Czech nation, constituted in the kingdom of Bohemia as well as in the margraviate of Moravia, greetings in the knowledge of salvation and observance of truth.

When the uncreated son of God who was forever in the spirit of the same eternal father, descended to earth not changing the place and not diminishing his majesty, assumed human form, he delivered the testimony of eternal life in speech and action. Of these he left these holy signs, four in number, for the imitation of the disciples and for exemplary behaviour the first of which is this. That the most divine sacrament of his body and blood would be celebrated by the servants of the church to the faithful. The second is that the word of the Lord would be preached by those freely and publicly and truthfully. Third, that civil dominion would be taken from the clergy as if it were a lethal virus. Fourth, that public and notorious sins would be eliminated from faithful people by the legitimate powers. Having humbly understood these inviolable truths, promoting the faith, building up hope, enlarging love, governing life and assuring eternal salvation, we have accepted them gratefully. In accordance with the measure of our strength we have followed them carefully and intend to follow them as long as life remains. Since the beginning we have also tended to their faithful recognition, love and observance as even now we intend for all God's people to come more fully to them.

Consequently we have spared no expense, work or cost in transmitting many letters over several regions of Christendom. We have visited the most Christian princes, the magnificent Friedrich, margrave of Brandenburg, the illustrious king of Poland [Władysław Jagiełło] and now the request of the most serene Sigismund, King of the Romans and of Hungary, that by his prominent envoys we have previously come to Bratislava and now to Cheb the imperial city so that it might be granted to us a free, secure and non hostile public audience before the general council of the church concerning the aforementioned articles in order to reveal, illuminate, declare, assert, justify, prove and defend [them] by Holy Scripture and by the statements of blessed doctors founded and established truly and unalterably in the same writings. [This shall be] in public, openly and manifestly a conspectus of these four redemptive articles in the whole council. For we hold to a faith which is free, without obstruction, so that the entire church of the living God might be reformed together with us in head as well as in member according to the teachings of Holy Scripture.

It is no wonder that the king communicated the advice of the princes, bishops, chief men and doctors the response that this limitation of the audience and the reform of the church would derogate the liberty and privilege of the general council standing out over all law inasmuch as we should accept the determination and decision of that council in all these matters, leaving aside the limitations and declarations of divine law and the writings of the holy doctors. What we have consequently considered meritoriously, reasonably, and properly inadmissible, insufficient, unworthy and entirely unequal, namely that divine truths, justified by themselves, should be judged by human arbitration, legitimized and allowed by its own will. In the end, the solid truth could be replaced by something false and deceptive. [This would mean] that those judging these truths and us are those who have no fear of God, have condemned them inequitably as notorious errors, as well as us because we observe them, always judging without cause, improperly and presumptuously. This then means that our enemies and our most ferocious foes who aspire to exterminate us would be the judges which all reverent healthy reason would refuse and human and divine laws would be shocked.

Therefore we neither wanted nor intended to agree with them in this matter, but we preferred first and foremost an equitable and righteous obligation so that the most certain and just rule of the Holy Scriptures, given in the earth by the most righteous judge, loving truth and justice who can neither deceive nor be deceived, be constituted in the midst of the council. [In this way] the conclusions of the blessed doctors, the correctness or error of these articles, along with ourselves, be founded, corrected or confirmed [on this basis]. However, they would not accept this in any event.

We ask that your intelligence condescend to consider the righteous equality we have offered to them and the arrogant contumacy from the malignant and cowardly pride of the opposite side which stands excessively out over itself and intends to submit to itself not only all the princedoms, kingdoms and dominions of Christendom but also to modify the inviolable doctrines of the divine truth confirmed only by the death of our Lord Jesus Christ. They esteem and judge them according to their own will in so far that what is believed truly and faithfully observed by those faithful to Christ is declined completely as error and superstition in their judgement and thus the Christian faith is established not on the most solid rock but on shifting sand. It is subjected to daily disintegration and the words of Christ supported by eternal affirmation that it is easier for heaven and earth to pass away then for his word to be modified will be changed through their censorship. What could be found more foolish than that arrogance, more irregular than that error, more pernicious than that plague? We ask you all, as people faithful to Christ, to think over and judge those things which we have told you and consider whether these bishops properly and worthily occupy the seat of the apostles who utterly oppose the life and behaviour of them. Certainly they walked through the lands of the world, ragged and despised by people, but faithfully announcing the Lord's truths to every tribe and nation, confirming these truths by their deaths. These [bishops] dressed in purple and fine linen, arrogant among the people, have become mute dogs, living quietly within castles and cities and despising these same truths and despoiling the faithful of their reputation, life and goods because of the faithful observance of them, not by themselves because they sleep with the dogs and not by the cruel elevation of the cross inciting, with deception, the secular arm to murder the faithful. These have released worldly wealth and decorated by all virtue have followed the Lord in poverty and need. [On the other hand] these owners of cities, castles, estates and regions, men instituted in wealth and full of vice do not follow the humble Christ, despised, but rather the proud Satan in pomp and vainglory and in the lusts of the flesh who as false prophets are revealed by the uncreated truth.

If they, as they propose, should invade our kingdom with their powerful armies seeking to destroy it with total extermination as is asserted, we, trusting in the virtue of the highest one, whose matter we follow, would be forced to defend ourselves with force as is permitted by all laws and all rights. Having diligently considered with open discussion the just and reasonable arguments written above, would you, intelligent and noble men, expose your souls and bodies to death in the dangers of warfare with the help of those criminal clergymen who speculate in the presumptuous and erroneous arrogance of the truths of almighty God and lying in the lusts of the world, in whoring, and in excrement as opposed to the righteous cause of Jesus Christ which we offer? Given on Saturday on the vigil of blessed Mary Magdalene [21 July], under the common seal of all adherents of the evangelical truth, near the border of the kingdom of Bohemia in the year 1431. To be presented to Nürnberg and the other imperial cities.

UB 2: 228–31.

160   Disputes over castles

[In this first of three letters, Sigismund gives full power to the lord of Rožmberk to deal with Kunát Kaplíř of Sulevice so that the castle of Zvíkov might be handed back to Sigismund. Control of castles and fortresses in Bohemia was crucial to the outcome of the crusades. The letter was written from Bamberg on 8 June 1431.]

We, Sigismund, by the grace of God, king of the Romans, ever Augustus, king of Hungary, Bohemia, Dalmatia, and Croatia, confess by this letter before all who see it or hear it read, that we have given full power and our will, signified by this letter, to our noble, faithful and dearly beloved Oldřich of Rožmberk, in order that he may negotiate in our name with the famous Kunát Kaplíř of Sulevice for the abdication of our castle at Zvíkov and the prisoners whom he has captured up to the present time, as well as other matters pertaining to that castle. Whatever the aforementioned Oldřich deals and gives assent to with the previously mentioned Kunát in this [matter] is according to our will and we intend this to be as firm as though we ourselves were negotiating it personally. To affirm this we have ordered the seal of our royal majesty to be appended to this letter. Given in Bamberg in the year 1431 since the birth of our Lord, on the Friday after St Boniface in the forty-fifth year of our Hungarian reign, the twenty-first of our Roman reign and the eleventh year of our Bohemian reign.

AČ 1: 32.

161   A call for aid for the crusading armies

[On 31 July 1431 Sigismund admonished Rožmberk to give aid in every way to the imperial army which was scheduled to invade them Czech lands through the Šumava [Bohemian Forest] on that day.]

We, Sigismund, by the grace of God, king of the Romans, ever Augustus, king of Hungary and Bohemia.

Dearly beloved. You know well that our princes and armies of Germany have been raised for the common welfare of ourselves, you and also of the entire land for the suppression of the enormous nuisance occurring in the land. We have already congregated before the forest in force and today, God willing, they shall invade through the forest with such power, with the help of God, to meet the enemy for the common good of the land as well. This is the time for everyone to give assistance with labour in order to be redeemed from that evil. Therefore we request diligently and admonish you to advise and provide assistance to our serene uncle Friedrich, margrave of Brandenburg, our supreme captain who has our full power as though he were us, to liberate the faithful for the consolation of the holy church and the peace of the land. If you have any truce or agreement with the enemy, you must renounce them at once, retaliate and destroy them for what you believe. We greatly hope that they are taken everywhere so that, if God wills, it will be the end of them. In this manner you serve the whole of Christendom and us and shall be remembered in all goodness. If this were not to happen, you and I might be regarded as failing to help in these matters and that would not be good. We have written also to all the other lords, knights and squires on our side and commanded them to help against the enemy as well.

Given in Nürnberg on Monday before St Peter in chains in the forty-fifth year of our Hungarian reign, the twenty-first of our Roman reign and the twelfth year of our Bohemian reign.

AČ 1: 32–3.

162   News about the crusader invasion of Bohemia

[In this letter, Sigismund expresses gratitude for the news and reports that the imperial army has marched into Bohemia. The date is 30 July 1431.]

We, Sigismund, by the grace of God king of the Romans, ever Augustus, and king of Hungary and Bohemia.

Dear faithful and noble one. We have understood well your letter delivered to us on Saturday in which you have written about the encampment of the enemy and how they turned up and divided themselves. We are grateful that you have apprised us of progress. We should let you know that we have also received reports from others that the enemy proceeded again and thus we pass this along. We have written at once about the negotiations to the margrave of Brandenburg and have sent your letter to him. He ought to be able to manage things from here and we hope that he is not tricked. Further, we let you know that our uncle, the aforementioned margrave has sufficient good people, cavalry and foot soldiers, enough cannon and other military preparation and his numbers are increasing. Today, if God wills, he is to march through the forest. He is much stronger than the enemy and can with high spirits take to the field against all enemies. They likewise have prepared their wagons as the enemies. Therefore we request that you be diligent in keeping abreast of progress and that you send us any information you might have about the Táborites and also to take action against them in your territory. By doing so you do us a special favour. We have already sent the fireballs, as you know. Given in Nürnberg on Monday before St Peter in chains, in the forty-fifth year of our Hungarian reign, the twenty-first of our Roman reign and the twelfth year of our Bohemian reign.

AČ 1: 33.

163   Report to the towns of upper and lower Lusatia

[This report, dated 5 August 1431, was written by Hans von Polenczk, governor of Lusatia, announces the progress of the fifth crusade. See the end of doc.173.]

I have written to you about the campaign into Bohemia. It should have one complete march which I shall be part of. After they march through the forest I wish to separate and together with those of Lusatia and your lands proceed to Lobaw according to the orders of my most gracious lord the king. I inform you that I will be with the princes and lords on next Wednesday having marched through the forest into Bohemia. I ask that you write to me concerning your opinion regarding Lobaw. Given in Senftenberg on Sunday before [St] Donatus.

UB 2: 233.

164   City of Basel apprised of crusade strength

[The fifth crusade was numerically the greatest ever assembled against the Hussite heretics. The bulk of the forces originated among the electors of Brandenburg and Saxony, the archbishop-electors of Mainz and Cologne, Count Louis of Württemberg and the cities of Frankfurt, Basel, Strasbourg, Cologne, Aachen and the Swabian towns. Notwithstanding, the Bavarian dukes had considerable personnel as did the Silesian and Lusatian armies and the Austrian troops under the command of Duke Albrecht, Sigismund's son-in-law. It is reported in the Latin chronicle of Bartošek of Drahonice that 40,000 cavalry and 90,000 infantry converged on Bohemia (FRB 5, p. 604). This is almost certainly a substantial exaggeration but the forces were considerable. This brief dispatch dated 14 August 1431 underscores quite well this renewed gathering strength of the crusade cause for another invasion of Bohemia.]

Dear friends. We have received with pleasure your letter requesting us to write discreetly about the business of the expedition into Bohemia. Up until now we have heard only that the powerful army of these lands with a great multitude of people passed through the forest on the way to Bohemia and in the course of fourteen days marched from Tachov to Domažlice, plundering, harrying and burning the land of Bohemia as much as they could (see map 2). In the same way our gracious lord of Austria, also with a powerful force, drew on towards our army, plundering and burning as well. We do not know how it will progress from here on. May almighty God grant his grace. We are committed to your honour with love and service. Given on the vigil of Our Lady's Assumption.

UB 2: 240.

165   Account of the fifth crusade fought at Domažlice

[This report on the crusade fought on 14 August was made at the Council of Basel which had opened on 23 July 1431. On 1 January 1431 Pope Martin V appointed Guiliano Cesarini as papal legate empowered to expedite the crusade. On 12 February Martin named Cesarini as president of the Council of Basel. Martin died on 20 February before the council actually convened. The crusaders followed their original plans and approached their target from the west and then veered south in the direction of Domažlice. From an assembled position west of Beroun, halfway between Prague and Plzeň, the Hussite armies, under the command of Prokop, marched on either the 11th or 12th of August at great speed. Their armies were divided into three divisions and marched around Plzeň to Chotěšov before veering southwest via Stod. They by-passed Horšovský Týn to the east and then marched directly south close to Rýzmberk Castle. They took up a defensive position on a hill near the road between Domažlice and Kdyně on 14 August. See maps 2–3.]

[While the council of Basel was getting underway] Guiliano [Cesarini] went through much of Germany personally preaching the cross against the Czechs. On account of this, as well as an imperial edict, a great army of the faithful assembled around the feast of John Baptist near Nürnberg where he himself likewise arrived at that time. He received in the same place 35,000 ducats from the pope through Leonard of Pescia, for the Czech matter. Letters of certification concerning the Council of Basel were received. Those gathered in Basel and especially the king of the Romans urged him to come to Basel to celebrate the council. He preferred to remain with the army of the faithful which was of considerable power and force. They invaded the kingdom of Bohemia on 1 August to exterminate the perverse heretics of that kingdom. He had then for a captain the Count of Blauo [?] in his brigade with 300 lancers. However, the general captain of the entire army had been given by the king of the Romans to the serene prince, Friedrich, margrave of Brandenburg and arch-chamberlain of the empire. Having passed through the forest, which surrounds the entire kingdom, its own best defence, they approached the town of Tachov which appeared not to be prepared, by supplies as well as by others, to sustain a conquest since they had no knowledge of the army's arrival from that direction.

Then Guiliano, who desired with his whole heart, to see the heretics exterminated and reduced by force and who worked very hard to assemble the army took the view that the town could be defeated easily and wished to conquer it that day. But those who led the army, in one voice, did not give their assent and decided rather that camp be set up on that day and that a conquest would be easier on the next day after the knights were refreshed from the weariness of the journey. Some of those in the army spoke with the leaders of the town. At daybreak, the town appeared to have been fortified by the delivery of supplies, dislocation of machines and a multitude of armed people. There was little hope it could be conquered. Therefore they removed themselves a distance of two miles where they captured by force a small town belonging to Duke Johannes of Bavaria and they burned all of the people there. After this they led the army to another [town] located nearby thinking it had not been informed. But they saw that it was already fortified and so they went off towards another one. However, they were unable to occupy any other town or castle along the way but as the army marched they burned villages and devastated the fatherland.

A few days had elapsed after their invasion when they were about a day's journey from Prague they heard a rumour in the camps that the priest Prokop, the leader of the Táborite army, together with a major force of armed Czechs was nearby and ready to do battle.[10] It was on the vigil of the assumption [14 August], an unhappy day for the army of the faithful, when the rumour spread through the camp that they were about to enter battle with the Czechs. In the third hour, Guiliano watching from a small hill saw wagons carrying food and military equipment retreating in the direction of the forest as though they were fleeing

---

[10] Despite the claim, the crusaders were considerably farther away from Prague than a days march. It is doubtful that the crusaders penetrated Bohemia any deeper than the village of Bezdružice, which lies six miles southeast of Teplá and some twenty miles northwest of Plzeň. In other words, the crusade forces were at least eighty miles from the capital at the peak of their invasion.

along with many armed men. Seeing this, as well as others including the duke of Saxony who had joined the army with a great force, a messenger was sent to the captain asking what this meant and why the goods should be lost in this manner. [The captain] answered that it was necessary to do this and therefore they were to obey. At that time there was suspicion of treason and having little or no confidence in each other they left their equipment and the people tried to escape as quickly as they could, attempting to make it to the forest before dark. During the flight of the lords the wagons carrying the equipment were captured by an attack of a few Czechs and were prevented from being taken out of the kingdom. Of 4,000 of them [wagons] barely thirty escaped into the forest before sunset. Thus it was, that without seeing any of the enemy they left all their military equipment and fled from the kingdom of Bohemia during the day and throughout the night. What is worthy of lamentation is that in addition, they lost a great amount of food and other goods to that kingdom.

Guiliano changed his clothes and, in disguise, on the night after the vigil of the assumption came out of that kingdom and forest without having eaten or drunk. He was placed under the protection of the bishop of Würzburg who escorted him as far as Nürnberg with 500 horse. Although many of the Germans reproached him with considerable acrimony on account of the flight of the army of the faithful which had invaded the kingdom of Bohemia, they strongly berated this Guiliano for some gave up hope and the victory.

On that day of darkness and smoke, of clouds and storm, men marked with the sign of the cross on their foreheads, deplored and regretted the abhorrence in the church. They confessed their sins and of the Christian people to the justice of the Lord God to our confusion and that of the priests saying, we have sinned before the Lord our God, with doubt we did not trust in him and we did not submit to him and we did not obey the voice of the Lord our God and walk in the commandments he has given to us. A curse has settled upon us, anathema is in the midst of the people who ran away, persecuted by no one, while the foe was in our heads our enemies got rich. How greatly the spirit of Guiliano turned from the idea of a hostile persecution of the Czechs under that storm and how decisively he turned to the celebration of the holy synod of Basel. His acts thereafter make this all the more certain.

Not wishing to blame its leader, who had been constituted president of the council, who coming near to Basel had entered Germany even though he was required by the Roman king to be present himself, to celebrate, did not do this for he regarded himself more useful to the military expedition against the Czechs than to the celebration of the council and impeded the convocation of the council rather than inhibit the expedition of the army. He decided to join himself and be personally present with the army rather than the council for it was determined that if he relinquished the supply of the army there was no hope for progress. He gave the primary letters of convocation not for the celebration of but for the arrangement of the council and certified it by the testimony of a letter to the pope and confessed to the Roman court that the appointment of legate to the council was disturbing and he regarded it as meaningless. After the grievous retreat from the kingdom of Bohemia, Guiliano continued with the proposal to reduce the heretics but through another means of prosecution towards its fulfilment through a general council which he had previously not attended on account of his hearty support for their destruction. He came to Nürnberg where he found the Roman king and he enjoyed his hospitality. Here the king, the electors, and other princes listened to the report of the flight of the army without being oppressed by a hostile force and were asked their advice on what to do further in this matter. They replied that it was not possible to make any conclusion but it seemed necessary to convoke the assembly of the whole holy empire which was scheduled in Frankfurt during the feast of St Gall [16 October].

At that time Guiliano expressed his conviction in the presence of the king and the others that the best remedy for the extermination of the heresies from the kingdom of Bohemia was in the celebration of the general council of Basel and not elsewhere. He persuaded the others to remain strong in faith because German people whom he had seen frightened and in panic at the flight of the army needed to be inspired and strengthened and given hope of support for the resistance of the heretics by means of the holy synod of Basel because the whole church was gathering there. The knowledge of the council and the hope of support was surely very useful because it encouraged many to stay away from the area of Bohemia and not to enter into any pact with them concerning their faith.

MC 2: 27–9.

166   An abbot files a chilling report

[This intelligence report written by the abbot of Waldsaßen, Brother Nicholas, on 15 August 1431, the day after the collapse of the crusaders, was directed to the civic authorities of Cheb. Its brevity does not detract from its grim foreboding. The report must have been received by the authorities in Cheb with a sense of dread and a good deal of fear and trembling and the shock of a fifth successive failure must have been heavy.]

Our prayers in advance, dear lord and friend. We advise you that our servant Ulrich Heint has just arrived at night fall and tells us that the army is fleeing through the forest and the Hussites are pursuing them with cavalry and infantry. He does not know whether or not the Hussites will proceed out of the forest entirely. We will let you know later. Given in Tirschenreut on the day of Our Lady's Assumption, during the night in the year of the Lord 1431.

UB 2: 240–1.

167   Hussite perspective on the campaign

[This incomplete Hussite report, summarizes the events and ascribes the victory to divine intervention. The report was written on 15 August 1431.]

When we were prepared early Tuesday morning and marched towards them, at the same time the enemy heard of it and drew up into formation with many strong troops. Those troops stood until we approached within a distance of about one mile. At that moment the Lord God sent into them such a strong fear that they abandoned their wagons in the forest in the morning while troops from other wagons protected them from our army. But when they saw that our army was pressing near and our entire force approaching towards Rýzmberk, they fled in different directions with their troops. We captured their wagons both in the forest and before the wood. When we drew up to the forest, at that moment, we dispersed, capturing nearly all of their wagons and chasing them through the forest through almost the entire night. I cannot say exactly how many wagons were taken but I would estimate them to be more than our own armies have. On them is considerable plunder and more than one hundred large cannon as well as other cannon. Through the forest some of them were killed and others captured.

The King of kings and Lord of lords, defends his own, rescues them, saves them, fights for them and wins. Men, brothers and sisters, together with the children, dearly beloved in the same King and Lord. This has been written to you about these enemies, especially how the cardinal, papal authorities, princes, bishops, secular empire with counts, lords, knights, with towns and other various nations and people have strongly invaded our land in order to oppress those gifts and the faithful Christians by which this land has been blessed by the Lord God. It was a great distress for you and for us. With great cruelty towards old and young, they burned, ruined and killed without mercy intending to exterminate the Czech language and to vituperate and extinguish their faith. But the Lord God who does not burden his faithful ones with more than they can endure, is a ready and faithful helper to those who call upon him in need. Now he has manifestly shown us sinners that when we are faithful, over all those enemies . . . .

AČ 6: 424.

168   An uninformed report of the battle

[This brief report, written two days after the events at Domažlice, is curiously incomplete. The report is dated 16 August 1431 and is addressed to Friedrich, count of Toggenburg, Brettegew and Thauas.]

Gracious lord! As your grace has written and desired that we write to you about the business of the campaign and the Hussites in Bohemia and so on, we have received your letter with pleasure. Up until now we have not heard much, except that the powerful army of these lands with a great force of people passed through the forest in the direction of Bohemia during fourteen days. They came from Tachov to Domažlice and plundered, harried, and burned as much of the land of Bohemia as they could and have taken some small dwellings and burned several houses in the suburbs of Domažlice and they remain before Domažlice. Similarly, our gracious lord of Austria, also with a powerful army, marched from his lands to join our army and he likewise plundered and burned. We do not know how it will go from here. May almighty God extend grace to this. Our most gracious Lord Sigismund, King of the Romans, is still with us. We do not know what to write now about what his royal grace is going to undertake. We are faithful to your grace with love and service. Given on Thursday after Our Lady's Assumption.

UB 2: 241.

169   Admission of crusader defeat and disaster

[While omitting specific details, this report admits disaster and contemplates apparent inscrutable divine providence. A sense of confusion and despair can also be detected. While many crusaders escaped with their lives almost all of Cesarini's 200 men were cut down by the Hussites. The report is dated 17 August 1431.]

To the honourable, discreet, dear lords and friends, our friendly service as before. We write to your favour, although we do not do so gladly. Nevertheless, we do not wish to conceal it. Unfortunately, may it be counted to almighty God, our lords the princes, lords and cities, who were there on behalf of Christendom, came off badly in the land of Bohemia so much so that unfortunately there was some movement within the forces and our entire army fled and retreated through the forest. Most of the wagons were left standing in the forest together with great equity on them. Many [of the crusaders] succeeded in escaping. The people emerged from the forest but the army was divided and everybody went home. Some of our people have come to say that neither they nor your people brought any wagons with them having lost them all unless any should be found of which we do not know. As for the people we hope that there are not too many which have been lost. Of course you cannot go out without any loss during such an escape as you can well imagine yourself. This has caused such damage to Christendom that it is grievous and must be taken to heart properly. We poor people around here on the border had rejoiced very much in the campaign but regrettably it has ended very badly and we do not know what will happen to us now, on what we can trust or on what to rely. It is not only around us but throughout Christendom that the almighty God arranges and causes things to pass according to his divine will. Whatever we can do for your favour and friendship will gladly be done. Given on Friday after Assumption.

UB 2: 242.

170   Hussite song of victory at Domažlice

[Following the battle of the fifth crusade the town secretary of Prague, Vavřinec of Březová, composed a lengthy triumphant poem in Latin extolling the virtues of Hussite invincibility. Nascent Czech nationalism and patriotism are clearly evident in the verses.[11] The 'song of victory' was also an expression of thanksgiving to God for the triumph of August 14 at Domažlice. Massive celebrations were held in Prague wherein the captured crusade banners were displayed in the Old Town square in front of the Týn Church. From here great crowds marched in procession to the Prague Castle. Vavřinec also composed a special order of service for the occasion which he included in the 'song of victory'. This poetic composition celebrating the fifth successive Hussite defeat of the crusading armies is comprised of more than 1,630 verses in eight syllable lines with epic fragments, monologues, dialogues and lyrics, together with numerous biblical quotations, totally approximately 3,500 words. Of note, amid the protracted celebration and expression of victory and defiance, is the desire for peace. The following verse from the epic poem makes this point.]

The swords will turn to ploughshares
The spears to sickles as God has promised
Weapons shall be made into bells
To welcome us.

---

[11]   The best study on this subject in English is František Šmahel, 'The idea of the "nation" in Hussite Bohemia', trans. R.F. Samsour *Historica* 16 (1968), pp. 143–247 and 17 (1969), pp. 93–197.

No longer shall nations raise swords
In war against their neighbours
But all shall live together
As brothers in peace.

FRB 5: 545–63 at p. 561.

171 A crusade commander admits defeat

[On 19 August 1431, Conrad of Kölbsheim wrote to the mayor and city council of Strasbourg about the power of the crusading army at Domažlice and what happened when the Hussite armies appeared. There are other relevant details in Juan of Segovia, '*Historia gestorum synodi Basiliensi*' in MC, volume 2.]

Honourable, discreet, wise, gracious and beloved lords! I commend my subject willing service to you. Dear Lords! As you had written to me to inform you in what measure the most gracious lord king accepted us, so I tell you that when I arrived in Nürnberg, I took on Heinrich of Mühlheim and Engelbert and went to our lord the king and relayed all the information to His Royal Grace which you had recommended to me and the others. We let you know that our most gracious lord the king accepted us and asked us when we wished to set off. We begged His Royal Grace to allow us one or two days to rest because we were in need of it. His Grace condescended to us graciously and said that he wished to commend us to those of Nürnberg that when we were in need they should help us. Then we set off from Nürnberg and drew into Bohemia.

Then our gracious lord the king came to us and spoke to us on a plain and gave his hand to all of us and graciously blessed us. Then we separated from him and joined the princes near a town called Weiden. We marched with them through the forest towards Tachov but we did not lay a siege against it but burned about four miles around us. Then we marched on to Domažlice and burned around us about 200 villages. On the next [day], the Assumption of Our Dear Lady [15 August], the princes set off from Domažlice and there came a warning to them that the Hussites were marching toward them and they began to prepare for battle and wished to move to a hill and there to set up a wagon fortress in order to prepare for the fight in expectation of it. About two hours after midday the Hussites marched up there and got ready for the battle. But at this moment the princes turned their backs around, and because of this gave it up and fled as if they wanted to be the first to get through the forest. So we and [those of] the other cities had to run after them because of the command of the princes and our banner was the last one through the forest. The Hussites have won more than 2,000 wagons from us and many assets there. Also, we let you know dear lords that your messenger Beinhein brought to me 400 guilders which I have divided among my companions. Given in Nürnberg on Sunday after Our Lady's Day in the year of the Lord 1431. Also you should know dear lords that our forces which went through the forest numbered 100,000 men, of these there were 14,000 cavalry and 8,000 wagons which carried food, cannon, and other weapons.

Neumann, pp. 122–3.

172 Poem on the fifth crusade

[Significant detail and unique information on the collapse of the fifth crusade can be gleaned from this poetic verse report written by the German poet and war reporter from Nürnberg, Hans Rosenblüt. The resolve of some crusade leaders proved insufficient to overcome the disunity which characterized this effort to defeat the heretics. The role played by Cardinal Guiliano Cesarini is downplayed and the supreme captain of the armies, Friedrich of Brandenburg, appears negligible. Of particular interest are the speeches made by several German barons and more significantly the revelation that the common foot soldiers were left to their fate by the panicked flight of the captains and who, according to Rosenblüt, were unaware of their dire plight until the Hussites were upon them and it was too late to flee. In the confusion which attended the flight of the crusaders, the papal legate Cesarini lost his robes, gold cross, cardinal's hat and the crusade bull itself entrusted to him by the pope naming him crusade legate as well as bearing ecclesiastical authority for the crusade itself (MC 2, pp. 27–8). These items were captured by the heretics and displayed in the town of Domažlice for 200 years.]

Lord, by your mighty power
May the complaint of this lament come to you
Of the awful disgrace
Which happened in the land of Bohemia
When many well-formed troops
Rode there to rescue the Christian name!

They came together at Tachov
Where they began and held council
The cardinal [Guiliano Cesarini] commanded all artillerymen to gather
To advise the supreme princes
On when the town could be conquered
And how many days they should camp before it.

Then eleven expert men gathered
To commence a special counsel
They considered it in short order
And brought their opinion to the princes
In order that they might be first allowed to see the town
The cardinal ordered it so and was amenable to it.

Then they rode round and round the town
They returned and reported
'We wish to conquer the castle by shooting
If you give us tools and shield
We can be inside on the sixth day.'

Then the captain went to one of the weapons
And prevented it from being fired saying:
'We must not rush.
If the enemy comes near

The weapons and powder should be preserved.'
The cardinal wished to know how much powder could be shot.

The gunners informed him they had thirty quintal
They could effect a great conquest.
The cardinal spoke to them
No powder would be spared
He would provide forty quintal and commanded them to shoot.

He wished for them to enjoy about one hundred ducats
Which he wanted to give to them as a bonus
To remember them and their goodness for God.

Then the prince of Brandenburg [Friedrich] said:
'Whoever is eager for the friendship of the king
I would advise not to conquer the towns.
We are here because of the war
It has not been ordered that we should murder townsfolk!'

Then one of the captains – a priest – said:
'Lord, is it not allowed?
A carpenter should carve in a cloister
With a sharp, newly-edged axe

If the abbot came and cut a stone with it
His rooms would probably be small
When his weapon became damaged.
Great infamy and vice will fall upon us
If we do not destroy towns!'

The young one from Meißen [Margrave Friedrich] listened to this and said:
'God must always be merciful
If I do not avenge the many poor people I have lost!
If I cannot soak my spurs in Hussite blood I will complain to God!
But if we wish to hold to the king's command
Then we will seek such honour
As though we have struck down a frog to death!'

When the people on foot were informed
That they did not want to allow them to conquer it
They began to curse the lords saying:
'What are we waiting for?'

When the princes heard of it
They turned their [equipment] from the town and marched to a nearby hill
Here they made a quick decision
On how best to approach the enemy
They plotted to advance with fire.

Then they set off and started a fire
Burning three miles of open country
[Planá, a small town about three miles northwest of Tachov]
And five times longer
As far as Hoštka.[12]

Then three gunners began and spoke to the people:
'Now, run through the open country
Before the princes try to prevent you
Whoever wishes to help will win honour and goods
We have found the nest full
Our enemies have retreated there
From the open country where they could not hide.'

---

[12] A village near Tachov, but it could also be a reference to the village of Hostouň which lay
between Tachov and Domažlice.

Then they brought three cannon
And created much excitement inside
Until a peace was arranged
The supreme captains called to them
Saying if they wanted to surrender the castle
Their lives would be spared.

Then the princes sent five knights inside
To take over the castle
They announced to the people outside
What assets and goods could be found within
And which they would hand over to them.

But those outside wanted to defraud them
And wished to be able to plunder the goods inside themselves
The foot soldiers evilly wanted the same thing
So they arose and marched to the moat
Breaking the peace and shooting inside.

This made the princes regret
That they did not wish to be obedient
Then the cavalry meddled and began to order the foot soldiers:
'You must remember and not forget what the princes order'
A secret messenger rode to the Hussites
And told them that they were divided
And there was great discord.

Then the Hussites said: 'This is good news!'
They arose and marched with all their strength
The messenger told them that they [the crusaders]
Were situated between Domažlice and Rýzmberk Castle.

Then the princes were apprised
That they were coming by the road
Hoping to find them in their encampment
Those of Prague and the Bohemian land.

Then the princes took counsel together
On whether to retreat or to remain
And whether they had sufficient numbers.
Then the cardinal spoke to the princes:

'Whoever among you takes to flight
Such a one is without grace and infamous
Shall lose his Christian name
And be recorded in the book of excommunication as a cursed man!'

Then Heinrich of Plavno stood up:
'Such a one shall be condemned to a sack
Whoever flees on this day
Regardless of whether he is a lord, knight or vassal
This is my opinion and it seems right to me!'

Then that young one of Meißen stood up again:
'I am in the forefront of everything!
Whoever sees me retreat
Must strike me down in anger
Run his sword and lance through me
This I command you. Do not hesitate!'

Then the young Margrave Johannes stood up:
'As my heart condemns it, as the tongue splits:
Whoever among us would run
When it comes [time] to meet the enemy
Such a one shall be condemned in front of all the world
His honour and knighthood is to be taken away from him
His banner to be trampled under foot in dung
This is my advice and my opinion!'

Then Duke Albrecht of Bavaria said:
'It is written that no one of my family has ever retreated from any battle!
If God gives us to fight today
Then I wish to be faithful to my father's guidance
Which is to turn ahead
This was his counsel which he gave to me
His opinion was that honour had never been taken from a Bavarian baron
Because they had won their swords by their faith.'

After this the bishop of Franconia [Johann II of Würzburg] spoke:
'That man is blessed who must fight for the Christian name
And must thank God
Because they shall all come to heaven
Who have spilled their blood

To such [warriors] heaven has never slipped away
As well as to those who are faithful here!'

Then one of the bishops from the Rhine [Archbishop Dietrich II of Cologne] said:
'Whoever would be faithless in these matters
Such a one goes deeper into the revenge of hell
Then Judas the traitor who betrayed the Lord
A great evil often brings small profit!'

There were two of the princes
Of whom no one knew their opinion
They spoke neither yes nor no
About whether to stay or march home
Or how to behave in these matters
However they ordered the ranks
Everyone was to prepare for battle
For it seemed to them that the enemy was not far off.

Then the old one of Brandenburg [Friedrich] made his stand on a high hill
With all of his knights and vassals
He intended to do battle with his enemies there
He sent for Duke Johannes [of Bavaria]
Who came running quickly to him
The bishop of Würzburg also drew up there with his troops.

Then they saw [from a distance of] half a mile
Their enemies marching forward at great speed
With three powerful armies
Wishing to oppose the Christians.

The margrave retreated a little
So that the enemy would not see them
And thus think that their numbers were smaller.

The margrave called upon the bishop:
'Lord', he said, 'do we want to confront the enemy?'
'Yes', he said, 'in the name of St Stephen
And also in the name of the holy knight St George
Who will help us to divide their wagon-fortress.'

Then one of the knights was sent to them
Holding the banner of St George
He said to them that they wanted to fulfil destiny
As they had heard previously many times.

He read many names from a letter
None of these people were there in the crowd
He knew this well enough but nevertheless called them up
[To inquire] if it was faithful or dangerous
God knows well [their reason for being absent]
And pronounces decision at the Last Judgement.

The margrave sent for two knights
One of whom was called Wilhelm of Rechberg
The other's name was Erkinger of Saunsheim
These he sent to the watch alone
He let them do as the pious ones do
In order that they should calculate the number of the enemy
And estimate them [accurately].

Then they hurried there with great haste
Running onto a hill
The enemy turned themselves against them
With three horrible groups
Which they intended to run and rush [against them] there.

The one of Rechberg said to Lord Erkinger:
'Ride away and report this matter to the margrave
Order him to flee!
There is no one around here
They outnumber us three to one!'

Then Erkinger said: 'Neither of us!
We must attack them hopefully
Even if there were four of them for each of us
Still we want to press them as good knights
We should undertake it gladly.
Should we put Christendom to shame?
It would be better to die today
We must act now as pious Christians
I hope that God will not forsake us!'

Then the one of Rechberg ran his way
He came in haste to the troops
He took the margrave's hand and shouted:
'Let everyone who is here, fly!
They outnumber us three to one!'
Then they set off and hurried away
Leaving everything there behind them
Those on horse and those on foot from the cities
That is the battle which they made!

All the foot soldiers remained behind
Because they had been positioned among the wagons
So that they should expect the enemy there
They intended nothing else but to do battle
They did not know that the princes had fled
Until the enemy drew up to them and stabbed and cut them [to pieces].

Those who retreated like the first ones
Were all very sorrowful
The grievous killing and murder
Remains not avenged by anything
Of those who were left behind in need
Their blood, for revenge, cries into heaven!

Blessed Omnipotent God
May you feed them all by the word of your grace
Who were killed during the retreat
Thus they were wrongly sold
Their lives and goods taken away from them
May you consider their innocent deaths
Allow them to obtain grace and favour.

Lord, through your death, which you have accomplished
Though you had never been guilty
May you incline your ear to the evil ones through the pious ones!
May they all come to confession and to penance
Who are guilty because of this retreat
Release them from their appetite of sin
In which they have indulged themselves!

You are the righteous judge of the living and the dead
Do not spare them to the Last Judgement
Because all of their iniquities must be judged
May you hear their cries and our lament
May your grace not pass us by
Lord, through your terrible wounds.

May you enable us here below, exalted Lord
To die in the right faith
May you cause us to lose life and goods
If only the soul might delight [in salvation].

If our sins have shamed you
Then may your blood, which you have shed,
Make you tender so that you might forgive
May you grant us to enjoy your innocent death
And the bloodshed of all the martyrs.

May you sprinkle your grace over us
Lord, through the great love of your son
And through the goodness of your Holy Spirit!

Liliencron 1: 334–9.

173   Troubles in the crusader camps

[A letter addressed to Paul of Rusdorf, the commander of the Teutonic Order in
Prussia by Kilian von der Mosel from Freiburg on 14 December 1431 underscores
the nature of conflict and disunity among the crusaders on the occasion of the fifth
crusade. Of particular note, is the high level of discontent with Sigismund who,
once again, declined to personally participate in the crusade. The Emperor's
absence raised numerous questions.]

Offering willingly the due service and commending [myself] to the protection of
your worthy grace. Worthy and magnificent dear gracious sir. As your grace
commanded me, when I separated from you, that I write the news to your grace,
I have not come to know anything yet of something true and original. However,
on the following Wednesday before St Laurence a friend of mine of the cavalry
of the force of Nigkil of Robis came here and informed me that the princes had
remained camped near Tachov for eight days. They intended to attack it but Duke

Hans of Bavaria had said that the town was the inheritance of his father and he did not wish for it to be burned down and not fired upon so that he would not earn the animosity of the common people. The princes became united and wanted four weeks not to attack. They set off on the same Wednesday, when he [Nigkil of Robis] marched toward Kladruby hoping to find the Táborites to fight wherever they might run into them. They had been entirely prepared to fight and had readied their force such that the Cardinal [Cesarini] joined my lord the duke of Saxony and commended to my lord the duke the Roman division. They stayed in the wagon fortress all night. The wagons go around five times and there are a hundred wagons in each line and they also have many empty wagons along with them and there are far too many of them. So the imperial cities joined my lord of Brandenburg and the Bavarian princes joined themselves and each group was about a mile from each other. The king wished to leave for the Latin lands [Italy, etc.] but the great count of Hungary came and had a sharp debate with him to the effect that if he did not wish to stay with the princes and be active in this matter he need not bother entering Hungary again. So he went off to Nürnberg. The Táborites also sent a message to the princes in the army about whether they would be able to [persuade] the king to come to the field where they hoped they could undertake fair negotiations. But the king wrote to the princes saying he wanted to go to Cheb or to Loket and did not wish to come farther. So the princes set off and went their way. Given in Freiburg, on the evening of Our Gracious Lady of the spice blessing, under my seal.

[Appendix] Also, these are the princes in the field: the Cardinal, bishop of Cologne, bishop of Würzburg, margrave of Brandenburg with his son, duke of Saxony, Duke Hans of Bavaria, Duke Heinrich of Bavaria, Duke Otto of Bavaria, also the one of Württemberg and the force of other princes with them, both ecclesiastical and secular. When they say they have a very great force it is my lord of Brandenburg who is the highest captain in the army. The one of Plavno [i.e. Heinrich of Plavno] is the cardinal's captain.

In the same way the duke of Austria has written to the princes. He wishes to keep the whole measure of what was agreed upon in Nürnberg. He departed with a great force to the land and moved also to the field. The heretics marched against him and wanted to fight and drew to within one mile. But the duke hid in the wagons and they made off at once too. They stayed four or five days against each other because the duke did not want to leave the wagons. The Táborites set off down the road and drew away. Thus the Táborites and Orphans gladly wanted to fight but the towns did not want to help them and did not wish to leave their towns and have had no occasion with any prince yet.

Also gracious and dear lord, I wish to make known to your grace that our lord the duke, the land and the towns with their powerless people marched into the land of Bohemia on Saturday and on the Sunday after St Laurence Day and with great force they continued to march on and drew near to Rýzmburk where they had a great collection of guns.

Also, I make known to your grace that Hans of Polenczk moved with great force to Lobaw with the towns of the land of Lusatia and with the [six towns].

Also gracious and dear lord, your grace sent me out into the land for people, although now I cannot gather any people. They do not want to ride for such money. The cardinal gives me two gulden for one horse and I want to continue until the day when I have instructed the people.

UB 2: 237–9.

174   Letter of Sigismund to Friedrich of Brandenburg

[This excerpt comes from a letter written from the emperor to the supreme commander of the armies of the fifth crusade. Sigismund downplays the obvious heavy losses but his crusading fervour against the heretics remains unabated. The letter is dated 26 August 1431.]

. . . As you know, the army has regrettably retreated from its positions inside Bohemia and has returned home. By the grace of God there has not been too much injury to the people. The situation, however, cannot be left as it now is. Christendom as well as the countries in the vicinity [of Bohemia] cannot be allowed to remain completely hopeless. Neither must the heretics be permitted any longer to maintain such delight and thereby be strengthened. . . .

UB 2: 243–5.

175   The Emperor expresses regret to Oldřich Rožmberk

[Sigismund writes to the lord of Rožmberk and expresses his great regret at the failure of the imperial army and its flight from Bohemia. He states his desire to arrange a new campaign during the assembly in Frankfurt. Written on 28 August 1431.]

We, Sigismund, by the grace of God, king of the Romans, ever Augustus, king of Hungary and Bohemia.

Dear faithful and noble [sir]. When you have written now of the flight of the princes and the army from Bohemia and so forth, we must tell you that we sorrow not a little. Although the princes and the cardinal are here with us and have given notice here and there, none of them have been able to explain, even though they too have wondered, why they fled from the land without being pressured to. Therefore, as you have written in your letter, there is no other reason than our sins. However, we intend neither to leave this matter in this fashion nor to fail again so easily but to undertake it again. Therefore we have called an assembly to Frankfurt on the next Day of St Gall [16 October]. Today we go from here to Augsburg and then on to Feldkirchen. Once we settle things with those of Milan, then we shall cross the mountains to Lombardy and send our advisor to Frankfurt to that assembly. If we are unable to come to an accord then we will personally come to the assembly. Do know that we, like God, will never forsake you, our dearly beloved. Also we let you know about Plzeň that we have now managed that matter as best we could so that they can go home happy. Concerning Budějovice we have written to our son so that he may be of assistance and whatever we can do we will gladly. Whatever news you receive, let us know. Given in Nürnberg on the day of St Augustine [28 August] . . . .

Rynešová 1: 127–8.

176   Orphan and Táborite expeditions abroad

[Buoyed by the overwhelming success at Domažlice against the crusaders, Hussite armies continued to send out sorties into Moravia, Silesia, Austria and Lusatia (see map 6). The first serious defeats suffered by the Hussites forces are herein recorded.]

At this time the priest Prokop with his followers set off for Silesia because his people were being harassed in the town of Němčí and they wished to support them with great cannon and machines for some weeks. When they heard that Prokop the priest was coming against them and had drawn near they fled from the fields into their towns and castles and he liberated his people. Then he proceeded against the other sects and sent Prokůpek, along with the Táborites and Orphans to Moravia. The aforementioned duke, aware that they and all their armies were marching against him ordered his people to enter the aforementioned towns and some of his castles while he rode with the rest into Austria. The previously mentioned Táborite sect at the time held the towns of Ivančice, Moravský Krumlov, Jevišovice, Tovačov and others in Moravia and in Austria a church called Tajov. King Sigismund spent the entire summer in Nürnberg but following the flight of the western Germans around the birth of the blessed virgin Mary [8 September] he rode with some princes towards the city of Basel to celebrate the general council.

In the same year, 1431, after the feast of the Assumption of the Blessed Virgin [15 August], the inhabitants of the land of Lusatia surrounded the town of Libavá, in which there were some Wyclifites, and after some weeks they took it by force with the help of some of the people inside. . . .

In the same year on the Saturday after the feast of St Gall, the captains from the sect of the Táborites, Tomáš of Vlašim and Mikuláš with the brother called Sokols and Leskovec, with their followers and 600 cavalry and 4,500 foot soldiers, so it is said, along with 360 wagons, rode towards Austria to collect wine and they obtained many barrels of wine and other items both on the way and on the return. The people of the duke of Austria, and also margrave of Moravia at the time, who had the daughter of King Sigismund as his wife, with his captain Lord Krajíř and 16,000 warriors, it is said, attacked the Wyclifites near the town of Waidhofen and they struggled mightily against each other but finally the people of the duke won and nearly 4,000 Wyclifites were reported to have been killed by them and seventy of the elite were captured and taken in chains to Vienna and they captured all of their wagons, cannon, wine and other things. Tomáš and Mikuláš Sokol, the captains, with a few men, escaped home on horse. Mikuláš Sokol at that time had control over the fortress of Řečice of the Prague archbishopric and the whole area through the help and power of the Wyclifites.

In the same year after the Assumption of the Blessed Virgin Mary [15 August] the priest Prokop with the sect of the Wyclifites and another priest Prokůpek, with the sect of the Orphans and with them Lord Hanuš and the son of Lord Bedřich of Kolovrat, already one of their adherents, marched from the district of Plzeň towards Silesia and there they freed those of their sect who had been surrounded in the town of Němči because the inhabitants of the land rode home from them without damage. Then they all turned toward Opava and then Hungary beyond the river Váh near the town of Nitra and there in that region they took from the houses and villages great plunder of horse, cattle and other things and created much damage. Here the priest Prokop the Great and Lord Hanuš of Kolovrat with their army separated from the Orphans in the direction of Uherský Brod. Then the priest Prokůpek and [Jan] Čapek [of Sány], at the time captain of the Orphans, the son of Lord Bedřich of Kolovrat of Libštejn, Jan of Žďár called Šmykouský and Sigismund Huler of Hořovice, with the citizens of Hradec Králové, and other people and warriors of that area with the sect and army of the Orphans remained in and around the town of Iľava in Hungary. They were commonly said to have 7,000 cavalry and foot soldiers, along with more than 300 wagons.

Then some Hungarians, Moravians, and Czechs gathered together, servants of the king Lord Sigismund, and marched against them and they struggled together for nine days so much so that the sect and army of the Orphans submitted themselves to flight and in that retreat they were said to have lost more than 250 wagons with cannon and various items and barely 2,000 of them were said to have returned with about fifty wagons. The others, namely Sigismund of Hořovice, were captured by the Hungarians and killed by the people of the king or drowned during the retreat across the aforementioned river. The march and return lasted through the whole of autumn until the feast around the birth of the Lord. Many of the Orphans died on account of the cold because at the time there was a continuous heavy frost since the feast of St Martin [12 November]. The sect of the Orphans returned to Prague at the birth of the Lord greatly diminished.

Then in the same year around the feast of St Catherine [25 November] the army of the priest Prokop the Great, with Táborites and those of Ostromeč, about 10,000 cavalry and foot soldiers, marched to Austria, invaded the town of Litschau and stayed in the area until the circumcision of the Lord and created much damage.

In the same year, the rest of the Orphans drew up soon after the birth of the Lord towards the property of Lord Zbyněk Zajíc of Házmburk, near Házmburk, and the people of this Lord Zbyněk, around forty horsemen, attacked some of the Orphans and killed seven of them and captured around twenty-five of them but they were released at the recommendation of Jan Zajíc of Budyně.

In the same year of the Lord 1432, on the Sunday after St Dorothy, there was a great gathering of the Wyclifites, Táborites, Orphans and their captains, namely the priest Prokop the Great, Priest Prokůpek, Čapek the Orphan captain, and Otík the Táborite captain, in Prague. At that time the very great coldness of the winter continued but they decided that the larger portion of them should march into Silesia. They rode first to Lusatia, then in the direction of Silesia and caused great damage.

In the same year during the first and second weeks of the fast [Lent] there was a great overflow of water on account of the fact that there had been an almost continuous snowfall all over Bohemia which had not been in more than fifty years. The aforementioned sects of the Táborites and Orphans marched toward the territory of Brandenburg and in the same fast they created much damage as far as Frankfurt and farther in the same territory as well as in the territory of Lusatia. They returned to Bohemia only at the feast of Stanislav [7 May].

In the same year and summer they marched to the town of Olomouc and there caused much damage. Obtaining information that the Silesians and those of Wrocław were holding a congress in the town of Strzelin they sent on those cavalry from Olomouc and then 600 cavalry with wagons and they conquered that town by assault and took 500 captives of Wrocław and of Silesia among which were four counsellors and the knight Nespor. They also took 300 pieces of armour and 415 horse. This happened around the feast of St James [1 May].

Chronicle of Bartošek of Drahonice, in FRB 5: 604–7.

177   Orphan invasion of Hungary

[The old Czech chronicler makes the error of ascribing this campaign to the command of Jan Žižka. This is, however, quite impossible. There is no evidence that Žižka ever undertook a campaign there even though some scholars once held the view that Žižka did invade Hungary in 1422. This has been refuted. However, the details of the account do resemble an Orphan expedition in November of 1431 and the detail concerning military tactics merits inclusion here. It also provides a sustained account of Hussite military activity outside Bohemia. See map 6.]

After the brethren had been in Moravia for a long period of time, they persuaded him [Žižka *sic*!] to embark upon an even more distant venture. So he prepared four wagon columns together with as many cannon as he could and crossed the hills marching into Hungary. The Hungarians did not make any effort to impede his progress or engage with him. The were hoping that some of his men would desert and then they would defeat him having gathered together a great cavalry against him. At length they engaged him having a number of cannon. When he saw that the odds were not good he turned his wagons in the direction of Moravia and headed that way. In the first instance he gathered all of his men close to the wagons and marched on with the wagons in closed formation. So he put the wagons at his flanks and put between the wagons two shields and behind each of the shields two or three men with guns. He did this so that if they [the Hungarians] tried to get into the wagons they would be unable to do it.

On that day the retreat was very difficult. Whenever he ordered a halt, he was fired upon. Since he could not stop them, he marched on until night fell. He did this so that they would not be certain of his camp and thus fire upon them and for this reason he did not allow any fire to be kindled in the camp. They [Hungarians] rode around his camp but since there was nothing to tie their horse to, they went to some of the villages nearby some distance away in order to be safe from him. After resting for a period of time as he thought adequate, they marched on to a lake by a hill. Here he took up position so that one flank went to the edge of the lake and the other to the side of the hill. This he did so that they would overshoot in their attempts to fire on the troops. He then proceeded to put some wagons up to the top and fashioned a bastion of them at one end and another at the other end. He created an entrenchment at this place and placed cannon on the bastions. This did not permit them [the Hungarians] to make any stand there. He remained camped here for the whole day and the next night. On the third day he marched from the lake to another river which flows in the direction of Narhid and pitched camp there. But he was afraid that he would come under assault when a crossing was attempted. So throughout the night he commanded that the wagons be secured by trenches from the bank of the river and surrounded with ditches so that his men could defend themselves while on the other side he put wagons and cavalry. He commanded that the ground on both banks be dug up in order that the river could be crossed with four wagon columns.

When they [Hungarians] saw that he was busy crossing the river with the wagons they began to attack the rear wagons but they were driven back by the cavalry and foot soldiers and many were killed and wounded. He crossed to the other side with all the wagons and his men. There he gave thanks to the Lord God because God had enabled him to cross the river. On he marched through the forest, marshes and valleys and made camp at a spot where it would be difficult to be fired upon. On the fourth day he drew on to some fish ponds near Tyrnau and here he repaired wagons changing their places in the columns because they [the Hungarians] had damaged some along the flanks and many horse had been killed. At this place they did not attack him. After repairing the wagons and in the encampment near the fish ponds he marched on to a hill on the fifth day. Again he was attacked by the cavalry and with cannon. He marched to the slope of the hill and secured one flank because it was easier to defend one flank than two. Realizing they could not harm him, they retreated from his army while he camped on the hill. Then it is said that considerable misery and distress arose in the camp and some would have given a lot of money for a green cabbage. This was on account of the fact that they [Hussites] did not go out of their wagons because the enemy had a strong cavalry and it was not possible to attack them on foot. Whenever the enemy attempted to attack him or engage him in battle he was always victorious and they wound up being beaten back. Cavalry are equipped differently than foot soldiers and for them it is not something easily done [fighting on horse?]. If one wishes to learn something, it is necessary to have both time and leisure in order to master it.

On the sixth day of the march he moved away from the slope in an effort to reach the hills but had to form the wagons into a single column for this was the only way forward. When the Hungarians saw this, they came after him with a large force in hopes that the men would have to leave the wagons in order to defend themselves and that his organization for battle would no longer be effective. He took up a position near a forest beneath a hill so that if they fired they would overshoot. With the artillery he took up position on the top of the hill. He gave orders that the horse should be unhooked from the wagons and had his men mount them armed with hatchets, shovels and spades. Then they went to inspect the road to see it was open. He did this so that the horsemen [Hungarians] could not attack his wagons from the sides and he ordered that the road be repaired. When he marched out with his men from the forest, he gave instructions that a new road be built about one-and-a-half hons away from the old one.[13] He did this so that if the

---

[13] The 'hon' is an old Czech distance measure consisting of about 125 paces.

enemy caught up with him he could take his men and guns to the old road and should his enemies attempt to impede his progress through the field when he intended to leave the forest he could shoot at them and kill them. This happened thereafter that while he was on this side of the forest he switched from a four-column wagon train to two. He had certain wagons broken apart and made from them a bastion from one side of the wood to the other ordering that [the planks] be tied together with ropes so that they could not be broken down easily. He did this so that if there was an attempt to jump into his wagons or take the cannon, the soldiers could defend themselves from behind these planks as though it were a wall. This happened afterwards as well. He sent into the forest the guns first of all, then the foot soldiers and fifty wagons from the right side. When those fifty wagons had entered the forest, he commanded that some of the infantry follow as seemed good to him. Then fifty more wagons from the left side and again some of the infantry. So in this way he sent on each occasion fifty wagons and in between foot soldiers as was necessary. He did this so that if they [Hungarians] attempted to kill those driving the wagons, or capture the wagons the foot soldiers marching in between would be able to prevent it.

When the last ones had passed, the Hungarians attacked the rear in an effort to seize the cannon. Coming down from the heights they attacked the wagons which had been placed there but they [the Hussites] stayed out of sight until the guns had entered the forest as well as the infantry. They were not afraid of the Hungarians and while they [Hungarians] captured the carts left behind they destroyed the road so that the cavalry were unable to follow. When they saw this and realized they could not harm him, some of them rode on ahead hoping to oppose him when he emerged from the forest. But others went home saying that this was not a man but rather a cunning devil since nothing prevailed against him. So he led his army out of the forest and through some fields between the hills. Arriving at the new road he had made, he commanded that fifty wagons proceed along this road which had been built on the right [of the old one]. When they proceeded through the fields they drove close to the slope so that there were foot soldiers on one side of the wagons and the slope on the other so he had no fear of the cavalry. He commanded that the other columns draw along the other road while he sent the artillery out of the forest on the old road and then into the fields. Gradually all of the wagons emerged from the forest and he put them in a single line and pulled them into a large circle. In this way he brought the two columns together and drove them [the Hungarians] from the field with a forceful arm. The number of wagons which left the forest increased until all were out in the open. This is how the Lord God helped him retreat from Hungary. From the time that Žižka [sic] had started to wage war this had been his most difficult undertaking.

SRB 3: 58–61.

178   Manifesto of the entire Czech land

[The following document constitutes a sustained argument aimed at undermining confidence in the official church and in her leaders. The manifesto is counter propaganda inasmuch as the Hussites depict the pope as a heretic, decry the injustice of the crusade and declare the worthlessness of the indulgences offered to the crusaders. The manifesto should be dated to 1431. The full Latin text appears in MC 1, pp. 153–70.]

Christ rules, Antichrist will be destroyed! May God open your hearts for his holy commandments and constitutions through his dear son Jesus Christ, according to the humanity of the son of the virtuous and pure Virgin Mary, may he strengthen your body and spirit in order that you may be able to complete your life in a pious and meritorious fashion according to his blessed will, amen! We wish this for your redemption, honourable, wise and dear lords and citizens. Let all of the community, rich and poor, listen with special attention to the words of this letter sent to you from the Czech land.

As it is known to you and to many other communities and kings, princes and lords, there has been a great division between us and you lasting several years. You have been provoked to fight against us in order to destroy us and, alas, many noble as well as ordinary men on your side and ours have lost their lives. Up to this point you have not heard clearly from us nor do you have knowledge of our beliefs or whether we can prove it from Holy Scripture or not. Beyond this, kings, princes and barons as well as cities have suffered great damage. Therefore, we wonder quite a bit that you trust and put confidence so firmly in the pope and his clergy who announce and serve you with a poisonous, blind and dubious hope in the remission of sins while asserting that your sins are forgiven but giving you much grace and indulgences so that you will fight against us and destroy us and our wives and children. But the grace and indulgences given by them to you are nothing but naked lies, great seduction and damnation of souls and bodies of all those who trust and depend on such things. . . . the pope reveals himself as an evident heretic, the prince of hypocrisy and the highest Antichrist to all pious and rational people through his false indulgences. Further, whoever could free his brother from death without his own destruction and does not do it is a murderer of his brother. If the pope could give the remission of the penalty and guilt to all people, then no one would be condemned and go to hell. If he can do this but does not he is the murderer of as many people who fall into judgement without indulgences. The false envoys of Antichrist travelling all over the world with indulgences committed to them for that purpose to strengthen the pope-crucifier, namely teach the people to have contempt for the truth of the gospel and thus they help Antichrist and his supporters kill the people unjustly. . . .

Should it be found and approved in Holy Scripture that they are correct and we are wrong and that we do not want to be taught, then they could accept the help of kings, princes, barons and cities and resist us according to the command of Holy Scripture. But such is the excuse and evasion of all the bishops, prelates and priests saying, 'Master Hus and Jerome, who were burnt to death in Constance, were convicted by the holy father and the whole council.' But you should know that they were not convicted by Holy Scripture but by wanton and unrighteous violence and God will punish all who assented to this through counsel or assistance. But if they say that this is not entirely possible to permit us to be heard in our faith. . . .

You dear and faithful lords and citizens, rich and poor! We inform you that in the year after our Lord's birth 1431, we enquired of the Polish king in Kraków [Władysław Jagiełło] ardently and humbly and of the Hungarian king [Sigismund] in Cheb for this hearing. But this was refused. Nevertheless the bishops have contrived to compel us by force to exterminate us but God did not permit them to fulfil their desire. . . . But they have on their conscience many thousands of men who were seduced and provoked by them to this struggle such that they suffered plunder and death. They will answer to God for this just as St Paul says in the epistle to the Romans, chapter one, verse thirty-two and to Galatians 5:19–21: 'all who do such things, deserve death, and not only these who do this, but also those who consent to it . . . .'

Husitské manifesty, pp. 177–83.

Chapter 7

New Tactics: Basel to Sión, 1432–7

179   Invitation to Hussites to attend the Council of Basel

[This tract, 'In what way the Czechs have been brought to the union of the church' was written by Jan Stojković of Dubrovnik. It outlines a formal invitation for the unvanquished heretics to attend the ecumenical council at Basel.[1]]

In order that all of those faithful to Christ, both contemporary as well as in the future, might know the devotion and diligence of the sacred council of Basel concerning the extirpation of heresies and the return of the Czechs, I will attempt to tell in this booklet, as briefly as I can, what has been done and acted upon in the said sacred council concerning the aforementioned [matter].

Following the outstanding army of Catholics, as frequently before on account of our sins, being forced to flee from Bohemia in the year of the Lord 1431 in the month of August, the most reverent father and lord in Christ, Lord Guiliano, the cardinal of St Agnolo, the legate who had been personally present with the army, came directly to Basel on the ninth of September. The sacred general council had already begun to be celebrated by his sub delegates who had been sent on by him previously, namely Lord Juan of Palomar, the auditor of the apostolic chamber, and the brother Jan of Dubrovnik, professor of sacred theology of the order of preachers. Not being without a special inspiration of the Holy Spirit and having undertaken negotiations and full advice previously, it was decided by the aforementioned most reverent lord legate and the other fathers present in the sacred council at that time in one accord, to invite and summon the Czechs with kindness and humaneness to the sacred council in order that those who could not be defeated through the power of weapons might be defeated by the gentleness

---

[1]   On the Hussites at Basel there are three important studies in English: Gerald Christianson, *Cesarini: The conciliar cardinal: The Basel Years, 1431–1438* (St. Ottilien: EOS-Verlag, 1979), Christianson, 'Wyclif's Ghost: The politics of reunion at the Council of Basel' *Annuarium historiae conciliorum* 17 (1985), pp. 193–208 and E.F. Jacob, 'The Bohemians at the Council of Basel, 1433', in *Prague Essays*, ed., R.W. Seton-Watson (Oxford: Clarendon Press, 1949), pp. 81–123.

and piety of friendly negotiations. Concerning the summoning of the aforementioned a letter was composed. The wording follows, namely this.

'This sacrosanct synod of Basel, lawfully assembled in the Holy Ghost, representing the entire church, to all ecclesiastical men, nobles and all the people of the kingdom of Bohemia, unity and peace in Christ Jesus our Lord. The love of Christ compels us to leave the lands of our recognition and come to the place which has been revealed to us by the Lord for the peace of the church and the redemption of Christian people. Why wonder that we decided to wander in a foreign territory when our Lord regarded it worthy to suffer a pilgrimage even to the most difficult death of the cross? If God loved the world so that he gave his only begotten son, so we also ought to worthily love as well that we would expose our souls for the sheep should it be necessary. This, certainly, as inspired by divine grace, we are ready to do towards everyone with a prompt spirit. Because of this we have come together to this sacred general council from every nation so that having exterminated the errors from Christian people, stilled wars, suppressed the wiles of vice, the unity of the faith, the concord of spirits and the discipline of holy customs were served everywhere and this mother church flourished in peace and unity spread throughout the lands of the world. Although there are many tasks to be addressed and necessary to solve in this sacred council nothing is more salutary before our eyes than for you to be joined with us in the same unity. If you knew by what affection we desire your salvation and peace, if you could see our hearts glowing with love for you, you would rush to us leaving aside everything, preparing without delay, trusting that you might find peace for your souls through us loving you like ourselves because of Christ. God may have permitted your dissension in the church for us to recognize through experience how many evils arise from brotherly division, but after it to love each other more perfectly. Consequently the unity, which cannot be compared with anything better among good people, shall be guarded more vigilantly. Jesus Christ prayed so that not only the apostles, but everyone who might believe through his name would be one, as much as they are one, father and son, and he said that his disciples were recognized thus, if they had love one for another. If we desire to be pleasing to Christ and if we want to be considered his disciples, we must work in the aspiration of being one and to have love and agreement with each other as is fitting for faithful Christians. According to the primitive church we show that it is to be one heart and one soul of the multitude of believers as well as God is one for us, one faith and one baptism. In this way we may be in one accord with the Son of the same Father, so that he would make us, of one demeanor, worthy to dwell in his house. How good and enjoyable it will be then, when in the same house of the holy mother the brethren dwell together in the concord of being one? How much joy and happiness will there be in heaven, when you, who have been divided from us for some time, will be reunited with us again in unity and love?

Behold, the Holy Spirit gathers brethren from every nation to live in love thus, as he himself is love, according to the promise of Christ to teach truth which is necessary for salvation. We know that our heavenly father sowed the good seed of faith in the earth, but the enemy of man came and sowed weeds. We think there is still much good seed and the root has not been damaged at all. We hope that the earth is still suitable for bearing fruit in the house of the Lord so long as the dew of the Holy Ghost waters it, causes it to blossom and dries up the noxious weeds.

'We believe you have been disturbed to see so many hardships, fires, depopulations and infinite evil which happen daily from this dissension and that you desire peace and quiet in your fatherland so that the Catholic faith might be advanced throughout the earth. This cannot be better provided for than in this sacred council where the universal church comes together. Here, whatever belongs to the truth of the faith, whatever to peace and concord, whatever to the purity of life and observation of the divine commands, is negotiated with all diligence and freedom. It will be permitted for all to see what they judge to be revealed in the Christian faith. It will be allowed to counsel and manage reform. The Holy Spirit, in whose name this holy synod is gathered, will be present. He will be a leader and an administrator of the council, perfectly illuminating the hearts of all to walk in the way of truth and peace. We have confidence in this that if you come with a pure heart and good intention, without doubt you will return to your fatherland happy and consoled, bringing peace, quiet and the grace of God with yourselves to your people. We have heard you complain frequently that you have not been given the free audience which you desired. The occasion for this complaint now recedes. Look, there is already a place provided and the possibility of a full audience. You are already invited and you shall be heard, not before a few but, before all, as many as you wish. May you also listen to us. The Holy Spirit will stand by as a mediator, judge and arbiter of what is to be observed and done in the church. We will remain together in the supplication and we will show our piety by fasts, prayers, tears, invocations and holy works as long and as fervently as the author of love and the teacher of truth will enlighten the hearts of all the people to recognize and to follow the path of truth and unity. On this account the Holy Spirit introduced into the church councils so that if any dissension in the faith arose among Christians, he would reveal the truth to those congregated together as one through the invocation of his name. Often a number of errors, opinions and schisms arose in the Christian religion but by means of the holy councils the Holy Spirit broke them completely and extinguished them. If you love the truth of the faith, if you desire peace, if you care about the honour of Christ, may you demonstrate the case. It can never and more effectively occur anywhere than here and in this way. Therefore we admonish, pray and appeal to you from our whole hearts and soul through the Holy Spirit, not to refuse to enter once you see the open door for so much good. May you come with confidence to this sacrosanct council in the name of Jesus Christ so that we might listen according to this word which the Holy Spirit made in the church of God. Although we appointed this place safe and free for all coming so that you should not be troubled perhaps from some cause, we offer ourselves ready to provide a full and sufficient safe-conduct in the name of the universal church for those coming, remaining and returning, whomever you wish to designate and to do everything to expedite their safety and security. Then we pray that you might send such men whom we hope the Holy Spirit will rest upon, namely moderate, [God] fearing, humble of heart, desiring peace and not requiring their own [interests] but those of Jesus Christ. May he condescend to grant peace and eternal life in the future age to us and to you and to all Christian people who live blessed throughout the ages. Amen.'

After this it was considered how the letter should be sent. It was advised that it ought to be sent to Brother Johannes of Gelnhausen, of the Cistercian Order and at one time a monk of the cloister in Maulbronn, now a truly meritorious abbot and father of the same cloister. He had been sent on other matters of negotiation on behalf of the sacred council to the most serene king of the Romans, Sigismund, who had been staying at Feldkirchen on his way to Italy at that time. So he delivered it to the royal majesty imploring his Serenity to transport this letter by available and secure means to the kingdom of Bohemia. And so it was done. The aforementioned Roman king, having accepted this letter respectfully in his hands, read and understood with great joy and provided the means whereby it could be suitably delivered to Bohemia.[2] It was delivered as will be evident from the following. There were then three copies of the letter, under the seal of the aforementioned legate, having been used at that time by the sacred council for all of its negotiations. One was designated to the aforementioned Roman king, the second to the city of Nürnberg and the third to the city of Cheb. All three were carefully and faithfully delivered to Prague. . . . Given in Basel on the twenty-sixth day of November in the year of the Lord 1431.

MC 1: 135–8.

180   Cheb Judge

[Five crusades had gone down to defeat with heavy losses. It was time for new tactics. The papal nuncio, Guiliano Cesarini, after the debacle at Domažlice, decided that diplomacy should be the next step. The meetings at Bratislava in

---

[2]   Winfried Eberhard, 'Der Weg zur Koexistenz: Kaiser Sigmund und das Ende der Hussitischen Revolution' *Bohemia* 33 (1992), pp. 1–43.

1429 had failed. Two months before Domažlice another meeting had floundered at Cheb. Cesarini was unable to attend that convocation and had dispatched Jan Stojković of Dubrovnik (better known as John of Ragusio) in late May as his representative. The Dominican hated the Hussites, however, and the meeting came to naught. The abysmal performance of the 1431 crusade caused Cesarini to try again. This document constitutes the agreement between representatives of the official church and Hussites regarding the basis upon which the heretics would be heard and judged at the Council of Basel. The agreement was reached in Cheb on 18 May 1432.]

In the name of the Lord Jesus Christ. In the year 1432 after the birth of the Lord, on the eighteenth of the month of May in the town of Cheb an agreement has been reached between the representatives and the ambassadors of the sacred council of Basel and the envoys of the Kingdom of Bohemia and the Margraviate of Moravia concerning the following articles and the formula of safe conduct.

First, in the name of the Lord Jesus Christ. It is granted to the ambassadors and envoys of the Kingdom of Bohemia and the Margraviate of Moravia who will be sent to the general council of Basel, as they have requested, a full and free audience before the complete gathering of this council as many times as they require, in complete and suitable conditions for negotiation, in order to present principally the four articles for which they are under question. Anything which might hinder the prosecution or resolution of this audience and matter shall be handled by the council during this said time without any fraud or deceit.

Second, in like manner, if requested, some important, good and erudite men of the council may be designated to kindly consult on the matters which have been proposed or which might be brought up later, in a brotherly fashion with their representatives as often as necessary.

Third, similarly there shall be designated for them an honourable and decent place for such an audience in the assembly before our mutual union. Following the union they will be provided a needful and honourable place according to the needs of their delegation.

Fourth, they should also be given a space of time of one, two or more days, depending upon how much they require, in order to thoroughly deliberate this hearing of theirs [their presentation] along with the responses and objections of their opponents.

Fifth, also, if requested, they shall be given a written copy of the proposals of the other side. They shall also provide the same written copy if requested.

Sixth, likewise neither the rules of canon law, the decrees nor the decretals or any statutes which were edited or might be written later, nor any other writings against wicked people, or directed against those of different beliefs, nor crusades or sentences of excommunication, regardless of how they are proclaimed against the aforementioned Czech and Moravian lords or their adherents of both ecclesiastical and secular state by anyone or through anyone, not by decrees or resolutions principally of the council of Constance and Siena, nor any delegations of them, regardless of use, may and can cancel, corrupt, weaken or annul the aforesaid safe conduct and audience.

Seventh, in the matter of the four articles which they advocate, the law of God, the practice of Christ, the apostles and the primitive church, with the councils and doctors truly established in it, will be accepted as the most true and indisputable judge in the Council of Basel.

Eighth, likewise, if desired, they, as we, may plead and object freely before the council any perverse conditions, moderately exposing deficiencies to one another which should be accepted in peace and good honour.

Ninth, also as the lords and representatives of Bohemia constituted that public crimes are to be eliminated from the church of God and especially from the place of the said council; we, the envoys of that council, will endeavour for this virtue in order that it might be implemented gradually and in agreement with the grace of God as well as the other matters which are to be reformed in the church of God.

Tenth, further, whenever they wish to come, go, stay or return during the time of the safe conduct, neither a break in divine service nor an interdict shall be observed on account of their presence.

Eleventh, likewise we will work by honourable command so they shall not be disturbed or interrupted during their divine services celebrated in their lodgings.

UB 2: 281–3.

181   Persistent anxiety over undefeated heretics

[The ever-present fear of Hussite expansion and invasion forms part of the anxious issue raised by Cardinal Cesarini in this letter written to Pope Eugenius IV several months after the debacle at Domažlice. The concerns underscored invite comparison to similar fears raised by Martin V in 1428 following the collapse of the fourth crusade. See doc.134. Cesarini's letter is dated 13 January 1432.]

... The laypeople will arise just as the Hussites in similar manner and exterminate us. They will believe that such action is pleasing to God. In the recent past, people in Magdeburg have driven the archbishop and the priests out of the town. In the manner of the Hussites they surrounded themselves with fortified wagons and it is rumoured that they have asked the Hussites for a captain. The matter is even more dangerous in other places nearby inasmuch as many of the towns have entered into agreements with them [the Hussites]. Similarly, the citizens of Passau expelled their bishop and laid siege to him in a castle. Both of these towns are close to Bohemia and should they be able to create an alliance with the Czechs, as we must expect, they will then gather together considerable help as well as disciples. . . .

MC 2: 95–107.

182 Armistice between Hussites and Silesian authorities

[Silesia had supported Sigismund and the crusade against the Hussite heretics from the beginning of the military period. Under the leadership of Prokop, the Hussites repeatedly invaded Silesia. On 24 June 1432, Konrad, bishop of Wrocław, one of the most intolerant enemies of the Hussites signed an armistice with the heretics. The following document is representative of the many agreements crusade supporters ratified on account of persistent Hussite success against the crusaders. The shifting influences in Silesia – Polish, German, Czech –bedevils efforts to find an accurate and consistent translation of proper names.]

We, Konrad, by the grace of God bishop of Wrocław, with our city of Nysa and with all of our lands, castles and cities, and all of our knights, vassals and dependents, both spiritual and secular, and we Bernard, Lord of Opila and Falkenberg, Konrad called Kantner, Konrad the White, brothers and lords of Oels and Kosel, Ludwig the younger, lords of Lobbes and Oława, by the same grace [of God] dukes of Silesia, with each and every baron, knight, citizen and inhabitant of our duchies, lands and cities; Hermann Ceteras, *Vicecapitaneus* of the duchies of Świdnica and Jawor with the barons, knights, vassals and natives, and also all of the civil magistrates, patricians and citizens of the cities and towns belonging to the duchies; the patricians of the city of Wrocław holding and administering the office of the duchy of Wrocław, together with the district and city of Środa Śląska [Neumarkt] and the remaining districts and territories belonging to the duchy, with the barons, knights, vassals and inhabitants of our aforementioned city of Wrocław and with the city and district of Namysłów, with the magistrate, patricians and inhabitants of the same district and city, whom we have bound to ourselves and whom we do bind to us through those present, and with all of the inhabitants, serfs, peasants and dependents, both spiritual and secular, of the aforementioned places, lands and districts, with no one missing or excluded from our records, which we acknowledge publicly to be seen, read and heard.

We freely undertake to avoid, on account of the common good and the opportunity for universal benefit, the irreparable injuries and devastation of lands and people henceforward with the noble and famous commanders Otík of Losa of the Táborites and Jan Čapek of Sány of the communities of Orphans, and with all of their followers and those belonging to their armies, wherever they are settled, and with the succeeding commanders of the aforementioned communities and armies in the future.

We accept with the approval of those present one true, Christian cease-fire and a good, stable truce. We promise to observe firmly and properly a stable truce and cease-fire under the good, Christian faith, without any interruption or wicked fraud by those named in the present document, for a two year period until sundown on the last day, under the particulars of the articles and limits written hereafter. We promise, in the name of all the people mentioned above, to preserve without complaints and to implement completely and without any altercation or addition each and every matter written and decreed (or matters yet to be decreed) by the holy and celebrated Council of Basel. Should, however, it occur that their [i.e. Hussite] legates dispatched to the Council of Basel dispute the final decision and conclusion of the Council regarding specific articles, by which their intentions might then be changed (may almighty God forbid it!); then the members of both parties of the truce mentioned above, following the return of the legates from the Council of Basel, will convene together within four months in the same place to detract or to conclude whatever will appear advantageous for the divine reverence and honour of almighty God, for the common good, for the honour of the Crown of the Kingdom of Bohemia, and for the betterment and utility of all.

In like manner, the said and recited cease-fire exists; if perchance some of the lords, namely Girzik of Weißinburg, Janko Cruschin of Hostinné, Matthias and Johannes (called the Salawi brothers) of Scall, Janko Holý of Porostle and of Náchod, Mikuláš Trčka of Lípa living in Homole, and Otík of Ogitcz and of Prziecztam, do not wish to adhere to this kind of cease-fire and stable peace, as indeed their refusal has been given to captains Otík and Jan Čapek of the armies mentioned previously, then the captains of the armies should inform us in their own correspondence to be sent to Świdnica. The captains of the armies are neither to undertake favours nor render aid to any lords refusing to accept and preserve the cease-fire, publicly or privately, for any reason. Should these lords who promise to speak against and violate our cease-fire perform acts of damage and plunder in our lands, districts and subjects, then the captains ought not give them approval, support or assistance during the two year duration of our truce. The captains shall not allow such men to enter or to gather within their castles or under their protection. We promise not to support any activities of these lords, nor to follow their judgement during the duration of the truce.

Similarly, the captains promise not to build any new castles, cities or towns for themselves in the lands and duchies of Silesia, nor to rebuild damaged structures for the duration of the cease-fire. We also promise to proceed in the same manner, erecting and building nothing new anywhere during the truce.

Likewise, it exists notably said and recited that should someone, who does not have a cease-fire with the parties, should pass with an army into an area protected by the truce, then in such a case the reception of food and necessities for people and horses ought not harm the cease-fire. The passing and receiving of food and drink during the cease-fire ought not be injurious or burdensome, and appropriate and passable victuals are to be made available as are necessary for the making of the journey. In the same way, if it happens that someone either by word of mouth or written agreement has made a promise involving a financial obligation or made an oath of security, then it is fitting that such an obligation be fulfilled. Nevertheless those persisting in holding onto the possessions and properties of Niemcza, Otmuchów and Kluczbork ought not receive or seize any necessities of the body for people or horses during the aforementioned cease-fire. Should someone from any of these properties or any other person break the cease-fire in any way, and should they be arrested and detained for pillage, homicide or another crime, then their punishment should be set in motion according to the law. Also under the terms of the treaty, all captives are to be released immediately and all confiscated goods returned, or complete satisfaction should be made for them. There shall be no refusals on this point, or the infringing side shall be obligated to pay the penalty of three thousand, sixty groschen of the Prague measure in hard currency. A violation [of these terms] should not hinder the other side from observing the terms of the cease-fire. But in the case that our side should break, violate or go against the articles of the treaty – may almighty God prevent it! – then we judge against ourselves for such an injury, and give the noble and healthy lords Bolko Ketthelicz of Holynsteyn, Pelko, marshal of the aforementioned duke, Bernard, and Ffranczko of Huguicz from our side [as guarantors]. The other side gives the noble lords Smil [Holický] of Šternberk in Brandýs, Aleš Vřešťovský of Rýzmberk and the famous Jan Černín of Vysoká. Thus we firmly promise to satisfy, to observe, to concur with and to fulfil what was concordantly decreed and recited by the judges from either side within the space of one month. Should we fail to fulfil the terms of the treaty, then we acknowledge that we would be breakers of honour and of faith with those whom we made this treaty. We acknowledge that by such events we would pay a fine of three thousand, sixty groschen of the same kind previously mentioned; the said fine is to be paid within the space of four weeks in good cash to the other side at the place of its choosing. If by chance God does not permit us to implement a solution of this kind, then we give to the other side complete power over us so that by the authority of these documents they might seize and fine any person under our protection and invade any location until the entire aforementioned sum of money is deposited at the proper place. All losses suffered by our side during such a time will be put aside by us, as the other side will have authority to act as indicated.

Also, it is notably said and recited that during the aforementioned cease-fire and truce should we or any of our men or dependents assault and occupy any city, town or castle in the other side's lands, or attack or kill one of the men who have a treaty with us, or one of their dependents in the open field or elsewhere, then we promise to restore the city, town or castle with everything that was taken from it, and to make complete satisfaction for the injury or attack according to the judgement of the other side under faith and honour, along with payment of the fine described above. Upon the faith and testimony of each and every person aforementioned, and upon the seal of the city of Nysa in the absence of the aforementioned Lord Konrad, bishop of Wrocław, in whose name and in the name of all his lands, cities, and vassals, together with the seals of the aforementioned dukes of Silesia, that is Bernard, Konrad Kantner, Konrad the White, and Ludwig, and in the name of all of their duchies and lands, and the seal of Hermann Ceteris, the aforementioned *Vicecapitaneus*, together with the provincial seal of the inhabitants of the duchies of Świdnica and Jawor, and also by the seal of the city of Świdnica, in duty and in place of all of the inhabitants, cities and towns of the duchies of Świdnica and Jawor, and also the seal of the inhabitants of the duchy of Wrocław together with the seal of the city of Wrocław in place and in the name of the inhabitants of the same duchy and the cities of Wrocław, Środa Śląska and Namysłów, all of which are attached below. Dated in Wrocław on the day of John Baptist in the year of our Lord, 1432.

Zeitschrift des Vereins für Geschichte und Alterthum Schlesiens 11 (1871), pp. 225–31.

183   Heretics arrive at the Council of Basel

[In early January 1433, Hussite delegates to the Council of Basel arrived in that city to great fanfare. The main envoys were greeted with a ceremonial welcome from the city fathers. The Hussites had a contingency of priests who waked in procession through the streets singing hymns and the commander of the Hussites armies, Prokop Holý, said a prayer for peace. There are several accounts of the Hussite arrival but Aeneas Sylvius seems to have captured some of the excitement on the streets, however contrived, as Prokop and his heretical colleagues arrived for an historically unprecedented appearance before an ecumenical council of all Christendom. Unlike other events he writes of, Aeneas was present in Basel.]

The citizens of the city climbed the walls and many members of the Council gathered in front of the city gates to watch the arrival of the delegates of this truly courageous and equally famous country. Multitudes thronged the streets through which they [the Hussites] were to ride. Women, children and young girls crowded in the windows and on roofs. Some pointed to one delegate and others pointed to another. There was admiration for the foreign clothing and mannerisms exhibited which they were unaccustomed to and never seen before. They looked at the awful and dreadful faces of the men and especially their wild eyes. Many claimed that it was probably true that such men had done the deeds rumoured of them. However, most of the people looked especially at one man: Prokop. It was this fellow who had often defeated the armies of the faithful, who had destroyed so many towns and killed many thousands of people. This man was feared by his foes as well as his own countrymen for he was the undefeated, brave and fearless leader who had shown himself invincible in the face of every test and terror.

Historia Bohemica, chapter 49, p. 150.

184   Speech of Prokop Holý

[The Hussite appearance at the Council of Basel ended inconclusively. The council sent representatives to Prague to continue the negotiations. Prokop addressed the envoys on 18 June 1433 in the Karolinum in Prague. It is one of the few speeches made by Prokop which have survived and it was his last address on an international platform. In one sense, the speech can be understood as a summation of Hussite philosophy about the crusade. Jan Rokycana chaired the sessions, assisted by Peter Payne and Mikuláš Pelhřimov.]

Concerning these wars we call almighty God to witness that although we did not deserve it, your side took up the bloody cross against us and thus began wars and attacks upon us. By fire and sword this brutally laid waste to the Kingdom of Bohemia. However, to this day, with the help of God we have stood against that unjust attack. Despite the fact that these years of war were cruel many spiritual benefits have arisen out of them and may we hope that by the will of God they will produce even more. Quite a number of those cruel enemies of the saving truth of the Four Articles were forced to give assent to them verbally. Afterwards they accepted them voluntarily and became ardent defenders until death. Likewise a great number of people have faithfully held to these truths and so have been protected from hostility and brutality. Was this not so they might have been moved by fear and become unfaithful to the Holy Ghost. We are also aware of several letters sent from the Council of Basel which referred to the great conflicts caused by the ecclesiastical fathers meeting in the city of Basel, but have granted us a hearing which we regard as a significant gift bestowed by God in order that these saving truths should be known to all nations. Beyond this, these storms of war and vice have been used by God to turn many to the truth which is a great victory for the militant church. Notwithstanding this, it is our opinion that before these storms can come to an end, these holy truths must be accepted and followed faithfully by each member of the church. We say these things to your Honours and we wish to assure you that we condemn the numerous evils which happen in war. But though we have sorrow for them we shall not cease to blame the ones who have caused them. We only tolerate the burdens of war so that we can establish these truths in their rightful place within the church and thereby lay hold upon the blessed peace and condition which, with the help of God, would cause the unity of the Church to flourish as well as the other matters which you desire such as better morality and brotherly love throughout the world.

MC 1: 419–20.

185   Gilles Charlier's undelivered reply to Prokop

[Prokop's speech of course generated several responses. Among them was the following document: 'Response to the proposal of Prokop Shaven, written by me, Aegidius Carlerius, deacon *Cameracensem*; however, it was not read before the congregation of the realm because of certain unexpected impediments.' Gilles Charlier was a former professor of theology at Paris, nephew of Jean Gerson, and at the time dean of Arras. He had confronted the Hussites at Bratislava in April 1429 and had written against them previously. He had been one of the official respondents at Basel and was among the ten delegates sent to Prague by the council.[3] His reply should be dated to late June 1433.]

Oh venerable men! Táborite men! Weighing our responses for your side, wishing to justify your wars as most beneficial, to you we say first, that we wish to judge rightly regarding the goodness or usefulness of this matter, not only as it affects one but all situations. As when something appears good or beneficial from one side and not from the other, then it is certainly not good. For the great Dionysius the Areopagite says: good comes from pure motive, evil from all sorts. Therefore the Master of Truth instructs us when he says, do not judge by appearances, rather judge rightly; for some matters appear to be good, which really are not. Therefore if good results sometimes come out of wars, these results are not good when many more evil results follow. Recognize the results, beloved men, not only as

---

3   On Charlier at Basel see Fudge, 'Crime, punishment and pacifism in the thought of Bishop Mikuláš of Pelhřimov, 1420–1452', in BRRP 3, pp. 88–91.

beneficial to those well-known to you, and you will see more evil than benefit. For regarding things that are advantageous to your side, more will be said below; but evils which result from these wars happen only to individuals, unless they are made manifest to everyone. You decide to destroy churches, to smash holy images, and to bring disorder, proscription and slaughter to the servants of God, i.e., the priests. You return virgins and religious women to the world, which we have no doubt is a great sacrilege. Additionally, you handle the body of our Lord, Jesus Christ, in the sacrament irreverently, which generates confusion in the ears of the faithful and causes offence to the pious. These and many other evils, which we omit as unworthy [of mention], follow wars. As well the perdition of souls and the filling of hell follow, and other things more than can be remembered by us, which are said to cause wars to be judged as simply beneficial, but are understood [by us] to be instead ruinous; and so we do not believe that these wars should be taken up lightly, if peace can be held otherwise. Since the end of war is peace, when it can be had by some reasonable manner, war should not be carried out; for when sanity can be held without bitter loss of power, then it [war] should not be assumed. Therefore how will you be able to justify the practice of the rest of your wars, when peace could be in your hands if you wished? No, friends! Do not be accustomed to such wars; instead leave it alone and arrange a peaceful compact!

However we do not simply damn wars, as long as the causes are just, according to a just order and a just mind. Are these present in your strife? Since a just order requires the authority of a prince, how without the authority of a superior prince are you allowed to wage war?[4] Again, how will the mind be just, when with a single word you can have peace, but you fail to accept it? Accordingly how will your cause be just when we offer peace to you, when we endeavour to lead you to the bosom of Mother Church, [and you refuse to accept our offers]? Perhaps you will say that you wish to undergo the dangers of wars for the sake of holding onto truths, and that you take the place of a prince. If you desire truths to be held by people, how can you use war as a suitable means for accomplishing this? Would not a gentle way be more useful? The apostle James says if you have a bitter zeal, and contention is in your hearts, do not be proud; such pride is not wisdom descending from above, but rather earthly, animal, and diabolical. For where there is zeal and contention, there is inconstancy and every perverse labour. Wisdom is from above and it is first virtuous, then peaceful, modest, pleasing, conscious of good, and following the fruit of justice begotten in

---

[4]   During the period between the death of King Václav and the formal accession of Sigismund to the throne the Hussites could appeal to the university masters (doc.12), the decisions and decrees of the national diet of Čáslav (doc.63) and to the regency of Zygmunt Korybut. Moreover the radical Táborites had already ruled that human laws were null and void and superceded by the law of God. *Historia Hussitica*, in FRB 5, p. 398.

peace for those making peace [James 3:14-18]. And so the truth of faith, because it is from above, is found in peace and modesty, not in contention and hostility, which are certainly a part of war. Because if by war someone is led to confess the truth, it must be presumed that he will not continue thus should the war cease; for violent dominions, where all safety is found in the sword, do not last long and will not cause someone to cling to [a belief] voluntarily. Then if you wish to follow the example of Christ, how can you be tempted to take up arms? For he sowed the beginning of his faith in peace; he did not select rich and powerful disciples, but poor, feeble and weak ones. If you judge truth to be in your eyes, it is not necessary to take refuge in arms, because he is stronger than regal power and all other forces, over which he triumphs. Those who take refuge in the sword admit that they are empty of truth, since it is conceded that the way of truth must be searched out. Therefore, lest you be deemed too far from the truth, relinquish your arms; convert to the inquisition of truth in the matters of your articles, which occurred long ago in the council! For it will be pleasing to you, in the presence of the Holy Council, as you wished very much, to inquire about these matters by way of disputation; and where few are considered to be doctors in the judgement of such a matter, we will send the dispute in writing to every famous university, as was ordained and is fitting. After all the declarations of the studies have been examined and nothing save the truth is known, following this the Holy Synod, will pronounce a decision over these matters, according to the instruction of the Holy Spirit, as to how these articles will be held by all Christians. This is the royal way, which will not lean to the right or the left. Walk on it! If by chance you do not wish to follow it, because you say that you are instructed best by these articles and because the Lord God revealed them to you, nevertheless you ought not despise this way. For if your revelation is from God, it will stand, nor will the Holy Spirit presiding over the general council ever dissolve it.[5] If He revealed these matters to a few in the Church [the Hussites], then you estimate that the whole Church and the council representing it will be forsaken, when all were certainly prepared to fulfil the will of God in their hearts.

Regarding the duties of the prince, the matters being considered should not be carried out by fighting even by a prince, as he is not permitted to make war unless he cannot pursue peace without violence. On that account, we do not see how you should be permitted to pursue war and the spilling of Christian blood, so that you might bring forth truths, as you see them, to the civilized world. Now let us say

---

5   Charlier perhaps has in mind the Hussite appeal to *revelatio* for aspects of their programme. The best example is Jakoubek of Stříbro's explanation for the reintroducing of the practice of utraquism. Jakoubek, 'Contra Andream Brodam pro communione plebis sub utraque specie', in Hermann von der Hardt, ed., *Magnum oecumenicum constantiense concilium*, 6 volumes (Frankfurt and Leipzig, 1697–1700), vol. 3, col. 566.

further that wars in themselves cause many injuries. For the hostile attacks of enemies leave behind lamentation, bring forth desolation, increase hatred and inflame wrath. The most Christian army is convulsed by these evils, which provoke the audacity of demons, causing innumerable other misfortunes.[6] If we had a hundred tongues and a hundred peoples as one iron voice, let us not see the shape of every wickedness in wars and the passing of every kind of punishment. Regarding which, when too many evils follow the upheavals of war, arms must be taken up, as doing so can occur too slowly. If through arms sometimes good results happen, but nevertheless too many evil things follow, how can the voluntary [use of arms] help?

Regarding the points mentioned before [in your proposal], where you show that through your wars certain men were forced to confess your truths, and afterwards [these men] spontaneously defended and protected those [same] truths against hostile attack, thereby increasing the number of those faithful to your truths, we respond thus: if you think to pass on your truths by force of arms, then likewise it stands even more to come forth well from an inquisition of the truth. For truly no one is constrained to believing something [in any way] as harshly as by evangelical truth, and no one can protect something better than by the protection of the truth; arms are also invalid against the most powerful of all truth. You profess this on your pictures, on which is written 'truth conquers,' and this we confess with great trust.[7] Because if truth conquers, why is it necessary to take up arms? Truth conquers, and it will conquer certainly; why therefore is it not placed before the inquisition? We inquire about your truth diligently, for we did it partially before now. Let us all honour truth openly, let us embrace and defend it. Indeed truth compels everyone to believe better than fierce wars. Truth will protect everyone better than iron weapons and walled cities. If you judge the holy, general Council of Basel, called together on account of the disturbance of your wars, and the audience presented there for you, we say to you that this should be reserved for divine judgement; we say likewise to you regarding what was decreed at the Holy Council of Constance, and at the celebrated Councils of Pavia and of Siena. And the place and form of a future council must be selected by decree, so that the Church may be steered by the divine office, and her sons might grow from virtue into virtue after long-standing failures are rejected.

---

[6]   It has been pointed out that the Hussite theory of just war went well beyond the provisions laid down in classic form by Augustine and Aquinas and even the exceptions enumerated by Wyclif. Ferdinand Seibt, *Hussitica: Zur Struktur einer Revolution* (Cologne and Graz: Böhlau Verlag, 1965), pp. 53–7.

[7]   On Hussite iconography see Horst Bredekamp, *Kunst als Medium sozialer Konflikte: Bilderkämpfe von der Spätantike bis zur Hussitenrevolution* (Frankfurt: Suhrkamp Verlag, 1975) and Fudge, pp. 226–51.

We believe indeed without a doubt, that the holy fathers of the Council of Basel called you to the council out of sincere love, desiring that you would want to be with them in one body of Christ, which is the Church, so that we might walk in unity in the house of the Lord. At the beginning of your proposal you say that our side chose conflict at the beginning; so we say. The Lord, to whose eyes everything is naked and open, knows that before our side moved against yours in war your side pillaged many of our monasteries following the death of King Václav.[8] Your people are for your articles, which they began to defend by arms. Therefore, when we saw your side assault the servants of the most high God and God's houses, this was counted against you. Thereupon you ought not give blame to our side as being the first to provoke [war]. Moreover, because you pray for deliverance from the evils of war with oppressed hearts, we freely hear you and we ask that you remember and recognize these matters of years ago. To this end we are led by the flesh of our merciful Lord, Jesus Christ, in which he visited us appearing from heaven, so that putting down contentions we will think as one and speak of peace. And may the peace of God, which overcomes every spirit, guard our hearts and our understanding, so that we are able to be moved from strife to peace, which is in heaven. Amen.

MC 1: 420–2.

186   Plans for a sixth crusade

[With the lack of definite agreement emerging from the Council of Basel, there were suggestions being discussed about the feasibility of a sixth crusade. The following document, dated 31 May 1433, reveals the lingering possibility entertained by some that the Hussite heretics might still be subdued militarily should the cross be preached a sixth time. I follow the transcription in Neumann, 'Francouzská husitika', pp. 138–41.]

In order to undertake an armed expedition against the Hussites it is essential to have the things which follow.

---

[8]   The accusation has merit. Numerous religious houses were sacked: Kartouzy, Břevnov, Strahov, Plasy, St Thomas Lesser Town, St Klement Old Town, Mother of God at the end of the bridge, St Benedict, St Mary Magdalene, St Ambrose, St Katherine, St Francis, Mother of God at Botiči and many others in Prague and elsewhere. Churches of non-utraquist leanings were attacked, organs and statues destroyed, iconoclasm was widespread and monks, priests and other religious were captured and abused. Accordingly, one Hussite source actually names 45 destroyed religious houses. *Historia Hussitica*, in FRB 5, p. 409.

First, that the prince who is in charge of the said army would be prepared to undertake [a campaign], if he had a letter from the king of the Romans calling to the attention of the electors (and) princes, prelates and good towns of the said empire containing, as the said king has established and required, the said prince as the most powerful of the Holy Empire to be willing to take and support the command of the said army as his own lieutenant. Along with this be contained in the same letters, that the said king commands the above cited that on obligation and oath that they have to him and for the benefit of Christianity they be very obedient to the said prince, and with those the money that has been raised and which they will raise be distributed all in all through the regulation of the prince.

Further, that the said king writes again to our holy father the pope [Eugenius IV], to the effect that because of the great affairs that he had in relation to the Turks who desired to destroy his Kingdom of Hungary, he cannot personally take up arms against the said Hussites, which is the reason he has chosen as his lieutenant the prince as the greatest of the said empire in order to be head of the said army. Thus he appeals to the pope that in the same way he should advise the aforementioned princes and everyone else, that they be truly obedient to the said prince, curse and excommunicate all those who are disobedient to the said prince and that they obey all the designated representatives. With this, that the said pope gives the tithe over to the empire and other neighbouring lands for the purpose of raising money for the army which will be employed by order of the said prince.

Also, being lieutenant of the said king, when I [sic] depart for Rome on this, would be for the purpose being crowned and to speak to the pope about these matters and however much this is that the said prince is willing to undertake this charge in passing, that the said king will do all the mountains, he will approach the country of Burgundy at two near frontiers and there the said prince could speak to him and could send some of his council to Rome with the said king if he does not wish to go there.[9]

Likewise, in order to know the strength of the said Hussites through the report of the knights of the country at present fugitive and from the homeland of the said king is certain that they could not find themselves in all strength more than 400 men at arms but of a community of 30 to 40,000 combatants, and so say these knights, that if a powerful prince comes to the country, that there are several fortresses and good towns which would be obedient to him and would help him against the said Hussites. However, without seeing the said power they would not dare move, for last year even though the Germans had assembled a great force

---

[9]   The French is quite precise in its shift to the first person, but it is erroneous nonetheless inasmuch as the one being crowned and speaking to the pope is neither Philip the Good nor his representative, but Sigismund who, after more than two decades, was finally attending a coronation ceremony as Holy Roman emperor.

they retreated in flight without daring to engage in battle. On this account, those who had been obedient to them were killed.

Similarly, that the said country is plentiful and one could lead wagons there to obtain all provisions and also that it is fertile in all good things except wine. In like manner, by common estimation of the population the said prince could have from the people of the lands of Germany 5000 to 6000 knights and squires. Further, it is hardly possible that any prince could undertake this matter without having the knowledge and consent of the said king for several reasons which the said prince could give.

Also, that from now on, large amounts of money shall be raised which will be deposited at the cathedral churches of the cities until it is announced who will be the leader for the said army at the coming season and to this prince each province will advise him in writing the sum of money which it is guarding. Likewise, if anyone could further advise the said prince of more things to which he would take charge, but who would wish to undertake it being that this is in God's time, for a great deed cannot be conducted if it is not put under an outstretched hand.

Similarly, it is not possible except by a prince of the German tongue that this thing can be conducted, the reason being that the king of the empire marches so to several great wars, by which he is rather detained, and does not have men among his subjects who know how to conduct such a business.

Further, that Duke Louis, Count Palatine of the Rhine, Lord of Heidelberg is chief of the electors, is very sick in body, that of him no more must make memory. Also, that the Duke of St Seigne, Margrave of Meißen [Friedrich of Wettin] who was the most powerful of the Germans and elector of the empire has recently passed away from life, and has left a son who is about sixteen years of age, who is too young to lead such a business. In like manner, that the Margrave of Brandenburg [Friedrich], who is the third elector, he is very ill in his person and also has not the strength in himself to lead this business.

Further, it will not be an expedient thing, that the Archbishops of Mainz, Cologne and Trier, who are the other electors, that one of them should be capable of being leader of the said army. Also, that the Duke Albrecht of Austria could not lead this matter, for neither the Dukes of Bavaria, nor the electors would obey him, as they say they are of a greater lineage than the said Duke of Austria, and also he has not the strength for this.

Likewise, for all conclusions, it is not at all a possible thing to believe that this matter could be led, will not take place in fact without a leader, of whom the king of the Romans is the one and the prince whose way of life is directed to the former, and to this opinion the largest party of the princes of Germany adhere and assert that one of the two must be the leader and personally always be present.

Paris, Bibliothèque Nationale MS. franç. 1278, fols. 145ᵛ–146ʳ.

187   An Orphan expedition in Great Poland and Prussia

[While negotiations and further crusade plans were contemplated, the Hussites left Bohemia in late April and entered Poland. After conquering numerous towns they advanced to Prussia where they laid siege to Chojnice [Konitz], the great fortress of the Knights of the Teutonic Order. Following an unsuccessful siege of several weeks duration, they marched east, then north to Gdańsk. On 29 August they overthrew the well-fortified Tczew which guarded the approach to Gdańsk. The city was shelled for four days [1–4 September] before the Hussites moved off to the Baltic Sea where, on 4 September, celebrations were held (see map 6). A peace treaty was reached with an eighteen year duration.]

In the year of the Lord 1433, when the term of the armistice [24 June] was fulfilled and on account of the fact that the aforementioned parties, namely the kingdom and the [Teutonic] Order, could not come to an agreement between each other, either through intermediaries, or legates and envoys of the Council of Basel and the pope, they appeared in Toruń at the feast of St George [23 April]. This was particularly because of Duke Swidrigal whom the Poles neither wished to receive into the Grand Duchy in any way nor to have him as grand duke. But the Order wanted to have him as grand duke and therefore assisted and supported him in terms of the confederations and leagues made between them and thus the conflict arose again between the two. Then, in support of the lord master and the Order, mercenaries from parts of Germany, Meißen, Lusatia and Silesia and other places came to help. However, their arrival was totally useless and in vain. First of all, they came only for the money, not for battle, and they executed no deed of force or knighthood for the salaries they were paid. They did take by force a castle in the district of Pomorze by name which had been occupied by villains and thieves, namely by Mandufel, for some time and they ejected them with force from that place.[10]

For assistance, the Poles brought for themselves the most outrageous rabble of Hussites, collected from the most damned mob of all lands. These Hussites and heretics were estimated to number about 5000 and came on foot with wagons and other military equipment. They entered the New March in the footsteps of the mercenaries named previously and they devastated the land reducing thirteen towns and villages to ashes. Those of Arenswald and barons of Wedelen made peace with the aforementioned heretics in the name of the king of Poland and defected from the Order in order to avoid destruction along with their forts and towns.

---

[10] Pomorze was a town between the Persante and Riga, north of New Stettin.

These enemies of the cross of Christ and the heretics, together with the Poles, entered the land of Prussia and laid siege to Chojnice [Konitz] with a hostile force and assaulted it cruelly for more than four weeks [July–August] undertaking many attacks against it. But their hostile weapons did little damage since [Chojnice] was defended by divine favour and their wild missiles rained down in vain since wise advice and strong resolve remained within. Thus, being preserved by the right hand of God the perfidious people laboured in vain moving off in confusion. The marshal of the Order, Lord Jodocus Strupberger, together with other captains and the lords Heinrich of Plavno, Otto of Donín, Friedrich of Bieberstein, barons and other feudal knights and mercenary vassals, along with domestic feudal knights and citizens, took up encampments near the village of Schwarzenwalde against the terrible persecutors of the Christian religion. Had they remained there with the army they might have preserved the land intact without any battle. But alas! Heeding unsound advice or confused by a spirit of uncertainty they dispersed like the movement of the grass and retreated from there, yielding up the area to the enemy to invade and destroy the land down to the roots.

When the hostile people [Hussites] saw the disorderly retreat they followed quickly burning the land of Pomorze in a tyrannical manner, reducing the very illustrious town of Dirsaw [29 August] and bringing the castle of Gesnitz to ashes. These perfidious people did not stop from this business until they reached the shores of the [Baltic] sea near Gdańsk. Here the great villain [Jan] Čapek, the leader of the Hussite army, entered the waters of the sea, as it is reported, and in a great show of wagging his proud head said: 'Behold! I say brethren, I proclaim to you that having reached the end of the earth at this point I cannot proceed any farther because of the hindering waters of the sea.' At the same place he filled some flasks with sea water which he said he would take to Bohemia in order that a great celebration of these crimes with even more pomp, with his companions, [might be carried out]. In accordance with the Scriptures, they delight in doing evil and they exult in the worst things [Proverbs 2:14].

SRP 3: 499–503.

188   Sorrowful lament on the evil Hussites

[This pessimistic monologue of the Hussite invasion to the Baltic Sea describes the heretics as the scum of the earth, who wreak destruction, kill the innocent and plunge the world into the darkness of everlasting night. Parallels within Hussite documents can easily be found describing the crusaders in a similar fashion.]

O, shining land of Prussia. Even though you are located almost in the extreme corner of the world you are not able to remain [apart from the] offence of the criminal sons of Belial or to avoid being lacerated by the grievous terror, after a good many lands and regions have been devastated most bitterly by them. O God, how much ignominy, how much scandal, how much pernicious misery which that villainous bunch of people have brought against your majesty: trampling so many regions, so many cities, so many castles and towns with churches and cloisters of the Christian religion, cruelly killing so many Christian people, both prominent citizens and common people without number by fire, sword, imprisonment and through other indiscriminate ways. Their fury has not been averted from these. They have not been satisfied with the depopulation of lands and the robbery of things, evilly they laid their sacrilegious and bloody hands on them and, what the ears of Christian men dread to hear, not sparing the priests or the monks or the nuns or the hermits. O wicked people, cruel people more tigerish than a tiger, more lionist than a lion, more atrocious than a witch, who is neither afraid of the Lord nor respectful of humankind, who is not ashamed to lay sacrilegious hands on the Lord's anointed.[11] Neither priestly dignity nor sacerdotal holiness or [even] fear of a harsh judgement diverts [them] from such nefarious audacities.

O lamentation! O impiety! O pernicious outrage! The Christian religion must undergo such ruin from these malignant people gathered together from the most squalid mob of all the nations and there is no one in the world who can impede and resist them. Love freezes, iniquity glows, peace has perished, justice is lost, all unity is dissolved. Here, like the eclipse of the sun, the quiet state of the world grows dark. [Thus] darkened one becomes afflicted; afflicted, one becomes subverted; subverted, one becomes irreversibly destroyed.

SRP 3: 503.

189 Commentary on the Hussite march to the Baltic Sea

[A town scribe, Conrad Bitschin, wrote at length about the Orphan expedition in his *Epistola Ecclesiae deplanctoria*. The document fairly bristles as a diatribe against those who either supported the Hussites or those who failed to resist them. The Teutonic Order is lauded for their resistance to the Hussite initiative. The

---

[11] The reference to *lamia* [witchcraft] is interesting inasmuch as a dozen years earlier Martin Talayero, Sigismund's envoy, wrote to the Polish king Władysław Jagiełło accusing the Hussites of using magic. The letter is dated 22 April 1421 and has been published in Jaroslav Kadlec, 'Magister Martin Talayero aus Tortosa im Kampf gegen die Hussiten' *Annuarium historiae conciliorum* 12 (Nos.1–2, 1980), pp. 297–308.

Hussites armies returned to Bohemia shortly after reaching the Baltic. It was to be their last expedition.]

A letter of lamentation from the church to all Christian lands and nations damnably assaulted by the ungodly Hussites and heretics. Following some common accusations the church speaks first to the lands most concerned with the Hussite wars, Bohemia itself, Moravia, Silesia and then Poland.

[A speech to Poland]

. . . Overcome completely by lament and deceit and by the enormity of injury and the infusion of great sorrow into distress, you, obdurate and ungodly Poland, wooded and barren country, being a miserable and hopeless nation, damned by pillage and other vices of depravity. How unstable and uncertain is the faith of the Poles which is often apparent and is experienced daily. Likewise it does not seem to be enough for them that for the completion of the evils of their inhumanity they have united quite wrongly the Lithuanians and the Tartars along with other barbarian and faithless nations who often assault the faithful people of Christ within the serene land of Prussia. Specifically [they] suppress and with hostility betray the venerable and eminent order of the German brothers of St Mary and other Christians and those dependent upon them who have shown themselves to be the brave knights of Christ and the fervent defenders of the Catholic faith up to the present time.[12] At the present time this ungodly nation prefers the war against Catholics to peace and has publicly allied with the perversity of the most outrageous gang of heretics and Hussites collected from the most damnable wombs of all nations in order to suppress the aforementioned confessors of the orthodox faith in the land of Prussia and in the neighbouring localities. O,

---

[12] This is a reference to the fact that the Poles had generally been sympathetic historically to the Hussite cause. It is also a commentary on the fact that the Hussite armies received equipment and a cavalry escort led by Piotr Sziafraniec. Other reinforcements from Poland and the Pomeranian duke Bohuslav were also added to the Czech force. These allied forces laid siege to the castle of the military and crusading order officially known as the Brothers of St Mary's Hospital of the Germans in Jerusalem, but in common parlance as the Knights of the Teutonic Order. The number and role of the Tartars was exaggerated by the Germans to give the impression that they were facing a foreign and pagan invasion. Already, the order had been seriously weakened by their defeat in the battle of Grünwald (Tannenburg) in 1410 when the troops of King Władysław Jagiełło consisting of Polish and Lithuanian knights, Czech mercenaries led by Jan Sokol of Lamberk, along with Tartars loyal to Witold, the governor of Lithuania, pushed the Knights back and marched on their capital, Malbork (Marienburg) situated on the Vistuła River and conquering several other strongholds belonging to the Knights. Of note for the subject of the crusades against the Hussites, is the fact that a Czech soldier named Jan Žižka was involved in these affairs in 1410.

wretched Poland! O, silly nation, insane country, how can you choose such an ungodly association without remembrance of your salvation? How can you adhere so imprudently to give advice, assistance and favour to such godless heretics [who have been] excluded from the bosom of mother church and condemned by the general verdict of the cross? How is it that obedience to the holy Roman Church, the reverence of the apostolic see and a holy zeal for the honour of the empire does not prohibit you from joining with such iniquity? How is it that the fear of God and the terror of horrible judgement does not turn you away from this? But I swear by God, that the lethal virus which you have carried secretly in your heart and which you can no longer conceal has been revealed and ejected now through public vomit. That is to say, you have been adhering to the aforementioned persecutors of Christ and the church secretly during the course of many years, supporting them, favouring them, feeding them and providing weapons and other necessities. Now, having thrown aside the garment of honour and taken up the gown of turpitude you go publicly against God and the church and the favour of the empire, together with the sons of Satan and you provide assistance through the lands and kingdoms against Catholics. It is no wonder since according to the testimony of wise men the similarity of attitudes causes the association of wills.

I am asking how it is possible that once you were an honoured mother whose virtue flourished once upon a time under your royal crown, that now you have fallen away to such an extreme that you prostitute yourself as an impure and criminal woman? What does the royal crown on your head mean to you which you have polluted so disgracefully through your perverse acts? I ask, does your conscience not convict you? It convicts you of the sin which has violated the venerable Catholic faith. Perpetual disgrace convicts you inasmuch as you have fallen down and in going astray as you have. What would be more telling about the wickedness of that nation than when the witness of its iniquity is well-known to the world and how to judge those nefarious deeds which are difficult to narrate and likewise horrible to hear and incredible to bear? Let no one regard the aforementioned depravity of the Poles to be recently fabricated or fictitious when in truth these distasteful conditions of them are reported in the oldest histories of the Slavs. It is thus told in the chronicle of the Slavs similarly that the form of weapons and the means of making war among the Czechs and Poles, namely that whenever they are summoned to an external war they are powerful in assembling but are most cruel in robbing and in murder. They spare neither monasteries nor churches nor cemeteries. Then it likewise happens that they misuse frequently the greed of the predators upon best friends just as the enemy. Such things and many others over a long time have been described long ago and can be found by any reader. [Then follows a speech to Hungary, Austria and Bavaria.]

May you weep and lament, poor Meißen, lacking in merit! Although you were plentiful in people and many things, fruit, cattle, and metals, as well as the finest cities and castles, you are lamentably ruined and afflicted by the iron, fires and rumours of the aforementioned disturbers of the peace and there is no one able to resist since you have but a boy for a prince with flippant advisors as supposed.[13] Therefore it is according to that which has been written: woe to the land whose king is a lad, woe, because you cannot survive. O, how inopportune was the death of the magnificent prince, Friedrich, duke of Saxony, who was recently called from this evil world to a higher place, who struggled powerfully against these heretics.[14] In the year of the Lord 1421, on the day of blessed Mary of the Snows, under the castle of Most, also known [in German] as Brüx, having been given the victory of the battle he inflicted the greatest possible defeat on those who disturbed the surrounding German lands which up to that time had been unmolested.[15] There is no prince in the world who would like [more] to break their inhuman iniquity! But I suppose that doubtless the Lord of heaven, not able to sustain their damnable contumacy by the will of God, determined those wayward people to you, bright knights of Christ and his glorious mother in Prussia, instituted by him for the extermination of the faithless, in order to establish the glory of his triumph, denied all the German princes until now, German friars of the holy house of Jerusalem, the extent of honour which everyone hoped confidently in you to redeem Israel. Woe, vain life of humankind! How useless is the wisdom of wise men. Certainly those whose protection and defence the land enjoyed have thrown away the sword of protection and exposed the people of the land to the pernicious dogs to be destroyed in keeping with that written by the prophet Ezekiel [7:18–19]: I lay my hand upon them and I make their land wasted. They shall be overwhelmed with fear, baldness on all their heads. Their silver shall be thrown into the squares and their gold will not suffice to set them free on the day of the Lord's wrath. Then he adds: the law will disappear from the priests and the council of the elders.[Then he says] why do you fool around like that, you wise men? Why do you sleep so soundly, glorious knights, before the force of such despicable rebels? O noble and fruitful country, why are you wounded so terribly by the serpentine teeth of such awful beasts? Why are you changed so miserably into the dust by such dirty villains without any resistence? Do you lack people or weapons? You teem with plenty of powerful warriors and horses and other military things. Why do you tolerate such calamities? On account of the

---

[13] Friedrich II of Saxony, son of the margrave of Meißen, often referred to in the sources as the 'young one of Meißen'.

[14] The reference is to Friedrich of Wettin, Margrave of Meißen.

[15] The reference is to the ill-fated Hussite campaign in Most under the command of Jan Želivský. The priest was ill-prepared and ill-qualified to lead the armies and the outcome was victory for the Germans. See doc.65. For further details see the *Chronicon veteris Collegiati*, in Höfler, vol. 1, p. 84 and *Historia Hussitica*, pp. 507–8.

indolence of your people or the idleness of your dukes? In truth, you have active people prepared to follow [the dukes] through the mountains and valleys, through the rocks and forests, through the thickets and stones, if they had clever and ingenious dukes. It is clear, with respect to the peace, that such an error is caused by the fixation of your dukes, because victory is not granted in body and in show but in battle together with the grace and bravery of the Lord of virtues. Valerius attests that to neglect the prosperous occasion of action is the greatest stupidity and the one compelled to fight in distress but who abstains from the battle is delivered up to ruin on account of such lethal cowardice. Why do you throw away so indiscreetly and imprudently the souls of yourselves and others, thus exposing yourselves to such dangers? How can you suffer such evil in your lands and nations? Who can watch with a stony heart and without many tears the painful destruction of the land, the sieges and ugly conquests of towns, the incineration of villages, damnable subversion of churches and monasteries, the unbelievable and execrable consumption of the harvests and fruits and other necessities? What can move you, the miserable need of the afflicted, the lamentation of the captives, the cry of the impoverished poor or the unheard of misery of the refugees? Will their wailing reach to you while the clouds vibrate and their cries fill the air? O, prudent and brave men, how can your ears remain deaf to such complaints of the suppressed and the poor? Why are you drunk with the spirit of dizziness? Who had caused you to go astray from the way just as the sons of Israel did penance for three days near the mountain of Seir after forty years of journey, not having entered the promised land? Surely, if it may be said, you have been properly repudiated by wisdom which you stubbornly refused. The righteous Lord in all his ways answers with worthy retribution everyone according to their merits. In like manner, as it has been said, you could have planted honourably a delicate garden with the treasure of wise men in former glory. But now, miserable country, by establishing the outstanding university with discretion and judiciousness, pursuing the will of reason, you are now said to have studied obstinately to impede. Because the country would have been fortified salutarily and liberated without any doubt by the advice and wisdom of wise men. As the outstanding man Peter Blezensis attests in some letter, the compendium of all prudence is comprehended in these writings. [To wit] whether the commonwealth is to be governed, whether battles are to be undertaken, whether castles are to be allocated, whether machines are to be erected, whether fences may be renovated, whether fortifications are to be made, and finally whether the peace of liberty, whether the veneration of justice, whether the reverence of law, whether friendship with neighbouring nations is to be retained, the books instruct profitably on all these matters.

The science is namely the spiritual sword in the hand of the powerful, this is the bag into which David put the three most transparent stones by which he knocked down Goliath. This is the zither through which the madness of Saul was reduced. Besides this, the writing is the furrowing plough of Sangar, by which the ground of our heart is cultivated, through which five hundred Philistines were petrified and others turned to flight. What is more? Even if it were carefully examined it cannot be seen. How would the princes persevere in authority or judge the people with equity without the supply of counsel and written erudition? Just as wisdom attests, the wise judge will judge his people and the princely domains will be stable once more. The king who will judge his people with verity and the poor with wisdom shall have his throne secured forever. According to the word of wisdom, the reign is transferred from one nation to another because of injustice, maltreatment and deception. Therefore the Lord speaks through the prophet: You who judge the land, be instructed and change to this and attach yourselves from injustice to the way of justice. If those also listened to the hard word of blessed Job who said, if the kings listen to the voice of the Lord they will fulfil their days, their goods and their years in glory. But if they do not listen they will perish by the sword and will be consumed by foolishness.

Wherefore, O glorious knights of Christ, meditate upon this and other things which pertain to God with a sincere heart, turning to God and putting your firm hope in him, the one we confess as creator of the world and for whom it is not difficult to rescue the little ones and who makes the faithful few more powerful than multitudes. Also, may you attend to the Catholic knights and soldiers who have come at this time from the most distant parts of the earth, that you receive a great recompense. May you attend, I pray, to your calling because you have been called up on account of the battle, not only for the reward, for the reward is given to you on account of the battle. Do not be idle partakers of bread and unworthy employees. I mean those who have offered no resistance against these public enemies of Christ within your own confines. They will likewise do nothing in foreign areas. Likewise, how could it be that the one who remembered not his own salvation remember the foreign one? If some zealots within the knights of Christ were not discouraged by your improper persuasion then they are admonished. In this sense, the public rumour in circulation now is that in cooperation with your despondence, after everything had already been destroyed by fire, the lords of Prussia wish to affirm an armistice with the aforementioned enemies of Christ, thinking those perfidious and unfaithful ones might serve the solid faith. We are failing, men of experience, we are failing because it has never been heard of, that unfaithfulness might provide a proper faith to anyone. Stand up, stand up, so that we might experience your bravery and see how you put your hands against the enemy. May you arise with confidence, not sparing work or expense and do not be afraid to expose your bodies for Christ who delivered himself voluntarily to death for us. Do not be fearful of the beatings and wounding, but be aware that more glory than blood flows from these wounds. Do not be frightened also to undergo glorious death for Christ for no one can circumvent the debt of death. In other words, we are all born for death and we yield up our sons to death for in truth the elected have been promised life in death as well as the glory which comes after death. May you carefully consider, you powerful knights and important men of Prussia how you were condemned by the numerous claws of the aforementioned Poles uniting themselves with the heretics, now with the Lithuanians and Tartars as well as other unfaithful people and barbarians not just in these matters but also in terms of wives and children. Likewise, you have seen with your own weeping eyes your dear wives and daughters violated at will, as well as your daughters and nieces and old men and old women dragged away and killed. You have seen captives taken off and no cruelty was spared on account of gender or age, there was no respect given to age or misery or condition. What hardened eyes can see such disgrace and evil and be dry and those who consider it have no desire to live after such distress!

Therefore, may you be moved by such iniquity and injury. May you be moved by such terrible affront! Why are you unmoving? Why do you yet remain? Stand up then! Stand up and raise up vengeance of such enormous violence against the aforementioned sons of Satan without sparing effort or expense. May you overpower them by force, with deceit, offence, iron, fire, fame and terrible bonds and set the country free from the hands of the worst enemy. Surely you, glorious and eminent Chojnice, will exult meritoriously in joy among so many great anxieties and tribulations. Beleaguered by the aforementioned sons of Belial and surrounded for two months, you resisted firmly in the Lord and were not paralysed by terror or threat. Therefore, it has been given to you the occasion of perpetual joy and praise. First, because the hostile weapons did not frighten you. The launching of severe swords and lances did not move you, neither did the rumble of the approaching cavalry nor the offence of the assaulting armies put fear within you to [cause you] to lower yourself to capitulate or [enter into some] disgraceful arrangement. Wherefore, for the immortal title of your praise and the enduring memory of this, the following song with verses has been edited.

Chojnice, noble place of sweet fragrance
Constant in bravery resisted the Czech nation
O, blessed lady, the help of weak penitent ones
Gave consolation to the sorrowful ones, protected those besieged
When the town was attacked by the troops of Czechs
She relentlessly resisted the perverse heretics
Holding fast to the true faith
The furious attacks did not wound you
The rumble of wagons and hostile lances did not frighten you
Walls were not broken down by their dangerous cannon

An impregnable barrier protected you
A praiseworthy agreement put out the flames
Various cries of wandering Czechs
Grim terrors of the Poles are confused
You firmly resisted with the Lord's virtue
In order to increase the praise of your name among them
May you stand up, mother of grace, halting the advance of the Czechs
[Stopping] the defiance and deceit of the Poles
May you stand by us, queen of glory, in such ruin
Give the palm of triumph from the thorn of the Hussites.

SRP 3: 512–18.

190   Compromise and settlement

[Near the end of 1433 the first draft of a compromise settlement aimed at ending the crusade and recognizing the Hussites was completed and signed by representatives of the Council of Basel and all Hussites parties: Praguers, Táborites and Orphans. In final form the Hussites adopted the agreements on 5 July 1436 at a solemn assembly of the Bohemian and Moravian estates when the provisions of the so-called *Compactata* were read publicly in the Moravian border town of Jihlava in the main town square in the presence of Emperor Sigismund. On 16 August, Sigismund pronounced the restoration of peace bringing to an end two decades of crusade. This concord was ratified by the Council of Basel in 1437. The excommunication of Bohemia as an heretical nation was thereby repealed. These agreements became part of the law of the Kingdom of Bohemia, even though Pope Pius II rescinded the 'compacts' on 31 March 1462 as being null and void. Every ruler from Sigismund to Maximilian II (†1576) affirmed the binding nature of the agreements. Not until 1567 was it removed from the royal confirmation oath. A critical edition of the agreements (Latin and Czech), based on several manuscripts, appears in AČ 3: 398–444. The original version of the *Compactata* is dated 26 November 1433.]

In the name of our Lord Jesus Christ. That which is written below has been brought to conclusion by the grace of the Holy Spirit, between the legates of the holy general Council of Basel and the general assembly of the illustrious Kingdom of Bohemia and the Margraviate of Moravia, in the city of Prague, in the year [1433].

First, the said assembly in the name of the said kingdom and the said margraviate, as well as for each and every one of those who are part of them, will receive and accept and conclude a good, solid and perpetual peace as well as the unity of the Church, and they will profess it and affirm it as is right.

This accomplished, the said legates, by the authority of the Council, will admit and accept this peace and unity, and will proclaim a general peace of all Christian people with the inhabitants and citizens of the said kingdom and margraviate. They will withdraw all sentences of censure and abolish them completely. They will admonish each and every Christian that none presume to disparage the said kingdom and margraviate, nor to invade them or do harm to them or to their inhabitants; that everyone, on the contrary, observe Christian peace towards them, regard them as their true brothers, as respectful and obedient sons of our Holy Mother Church, and be motivated towards them with brotherly affection.

On the matter of the first article, which the ambassadors of the kingdom and margraviate presented to the holy council under this form: 'That the communion of the very divine eucharist, useful and necessary for salvation, under the two kinds (of bread and wine), be administered freely by the priests to all the faithful of the Kingdom of Bohemia, and of the Margraviate of Moravia and of such places where they have adherents', it has been decided as follows: The Bohemians and Moravians who truly and honestly accept ecclesiastical unity and the peace, and who conform to the faith and the rites of the Catholic Church in all things, with the exception of communion in both kinds, those (male and female) who follow these practices will communicate through the authority of our Lord Jesus Christ and the church, his true bride. This article will be discussed at length in the holy Council concerning the rule, and one will see from its intention that which must be held for catholic truth and accomplished for the usefulness and salvation of the Christian people.

When this question has been dealt with maturely and methodically, if nevertheless they persevere in the desire of having this communion under the two kinds and that their ambassadors express this, the holy Council will agree that the priests of the said kingdom and margraviate may give communion in both kinds to the people, that is to say to persons who, having reached the age of discretion, shall ask for them with reverence and devotion, and this for their usefulness and salvation in the Lord.

But it shall always be the practice that the priests always say to those who are going to communicate thus that they must firmly believe that under the species of the bread that it is not only the flesh, nor under the species of the wine only the blood, but that the entire Christ is integral in both kinds. The legates of the holy Council will make known by their letters, by virtue of the authority of the holy Council, to each and every one of whatever estate or condition he may be, that no one should have the audacity to reproach the Bohemians and the Moravians when they use communion under both kinds, or attack either their reputation or their honour. The holy Council will do likewise when it reaffirms the concession of this liberty.

Concerning the matter of the three following articles, that which follows has been decided by the legates of the holy Council. Since on the doctrine of true Catholicism one must proceed with very great care and prudence, above all in a holy general Council, to the end that the truth be declared through words so well considered and so well ordered that they will not in the future constitute for anyone a stone on which one could stumble, nor give occasion for error and, to use the words of the blessed Isidore [of Seville] in order to avoid some obscurity becoming a pitfall.

On the subject of the prohibition and the correction of sins, about which your article is compiled: 'That all mortal sins, especially if they are public, be stopped, corrected and eliminated reasonably and according to the law of God by those whom it concerns', these words 'by those whom it concerns' are of too general an order and could be an obstacle. Beyond this, according to the teaching of Scripture, one must not put an obstacle in front of the blind and that one must fill in the pits for fear that one's neighbour's cattle does not injure itself there, all chance of this kind must be removed. We say then that, according to the teaching of Holy Scripture and the writings of the holy doctors, here is what must be held as catholic. All mortal sins, above all those that are public, must, as far as it is reasonable to do, according to the law of God and the prescriptions of the Holy Fathers, be stopped, corrected and eliminated. However, the power to punish criminals does not belong to private persons, but only to those who have jurisdiction over them, the distinction of the courts and the order of law and of justice being observed.

On the subject of the preaching of the Word of God, for which your article directs: 'That the Word of God be freely and faithfully preached by priests and clerics who are capable of it', for fear that one does not draw from the word 'freely' the opportunity of a rash and harmful liberty that you yourselves have often declared you do not have in mind, it is necessary to be circumspect. We say [then] that, according to the teaching of Holy Scripture and the writings of the holy doctors, here is what should be held as catholic. That the Word of God should be preached by priests and Levites who are capable, approved and sent out by their superiors to whom this comes back; that it be, we say, preached freely, which is not wishing to say no matter how, but with order and faithfulness, being, save for the authority of the Pontiff who is first in all things, according to the Holy Fathers.

On the subject of the last article, expressed in these terms: 'It is not permitted to clerics in the time of the law of grace, to exercise a right of property like secular people over temporal goods', we recall that, when a public and solemn discussion on this point took place at a holy Council, he who was appointed by the holy

Council for this discussion [Juan Palomar] established two conclusions in these terms. First, that non-religious clerics, that is to say those not so bound by oath, can legitimately have and possess all sorts of temporal goods, inheritance from their parents or others if they have left them some, and other goods justly acquired by gift or other legal contract, or again by other legal means, Secondly, that the Church can legitimately have and possess temporal goods, movable and immovable, houses, endowments, small holdings, fortified towns, fortresses, cities, and exercise over them a private and civil right of ownership.

Now your ambassador [Peter Payne] who took part in this discussion granted these same points saying that they do not contradict the sense of the article if it is well understood, since he himself formally accepted the rights of civil property. From this fact and others one could clearly understand that the words 'exercise a right of property like secular people' put in the aforementioned article seem to relate to what manner or particular way of owning. Nevertheless, as the doctrine of the Church must not be deep with ambiguous words but clear, for this motive, we have judged it necessary to express in the following manner that which should be held as catholic according to the law of God and the writings of the holy doctors. The two conclusions mentioned above are true and the men of the Church must faithfully manage the goods of the Church of which they are administrators, according to the salutary prescriptions of the Holy Fathers, and these same goods of the Church cannot be withheld [that is to say, 'usurped'] by others.

The said assembly receives and accepts the declaration of the three articles, which lean on the truth of Holy Scripture. Nevertheless, it seems that in relation to these three articles, a number of abuses and some disorder has been created. It is the intention of this assembly to insist in an urgent manner to the holy Council, through its ambassadors, on the reform of these abuses and these disorders. If certain individual people wish to promote such reforms in the holy Council as is right and good, this should be permitted and the means be extended to them. As for the legates of the holy Council, they have signified their agreement with that which has proceeded, as the holy Council aims to reform morals and desires, with the help of the Lord, to apply and employ itself. These same legates, desiring with all their soul that all reform be well accomplished in the Church of God, wish and commit themselves to help and co-operate with everything relating to a positive reform of the Church, etc.

Finally, after which, by the grace of God, all war over the question of faith will have ceased and that a good peace will reign, which all should diligently commit themselves to maintain, it seems very expedient that also for the other questions that do not concern faith, if any exist with immediate neighbours, all parties cease to use force and end the controversies by assemblies agreed by all or by others, in the holy Council or outside, through concord, through amicable arrangements or by a judgement. For the strength and the observation of this peace, the legates of the holy Council will give every guarantee, and the bull and the instructions of the holy Council will be obtained for all princes and neighbouring communities, as well as all that is necessary and appropriate. On the side of the aforementioned kingdom and margraviate, letters will be given with seals and appropriate guarantees, peace will be proclaimed, it will be required to be observed and all that is necessary and appropriate will be done for the observation of the said peace and of unity etc.

MC 1: 495–8.

191   Prokop's last letter

[During the second half of 1433 and early 1434 the conciliar fathers, principally through the mediation of Juan Palomar, sought further ways to subdue the Hussites. Commencing in July 1433, Hussite armies laid siege to Plzeň, the Catholic-Royalist stronghold in west Bohemia. Twice, Přibík of Klenové, a traitorous Táborite captain, brought supplies to the besieged town, thus averting Hussite victory. This is attested both by Bartošek of Drahonice (FRB 5, p. 612) as well as the records of the Council of Basel. Meanwhile, the New Town of Prague fell to a coalition of barons on 5 May, the same day Plzeň was relieved. Prokop Holý and Jan Čapek of Sány, an Orphan captain, managed to escape. After consulting with Čapek, Prokop wrote to the priest Prokůpek encamped outside Plzeň. The very dire situation is underscored in this short missive and the field armies were summoned for one last stand. The letter is dated 6 May 1434 just before the Battle of Lipany.]

Brother Prokůpek, commander of the Orphan army, etc. The Almighty Lord who brings peace to the storm and comfort to the afflicted, be also with you dear brother in Christ. Be assured that with the permission of God the false barons and those of the Old Town have attacked our brethren in the New Town, killing some and taking over the town. It seems good to us that you should abandon everything and move from Plzeň to Sedlčany. Čapek is in the process of getting troops together and we Táborites are as well. It is better to die than not avenge the innocent blood of our friends so treacherously shed. Be strong in the Lord and in the knowledge that He gives comfort to those who are punished.

Rudolf Urbánek, *Lipany a konec polních vojsk* (Prague: Melantrich, 1934), p. 261.

192　Report on the battle of Lipany

[On 27 May the enemies of the Hussite armies shelled the Orphan town of Český Brod. The next day the two sides faced each other on a hill near the village of Lipany (see map 3). For two days tension built. Negotiations broke down. Information on the events of 30 May are sketchy and must be drawn almost entirely from intelligence on the anti-Hussite side. The battle of Lipany marked the virtual end of Hussite field armies. Ironically, Czech defeated Czech in the interest of the crusade. What five Imperial backed expeditions over a dozen years and an intermittent daily war could not achieve – dislodging the Hussites militarily – an encounter between Bohemian forces on a single afternoon accomplished. Though not named, the principal commander of the forces opposed to the Hussite armies was Diviš Bořek of Miletínek, a man who years earlier had learned military strategy from Jan Žižka. This report was written from Plzeň to certain Franciscan and should be dated either June 1 or 2, 1434.]

To the honourable man, Lord Mikuláš, custodian of the Order of the Friars Minor, and to Prokop Ferigel Segel, our dearest friends, the council and community of the town of Nová Plzeň.

Promising our services, dearest friends, we announce to you the good and joyful news that all of our enemies are bowed down and have been defeated. We send this written report to the sacred council [of Basel] and to the Imperial majesty. The proceedings of the struggle occurred in this manner. When both encampments had been settled against each other, the army of the Hussites disrupted and frightened our forces with large and small cannon. Then the people called out against the barons murmuring and saying: why do we lose our lives and get killed like this and spend this time in vain? Let us proceed toward them. It is better to die fighting than to perish miserably like this. At that time the lords and captains stood up and put the ranks in order and then proceeded to fight. When the hour of battle had come and the forces advanced against each other, we were ordered to turn about and our forces retreated in accordance with previous instruction and we pretended to be in flight so that we who were formerly in the rear were now in the front. When our enemies saw this, namely that we had turned our backs, they cried horribly in a great voice with the sound of bugles: arise, stand up and let us pursue them. Look, they are running away. And thus all of our adversaries arose from their encampment and emerged from their wagons, [both] cavalry and foot soldiers followed us. Then we who had been in the rear, seeing that they moved out from their encampment and wagons, arose in the name of the Lord, on whose cause we acted, attacked them from behind and prevented their retreat to their encampment and wagons. Other barons and lords, arose with all of the multitude from the front and they attacked them in one accord as though a single man and knocked them down from behind and from the front like sheaves, even though they had surrendered and were surrendering as prisoners. There was no time for taking captives, only a time of killing. Some who were taken prisoner by us were snatched from our hands by force and killed. Thus, with the Lord God's [aid] we have defeated all the enemies in this way and only few escaped. For this victory may God be praised. All their wagons, cannon, military tools and defensive weapons were seized because they had left them all there. May you also know that the barons and lords stood in the field with powerful force and did not leave until that which had been started was brought to a close. . . . Given in Nová Plzeň on Tuesday after the feast of Corpus Christ in the year of the Lord, 1434.

UB 2: 414–15.

193   Annihilation of the Hussite field armies

[This anonymous report was brought from Lipany by an otherwise unknown man named Matěj of Husinec on either the second or third day of June. Thousands of heretics were slaughtered, including the commanders Prokůpek and Prokop Holý, in the carnage which went on into the night.]

On Sunday after Corpus Christi the lords struggled with the Hussites, Prokop's army and the army of the Orphans, and all of their forces were in the field. Then the lords wounded, defeated and killed all of the army of the Hussites. Scarcely 500 enemies escaped. Our [ranks] took their wagons, cannon, and all their tools and necessities. The Hussites cannot take to the battle field in force any more.

The lords wrote to all of the towns on the Hussite side and commanded them to be obedient to the emperor and to join our side. Whoever wishes to do this should be received. Those who do not wish to, may be compelled by force to do it. They intend also not to draw back from the field to make peace first. When they are united as one man they intend to ride to the emperor and bring him to the land.

The lord Mikuláš Krchlebec of Klingenberk, who led the vanguard, took to himself the servants of his lord and the oldest from the district of Plzeň and the barons Menhart of Jindřichův Hradec and other noble lords were disposed to it. They dispatched the wagons to the vanguard in eleven rows. The Hussites ranked theirs into six rows. Then our people added four cannon to the flanks. Then they, our vanguard and the vanguard of the Táborites, rode against each other. We shot from the most forward cannon into their vanguard and later stopped for a little while and pretended as though they had been urged and they turned back as if they wished to leave the field. Then the Hussites shot off their cannon like ours. Lord Mikuláš came again towards their vanguard and commanded the lords on our flanks to shoot the cannon into the sides of the Hussite army. But then Lord Mikuláš returned and drew back a short distance from them as though he had given the order to retreat. When the Hussites saw this, they left their wagon-fortress and hurried after our troops. Then Lord Mikuláš with his people turned again and entered the wagon-fortress and fought with the enemy until they locked him into the wagon-fortress. Thereafter, Lord Menhart of Jindřichův Hradec and the one of Rožmberk and other lords moved the best armed people among those of our forces into the wagon-fortress to help while others assaulted the enemies and upset the wagons of the fortress in order to get inside to help our people so that they were able to win the battle and defeat all of the enemies.

Some of them came to the lords on our side and others in the field, especially those of Žatec, Louny, Litoměřice, Český Brod and some other towns. Other Hussite barons rode to the lords in our army wishing to unite and join with us. The battle occurred close to old Kolín and near to new Kolín between the hills and quite a few of our [troops] were killed and quite a number of theirs. And our lords took the Hussite wagon-fortress into our own wagon-fortress and equipped it.

UB 2: 416–17.

194   The end of Prokop Holý

[This account of the disaster of Lipany recounted by Aeneas Sylvius is a rather poetic version of the final moments in the lives of many Hussite warriors and especially of the commanders Prokůpek and Prokop Holý. Despite the contempt with which Aeneas regarded the heretics there is no mistaking his admiration for the courage of Prokop. This version is accurate in its main themes. What can be added here is that once the Hussites were tricked into leaving their wagon fortress and were caught out, they were doomed when one of the captains, Jan Čapek of Sány fled from the field to Kolín with his cavalry leaving the foot soldiers to their fate. Prokop Holý gave his last orders to open the wagon fortress so that some of his men could escape the carnage. He chose not to take advantage of this opportunity and died sword in hand. Two notable survivors were Peter Payne and Jan Roháč of Dubá. Čapek's conduct brought him disgrace and he was later exiled from the country.]

They arrived at a place on spacious fields between Český Brod and Kouřim, four thousand, five hundred paces from Prague. Here, wagons clashed with wagons and people shouted at each other, hurling degrading names. Prokop decided not to provide any opportunity for a fight unless the circumstances were in his favour. He intended to go to Prague where he had no doubts that the New Town would open their gates. However, when the cavalry of the barons went around the wagon barricade they found that it was open at the rear. They penetrated the fortress and caused great bloodshed. This unexpected disaster took the enemies by surprise and they did not know what to do. There was confusion throughout the camp and the strangeness of the situation increased the horror. Previously, they had never experienced an intrusion of cavalry into the wagon barricade. Foot soldiers were slaughtered everywhere. The barricade was opened on the other side. Everyone tried to flee but the barons attacked and those who attempted to escape were killed everywhere.

Prokop was unable to hold back his warriors. Fear and danger prevented them from hearing his commands so he charged into the thickest enemy line with a group of his men whom he had selected among the strongest ones rather than from the most devoted and he was able to contain the enemy attack for some time. He killed many of the enemies and almost took their victory from them. Surrounded by a great number of horsemen he was hit by a stray arrow and fell wearied with conquering, rather than conquered himself. Like him, the other Prokop, who as mentioned previously was called 'the smaller' [Prokůpek], fought bravely in the same battle and was killed. This was the end of the two most harmful and heinous monsters. Thus the previously undefeated army of criminal Táborites and Orphans were defeated and annihilated.

Aeneas Sylvius, *Historia Bohemica*, chapter 51, p. 161.

195   Defiance by the Hussite remnant

[Having survived Lipany, Jan Roháč of Dubá, now the preeminent Hussite military personality, had ridden with Žižka from the beginning among the early 'warriors of God'. His spirit and attitude mirrored that of Žižka. Neither man ever countenanced the thought of meeting Sigismund anywhere but on the field of battle. While other Hussites were prepared for negotiation, despite the debilitating results of Lipany, Roháč and his men dug in once more against crusaders and the despised emperor. This manifesto, dated 21 December 1434, reveals that resolve.]

In the name of almighty God and for the honour, praise and propagation of his holy truths! We, Jan Roháč of Dubá, captain of the town of Hradiště, known as Tábor, the mayor, counsellors and elders of the same town of Hradiště, and the community of the towns of Písek, Prachatice, Vodňany, Hradec nad Labem, Dvůr Králové, Jaroměř, Čáslav, Nymburk, Mladá Boleslav, Třebíč, Ivančice with some adherents of ours, have carefully noted and understood through the frequent and numerous warnings from the friends of the holy truths and also from those who are on the side of the adversaries, how that emperor, the principal enemy of the truth of God, along with his helpers, both open and secret, have tried and studied deception cleverly and quite willingly [with the purpose] of separating us from the faithful ones of God's truth through glib speeches and instructions [aiming] to deceive, suppress and, in the end, exterminate us.

At the time of the year since the birth of the son of God, 1434, on the day of St Thomas [21 December], God's apostle, we held an assembly in the town of Hradiště, called Tábor, in order to be able with the faithful to eschew and avoid, with the help of almighty God, the deceit, intrigue and infidelities and to remain in God's truths with all of the faithful. At this assembly we united on these articles written and constituted below.

First, we have refreshed among us the former obligations of all the communities of the faithful to the Four Articles, received in the beginning and we have committed, vowed and solemnly affirmed through the offering of the hand, that we shall help each other faithfully, until loss of goods, assets and lives, against that emperor and against everyone who would oppress us against our will away from that which is good or those who wish to oppress us.

Noting and considering how especially our Lord God takes vengeance on every sin and disorder among the enemies of the divine truths, as well as the hypocrites and we ourselves, and wishing to avoid another vengeance and to avert his terrible anger against us, we have agreed and are consenting to put to an end, with the help of God, open and secret sins among us as well as in others as far as we are able. We would repent of these sins which we have not avoided, faithfully every time and lower ourselves before his holy face as much as possible, rejecting all pride. Expecting especially that we may be stricken with difficult tests now we have decided to fast and pray together one day of every week, in addition to Friday, at least in this time up until the fast [Lent].

We have consented further, that if any community would be disrupted in itself or divided, which God does not wish and there is not a means for unity then it should call itself to peace and unity with the neighbouring communities standing up with us in this holy unity. Also that it should be spoken at the next assembly of all the adherents of the law of God that it has been decided how to proceed on it, especially so that we have one common hand on such assemblies and we can give the same answers from one will and advice like one man without division.

Lastly, when we were still together in that assembly, at the time we were given to know through messengers, as well as by the letters from the noble, brave, wise and discreet ones, particularly from Lord Vok of Holštejn and other good people of Bohemia and also from Moravia, and after your message, the lords and brothers of Žatec, that they wish to hold with what has been constituted here together by us and by other faithful ones according to God's truths, and to advise and help us with their goods and their lives.

A caution has been sent to us from one friend of the truth of God in a letter from the other side. 'May almighty God the Lord condescend to be with you as well as with us in your sorrow which he has allowed because of our sins. Dear brothers, I am frightened because of the greater sorrows which I hear of. I have been informed by those who favour us that our enemies and those of God, and for a long time suppressors of his clear truths which they are oppressing and which they want to finally oppress, are already delighted and have sent letters to each other saying we have what we wanted. When we have not overcome the walls of the towns of those black pudding eaters, we did not have the courage to fight them because since the beginning the towns were led into the war against us. We have already caught the bird. Let us be encouraged to pluck the feathers off of it as quickly as possible without delay. Let us no longer be troubled by those four articles with which they have bidden us for so long. Let us receive them from them, then everything will be easier. Let us eat the four articles, then we shall eat them too. They will gladly stand by us, they will peck the little townsfolk, they will gladly leave our houses and our goods, they will return castles and forts to the lords, the cloisters and payments to the monks in which they now rest. Do not let us delay, let us be good. So if they wish to be good in their wrath, why not us, dear brothers, who have the truth and the holy cause and our restoration is in God and in the power of his virtue?'

Let us be faithful to ourselves and the power of the town to the praise of God. Consult bravely together with the priests in all places for God and those pure truths. It concerns both you and God if it were not for the help of God and your solicitous care. Let God be the consolation of you as well as of us. Amen.

Husitské manifesty, pp. 214–17.

196   Heretics' philosophy of resistance

[This lengthy chronicle by the Táborite bishop Mikuláš Pelhřimov, nearly 350 printed pages, does not constitute a history of deeds but rather a doctrinal history documenting the Táborite agenda. A history of radical Hussite ideas emerges providing a theoretical foundation for resistance to the crusades.[16]]

In the kingdom of Bohemia and in the Margraviate of Moravia many sincere disciples were attracted and brought to a place of righteousness through the

---

[16] On Mikuláš, see Kaminsky, 'Nicholas of Pelhřimov's Tábor: An adventure into the eschaton' and Thomas A. Fudge, 'Crime, punishment and pacifism in the thought of Mikuláš of Pelhřimov, 1420–1452', in *BRRP* 3, pp. 69–103.

perseverance of Master Jan Hus and Jerome of Prague together with divine visitation. . . .

However, the Devil, the enemy of the truth and of human salvation. . . . agitated certain of his followers. . . . Because of this, violence and cruelty was perpetuated both by the laity as well as the clergy including the pope and prelates, Sigismund, who at that time was the king of Hungary, by Germans as well as other nations and compatriots who assisted in this because they were looking for ways in which to condemn, vilify and destroy those rights which had begun to say nothing of the language of the Bohemian nation. But the people were unified in the cause of the four articles, as enumerated above, and were unwilling to forfeit these rights and stray from the orthodox faith despite the preponderance of violence and cruelty. On the authority of the unanimous assent and advice of the masters of Prague and of the other priests who at that time were recognized as legitimate authorities, they hesitantly accepted war as a necessary option principally for this reason: to defend the aforementioned truths and to protect the faithful who supported it. This was undertaken in order that all errors of Antichrist might be destroyed through war, even though these errors were disguised and the faith of Christ, order, justice and truth might be advanced through proper means and methods according to the law of God for the exclusion of all disorder.

The war was organized, prepared and supported according to the model and rules of the old, righteous warriors. Much attention was paid to this by the previously mentioned masters of Prague and the priests in the Kingdom of Bohemia who at that time joined themselves to the people we have been speaking about. Nevertheless, at that time, alas, the war came to an end falling into serious disorder on account of many who had committed themselves under false pretensions having other motivations which were contrary to the purpose and desire of the faithful who steadfastly contended for what was right on the basis of a true Catholic idea. . . .

FRA 1, vol. 6: 477–81.

197 Hussites denounce Hussites

[A criticism of the Czech masters by Chelčický in his 'Reply against Master Rokycana' written in the mid-1430s is a denunciation of war judging Rokycana and the conservative Hussites of having abandoned the law of God, of having drunk of the poison of the Great Whore, and thus of violating Christian faith. Comparison can usefully be drawn to doc.41.]

You oppose me, using our masters to prove through their writings that purgatory is in hell. As far as I am concerned, I only accept their knowledge to the extent that it strengthens my faith in the law of God. They taught me themselves to think in this manner, and I say this, without contempt, that what they have done well or taught accurately in their edifying sermons or elsewhere. I assert, however, that they also have drunk of the wine of the great whore with which she has overwhelmed all the people, and this poison has contaminated all of the nations. In saying this, I refer to the scandalous propositions which they have in their writings in order to seduce the people, especially the sayings of Jan Hus with respect to murder, the taking of oaths, images, and other weaknesses which have been drawn out not in the spirit of Jesus, but in the wineskins of the great whore, mother of adulterers and earthly abominations, who has plunged the world into blood while getting drunk on the blood of the saints and the martyrs of Jesus.[17] I can not in any way approve of these propositions which the masters have left us, to the scandal and indignation of quite a number of people. Some are so outraged by these writings that they despise them as though they were pagan books. Many others are strengthened in murder to the point that if even an angel were to come to teach them, they would only believe Hus.

It is a serious fault to contravene the commandment 'you should not kill' in such a way that one requires the people, through comments of complete falsehood, to commit the very crime which it prohibits, by providing them with an interpretation that is cruel and scandalous. What a shame that this man, who originally explained it in a sense so faithful, suddenly changed tone and came to hold the opposite, as though he pointed the sword against his own chest. He was aware initially of the danger of killing people according to human law and that divine law provides no such example.

Only God alone can create the soul, join it to a body or separate it on account of sin. A murderer usurps the law of prosecution and knowledge of sin which belongs to God alone. All the commandments of the second table indicate how we are to love our neighbours. Nothing is more contrary to this than homicide. . . .

If he had left it there, without commenting further on this principle, he would have bequeathed to us a good thing. Nevertheless, he took issue with all this in admitting that, following the law of love, in the name of faith and justice – linking to them sixteen motives of charity – love is in harmony with homicide like a lance thrust into a beating heart. These masters would not have drunk of the poisoned cup, if this whore had not given it to them with her own hand. It is she who possesses barrels of poison, with her apostles and her doctors who drink of

---

[17] The reference is to Hus' 'Výklad viery', chapters 45–8 where he discusses homicide and war. Karel J. Erben, ed. *Mistra Jana Husi Sebrané spisy české*, 3 volumes (Prague, 1865–8), vol. 1, pp. 156–84.

it and lavish their gifts on all who come near. From where does Hus draw, when he affirms this: 'I admit that the holy church has two swords', if not from St Augustine who claims that the lord commanded his disciples to carry his sword. Similarly, the holy church always has two swords, one spiritual and the other temporal. . . .

If it occurred to me to discuss this in person *viva voce* you would say to me that these pages from Hus are relevant for knights and would argue that this must be the military order according to the teaching of the doctors. Of course, I am not unaware that in preparation for martyrdom, he would have taken the side of armed force had he found in their favour more than an authority among the doctors. However, I shall ask you a question. To which type of knights, in your opinion, does the military state belong? Is it to the whippersnappers, in our castles and manors, who cover their shoulders with long hair and who wear clothes so short that they cannot decently cover their backsides? If it is for them to wage war, then tell me what are the burghers and the peasants doing on the fields of battle? You see, you and yours, how your discourses are full of lies, when in time of war you make warriors of tanners, shoemakers, carpenters, in short all those who are capable of wielding a sword. In your sermons, you refer only to princes and knights but, in fact, you involve everyone.

That is why I say that Hus, in baldly explaining the divine commandment 'you shall not kill' and in allowing princes and knights to go and fight, plunges the people into blood. This has been proven in practice. Far from waging war personally, the king and princes see the poor pages, expel the peasants from their cottages and force each of them to take a crossbow, a helmet, a shield. See how Hus and all the others imbibe long drinks of human blood in praising what is in opposition to the truth of the original holy church, and recognizing that it is not without reason that they require help from the temporal power. At the moment of (the furnishing) of a magistrate's evidence he appeals, according to Psalm [109:6], to royal power and certifies that he is more confident, in the trial to summon the help of warriors and kings. He is able without difficulty to cast aside the acts of the apostles and finds himself better off in the company of kings. And it seems to him that from this moment, Christians are no longer obligated to follow with perseverance the apostles and the holy primitive church, seeing that kings have been introduced among them.

Now the original church followed the apostles with perseverance for 320 years, passing through great persecutions among the pagans, without appealing to temporal power, but in being subjugated, on the contrary, to the pagan authority until Constantine. When this man, who had committed cruelties without number, wished to take advantage from Christ, he mixed Christians with his pagan lordship. The poor priest [i.e. Silvester] who hid from him in caves and in the woods having received from him honour and imperial power, fell away from the faith. Also, when this thing happened, one heard this sinister (saying): 'Today, poison has been poured into the holy church. Is it then because of these two rich lords, the temporal and the spiritual, that the faith will cease to exist that suffering will be eradicated, in such a way that the temporal lord shoulders the spiritual and carries the testimony for him by the cutting edge of his sword, while the other sings apostolic acts?'

The doctors even served the temporal lord by establishing him with the use of references from the old and the new testaments – in the faith of Christ, both he and his sword, as much as an apostle and representative of God. They advised him to maintain in peace holy mother church, to protect her so that she could rest while he pleased himself, serving God with pious cruelty, to the point of putting to fire and blood entire regions and bringing through his good offices thousands of people (to the faith). So the doctors write that the holy church indubitably possesses two swords, since she has drunk this poison with them. Since she has abandoned the commandments and the inheritance of Jesus Christ and ceased following him, she wallows in blood and renders evil for evil.

It came to pass that your master Jakoubek, in his room at Bethlehem [Chapel in Prague] called me a heretic because we were not in agreement on the subject of authority, I said to him thus. 'In your opinion, if force agrees with the faith, can you find in the gospel proof to justify its sins, wars and other cruelties?' He replied to me: 'No, but this is the conviction of saints in the past.' When the king left Prague, and when many people were massacred on both sides he excused again the murderers saying: 'I cannot burden their conscience with these killings because this would bring shame on the entire estate of the knights.'[18] From where does he know this, this man of great humility and holy morals? Where did he imbibe this idea? Was it of himself that he spoke thus? By this commandment 'you shall not kill', St Gregory tells us, that it is forbidden to kill anyone voluntarily, but not to put to death those who are guilty according to the law.[19] Whoever makes use of force, by order of the law to punish the wicked, does not transgress by this commandment and will not be excluded from the eternal kingdom. In the same sense was St Augustine.[20] A knight who kills another man

---

[18]   This is a reference to the events which occurred in Prague in the summer of 1419 after King Václav had retired from the city to his country residence. On 30 July, a Hussite mob led by Priest Jan Želivský and in the company of Jan Žižka overthrew the city government and killed the officials by defenestration. When the king learned of the coup his rage knew no bounds but he died shortly thereafter of apoplexy. The reference might likewise include the first crusade.

[19]   According to the *Glossa Ordinaria* on Exodus 20:13, Migne, *Patrologia Latina,* volume 113, col. 254.

[20]   There are several texts among the writings of Augustine which are relevant here: 'Contra Faustum Manicheum' in PL 42: 444–5, 447–8; 'De libero arbiterio' PL 32: 1227–8, 1259;

by order of the power to which he is in subjection, does not violate any law of his city.

These doctors could then pardon more sins than the Lord Jesus who said that according to the ancients you must not kill. The one who kills deserves to be punished by the judge [Matthew 5:21–2]. I tell you, whoever gets angry with his brother will answer for it before the judge. For these doctors, there is neither guilt nor remorse after the murder, leaving no need for repentance or purification. The ancient law tormented the conscience much more than does the pardon of these doctors, as was demonstrated after the massacre of the Midianites who were killed on the order of God. For Moses gave the combatants the following order that whoever kills a person or touches a body will purify himself the third and seventh day; you will wash your clothes the seventh day, then you will enter into the sanctuary [Numbers 30:19–20].

The voice of conscience did not cease speaking to them strongly, even though God himself had ordered them to fight. Now, the law of perfect liberty opens the door to this licence, so much so that after having exterminated lots of people, the killers hurry to the altar, with their pikes all bloodied, to receive the holy sacrament. If someone had eaten a pork sausage one Friday, he would blame him – and how! – your master Jakoubek. Yet see how spilt blood raises no obligation in his conscience. Who then has taken it away from him? The saints of old who were full of the holy spirit? Advise him not to be in too much haste with permission to kill, for his authority is indeed limited. Thus when a lord puts on foot a large army of peasants, making them into knights, and these have full power to kill, are these not assassins, or men who must repent of their crimes? Indeed on the contrary, they boast of conducting themselves bravely and having massacred heretics. This poison was poured into Christianity by the doctors, who were certainly not present at the council of Jesus the poor, but indeed at the council of the great whore, who has filled the earth with blood and abomination. Or rather, by chance did the Holy Spirit settle upon these doctors, while they were writing so many books about it? Faith has not been abolished, nor the New Testament. Men are bound to conform to it and to obey Christ in loving their enemies and in doing good to them. They are bound to feed them and give them drink when they are hungry and thirsty; to pray to God for them and to render to no one evil for evil. It is impossible that the Holy Spirit has revoked, through the intermediary of these doctors, the commandments which was announced to all people through the voice of the apostles. . . . The sword which serves to spill blood, it is the church which has won it over; Christ has never stopped wanting the opposite. Also is it not astonishing that our masters have proved the existence of purgatory situated

'Enarrationes in Psalmos' PL 37: 1653–4; 'De civitate dei' PL 41:35 and Ep. 47.5 in PL 33: 186–7.

in hell, in the same way as these doctors; because after having approved of murder, their conscience was subdued by their teaching, and the divine commandments which no longer had authority over them gave them away to this Holy Spirit which was at home with the doctors.

Karel Černý, 'Klasobraní po rukopisích' *Listy filologické* 25 (1898), pp. 391–5.

198   Demands of the St Valentine's Day assembly

[Convened on St Valentine's day, 1435, the diet had been called chiefly to negotiate the terms under which Sigismund would be recognized as king of Bohemia. A series of issues caused the assembly to drag on into the month of March. The militarily defeated Hussites still attempted to have a voice in public affairs in the Czech kingdom. It is not without significance that in these demands communion under both kinds – *sub utraque specie* – is mentioned ten times. In all, there were twenty-seven conclusions promulgated.]

First, the cities should retain their rights and liberties. Second, mortal sins, such as a game of dice or dancing, should not be made public knowledge. Third, no one ought to be received by any city, unless he takes communion *sub utraque specie.* Fourth, those who were expelled from cities and communities because they take communion *sub utraque specie*, ought not be received back by that city or community, unless the person is received unconditionally. Fifth, those who left behind their property in any city ought not to return to their property, unless the same city or community receives them unconditionally. Sixth, no official ought to be placed in office, unless he takes communion *sub utraque specie.* Seventh, Germans ought not to be received in any city or office, unless previously they took communion *sub utraque specie.* Eighth, the judgements of the clergy or of secular men should not be challenged or overturned. Ninth, the emperor should have no advisors in his counsel, who do not take communion *sub utraque specie.*

Tenth, no barons opposed to the law of God should be in any office. Eleventh, only the communities and cities should intervene in the judgement of widows and orphans. Twelfth, the emperor or anyone else ought not have a chaplain, unless he takes communion *sub utraque specie.* Thirteenth, judgements being withheld should be made, and freedom should be given to those owing rents so that their debts are not discharged, and no unusual taxes are imposed. Fourteenth, proscriptions and the alienation of goods of the emperor and indeed King Václav ought to be discharged, and should not be taken as valid. Fifteenth, Moravia should be restored to the Kingdom of Bohemia. Sixteenth, the imperial relics and the revenues of the Kingdom of Bohemia should be restored. Seventeenth, religious orders ought not return to the cities of Bohemia. Eighteenth, no one should be compelled to rebuild monasteries, unless perchance a city rebuilds it out of good will.

Nineteenth, the emperor ought not confiscate any property for an official or burgrave, namely cities or castles. Twentieth, the emperor with his officials shall take communion *sub utraque specie* so that one does not make another a heretic over it. Twenty-first, whoever does not take communion *sub utraque specie* shall be compelled by the emperor to do so. Twenty-second, servants of the emperor ought not obtain the property of orphans or take their inheritance; rather they should pass to relatives. Twenty-third, the emperor should not appoint powerful captains in the cities. Twenty-fourth, if a community should happen to not hold any of these conclusions, then the other communities shall rise up against it, and the emperor shall not speak against this. Twenty-fifth, if some community should be oppressed by the emperor or his officials because of receiving communion *sub utraque specie*, then the other communities should provide assistance against the oppressors. Twenty-sixth, no one should ride in the legations except those who are nominated, whether they are masters or priests. Twenty-seventh, in each and every city, castle, fortified place, town and village the laity should take communion *sub utraque specie*, and their names should be entered on a list and noted.

UB 2: 440–1.

199   The king's concessions to the heretics

[In response to the demands of the Czechs, Sigismund met with envoys in the Moravian city of Brno in July 1435 to consider a reply. Among the notable attendees were, in addition to Sigismund, Duke Albrecht, Juan Palomar, Philibert, Bishop of Coutances, Menhart of Hradec, Hynek Ptáček of Pirkštejn, the fifteen-year-old Jiří of Poděbrady (the future Hussite king of Bohemia), Vilém Kostka of Postupice, Matěj Louda, Jan Rokycana, Martin Lupáč, Ulrich of Znojmo, Václav Koranda of Plzeň, Mikuláš of Pelhřimov, Peter Payne, Křišťan of Prachatice, Prokop of Plzeň, Oldřich Rožmberk, and others. The following document outlines the king's concessions and his decisions.]

Sigismund, Emperor of the Romans by the grace of God, etc. Our Lord Jesus Christ, the mediator between God and humankind, while bearing care for the salvation of humanity from the highest order, endured his cruel labour, for which he also wished at the same time to suffer curses, and did not scorn to sink down into a most disgraceful death, in order to restore each side to one. Indeed by Christ's example, for he is the lord of all and the best teacher and leader, and out of the imperial dignity we are disposed and committed to embracing the good of peace, unity and concord. After certain compacts between the legates of the holy Council of Basel, the Kingdom of Bohemia and the Margraviate of Moravia were written and sealed in Prague, it remained that the parties were well-disposed to the vindication of the Kingdom of Bohemia and the Margraviate of Moravia by our holy Council of Basel and also by our imperial prudence for the purpose of improving the situation in those lands.

Nevertheless, there were still various disagreements among the legates of the holy Council of Basel on one side, and the nobles, the city of Prague, both energetic and famous, and the reverend and prudent messengers of the Kingdom of Bohemia, long ago sent to us in Brno, on the other side. We placed our mind and heart, and at the same time the humours to diligent care and anxious disquiet, bearing the weight of the day and of anxiety so that we might lead back the divided into one, the adverse into harmony, the scattered and distant into unity, and at the same time bring all equally into a holy and blessed union. Indeed, we have always loved the peace and tranquillity of this realm, and we have cultivated both of these cordially, wishing to reach agreeable solutions for future dissension and controversies, by which the subjects can so often be excited. And for those matters which the compacts for the concord of the realm do not appear sufficient, we wish to provide peace salubriously, with the aforementioned ambassadors of the kingdom and margraviate to the praise of God, for that realm, all the adjacent nations, all Christian people, and also for the salvation of countless souls.

In the name of the Lord we make known to one and all that we consent immediately to the conclusions written below: first, benefices in the Kingdom of Bohemia and the Margraviate of Moravia ought not be conferred upon foreigners, but the law of collation will pertain there to the kings and inhabitants of the Kingdom of Bohemia and the Margraviate of Moravia by perpetual right. Also, secular and spiritual persons outside of the kingdom and margraviate ought neither be appealed to nor be judged [by someone in these places]; but any person in the jurisdictions of the prefect-commander of the aforementioned kingdom or margraviate will be subject, and he will be content and praise the same place. The liberties moreover of the archbishopric of Prague, and the privileges in the way of naming for himself subject bishoprics are preserved as sound and without loss. As well, those who take communion *sub una specie* in the aforementioned kingdom and margraviate, lest confusion follow a mixture, will not be restrained against their will and freedom; but their places, in which communion *sub utraque specie* was not previously protected, will be sustained. And so that the matter and opportunity for contention [should not arise], all of the churches, peoples, and parishes will be indicated, in which and from which communion *sub utraque specie* was served in safety, as it will be served in the future in these same places perpetually. Indeed, those recorded in the special letter will be secured as valid in the public memory by the seal of our majesty.

We also wish, however, that these places be selected by the Bohemian lords, nobles, men of renown, Prague, and the other cities together with the clergy of the archbishopric of Prague and the other titular and suffragan bishops. Indeed those chosen will be confirmed by our equally responsible and concerned disposition, and will be consecrated by the bishops without exhibition of the pallium for confirmation, or payment to his chancery. The entire clergy of the diocese of Prague, subjected to the archbishop elected by the aforementioned lords, will be obedient. Scholars of the diocese of Prague whether they take communion *sub una specie* or *sub utraque specie*, their aptitude and suitability presupposed, should be compelled and ordered into holy orders; their right to take communion, however, not being diminished by this. As well, because freedom is given to all by the sacred Council of Basel in the kingdom, so in the margraviate will the taking of communion *sub utraque specie* be constituted, namely for the people in the bishoprics of Olomouc and Litoměřice desiring to take communion *sub utraque specie*. Scholars there will be compelled into holy orders and consecrated, their aptitude and suitability presupposed, and priests wishing the laity to take communion *sub utraque specie* will be held to their dioceses in which the aforementioned communion was served in former years. If common people, who take communion in the said manner, wish to return to their appropriate parishes with the decree and consent of the diocese, such people will take communion in the aforesaid manner only in places where it was previously served. Otherwise people taking this sort of communion must not be tolerated, as they must find substitute places to go for communion.

We assert these matters before those present, and we promise on our imperial word to the aforementioned ambassadors and to the Kingdom of Bohemia and the Margraviate of Moravia that we will maintain each and every one of the above written points. We also wish that both by us and our successors in the future for perpetuity each of these be held and fully preserved. We, with the holy council and our lord, the highest pontiff, desire that the aforementioned articles shall receive a real effect, and we will not permit it to be otherwise in our realm or margraviate. On the contrary, if someone should attempt in any way to disturb the realm or margraviate in these matters, we will stand by them [i.e. the articles] effectually so that they are carried out, and any fraud or deceit is stopped. This was written in Brno after [the day] of the apostle James.

UB 2: 445-8.

200   Pact made by the emperor with Tábor

[One of the outcomes of the crusade period against the Hussites was the treaty granted by Sigismund to the town of Tábor, recognizing its independence, rights and privileges. The agreement was reached and ratified in the town of Třeboň on 16 October 1436.]

In the year 1437 [sic] after the birth of the son of God, on the day of St Gall [16 October], a treaty was ratified in Třeboň [mediated] through the noble baron Lord Oldřich Rožmberk and Lord Přibík of Klenové between the most invincible prince and lord Sigismund, by the grace of God, Roman emperor, ever Augustus, king of Hungary and Bohemia, on one side, and the honourable priest Bedřich of Strážnice and the discreet mayor, councillors and community of the mountain Tábor on the other side. First, [this agreement was made] so that the priest Bedřich, together with the aforementioned community would not be compelled away from the law of God and if it seemed to anyone that he, along with the community, held anything against Scripture or the law of God, then it must be proven by Holy Writ and they would correct it.

Item, the emperor's grace [has agreed] to free the town of Tábor from any claim along with the town of Sezimovo Ústí with their villages and their equipment belonging to that town which have belonged to Ústí for a long time.

Likewise, it is agreed that councillors will not be placed in that town either by the grace of the emperor or by his officers but the town shall [constitute] itself. In six years the grace of the emperor or the future king of Bohemia shall install councillors but these shall not take the rights which sub-chamberlains usually do.

Similarly, it is agreed that they shall not be compelled to take part in any wars by the grace of the emperor nor his successors. But if it is necessary for [the good of] the land and other towns then they might assist His Grace according to their ability. It is also agreed that during the next two years they shall not make any war unless it be against foreigners or on behalf of the land. Also, that all prisoners shall be released from both sides in Bohemia, Moravia and Austria.

In like manner, it is also agreed that His Grace shall give them proper and equitable rights and shall confirm [the legitimacy of] their seal. If he wishes to add anything to the seal which they normally use, he may do so as he would to his own town. Also, it is further agreed that they shall pay a rent of five threescores on St George's day [23 April] and five threescores on the day of St Gall to His Grace and to his successors and they shall begin on the next day of St George.

Likewise, the markets and annual fairs which they have and those which Ústí used to hold, shall remain theirs as well as the town books which they possess. The judgements and the records therein shall remain and be confirmed. Similarly, it is settled that His Grace the emperor has added to them the estate of Louňovice together with the courts, ponds, forests and all equipment which belong to the area of Louňovice so that they might serve His Grace even better. He shall affix a debt of 2,500 threescores of groschen on that estate. If His Grace or a future king of Bohemia wishes to pay them off, then he shall make this known a year in advance so that they may collect the fruits and interests from the ponds and the fields.

In like manner, it is agreed that the aforementioned community is to promise to be faithful and obedient to His Grace. If it seems insufficient to His Grace then they shall make such declaration to His Grace by a worthy and honest written statement. Also, it is agreed that they are to leave all the estates which they possess, either through heredity or conquest in Bohemia, Moravia or in Austria by the forthcoming day of St Gall including interest which they collect. This applies also to the domains used by their servants. Likewise, it is also agreed that the community shall not punish anyone through self-will. But if one is convicted by guilt such a one shall be regarded according to the proper order of the law as in other towns of the land. Also, His Grace the emperor shall not allow them to be oppressed by anyone else His Grace shall help and defend them as their lord against such a one who would attempt to compel them beyond these agreements.

These written agreements shall be confirmed and assured by His Grace and Majesty the emperor in so far as possible concerning both sides. Conscientiously we, Oldřich Rožmberk and Přibík of Klenové, the mediators of these matters, the priest Bedřich of Strážnice, the major and councillors of the mountain of Tábor, have affixed our seals to this letter which is given as written above.

AČ 3: 450–1.

201 Hradec Králové falls to Sigismund

[Despite diplomacy, negotiations and the devastation of Lipany, the crusade and resistance to crusade had not ended. At the time of the first crusade Sigismund and his crusaders conquered Hradec Králové. Shortly thereafter the Hussites reclaimed it with a surprise military assault (doc.29). Nearly seventeen years later it was again claimed by the king. The event took place on the night of 3–4 March 1437. It marked the beginning of the last phase of Hussite military activity in Bohemia and the last chapter of the repression of the crusading era.]

In the same year on the third Sunday of Lent the citizens of Hradec Králové became aware that armed men and hired soldiers were gathering together in a conspiracy against them. A plan was afoot to search the cellars. Surrounding themselves with men they regarded as reliable they waited until the eighth hour of the evening and then began to cry out as they seized power within the city.

They attacked the homes of the priests. Priest Ambrož broke his leg as he climbed down a wall. His followers were arrested and locked up in the jail. So the citizens regained control over their lives and goods. About 300 mercenary cavalry men and about 700 infantry were inside the city. The townspeople who had formerly been banished were allowed to return. Priest Martinék Prostředek gathered together those who now fled from the city and brought them to Lord Roháč of Dubá to the castle of Sión. Lord Roháč refused to recognize Sigismund as king and had no wish to know anything about him. As a result he engaged in war against everyone who acknowledged the emperor as their king.

SRB 3: 99.

202   The emperor declares war on the Roháč resistance

[After the fall of Hradec Králové, the Hussite resistance, led by Roháč, went to an old fortress near Kutná Hora which they called Sión and here they established their headquarters. Opposition to the king from various parts of the country began to congregate there. Sigismund could not tolerate this affront. He went to Cheb to confer with the imperial electors but at the same time he sent troops to conquer Sión. The following letter, addressed to Oldřich Rožmberk, is dated 29 June 1437.]

Sigismund, by the grace of God, Roman emperor, ever Augustus, king of Hungary, Bohemia, etc. Dear high-born and faithful one. The war against Sión and Roháč, that plague of the land, has been arranged and declared with the consent of the entire land and with your agreement as well. We have already raised a siege against that castle [Sión] some time ago, but that is no secret to you inasmuch as we wrote about it to you previously and we have dispatched some of our Hungarian and Czech courtiers. We request and desire diligently of you to send to Sión at once some of your cavalry and foot soldiers as soon as you can without delay. Do this for the common good and for our honour. If you do not do this, others will become suspicious. We are confident that you are discreet enough [to know] not to bring shame on the land and dishonour to us. Given in Prague on the day of SS Peter and Paul the apostles in the fifty-first year of our Hungarian reign, the twenty-seventh year of our Roman reign, in the seventh year of our Bohemian reign and in the fifth year of our Imperial reign. We have also sent a message through your servant Chval to which you have made no reply.

Rynešová 1: 222.

203 Gathering of force for the last fight

[There seems to have been some lack of enthusiasm for the emperor's initiative to put down the Hussites utterly. For several months, the siege against Sión Castle had been ineffective. Sigismund urged powerful Czech barons like Oldřich Rožmberk to support the war. His second letter to the baron is dated 9 July 1437.]

Sigismund, by the grace of God, Roman emperor, ever Augustus and king. Dear noble and faithful one. It is no secret to you that we have assembled with the princes and electors in Cheb. We are flourishing with them and in accordance with our wishes. We will soon return to Bohemia again with good news. But those who are encamped near Sión have saddened us very much with their letters in which they write about their many labours and the danger because they are few in number. In addition to this, others are arranging assemblies in the same area and are sending letters to the towns and wherever they can saying that much good may come from the siege so much so that we do not understand this. It is not easy for us to leave what we have entered into here and you would not think it was good either. Therefore, for God's sake, have regard for our honour and for the land as well and do not delay to dispatch your people to Sión. It is essential that these wicked people must not obtain praise through our weakness and indolence and thus come to shame and loss together with you. Thus, we do not believe that you will delay for any reason.

Meanwhile, we shall conclude matters here and come again to Bohemia and will oversee everything diligently with the help of God and with gratitude for the good and obedient ones but taking action against the others according to their behaviour in consultation with you and others. We are confident that you will not neglect to send your people to Sión in good will for our honour and the good of the land. Given in Cheb on the Tuesday before [the day of] St Margaret [20 July].

Rynešová 1: 226.

204 Fall of the heretics' fortress

[Sigismund did not trust, with some justification, in the sincerity of the Czech commanders who had been placed in charge of the siege against the heretics so the Emperor hired Hungarian mercenaries to bolster the offensive. In early September Michael Ország and the Hungarians arrived at Sión and shortly thereafter the fortress was taken after fierce fighting during which most of the defenders were killed.]

In the same year [1437], [forces from] both [towns of] Prague went out to help against Sión Castle and Roháč with the courtiers of the emperor. The emperor himself accompanied them out of the city personally but then he returned. [Roháč assumed the stance he did] because he did not wish to be in subjection to His Grace. Afterwards on the Friday [6 September] before the birth of the Mother of God, Roháč was captured along with six others and then the castle was taken as well as other [prisoners]. Lord Ptáček sent word to the emperor who was relieved and he ordered the bells rung in the castle and in churches everywhere in Prague to give thanks to God for such a victory.

Following this, on the Sunday after the birth of the Mother of God, Lord Ptáček and the other barons returned to Prague with the entire army having destroyed Sión Castle. They escorted with them Lord Jan Roháč and the Polish knight Vyšek, the priest Martinék Prostředek, Zelený the gunner, and many others. The brave knight Roháč was led immediately to the town hall and tortured so horribly that his intestines fell out.

On the following day, Monday [9 September], he was escorted together with all of his people to the gallows. Although he was a banner lord and the uncle of Lord Ptáček, nevertheless he was obliged to hang on the gallows at the behest of the emperor along with forty or so of his followers. Roháč [was hanged] on the highest [gallows] with three under him on another gallows and the others on the common gallows. There was a very great lamentation among the people. Whenever it was mentioned thereafter people wept greatly as the older ones have testified.

SRB 3: 103–4.

205   Last stand at Sión Castle

[The following document extract reveals the importance of Jan Roháč of Dubá in the last chapter of the Hussite struggle against the crusade mentality aimed at the extermination of heresy in Bohemia. The author, Eberhart Windecke, is not writing from first hand knowledge of the events and thus there are gaps and errors in his account. The fact that he does not know the name of Roháč's castle is suggestive of this and the references to Jan Rokycana are completely erroneous. The person in question referred to as Rokycana is most likely Martinék Prostředek. The idea of an assassination plot is also dubious.]

At the same time that the Roman emperor Sigismund made war on Prague, there was a knight there called Roháč who caused many irregularities in Prague against the faith and the emperor until the time the emperor came to Prague. This same

Rohač renounced the emperor. There was also another, a priest in Prague, called Rokycana, who likewise had created many problems. He lived in Prague. The emperor tolerated them as long as he could but they opposed him to the end. Nevertheless, these two, Rohač and Rokycana, saw that the power of the emperor became greater and greater because the landlords, nobility and all the common people had become weary of the conflict. One night, these two, Rohač and Rokycana, with their helpers, wanted to murder the emperor. But one pious Czech, aware of this, warned the emperor. The emperor allowed their plan to be attempted – their crime against him – but he was careful in order to save his life. However, Rohač and Rokycana realized they could not achieve their goal so they fled from Prague to one strong castle where they remained until the emperor came against it and conquered it. I do not know the name of the castle [Sión].

After the emperor took the castle he had these men brought before him. Rohač would not look at the emperor and wished rather that his eyes would be put out since he preferred to suffer that [fate] rather than gaze upon the emperor. The emperor spoke to him in a peaceful manner: 'something else will happen to you other than putting your eyes out.' He then had a gallows built with two other gallows above it so that there were three gallows. Then he hanged Rohač in a red gown on the highest gallows and on the other were hanged Rokycana who was one of the Hussite priests and on the third gallows he hanged another evil master, a very great criminal [Wyšek Racziniski].[21]

Windecke, pp. 434–5.

206   Execution, Effrontery, Exodus

[There were three important events in the aftermath of the fall of Sión Castle in the autumn of 1437. First, the Hussite garrison were executed in Prague. Secondly, residual resistance to the emperor remained and further sorties were carried out against Royalist positions. Third, the emperor left Prague never to return. The following chronicle extract reports briefly on all three events.]

In the year 1437, on Sunday, on the day of the birth of the Blessed Virgin Mary [8 September], Rohač was brought, along with the Wyšek Racziniski, a Polish knight, the priest Martinék Prostředek and someone named Zelený, the best

---

[21] There is an illustration of this event in Eberhart Windecke, *Historia imperatoris Sigismundi germanica*, Vienna, Österreichische Nationalbibliothek ms 13975 fol. 430ʳ and reproduced in Fudge, p. 119.

artilleryman, and the burgrave of the mountain of Sión, together with forty-six prisoners, to Prague by the people of the lord emperor and led them to the town hall where they were tortured cruelly. On the following day, Monday, Roháč was hanged with a golden noose and rope and the others with red nooses. Five of those hanged were dressed in red gowns. Altogether fifty-three were hanged [including] seven of his [Roháč] men who were captured previously, namely Jindříšek, Baba, Hrdinka, Žídek and their accomplices.

In the same year, 1437, in the week prior to the feast of St Martin, an individual named Pardus, formerly a captain of the Orphan sect, with more than 300 horsemen and an unknown number of foot soldiers, invaded the town of Litovel in Moravia and nearly succeeded in victory. But some of the citizens climbed into a tower and others from Olomouc entered the town using ladders on the same day and they took 293 horses and killed many and captured about 150 of them, twenty more were captured three days later. Pardus himself, with nineteen others, had escaped but was captured with all of his accomplices under the castle and the people from Olomouc took horses, weapons, silver, clothes and wagons for themselves. The captives were the son of Jeník [..] on Sunday during the vigil of St Martin, 10 November.

In the same year, on the Sunday morning before St Martin, the aforementioned lord emperor [Sigismund] went out from Prague towards Znojmo with a large retinue, Lady Barbara, the Queen of Hungary and Bohemia and those from Cilly rode with them. There were a thousand horsemen, more than 100 wagons and hundreds of people of foot.

Bartošek of Drahonice, FRB 5: 620–1.

207   Poem about Roháč

[Jan Roháč of Dubá, commander of the Sión garrison, former lieutenant of Jan Žižka and the last warrior of the Hussite crusades, was hanged in Prague on 9 September 1437 by order and under the supervision of Emperor Sigismund. The poem is contemporary with the events it portrays. In these verses, the fate of Roháč is bewailed but not without the criticism that he should have submitted to the authority of the emperor. In this poem Sigismund is compared to the Biblical Samson who died in the house he destroyed. The parallel is somewhat ambiguous. Militarily, there was no one remaining within the Hussite ranks to rival the stature and importance of Roháč. For the Latin text and commentary see Emil Pražák, 'Otázka významu v latinské písni o Roháčovi' *Česká literatura* 32 (No. 3, 1984), pp. 193–201.]

In order to preserve in writing to be examined by those to come
What has been done by the disastrous weapons and fatal wounds
To be revealed to the multitudes of coming generations.

So that such deeds would not evoke great consternation
Anyone close to you could see in such acts
So that the heart may be enlightened by inner light
And watered from without, let them listen now to what has been done.

In the year of the Lord one thousand
In addition four hundred and thirty seven
During the days of the month of September
On the third day [came] the great rank of troops.

[In] the famous city of Prague
Michael Ország, splendid governor,
With a retinue of barons in attendance with warriors
[Came] to besiege that terrible place.

Under God as leader they [sought] to destroy the Castle of Sión
And thus they set out with great force
Under pious command against the man named Roháč
The mad one who caused faces to frown.

Before this multitude and soldiers reached the castle
The baron of the emperor
The warlike Lord [Hynek] Ptáček [of Pirkštejn]
Captured the wicked Roháč.

The hearts of the soldiers are weakened
Of those taken within the castle
When their captain is taken away they are sorrowful
Dread is in all their minds before the gleaming soldiers.

They had no other hope
So they chose to flee by night in order to save the garrison
They were quite surprised
When our men captured them
And set the castle on fire.

This was unsettling for them and they lifted their voices
Mary! May you be the shield of the defenders
The castle being wasted
The prisoners were escorted in chains to the town hall in Prague.

They listened about the upraised cross
And how they would be put to a difficult death
From the circle of the executioners
A voice in Rama was heard when they were questioned and tortured
By the gathered officials.

On the ninth day of the month of September
Worthy compensation was given to them as reward for their [crimes]
They were handed over to the power of the executioners
And given up to be hanged upon the gallows.

Mad with confusion they were carried in chains
In procession to the gallows
Their guard came ahead of them
Roháč was also brought by the neck as a sign of merit.

Having been awarded the highest place with a golden rope
With a golden rope about his neck
He is hung up and they are all hanged
The honour of robbers is paid to them
Woe, what a laurel garland!

O, miserable ones, O unhappy ones
What retribution you have reached as a reward for your merits!
Why did you rob the travellers?
How dishonourably you fought for life in the race of the world.

Why did you not obey the emperor?
Why did you reject his grace?
Now you dangle ignobly
On account of vainglory and because of your stubbornness.

O, unhappy Roháč, foolish indeed
You acted poorly without discretion
Who seduced you into such devilry?
Or did your own stupidity powerfully pervert you?

Because you offended them in this manner
Insulting the emperor and attacking his people
You have received a worthy payment
Hitched up on a high scaffold drinking the cup of death.

You who might have conversed
Enjoyed and feasted with dukes and lords
Are thrown away like a rotted member
Deformed, disdained dishonoured, you hang with villains.

O, how good and cheerful it would have been for you
To have had Sigismund as lord!
Did you not know, O, ignorant one,
That it is hard to kick against the stinging pricks?

How could the frightened rabbit
Measure up to the lion
Or the tiny pygmy to Samson?

Frankfurt am Main, City Library MS. 62 fol. 169^r.

208   Death of the crusading king

[Sigismund was a man of many faces. Hussite heretics regarded him as 'the great enemy of Bohemia' (doc.27), an atrocious criminal (doc.43), a heretic and a deviant (doc.49). Admirers described him as 'the finest sight of all. For his expression is very kind and benevolent and his face is humorous and generous; his beard is nearly white and thick; there is such affability and majesty in his expression that people who do not know him can tell by his appearance and distinguished expression that he is king over others.'[22] Perhaps more balanced is this portrait given by Aeneas Sylvius: 'He was tall, with bright eyes, a broad forehead, pleasantly rosy cheeks and a long thick beard. He possessed a great mind and had many ideas but he was always changing. He possessed great wit in conversation but was given over to wine and women and is suspected of thousands of clandestine love affairs. He had a quick temper but was also quite forgiving. He was unable to keep money but spent it in great sums. He promised more than he

---

[22]   Poggio Bracciolini, letter to Nicolaus de Niccolis, 6 June 1433, describing Sigismund's arrival at the Council of Basel, in Phyllis Walter Goodhart Gordan, trans., *Two Renaissance Book Hunters* (New York: Columbia University Press, 1991), pp. 176–81 at p. 178.

could ever deliver and was often deceptive.'[23] The following document portrays Sigismund as a great crusader who liberated Prague from heresy before dying in peace. The history of Sigismund's last days are a bit more complex. The execution of Roháč caused great resentment towards the emperor. The illegality of the event was politically motivated. Three months after the execution of the Sión garrison, Sigismund hurriedly left the capital hoping to evade his enemies and reach his beloved Hungary before death overtook him. He made it as far as Znojmo in southern Moravia. As one of the main promoters of military action against the Czech heretics, his death brought the period of the crusade against the Hussites to a definitive conclusion. I have reversed part of the text in the interests of logical progression and readability.]

You should know, as you have read, how the Emperor Sigismund went to Prague and happily reduced the evil Bohemian heretics to the right faith, to the extent that he [converted] most of them. In the meanwhile he fell ill and was carried towards the Moravian town of Znojmo. . . . May you hear how Emperor Sigismund is said to have died and in what excellent manner he expired. On the day of his death he ordered that he be dressed as a Roman emperor in his rochet, other gowns, his electoral cap and imperial crown. In the morning he heard mass and following mass he ordered that this should be done: 'Do to me now as I should be buried.' Thus it was done. [Grave clothes were put on over the imperial regalia.] Then he sat upon a chair and was dying. You should notice that he ordered them prior to his death that after he died he should remain there two or three days so that everyone could see that the lord of the world had died and was gone. . . . Thus he rested in Znojmo and died on the following Monday after the conception of the Virgin Mary, as it was written in the year 1437 on the ninth day of December.

Windecke, pp. 446–7.

209   Survivors of the crusades

[Aeneas Sylvius Piccolomini, from 1458 Pope Pius II, visited Tábor twice in the summer of 1451. His account is significant for its witness to persistent heresy in Bohemia and the failure of the repeated crusades to eradicate it. The letter of 21 August was addressed to Juan Carvajal the cardinal of San Angelo.]

---

[23]   The relevant manuscript from the Vatican was published in František Palacký, *Italienische Reise* (Prague, 1838), p. 113.

Travelling from New Town [Jindřichův Hradec] to Prague in the company of the noble baron Albrecht Eberstorf and the knights Prokop of Rabštejn and Enrico Truscers it seemed best to us to stay overnight with the Táborites rather than in unprotected villages due to the danger of ambush by bandits. Thus we elected to follow the example of the wolf rather than the rabbit. So we dispatched some messengers to the Táborites to ask them if they would grant us hospitality. This they agreed to most willingly and extended good will towards us for our arrival.

The sight was worth seeing. A great throng of rustic and indecent people, in spite of their efforts to appear civil, appeared. The weather was cold and rainy but in Bohemia it is often the case that summer and winter mix together. Some of them were wearing only a long vest while others wore fur coats. Some did not have saddles or bits for their horse or spurs. Others had their legs protected by [jambeau] while others had them uncovered. Some had only one eye, others were missing a hand. Using the words of Virgil it was something terrible to see those wasted faces with ears cut off and noses mutilated with obscene scars.[24] They were wandering about lacking all order and talking without any restraint. They welcomed us with an unseemly and uncouth ceremony but offered us fish, beer and wine as gifts. We arrived at the entrance of the fortress, but if I were not able to call it a bulwark or refuge of heretics I would not know how to describe it. In this place are all the monsters of impiety and blasphemy among Christians. They escaped here to find protection. In order to find out how many heretics are in this place, it is sufficient to count heads. Freedom here consists in everyone believing whatever they wish.

Outside the fortress entrance hang two rectangular shields. On one an angel has been painted holding a chalice in his hand as if to convince the people to receive communion in the form of wine. On the other Žižka, an old man blind in both eyes, has been painted. For a long time he had been leader of the Táborites. He lost his first eye when he was a child and the other was lost to an enemy arrow.

It is said that his followers were incited by him frequently to shed the blood of Christians, to burn numerous towns, destroy monasteries, burn holy buildings, prostitute virgins and kill priests. It is significant that the Táborites followed not a one-eyed person but a blind man. In fact what sort of leader but a blind person would be suitable for people like this who understand nothing of divinity, have no religion and know nothing of equity and justice? The saying of the Saviour comes true: 'If a blind person guides another blind person both of them will fall into the ditch' [Matthew 15:14]. When this military leader was about to die, he told the Táborites who had come to ask him whom they should elect in his place: 'When the soul has departed from me, skin my corpse and give the flesh to the birds.

---

[24] Aeneid, 6.496–7 in H. Rushton Fairclough, *Virgil: Ecologues, Georgics, Aeneid 1–6* [Loeb Classical Library, 63] (Cambridge, MA: Harvard University Press, 1999), p. 566.

With the skin make a drum which shall be your guide in battle. Wherever the Germans hear its sound they will lift up their legs and run away because of their fear of Žižka in the drum.'[25]

After his death some of the Táborites chose Prokop as captain while others maintained a fervent respect to his memory to the extent that they regarded no one worthy enough to succeed such a great leader. Declining to have a leader they took the name of Orphans since they did not have a father. These blind people considered this blindness deserving of veneration not only during his lifetime but also after his death and so followed it all the way to hell. So, he is considered by the Táborites as their god and while they eschew pictures and sacred paintings they venerate religiously his image giving to Žižka the honour they deny Christ.

Their sect is deadly, detestable and deserves the maximum punishment. They do not believe that the Roman Church is supreme nor that any of its clergy are. They destroy images of Christ and of the saints and suggest doubt about the fire of purgatory. They affirm that the prayers of the saints who rule with Christ are not necessary for living people. They have no holidays except Sunday and Easter Day. They scorn fasting and do not accept the canonical hours. They administer the Eucharist under the forms of bread and wine even to children and the insane.

The celebrants during the consecration of the sacrament do not pronounce any other words save those of the 'our father' and those of the rite of consecration. They neither change their clothes nor wear vestments. Some of them, in their folly, affirm the Mass is but a representation following in the error of Berengar.[26]

With respect to the ecclesiastical sacraments they accept only baptism, the Eucharist, marriage, and ordination. They accept the sacrament of penance only partially and reject all together confirmation and extreme unction. They are exceedingly hostile to monasticism affirming that the monastic rules are inventions of the Devil. They do not bless the water when they desire to baptise a simple person, they have no consecrated cemeteries but bury the bodies of the dead in fields with animals. In reality this is appropriate for people such as them. They consider prayers for the dead useless. They deride the consecration of churches and celebrate the sacrament anywhere at all without distinction.

They pay most attention to hearing sermons. During the preaching if someone is negligent and remains at home or is otherwise preoccupied with business or pleasure, that individual is beaten and forced to go and listen to the 'word of God', as they call it. They have a type of wooden building similar to a granary which they refer to as a temple. Here they preach to the people and daily explain the Law

---

[25] Probably a version of a folk tale, told again with some variation in the *Historia Bohemica*, chapter 44, p. 138. See doc.106.

[26] French theologian from Tours (*c*.1000–1088) who opposed the eucharistic theology of Paschasius Radbertus whose doctrine had strong affinities to transubstantiation.

[of God]. They have an unconsecrated altar, which they say need not be consecrated, from which they show the sacrament to the people.

Their priests do not have a tonsure nor do they shave. Their houses are supplied through the Táborite community with grain, beer, bacon-fat, vegetables, wood and other necessary items. Additionally they receive from the members every month about sixty groschen with which they can buy fish, fresh meat and, if they so desire, wine. They do not offer anything on the altar, they condemn tithing and first fruits, of which they retain neither the name nor the meaning. At any rate not all of them agree on the same faith, some follow one, while others another. Everyone then follows their own will since there is no common will.

Emperor Sigismund granted to these sacrilegious and wicked people this town and made them free [see doc.200]. He was satisfied to receive from them a small tax. However, they deserve to be exterminated or confined in quarries away from the human race and made to dig and break stone. Sigismund committed an extremely dishonourable act in this respect not only towards himself but also towards his entire kingdom. In fact, now, a small quantity of yeast corrupts the entire mixture so this human scum contaminates the name of all the people in Bohemia. . . . They have numerous war machines taken from their vanquished foes and conquered towns. They show them in the square for the purpose of striking terror into the neighbouring people. . . . They have. . . . great riches being the collected booty of their military expeditions. . . . When they did not find any more plunder, they invaded the estates of the nobility as well as monasteries. Later on Sigismund granted them ownership of those possessions for life. I do not know if he contravened divine law or human law more in this. . . .[27]

FRA II, vol. 68: 23-7.

---

[27] Aeneas travelled to Bohemia to attend the national diet to report to the Czech Estates that Emperor Frederick III was prepared to keep the heir to the throne, the eleven year old Ladislav, in Vienna. There are three relevant sources. Kaminsky, 'Pius Aeneas among the Táborites' Church History 28 (1959), pp. 281-309, Hans Rothe, 'Enea Silvio de Piccolomini uber Böhmen', in Studien zum Humanismus in den Böhmischen Lander, eds., Hans Rothe and Hans-Bernd Harder (Cologne: Böhlau Verlag, 1988), pp. 141-56 and František Šmahel, 'Enea Silvio Piccolomini and his Historia Bohemica', in Historia Bohemica, pp. liii-xcvii.

Select Bibliography

Primary Sources

Bartoš, František M., ed. *Listy Bratra Jana a Kronika velmi pěkná a Janu Žižkovi.* (Prague: Blahoslav, 1949).

Codex Diplomaticus Lubecensis, part 1. In *Urkunden-Buch der Stadt Lübeck*, vol. 6. (Lübeck: Ferdinand Grautoff, 1885).

Goll, Jaroslav, ed. *Fontes rerum bohemicarum*, vol 5. (Prague: Nákladem nadání Františka Palackého,1893).

Grünhagen, Colmar, ed. 'Geschichtsquellen der Hussitenkriege [1420–37]'. In *Scriptores rerum Silesicarum*, vol. 6. (Breslau: Josef Max & Co., 1871).

Hall, Bert S. *The Technological Illustrations of the so-called 'Anonymous of the Hussite Wars'.* (Wiesbaden: Reichert, 1979).

Hardt, Hermann von der, ed. *Magnum oecumenicum constantiense concilium*, 6 vols. (Frankfurt and Leipzig: C. Genschii, Helmestadi, 1697–1700).

Hartlieb, Johannes. *Liber de arte bellica germanicus.* Vienna, Österreichische Nationalbibliothek MS 3062 fols. 27^r-240^r.

Havránek, Bohuslav, Hrabák, Josef and Daňhelka, Jiří eds. *Výbor z české literatury doby husitské*, 2 vols. (Prague: Československá akademie věd, 1963–4).

Hegel, Karl, ed. 'Die Magdeburger Schöppenchronik'. In *Die Chroniken der deutschen Städt*, vol. 7. (Leipzig: Hirzel, 1869).

Hirsch, Theodor, Töppen, Max, Strehlke, Ernst, et al., eds. *Scriptores rerum Prussicarum*, 6 vols. (Leipzig: Hirzel, 1861–74).

Höfler, Konstantin von, ed.'Geschichtschreiber der Husitischen Bewegung in Böhmen', 3 vols. In *Fontes rerum austriacarum*, vol. 1, parts 2,6,7. (New York: Johnson Reprint Co., 1969–70).

Housley, Norman. *Documents on the Later Crusades, 1274–1380.* (New York: St Martin's Press, 1996).

Kerler, Dietrich, ed. *Deutsche Reichstagsakten*, vols. 8–9. (Gotha: Friedrich Andreas Perthes, 1883, 1887).

Liliencron, Rochus von, ed. *Die historischen Volkslieder der Deutschen vom 13. bis 16. Jahrhundert,* 2 vols. (Hildesheim: Georg Olms Verlagsbuchhandlung, 1966).

Loserth, Johann, ed. Ludolf of Żagan, 'Tractatus de longevo schismate'. In *Archiv für österreichische Geschichte*, vol. 60. (Vienna: Carl Gerold's Solin, 1880), pp. 402–561.

Martínková, Dana, Hadravová, Alena and Matl, Jiří, eds. *Aeneae Silvii Historia Bohemica.* [Fontes rerum Regni Bohemiae, vol. 1]. (Prague: Koniasch Latin Press, 1998).

Molnár, Amedeo, ed. *Husitské manifesty.* (Prague: Odeon, 1986).

Nejedlý, Zdeněk. *Dějiny husitského zpěvu*, 6 vols. (Prague: Československá akademie věd, 1954–6).

Neumann, Augustin, ed. 'Francouzská Hussitica'. In *Studie a texty k náboženským dějinám Českým* 3 (Olomouc, 1923), pp. 11–151.

Nicolas, Harris, ed. *Proceedings and Ordinances of the Privy Council of England*, vol. 3. (London, 1834).

Palacký, František, ed. 'Staři letopisové češti od r. 1378 do 1527'. In *Scriptores rerum bohemicarum*, vol. 3. (Prague: J.S.P, 1829).

_____. *Archiv český čili staré písemné památky české i moravské*, vols. 1–6. (Prague: Kronberg and Riwnáče, 1840–72).

_____ and Birk Ernest, eds. *Monumenta conciliorum generalium seculi Decimi Quinti*, vols. 1–2. (Vienna: C.R. Officinae typographicae, 1857–73).

_____. *Documenta Mag. Joannis Hus vitam, doctrinam, causam in constantiensi concilio actam et controversias de religione in Bohemia annis 1403–1418 motas illustrantia*. (Prague: Friedrich Tempsky, 1869).

_____. *Urkundliche Beiträge zur Geschichte des Hussitenkrieges*, 2 vols. (Prague: Tempsky, 1873).

Przeździecki, Alexander, ed. Jan Długosz. 'Historia Polonicae'. In *Opera Omnia*, vol. 13. (Kraków: Kirchmayer, 1877).

Rynešová, Blažena and Pelikán, Jan, eds. *Listináře Listář Oldřicha z Rožmberku*, 4 vols. (Prague: Ministerstva školství a národní osvěty tiskem státní tiskáry, 1929–54).

Siegl, Karl, 'Briefe und Urkunden zur Geschichte der Hussitenkriege aus dem Egerer Stadtarchive'. *Zeitschrift des Deutschen Vereins für die Geschichte Mährens und Schlesiens*. Vol. 22 (1918), pp. 15–58, 167–196 and Vol. 23 (1919), pp. 1–38.

Tanner, Norman P., ed. *Decrees of the ecumenical councils*, 2 vols. (London and Washington, DC: Sheed & Ward and Georgetown University Press, 1990).

Twemlow, J.A., ed. *Calendar of Entries in the Papal Registers*, vol. 7. (London: Mackie & Co., Ltd., 1906).

Vavřinec of Březová. 'Historia Hussitica'. In Jaroslav Goll, ed. *Fontes rerum bohemicarum*, vol. 5. (Prague: Nákladem nadání Františka Palackého, 1893), pp. 329–541.

Wagner, Eduard, Drobná, Zoroslava and Durdík, Jan. *Medieval Costume, Armour and Weapons*, Jean Layton (trans). (London: Andrew Dakers, 1957).

Windecke, Eberhart. *Denkwürdigkeiten zur Geschichte des Zeitalters Kaiser Sigmunds*, ed., Wilhelm Altmann. (Berlin: R. Gaertners Verlagsbuchhandlung, 1893).

_____. *Geschichte Kaiser Sigismunds*. Vienna, Österreichische Nationalbibliothek MS 13.975. fols. 155^r–430^i.

Secondary Sources

Bailey, Michael David. 'Heresy, Witchcraft, and Reform: Johannes Nider and the Religious World of the Late Middle Ages.' (Unpublished PhD dissertation, Northwestern University, 1998).

Bartoš, František M. 'An English Cardinal and the Hussite Revolution'. *Communio Viatorum* vol. 6 (1963), pp. 47–54.
_____. *The Hussite Revolution 1424–1437*. John Klassen, ed. (New York: Columbia University Press, 1986).
Blind Courage: The unique genius of Jan Žižka, [documentary film]. (Redding, CA: Cartesian Coordinates, 1999).
Christianson, Gerald. *Cesarini: The Conciliar Cardinal – The Basel Years, 1431–1438*. (St Ottilien: EOS Verlag, 1979).
Fudge, Thomas A. 'The state of Hussite historiography'. *Mediaevistik: Internationale Zeitschrift für interdisziplinäre Mittelalterforschung* vol. 7 (1994), pp. 93–117.
_____. *The Magnificent Ride: The First Reformation in Hussite Bohemia*. (Aldershot: Ashgate, 1998).
_____. '"More glory than blood": Murder and martyrdom in the Hussite crusades'. In *BRRP*, vol. 5. (Prague: Academy of Sciences of the Czech Republic, forthcoming).
_____. 'Žižka's Drum: The political uses of popular religion', forthcoming.
Hall, Bert S. *Weapons and Warfare in Renaissance Europe*. (Baltimore: Johns Hopkins University Press, 1997).
Heymann, Frederick G. 'The national assembly of Čáslav', *Medievalia et Humanistica* vol. 8 (1954), pp. 32–55.
_____. 'The role of the towns in the Bohemia of the later Middle Ages'. *Cahiers d'Histoire Mondiale* vol. 2 (1954), pp. 326–46.
_____. 'City Rebellions in 15th century Bohemia and their ideological and sociological background'. *Slavonic and East European Review* vol. 40 (1962), pp. 324–40.
_____. *John Žižka and the Hussite Revolution*. (New York: Russell & Russell, 1969).
_____. 'The Crusades against the Hussites', in Harry W. Hazard, ed. *A History of the Crusades*, vol. 3. (Madison: University of Wisconsin Press, 1975), pp. 586–646.
_____. 'The role of the Bohemian cities during and after the Hussite Revolution', in Béla K. Király, ed. *Tolerance and Movements of Religious Dissent in Eastern Europe*. (New York: Columbia University Press, 1975), pp. 27–41.
Holmes, G.A. 'Cardinal Beaufort and the Crusade against the Hussites'. *English Historical Review* vol. 88 (1973), pp. 721–50.
Housley, Norman. 'Explaining Defeat: Andrew of Regensburg and the Hussite Crusades'. In Michel Balard, Benjamin Z. Kedar and Jonathan Riley-Smith, eds. *Dei gesta per Francos: Etudes sur les croisades dédiées à Jean Richard*. (Aldershot: Ashgate, 2001), pp. 87–95.
Hruza, Karel. 'Schrift und Rebellion: Die hussitischen Manifeste aus Prag von 1415–1431.' In František Šmahel, *Geist, Gesellschaft, Kirche im 13.–16. Jarhrhundert*. (Prague: Centre for Medieval Studies, 1999), pp. 81–108.
Jacob, E.F. 'The Bohemians at the Council of Basel, 1433'. In R.W. Seton-Watson, ed., *Prague Essays*. (Oxford: Clarendon Press, 1949), pp. 81-123.
Kaminsky, Howard. 'The Prague insurrection of 30 July 1419'. *Medievalia et Humanistica* vol. 17 (1966), pp. 106-26.
_____. *A History of the Hussite Revolution*. (Berkeley: University of California Press, 1967).

Klassen, John M. *The Nobility and the making of the Hussite revolution.* (Boulder: East European Monographs, 1978).

_____. *Warring Maidens, captive wives and Hussite queens: Women and men at war and at peace in fifteenth century Bohemia.* (Boulder: East European Monographs, 1999).

Lacaze, Yvon. 'Philippe le Bon et le problème hussite: Un projet de croisade bourguignon en 1428–1419'. *Revue historique* vol. 241 (1969), pp. 69–98.

Lützow, Franz. *The Hussite Wars.* (London: J.M. Dent and Sons, 1914).

Macek, Josef. *Husité na Baltu a ve Velkopolsku.* (Prague: Rovnost, 1952).

_____. *The Hussite movement in Bohemia.* Vilém Fried and Ian Milner (trans). (London: Lawrence and Wishart, 1965).

Magosci, Paul Robert. *Historical Atlas of East Central Europe.* (Seattle: University of Washington Press, 1993).

Petrin, Silvia. *Der österreichische Hussitenkrieg 1420–1434.* (Vienna: Österreichischer Bundesverlag, 1982).

Polívka, Miloslav. 'The idea of peace in the Hussite movement'. In Jaroslav Purš, ed., *Jointly in the struggle for peace against war.* (Prague: Institute of Czechoslovak and World History of the Czechoslovak Academy of Sciences, 1984), pp. 31–46.

_____. 'La transformation de l'armée populaire pendant la révolution hussite dans les armées 1419–1434', unpublished paper, 1984.

Rychterová, Pavlína. 'Frauen und Krieg in Chroniken über die Hussitenkriege.' In František Šmahel, *Geist, Gesellschaft, Kirche im 13.–16. Jarhrhundert.* (Prague: Centre for Medieval Studies, 1999), pp. 127–143.

Schlesinger, Gerhard. *Die Hussiten in Franken: Der Hussiteneinfall unter Prokop dem Großen im Winter 1429/30, seine Auswirkungen sowie sein Niederschlag in der Geschichtschreibung.* (Kulmbach: Stadtarchiv, Freunde der Plassenburg, 1974).

Šmahel, František. *Husitská revoluce,* 4 vols. (Prague: Historický ústav, 1993). German edition, *Hussitische Revolution* (2002).

Stöller, Ferdinand. 'Österreich im Kriege gegen die Hussiten (1420–1436).' *Jahrbuch für Landeskunde von Niederösterreich* vol. 22 (1929), pp. 1–87.

Theobald, Zacharias. *Hussitenkrieg.* (Hildesheim: Georg Olms Verlag, 1609/1981).

Zeman, Jarold K. *The Hussite Movement: A Bibliographical Study Guide.* (Ann Arbor: University of Michigan, 1977).

Index

There are no general or comprehensive entries for Bohemia, Hussites, Prague, Tábor or the crusade in general as these are too many to list. Likewise, on the grounds of relevance, there are no comprehensive entries for obscure names of individuals appearing in lists of attendees at meetings or those named as being killed in pitched battles. Entries for heresy, Sigismund, Táborites and topics relating to the eucharist are selective inasmuch as these are very numerous. The names of medieval people are normally listed under their places of origin. The names of specific churches, monasteries and convents are listed in alphabetical order under the headings 'churches' and 'religious houses.' Unless otherwise noted, the listed churches are located in the immediate vicinity of Prague. Czech names are given in the Czech form with the single and notable exception of Prague. The use of abbreviations has been avoided.

Albrecht, Bishop of Bamberg 109, 111, 224
Albrecht, Duke of Austria 137, 151, 186, 256, 264, 313, 319, 358, 385
Annalists, Old Czech 12, *see* historiography
Antichrist 8, 25, 43, 66, 70, 102, 123, 295, 339, 379
  pope as 19
Anticlericalism *passim*
Apocalyptic 8, 32–3
Aquileia, Patriarch of 74
Arc, Joan of 10, 284–5
Archers 78, 242, 254, 268, 269, 272, *see also* troops
Armour, *see* weapons and armour
Arnoštovice, Priest Václav of 76
Arnoštovice, town of 76
Arundel, Thomas (†1414), Archbishop of Canterbury 259
Atrocities of the crusades 128–9, 139, 141, 142, 145, 155, 200, 211, 315, 318, 329, 351, 361, *see also* blood, mass destruction, murder, rape
Augustine, St 35, 294, 355, 381, 382, *see also* authorities
Austria 45, 72, 75, 103, 137, 196, 278, 331, 333, 389
Authorities 2, 10–11, 61
  patristic medieval 61, 294, 352, 370
see also St Augustine, canon law, Chrysostom, and Jerome

Baltic Sea 9, 190, 359, 360
Bamberg 45, 210, 280, 282
Banners 4, 30, 40, 79, 147, 156, 157, 158, 159, 169, 180, 190, 205, 208, 230–1, 235–7, 300, 302, 321, 328
Banská Bystrica, town of 115
Bartoš, František M. 12
Basel, Council of 5, 7, 9, 124, 296, 314, 333, 341, 348, 350–1, 359, 372, 385, 387, 397
Bayreuth, city of 238, 280
Beaufort, Henry 7, 9, 225–7, 230–1, 234, 240, 241–2, 243, 244–6, 249, 251–5, 268, 275–8, 284
  abandons the field 230
  advises Lübeck of crusade 241–2
  curses the crusaders 232
  Hanseatic League and 277–8
  Joan of Arc and 284
  petitions English Privy Council 251–3
  Privy Council replies to 275–6
  reputation of 268
  Sigismund encourages 244–6
  uses different tactics 225–7
Beheimstein, castle of 279
Bělá, town of 115
Belgrade 245
Bělobožka 97
Benešov, town of 26, 39
Beroun, town of 89, 91, 115, 187, 314
Besançon 174, 228

Bible 9, 28, 32, 63, 68, 76, 86, 118, 127, 135, 192, 286, 309
  as authority 2, 63, 70, 84, 339, 370
Bílina, Jakoubek of 199, 200, 231
Bílina, town of 115, 130
Bitschin, Conrad 361
Blood and bloodshed 9, 35, 59, 71, 72, 76, 93, 127, 139, 144, 147, 155, 181, 200, 201, 204, 211, 224, 226, 263, 264, 267, 304, 324, 326, 329, 330, 351, 354, 361, 366, 372, 376, 380, 381, 382, 383, 399
Bohemian Diet 9, 26–9, 86, 117–21, 192, 353, 384–5, 401
Bohemian Forest 128, 227–8, 311–12, 313, 317, 318, 319, 321–2
Boskovice, town of 182
Bracciolini, Poggio 397
Branda, see Castiglione, Branda of
Brandenburg, Friedrich of 7, 52–3, 156, 158, 159, 160, 224–5, 230–1, 237, 238–41, 267, 280, 300, 309, 312–13, 315, 322, 323, 327, 331, 332, 358
  disagrees with crusade 228, 239
  efforts to galvanize crusaders 158
  frustration of 237, 240, 300–1
  illness 301, 388
  meets with Hussites 279, 280
  opposes crusade 52–3
  refuses to go to Stříbro 228
  relation to Sigismund 264–6
  reports to Sigismund 238–41
  role in fifth crusade 322
  supreme commander of crusade 157, 300, 331
  tactics of 240–1, 301, 323, 327
Brandenburg, Margraviate of 61–2, 71
Branković, Djuradj 245
Bratislava 6, 9, 256, 262, 305, 351
Breslau, see Wrocław
Březnice, town of 29
Březová, Vavřinec of 11–12, 14, 41, 74, 75, 126, 141, 218, 320, see also historiography
Brno, city of 115, 134, 137, 148, 149, 184, 265, 266, 385
Brod, Ondřej of 73
Brumov, town of 134
Bruska 74
Buchov, Zbyněk of 40, 97, 98, 117, 119, 153
Buda, city of 178

Budyšín, town of 42, 54, 57, 114, see also six towns
Bulls 5, 6, 7, 8, 10, 27, 59, 270, 322
Bystřice, town of 76
Bzdinka, see Vícemilice, Jan Hvězda
Bzí Hora 25–6

cannon 31, 36, 125, 129, 146, 156, 166, 200, 222–3, 231, 263, 312, 318, 322, 325, 334, 373, 374, see also weapons and armour, and war wagons
Canon law 382
Čapek, Jan 7, 66, 78, 80, 181, 360
Carvajal, Juan 398
Čáslav, town of 89, 115, 116–17, 140, 145, 153, 167, 182, 187, 192, 376
  Diet of (1421) 9, 86, 117–21, 353
Castiglione, Branda of 7, 106, 156, 173, 174, 175–7, 196
Castles and fortresses 29, 53, 86, 96–7, 105, 107, 155, 168, 193, 279, 310, 348, 359, 385
Častolovice, Půta 103, 133, 139, 167, 179, 256, 267
Cathars 3, 193
Catherine, Princess of Meißen 201, 206–7
Cavalry 39, 88, 122, 124–6, 131, 140, 180, 231, 263, 278, 312, 313, 317, 325, 335, 337–8, 373, 390, see also troops
Cerretano, Jacob 251
Cesarini, Giuliano 5, 7, 296–300, 303–4, 316, 319, 322, 325–6, 331, 332, 341, 344–5
Česká Lípa, town of 115
České Budějovice, town of 76, 100, 265, 278, 333
Český Brod, town of 115, 142, 187, 191, 256, 373, 375
Chalice 1, 2, 16, 40, 74, 76, 79, 154, see also eucharist and utraquism
  banned by Council of Constance 2–3, 4, 69
  defended by barons 4
  heresy and 74, 399
  King Václav IV and 27
  lack of lay observation 1–2
  on banners, clothes and weapons 79, 154, 399
  persecution on account of 40–1, 55, 56, 74, 76–7
  symbol of Hussite cause 2, 74, 79, 154, 399
Chalice, Žižka's fort 124, 130, 165, 166, 399

Charles IV, Emperor 1, 15, 53, 61, 71, 183, 190
Charlier, Gilles 356
Cheb Judge 344–6
Cheb, town of 124, 128, 130, 212, 219, 224, 304, 317, 340, 390, 391
Chelčice, town of 76
Chelčický, Petr 7, 9, 85, 379
Children 23, 24, 26, 33, 34, 37, 39, 47, 72, 76, 78, 80–2, 96, 104, 105, 139, 142, 145, 161, 167–8, 179, 199, 206, 225, 247, 288, 318, 339, 351, 367, 400
  among the armies 37, 39, 124
  as martyrs 76, 79
  illegitimate of priests 291–2
  in danger from crusaders 72, 121, 128, 139, 145
  murdered by crusaders 93, 202
  praying 78
  receive communion 167, 400
  singing 78, 80–2
  spared by Žižka 95, 96
  taxed for crusade funding 247
Chlum, Jan of 56, 117
Chojnice, fortress of 359–60, 367–8
Chomútov, town of 115, 130, 187
Chotěboř, town of 103–4
Chotěmice, Janek of 40
Chotěšov, town of 187, 314
Chrudim, town of 103, 133, 187
Chrysostom, John St 24, 294
Churches
  Bethlehem Chapel 2, 85, 382
  of the Holy Ghost (Hradec Králové) 182
  Our Lady at Botiče 39
  Our Lady before Týn 20, 213, 216, 320
  Our Lady of the Snows 3, 21
  St Adalbert 2
  St Ann (Hradec Králové) 167
  St Apollinaris 28
  St Gothard (Hořice) 166
  St John (Kutná Hora) 138
  St Martin-in-the-Wall 2
  St Martin (Kutná Hora) 41
  St Michael 2, 78, 217
  St Nicholas 214–15
  St Pankrac 89–92
  St Peter 215
  St Peter and St Paul (Čáslav) 182
  St Sebald (Nürnberg) 156, 300

St Stephen 184
St Valentine 74
St Vitus 82
Chvalkovice, Jiřík 64
Cologne, Dietrich of 105, 107, 109, 111, 112, 223
Common chests 38
Compactata of Basel 368–72
Conrad, Archbishop of Mainz 105, 107, 109, 111, 112, 223
Constance, Council of 2, 4, 5, 8, 14, 40, 45, 47, 59, 62, 70, 136, 172, 197, 250, 257, 299, 340, 355
  and Hus 40, 45, 47, 62, 172
  and Sigismund 62
  and utraquism 2, 40, 69
  and Wyclif 46
  resolutions against Hussites 2, 17–20
Counter-crusades 5, 333–5
Crime 16, 86, 105, 170, 285, 360, 396
Crusade rhetoric and ideology 8, 49–52, 59, 326–7, 366–7
Crusades against the Hussites
  Fifth 314–17
  First 5, 74–80
  Fourth 230–8
  Second 5, 129–32
  Third 155–6
Czech language 28, 59–60, 61, 63, 70, 72, 93–4, 118, 318

Dalmatia 51, 73
Defenestration of Prague (1419) 3, 6, 8, 126, 184, 382
Devil 4, 45, 56, 85–6, 113, 115, 175, 183, 209, 218, 226, 232, 286, 379, 400
Diplomacy 5, 6, 7, 9, 69–73, 79, 176, 196–8, 243, 264–6, 296, 389
Diváček, mint master at Kutná Hora 55
Długosz, Jan 142, 144, 196
Domažlice, town of 5, 6, 9, 29, 115, 133, 262, 280, 314, 319, 325, 346
Dominici, Jan 7, 21, 45
Donínsky, Václav 40
Dorpat, see Tartu
Dragon, Order of 56, 60
Drahonice, Bartošek of 313, 372
Dubá, Václav of 39, 53, 56
Dubrovník, Jan Stojković of 296–300, 341, 345
Dvůr Králové, town of 115, 168, 187, 376

Ecclesiastical corruption 4, 22, 26, 27, 86, *see also* simony
Economic blockade of Bohemia 7, 171–3
Eggenburg, Castle of (Austria) 264
Elsterburk, Jindřich of 53, 101
England 198, 218, 250, 275–6, 278
Erik, Scandinavian king 174
Eschatology 8, 246
Eucharist 1, 19, 22, 36, 385–7
  and children 400
  and reform, revolt 1, 3
  Hussite practice of 103
  lay participation in 1
  necessary for salvation 369
Eugenius IV, Pope 300, 346–7, 357
Excommunication 5, 19, 113, 136, 177, 203, 249, 288, 290, 326, 367
Execution of heretics 40–1, 61, 63, 72, 95, 103–4, 392, 393–7
Expulsion of Catholic priests 4, 15, 18, 33
Ezstergom, town of 192, 256

Fear 31, 78, 84, 85, 89, 92, 100, 103, 104, 105, 121, 135, 144, 152, 186, 194, 203, 218, 231, 235, 240, 247, 279, 261, 299, 303–4, 316, 317, 318, 346–7, 376, 400
Fictum, Boso of 207–8, 209
Fidei catholicae fundamento 174–5
Filippo Scolari, Count of Ozoro (Florentine condottiere), *see* Spano, Pipo
Fire, death by 21, 72, 76, 79, 82, 83, 95–6, 102–3, 103–4, 104–5, 129, 139, 159, 166, 182, 318, 361
  uses of 38, 39, 76, 82, 88–9, 101, 114, 131, 139, 143, 144, 149, 156, 186, 231, 278, 281, 321, 324, 336, 351, 360, 361, 399
Fleming, Richard, Bishop of Lincoln 250
Food 75, 88, 123, 124, 125, 138, 141, 172, 176, 186, 209, 220, 220–1, 290, 315, 316, 322, 349
Foot soldiers 92, 122, 124–6, 131, 166, 180, 231, 263, 312, 325, 334, 337–8, 373, 390, *see also* troops
Force, use of 16, 33–6, 58, 91, 257
  university masters ruling on 33–6
Four Articles of Prague 4, 8, 72, 80, 83, 98, 99, 101, 115, 116, 118, 133, 135, 137, 167–8, 184, 285, 293, 308, 309, 351, 369–71, 377, 379, 384

basis for Hussite military action 4, 68, 80, 99, 101, 133, 135, 285, 293, 294, 379
common denominator in Hussitism 115, 116, 135, 285, 377, 379
discussed at Council of Basel 345, 346
nobility and 137, 184–5
relation to salvation 120, 351
sent to the crusaders 80
Sigismund and 135–6
summary of Hussite theology 4, 8, 83–4, 99, 285, 294–5, 377
France 3, 198, 278
Frankfurt am Main 150, 228, 244, 317, 332
Funding for the crusades 8, 56–7, 158, 174, 247, 248 50, 272

Garbów, Black Záwiš of 142–5, 189
Gdańsk, city of 190, 359, 360
Georgii, Duke of Smolensk (Russia) 88
German bishops, League of 105–13
Germans 27, 41, 45, 59, 60, 72, 82, 93, 104, 123, 130, 142, 184, 186, 188, 198, 203–4, 279, 359, 384
  conflict with Czechs 27, 41, 58, 60, 79, 82, 130, 142, 184, 185, 186, 384
  crusade and 4, 52, 58, 75, 93, 129–31, 143, 146, 166, 188, 279–80, 297
  defeat at Ústí 198–207
  mercenaries 359
  protected by Sigismund 93
  Sigismund ruler of 21, 72
  vilified by Pipo Spano 142
  won the battle at Most 122–3, 364
Gerson, Jean 351
Greeks 70, 305
Grimma, town of 278, 279, 281
guerilla warfare 159, 194

Habry, town of 137, 145, 146, 188
Hans, Duke of Bavaria 71
Hanseatic League 277–8
Haselbach, Thomas Ebendorfer of 82
Heinrich, Duke of Glogów 115
Heresy and heretics 3, 4, 6, 15, 68–9, 83, 136, 152, 392, 399, *see also* plague, heresy as
  and utraquism 61, 74, 75, 135, 184, 185, 385
  Archbishop of Prague embraces 113–14
  as category of abuse 75, 79, 83, 93, 286, 360, 362
  at Basel 5, 341–4, 350–1

concessions to 5, 368–72, 385–7
converts to 196
Council of Constance and 15, 62, 70, 94, 172
crusade directed at 3, 20, 42, 103, 139, 195,
    210–13, 271, 296–300, 315, 317, 356–8
endemic in Bohemia 16, 18, 45–6, 48, 68–9,
    105, 107, 109, 249, 250, 268, 332, 368
growth of in Bohemia 4, 6, 37, 48, 105, 224,
    242, 249, 250, 262, 304, 332
Hus and 3, 19, 49, 136, 183
iconography of 41
Lateran Council's ruling on 46
leaders of 19, 49, 136
Polish support for 149, 304, 306
resolutions against 8, 17–20, 45–9, 49–52
result of reform efforts 1, 2, 4, 101
Sigismund's attitude towards 50, 53–4, 57–8,
    71, 82, 93, 114–15, 134, 262–3, 332
Sigismund as a heretic 65, 83, 101, 138, 397
social implications of 3, 38, 152, 171–3,
    175, 198
songs about 19
subject to canonical sanctions 48, 49, 69,
    175–7
supported by Czech nobility 60–3
suppression of 2, 20, 21, 40–1, 42, 45–9, 71,
    76–7, 97, 103, 107–12, 139, 150, 151,
    173, 210–13, 220, 242, 271, 315
Hermann, suffragan Bishop of Prague 19, 80,
    96–7
Heštejn, Castle of 135
Historiography 11–13
Holštýn, Vok of 92
Horažd'ovice, town of 115, 153
Hořice, town of 165–7
Horky, town of 104
Horses 36, 37, 38, 40, 61, 73, 76, 82, 89, 125,
    145, 166, 178, 186, 200, 229–30, 240,
    256, 265, 329, 335, 394, 399
Horšovsky Týn, town of 314
Hospital Field 77, 180, 190
Hospital of our Lady of the Germans, see
    Teutonic Knights
Hradčany, see Prague Castle
Hradec Králové, town of 31, 53, 64, 91, 115,
    121, 137, 166, 182, 186, 190, 196, 334,
    389–90
Hradec, Ambrož of 7, 31, 64, 121, 173, 182,
    390
Hradec, Jindřich of 37

Hradec, Marek of 19
Hradec, Menhart of 374–5, 385
Hradiště 37, 39, 376
Hromádka, Jan 37, 103–4
Hrbovice, town of 200, 201
Hrzek 76
Humpolec, town of 134, 139
Hungary and Hungarians 72, 81, 91, 93, 102,
    115, 116, 135, 137, 142, 147, 185, 188,
    198, 226, 245, 331, 336–8, 379, 390, 391,
    see also Sigismund
among principal crusaders 72–3, 81, 91,
    137, 142, 143, 188, 279
army of 102–3, 135, 142, 146, 186, 188,
    267, 279
brutality of 137, 145
Hussites in 334–5, 336–8
mercenaries of 391
papal legate sent to 45
Sigismund protects 93
Hus, Jan 2–3, 4, 17, 18, 19–20, 27, 40, 41, 43,
    44, 45, 49, 56, 62, 71, 85, 117, 136, 183,
    204, 214, 256, 285, 286–7, 340, 379, 380,
    381
as heretic 2–3, 17, 18, 19, 20, 45, 46, 47, 49,
    75, 79, 136, 184–5, 286–7
as martyr 3, 41
charges against 10, 45, 48
death of 3, 14, 33, 40, 41, 62, 71, 136, 340
in iconography 3
in songs 3, 19
reformer 2
as saint 3, 20
sermons of 11, 85, 136, 184
Sigismund and 4, 62, 71
support for 4, 27
theology of 46
vilified 15, 46, 47, 49
Hus, Mikuláš of 31, 40, 89, 90, 92
Hussites
at Basel 6–7, 9, 341, 350–1
demonized 42, 149–50, 195, 197, 242, 361,
    367, 376, 390, 399–401
heresy of 1, 2, 8, 45, 113, 149, 155, 172,
    176, 242, 244, 268, 271
influence of 3, 346–7
term of opprobrium 2, 15, 57, 155, 184, 204,
    359, 362
theology of 85, 247, 285–94, 308–11, 339–40,
    378–9, see also Four Articles of Prague

Iconoclasm 33, 35, 57–8, 79, 95, 114, 184, 284, 356
Illness and disease 82, 89, 236
Imperial Diet, see Reichstag
Indulgences 49, 52, 131, 172, 185, 249, 270, 272, 286, 288, 339
  denounced by Hussites 59, 74, 286, 288, 289, 339
  plenary indulgences for crusaders 8, 49, 139, 172, 185, 248
Infant communion 2, 16
Infantry 39, 278, 313, 317, see also troops
Innocent III, Pope 103, 193
Inquisition and inquisitors 4, 10, 45, 355
Intelligence reports 7, 36–7, 317
Inter Cuntus 10, 45–9, 50, 172, see also bulls
Interdict 16, 113, 136
Iron, Jan the, see Železný, Jan
Iron Lords 37–8, 195
Isenburg, Heinrich of 78
Ivančice, town of 182, 333, 376

Janov, Matěj of 1
Jaroměř, town of 64, 115, 168, 376
Jawor, town of 114, 149, 350
Jemniště, Mikuláš of 88
Jerome, St 23
Jesenice, Jan of 16, 19
Jevišovice, town of 333
Jews 7, 10, 28, 38, 104–5, 146, 246–8
Jihlava, town of 134, 137, 139, 142, 167, 265, 368
Jílové, town of 30
Jindřichův Hradec, Oldřich Vavák of 86
Jindřichův Hradec, town of 86, 399
Jistebnice kancional 66
Johannes, Bishop of Würzburg 109–110, 211
Just war theory 35, 355

Kadaň, town of 115, 130, 239
Karlštejn Castle 88, 155, 189
Kavel Hill 89
Kingdom of God 1, 34, 85, 210, 291, 382
Kladruby 118, 187, 331
Klatovy, town of 29, 55, 80, 115, 153, 180
Klem 62
Klenové, Přibík of 372, 388, 389
Kněžov, town of 89
Knights of the Cross 167
Knights of St John, Order of 37

Knín, town of 29
Kölbshcim, Conrad of 321
Kolditz, Albrecht of 114
Kolín, town of 103, 115, 145, 187, 188, 375
Kolštejn, Hynek of 89
Konopiště, Castle of 180
Konopiště, Petr of 29–30
Koranda, Václav, of Plzeň 25, 29, 36, 78–9, 96–7, 187, 294, 385
Korybut, Zygmunt 122, 149, 153–4, 155, 164, 180, 182, 189, 196, 198, 199, 202, 203, 204, 213–14, 304, 306, 353
Kostelec-nad-Labem, town of 115, 177–8, 179, 189
Kouřim, town of 115, 140, 187, 191, 192, 375
Kozojedy, Castle of 166
Krajíř 100
Kraków, 45, 306, 340
Krása, Jan 37, 61, 71, 185
Krasikov, Castle of 134, 155, 187
Kroměříž, Jan Milíč of 1
Krumlov, town of 99, 333
Küchmeister, Michael 151
Kunratice (New Castle) 30, 31
Kunštat, Viktorin 89, 94, 117, 205
Kutná Hora, city of 9, 30, 40, 42, 55, 61, 86, 88, 89, 92, 103, 115, 117, 127, 133, 137, 142–3, 144, 145, 146, 147, 178–9, 187, 188, 190, 390
  battle of 137–41
  persecution of Hussites at 40, 41, 61, 103, 178–9
Kynžvart, town of 128

Labe River 103, 177, 179, 198
Laboun, Zdeněk of 19
Ládvím, town of 26
Languedoc 3
Last Judgement 328, 330
Lateran Councils 45–6, 48
Law of God 4, 25, 29, 36, 40, 41, 61, 64–5, 66, 83, 91, 94, 102, 118, 138, 152, 170, 218, 370, 371, 379–80, 400–1
  antichrist is opposed to 25
  basis of Hussite cause 25, 68, 118, 120, 123, 165, 166, 171, 184, 187, 199, 260, 307, 346, 370, 377, 379, 388
  crusade opposes 32
  defence against crusade according to 4, 26, 66, 84, 94, 123, 138, 139, 166, 171, 185

Four Articles of Prague is 83, 118
  Hussites persecuted because of 41, 95
  monks and priests opposed to 64
  secular law should honour 27, 353, 384
  Sigismund asked to defend 27, 29
  utraquism is 27
Ledeč, town of 134, 139
Lefl, Jindřich of 92
Legates, papal 6, 7, 9, 15, 19, 61, 62, 63, 68,
  70, 80, 106, 117, 135, 136, 138, 172, 174,
  175, 196, 198, 225, 229, 230, 241–2, 243,
  244, 249–50, 251, 253, 259, 263, 268,
  269, 270, 278, 284, 296, 297, 300, 303,
  314, 317, 322, 341, 344, 348, 359, 368,
  369, 372, 386, see also Beaufort, Branda,
  Cesarini, Dominici, Lucena, Ferdinand of
  and Železný, Jan
Lèsé majesté, see treason
Leštno, Václav of 40
Letovice, town of 182
Lichtenburk, Hynek Krušina of 88, 89, 90, 91,
  94, 117, 119, 121
Lichtenburk, Jan of 89, 94
Lípa, Mikuláš Trčka of 348
Lipany, Battle of 5, 191, 196, 214, 372, 373–6,
  389
Lipé, Hlaváč of 54
Lipnic Castle 80, 96–7
Litoměřice, town of 55, 115, 130, 167, 375,
  387
Litomyšl, town of 45, 115, 187
Liturgy 3, 7, 78, 156–8
Loket, town of 128
London 242
Louda, Matěj 385
Louny, town of 63, 105, 115, 180, 375
Lübeck 241–2
Lucena, Ferdinand of 7, 49, 61, 63, 68, 136
Ludwig, Count Palatine of the Rhine 105,
  107, 109, 111, 112, 223
Lupáč, Martin 214, 385
Lusatia 52, 54, 137, 199, 266, 280, 296, 313,
  333, 335, 359
Lužnice River 97, 98
Lužnice Valley 96

Machovice, Chval of Řepice and 37, 40, 98,
  100, 101, 117, 153
Mainz, Conrad of 105–19, 111, 112, 224
Makotřasy, town of 105

Malenice, Michael (called Čížek) 19
Maleňovice, Hynek of 92
Malešov, town of 179–80, 189
Malín, town of 72
Manifestos 8, 10–11, 25–6, 58–60, 60–3,
  69–73, 93–4, 210–13, 285–94, 308–11,
  339–40, 376–8
  anti-Hussite 210–13
  diplomatic 9
  Prague 58–60, 93–4
  Táborite 8, 100–1, 285–94, 376–8
Martin V, Pope 3, 7, 8, 17, 18, 20, 45–9,
  49–52, 136, 149, 151–3, 156, 158, 172,
  174–5, 225, 243, 250–1, 297, 300, 314, 346
  authorizes crusade 20, 49–52
  blesses crusader banner 156
  bulls and writings against Hussites 3, 8,
  45–9, 49–52, 151–3, 172, 174–5, 175–6,
  243, 250–1
  crusading bull of 49–52
  death of 300, 314
  orders taxation to fund crusade 158
  secret negotiations of 213
Martyrs and martyrdom 3, 16, 34, 76, 98, 106,
  109, 111, 127, 214, 330, 380
Mass 16, 27, 30, 74, 76, 97, 146–7, 190, 220,
  297, 398, 400
Mass destruction 95–6, 103–4, 104–5, 128,
  129, 137, 147, 351
Mašt'ov, town of 128–9, 239
Meißen 45, 59, 77, 122, 279, 363–5
  margraves of 42, 71, 73, 122, 154, 156, 186,
  187, 206
Mělník, town of 43, 89, 117, 177, 179
Memmingen 112, 163, 230
Mercenaries 30, 84, 86, 88–9, 128, 359
Městecký, Jan 103–4, 133
Mezilesí, town of 129
Meziříčí, town of 136
Mikuláš 'the butcher' 55
Mikuláš 'the fierce', Mint Master in Kutná
  Hora 103
Miletínek, Diviš Bořek of 155, 166, 373
Miličína, town of 75
Military Ordinances 7, 167–71, 219–23
Mint in Kutná Hora 86, 88, 103, 117, 140
Miracles 75, 178, 247
Mladá Boleslav, town of 115, 376
Mladoňovice, Petr of 213, 217
Mohelnice, town of 182

Mokrovousy, Beneš of 64, 168
Monasteries and convents, *see also* religious
    houses
  Břevnov 356
  Emmaus 38
  Holy Cross 75
  Kartouzy 356
  Kladruby 118, 187, 331
  Mother of God at the end of the Bridge 356
  Plasy 356
  Strahov 39, 356
  St Ambrose 40, 79, 356
  St Benedict 356
  St Catherine 356
  St Francis 356
  St Klement 356
  St Mary's on the Sand (Silesia) 278
  St Mary Magdalene 356
  St Nicholas 39
  St Thomas 39, 356
  Třebíč 182, 376
  Velehrad 102–3
  Zbraslav 184, 186, 187
Monstrances, public use of 40, 184, 190
  during battles 167
  in Hussite processions 40, 184
Moravia 19, 45, 62, 102–3, 115, 134, 137,
    152, 155, 177, 182, 193, 265, 333, 359,
    377, 384, 388, 394
Moravský Krumlov, town of 333
Most, town of 122–3, 129, 187, 364
Můcha, 'the fisherman' 187, 189
Murder 36, 40, 41, 55, 101, 103–4, 104–5,
    129, 137, 140–1, 185, 194, 339, 361, 380

Na Křížkach 26
Náchod, town of 53, 121, 165
Namysłow, town of 114, 148, 296, 347, 350
Nationalism 320
Nationalities in the First Crusade 74–5
Nebovidy, town of 137, 142, 146
Nedakunice, town of 102
Někmeř, Hynek of 32
Někmeř, town of 31
Německý Brod, town of 103, 137, 142, 144,
    164, 188
Nitra, town of 45, 334
Nobility 3–4, 31, 37, 48, 50, 60–3, 71, 79–80,
    89, 91, 93, 99, 107–8. 121, 130, 136, 140,
    153, 159, 183, 201–2, 340, 374, 375, 376

defend Hussites 4, 14, 26, 37, 60–3, 64, 86,
    102, 115, 118, 119, 121, 133, 134, 136,
    137–8, 170, 184, 186, 199, 207, 296, 307
  faithful to Sigismund 29, 72, 79–80, 90, 91,
    92, 98–9, 101, 103, 133, 134, 137, 166,
    178, 179, 256, 300, 376, 384, 391
Nürnberg 53, 128, 160, 174, 198, 199, 225,
    247, 248, 296, 314, 331, 344
Nymburk, town of 89, 115, 179, 187, 376

Odolem, prison guard 97
Okoř, town of 105
Olomouc, city of 45, 71, 102, 149, 265, 387,
    394
Omnium plasmatoris domini, *see* Martin V,
    Pope
Ondřej, Abbot at Třeboň 100
Opole, Bolek of 256
Orebites 115, 126, 144, 167, 168, *see also*
    Orphans
  and vestments 144
Orlík, Castle of 123
Orphans 9, 167, 182, 190, 195, 196, 198, 199,
    204, 231, 279, 282, 304, 331, 333–5, 336–
    8, 348, 359–62, 368, 372, 373, 374, 376,
    394, 400, *see also* Orebites
  and counter-crusades 279, 333–40, 359–68
  armies of 196, 198, 204, 231, 279, 282,
    374–6
  demonized 195
  hardships among 335
  occupied Tachov 241
  origin of their name 182, 190, 400
Orsini, Giordano 6, 7, 9, 196, 198
Ország, Michael 391, 395
Osek, Castle of 199
Ostrov, Lacek of 135
Ostroh, town of 135, 137
Otík, Táborite commander 335, 347–8
Ovenec, town of 74

Pacifism 9, 85–7, 320–1, 352, 379–84
Palacký, František 6, 12, 284
Palomar, Juan of 303, 341, 371, 372, 385
Papacy, *see also* Martin V, legates, bulls,
    indulgences
  backing for crusade 9, 74, 130–1, 174–5,
    248
  Hussites opposed to 99, 288, 318
Pardubice, Arnošt of 1

Pardubice, town of 64, 103
Passau 21, 45, 225, 346
Pavia-Siena, Council of 171, 175, 176, 299, 355
Payne, Peter 218, 256, 259–60, 262, 355, 371, 375, 385
Peasants, see vassals
Pelhřimov, Mikuláš of 9, 351, 378, 385
Philibert, Bishop of Coutances 385
Philip the Good, Duke of Burgundy 10, 256, 268–75, 282–4, 296, 303, 357
Pictures 144, 167, 355, 400
Pikarts (Adamites) 188, 247
Pilgrims and pilgrimages 29, 30
Pirkštejn, Hynek Ptáček of 385, 392, 395
Písek, town of 53, 55, 84, 98, 115, 153, 376
Pius II, Pope 368, see also Aeneas Sylvius
Plague 88, 190, see also illness and disease
  heresy as 46, 174, 244, 249, 250, 278, 307, 310
  Roháč as 390
Plassenburg, Castle of 238, 241
Plavno, Heinrich of 133–4, 207, 228, 233, 240, 266, 279, 326, 331, 360
Plumlov, Jindřich of 88, 91–2
Plundering 14, 78–9, 104, 122, 135, 165, 247, 281, 314, 319, 356
Plzeň Alliance 100–1, 133, 177, 196
Plzeň, Prokop of 213, 217, 385
Plzeň, town of 29, 31, 36, 37, 53, 55, 187, 189, 194, 231, 265, 314, 333, 372, 374
Poděbrady, Jiří of 385
Podlažice, town of 64
Poland 10, 45, 143, 149, 189, 215, 304, 306, 359–68
Polička, town of 115, 121, 137, 187
Poříčí, battle at 6, 39
Poznán, town of 45
Prachatice, Křišťan of 19, 213, 217, 376
Prachatice, town of 94–6, 115, 153
Prague, passim
  New Town of 14, 30, 31, 37, 38, 40, 55, 58, 60, 77, 89–90, 94, 117, 180, 189, 218, 304, 372, 375–6
    agreement reached with Vyšehrad 89
    attacked 372
    loyal to Hussites 115
    manifesto from 93–4
    radical tendencies in 21, 184, 375–6
    Sigismund flees from 90
  streets chained off 185
  Old Town of 20, 30, 55, 77, 125, 215, 217, 218, 356, 373
    captured banners displayed in 320
    conservatives in 217
    important meeting in 59
    radicals plunder 78
    streets chained off 185
    under siege 189
  Lesser Town of 30–1, 356
    besieged 30
    burned 30, 92
    monasteries destroyed in 39
    plundered 31, 92
Prague Castle 39, 60, 77, 80, 82, 86, 90, 92, 184, 187, 190, 320
Prague, Jerome of 3, 19–20, 27, 33, 40, 45, 46–9, 62, 71, 183, 285, 286–7, 340, 379
  as heretic 19, 20, 46, 47, 49, 287
  as martyr 3
  as saint 20
  death of 3, 33, 40, 71, 183–4, 340
  in iconography 3
  in songs 3, 19
Přelouč, town of 103
Přibenice, fortress of 96–7, 155
Přibram, Jan 120, 213, 217
Přibyslav, town of 115, 182, 183, 190
Priesthood 289–90
  abused by Hussites 16, 33, 35, 127, 262, 353, 361, 399
  ordination of Hussites to 4, 19, 80, 96–7
  regarded as evil 41, 43, 46, 59, 99, 127, 217, 288, 294
  relation to secular power 27, 83, 99, 118, 295
  supported Hussites 41, 56, 102, 184
Prisoners 73, 76–7, 82–3, 92, 96, 129, 131, 146, 231–2, 301–2, 335, 361, 374, 390
Prokop Holý 7, 190, 195–6, 198, 230, 256, 258, 259, 262, 278, 280, 281–2, 285, 294, 296, 333–5, 347, 350–1, 351–2, 372, 374, 375–6, 400
  among the warriors 7, 335, 347, 375
  as commander 190, 198, 278, 282, 314, 335, 347, 374, 400
  at Basel 350–1
  authority of 281–2
  correspondence of 372
  counter crusades and 333–5, 347

death of 196, 374–6
diplomacy and 256, 258, 259, 262
fifth crusade and 314
fourth crusade and 230–1
friend of Žižka 196
manifesto of 288–94
policies of 196, 278
rise to prominence 195–6
speeches of 351–2
Prokůpek 182, 190, 196, 279, 333–5, 372, 374, 376
Propaganda 7, 125–6, 284, 339
Prostředek, Martinék 390, 392, 393
Prussia 10, 59, 190, 359–68
Puchala, Dobeslav 306
Postupice, Vilém Kostka of 280, 385

Rabann, Bishop of Speyer 109
Rabí Castle 126, 187
Rabštejn, Prokop of 124, 399
Racziniski, Wyšek 393
Ragusio, John of, see Dubrovnik, Jan Stojković of
Rape 36, 63, 64, 137, 139, 145, 146, 188
Recruitment into armies 8, 84, 123–4
Reforms, ecclesiastical 1, 3, 15, 172, 257, 294, 309, 346, 371
    radicalism of 3
    Sigismund supports 15
    university masters support 4
Regensburg 45, 150–1, 171, 175, 195
Regensburg, Andreas of 158
Reichstag 9, 52, 106, 150, 171, 173, 201, 219, 239, 248, 300, 317
Rejnštejn, Jan Cardinal of 19
Relics 19
Religious houses, destruction of 33, 35, 39, 102, 114, 186, 187, 224, 278, 289, 356, 363, 365, 399, 401
Retz, Castle of (Lower Austria) 196
Revolution 1, passim
Rewards offered for arrest of heretics 40–1, 72, 127
Rhine 59
Roháč, Jan, of Dubá 7, 102, 168, 198, 375, 376–8, 390, 392–7, 398
Rokycana, Jan 213, 214, 216, 218, 351, 379, 392–3
Rokycana, Šimon of 19
Rokycana, town of 115, 385

Roman Church 3, 16, 20, 50–2, 58, 93, 136, 177, 353, 400
Rosenblütt, Hans 232–8, 322
Roudnice, town of 113, 114, 177
Roupov, Castle of 232
Rožmberk, Oldřich 7, 31, 61, 84, 94, 96–7, 98–9, 100, 102, 117, 119, 139, 178, 186, 192, 193–4, 197, 256, 311, 332–3, 375, 385, 388, 389, 390, 391
    at Čáslav 117, 118, 192
    court books of 194
    flees Prague 31
    key crusader ally 94, 98, 178, 186, 193–4, 197, 256, 311–12, 375, 390, 391
    opposes Sigismund 61, 192
    truce with Hussites 98–9, 388–9
    warned by Sigismund 192–3
Rusdorf, Paul of 150, 330
Russia 74, 88
Rýzmberk, Castle and family of 33, 314, 325, 332, 349

Salzburg 45, 223, 225, 248
Sány, Jan Čapek of 334–5, 348, 372, 375
Saxon House 31, 92
Saxony 32, 77, 90, 160, 163, 199, 208, 220, 236, 278
Sázava River 30, 39, 133, 146
Scandinavia 74
Schlink, Kaspar 124
Sermons, preaching 4, 7, 11, 19, 21–5, 29, 40, 56, 63, 64, 195, 272, 400
    Ambrož 64
    Koranda 29
    urging utraquism 40
    Želivský 21–4, 56
Sex, brothels and prostitution 28, 236, 291–2, 310
Sezimovo Ústí, town of 29, 37, 39, 185, 388
Sieges 159, 245, 264, 271, 301, 321, 346–7, 365
    Chojnice 359–62, 367–8
    Chomútov 104
    Chotěboř 103
    Chrudim 133
    Karlštejn Castle 155–6, 189
    Kladruby 187
    Krasikov Castle 134
    Most 122
    near Kostelec-nad-Labem 178

Německý Brod 142–4
Prague 72
Prague Castle 186
Plzeň 187, 372
Přibyslav 190
Rabí Castle 126, 187
Sión Castle 390–2, 395
Stříbro 243
Tachov 227, 230
Ústí-nad-Labem 198–9
Vožice Castle 196
Vyšehrad 88–90, 186
Žatec 129–31, 156, 188
Zbraslav Monastery 186–7
Siena, see Pavia-Siena, Council of
Sigismund 3, 5, 8, 9, 14–17, 31, 37, 52–4, 57,
    60–3, 65–6, 69, 70, 74–5, 78, 88, 94, 96,
    100, 101, 114, 122, 131,171,174, 177,
    181, 183–5, 195, 200, 207, 213, 214, 224,
    262–4, 284, 296, 297, 300, 307, 308, 319,
    330, 333, 334, 340, 344, 347, 361, 368,
    379, 392, 394, 401
    administrator of the crusade 50–2, 398
    at Vyšehrad 88–93
    atrocities of 37, 60–3, 93, 101, 135, 139
    coronation of 82, 83, 186, 353, 357
    Council of Constance and 14, 17, 41
    death of 5, 7, 397–8
    deception of 55–6, 63, 82, 93
    declines to bombard Prague 82
    demands made of 8, 26–9, 385–7
    diplomacy 6, 196–7, 201, 256–61, 264–6,
        309, 384
    his cannon 231
    in apocalyptic imagery 32, 56, 65–6
    injured 300
    key crusader 4, 6, 7, 20–1, 29, 31, 49, 52–4,
        70, 103, 121, 131, 137–42, 143–8, 151,
        156, 158, 177–8, 238–41, 266–7, 300
    letters of 9, 42, 52–4, 57–8, 121, 148–9,
        149–50, 158–60, 192–3, 244–6, 262–4,
        266–7, 300–2, 304–7, 311–13, 332–3,
        390, 391
    on the battle field 75–7, 88–93, 134, 135–6,
        137–42, 143–8, 376
    opposed by Czech barons 60–3
    prepared to crusade 42, 52–4
    rejected as king 9, 115, 116–19, 153, 390
    reluctant to invade Bohemia 14–17
    role in Hus' death 4, 41, 183

    swears obedience to Martin V 17
    view of heresy 4, 55, 57–8, 121, 262–4
    vilified 32, 65–6, 93–4, 100–1
Silesia 45, 52–3, 115, 121, 133, 137, 149,
    171, 265, 266, 278, 306, 333, 335, 347,
    359, 363
Simony and other abuses 23, 26–8, 44, 86,
    183, 289–90, see also ecclesiastical
    corruption
Šindel, Jan Ondřejův 124
Sins, punishment of 4, see also Four Articles
    of Prague
Sión, Castle of 341, 390, 391–4
Six Towns of Upper Lusatia 54, 114, 265
Škaredý pond 38
Slaný, town of 63, 105, 115, 130
Slovakia 115, 279
Soběšín, Aleš Krk 92
Soběslav, Jan Papoušek of 2, 124
Soběslav, town of 97
Songs 7, 11, 19, 43–4, 65–6, 66–8, 74, 78,
    80–2, 147–8, 200–7, 232–8, 287, 320–1,
    322–30, 367–8
    about Hus 19
    about Zbyněk 43–4
    as historical sources 147–8, 200–7, 214–19,
        367–8
    battle 66–8
    children and 78, 80–2
    political 65–6, 147–8
Spano, Pipo 39, 40, 135, 137, 142–5
Šróda Šląska, town of 114, 148, 347, 350
Štěkeň, town of 37
Štemberk, Petr of 92
Šternberk, Petr of 29, 40, 88, 92
Stöffel, Heinrich of 227–8, 229
Strachův Dvůr, town of 165–7
Strakonice, town of 37
Strasbourg 321
Strážnice, Bedřich of 103, 388, 389
Strážnice, Petr of 135, 137, 140
Strážnice, town of 102–3
Strážnice, Václav of 135, 137
Stříbro, Jakoubek of 2, 11, 19, 80, 85, 214,
    246, 354, 382, 383
Stříbro, town of 115, 230–2, 240
Štvanice Island (Vltava River) 40
Sudoměř, battle at 6, 36–8, 123, 195
Šumava, see Bohemian Forest

Supplies 88, 89, 134, 172, 176, 270–1, 315, 322

Sušice, town of 29, 115, 153

Švamberk, Bohuslav of 31, 101, 155, 166, 187, 196

Švihovský, Břeněk 33, 36
killed at Sudoměř 38

Svojšín, Petr of, mint master, 117

Świdnica, town of 60, 114, 267, 348, 350

Sylvius, Aeneas 74, 124–6, 181, 183, 196, 350, 368, 375, 397–398, *see* historiography

Sziafraniec, Piotr or Jan 306, 362

Tábor, town of and Táborites 9, 12, 33, 38, 39, 66, 68, 75, 76, 78, 80, 82, 92, 95–6, 96, 100, 102, 115, 118, 124, 130, 137, 138, 139, 141, 143, 153, 155, 164, 167, 185, 189, 190, 194, 195, 199, 202, 204, 231, 246, 256, 259, 281, 285–94, 296, 313, 315, 331, 333–5, 352, 368, 372, 376, 377, 388–9, 398 401
apocalyptic views of 32
armies or warriors of 31, 39, 40, 76, 82, 90, 95, 103, 115, 126, 130, 137–8, 138, 139, 179, 189, 190, 194, 196, 198, 199, 200, 202, 204, 231, 232, 256, 259, 278, 282, 296, 313, 315, 331, 333–5, 348, 372, 374
enemies of 33
founding of 37
godless by accusation 68, 141, 195
heretics 143, 155
in Moravia 102–3
killed 103–4, 373, 374–5, 376
leaders of 40, 76, 99–101, 124, 154, 167, 196, 198, 231, 281, 315, 334, 335, 376, 378, 399, 400
'Little' Tábor 164
manifestos of 8, 25–6, 285–94
mine shaft 41
revolutionary activities of 39, 77, 78–9, 95–6, 335
priests of 36, 39, 92, 97, 138
privileges of 9, 388–9
programme of 12, 85, 246–7, 285–94, 353, 378–9
town of 36, 37, 39, 96–7, 119, 124, 153, 154, 164, 185, 376, 377, 388, 398–401
women of 31, 39, 40, 78–9, 105

Tachov, town of 9, 227, 230–2, 240, 314, 319, 321, 322

tactics, military 7, 77–8, 82, 95, 104, 124–6, 129, 134, 141, 146–7, 155–6, 165–7, 178, 179–80, 188, 196, 231, 336–8, 373–4

Tartu, town of 149

Tata Castle (Hungary) 192–3

Teplá, town of 228, 315

Teutonic Order, Knights of 71, 130, 149, 228, 242, 330, 359, 361, 362

Theology 1,2, 3, 8, 10–11, 12, 32, 74, 80, 85, 89, 278, 303, 368–72, 400

Tišnov, Šimon of 19

Tovačov, town of 333

Towns, Hussite 9, 115–17

Treason 69, 152, 177

Třebíč, fortified monastery of 182, 376

Třeboň, town of 100, 388

Trenčín, town of 115, 134

Trier, Otto of 105, 107, 109, 111, 112, 223

Trnava, town of 264, 279

Troops, numbers of 74, 131, 146, 160–3, 200, 231, 266, 269, 271, 272, 275, 322, 328, 357–8, 359
Chrudim 133
Domažlice 316, 322
Hradec Králové 390
Hussites in Austria 334–5
Hussites in German territories 278–9, 280
Hussites in Poland 359
Kostelec-nad-Labem 178
Kutná Hora 137
Lipany 374
Malešov 189
Most 122
Poříčí 39
Sázava Valley 145, 147
Stříbro and Tachov 230–2
Sudoměř 36–7
Ústí-nad-Labem 199–201
Vítkov 74–5, 77–8
Vladař mountain 134
Vyšehrad 88, 90–1, 92
Žatec 129, 131
Živohošť' 29–30, 31

Truces and peace treaties 63, 88, 98–9, 194, 347–50, 368–72

Trutnov, town of 115, 121

Turks 245, 267, 357

Tuřov, town of 76

Týn Horšův, town of 73, 189

Uherské Hradiště, town of 142, 334
Újezdec Castle 38
Ulm 128, 145, 199, 227
University in Prague 2, 4, 19
  supports utraquism 2, 4
  Hussites in 19
Ústí-nad-Labem, battle at 6, 115, 198–207,
  278
Ústí, Prokop of 89, 94
Ústí, town of (south Bohemia) 37, 39
Utraquism 1, 2, 4, 19, 25, 40, 55, 61, 63, 69,
  70, 83, 154, 183, 189, 203, 356, 369, 384,
  386–7
  Jakoubek's writings on 19
  practice forbidden 55, 63, 70, 95

Václav IV, King 4, 14, 15, 18, 43, 53, 71, 183,
  187, 189, 278, 353, 356, 382, 384
  death of 4, 26
  ratified utraquism 27
Václav, St 60
Váh River 115
Vartenberk, Čeněk of 7, 19, 26, 31, 39, 53,
  60–1, 97, 117, 119, 121, 139, 164, 166–7,
  205
Vartenberk, Sigismund of Děčín and 60
Vassals and peasants 38, 42, 64, 72, 76, 77,
  79, 84, 91, 101, 102, 125, 129, 137, 147,
  150, 159, 168, 169, 170, 171, 193, 208,
  215, 261, 347, 381
  as martyrs 76, 89
  in Hussite armies 78, 84, 91, 125, 130, 203,
  260–1, 381, 383
Vechta, Konrad of, Archbishop of Prague 4,
  16, 113–14, 117, 184
Vejrov, Ondráček of 95
Velehrad Monastery 102–3
Věnečký, Jan 37
Venice 9, 69–73
Veselí, Burgrave of Prague Castle 39
Veseli, Jaroslav 92
Vestments 138, 144, 190, 400
Věžonice, Tomáš of 103
Vícemilice, Jan Hvězda (Bzdinka) 182, 195
Vienna 82, 278
Vienne, Council of 176
Vílemov, town of 164, 165
Virgin, Castle of the 166

Vítkov hill 9, 74–5, 77–80, 84, 100, 123, 186
Vladař mountain 133, 188
Vltava River 29, 77, 177
Vodňany, town of 84, 376
Vojtěch, Dean of the Týn Church 20
Vojtěch, priest in Chelčice 76–7
Vožice, town of 38
Vřesov, Aleš of 64
Všemberk, Jan 89–90
Vyšehrad 31, 38, 57, 77, 88–93, 100, 185
  battle at 6, 9, 88–92, 100, 186
  controlled by Sigismund 31, 39, 185
  fortifications strengthened 38–9
Vysoké Mýto, town of 115

Wages for crusaders 252, 255, 272
Waldensians 3
Waldhauser, Konrad 1
War wagons 10, 29, 30–31, 36, 37, 38, 39, 40,
  124–6, 138, 140, 144, 146, 166, 178, 179,
  180, 181, 188, 199, 200, 209, 222, 230,
  231, 240–1, 263, 267, 274, 278, 279–80,
  300, 313, 315, 316, 318, 320, 321–2, 327,
  329, 331, 334, 335, 336–8, 358, 359, 367,
  373, 375, 394
  carrying cannon 31, 36, 124, 125, 200,
  232–3, 322, 334
  strategic use of 38, 39, 124–6, 134, 140,
  143, 166, 178, 179–80, 186, 188, 230,
  233, 240, 241, 300, 313, 318, 321, 327,
  329, 331, 336–8, 346, 375, 376
Warriors of God, Hussites as 5, 66–8
Wealth, divesting of ecclesiastical 4, 18, 83,
  101, 168, 290, 291
Weapons and armour 30, 37, 40, 67, 73, 75,
  82, 90, 95, 100, 123–4, 124–6, 128, 130,
  140, 147, 155–6, 180, 204, 222–3, 273–4,
  300, 322, 323, 332, 335, 355, 374, 394,
  401
Weather 38, 82, 134, 141, 166, 198, 335, 399
Wesel, town of 109
Wilhelm, Landgrave of Thuringia 42
Windecke, Eberhart 74, 88, 141, 143, 189,
  279, 392
Witchcraft and magic 361
Witold, Grand Duke of Lithuania 149, 150,
  151, 362
Władysław Jagiełło, King of Poland 142, 144,
  151, 175, 195, 304–7, 309, 340, 361, 362

Women 7, 20, 30, 37, 38, 39, 40, 63, 72, 73,
   77–8, 79, 96, 101, 104, 105, 121, 124,
   128, 131, 138, 139, 142, 145, 168, 170,
   177, 179, 188, 199, 201, 204, 207, 208,
   220, 233, 249, 260, 318, 350, 351, 353,
   367, 397
   abused by crusaders 63, 64, 72, 79, 101,
      121, 130, 137, 139, 145, 188, 203
   among armies 31, 38, 39, 74, 77–8, 79, 105,
      124
   as heretics 33, 78–9, 107, 112, 177, 199
   preaching by 20
   spared by Žižka 95, 96, 104, 179
   violence and iconoclasm by 78–9, 105
Wrocław, Conrad, Bishop of 137, 347
Wrocław, city of 37, 45, 49, 52, 59, 60, 62,
   71, 114, 148, 185, 194, 224, 248, 256,
   266, 278, 335, 350
Wyclif, John 18, 19, 45, 46, 47, 48, 136,
   140–1, 250, 355
Wyclifism (as synonym for Hussites) 2, 15,
   16, 18, 20, 27, 42, 46, 50, 55, 57, 113,
   114, 122, 127, 148, 155, 159, 172, 176,
   184, 231, 334

Žagan, Ludolf of 113–14, 122, 127, 154
Žatec, town of 9, 53, 54, 57, 105, 115, 128,
   137, 180, 188, 265, 375, 377
Zbraslav Monastery 184, 186, 187
Zbraslavice, Markold of 36, 294
Zbyněk, Archbishop of Prague 43–4, 183
Železný, Jan 7, 49, 62, 137, 256
Želiv, town of 56
Želivský, Jan 3, 7, 11, 21–5, 55, 56, 58, 80,
   120, 122–3, 129, 184, 217, 364, 382
Žinkovy, town of 29
Živohošt', battle of 6, 29–32
Žižka, Jan 7, 31–2, 33, 36–8, 66, 75, 77–9,
   82, 84, 85, 86, 88, 94, 99–100, 101, 102,
   117, 119, 122, 123–4, 126, 127, 129,
   133–4, 137–41, 143–5, 153, 155, 164–5,
   173, 177–8, 179–80, 181, 183–90, 198,

219, 336, 338, 362, 373, 376, 382, 394,
   399–400
   assassination target 123
   attends Diet of Čáslav 117, 119
   battle at Kutná Hora and 134, 138, 139–40,
      145–6, 188
   blindness 126, 134, 138, 143, 187, 188
   courage of 40, 78, 155, 185
   death of 6, 182–3, 190, 192, 195
   drum 182–3, 399–400
   Hussite leader 31, 38, 78, 79, 94, 98, 99–
      100, 122, 126, 166, 178, 179–80, 181,
      195–6
   iconography of 190, 399, 400
   leaves Prague 88
   letters of 98–100, 101, 123–4, 153–4,
      154–5, 164–5, 167–71, 190
   Malešov and 179–80, 189
   military rule of 9, 167–71, 219
   policy on women and children 95, 96, 104,
      179
   recruits forces 84, 123
   reputation of 37, 40, 85, 138, 144, 147, 155,
      166, 178, 185, 189, 376
   Sázava Valley battles 146–7, 188–9
   Sudoměř and 36–8
   tactics of 38, 124–6, 134, 166, 178, 179–80,
      196, 278, 373
   Vítkov and 75, 77–8, 185–6
   Vladař and 133–4
   wrath of 95–6, 127, 154–5, 167, 186
Zlíchov, town of 88
Žlutice, town of 115, 133, 189, 230, 239
Znojmo, town of 265, 394, 398
Znojmo, Ulrich of 385
Žofie, Queen, Regent of Bohemia 4, 26, 30,
   31, 64, 143, 144
Zvíkov, Castle of 311
Zvířctice, Zdislav of 19
Zvole, Kuneš of 251–2, 255, 300
Zwettl, town of 278